We dedicate this book
to our daughters
Jenny and Nicole

© Copyright 1997, 2001/2002
    MERGUS Verlag GmbH, P.O. Box 86, 49302 Melle, Germany.
    Email: info@mergus.de   Internet: http://www.mergus.de
® MERGUS is a registered trademark in USA

ISBN 3-88244-083-X

Second English Edition, 2001/2002 - Hardcover

Distribution: Aqua Medic, Inc.
                       25003 Pitkin Road # A300,
                       Spring, Texas 77386
                       aquamedic@ev1.net

Publisher: Hans A. Baensch
Editor: Dr. Rüdiger Riehl
Translated and revised by: Gero W. Fischer, Ph.D.
                       Shellie E. Borrer, M.S.

Printed in Spain

Hans A. Baensch   Dr. Gero W. Fischer

AQUARIUM ATLAS

PHOTO-INDEX
1-5

Hardcover Edition

Translated and revised by:

Gero W. Fischer, Ph.D.
Shellie E. Borrer, M.S.

MERGUS

Publishers of Natural History and Pet Books
Hans A. Baensch • Melle • Germany

Preface

A long time has passed since the conception and publication of the first AQUARIUM ATLAS. Since then, the MERGUS AQUARIUM ATLAS has expanded. There are now five, autonomous volumes. The PHOTO INDEX 1–5 presents all the fish species of the 5 AQUARIUM ATLASES—approximately 4000—and a comprehensive index in one convenient book.

The approximately 4500 color photographs are accompanied by brief, concise information on natural distribution, social behavior, dietary requirements, breeding, etc. The data are conveyed through intuitive abbreviations and keywords to provide the absolute maximum amount of information for the multitude of fishes contained within the book. Orders and families of all species are presented in chapter introductions. Behind the scientific name, a volume and page number reference are given, indicating where more detailed information can be found. The comprehensive index includes all the scientific names, common names, and synonyms. The entries are alphabetized by genus/species and species/genus. With minimal information, any fish of the various volumes of the AQUARIUM ATLAS can be found. As is customary for the AQUARIUM ATLAS, the table of contents is subdivided in groups—and an additional systematic list of taxons (in alphabetic order) eases the finding of taxonomic groups, often to subfamily.

With fishes, like other areas of systematics, there are many opinions in regard to the proper classification of species in orders, families, subfamilies, and genera: we largely followed the reference volume "Fishes of the World" by JOSEPH S. NELSON (3ed ed., 1994). However, classifications used in the AQUARIUM ATLAS series were taken into account. Every AQUARIUM ATLAS user will be able to locate the taxon with which he/she is familiar. Most alterations were made at the family and subfamily level.

The world is becoming smaller every day and the tropics are progressively more accessible. As aquarists we can bring the tropics into our living rooms. This INDEX is a compact "take along reference," invaluable to accompany you to your aquarium store around the corner or to the river around the globe to provide reliable information for all those interested in ichthyofauna. Page through it and plan your next travel destination. Collectors and importers have now a standard reference that provides current scientific names, common names, and synonyms. As this book becomes translated, more and more people around the world gain access to a common reference, further easing international commerce.

Whether you are an advanced hobbyist or a beginning aquarist, the PHOTO INDEX will prove a useful tool. The specialist will encounter new challenges, and the beginner will be able to easily choose hardy fishes which will forgive the many small errors of the novice aquarist.

A "Redlist" of species subject to various degrees of threat is part of the appendices.

If we consider that the PHOTO INDEX presents about 4000 freshwater and brackish water species of the more than 10000 described species from those biotopes, we realize that there is a long road to travel to reach our goal—to present all fishes of freshwater and brackish water biotopes.

As part of this endeavour we appreciate further contributions from photographers and aquarists throughout the world to better the information for all. We extend our thanks in advance.

Our address is listed at the beginning of this book.

All under the motto: "Information is the first step to effective species preservation."

Hans A. Baensch   *Dr. Gero W. Fischer*
Melle – Germany   Quito – Ecuador

September, 1997

Table of Contents

Fishes

Table of Contents

Table of Contents

Table of Contents

Table of Contents

Table of Contents

List of Orders, Families, and Subfamilies

List of Orders, Families, and Subfamilies

List of Orders, Families, and Subfamilies

List of Orders, Families, and Subfamilies

List of Orders, Families, and Subfamilies

List of Orders, Families, and Subfamilies

Symbology

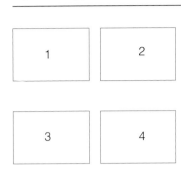

Page Layout:

Moving from left to right and top to bottom, the photos are consecutively ordered. The numerical equivalent is used for family and subfamily designations in the page headings as well as to identify the species matching the synonyms listed in the comprehensive index.

Just beneath the photographs of the approximately 4000 species, concise information concerning the fish can be found based on the 1996/97 editions of the AQUARIUM ATLAS, Volumes 1–5.

Scientific name	AQUARIUM ATLAS Volume/Page
Common name	
H: Habitat.	Fw,Bw,Mw
SD: ♂ or ♀: Sexual differences.	**S**: Social behavior
B: Breeding.	**F**: Feeding
T: Temperature, **L**: Length, **pH**: Acidity/Alkalinity, **D**: Difficulty	

Scientific name: This is the current valid Latin taxon for the species. Other scientific names for the same species—usually the result of changes in classification or subsequent descriptions—are listed in the comprehensive index as synonyms.

Common name: Unfortunately, common names have a limited applicability unless there is a grand consensus on what name should be applied to what species. Frequently, common names vary from region to region and many species do not have one. Scientific names are regulated and therefore offer a much more reliable standard.

Symbology

Aquarium Atlas **Volume/Page:** These are the reference numbers corresponding to the volume and page where the species was introduced. More in-depth information can be found there.

Habitat: This is the natural geographic distribution of the species. An "E" (endemic) following the designation indicates that the distribution is limited to that area.

Fw, Bw, Mw: Freshwater (only indicated in cases of possible doubt), brackish water, and marine water, respectively. The order of the terms indicates preference.

Sexual differences (SD): The most obvious external characteristics that permit the determination of gender. A ripe female (♀) can normally be distinguished from the male (♂) by a distended ventrum, barring the presence of other distinguishing features. Sexing juveniles is typically difficult to impossible.

Social behavior: The general social behavior of the species, whereby the size of the specimen is clearly of paramount influence. The symbols [!, −, (−), =, +] stand for the following:

! **Caution. This species presents a danger to aquarists (e.g., bites, toxic spines)!**

− Species tank/individual maintenance is suggested. Most of these fishes are very large and/or predators.

(−) Due to the delicate nature of the fish, a species tank is recommended. Rare species in which offspring are desired are included herein.

= A "specialized" community aquarium is appropriate, e.g., a community of certain types of cichlids or a group of large, peaceful fishes. Oftentimes intraspecific aggressions are very pronounced, while heterospecifics are ignored.

+ A "normal" community aquarium is appropriate. These peaceful fishes can fall prey to fishes more aggressive than themselves. Respect the basic rules for association: no extreme size differences, similar temperament, similar water requirements, appropriate size aquarium and decoration, etc.

? Unknown. There is no information available concerning its social interactions. Dedicated aquarists can make a significant contribution by reporting their observations.

Double symbols (e.g., +,−) signify a change in demeanor over the lifespan of the fish.

Symbology

Breeding: Basic type and facts on the reproductive biology. More information can be found in the respective introductions. If the reports are based on observations in its natural habitat, aquarium breeding has not been successful. In the interest of species preservation, aquarium reproduction is desired (use a species aquarium). Often the expected number of eggs (e) or young (y) is also indicated.

Feeding: Nutrition of the species. (A detailed explanation can be found in the AQUARIUM ATLAS Volume 1, pp. 200 f.)

H   Herbivore = plant-eater
In nature, these species feed on fruits, seeds, leaves (of aquatic plants as well as terrestrial plants that extend into the water), and algae. Many also accept foods of animal origin, but predators do not rank among their numbers.
Because they have a reduced stomach and a long intestine, they must be fed small quantities 3–4 times every day.

C   Carnivore = meat-eater
The majority of these species are predators, but fishes which consume animal-based commercial diets are also included herein. Although live foods are in some instances a necessity, freeze-dried foods (FD) and frozen foods often offer a suitable alternative. The stomach is well-developed, and the intestine is short. In the aquarium, feeding once a day is usually adequate.

C! Cannot, or only with great difficulty, be trained to dry commercial diets (e.g., FD, flakes).

L   Limnivore = aufwuchs-eater
Similar to the herbivores, these species have a reduced stomach and a long intestine. They graze the biocover (aufwuchs) of the decorations and the aquarium panes. The algae with the small animals and microorganisms contained therein are grazed throughout the day. This must be taken into consideration when establishing the feeding regime (tablet foods let the fish feed leisurely).

O   Omnivore = meat- and plant-eater
These species are the least problematic to feed. Predators and specialized herbivores are absent from their ranks. Normal flake foods admirably fulfill their needs.

P   Facultative parasite.
Although these species are parasites in nature, in the aquarium they will readily accept normal diets.

P! Obligatory parasite.
These species continue their parasitic lifestyle in the aquarium even when offered alternative diets. They include scale-eaters, eye-biters, and blood-suckers.
A qualitative and quantitative optimal feeding regime—given appropriate water values—is often the decisive factor when breeding a species.

Temperature: The range of the most favorable temperatures. Species from northern or southern latitudes normally require seasonal variations in temperature for continued vitality and reproductive success in captive environments.

Length: The total length (tip of snout to the end of the caudal fin) of the species is a decisive criterium in the selection of tankmates and the stocking density as well as the required size of the aquarium.

pH: The recommended acidity or alkalinity for maintenance (and usually for breeding).
   $\ll 7$ $\cong$ strongly acid (below 6.0)
   < 7 $\cong$ slightly acid to neutral (from ca. 6.0 to 7.0)
   7 $\cong$ around neutral or no specific requirement
   > 7 $\cong$ neutral to alkaline (from ca. 7.0 to 8.0)
   $\gg 7$ $\cong$ strongly alkaline (above 8.0)
Normally, the pH infers the preferred water hardness:
   strongly acid $\cong$ very soft,
   acid $\cong$ soft,
   neutral $\cong$ moderate values, no particular demands,
   alkaline $\cong$ hard,
   strongly alkaline $\cong$ very hard.

Difficulty: The degree of difficulty involved in maintenance. (See AQUARIUM ATLAS Volume 1, pp. 203 f.)
  1 Species in this group are robust, tolerating all but the most blatant errors. They are apt for beginners.
  2 A certain amount of experience is required.
  3 Species for advanced hobbyists.
  4 Only experts and specialists should attempt to care for these problematic species. It includes large, rare, delicate, and even toxic or dangerous species.

Lampetra fluviatilis

Group 0

Origin/Taxonomy

The lamprey family (Petromyzontidae), part of the subclass Cyclostomata, originated during the Pennsylvanian, or Upper Carboniferous, period about 325 million years ago. Since they lack a bony skeleton, there is no fossil record. The lack of mandibles affirms their classification into Agnatha, the jawless fishes (NELSON, 1994).

Taxon	Members	Page
Class Cephalaspidomorphi		
PETROMYZONTIFORMES	41 of 41 (32)*	
Petromyzontidae	6 G, 41 S**	25

Geographic Distribution

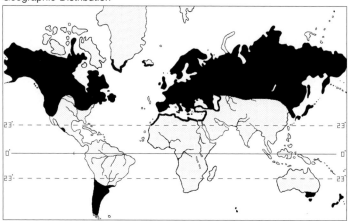

Area of distribution of the family Petromyzontidae.

Breeding

Reproduction in the aquarium has not been successful, largely due to their complex lifecycle and dietary requirements which are very difficult to satisfy in an aquarium.

In nature, oviposition occurs in freshwater at 12–16°C. Up to 3000 eggs are laid in shallow depressions.

---

* 41 of a total of 41 species in this order require freshwater at least part of their life. (32 species inhabit freshwater exclusively.)
** A total of 41 species are recognized in 6 genera.
(NELSON, 1994)

Lifecycle

The larval stage lasts for up to 6 years. During this time, the larvae—called *Ammocoetus*—remain in freshwater. This is a period of slow growth, mostly spent buried in the substrate. After metamorphosis, some species migrate to the sea and remain there for an additional 3 years. Growth is fast during that time. They return to freshwater to spawn, and within a few days of spawning, they die.

Nutrition

Larvae are filter-feeders, obtaining their nourishment from suspended matter which drifts by in the current. To feed, the head is extended forth from the fine-grained substrate where they are buried. Following metamorphosis, they adopt a semiparasitic lifestyle. Using their oral disc (see below), they latch onto a host, rasping tissue and sucking blood. They cease to feed at the onset of the spawning migration.

Behavior

Larvae are harmless, whereas adults are oftentimes parasites, even attacking conspecifics. Parasitic species feed after metamorphosis; nonparasitic forms reproduce after metamorphosis without ever feeding.

Particularities

The body is scaleless and eel- to worm-shaped. Pectoral and ventral fins are lacking. The mouth is round and closes like a shutter.

Entering Lake Ontario in 1890, the sea lamprey (*Petromyzon marinus*) migrated through the Welland Canal, appearing about 30 years later in Lake Erie. Twenty five years later it had reached Lake Superior. As a consequence, the fisheries in the lakes collapsed (lake trout, burbot, lake whitefish). Only through continued management with specific poisons have the native fish populations been able to recover (MOYLE and CHECH, 1988).

Lampetra planeri oral disc   2/201

Lampetra wilderi ♀ with eggs   4/8

> Aquarium maintenance of this entire family is not recommended.

Lampetra fluviatilis 4/7
River lamprey
H: Europe.
SD: Urogenital papilla. S: –
B: Artificial insemination. F: O,C
T: 5–18°C, L: ca.100 cm, pH: 7, D: 4

Lampetra planeri 2/201, (5/8)
Brook lamprey
H: Europe.
♀: Red, swollen anal region. S: –
B: Nature: March–June. F: C
T: 4–16°C, L: 19 cm, pH: 7, D: 4

Lampetra wilderi 4/8
American lamprey
H: USA: Great Lakes.
♀: "Anal fin." S: –
B: Unsuccessful. F: C
T: 5–20°C, L: 20 cm, pH: 7, D: 4

Lethenteron japonicum 4/11
Arctic lamprey, Japanese lamprey
H: North America, Russia, Japan.
♀: "Anal fin." S: –
B: Unsuccessful. F: C
T: 5–18°C, L: 18–54 cm, pH: 7, D: 4

Lethenteron kessleri 4/12
Kessler's lamprey
H: Russia, Japan; w/o connection to sea.
♂: Longer; taller dorsal fin. S: –
B: Nature: May–July. F: C
T: 5–25°C, L: 35 cm, pH: 7, D: 2–3

Lethenteron zanandreai 5/8
Lombardian lamprey, ciriola
H: Europe: Italy. Endangered
♂: Oral disc larger; tail bent down. S: =
B: Nat.: Jan.–Jun. (March); 2000e. F: C
T: 5–19°C, L: 22 cm, pH: 7, D: 4

Group 1   Pseudo-Bony and Cartilaginous Fishes

From an evolutionary standpoint, Group 1, like Group 0, is composed of primitive fishes; i.e., they are not true bony fishes (Teleostei). Subfamilies are not arranged in alphabetic order.

---

*   26 of the 26 species in this order require freshwater at least part of their life.
(14 species inhabit freshwater exclusively.)

** A total of 24 species are recognized in 4 genera.
(NELSON, 1994)

Class: Actinopterygii

Subclass: Chondrostei

Ray-Finned Fishes

Geographic Distribution

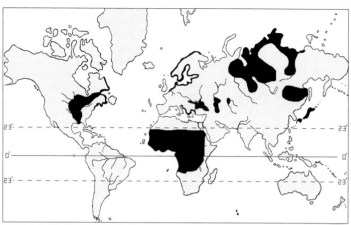

Area of distribution of the subclass Chondrostei.

Order ACIPENSERIFORMES (Sturgeons and Paddlefishes)

Many species within this order are appreciated worldwide as sources of caviar and fine meat (family Acipenseridae). Unfortunately, some are endangered due to overfishing, environmental pollution, and hydraulic construction projects interrupting their spawning rivers (most are anadromous migratory species). Thanks to success in captive breeding programs, heightened environmental awareness, and enforced fishing quotas, the outlook for the future is steadily improving.

The Mississippi River basin is home to the paddlefish (family Polyodontidae). Efforts are being made to breed this enormous fish in captivity to augment native populations through release programs as well as to produce fingerlings for aquaculture.

Both sturgeons and paddlefishes achieve sizes that far exceed the spatial limitations of "normal" aquaria. Prior to purchasing a juvenile, aquarists must consider what will become of their pet once it has outgrown the aquarium.

Order POLYPTERIFORMES (Lobe-Finned Pikes)

Lobe-finned pikes are strictly inhabitants of tropical Africa. They breathe atmospheric air: the two-part, ventrally located, lunglike swimbladder is connected to the esophagus and serves as an accessory respiratory organ. If lobe-finned pikes are precluded from reaching the surface to breathe, they will drown, even in oxygen-rich waters. Intraspecific aggressions are pronounced and heterospecifics which fall into the category of "suitable prey" are in mortal jeopardy. They often "sit" on their ventral fins.

CARTILAGIN.

Acipenser baeri   3/74
Sandpaper sturgeon, Siberian sturgeon
H: Asia: CIS States.
SD: Unknown.   S: =
B: Anadromous and local.   F: C
T: 10–20°C, L: >200 cm, pH: >7, D: 3–4

Acipenser gueldenstaedti   3/74
Plated sturgeon
H: Europe, W Asia: land-locked seas.
SD: Unknown.   S: =
B: Anadromous; caviar.   F: C
T: 10–20°C, L: <400 cm, pH: >7, D: 3–4

Acipenser medirostris   3/76
Green sturgeon
H: America and Asia.   Rare
SD: Unknown.   S: ?
B: Anadromous.   F: C
T: 10–20°C, L: <210 cm, pH: >7, D: 3–4

Acipenser nudiventris   3/76
River sturgeon
H: Europe and Asia: land-locked seas.
SD: Unknown.   S: =
B: Anadromous.   F: C
T: 10–20°C, L: 200 cm, pH: >7, D: 3–4

Acipenser ruthenus   1/207
Sterlet
H: Europe and Siberia.
SD: Unknown.   S: =
B: Nature: May, June.   F: C
T: 10–18°C, L: 100 cm, pH: >7, D: 2–3

Acipenser schrencki   3/78
Amur sturgeon
H: Asia: CIS States, China.
SD: Unknown.   S: =
B: Anadromous: June–Sept.   F: C
T: 10–20°C, L: <290 cm, pH: >7, D: 3–4

CARTILAGIN.

Acipenser stellatus   3/78
Star sterlet
H: Europe and W Asia.
♀: Fuller at spawning time.   S: =
B: Anadromous: June–September. F: C
T: 10–20°C, L: <190 cm, pH: >7, D: 3

Acipenser sturio   3/81
Sturgeon
H: European coasts.
SD: Unknown.   S: =
B: Nat.: June, July; anadromous.   F: C
T: 10–18°C, L: 600 cm, pH: >7, D: 4

Huso dauricus   3/82
Kaluga sturgeon
H: Asia: CIS States, China.
SD: Unknown.   S: –
B: Nature: May, June.   F: C
T: 10–20°C, L: 560 cm, pH: >7, D: 4

Huso huso   3/82
Beluga sturgeon
H: Europe and Asia.
SD: Unknown.   S: =
B: Fall, spring; Beluga caviar.   F: C
T: 10–20°C, L: 900 cm, pH: >7, D: 4

Pseudoscaphirhynchus kaufmanni   3/84
Kaufmann's sturgeon ♂
H: CIS States.
♂: Elongated C fin; pointed mouth. S: ?
B: Nature: April.   F: C
T: 10–20°C, L: 75 cm, pH: >7, D: 3–4

Scaphirhynchus platorhynchus   2/204
Shovelnose sturgeon
H: North America.
SD: Unknown.   S: =
B: Nature: April–June.   F: C
T: 10–20°C, L: 150 cm, pH: >7, D: 4

Aᴄɪᴘᴇɴsᴇʀɪꜰᴏʀᴍᴇs
Polyodontidae[1]
Pᴏʟʏᴘᴛᴇʀɪꜰᴏʀᴍᴇs
Polypteridae[2-6]

Paddlefishes

Lobe-Finned Pikes

CARTILAGIN.

Polyodon spathula　　　　2/215
Paddlefish
H: North America.
SD: Unknown.　　　　　　　　S: =
B: Nat.: Feb.–May; aquaculture.　F: C
T: 10–18°C, L: 200 cm, pH: 7, D: 4

Erpetoichthys calabaricus　　1/210
Snakefish
H: Western Africa.
♂: 12–14 anal fin rays (♀ 9).　　S: =
B: Unsuccessful.　　　　　　　F: C
T: 22–28°C, L: 40 cm, pH: <7, D: 3

Polypterus delhezi　　　　2/216
Armored bichir
H: Africa: Zaïre.
SD: Unknown.　　　　　　　　S: –
B: Unsuccessful.　　　　　　　F: C
T: 26–28°C, L: 35 cm, pH: 7, D: 3–4

Polypterus ornatipinnis　　　1/210

H: Central Africa: upper & central Zaïre.
♂: Borader anal fin? Narrow head? S: –
B: Plant thicket; 200–300 eggs.　F: C
T: 26–28°C, L: <46 cm, pH: 7, D: 4

Polypterus palmas palmas　　2/216
Marbled bichir
H: Africa: Guinea, Sierra L., Lib., Zaïre.
♂: Anal fin has twice as many rays.　S: –
B: Egg scatterer.　　　　　　　F: C
T: 26–28°C, L: 30 cm, pH: 7, D: 3

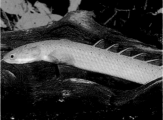

Polypterus senegalus　　　2/218
Senegal bichir, Cuvier's bichir
H: Africa: White Nile.
SD: Unknown.　　　　　　　　S: –
B: Unsuccessful.　　　　　　　F: C
T: 25–28°C, L: 30 cm, pH: 7, D: 3–4

Class: Actinopterygii
Subclass: Neopterygii

Ray-Finned Fishes

Geographic Distribution

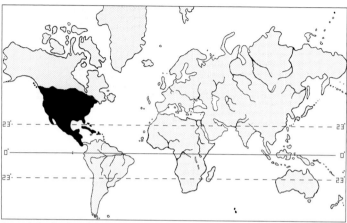

Area of distribution of the class Neopterygii.

Order Amiiformes (Bowfins)

During the Cretaceous and Jurassic periods (100 and 190 million years ago), the Amiiformes had numerous representatives. Today, the bowfin (family Amiidae) is the sole survivor. It inhabits the Mississippi Basin and Florida.

Its lung—a modified swimbladder—allows it to survive periods of heat and drought. Beginning at 10°C and increasing in direct proportion to temperature, part—or even all—of its oxygen requirement is fulfilled by atmospheric oxygen processed through the lung. The bowfin is capable of surviving the drought in a muddy cave (Moyle and Cech, 1988).

In nature, several pairs often spawn next to each other, creating breeding colonies. The bowfin is very prolific; an estimated 70,000 eggs are laid within plant thickets.

Only juveniles can be properly housed in a home aquarium. The monstrous proportions attained by adults as well as their predaceous lifestyle make them absolutely inappropriate aquarium residents.

Order Semionotiformes (Gar Pikes)

Gar pikes (family Lepisosteidae) climaxed in the same period as the bowfins (see above); today only seven species remain. Their area of distribution overlaps that of the bowfin, but extends southward into southern Central America.

The slim body is covered by armorlike ganoid scales, and the joints of the

31

AMIIFORMES
Amiidae[2]
SEMIONOTIFORMES
Lepisosteidae[3–6]

Bowfins

Gar Pikes

CARTILAGIN.

spinal column allow nodding movements of the head. The swimbladder functions as an accessory breathing organ and is particularly important during the warmer times of the year.

Gar pikes are ambush predators. The caudal fin and the posteriorly positioned dorsal and anal fins provide the bursts of speed necessary to capture its prey.

Because of their rapid growth and large mature size, large public aquaria are much more apt environments than home aquaria.

Amia calva   2/205
Bowfin, American mudfish
H: North America: USA.
♂: Spot on C peduncle; smaller.   S: –
B: Nature: May, June.   F: C
T: 15–20°C, L: 75 cm, pH: 7, D: 4

Lepisosteus oculatus   2/210
Spotted gar
H: North America: USA.
SD: Unknown.   S: –
B: Too large for aquarium breeding. F: C
T: 12–20°C, L: 125 cm, pH: 7, D: 4

Lepisosteus osseus   2/210
Longnose gar
H: North America: USA.
SD: Unknown.   S: –
B: Nature: March–May.   F: C
T: 12–20°C, L: 150 cm, pH: 7, D: 4

Lepisosteus platostomus   2/212
Spotnose gar
H: North America.
SD: Unknown.   S: –
B: Unsuccessful.   F: C
T: 10–18°C, L: 60 cm, pH: 7, D: 2

Lepisosteus tristoechus   2/212
Alligator gar
H: America: S USA, Cuba, N Mexico.
SD: Unknown.   S: –
B: Unsuccessful.   F: C
T: 18–23°C, L: >300 cm, pH: 7, D: 3

Class: Chondrichthys
Subclass: Elasmobranchii

Cartilaginous Fishes

Geographic Distribution

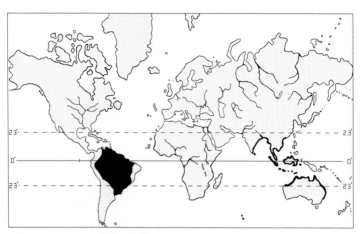

Area of distribution of the order Rajiformes (fresh-/brackish water).

Order RAJIFORMES

Several stingrays of the family Dasyatidae—especially those of the subfamily Potamotrygoninae (river stingrays)—are relicts of species of the Pacific Ocean which adapted to freshwater at the time of the formation of the Andes Mountains, which were created by the forces of continental drift and the collision of continental plates. Prior to that time (15 million years ago) the Amazon flowed into the Pacific. Five million years were required for the resulting accumulation of freshwater—the largest ever!—to forge through the eastern plateau and begin draining into the Atlantic. In comparison to their marine counterparts, freshwater stingrays have a low concentration of uric acid in their blood and their rectal gland is vestigial.

Fertilization is internal—these rays are livebearers. Occasionally, newly captured pregnant females give birth to approximately 12 offspring as they are brought into the boat. The (premature?) newborns are miniature adults, about 10 cm diameter, and have a huge yolk sac hanging from their central "navel." Rays have bred in the aquarium (see AQUARIUM ATLAS Vol. 5, p. 10).

Close to the tip, the whiplike tail has one or more poisonous barbed spines which are replaced every 6–12 months. These spines are employed as defensive weapons. When bathers or fishermen inadvertently step on a resting stingray, the tail whips up and plunges the spine into the offending object, i.e., the ankle or lower leg of the person. The injury is painful due to the physical aspects of the wound as well as the toxin. Furthermore, since innumerable decaying organics are embedded in the spine's convoluted sur-

33

face, the risk of infection is high. When walking in areas suspected of harboring rays—usually sand- or mud-bottomed lowland waters—scuffle your feet as you walk to warn stingrays of your approach, thereby allowing them to flee.

The likelihood of injury is much less in the aquarium. Nevertheless, stingrays must be respected and treated with caution in view of their potential danger. Keep a wary eye when carrying out tank maintenance.

Provided the aquarium is long and wide, stingray husbandry is quite feasible. However, it is still considered difficult and best left to experienced hobbyists.

Sawfishes (family Pristidae) are mostly marine inhabitants of Southeast Asia, but *Pristis microdon* (p. 36) is found up to 400 km (250 mi) inland in Australian rivers. Despite its sharklike appearance, the northern sawfish is more closely related to rays. It is not prolific, giving birth to only about 20 live offspring.

Of course, with a length of 5 m, it is entirely too large for an aquarium.

Himantura oxyrhynchus   4/14
Indo-Australian ray
H: NW Australia, S Indonesia.   Bw
♂: Thickened ventral fins.   S: !
B: Unknown.   F: C
T: 23–26°C, Ø: 250 cm, pH: >7, D: 4

Paratrygon orbicularis   4/14
Ring ray
H: South America: Brazil.
♂: Thickened ventral fins.   S: !
B: Nature: livebearer.   F: C
T: 22–28°C, Ø: 50 cm, pH: <7, D: 4

Potamotrygon henlei   4/16
Fire stingray
H: South America: Brazil.
♂: Thickened ventral fins.   S: !
B: Nature: livebearer.   F: C
T: 23–28°C, L: 35 cm, pH: <7, D: 3–4

CARTILAGIN.

Potamotrygon hystrix 4/16
Mottled freshwater stingray
H: South America.
♂: Thickened V fins. More contrast? S: !
B: Nature: livebearer, 6–12 young. F: C
T: 24–26°C, Ø: 70 cm, pH: <7, D: 4

Potamotrygon hystrix (?) ♀ 5/11
Mottled freshwater stingray
With young.

Potamotrygon laticeps 1/209
Common freshwater stingray
H: South America.
♂: Thickened V fins; more contrast? S: !
B: Nature: livebearer. F: C
T: 23–25°C, L: 70 cm, pH: <7, D: 4

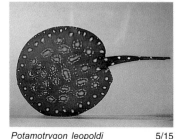

Potamotrygon leopoldi 5/15
Leopold's freshwater stingray
H: South America: Brazil: Rio Xingú.   E
♂: Appendage behind gen. papilla. S: !
B: Unsuccessful. F: C
T: 20–25°C, Ø: 25 cm, pH: <7, D: 4

Potamotrygon motoro 2/219
Ocellated freshwater stingray
H: South America.
♂: Thickened ventral fins. S: !
B: Nature: livebearer. F: C
T: 24–26°C, Ø: 30 cm, pH: <7, D: 3

Potamotrygon motoro ♂ 5/11
Ocellated freshwater stingray
Breeding report in AQUARIUM ATLAS 5.

Potamotrygon sp. aff *reticulatus*   4/20
Reticulated freshwater stingray

Potamotrygon reticulatus   4/18
Reticulated freshwater stingray
H: South America.
♂: Thickened ventral fins.   S: !
B: Nature: livebearer.   F: C
T: 24–26°C, Ø: >30 cm, pH: 7, D: 4

Potamotrygon schroederi   5/16
Schroeder's freshwater stingray
H: South America: Venezuela.   Very rare
♂: "Testicles" behind the anus.   S: !
B: Nature: livebearer.   F: C
T: 18–25°C, Ø: 40 cm, pH: <7, D: 4

Potamotrygon sp.   4/20

Pristis microdon   2/220
Northern sawfish
H: SE Asia, Australia.
♂: Ventral fin is copulation organ.   S: ?
B: Nature: livebearer; <20 young.   F: C
T: 24–26°C, L: 500 cm, pH: 7, D: 4

Class: Sarcopterygii
Subclass: Dipnoi

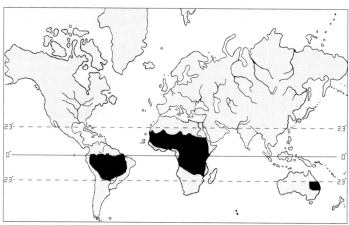

Area of distribution of the subclass Dipnoi.

CERATODONTIFORMES
Ceratodontidae

Australian Lungfishes

Order CERATODONTIFORMES

The family of Australian lungfishes (Ceratodontidae) is comprised of only one species, *Neoceratodus forsteri*. In comparison to the Lepidosireniformes (below), their lung activity is little developed. It burrows in the mud, but should the water dry up, it dies. The mature size of the species demands a large aquarium.

Neoceratodus forsteri   2/206
Australian lungfish
H: Australia: Queensland.
SD: Unknown.   S: –
B: Nature: froglike egg mass.   F: C
T: 22–28°C, L: 180 cm, pH: 7, D: 4

LEPIDOSIRENIFORMES

Order LEPIDOSIRENIFORMES

American and African lungfishes (families Lepidosirenidae and Protopteridae, respectively) have a lunglike modified swimbladder into lungs, allowing them to survive the dry season. As the water begins to disappear, the fish forms a cocoon of mud and mucus. An air hole is left next to their mouth. All of these fishes grow too large for the average home aquarium.

37

Lepidosiren paradoxa 2/207
South American lungfish
H: Central South America.
SD: Unknown. S: =
B: Nature: constructs tunnels. F: C
T: 24–28°C, L: 125 cm, pH: 7, D: 4

Lepidosiren paradoxa juv. 2/207
South American lungfish

Protopterus annectens annectens 2/221, 3/86
African lungfish
H: Africa: from Senegal to Nigeria.
SD: Unknown. S: –
B: Nature: paternal family. F: C
T: 25–30°C, L: 82 cm, pH: 7, D: 2

Protopterus dolloi 1/208

H: Africa: Zaïre Basin.
SD: Unknown. S: –
B: Nature: paternal family. F: C
T: 25–30°C, L: 85 cm, pH: 7, D: 4

Protopterus aethiopicus aethiopicus 3/86
Ethiopian lungfish white color morph
H: Africa: Nile.
SD: Unknown. S: –
B: Nature: paternal family. F: C
T: 25–30°C, L: 200 cm, pH: 7, D: 4

Protopterus aethiopicus aethiopicus 3/86
Ethiopian lungfish

Hyphessobrycon columbianus; top ♀, bottom ♂ (p. 99).

CHARACINS

Origin/Taxonomy

The characins are among the oldest fish orders, probably originating during the Mesozoic Era 80–150 million years ago, prior to the separation of Africa and America. This theory is supported by the presence of very similar groups on both continents, i.e., *Hydrocynus* vs. *Hoplias* or *Erythrinus* and Citharinidae vs. Hemiodidae and Curimatidae (GÉRY, 1977).

Characins were previously classified into the suborder Characoidei of the carplike fishes (Cypriniformes). Today they have been placed into an autonomous order, the Characiformes. Similar changes have taken place in the familial divisions in response to new discoveries and changes in taxonomic criteria. This book strives to follow a modern classification without abandoning our loyal owners of older editions of the AQUARIUM ATLAS. The table of contents and the alphabetical list of orders, families, and subfamilies as well as the comprehensive index at the end of this book are presented in great detail to bridge the old and the new classification schemes.

According to the newest criteria, characin families now conform to the following classification arrangement (NELSON 1994; MOYLE and CECH, 1988):

- Africa: Characidae (including Alestiinae, previously Alestidae), Citharinidae (including Distichodontinae, previously Distichodontidae), and Hepsetidae.
- America: Anostomidae, Hemiodontidae (also called Hemiodidae), Ctenoluciidae, Curimatidae, Erythrinidae, Gasteropelecidae, Lebiasinidae, and Characidae (encompassing what are now the subfamilies Characidiinae, Crenuchinae, Serrasalminae, and Rhoadsiinae).

The classification for Group 2 is given below. Subfamilies without page numbers have not been listed. The relative position of families and subfamilies is, of course, subject to future change.

Although for aquarists this means a time of adjustment and confusion, it bears little impact on how a fish should be maintained, fed, or its requirements for breeding.

CHARACINS

Geographic Distribution

With the exception of *Astyanax fasciatus mexicanus* (p. 98) which can be found as far north as Texas (North America), the area of distribution of the

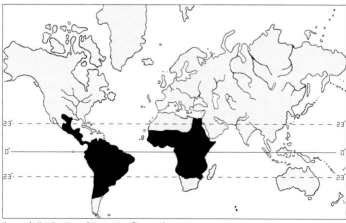

Area of distribution of the order Characiformes.

order Characiformes is restricted to Central and South America (over 1100 species) and Africa (over 175 species).

Sexual Differences

It is impossible to ascertain the sex of juvenile characins. In many species, sexual differences are only manifest once the animals attain sexual maturity, if at all. Frequently the genders are only distinguishable when the female's ventrum becomes distended with eggs. Since the sexual differences of many species are listed as "unknown," the table below will help the aquarist look for any possible differences which might be discerned under close scrutiny. Naturally, no single species will show all of these characteristics, and some will not be recognizable even under the most minute inspection.

Some traits such as longer fins, coloration, and size differences can only be used with certainty once the aquarist has maintained the fish for considerable time. Then it can be deduced with confidence that the fins are short

Possible External Sexual Differences of Characins

| Characteristic | Sex | | Exceptions (E)/Comments |
	male	female	
Size	smaller	larger	E: *Phenacogrammus, Pseudochalceus, Nematobrycon* Same age?
Body	more color	simpler	E: *Megalamphodus*. Good diet?
Figure	slimmer	fuller	Is it mature? Diet?
Fins	elongated	"normal"	Mainly anal, dorsal, and caudal fins.
Fins	ragged	clean-edged	Presence of predators?
Fins	more color/design	plain/transparent	E: *Megalamphodus*.
Anal fin	straight, convex, lobed	concave or straight	Age?
	w/ hooklets	w/o hooklets	In Tetragonopterinae.
Dorsal fin	w/ dots	plain	In Characidiinae.
Swimbladder	inferiorly pointed	inferioirly rounded	E: *Gymnocorymbus ternetzi, Hyphessobrycon bifasciatus*. Only visible in transparent species.
Ventral region	straight or concave	convex	Clearly notable when ripe.
From above	slimmer	rounder	In Gasteropelecidae (hatchets).
Behavior	rival aggressions	courtship	Requires a long period of observation of acclimated fishes (pairs?).

due to genetics versus nipped by a predator, broken from rough handling, or shortened by disease; the coloration is dull because of its gender and not poor nutrition or a sign of submission; and the small stature is a product of gender rather than poor nutrition or age.

Behavior

The great majority of characins is diurnal. Most tend to be predators, but many species are too small to present a problem in the aquarium. Even piranhas are remarkably docile under certain conditions: they hunt in schools, but when well-fed, they are rather calm and generally do not molest tank-mates. A species aquarium is recommended, however.

Typically, characins are schooling fishes. They significantly enliven community aquaria as they energetically swim through mid-water.

Characins have adapted to a wide range of biotopes, including rapids (e.g., Citharinidae, Hemiodontidae, and Characidiinae) and water remnants (e.g., Lebiasinidae and Erythriniidae).

Nutrition

As most characins are omnivorous, they are easily maintained on a diet of flake foods; even piranhas (e.g., *Serrasalmus nattereri*, p. 95) can be trained to trout pellets. Of course, dry commercial diets are generally insufficient to bring breeders into spawning condition. Most species demand a dietary regime of live and/or frozen foodstuffs for successful reproduction.

Some species, such as *Hoplias malabaricus* (p. 130), are such pronounced predators, they starve as soon as they have devoured their last tankmate—not even conspecifics are exempt from their hungry eye. Predatory characins are easily recognized by their dentition. The teeth of the tiger characins of the African genus *Hydrocynus* (pp. 51 f.), South American trahiras (Erythrinidae, p. 130), piranhas within the subfamily Serrasalminae (pp. 91 ff.), and the genus *Hydrolycus* of the Rhaphiodontinae (p. 91) in the family Characidae are especially prominent. Caution is advised when handling any of these fishes; all are capable of inflicting serious injury with their bite!

Herbivores and detritivores (aufwuchs-feeders) are more difficult to maintain in aquaria. The presence of herbivores virtually precludes plants from the decor. Even toxic Java moss is frequently devoured by hungry fishes—often with fatal consequences—and detritivores eventually exhaust surfaces to "graze." Fortunately, the diet of many herbivores and detritivores is quite plastic in the aquarium, and many will accept vegetable flake foods. Fishes of these trophic levels are largely members of the African family Citharinidae (*Distichodus* spp., pp. 56 f.) and the South American families Anostomidae (pp. 66 ff.), Chilodontidae (p. 125), Curimatidae (pp. 127 ff.), and Prochilodontidae (p. 144) as well as the subfamily Serrasalminae (*Myleus* spp. and others, pp. 93 f.).

Generalities

With the exception of catfishes, characins are the most common fishes of South America. In Africa, they are subjected to strong competition by cyprinids and are surpassed in species diversity by several fish groups; cichlids dominate the lake biotopes of Africa, while characins are by and large limited to slow-flowing, lowland waters (MOYLE and CECH, 1988).

Characins have highly developed senses, and as it so happens, they are the first fishes to arrive at the feeding site. Even the blind cave tetra (*Astyanax fasciatus mexicanus*, p. 98) detects the presence of food almost as fast as species with sight, thanks to its well-developed olfactory sense. It is by the sense of smell that the school detects an injured member, triggering the instinct to flee. Characins also react to visual and acoustic stimuli. The latter are detected with the aid of the "Weber's apparatus." It connects the auditory organ with the swimbladder which acts as a resonance body (GÉRY, 1977).

Often silver in color, the body is covered with cycloid scales. Numerous species have a dark spot on the caudal peduncle, a typical signal design of schooling fishes. All characins, except cave dwellers, have large eyes. An adipose fin is the norm.

Some fishes, e.g., species within the Hemiodontidae and Curimatidae, easily loose their scales. Such species are characteristically very nervous and sensitive, requireing careful handling. Those specimens that have survived the commercial chain, however, are much more tolerant of stressful situations than their cognates in the wild.

The order Characiformes contains many of the most popular aquarium species. One only need think of the neon tetra, the cardinal tetra, the head-and-tail-light tetra, the various rummy-noses, and the Congo tetra to realize the impact these species have on the hobby. Millions are collectively sold each year. Rare is the aquarist who can claim to have never maintained at least one of these species.

From a touristic point of view, piranhas are arguably the best known freshwater fishes of all. To capture such a fish is part of the "must do" activities of every Amazon adventure vacation.

In aquaculture, too, characins have their representatives, although their potential is far from being fully exploited. The omnivorous pacus of the genus *Colossoma* (pp. 91 f.) are presently the most commonly cultured characins. Their combined attributes of rapid growth, acceptance of dry pelleted diets, tolerance towards high stocking densities, robustness, and superior meat make them desirable aquaculture subjects. Since they are migratory fishes, however, they do not spawn naturally in ponds. Injection protocols with pituitary extract, or synthetic analogues, are essential to induce spawning. That procedure demands intensive handling of the mature breeders—in this case 3–4 year old fish weighing between 3 and 7 kg—certainly not an easy task.

CHARACINS

Family	Origin	Behavior	Diet	Reproduction	Remarks
Anostomidae	SA, (CA)	loners; peaceful to heterospecifics	L,H	in ponds; difficult; among plants	Some species headstanders.
(Characidae) Alestiinae	Af,(CA,SA)	community fishes predators	O,C C	among fine-leaved plants	Heterogenous; see p.71. Most beautiful characins of Africa
Chilodontidae	SA	peaceful; slight schooling behavior	O,H,L	egg scatterers	Peat filtration eases breeding; headstander.
Citharinidae	Af	peaceful predators	H C	egg scatterers; many unknown	Ichthyoborinae: mobile upper mandible.
Ctenoluciidae	SA	ambush predators; singly or group	C	egg scatterers; rare	Middle/upper water strata; tip of mouth sensitive.
Curimatidae	SA	peaceful, certain group formation	L,H	among flooded plants	Many similar species.
Erythrinidae	SA	pronounced predators	C	unknown; in ponds	Able to breathe atmospheric oxygen.
Gasteropelecidae	SA	peaceful schooling fishes	C,O	difficult; on fine-leaved plants	Surface fishes: can "fly."
Hemiodontidae	SA	active schooling fishes	H,O,L	unknown	Lose scales easily; sensitive in nature.
Hepsetidae	Af	ambush predators	C!	bubble nest with brood care	Monotypic family.
Lebiasinidae	SA	Leb.: small predators Pyrr.: peaceful	C O,C	unknown substr./egg scatterers	Snake over land. Some of most beautiful characins.
Prochilodontidae	SA	large, peaceful schooling fishes	L,H	migrate upriver to spawn	Limnivores difficult to feed in an aquarium.

CHARACINS

Phenacogrammus interruptus (Congo tetra), top ♂, bottom ♀; see p. 54.

Subfamily Alestiinae

This taxon, now considered a subfamily of the Characidae, holds the most popular African characins, e.g., the Congo tetra. A total of 18 genera and 109 species are recognized. With the exception of the genus *Hydrocynus* (see below), most can be maintained in "normal" aquaria. They are moderate-sized, peaceful, and relatively undemanding in regard to water quality. Aquaria that have numerous hiding places, abundant vegetation, and a dark substrate emphasize their coloration and minimize their timidness.

The reproductive biology of Alestiinae is typical for characins: The eggs are scattered among fine-leaved plants. As they sink through the water column, they are immediately fertilized by the accompanying male. The entire spawning sequence can take several days. Peat-filtered, soft, slightly acid water is recommended. Successful reproduction is contingent upon the breeders being conditioned on a varied diet. Some species prey upon their spawn.

As indicated by their common names—e.g., tiger characin and wolf tetra (pp. 51 f.)—the genus *Hydrocynus* contains infamously vicious fishes. They are large predators with impressive dentition, demanding solitary maintenance or significantly larger tankmates. However, size alone is sufficient reason to bar them from home aquaria.

Alestes baremoze   5/18

H: Lower Nile, L. Albert, Rudolf, Chad B.,...
♂: Elongated dorsal fin.   **S:** =
B: N.: scatters eggs among plants.   **F:** O
T: 20–26°C, **L:** 31 cm, **pH:** 7, **D:** 3–4

Alestes imberi   1/216
Red Congo tetra

H: Cameroon, Zambia, Zaïre, L. Malawi.
SD: Unknown.   **S:** +
B: Nature: 14 000 eggs.   **F:** C,O
T: 22–26°C, **L:** 10 cm, **pH:** 7, **D:** 2–3

Alestes longipinnis   1/218
Long-finned characin

H: Niger D., Gold C., Sierra L., Ghana, Togo.
♂: Very elongated dorsal fin rays. **S:** +
B: Egg scatterer: <300 eggs.   **F:** C,O
T: 22–26°C, **L:** 13 cm, **pH:** 7, **D:** 2

Alestes nurse   2/224
Nurse tetra

H: From the Nile to the Niger River.
♂: Concave anal fin.   **S:** +,=
B: In flooded grasslands.   **F:** O
T: 23–27°C, **L:** 25 cm, **pH:** 7, **D:** 1

Alestopetersius smykalai ♂   4/22
Blue diamond characin

H: Nigeria.
SD: See photos.   **S:** +
B: Among fine-leaved plants.   **F:** C,O
T: 23–27°C, **L:** 10 cm, **pH:** 7, **D:** 2–3

Alestopetersius smykalai ♀   4/22
Blue diamond characin

CHARACINS

Arnoldichthys spilopterus 1/216
African red-eyed characin
H: Lagos to the Niger Delta.
♂: Convex and tricolored anal fin. S: +
B: Eggs scattered: 1000 eggs. F: C,O
T: 23–28°C, L: 8 cm, pH: <7, D: 2–3

Bathyaethiops breuseghemi 3/94
African moon characin
H: Zaïre Basin.
♂: Intensely colored dorsal fin. S: +
B: Egg scatterer. F: C,O
T: 22–25°C, L: 7 cm, pH: 7, D: 2–3

Bathyaethiops caudomaculatus ♂ 4/24
African moon-tetra
H: Congo region.
♂: Larger red spot. S: +
B: Unknown. F: C,O
T: 23–27°C, L: 7–8 cm, pH: 7, D: 2–3

Bathyaethiops caudomaculatus 3/92
African moon-tetra
H: Zaïre.

Bathyaethiops caudomaculatus juv 4/26
African moon-tetra

Bathyaethiops greeni 4/26
Green's characin
H: Zaïre.
♂: Pointed dorsal and anal fins. S: +
B: Unknown. F: C
T: 22–28°C, L: 6 cm, pH: <7, D: 2

Bathyaethiops sp. ♂   3/93

H: Zaïre.

Brycinus affinis   4/28

H: E Africa: Tanzania.
♂: Concave anal fin.   S: +,=
B: In flooded areas.   F: C,O
T: 22–28°C, L: 28 cm, pH: 7, D: 2

Brycinus leuciscus   4/30

H: E Nigeria.
♂: Larger and lobed anal fin.   S: =
B: Flooded areas.   F: O
T: 22–27°C, L: 30 cm, pH: 7, D: 3

Brachypetersius pseudonummifer   4/26

H: Upper Zaïre.
♂: More slender.   S: +
B: Unknown.   F: C
T: 20–27°C, L: 8 cm, pH: <7, D: 2–3

Brycinus brevis   4/28
Silver big-scale tetra

H: Gold Coast, Lagos, E Nigeria.
♂: Concave anal fin.   S: +,=
B: In flooded areas.   F: C,O
T: 23–27°C, L: 22.5 cm, pH: 7, D: 2–3

Brycinus macrolepidotus   4/30
True big-scale tetra

H: W Africa.
♂: Concave anal fin.   S: +,–
B: Too large for aquar. breeding.   F: C,O
T: 23–27°C, L: 42 cm, pH: 7, D: 3

CHARACINS

49

Brycinus schoutedeni 4/32
Large-scale brycinus
H: Lower Congo Basin.
♂: Large red spot. S: +,–
B: Unknown. F: C,O
T: 22–27°C, L: ca. 25 cm, pH: 7, D: 3

Bryconaethiops boulengeri 5/18
Boulenger's featherfin characin
H: Zaïre: Congo Basin.
♂: Very elongated dorsal fin. S: +,=
B: Unknown. F: O
T: 22–27°C, L: 25 cm, pH: 7, D: 3

Bryconaethiops macrops 4/32

H: Cameroon, Congo.
♀: Fuller at spawning time. S: +
B: Groupwise among plants? F: O
T: 23–26°C, L: 12 cm, pH: 7, D: 2–3

Bryconaethiops microstoma 2/224
Filament tetra, small-mouthed featherfin .
H: Lower Zaïre.
♂: Colorful, longer dorsal fin? S: +
B: Unknown. F: H,L
T: 24–28°C, L: 15 cm, pH: 7, D: 2

Hemigrammopetersius barnardi ♀ 3/89

H: Tanzania: coastal basin.
♂: Rounded lobelike anal fin. S: +
B: Unknown. F: C,O
T: 24 27°C, L: 6 cm, pH: 7, D: 2

Hemigrammopetersius caudalis 1/218
Yellow-tailed Congo tetra
H: Stanley Pool, Zaïre tributaries.
♂: White-tipped V and A fins. S: +
B: Egg scatterer; <300 eggs. F: C,O
T: 22–26°C, L: 7 cm, pH: 7, D: 3

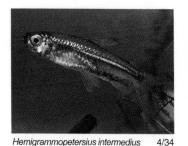

Hemigrammopetersius intermedius   4/34
Short-finned Congo tetra
H: Lake Chad, Niger, Ivory Coast.
♂: Lobed anal fin.   S: +
B: Flooded regions.   F: C,O
T: 22–28°C, L: ca. 8 cm, pH: 7, D: 1–2

Hemigrammopetersius cf. *pulcher*   5/20
H: Zaïre.
♂: Long and convex anal fin.   S: +
B: Unknown.   F: C
T: 22–25°C, L: 4 cm, pH: 7, D: 2–3

CHARACINS

Hemigrammopetersius cf. *pulcher*   5/20

H: SE Nigeria: Kwa Falls.

Hemigrammopetersius septentrionalis   4/34
H: Gambia, Senegal, Cameroon, Guinea.
♂: Convex anal fin.   S: +
B: Eggs sink to the bottom.   F: C,O
T: 23–27°C, L: 6 cm, pH: 7, D: 2–3

Hemigrammopetersius tangensis ♂   4/36
Tanga characin
H: E Africa.
♂: White anal fin.   S: +
B: Eggs sink to the bottom.   F: C,O
T: 23–27°C, L: 5.5 cm, pH: 7, D: 2–3

Hydrocynus goliath   2/226
African tiger fish, wolf tetra
H: Zaïre River.
SD: None.   S: –
B: Impossible in the aquarium.   F: C
T: 23–26°C, L: 40/150 cm aq/nt, pH: 7, D: 4

Hydrocynus vittatus   4/42
Tiger charatin
H: Tropical Africa.
♂: Smaller and slimmer.   S: –
B: Nature: winter months.   F: C,O
T: 22–28°C, L: 65 cm, pH: 7, D: 4

Ladigesia roloffi   1/220
Sierra Leone dwarf charatin
H: Liberia, S. L., Ivory Coast, Gold Coast.
♀: Straight anal fin.   S: =
B: Among spawning fibers.   F: C,O
T: 22–26°C, L: 4 cm, pH: <7, D: 2–3

Lepidarchus adonis signifer ♂   1/220
Adonis charatin
H: W Africa.
♀: Virtually transparent.   S: +
B: Among spawning fibers; <30 e. F:C,O
T: 22–26°C, L: 2 cm, pH: <7, D: 3

Micralestes acutidens   1/222, 4/36
Sharp-toothed tetra
H: Nile, Niger, Zaire, Zambezi, Togo, Ghana.
♂: Slimmer; different anal fin.   S: +
B: Not described.   F: C,O
T: 22–26°C, L: 6.5 cm, pH: 7, D: 2

Micralestes elongatus   4/38

H: W Africa: Atlantic streams.
♂: Broader anal fin.   S: +
B: N.: e scattered among plants.   F: C,O
T: 22–26°C, L: 6 cm, pH: 7, D: 2

Micralestes humilis   2/226, 4/38
African redfin tetra
H: Zambezi, Zaïre, Chad, etc.
♂: Rounded anal fin?   S: +
B: Unknown.   F: C,O
T: 24–28°C, L: 9 cm, pH: <7, D: 2

Micralestes occidentalis   4/40

H: Ivory Coast, Ghana, Liberia, Sierra L.
♂: Round anal fin; pink hue.   S: +
B: Unknown.   F: C,O
T: 22–26°C, L: 8 cm, pH: 7, D: 2–3

Micralestes sp.   (2/226)
African redfin tetra

H: Togo, Ghana, Chad.
♂: Slimmer; longer anal fin.   S: +
B: Unknown.   F: O
T: 23–27°C, L: 12 cm, pH: 7, D: 1

Micralestes stormsi ♀   3/90
True red Congo tetra

H: Zaïre Basin, S Lake Chad.
♂: Red adipose fin and iris.   S: +
B: Unknown; egg scatterer?   F: C,O
T: 22–26°C, L: 7.5 cm, pH: 7, D: 2

Petersius conserialis ♂   3/90

H: Tanzania.   Rare
♂: Convex anal fin.   S: +
B: Unknown.   F: O
T: 22–26°C, L: 14.5 cm, pH: 7, D: 3

Phenacogrammus altus ♂   3/92

H: Zaïre Basin.
♂: More colorful and slimmer.   S: +
B: Unknown; like *P. interruptus*?   F: C,O
T: 24–27°C, L: 6.5 cm, pH: <7, D: 3

Phenacogrammus ansorgii   3/94
Ansorg's blue Congo tetra

H: Gabon, Zaïre, Angola.
♂: Shoulder spot; threadlike D & A.   S: +
B: Rare; as for *P. interruptus*.   F: C,O
T: 24–28°C, L: 7.5 cm, pH: <7, D: 2–3

Phenacogrammus sp. "Congo I" ♂   5/22
Bleher's Congo tetra
H: Zaïre region: "Boma."
♂: Larger dorsal and anal fins.   S: +
B: Egg scatterer; <300 eggs?   F: C,O
T: 22–26°C, L: 6 cm, pH: <7, D: 2–3

Phenacogrammus deheyni   4/40
Deheyn's Congo tetra
H: Central Congo.
♂: More colorful; larger fins.   S: +
B: Like *P. interruptus*?   F: C,O
T: 24–27°C, L: 7 cm, pH: 7, D: 2–3

Phenacogrammus huloti   5/22
Black-banded Congo tetra
H: Zaïre, NW Gabon.
♂: Pointed dorsal and anal fins.   S: +
B: Egg scatterer; <300 eggs?   F: C,O
T: 22–25°C, L: 6–7 cm, pH: <7, D: 2

Phenacogrammus interruptus   1/222
Congo tetra
H: Zaïre region.
♂: Larger fins; more colorful.   S: +
B: Egg scatterer; <300 eggs.   F: C,O
T: 24–27°C, L: 8.5 cm, pH: <7, D: 2–3

Phenacogrammus "Congo II" ♂   5/24
Lime Congo tetra
H: Zaïre.
♂: Longer dorsal and anal fins.   S: +
B: Egg scatterer; <300 eggs?   F: O
T: 23–26°C, L: 6 cm, pH: <7, D: 3

Phenacogrammus "Congo II" ♀   5/24
Lime Congo tetra

Family Citharinidae

The Citharinidae are a diverse family. It contains both deep-bodied herbivores and aufwuchs-feeders (subfamily Distichodinae) as well as slender, elongated predators with a movable lower mandible (subfamily Ichthyoborinae). A total of 20 genera and about 98 species are recognized within this family.

There is a gamut of sizes. Some species grow too large for normal home aquaria, requiring large public or show aquaria; some are moderate-sized; and others are so small that they require a species aquarium to prevent constant harassment from stouter tankmates.

The aquarium's decor should follow "normal" parameters for mid-water inhabitants, taking into account the herbivorous tendencies of some species. Since it foments algae growth, intense illumination is beneficial for aufwuchs-feeders.

Offer predators subdued illumination and numerous hideouts among plants, roots, and rocks.

Breeding citharins has met with sporadic success. They have been observed scattering their eggs among fine-leaved plants. The spawns of some species are extremely susceptible to microbial attack. When transferring the breeders, ensure that the water of the recipient container is very similar to he origin.

Nannocharax species are very similar to the bottom-oriented South American subfamily Characidiinae. The obvious ties between these two characin groups is one of the key pieces of evidence used to date the origin of characins to the time of initial continental drift (see introduction of the group).

Belonophago tinanti   2/228
Needle fin-eater
H: Lower Congo.
SD: Not described.   S: –
B: Unknown.   F: C!
T: 24–26°C, L: 20 cm, pH: <7, D: 4

Citharinus citharus   3/96

H: Senegal to Nile Basin.
SD: Unknown.   S: –
B: Unknown; too large.   F: O
T: 22–28°C, L: 50 cm, pH: 7, D: 3

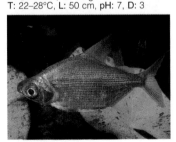

Citharinus congicus   4/43
Congo citharin
H: Zaïre Basin, Tanzania.
SD: None.   S: +,=
B: Swamps during rainy season. F: H,O
T: 22–26°C, L: >43 cm, pH: 7, D: 4

CHARACINS

Distichodus affinis   1/226
Red-finned distichodus
H: Lower Zaïre.
SD: Unknown.   S: +
B: Egg scatterer.   F: H,L
T: 23–27°C, L: 21 cm, pH: 7, D: 3

Distichodus decemmaculatus   1/224
Dwarf distichodus
H: Central Zaïre Basin.
SD: Unknown.   S: +
B: Unsuccessful.   F: H
T: 23–27°C, L: 7.5 cm, pH: 7, D: 2

Distichodus fasciolatus   1/224
Shark-tailed distichodus
H: Zaïre: Katanga. Cameroon, Angola.
SD: Unknown.   S: =
B: Unknown.   F: H
T: 23–27°C, L: 60 cm, pH: 7, D: 3

Distichodus lusosso   1/226
Long-nosed distichodus
H: Zaïre Basin, Angola, Cameroon.
SD: Unknown.   S: +
B: Unknown; too large.   F: H
T: 22–26°C, L: 40 cm, pH: 7, D: 3

Distichodus notospilus   2/228
Lead distichodus
H: S Cameroon to Angola.
SD: Unknown.   S: =
B: Unsuccessful.   F: H,O
T: 23–27°C, L: 15 cm, pH: 7, D: 3

Distichodus rostratus   4/45

H: W and N Africa.
SD: Unknown.   S: =
B: Swamps during rainy season. F: H,O
T: 22–28°C, L: 75–80 cm, pH: 7, D: 4

CHARACINS

CHARACINS

Distichodus sexfasciatus　　1/228
Six-barred distichodus

H: Zaïre Basin, Angola.
SD: Unknown.　　　　　　　　　　S: =
B: Nature: egg scatterer.　　　　　　F: H
T: 22–26°C, L: 1 m (nat.), pH: 7, D: 4

Eugnathichthys macroterolepis　　5/32
Checkerboard African darter tetra

H: Zaïre Basin.
SD: Unknown.　　　　　　　　　　S: –
B: Unknown.　　　　　　　　　　　F: C
T: 23–27°C, L: 15 cm, pH: 7, D: 3–4

Hemigrammocharax sp. aff. *lineostriatus*
5/26

H: Angola.
♂: Somwhat more slender.　　　　　S: +
B: Territorial.　　　　　　　　　　F: C
T: 22–26°C, L: 3.5 cm, pH: 7, D: 2

Hemigrammocharax multifasciatus　　5/26
Checkerboard African darter tetra

H: Upper Zambezi, N Zaïre Basin, Gabon.
♀: Fuller during spawning season.　S: (–)
B: Not described.　　　　　　　　　F: C,O
T: 22–26°C, L: 6 cm, pH: 7, D: 2

Ichthyborus monodi　　4/57

H: S Nigeria, W Cameroon.
♀: Larger; rounder ventral region.　S: –
B: Unknown.　　　　　　　　　　　F: C!
T: 24–27°C, L: 20 cm, pH: 7, D: 3–4

Ichthyborus ornatus　　3/99
Ornate fin-nipper

H: Zaïre Basin.
SD: Unknown.　　　　　　　　　　S: –
B: Unknown.　　　　　　　　　　　F: C!
T: 22–26°C, L: 20 cm, pH: <7, D: 4

57

Ichthyborus quadrilineatus 4/58
Four-line fin-nipper
H: From Gambia to Guinea-Bissau.
SD: Unknown. S: –
B: Unknown. F: C?
T: 22–27°C, L: 12 cm, pH: 7, D: 3–4

Nannaethiops unitaeniatus ♀ 1/228
One-striped African characin
H: Zaïre to Niger; the White Nile.
♂: Slimmer; more colorful. S: +,–
B: Egg scatterer. F: C
T: 23–26°C, L: 6.5 cm, pH: 7, D: 2–3

Nannaethiops unitaeniatus ♂ 3/96
One-striped African characin

Nannocharax ansorgei ♂ 5/28
Ansorge's African darter
H: Gam.,Sen.,Niger,Volta R.,Chad,Sierra L.
♂: Slightly larger and brighter. S: +
B: In pairs or more ♀♀. F: C
T: 22–26°C, L: 4.5 cm, pH: 7, D: 2

Nannocharax brevis 4/46
Small African darter
H: Central Zaïre Basin.
♀: Fuller during spawning season. S: =
B: Not described. F: C,O
T: 23–27°C, L: 4.5 cm, pH: 7, D: 2–3

Nannocharax fasciatus 1/230
Striped African darter
H: Cameroon, Volta, Niger, Gabon, Guinea.
SD: Not described. S: +
B: Unsuccessful? F: C
T: 23–27°C, L: 7–8 cm, pH: 7, D: 3

CHARACINS

Nannocharax latifasciatus t.♂, b.♀ 4/46
African broad-band darter   5/29

H: S Nigeria on border with Cameroon.
♂: Slightly slimmer.   S: +
B: Peat fibers.   F: C,O
T: 23–26°C, L: 5 cm, pH: 7, D: 2–3

Nannocharax macropterus   4/48

H: Zaïre Basin.
♂: Smaller, slimmer, more colorful. S: +
B: Unsuccessful.   F: C
T: 24–28°C, L: 6 cm, pH: <7, D: 2–3

Nannocharax occidentalis   4/48

H: Central and lower Niger.
♂: Slimmer; pale brown D,A,C fins. S: +
B: Unknown.   F: C
T: 22–27°C, L: <7.5 cm, pH: 7, D: 2–3

Nannocharax parvus   (5/29), 2/230
African broad-band darter   t.♂, b.♀

H: Niger to Ogove.
♂: Slimmer.   S: +
B: Unknown.   F: H,O
T: 22–26°C, L: 5 cm, pH: 7, D: 1–2

Nannocharax parvus   (5/29), 2/230
African broad-band darter

Nannocharax procatopus   5/30
Backgammon African darter

H: Central Zaïre Basin: Stanley Falls.
♀: Fuller during spawning season. S: (–)
B: Unknown.   F: C,L
T: 20–24°C, L: 8 cm, pH: >7, D: 2–3

CHARACINS

Nannocharax sp. cf. *fasciatus* 5/30
Seybold's African darter tetra
H: Liberia: St. Paul and Cess rivers.
♀: Fuller during spawning season. **S:** +
B: Unknown. **F:** C,L
T: 22–26°C, **L:** 7 cm, **pH:** 7, **D:** 2

Neolebias ansorgii b.♂, t.♀ 1/230
Ansorge's neolebias
H: Cameroon, Angola, central Africa.
♂: More colorful (see photo). **S:** (–)
B: Peat fibers, Java moss; <300 e. **F:** C,O
T: 24–28°C, **L:** 3.5 cm, **pH:** <7, **D:** 2–3

Neolebias ansorgii red morph 3/98
Red Ansorge's neolebias ♀ top
H: Cameroon, Angola, central Africa.
♂: Darker. **S:** (–)
B: Not easy; peat fibers. **F:** C,O
T: 24–28°C, **L:** 3.5 cm, **pH:** <7, **D:** 2–3

Neolebias axelrodi ♂ 4/50
Axelrod's neolebias
H: S Nigeria, SE Benin.
♂: More colorful; red anal fin. **S:** +
B: Peat fibers or Java moss; 60 e. **F:** C
T: 22–26°C, **L:** <3 cm, **pH:** <7, **D:** 3

Neolebias axelrodi ♀ 4/50
Axelrod's neolebias

Neolebias kerguennae 4/50

H: W Gabon.
♂: Brighter, smaller, slimmer. **S:** (–)
B: Rare; peat fibers, Java moss. **F:** C,O
T: 24–28°C, **L:** <3 cm, **pH:** 7, **D:** 3

Neolebias powelli 1 spot   4/52
Domino neolebias
H: Niger Delta; S Nigeria.
♂: Somewhat redder.   S: (–)
B: Difficult; peat fib., Java moss. F: C,O
T: 23–26°C, L: <3 cm, pH: <7, D: 3

Neolebias powelli 2 spots   4/52
Domino neolebias

Neolebias powelli 3 spots   4/52
Domino neolebias

Neolebias trewavasae ♂   4/54
Trewavas' neolebias
H: Zaïre Basin. Nile?
♂: Smaller, slimmer, darker.   S: +
B: Peat fibers or Java moss.   F: C,O
T: 24–28°C, L: 5 cm, pH: <7, D: 3

Neolebias trewavasae ♀   4/54
Trewavas' neolebias

Neolebias trilineatus   2/230
Three-lined neolebias
H: Zaïre Basin.
♂: Reddish fins.   S: +
B: Fine-leaved plants; <250 e.   F: C,O
T: 23–26°C, L: 5 cm, pH: 7, D: 2

61

CHARACINS

Neolebias unifasciatus 4/54
One-banded neolebias
H: W Africa.
♂: Brick red when sexually active. **S:** =
B: Peat fibers or Java moss. **F:** C,O
T: 24–28°C, L: 5 cm, pH: <7, D: 2–3

Paraphago rostratus 2/232
Striped fin-eater
H: Congo Basin.
SD: Unknown. **S:** –
B: Unsuccessful. **F:** C!
T: 23–26°C, L: 18 cm, pH: <7, D: 4

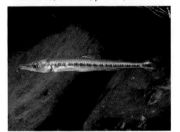

Phago loricatus 4/58

H: Nigeria: Niger Delta.
SD: Unknown. **S:** –
B: Not described. **F:** C
T: 22–27°C, L: 12 cm, pH: 7, D: 3–4

Phago maculatus 1/232
Spotted fin-eater
H: W Africa: Niger Delta.
SD: Unknown. **S:** –
B: Unsuccessful. **F:** C!
T: 23–28°C, L: 14 cm, pH: 7, D: 3–4

Family Hepsetidae

This is a monotypic family. Although the African pike characin is a predator, it can still be associated with conspecifics and equal-sized heterospecifics. Its size and custom of "ambushing" sinking foods with great bursts of speed make a generously proportioned aquarium a necessity.

Maintenance should be reserved for specialists who are willing to offer feeder fishes on occasion.

Hepsetus odoe 2/233
African pike characin
H: Tropical Africa except Nile Basin.
SD: Unknown. **S:** –
B: N.: free bubble nest; brood care. **F:** C!
T: 26–28°C, L: 70 cm, pH: 7, D: 4

Hyphessobrycon loretoensis, H. metae, or *H. peruvianus?* The pictured fish bears great similarity to the aforementioned species (see pp. 112 and 113). In contrast, the superior part of its eye is intensely red. It was captured in the creeks of the upper Rio Napo Basin, Ecuador.

Brachychalcinus sp. aff. *orbicularis* (p. 96). Following several generations of selection, the red coloration of the fins is retained by most subadults and some adults. In nature, only juvenile specimens have red fins (original stock captured in the upper Rio Napo Basin, Ecuador).

The Biotope

The primary area of distribution of characins in the world is inarguably the Amazon Basin, which superficially presents itself as a defined system of rivers and lagoons. The hydrographic reality, however, is different. With the cyclic alternation of rainy and dry seasons, extensive areas of the basin are subjected to extreme fluctuations in water level, some up to 12 meters! Even the slight variations of "just" 2 m which occur on the western fringe of the basin (at 200 m elevation, yet still a linear distance of 2800 km from the Atlantic Ocean) decisively influence the aquatic fauna. During the rainy season, lagoons with relatively defined shores turn into large, undefined flood plains, inundating several square kilometers of rain forest. The same bodies of water shrink to just a few hectares at the peak of the dry season.

These ecological changes are of clear consequence to the fishes. During the rainy season, there is an excess of food and living space—a time of plenitude for herbivores and limnivores. Predators, in contrast, are presented with a cornucopia of food during the dry season, when the population density increases exorbitantly. Along the shores, one pound *Hoplias malabaricus* lurk, waiting for their prey. Not uncommonly they leap into dugout canoes at night when startled by a spotlight. Similar occurrences on the open lagoon waters can be experienced with various members of the Prochilodontidae, such is the fish density during this season.

The water quality changes concurrently. As the water recedes, the oxygen-depleted waters of the flood plains drain into the lagoons and then into the rivers. In the lagoons during this time only a thin surface film contains higher oxygen concentrations due to wind and some wave action. *Colossoma* spp. have certain adaptations which allow them to survive such inhospitable environs. Under oxygen-deficient situations, their lower lip swells, turning into a kind of scoop. This temporary anatomical modification allows the fish to "inhale" the surface layer more efficiently. Other characins utilize atmospheric oxygen with their modified swimbladder (e.g., Erythrinidae).

The riverine biotopes can basically be divided into white (clear) and black water rivers. The following table summarizes their characteristics. For aquarium care, especially breeding, the differences in pH and mineral concentration (hardness, conductivity) are of particular interest.

	White/Clear Water	Black Water
Example	Amazon, Napo, Ucayali	Rio Negro
Origin	young mountains	weathered mountain ranges
Color	gray turbid or greenish	tea-colored/transparent
pH	around neutral	acid to very acid
Hardness	soft	very soft to immeasurable
Nutrients	much suspended matter	little suspended matter
Biology	rich in bacteria	slightly antiseptic

t.l.: Floodwaters. Large amounts of precipitation keep the rivers swollen. The lagoons cannot drain, and several square kilometers of their surroundings become inundated. Herbivores have an unlimited supply of food and the overall fish density is very low.

t.r.: The dry season has begun, and the rivers are once again contained within their banks. Because rainfall has diminished appreciably, the flooded forests fall dry and the lagoons shrink. The fish density in the lagoons rises to amazing levels; predators are literally swimming in food. Water remnants are virtually devoid of oxygen due to the returning "forest water" and the large quantity of decaying organic matter contained therein. Fishes unwary enough to become trapped in such waters soon perish.

b.: The last open water has disappeared and terrestrial plants are now growing on the moist bottom. With the next rainy season everything will be flooded once again and the cycle repeats (Vol. 5, p. 686).

Family Anostomidae

Most Anostomidae are small schooling fishes. Despite their amiable nature in front of heterospecifics, they are often hostile towards conspecifics. Juveniles are typically very attractive, progressively becoming green/brown with age. Headstanders are especially interesting aquarium charges. Due to their size and active lifestyle, *Leporinus* and some of the other genera require large aquaria. Plastic plants are the only "vegetation" respected by these herbivores and limnivores.

Abramites hypselonotus   1/233
High-backed headstander
H: Amazon and Orinoco basins.
SD: Unknown.   S: =
B: Unsuccessful (?).   F: L,H
T: 23–27°C, L: 13 cm, pH: 7, D: 2–3

Abramites solarii   3/100

H: Rio Paraguay Basin.
SD: Unknown.   S: =
B: Unknown.   F: L,H
T: 22–25°C, L: 12 cm, pH: 7, D: 3

Anostomus anostomus   1/234
Striped anostomus, striped headstander
H: Colombia, Venezuela, Guyana, Brazil.
SD: Unknown.   S: +
B: With pituitary hormones.   F: L
T: 22–28°C, L: 18 cm, pH: <7, D: 2–3

Pseudanos gracilis   2/234
Four-spotted headstander
H: Brazil.
SD: None.   S: +
B: Unsuccessful.   F: C,O
T: 24–26°C, L: 14 cm, pH: <7, D: 3

Anostomus plicatus   3/100
Odd-lip anostomus
H: Guyana, Suriname.
SD: Unknown.   S: +
B: Unsuccessful.   F: H,O
T: 24–28°C, L: 15 cm, pH: <7, D: 2–3

CHARACINS

Anostomus spiloclistron 3/102
False three-spotted anostomus
H: Guyana, Suriname.
SD: Unknown.   S: +
B: Unknown.   F: H,O
T: 24–28°C, L: 16 cm, pH: <7, D: 3

Anostomus taeniatus t. day, b. night 1/234
Lisa
H: Central Amazon, Rio Negro.
SD: Unknown.   S: +
B: Unknown.   F: L,O
T: 24–26°C, L: 20 cm, pH: <7, D: 3

Anostomus ternetzi 1/236
Ternetz's anostomus
H: Brazil.
SD: Unknown.   S: +
B: Unknown.   F: L
T: 24–28°C, L: 16 cm, pH: <7, D: 2–3

Leporellus vittatus 2/234
Leporellus
H: Amazon, Orinoco, Paraná.
♀: Fuller through ventrum.   S: +
B: Unknown.   F: L,H
T: 22–25°C, L: 12 cm, pH: <7, D: 2–3

Leporellus vittatus 2/234
Leporellus

Leporinus affinis 1/238
Many-banded leporinus
H: Col., Venezuela, Brazil, Peru, Paraguay.
SD: Unknown.   S: =
B: Unsuccessful.   F: H
T: 23–27°C, L: 25 cm, pH: <7, D: 3

67

CHARACINS

Leporinus desmotes 2/236
Black and yellow leporinus, trunk leporinus
H: Guyana, Amazon Basin.
SD: None. S: +
B: Unknown. F: L,H
T: 22–26°C, L: 18 cm, pH: 7, D: 2–3

Leporinus fasciatus fasciatus 1/238
Black-banded leporinus
H: Venezuela, Amazon tributaries.
SD: Unknown. S: =
B: Unsuccessful. F: H
T: 22–26°C, L: 30 cm, pH: <7, D: 3

Leporinus friderici 2/238
Frideric's leporinus
H: Amazon, Guyana.
♂: V and P fins red when spawning. S: =
B: Too large? F: H,O
T: 23–26°C, L: 50 cm, pH: <7, D: 2–4

Leporinus granti 3/102
Grant's leporinus
H: Guianas, Amazon Basin.
SD: None. S: +
B: Unsuccessful. F: H
T: 22–26°C, L: 20 cm, pH: <7, D: 2

Leporinus cf. *jamesi* 4/60
James' leporinus, faded leporinus
H: Brazil: Amazon region.
SD: None. S: =
B: Too large (?). F: H,O
T: 22°C, L: 30 cm, pH: 7, D: 3–4

Leporinus lacustris 3/104
Lake leporinus
H: Brazil, Paraguay.
SD: None. S: +
B: Unsuccessful. F: H,O
T: 22–27°C, L: 20 cm, pH: 7, D: 2

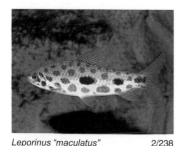

Leporinus "maculatus" 2/238
Spotted leporinus
H: Guianas, Amazon Basin.
♂: Slimmer and slightly smaller. S: +
B: Coincidental; among plants. F: H,O
T: 22–26°C, L: 18 cm, pH: <7, D: 2

Leporinus megalepis 3/104
Large-scaled leporinus
H: Guyana, Amazon Basin.
SD: None. S: +
B: Unknown. F: H,O
T: 22–27°C, L: 30 cm, pH: <7, D: 3

Leporinus moralesi 4/60
Mulberry leporinus
H: Venezuela, Brazil, Peru.
♀: Fuller at spawning time. S: +
B: In flooded areas. F: O,H
T: 22–26°C, L: 30 cm, pH: 7, D: 3–4

Leporinus nigrotaeniatus juv. 1/240
Black-lined leporinus
H: Guyana, Brazil.
SD: None. S: +
B: Unknown. F: H
T: 23–26°C, L: 40 cm, pH: 7, D: 4

Leporinus nigrotaeniatus adult 3/106
Black-lined leporinus

Leporinus octofasciatus 2/240
Red-finned or eight-banded leporinus
H: Brazil.
SD: None. S: =
B: Unknown. F: H
T: 23–26°C, L: 22 cm, pH: <7, D: 3

CHARACINS

Leporinus pellegrini   2/240
Pellegrin's leporinus, belted leporinus
H: Guianas, upper Amazon.
SD: Unknown.   S: +
B: Unsuccessful.   F: H,O
T: 25–26°C, L: 12 cm, pH: <7, D: 2

Leporinus steyermarki   3/106
Gray leporinus
H: Venezuela? Paraguay.
SD: None.   S: +
B: Unsuccessful.   F: H,O
T: 22–26°C, L: 30 cm, pH: <7, D: 3

Leporinus striatus L. arcus below   1/240
Striped leporinus
H: Col., Ven, Ecuador, Bolivia, Paraguay.
SD: Unknown.   S: +
B: Unknown.   F: H
T: 22–26°C, L: 25 cm, pH: <7, D: 3

Leporinus wolfei   4/62
Wolf's leporinus
H: Peru: Amazon Basin.
SD: Unknown.   S: +
B: Unsuccessful.   F: H,C
T: 23–28°C, L: <30 cm, pH: 7, D: 2–4

Pseudanos trimaculatus   1/236
Three-spot headstander
H: Brazil, Guyana.
SD: Unknown.   S: +
B: Unknown.   F: L,O
T: 23–27°C, L: 12 cm, pH: 7, D: 3

Schizodon fasciatus   2/242
Banded schizodon
H: Amazon Basin.
SD: Unknown.   S: =
B: Unsuccessful (due to size).   F: H
T: 22–28°C, L: 40 cm, pH: <7, D: 4

CHARACINS

Subfamily	Origin	Behavior	Diet	Reproduction	Remarks
Aphyocharacinae	SA	peaceful schooling fishes	C,O	egg scatterers; peat extract required	Spawn predator.
Bryconinae	SA	peaceful, later bellicose	C,O	egg scatterers; on flooded grasses	Schooling fishes for large aquaria.
Characidiinae	SA	bottom-oriented	C,O	little known; egg scatterers	All species are very similar.
Characinae	SA	predatory inclination	C,O	egg scatterers	Dog characins are inapt for aquaria.
Cheirodontinae	SA	peaceful schooling fishes	C,O	little success	Many small and delicate species.
Crenuchinae	SA	peaceful, but slightly territorial	C	cave-spawners w/ brood care (♂)	Live foods are required for extended care.
Glandulocaudinae	SA	peaceful schooling fishes	C,O	eggs on broad leaves; very small larvae	♀ stores sperm for weeks, ♂ has gland on caudal peduncle.
Iguanodectinae	SA	schooling fishes	C,O	egg scatterers	*Piabucus dentatus* perhaps a Tetragonopterinae.
Paragoniatinae	(CA),SA	peaceful schooling fishes	C,O	often difficult, egg scatterers	*X. bondi* similar to glass catfish.
Rhaphiodontinae	SA	very predatory	C	egg scatterers	Teeth several centimeters long.
Rhoadsiinae	CA,SA	territorial	C,O	egg scatterers; care	Coloration acquired with age.
Serrasalminae	SA	schooling fishes	C,O,H	egg scatterers; some need hormone treatment	Carnivorous piranhas and peacefulherbivores.
Stethaprioninae	SA	schooling fishes	C,O	eggs laid among fine-leaved plants	Non-herbivorous "substitute silver dollars."
Tetragonopterinae	CA,SA	schooling fishes	C,O	condition with live food, among fine-leaved plants	See p. 74.

CHARACINS

Subfamily Aphyocharacinae

Hardy and long-lived, Aphyocharacinae are modest-sized fishes of the upper and middle water column. Water chemistry is of secondary importance. Even for breeding, their demands on water chemistry are not particularly stringent. However, soft, slightly acid water is preferred.

The gametes are expelled close to the water surface. Frequently, the parents devour the eggs before they have sunk to the bottom. Shallow water (about 15 cm) and a spawning grid in the breeding aquarium greatly improve yields.

Subfamily Bryconinae

On average, these large, silver fishes hold little appeal for hobbyists. With the exception of the endangered Patagonian characin (p. 77) which excavates a spawning pit in the gravel substrate, all the Bryconinae are egg scatterers. In nature, they spawn among inundated grasses.

Subfamily Characidiinae

This subfamily contains small, modestly attractive, elongated, bottom-oriented species. Little is known about their reproductive biology, but they have been repeatedly bred in densely planted aquaria.

Subfamily Characinae

Numerous species within this subfamily are predators, e.g., the large dog characins (p. 81), which are not recommended for aquaria; *Exodon paradoxus* (p. 82), an attractive, but belligerent gem; and small glass headstanders. The relatively small stature of the glass headstanders facilitates the choice of tankmates. All species are egg scatterers.

Subfamily Cheirodontinae

With the exception of a few very small species, Cheirodontinae are good candidates for community aquaria. The delicate nature of the tiny species calls for a species aquarium. Most species have not been bred in the aquarium.

Subfamily Crenuchinae

Unique among the characins, Crenuchinae spawn in caves or similar secluded areas and the male practices brood care. The number of eggs is quite modest. Unfortunately, long-term aquarium care is contingent upon a diet of live foods.

Subfamily Glandulocaudiinae

The reproductive biology diverges from the "norm:" subsequent to internal fertilization, the female deposits the eggs on the underside of a broad leaf or among fine-leaved plants. Since the female is able to store the sperm, the male is superfluous during oviposition.

With the exception of the tiny *Tyttocharax atopodus* (p. 88), all species are suitable for the community aquarium.

Subfamily Iguanodectinae
Plain, elongated species constitute this small subfamily. So far, they have not become widely distributed in the hobby.

Subfamily Paragoniatinae
All of these fishes require swimming space. When they are maintained in a school, their timidness diminishes. They are undemanding omnivores. Given their flexibility in regard to water chemistry, size is the only criterium that must be taken into consideration when choosing tankmates.

Success in breeding is highly species-specific, but the methodology is "typical" of that of characins.

Subfamily Rhaphiodontinae
These predators have teeth which are several centimeters long. Even unsuspecting aquarists are not exempt from their dangerous bites. Aquarium maintenance is strongly discouraged.

Subfamily Serrasalminae
This subfamily—frequently given the rank of family—contains both the herbivorous silver dollars as well as the infamous and feared carnivorous piranhas. All are medium- or large-sized schooling fishes that require generously dimensioned aquaria.

Herbivores are absolutely peaceful; however, plants must be waived from the decor.

The maintenance of piranhas is greatly simplified if the time and effort is invested to train them to pelleted foods. When well-fed, aggressions are dampened, but caution must always be observed during handling! Be prepared to sacrifice any cloth or plastic nets used.

To date, all species successfully bred in the aquarium have been egg scatterers. Fine-leaved aquatic vegetation or hanging roots of floating plants are used as spawning substrates. Large migratory species have only been bred in captivity with hormone injections.

Before the invention of synthetic hormones, pituitary extract was the only option. Pituitary glands—usually from common carp or ripe, wild-caught specimens of the corresponding species—are collected, treated with acetone, ground, and then mixed with saline solution and injected. Not all hormones work equally well with all species. Likewise, the number and volume of the doses varies, depending on the hormone as well as the fish species and gender of the recipient. Since the treatment merely induces the release of eggs, success is contingent on the ripeness of the fish. Artificial reproduction is chiefly used in aquaculture to breed food fishes. Neither of the giant pacus, *Colossoma macropomum* (p. 92) or *C. brachypomus* (p. 92) have ever been bred in captivity without such hormone treatments (ESTEVEZ, 1990).

Subfamily Stethaprioninae
Most community aquaria are apt environments for the members of this small subfamily of deep-bodied characins. Although plain in color, they have an

CHARACINS

appealing discoid shape and are significantly more respectful of plants than silver dollars. Juvenile *Brachychalcinus* sp. aff. *orbicularis* (p. 63) have bright red unpaired fins, but the coloration is rarely retained into adulthood.

Subfamily Tetragonopterinae

This species-rich subfamily contains the "typical characins" of the aquarium hobby. Small- to medium-sized, the great majority of these schooling fishes are suitable additions for the community aquarium.

For most, breeding is contingent upon a varied diet of live foods. Flake foods are inadequate to bring the large majority of species into spawning condition. Soft, slightly acid water is always favorable. Some species require extreme values, lest their eggs fungus.

With few exceptions (see below), the Tetragonopterinae are egg scatterers. Oviposition occurs in the morning hours, and the breeders should be transferred soon after. To a certain degree, all will hunt their eggs from among the fine-leaved vegetation. This regrettable tendency may be circumvented or curtailed by using a spawning grid, densely planting the aquarium, or feeding a good diet.

Oddities of this subfamily include the ability of female *Creacrutus beni* and *C. brevipinnis* (p. 103) to store sperm, the intolerance of light by the eggs of species such as the neon and cardinal tetras (pp. 121, 122), the paternal family of *Nematocharax venustus* (p. 121), and the fact that *Pseudochalceus kyburzi* (p. 123) is an adhesive spawner which practices brood care.

Aphyocharax alburnus   1/242
False flame-tail tetra
H: S Brazil, Paraguay, Argentina.
SD: Unknown.   S: +
B: Egg scatterer; plants; <500 e. F: O,C
T: 22–28°C, L: 7 cm, pH: <7, D: 1–2

Aphyocharax anisitsi   1/242
Bloodfin, Argentine bloodfin
H: Argentina.
♂: Tiny hooklets on anal fin.   S: +
B: Egg scatterer; plants; <500 e. F: O,C
T: 18–28°C, L: 5 cm, pH: 7, D: 1

Aphyocharax dentatus ♂   2/243
False bloodfin
H: Colombia, Brazil, Paraguay.
♂: Hook-shaped anal fin.   S: =
B: Schooling egg scatterer.   F: C,O
T: 15–22°C, L: 12 cm, pH: 7, D: 2

Aphyocharax erythrurus 4/80
Flame-tail tetra
H: Venezuela.
♀: Somwhat larger and fuller. S: +
B: Egg scatterer; <500 e. F: C,O
T: 22–26°C, L: 7 cm, pH: <7, D: 2

Aphyocharax paraguayensis 1/284,2/244
White-spot tetra
H: Rio Paraguay Basin.
♂: Slimmer. S: +
B: Eggs scattered on plants. F: O
T: 22–27°C, L: 4 cm, pH: <7, D: 1–2

Aphyocharax rathbuni t.♂, b.♀ 2/244
Rathbun's bloodfin
H: Rio Paraguay.
♂: White-tipped fins. S: +
B: Eggs scattered among plants. F: C,O
T: 20–26°C, L: 5 cm, pH: <7, D: 2

Aphyocharax cf. *rathbuni* b.♂, t.♀ 5/34
possibly *Aphyocharax avary*
H: Rio Paraguay.
♂: White-tipped fins. S: +
B: Eggs scattered among plants. F: C,O
T: 18–24°C, L: 4.5 cm, pH: 7, D: 1–2

Aphyocharax sp. aff. *rathbuni* 5/34
Rathbun's bloodfin
See the photo on p. 5/38.

Brycon cephalus 3/108
South American trout
H: Amazon Basin.
SD: Indiscernible. S: +,–
B: Unknown. F: C,O
T: 22–26°C, L: 22 cm, pH: 7, D: 3

75

CHARACINS

Brycon falcatus 1/244

H: Guianas, Brazil.
SD: Unknown. S: +,–
B: Not attempted? F: C,O
T: 18–25°C, L: 25 cm, pH: <7, D: 3

Brycon melanopterus 2/246
Sickle-band brycon

H: Amazon Basin; broadly distributed.
SD: Unknown. S: +,–
B: Not described. F: C,O
T: 22–26°C, L: >18 cm, pH: <7, D: 2–3

Brycon cf. *rubricauda* 5/35
Redfin brycon

H: Brazil; primarily white water.
SD: Unknown. S: –
B: In flooded areas. F: C,O
T: 20–28°C, L: 30 cm, pH: <7, D: 4

Bryconops affinis 2/246

H: E Brazil.
SD: Unknown. S: +,–
B: Eggs scattered among plants. F: C,O
T: 22–28°C, L: 12 cm, pH: <7, D: 3

Chalceus erythrurus 3/108
Yellow-finned chalceus

H: Amazon Basin.
SD: None. S: =
B: Unknown. F: C,O
T: 22–26°C, L: 25 cm, pH: 7, D: 3

Chalceus macrolepidotus 1/244
Pink-tailed chalceus

H: Guianas, Amazon.
SD: Unknown. S: –
B: Unsuccessful. F: C
T: 23–28°C, L: 25 cm, pH: 7, D: 4

CHARACINS

Gymnocharacinus bergi ♂ 3/110
Patagonian characin
H: Argentina: N Patagonia. E
♂: Smaller; white-fringed C fin. S: +
B: In gravel. F: O
T: 18–22°C, L: 6 cm, pH: <7, D: 3

Gymnocharacinus bergi ♀ 3/110
Patagonian characin
Critically endangered species! There are only an estimated 250 specimens left on the wild!

Salminus maxillosus 5/36
Trout characin
H: La Plata Basin. Amazon?
SD: Unknown. S: –
B: Unknown. F: C
T: 20–26°C, L: >60 cm, pH: 7, D: 4

Triportheus albus 2/248
Yellow-finned hatchetfish
H: Brazil.
SD: Difficult to recognize. S: =
B: Eggs scattered among plants. F: C,O
T: 22–28°C, L: 11 cm, pH: <7, D: 3–4

Triportheus angulatus 1/244
Dusky narrow hatchetfish
H: Amazon Basin.
SD: Unknown. S: =
B: Unknown. F: C
T: 22–28°C, L: >10 cm, pH: 7, D: 2

Triportheus pictus 2/248
Colored hatchetfish
H: Amazon Basin.
♂: More elongated and slimmer. S: =
B: Unsuccessful. F: O
T: 22–28°C, L: 16 cm, pH: <7, D: 2–3

CHARACINS

Triportheus rotundatus   2/250
Black-winged hatchetfish
H: Guianas, Venezuela.
♀: Ventrally fuller.   S: +
B: Not described.   F: C,O
T: 24–27°C, L: 15 cm, pH: 7, D: 2

Ammocryptocharax elegans   4/116
H: Brazil.
SD: None.   S: –
B: Unknown.   F: C
T: 23–27°C, L: 7 cm, pH: ≪7, D: 3–4

Ammocryptocharax cf. *minutus*   4/118
H: Upper Orinoco and Rio Negro.
SD: Unknown.   S: +
B: Unknown.   F: C,O
T: 23–26°C, L: 5 cm, pH: ≪7, D: 3

Ammocryptocharax vintonae   4/116
H: Guyana: Membaru River.
♀: Fuller at spawning time.   S: +
B: Unknown.   F: C
T: 23–27°C, L: 4 cm, pH: <7, D: 2–3

Characidium brevirostre   4/118
Blunthead characidium
H: Colombia, Peru.
♂: Larger dorsal fin.   S: +
B: No breeding reports.   F: C,O
T: 22–26°C, L: 5.5 cm, pH: <7, D: 2

Characidium fasciatum   1/314
Banded characidium
H: Ubiquitous South America.
♂: Base of dorsal fin dotted.   S: +
B: Egg scatterer.   F: C
T: 18–24°C, L: 8–10 cm, pH: <7, D: 2

Characidium sp. aff. *fasciatum* 2/295
Rio Negro darter tetra
H: Brazil: Rio Negro.
SD: Not described. S: +
B: Egg scatterer. F: C,O
T: 22–24°C, L: 8–10 cm, pH: <7, D: 2

Characidium sp. aff. *fasciatum* 2/295
Peru darter tetra
H: Peru.

Characidium rachovii ♂ 1/314
Rachow's darter tetra
H: S Brazil.
♂: Dotted dorsal fin. S: +
B: Egg scatterer? F: C,O
T: 20–24°C, L: 7 cm, pH: <7, D: 2

Characidium sp. 4/120
C. purpuratum group
H: Brazil: São Paulo (Itanhaèm).
♀: Somewhat fuller. S: +
B: Unsuccessful. F: C,O
T: 20–25°C, L: 10 cm, pH: 7, D: 2–3

Characidium sp. 4/120
C. purpuratum group
H: Brazil: São Paulo (Cuiaba).

Characidium sp. ♂ 4/122
C. purpuratum group
H: Brazil: São Paulo.

CHARACINS

Characidium sp. ♀   4/122
C. purpuratum group
H: Brazil: São Paulo.

Characidium steindachneri   4/123
Spotted characidium
H: Peru, Colombia: Amazon Basin.
SD: Unknown.   S: +
B: Unknown; egg scatterer?   F: C,O
T: 22–25°C, L: 6 cm, pH: <7, D: 2–3

Elachocharax georgiae   2/297
Dwarf darter tetra
H: Brazil: Rio Negro, Rio Madeira.
SD: Unknown.   S: +
B: Nat.: occasional pop. explosions. F: C
T: 24–30°C, L: 3 cm, pH: ≪7, D: 2–3

Klausewitzia ritae   5/72
Rita's dwarf darter tetra
H: Brazil: Tapajos Basin.
SD: Unknown.   S: +
B: Aquarium w/ dense vegetation. F: C
T: 23–28°C, L: 4 cm, pH: ≪7, D: 3

Melanocharacidium dispilomma   5/72

H: N Brazil, S Venezuela.
♂: Smaller, slimmer.   S: +
B: Unsuccessful.   F: C
T: 22–29°C, L: 7 cm, pH: 7, D: 2

Odontocharacidium cf. *aphanes*   2/298
Green dwarf darter tetra
H: Brazil: Tapajos Basin.
SD: Unknown.   S: +
B: Unknown.   F: C
T: 24–28°C, L: 4 cm, pH: ≪7, D: 3

Odontocharacidium aphanes   3/146

H: Brazil: Negro and Amazon rivers.
SD: None.   S: +
B: Java moss.   F: C,O
T: 22–26°C, L: 2 cm, pH: ≪7, D: 3

Asiphonichthys condei   1/248
Small-scaled glass headstander

H: Venezuela, Paraguay.
♂: Slimmer, more yellow, smaller.   S: –
B: Egg scatterer?   F: C
T: 23–25°C, L: 7 cm, pH: 7, D: 3

Charax gibbosus   2/252
Glass headstander

H: Guyana, Amazon Basin, Rio Paraguay.
♂: Yellowish. ♀: Larger.   S: =
B: Egg scatterer.   F: C,O
T: 24–27°C, L: 15 cm, pH: 7, D: 2

Charax pauciradiatus ♂   3/112
Glass headstander

H: Amazon Basin, Paraguay.
♀: Larger.   S: =
B: Egg scatterer?   F: O
T: 22–27°C, L: 15 cm, pH: 7, D: 2

Charax tectifer   4/63

H: Upper Amazon, Ecuador.
♀: Fuller and somewhat larger.   S: =
B: Eggs scattered among plants.   F: C,O
T: 23–28°C, L: 14 cm, pH: 7, D: 3

Cynopotamus argenteus   2/252
River dog, silver dentudo

H: Paraguay.
SD: Unknown.   S: –
B: Unsuccessful.   F: C
T: 20–24°C, L: 12 cm, pH: <7, D: 4

CHARACINS

Exodon paradoxus 1/246
Bucktoothed tetra
H: Brazil, Guyana.
♀: Ventrally fuller. S: –
B: Among aquatic plants. F: C
T: 23–28°C, L: 15 cm, pH: <7, D: 3

Gnathocharax steindachneri 1/246
Biting tetra
H: Brazil: Rio Madeira.
♀: Black spawning spot. S: =
B: Egg scatterer. F: C,O
T: 23–27°C, L: 6 cm, pH: <7, D: 2

Roeboexodon guyanensis 4/66
Shark-mouth characin
H: Guianas, Brazil: Rio Xingú.
SD: Unknown. S: =
B: Unknown. F: C
T: 23–26°C, L: 10 cm, pH: <7, D: 3

Roeboides caucae 1/248
Cauca humpback
H: Colombia: Rio Cauca.
♂: More elongated. S: –
B: Eggs scattered among plants. F: C
T: 22–26°C, L: 6 cm, pH: 7, D: 3

Roeboides dayi 4/68
Day's humpback
H: Venezuela, Trinidad.
♀: Fuller when ready to spawn. S: –
B: Egg scatterer. F: C
T: 22–28°C, L: 5 cm, pH: 7, D: 2–4

Roeboides descalvadensis 4/68
Descalvado-humpback
H: Brazil.
♀: Fuller when ready to spawn. S: =
B: Egg scatterer? F: C
T: 22–26°C, L: 5 cm, pH: 7, D: 3

CHARACINS

Roeboides meeki   3/114
Meek's predatory characin
H: Colombia: Rio Cauca.
♂: More slender.   S: –
B: Egg scatterer?   F: C
T: 22–26°C, L: 6 cm, pH: 7, D: 3

Roeboides paranensis   3/114
Paraguayan predatory characin
H: Paraguay.
SD: Unknown.   S: –
B: Egg scatterer?   F: C
T: 22–26°C, L: 6.5 cm, pH: 7, D: 3

Roeboides thurni   5/37
Thurn's glass headstander
H: Guyana.
SD: Unknown.   S: –
B: Pairwise in fine-leaved plants.   F: C
T: 22–25°C, L: 5 cm, pH: 7, D: 2–3

Brittanichthys myersi   3/116
Myers' blood tetra
H: Rio Negro, Rio Xeriuni.
♂: Anal fin rays have hooklets.   S: +
B: Unknown.   F: C,O
T: 22–24°C, L: 4 cm, pH: ≪7, D: 3

Brittanichthys sp.   4/104

H: Peru.
SD: Unknown.   S: (–)
B: Unknown.   F: C,O
T: 23–27°C, L: 3 cm, pH: <7, D: 3

Holoshestes pequira   3/116
Orange spot characin
H: Rio Guaporé, Rio Paraguay.
♂: More colorful and slimmer.   S: +
B: Like *Paracheirodon innesi*?   F: C,O
T: 22–26°C, L: 5.5 cm, pH: 7, D: 2

CHARACINS

Odontostilbe fugitiva   3/118
Fugitive characin
H: Amazon Basin, Colombia.
♂: More slender.   S: +
B: Unknown.   F: C,O
T: 22–26°C, L: 5 cm, pH: <7, D: 2–3

Odontostilbe piaba   2/269
Piaba tetra
H: Brazil.
♂: Concave A fin; long swimbladder.S:+
B: Unknown.   F: O
T: 20–27°C, L: 5 cm, pH: 7, D: 2

Odontostilbe pulchra   5/40

H: Trinidad, Venezuela.
♂: Slimmer and smaller.   S: +
B: Unknown.   F: C,O
T: 22–25°C, L: 3.5 cm, pH: 7, D: 2–3

Phenacogaster megalostictus   5/41
Large-spot glass tetra
H: Guyana to the Rio Negro.
♀: Short and round swimbladder.   S: =
B: Schoolwise among plants.   F: C,O
T: 22–27°C, L: 4.5 cm, pH: <7, D: 2–3

Phenacogaster pectinatus   3/118
Pectinatus
H: Upper and central Amazon Basin.
♂: Anteriorly lobed anal fin.   S: +
B: Like *Hemigrammus*?   F: O
T: 23–27°C, L: 8 cm, pH: 7, D: 1

Saccoderma hastata   4/66

H: Colombia.
♂: Adults have a caudal fin gland.   S: +
B: Unknown.   F: O
T: 23–27°C, L: 3.5 cm, pH: <7, D: 2–3

Saccoderma melanostigma ♂ 5/38

Saccoderma melanostigma ♀ 5/38

CHARACINS

H: Venezuela: Lake Maracaibo.
♂: Larger; longer fins. S: +
B: Unknown. F: O
T: 25–28°C, L: 5 cm, pH: 7, D: 2

Crenuchus spilurus 1/317
Sailfin characin
H: Guyana.
♂: Pointed and red dorsal fin. S: =
B: Cs; ♂ tends spawn;<60e. F:C,O
T: 24–28°C, L: 6 cm, pH: <7, D: 3–4

Poecilocharax bovallii ♂ 5/74
H: Guyana: Poloro River.
♂: Slender; reddish anal fin. S: =
B: Brood care by the ♂? F: C
T: 23–27°C, L: 5 cm, pH: 7, D: 2–3

Poecilocharax bovallii ♀ 5/74

Poecilocharax weitzmani ♂♂ 3/147
Black darter tetra
H: Amazon Basin.
♂: Slender to "skinny." S: =
B: Brood care by the ♂. F: C!
T: 24–28°C, L: 4 cm, pH: ≪7, D: 3

Coelurichthys microlepis t.♀,b.♂   3/120
Croaking tetra, small-scaled tetra
H: SE Brazil.
♂: Larger and more colorful.   S: +
B: Spawns on plants.   F: C
T: 18–23°C, L: 6 cm, pH: 7, D: 3–4

Coelurichthys tenuis t.♀, b.♂   3/120
Barberos characin, tenuis tetra
H: SE Brazil, Paraguay, N Argentina.
♂: Elongated & pointed anal fin.   S: +
B: Int. fertilization; among plants.   F: C?
T: 19–22°C, L: 5 cm, pH: <7, D: 3–4

Coelurichthys tenuis ♂   2/254
Barberos characin, tenuis tetra

Corynopoma riisei ♂   1/250
Swordtail characin
H: Colombia, Rio Meta.
♂: Long, paddlelike pectoral fins.   S: +
B: Sperm stored by ♀.   F: O
T: 22–28°C, L: 6–7 cm, pH: 7, D: 2

Gephyrocharax chapare   4/70
Chapare gland-characin
H: Bolivia. Colombia?
♂: Gland on caudal peduncle.   S: +
B: ♀ stores sperm; among plants.   F: C,O
T: 20–24°C, L: 4.5 cm, pH: 7, D: 2–3

Gephyrocharax valencia   2/256
Mountain minnow tetra, Valencia tetra
H: Venezuela: Lake Valencia.
♂: Raglike anal fin.   S: +
B: ♀ stores sperm; among plants.   F: O
T: 23–26°C, L: 5 cm, pH: 7, D: 1

Gephyrocharax venezuelae 4/70
Venezuela gland-characin
H: Venezuela.
♂: Special scale on caudal peduncle. S: +
B: Like *G. chapare*? F: C
T: 20–24°C, L: 5 cm, pH: 7, D: 2

Mimagoniates lateralis ♂♂ 5/42
H: Brazil: São Paulo, Santa Catarina.
♂: Gland; larger and slimmer. S: +
B: Internal fert.; on broad leaves. F:O
T: 23–26°C, L: 5 cm, pH: <7, D: 2–3

Mimagoniates lateralis ♀ 5/42

Mimagoniates microlepis ♂ 5/45
Croaking tetra
H: SE Brazil: coastal rainforest.
♂: Larger; brighter; longer fins. S: +
B: Among plants. F: C
T: 18–25°C, L: 5–7 cm, pH: 7, D: 2–3

Mimagoniates microlepis ♂ 5/45
Croaking tetra

Mimagoniates microlepis ♀ 5/45
Croaking tetra

Mimagoniates microlepis 3/120
Croaking tetra "Joinville"

Pseudocorynopoma doriae ♂ 1/250
Dragon-finned characin, dragon-fin tetra
H: S Brazil, La Plata region.
♂: Long dorsal and anal fins. S: +
B: Egg scatterer, plants; 1000 e. F: O
T: 20–24°C, L: 8 cm, pH: 7, D: 1

Pterobrycon myrnae ♂ 2/256
Blotched arrowhead tetra
H: Costa Rica.
♂: Long V fins; "paddle scale." S: =
B: Unsuccessful. F: C,O
T: 23–26°C, L: 6 cm, pH: <7, D: 2

Tyttocharax atopodus 4/72
Bristlemouth dragon-fin tetra
H: Peru.
SD: Unknown. S: –
B: Underside of leaves? F: C,O
T: 20–24°C, L: 2.5 cm, pH: <7, D: 3

Xenurobrycon macropus 3/122

H: Rio Paraguay.
♂: Conspicuous A and C fins. S: =
B: Unknown. F: O
T: 22–28°C, L: 5 cm, pH: 7, D: 2

Iguanodectes spilurus 1/296
Iguana characin, slender tetra
H: Guyana, Brazil.
♂: First rays of anal fin longer. S: +
B: Use a spawning grid. F: C,O
T: 23–27°C, L: 5–6 cm, pH: <7, D: 2

Piabucus dentatus 2/292
Toothed Piabuco tetra
H: Guianas, central and lower Amazon.
SD: Not described. S: =
B: Unsuccessful. F: C
T: 20–25°C, L: 18 cm, pH: 7, D: 2

Paragoniates alburnus 1/252
Pasca
H: Central and upper Amazon, Venezuela.
SD: Unknown. S: +
B: Eggs scattered among plants? F: C,O
T: 23–27°C, L: 6 cm, pH: 7, D: 2

Phenagoniates macrolepis 2/258
Barred glass tetra
H: S Panama.
SD: Unknown. S: =
B: Unsuccessful. F: C
T: 22–24°C, L: 6 cm, pH: <7, D: 3–4

Prionobrama filigera 1/252
Glass bloodfin
H: Argentina, S Brazil: Rio Paraguay.
♂: Longer anal fin. S: +
B: Floating plants required. F: O
T: 22–30°C, L: 6 cm, pH: 7, D: 1–2

Prionobrama sp. (*filigera*?) 4/72

H: Amazon, Paraguay, Paraná, Uruguay.
♂: Longer dorsal and anal fins. S: +
B: Unknown. F: C
T: 23–26°C, L: 5–6 cm, pH: 7, D: 2

Rachoviscus crassiceps ♂ 3/123
Thick-head characin
H: Rio de Janeiro, Paraná.
♂: White-fringed fins with hooklets. S: =
B: Unknown. F: C,O
T: 20–25°C, L: 4.5 cm, pH: <7, D: 1–2

Rachoviscus crassiceps ♀ 5/48
Thick-head characin, golden tetra

Rachoviscus graciliceps ♂ 5/48

H: Brazil: Bahía.
♂: Larger; more colorful; hooklets. S: =
B: Continous spawner; use grid. F: C,O
T: 22–25°C, L: 5 cm, pH: <7, D: 2

Rachoviscus graciliceps ♀ 5/48

Xenagoniates bondi 1/252
Long-finned glass tetra
H: Colombia, E Venezuela.
SD: Unknown. S: +
B: Unsucessful. F: C,O
T: 20–26°C, L: 6 cm, pH: 7, D: 2–3

Acestrorhynchus altus 3/112
Red dog characin
H: Amazon and Paraguay basins.
SD: Unknown. S: –
B: Unknown. F: C!
T: 22–26°C, L: 35 cm, pH: <7, D: 4

Acestrorhynchus falcirostris 2/251
Dog characin, Amazon cachorro
H: Amazon Basin, Orinoco, Guyana.
SD: Unknown. S: –
B: Unknown. F: C!
T: 24–26°C, L: 40 cm, pH: <7, D: 4

CHARACINS

CHARACINS

Acestrorhynchus cf. *microlepis*   5/50
Small-scaled dog characin
H: Amazon region.
SD: Unknown.   S: –!
B: In flooded areas.   F: C!
T: 18–28°C, L: >30 cm, pH: <7, D: 4

Hydrolycus scomberoides   4/74, 5/50
Tiger characin
H: Amazon, Orinoco, Rio Paraguay.
SD: Unknown.   S: –!
B: Unknown.   F: C!
T: 20–28°C, L: <60 cm, pH: 7, D: 4

Hydrolycus scomberoides   4/74, 5/50
Tiger characin

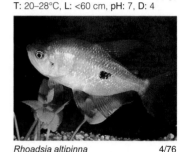

Rhoadsia altipinna   4/76
Rainbow tetra
H: W Ecuador.
♂: Sickle-shaped D; A w/ red edge.   S: –
B: Egg scatterer; territorial.   F: C
T: 22–25°C, L: 17 cm, pH: 7, D: 3–4

Acnodon normani   1/350

H: Brazil: Rio Xingú, Rio Tocantins.
SD: Unknown.   S: +
B: Unknown.   F: H
T: 22–28°C, L: <15 cm, pH: <7, D: 3

Catoprion mento   2/328
Wimple piranha
H: Guyana. Brazil: Mato Grosso.
SD: Unknown.   S: +,–
B: There are no reports.   F: C!
T: 23–26°C, L: 15 cm, pH: ≪7, D: 4

CHARACINS

Colossoma brachypomus   2/328
Silver pacu
H: Upper Amazon.
SD: Unknown.   S: +
B: Unknown.   F: H,O
T: 23–28°C, L: 45 cm, pH: <7, D: 4

Colossoma macropomum   1/350
Gamitana, giant pacu, black pacu
H: Amazon region.
♂: Ponted D fin? Dentate A fin?   S: +
B: Migratory; hormone injections.   F: H
T: 22–28°C, L: >60 cm, pH: 7, D: 3

Metynnis argenteus   1/352
Silver dollar
H: Guyana, Brazil.
♂: A fin anteriorly longer & reddish.   S: +
B: Floating plants; <2000 eggs.   F: H
T: 24–28°C, L: 14 cm, pH: <7, D: 3

Metynnis argenteus   4/136
Silver dollar, "cut throat" silver dollar
Possibly a ♂ in breeding colors.

Metynnis hypsauchen ♀   1/352
Plain metynnis
H: Venezuela, Guianas, Brazil, Paraguay.
♂: A fin more colorful and longer.   S: +
B: Floating plants; <2000 eggs.   F: H
T: 24–28°C, L: 15 cm, pH: <7, D: 3

Metynnis hypsauchen ♂   1/352
Plain metynnis
Spawning coloration (photo 3/163).

92

CHARACINS

Metynnis hypsauchen fasciatus   2/330
Striped metynnis
H: Amazon Basin.
♂: Anal fin longer and hook-shaped. **S**: +
B: Among floating plants.   **F**: H,O
T: 23–26°C, **L**: 14 cm, **pH**: <7, **D**: 3

Metynnis lippincottianus   1/354
Spotted metynnis
H: Amazon Basin: white waters.
♂: Anal fin red and longer anteriorly. **S**: +
B: Floating plants; <2000 eggs.   **F**: H
T: 23–27°C, **L**: 13 cm, **pH**: 7, **D**: 2

Metynnis maculatus   3/160
Red-bellied pacu
H: Brazil, Bolivia.
♂: A fin brighter & anteriorly longer. **S**: +
B: On Java moss; 150 eggs.   **F**: H
T: 20–28°C, **L**: 18 cm, **pH**: <7, **D**: 2–3

Metynnis mola juvenile   3/160

H: Rio Paraguay Basin.
♂: Broad and round anal fin.   **S**: +
B: Unknown.   **F**: H
T: 20–26°C, **L**: 15 cm, **pH**: <7, **D**: 2–3

Myleus gurupyensis   3/162

H: Guianas, Amazon Basin.
SD: None?   **S**: +
B: Unknown.   **F**: H
T: 23–27°C, **L**: ca. 25 cm, **pH**: 7, **D**: 3

Myleus pacu   3/162
Brown pacu
H: Guianas, Amazon Basin.
SD: None.   **S**: +
B: Unknown.   **F**: H
T: 22–28°C, **L**: <60 cm, **pH**: 7, **D**: 3

Myleus rubripinnis luna ♂   2/330
Moon redhook
H: Brazil: central Amazon.
♂: More colorful; bilobed anal fin.   S: +
B: Among plants.   F: O
T: 23–25°C, L: 12 cm, pH: <7, D: 3–4

Myleus rubripinnis luna "yellow"   4/136
Moon redhook
H: Brazil: lower Rio Tocantins.
♂: Brighter; A fin anteriorly longer. S: +
B: Unsuccessful.   F: O,H
T: 22–27°C, L: 12 cm, pH: <7, D: 2–3

Myleus rubripinnis rubripinnis   1/354
Redhook
H: Guyana, Amazon region.
SD: Unknown.   S: +
B: Unknown.   F: O
T: 23–27°C, L: <25 cm, pH: <7, D: 3–4

Myleus schomburgkii   2/332
Black-barred myleus
H: Venezuela, Brazil.
♂: Bilobed A fin; pointed D fin.   S:+
B: Unsuccessful.   F: H,O
T: 23–27°C, L: 12 cm, pH: <7, D: 2–3

Mylossoma aureum   4/138
Silver dollar
H: Orinoco and Amazon basins.
♂: Anal fin anteriorly longer.   S: +
B: Nat.: pairwise egg scatterer.   F: H,O
T: 22–28°C, L: 20 cm, pH: <7, D: 2–3

Mylossoma duriventre   1/356
Hard-bellied silver dollar, silver mylossoma
H: S Amazon Basin to Argentina.
SD: Unknown.   S: +
B: Unknown.   F: H
T: 22–28°C, L: >20 cm, pH: <7, D: 4

Ossubtus xinguense   4/138
Eagle-beak pacu
H: NE Brazil: Rio Xingú, Altamira.   E?
SD: Unknown.   S: +
B: Unknown.   F: H,O
T: 22–25°C, L: ca.15 cm, pH: <7, D: 3

Serrasalmus calmoni   2/332, 5/80
Tail-light piranha, dusky piranha
H: Venezuela, Guyana, lower Amazon.
♂: Darker; anal fin more curved.   S: +
B: Schoolwise among plants.   F: O
T: 23–28°C, L: 15 cm, pH: 7, D: 1–2

Pygocentrus nattereri adult ♂   1/356
Red piranha
H: Guyana to the La Plata Region, Paraguay
♂: Red throat. ♀: More yellow.   S: !
B: Eggs scattered among plants.   F: C
T: 23–27°C, L: 28 cm, pH: <7, D: 4

Serrasalmus nattereri juvenile   1/356
Red piranha
See photo on page 1/359.

Pygocentrus caribe   2/334
Shoulder-spot piranha, black-eared piranha
H: Venezuela, Guianas.
♂: Head more massive; slimmer.   S: !
B: Eggs scattered among plants.   F: C
T: 22–27°C, L: 28 cm, pH: <7, D: 3–4

Serrasalmus rhombeus   1/358
Spotted piranha, white piranha
H: Guianas and Amazon Basin.
♂: A fin anteriorly pointed & longer. S: !
B: Accomplished.   F: C
T: 23–27°C, L: 38 cm, pH: <7, D: 4

95

CHARACINS

Serrasalmus sp. juv.   5/82
Piranha
H: Amazon Basin.
SD: Unknown.   S: !
B: Unknown.   F: C
T: 22–28°C, L: ca. 25 cm, pH: <7, D: 3

Serrasalmus spilopleura   1/358
Dark-banded piranha, fire-mouth piranha
H: Orinoco, Amazon Basin, La Plata.
♀: Caudal fin more deeply forked.   S: !
B: Among aquatic vegetation.   F: C
T: 23–28°C, L: 25 cm, pH: <7, D: 4

Pygocentrus natteri   2/334
Diamond piranha
H: Paraguay, until Venezuela.
SD: Unknown.   S: +
B: Unknown; schoolwise.   F: H
T: 20–25°C, L: 25 cm, pH: <7, D: 4

Utiaritichthys sennaebragai   4/140
H: Brazil.
♂: Ventral fins more intensely red.   S: =
B: Unknown.   F: H
T: 23–28°C, L: 25 cm, pH: <7, D: 4

Brachychalcinus orbicularis   1/254
Silver dollar tetra
H: Northern and central South America.
SD: Unknown.   S: +
B: Egg scatterer.   F: H,O
T: 18–24°C, L: 12 cm, pH: 7, D: 3

Poptella longipinnis   4/78
H: Venezuela.
♀: Fuller during spawning season.   S: =
B: Unknown.   F: C,O
T: 25–28°C, L: 10 cm, pH: 7, D: 2

Stethaprion erythops   4/78
Bumpy-back silver dollar
H: Upper and central Amazon Basin.
SD: Unknown.   S: +
B: Unsuccessful.   F: C
T: 24–28°C, L: 8 cm, pH: 7, D: 2–4

Tucanichthys tucano ♂   5/58
Tucano tetra
H: Brazil: Rio Uaupés.
♂: Smaller and slimmer.   S: =
B: Rearing has been unsuccessful.   F: C
T: 21–27°C, L: 2 cm, pH: ≪7, D: 4

Tucanichthys tucano ♀   5/58
Tucano tetra

Tetragonopterinae sp. nov.   5/61

H: Brazil: Rio Uaupés.
♂: Deeper-bodied.   S: =
B: Unknown; turns very aggressive.   F: C
T: 24–30°C, L: 7 cm, pH: <7, D: 2–4

Tetragonopterinae sp. nov. ♂   5/63

H: Brazil: Rio Uaupés.

Astyanax abramis   5/52
Straw-colored astyanax
H: E Andean South America to Paraguay.
♂: Smaller and slimmer.   S: +
B: Surely possible.   F: C,O
T: 23–26°C, L: 5 cm, pH: 7, D: 2–3

CHARACINS

CHARACINS

Astyanax bimaculatus   1/255
Two-spot astyanax
H: E South America to Paraguay.
♂: Red/yellow A and C fins.   S: +
B: Surely possible.   F: C,O
T: 20–28°C, L: 15 cm, pH: <7, D: 2

Astyanax daguae   5/52
Plain-tailed astyanax
H: Colombia.
♂: Slimmer.   S: +
B: Among plants.   F: C,O
T: 24–27°C, L: 4 cm, pH: 7, D: 2–3

Astyanax fasciatus mexicanus   1/256
Blind cave tetra
H: Texas to Panama.
♂: Slimmer.   S: +
B: Relatively simple.   F: C,O
T: 20–25°C, L: 9 cm, pH: 7, D: 1

Astyanax brevirhinus   4/80
Blunt-nose astyanax
H: E Brazil.
♂: More intensely colored.   S: +
B: Unsuccessful.   F: C,O
T: 23–27°C, L: 10 cm, pH: 7, D: 2

Astyanax fasciatus fasciatus   3/124
American stripe tetra, silvery tetra
H: Mexico to Argentina: not everywhere.
♂: Slimmer.   S: +
B: Among plants.   F: C,O
T: 20–25°C, L: 14 cm, pH: 7, D: 1

Astyanax giton   3/124

H: E Brazil.
SD: Unknown.   S: +
B: Unknown.   F: C,O
T: 20–25°C, L: 8 cm, pH: 7, D: 1

CHARACINS

Astyanax guianensis   3/126
Guyana tetra
H: Guyana, Venezuela.
♂: More curved anal fin.   S: +
B: Schoolwise among plants.   F: C,O
T: 23–27°C, L: 6 cm, pH: 7, D: 1–2

Astyanax cf. *maximus*   4/82
H: Peru.
♂: More slender.   S: ?
B: Unknown.   F: C,O
T: 20–22°C, L: ca. 20 cm, pH: 7, D: 2–3

Astyanax cf. *ribeirae*   4/82

H: SE Brazil.
♂: Longer dorsal fin.   S: +
B: Pairwise among plants.   F: C,O
T: 23–27°C, L: 8 cm, pH: 7, D: 2

Astyanax scabripinnis   3/126
Rough-finned tetra
H: E and SE Brazil.
♀: Distinctly fuller.   S: +
B: Schoolwise among plants.   F: O
T: 22–26°C, L: 10 cm, pH: 7, D: 2

Hyphessobrycon columbianus   5/54

H: Colombia: Darien region.
♂: Slimmer. Larger dorsal fin?   S: +
B: Scatterer, even on bare glass.   F: C
T: 24–27°C, L: 5 cm, pH: <7, D: 2

Astyanax sp. "Cabruta"   5/54
Cabruta tetra
H: Venezuela: around Cabruta.
♂: Longer anal fin?   S: +
B: Unknown.   F: O
T: 22–28°C, L: 7 cm, pH: 7, D: 2

CHARACINS

Astyanax sp. "Lago Tefé"   4/84
Gold fin tetra
H: Brazil: Lake Tefé and surroundings.
♂: Much smaller and slimmer.   S: +
B: Unsuccessful.   F: C,O
T: 24–27°C, L: 4.5 cm, pH: 7, D: 2–3

Astyanax sp. "Lago Tefé"   4/84
Gold fin tetra
top ♀, bottom 2 ♂♂

Astyanax zonatus   2/260
Diamond tetra, false Kennedy's tetra
H: Paraguay. Upper Amazon?
♂: Slimmer and somewhat larger.   S: +
B: Schools among plant clumps.   F: C,O
T: 20–25°C, L: 8 cm, pH: 7, D: 1

Astyanax riesei ♀   1/256
Ruby tetra
H: S Colombia: Rio Meta.
♂: More slender.   S: +
B: Unsuccessful.   F: C
T: 20–26°C, L: 4 cm, pH: 7, D: 3

Axelrodia stigmatias   2/261
Pepper tetra, white star tetra
H: Amazon Basin.
♂: Slimmer; more intense white lines. S: +
B: Unsuccessful.   F: C,O
T: 22–26°C, L: 3 cm, pH: ≪7, D: 2–3

Boehlkea fredcochui   1/258
Cochu's blue tetra
H: Peru, Colombia.
SD: Unknown.   S: +
B: Successful.   F: C,O
T: 22–26°C, L: 5 cm, pH: <7, D: 2–3

CHARACINS

Bryconamericus iheringi   5/56

H: S Brazil, N Argentina.
♂: Smaller and more slender.   S: +
B: Eggs scattered among plants? F: C,O
T: 18–23°C, L: 10 cm, pH: 7, D: 2

Bryconamericus scopiferus   4/86
Rust-brown tetra
H: Colombia.
SD: Unknown.   S: +
B: Eggs scattered among plants? F: C,O
T: 23–27°C, L: 10 cm, pH: <7, D: 2

Bryconamericus sp. aff. *stramineus*
3/128
H: Paraguay.
SD: Unknown.   S: +
B: Eggs scattered among plants? F: C,O
T: 22–26°C, L: 6 cm, pH: <7, D: 2

Bryconella pallidifrons   4/86

H: Peru.
♂: 0.5 cm smaller; slimmer.   S: +
B: Unsuccessful.   F: C,O
T: 26–28°C, L: ♀ 3.5 cm, pH: <7, D: 2–4

Bryconops caudomaculatus ♂   2/262
Red cross tetra
H: Guyana, Brazil, Colombia.
♂: More pointed caudal fin lobes.   S: +
B: Unsuccessful.   F: C,O
T: 23–26°C, L: 13 cm, pH: 7, D: 2–3

Bryconops caudomaculatus ♀   2/262
Red cross tetra

CHARACINS

Bryconops (Creatochanes) inpai　　4/88

H: Brazil, Peru.
♀: Fuller when ripe.　　　　　　　　　S: +
B: Unknown.　　　　　　　　　　　　　F: O
T: 24–27°C, L: 10 cm, pH: <7, D: 2–4

Bryconops melanurus　　2/264
Tail-light tetra

H: E Brazil.
♂: More slender.　　　　　　　　　　S: +,=
B: Nature: egg scatterer.　　　　　　F: C,O
T: 23–26°C, L: 10 cm, pH: <7, D: 2–3

Carlastyanax aurocaudatus　　1/258
Goldentail astyanax

H: Colombia: Rio Cauca.　　　　　　　E
SD: Unknown.　　　　　　　　　　　　S: +
B: Unknown.　　　　　　　　　　　　F: C,O
T: 22–25°C, L: 5 cm, pH: <7, D: 2–3

Ceratobranchia obtusirostris　　3/128

H: Colombia, Peru.
SD: Unknown.　　　　　　　　　　　　S: +
B: Unknown.　　　　　　　　　　　　F: O
T: 20–24°C, L: 7, pH: <7, D: 2

Cheirodon affinis　　2/264
Black-base tetra

H: Costa Rica, Panama.
♂: Thicker rays; hooklets.　　　　　　S: +
B: Unknown.　　　　　　　　　　　　F: C,O
T: 22–24°C, L: 4.5 cm, pH: 7, D: 2

Cheirodon galusdae　　2/266
Chile tetra

H: Central Chile.
♂: Slimmer.　　　　　　　　　　　　S: –
B: Unsuccessful.　　　　　　　　　　F: C
T: 18–22°C, L: 6 cm, pH: 7, D: 3

Cheirodon kriegi   2/266
Three-spot tetra
H: Brazil: Rio Paraguay Basin.
♀: Ventrally fuller.   S: +
B: Eggs scattered among plants.   F: C,O
T: 24–27°C, L: 5 cm, pH: <7, D: 2

Cheirodon parahybae ♀   1/260
H: SE Brazil.
♂: Slimmer; hooklets.   S: +
B: Unknown.   F: C,O
T: 23–27°C, L: 4.5 cm, pH: 7, D: 2

CHARACINS

Creagrutus beni ♀   2/270
Benny tetra
H: Venezuela, Brazil, Peru, Bolivia.
♀: More colorful (!).   S: +
B: ♀ stores sperm; 50–70 eggs.   F: O
T: 22–26°C, L: <8 cm, pH: <7, D: 1–2

Creagrutus brevipinnis   4/88
H: Colombia: Rio Cauca.   E
♀: More colorful (!).   S: +
B: Short-term sperm storage (♀).   F: C
T: 23–27°C, L: 6 cm, pH: <7, D: 3

Creagrutus lepidus   5/56

H: N Venezuela.
♂: Slimmer; brighter; longitu. band.   S: +
B: Unknown.   F: C
T: 25–30°C, L: 7–8 cm, pH: >7, D: 2

Ctenobrycon spilurus hauxwellianus
Silver tetra   1/262
H: Amazon.
♂: Brighter coloration.   S: =
B: Eggs scattered among plants.   F: C,O
T: 20–28°C, L: 8 cm, pH: 7, D: 2

103

CHARACINS

Gymnocorymbus socolofi 2/270
Socolof's tetra
H: Colombia: Rio Meta.
SD: Not described. S: +
B: Unknown. F: O
T: 23–27°C, L: 5.5 cm, pH: <7, D: 2

Gymnocorymbus ternetzi 1/262
Black tetra, black widow
H: Bolivia: Rio Paraguay, Rio Guaporé.
♂: Pointed D fin and broader A fin. S: +
B: Eggs scattered among plants. F: O
T: 20–26°C, L: 5.5 cm, pH: 7, D: 1

Gymnocorymbus thayeri 1/264
Straight-finned black tetra
H: Amazon and Orinoco basins.
♂: Concave anal fin. S: +
B: Unknown. F: C,O
T: 23–27°C, L: 6 cm, pH: <7, D: 2

Hasemania nana 1/264
Silver-tipped tetra
H: Brazil.
♂: Brighter; white-tipped anal fin. S: +
B: Eggs scattered among plants. F: C,O
T: 23–28°C, L: 5 cm, pH: <7, D: 1

Hemibrycon jabonero 4/90
Jabonero tetra
H: Venezuela, Ecuador. Colombia?
♀: Somewhat larger and fuller. S: =
B: Unknown. F: C
T: 22–26°C, L: <10 cm, pH: <7, D: 2 3

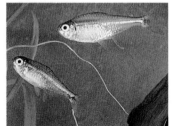

Hemigrammus barrigonae b.♂,t.♀ 4/92
Henn's Meta pink, Barrigona tetra
H: Colombia.
♂: More slender and smaller. S: +
B: Fine-leaved plants. F: C,O
T: 22–26°C, L: 4.5 cm, pH: <7, D: 3

CHARACINS

Hemigrammus bellottii   3/130
Dash-dot tetra
H: Guianas, Amazon.
♂: More slender and smaller.   S: +
B: Among fine-leaved plants.   F: C,O
T: 23–27°C, L: 4 cm, pH: <7, D: 2

Hemigrammus bleheri   1/272, 3/130
Rummy-nose tetra, red-nose
H: Colombia, Brazil.
♂: More slender.   S: +
B: Eggs scattered among plants. F: C,O
T: 23–26°C, L: 4.5 cm, pH: <7, D: 2–3

Hemigrammus boesemani   2/272
Boeseman's tetra
H: Guianas, Amazon.
♂: Swimbladder inferiorly pointed. S: +
B: Among fine-leaved plants.   F: C,O
T: 23–26°C, L: 4.5 cm, pH: <7, D: 2

Hemigrammus caudovittatus   1/266
Buenos Aires tetra
H: Argentina, Paraguay, SE Brazil.
♂: Fins are more red or yellow. S: +
B: Fine-leaved (hard) plants.   F: C,O
T: 18–28°C, L: 7 cm, pH: 7, D: 1

Hemigrammus cupreus   4/92
Shiny copper tetra
H: Amazon Basin.
♂: Brighter.   S: +
B: Among fine-leaved plants.   F: C,O
T: 23–27°C, L: 3.5 cm, pH: 7, D: 2

Hemigrammus elegans   1/266

H: Amazon.
♂: Slimmer.   S: +
B: Among fine-leaved plants.   F: C,O
T: 23–27°C, L: 3.5 cm, pH: 7, D: 2

Hemigrammus erythrozonus   1/268
Glowlight tetra
H: Guyana: Essequibo River.   E
♂: Slimmer and smaller.   S: +
B: Among fine-leaved plants.   F: C,O
T: 24–28°C, L: 4 cm, pH: <7, D: 2

Hemigrammus guyanensis   2/272
Red dot tetra, Guyana tetra
H: French Guiana.
♂: Pointed swimbladder.   S: +
B: Among fine-leaved plants.   F: C,O
T: 20–24°C, L: 4 cm, pH: <7, D: 1–2

Hemigrammus hyanuary   1/268
January tetra, Costello tetra
H: Brazil: Amazon.
♂: Barbed anal fin.   S: +
B: Among fine-leaved plants.   F: C,O
T: 23–27°C, L: 4 cm, pH: <7, D: 1–2

Hemigrammus sp. aff. *hyanuary* ♂ 4/96

H: Colombia.
♂: More slender (see photos).   S: +
B: Among fine-leaved plants.   F: C,O
T: 23–27°C, L: 4 cm, pH: <7, D: 2

Hemigrammus sp. aff. *hyanuary*   4/96
Two ♀♀.

Hemigrammus levis   1/266
Golden neon tetra
H: Central Amazon.
♂: More slender.   S: +
B: Among fine-leaved plants.   F: C,O
T: 24–28°C, L: 5 cm, pH: 7, D: 1–2

Hemigrammus marginatus 1/266
Bassam tetra
H: Colombia, E Brazil, Paraguay.
♂: More slender. S: +
B: Among fine-leaved plants? F: C,O
T: 20–28°C, L: 8 cm, pH: 7, D: 1

Hemigrammus mattei 4/98
False ocellifer, false head-and-tail light
H: Argentina.
♀: Blunt swimbladder; deep body. S: +
B: Among fine-leaved plants. F: C,O
T: 22–26°C, L: 4.5 cm, pH: 7, D: 1

Hemigrammus micropterus 3/132

H: Venezuela.
♂: More slender and smaller. S: +
B: Among fine-leaved plants? F: C,O
T: 23–27°C, L: 3.5 cm, pH: <7, D: 2

Hemigrammus ocellifer 1/270
Head-and-tail light tetra
H: French Guiana, Amazon, Bolivia.
♂: More slender. S: +
B: Among fine-leaved plants. F: C,O
T: 24–28°C, L: 4.5 cm, pH: <7, D: 1–2

Hemigrammus pulcher 1/270
Pretty tetra, black wedge tetra
H: Peru, Brazil.
♂: Smaller; pointed swimbladder. S: +
B: Compatible pairs required. F: C,O
T: 23–27°C, L: 4.5 cm, pH: <7, D: 2

Hemigrammus rhodostomus 1/278
Ahl's rummy-nose tetra
H: Lower Amazon.
♂: Slimmer. S: +
B: Among fine-leaved plants. F: C,O
T: 24–27°C, L: 5 cm, pH: <7, D: 1–2

CHARACINS

Hemigrammus rodwayi   (1/266), 1/272
Golden tetra
H: Guyana.
♂: Anal fin anteriorly white and red.   S: +
B: Among fine-leaved plants.   F: C,O
T: 24–27°C, L: 5 cm, pH: <7, D: 2

Hemigrammus rodwayi   (1/266), 1/272
Golden tetra
Normal coloration. Golden specimens are almost always ♂ (photo on p. 1/267).

Hemigrammus schmardae   2/274
Schmard tetra
H: Brazil.
♂: Slimmer.   S: +
B: Among fine-leaved plants.   F: C,O
T: 24–27°C, L: 5 cm, pH: <7, D: 2

Hemigrammus stictus ♀ adult   2/276
Red-base tetra
H: Guianas, Amazon, Colombia.
♂: Slimmer.   S: +
B: Among fine-leaved plants.   F: C,O
T: 23–27°C, L: 6 cm, pH: <7, D: 2

Hemigrammus stictus ♂ juv.   2/276
Red-base tetra

Hemigrammus tridens ♂   3/132
Cross-spot tetra
H: Paraguay.
♂: Slimmer and smaller.   S: +
B: Among fine-leaved plants?   F: C,O
T: 23–25°C, L: 3.5 cm, pH: <7, D: 2

CHARACINS

Hemigrammus ulreyi   1/274
Ulrey's tetra
H: Upper Rio Paraguay.
♂: Slimmer and smaller.   S: +
B: Unsuccessful.   F: C,O
T: 23–27°C, L: 5 cm, pH: <7, D: 1–2

Hemigrammus unilineatus   1/274
Featherfin
H: Guianas, Rio Paraguay, Amazon.
♂: Slimmer; pointed swimbladder.   S: +
B: On fine-leaved plants; <300 e.   F: C,O
T: 23–28°C, L: 5 cm, pH: 7, D: 1

Hemigrammus sp. aff. *unilineatus*   4/104

H: Peru.
SD: Unknown.   S: +
B: Among fine-leaved plants.   F: C,O
T: 23–27°C, L: 5 cm, pH: <7, D: 2

Hemigrammus vorderwinkleri   2/274
Vorderwinkler's tetra
H: Brazil.
♂: More hook-shaped anal fin.   S: +
B: Among fine-leaved plants.   F: C,O
T: 23–27°C, L: 4 cm, pH: <7, D: 2

Hyphessobrycon amandae   4/91
Ember tetra
H: Brazil.
♂: More intensely colored.   S: +
B: Not described.   F: O
T: 24–28°C, L: <3 cm, pH: <7, D: 2

Hyphessobrycon bentosi bentosi   1/280
Rosy tetra, Bentos' tetra
H: Guyana, lower Amazon.
♂: More pointed dorsal fin.   S: +
B: Among fine-leaved plants.   F: C,O
T: 24–28°C, L: 4 cm, pH: <7, D: 1–2

CHARACINS

Hyphessobrycon bentosi rosaceus
Rosy tetra   1/280
H: Guyana, lower Amazon, Paraguay.
♂: Brighter; longer dorsal fin.   S: +
B: Among fine-leaved plants.   F: C,O
T: 24–28°C, L: 4 cm, pH: <7, D: 1–2

Hyphessobrycon bifasciatus gold 1/282
Yellow tetra
H: E Brazil.
♀: Fuller.   S: +
B: Among fine-leaved plants.   F: O
T: 20–25°C, L: 4 cm, pH: 7, D: 1

Hyphessobrycon bifasciatus   1/282
Yellow tetra
Normal coloration.

Hyphessobrycon eques   1/282
Serpae tetra
H: S Amazon and Paraguay basins.
♂: Pointed swimbladder.   S: +
B: Pairwise in fine-leaved plants. F: C,O
T: 22–28°C, L: 4 cm, pH: 7, D: 2

Hyphessobrycon compressus   3/134

H: Mexico, Guatemala, Honduras.
♂: Somewhat larger and slimmer. S: +
B: Among fine-leaved plants.   F: C,O
T: 23–26°C, L: 3.5 cm, pH: <7, D: 2

Hyphessobrycon copelandi   1/280
Copeland's tetra
H: Upper and central Amazon Basin.
♂: Much longer D and A fins.   S: +
B: Among fine-leaved plants.   F: C,O
T: 24–28°C, L: 4.5 cm, pH: <7, D: 2

110

CHARACINS

Hyphessobrycon elachys   3/134
Reed tetra
H: Brazil, Paraguay.
♂: Elongated D, V, and A fins.   S: +
B: Among fine-leaved plants.   F: C,O
T: 24–27°C, L: 5 cm, pH: <7, D: 2

Hyphessobrycon erythrostigma   1/284
Bleeding heart tetra
H: Peru: upper Amazon Basin.
♀: Top. ♂: Bottom.   S: +
B: Among fine-leaved plants.   F: C,O
T: 23–28°C, L: 6 cm, pH: <7, D: 2

Hyphessobrycon flammeus   1/286
Flame tetra
H: E Brasil.
♂: Red A fin. ♀: Black-tipped V fins. S: +
B: Among fine-leaved plants.   F: O
T: 22–28°C, L: 4 cm, pH: 7, D: 1

Hyphessobrycon georgettae   4/94
Georgett's tetra
H: Suriname.
♂: Longer; pointed swimbladder.   S: +
B: Among fine-leaved plants.   F: C,O
T: 23–27°C, L: 4 cm, pH: <7, D: 2

Hyphessobrycon griemi   1/286
Griem's tetra
H: Central Brazil.
♂: A fin blood red w/ white fringe. S: +
B: Easy; on fine-leaved plants.   F: C,O
T: 23–28°C, L: 4 cm, pH: 7, D: 1–2

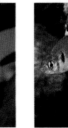

Hyphessobrycon haraldschultzi   4/94
Schultz's tetra
H: Brazilian/Colombian border.
♀: Fuller at spawning time.   S: +
B: Among fine-leaved plants?   F: C,O
T: 22–26°C, L: 3.5 cm, pH: <7, D: 2–3

111

CHARACINS

Hyphessobrycon herbertaxelrodi 1/288
Black neon

H: Brazil, Paraguay.
♀: Ventrally fuller. S: +
B: Fine-leaved plants; peat filter. F: C,O
T: 23–27°C, L: 4 cm, pH: <7, D: 2–3

Hyphessobrycon heterorhabdus 1/288
Flag tetra

H: S tributaries of the central Amazon.
♀: Fuller and somewhat larger. S: +
B: Among fine-leaved plants. F: C,O
T: 23–28°C, L: 4–5 cm, pH: <7, D: 2

Hyphessobrycon igneus 3/136
Firefin tetra

H: Argentina, Paraguay.
♂: More colorful and slimmer. S: +
B: Unknown. F: C,O
T: 20–24°C, L: 5 cm, pH: 7, D: 2–3

Hyphessobrycon inconstans 1/290,3/136
Fickle tetra

H: E Brazil, Paraguay, Colombia.
♀: More convex ventrally. S: +
B: Egg scatterer. F: C,O
T: 22–28°C, L: 4.5 cm, pH: 7, D: 1

Hyphessobrycon loretoensis 1/290
Loreto tetra

H: Peru: upper Amazon Basin.
♂: More slender. S: +
B: Unsuccessful? F: C,O
T: 22–26°C, L: 4 cm, pH: <7, D: 2–3

Hyphessobrycon loweae ♀ 5/64

H: Brazil: Mato Grosso.
♂: Longer anal and dorsal fins. S: +
B: Unknown. F: O
T: 25–28°C, L: 4.5 cm, pH: 7, D: 2

Hyphessobrycon luetkeni　　　3/138

H: Paraguay, SE Brazil.
♂: More slender.　　　　　　　　S: +
B: Among fine-leaved plants.　　F: O,C
T: 22–26°C, L: 6 cm, pH: 7, D: 2

Hyphessobrycon metae　　　2/278
Rio Meta tetra, purple tetra

H: Colombia: Rio Meta.
♀: Fuller and deeper-bodied.　　S: +
B: Among fine-leaved plants.　　F: C,O
T: 22–26°C, L: 5 cm, pH: <7, D: 2–3

Hyphessobrycon minimus　　　4/98
Mini tetra

H: Peru, Guyana.
♀: Blunt swimbladder; taller.　　S: +
B: Among fine-leaved plants?　　F: C,O
T: 23–27°C, L: 3 cm, pH: <7, D: 3

Hyphessobrycon minor　　　1/290
White minor

H: Guianas.
SD: Unknown　　　　　　　　　S: +
B: Among fine-leaved plants?　　F: C,O
T: 23–27°C, L: 3 cm, pH: 7, D: 2

Hyphessobrycon newboldi　　　5/64

H: Venezuela.
♂: 1 cm smaller; slimmer.　　　S: +
B: Unsuccessful; large tank.　　F: O
T: 25–29°C, L: ♀ 5 cm, pH: 7, D: 2–3

Hyphessobrycon peruvianus　　　3/138
Peruvian tetra, blue Loreto tetra

H: Peru: Iquitos.
♂: More slender.　　　　　　　S: +
B: Among fine-leaved plants.　　F: C,O
T: 24–26°C, L: 4.5 cm, pH: <7, D: 2–3

CHARACINS

Hyphessobrycon pulchripinnis   1/292
Lemon tetra
H: Central Brazil: Tocantins tributaries.
♂: Black-fringed anal fin.   S: +
B: Egg scatterer.   F: C,O
T: 23–28°C, L: 4.5 cm, pH: <7, D: 1–2

Hyphessobrycon pyrrhonotus   5/66
Redback bleeding heart tetra
H: Brazil: central Rio Negro.
♂: Longer dorsal fin.   S: +
B: Soft, neutral water.   F: C
T: 24–27°C, L: 6 cm, pH: 7, D: 2–3

Hyphessobrycon reticulatus   2/280
Netted tetra
H: SE Brazil: La Plata Basin.
SD: Unknown.   S: =
B: Among fine-leaved plants?   F: C,O
T: 15–25°C, L: 8 cm, pH: 7, D: 2–3

Hyphessobrycon "robertsi" ♂ ♂   1/292
Sicle tetra
H: Peru: Iquitos.
♂: Elongated dorsal fin.   S: +
B: Difficult; peat-filtered water.   F: C,O
T: 23–28°C, L: 5 cm, pH: <7, D: 2

Hyphessobrycon robustulus   1/290

H: Peru: Amazon Basin.
SD: Unknown.   S: +
B: Among fine-leaved plants?   F: C,O
T: 23–26°C, L: 4.5 cm, pH: <7?, D: 2

Hyphessobrycon "saizi"   5/66
Saiz's tetra
H: Colombia: Rio Meta. Suriname.
♀: Fuller and deeper-bodied.   S: +
B: Unsuccessful.   F: C,O
T: 22–26°C, L: 4.5 cm, pH: <7, D: 3

CHARACINS

Hyphessobrycon scholzei   1/294
Black-lined tetra
H: E Brazil, Paraguay.
♂: Smaller; deeply forked C fin.   S: +
B: Among fine-leaved plants.   F: O,H
T: 22–28°C, L: 5 cm, pH: 7, D: 1–2

Hyphessobrycon serpae   4/100
Serpae tetra
H: Brazil, Paraguay.
♂: Pointed D fin and redder C fin.   S: +
B: Among fine-leaved plants.   F: C,O
T: 22–26°C, L: 4.5 cm, pH: 7, D: 1

Hyphessobrycon socolofi t.♀ b.♂ 2/280
Socolof's cherry-spot t., lesser bleeding heart
H: Brazil: Rio Negro.
♂: Slightly larger dorsal fin.   S: +
B: Egg scatterer; spawning grid. F: C,O
T: 23–27°C, L: 4.5 cm, pH: <7, D: 2–3

Hyphessobrycon stegemanni   4/100
Stegemann's tetra
H: Brazil: lower Rio Tocantins.
♂: Slimmer.   S: +
B: Among fine-leaved plants.   F: O
T: 23–28°C, L: 3 cm, pH: <7, D: 2–3

Hyphessobrycon tropis   4/102

H: Brazil.
♂: Anal keel.   S: +
B: Among fine-leaved plants?   F: C,O
T: 21–26°C, L: 3–4 cm?, pH: 7, D: 1–2

Hyphessobrycon tukunai   4/102
Tukuna tetra
H: Upper Amazon region.
♂: 1st ray of A fin thick, w/ hooklets. S: –
B: Unsuccessful.   F: C,O
T: 21–24°C, L: 2–3 cm?, pH: 7, D: 2

CHARACINS

Hyphessobrycon vilmae   1/290
Vilma's tetra
H: Brazil: Mato Grosso.
♀: Larger and fuller.   S: +
B: Unsuccessful.   F: C,O
T: 22–26°C, L: 4 cm, pH: 7, D: 2–3

Hyphessobrycon werneri   3/140
Werner's tetra
H: Brazil.
♂: Larger dorsal fin; more colorful.   S: +
B: Unknown.   F: C,O
T: 22–27°C, L: 4 cm, pH: <7, D: 1–2

Hyphessobrycon "white fin"   5/62

Inpaichthys kerri t.♀, b.♂   1/296
Blue emperor
H: Amazon region.
♂: Larger and more colorful.   S: +
B: On Java moss; <400 eggs.   F: C,O
T: 24–27°C, L: ♂ 4 cm, pH: <7, D: 2

Markiana nigripinnis   4/106
Blackfin tetra
H: Paraguay.
♂: Orange to red fins.   S: =
B: Successful.   F: O
T: 20–26°C, L: 15 cm, pH: 7, D: 2

Hyphessobrycon axelrodi   4/106
Calypso tetra
H: Trinidad.
♂: Smaller and slimmer.   S: +
B: Egg scatterer.   F: C,O
T: 22–23°C, L: 4 cm, pH: 7, D: 2–3

CHARACINS

Hyphessobrycon megalopterus   1/298
Black phantom tetra
H: Central Brazil.
♀: Brighter: red adipose, P, A fins. S: +
B: Egg scatterer; dark tank.   F: C,O
T: 22–28°C, L: 4.5 cm, pH: <7, D: 2

Megalamphodus micropterus   5/68
H: Brazil: Rio São Francisco.
♂: Slimmer; broader swimbladder. S: +
B: Unsuccessful.   F: C,O
T: 23–27°C, L: 3.5 cm, pH: <7, D: 2–3

Hyphessobrycon roseus b.♂, t.♀ 2/282
Golden phantom tetra
H: Guianas: Maroni Basin.
SD: See photo.   S: +
B: Egg scatterer.   F: C,O
T: 23–27°C, L: 3 cm, pH: <7, D: 2

Megalamphodus sp. ? bred?   2/282
H: ?
♂: D fin larger, usually w/o black. S: +
B: ?   F: C,O
T: 23–27°C, L: 4 cm, pH: <7, D: 2–3

Hyphessobrycon sweglesi t.♀,b.♂ 1/298
Red phantom tetra
H: Colombia.
♀: Red/black/white dorsal fin.   S: +
B: Egg scatterer; darkened tank.   F: C,O
T: 20–23°C, L: 4 cm, pH: ≪7, D: 2–3

Moenkhausia ceros   2/284
Ceros tetra
H: Peru: Rio Ucayali.
♂: Pointed swimbladder.   S: +
B: Not described.   F: C,O
T: 24–26°C, L: 6 cm, pH: 7, D: 1–2

Moenkhausia chrysargyrea ♂   4/108
Question mark moenkhausia

H: Guianas, Brazil.
♀: Fuller and somewhat larger.   S: +
B: Perlon fibers; peat water.   F: C,O
T: 23–28°C, L: 7.5 cm, pH: <7, D: 2

Moenkhausia chrysargyrea ♀   4/108
Question mark moenkhausia

Moenkhausia collettii   1/300
Colletti tetra

H: Amazon Basin, Guianas.
♂: Elongated anal fin.   S: +
B: Java moss; dark; 150 eggs.   F: C,O
T: 23–27°C, L: 3 cm, pH: <7, D: 2

Moenkhausia comma   2/284
Comma tetra

H: Lower Amazon.
♂: Ventrally slimmer.   S: =
B: Among plant bunches.   F: C,O
T: 23–28°C, L: 8 cm, pH: <7, D: 2

Moenkhausia copei   2/286
Cope's moenkhausia

H: Amazon Basin and Guianas.
♂: More curved anal fin.   S: +
B: Among fine-leaved plants.   F: C,O
T: 22–26°C, L: 6.5 cm, pH: <7, D: 2–3

Moenkhausia dichroura   3/140
Spot-tailed moenkhausia

H: Guyana, Brazil, Paraguay.
♂: Pointed swimbladder.   S: +
B: Unsuccessful.   F: C,O
T: 22–26°C, L: 4.5 cm, pH: <7, D: 2–3

CHARACINS

Moenkhausia sp. aff. *dichroura*   5/62
Spot-tailed moenkhausia

Moenkhausia eigenmanni   4/110
Eigenmann's tetra
H: Colombia: upper Rio Meta.
♀: Fuller during spawning season.   S: +
B: Unknown.   F: C,O
T: 23–27°C, L: 5 cm, pH: <7, D: 2

Moenkhausia grandisquamis   4/110
Large-scaled moenkhausia
H: Guyana and Amazon Basin.
♂: Slightly smaller and slimmer.   S: =
B: Unsuccessful.   F: O,H
T: 21–25°C, L: <8 cm, pH: <7, D: 2–4

Moenkhausia hemigrammoides   3/142
Signal tetra
H: Guianas.
SD: Unknown.   S: +
B: Unknown.   F: O
T: 22–25°C, L: 3.5 cm, pH: 7, D: 1

Moenkhausia intermedia   1/300
False spot-tailed tetra
H: Amazon Basin, Rio Paraguay.
♂: Longer A fin; pointed swimbladr.   S: +
B: Pairwise in a dark aquarium.   F: C,O
T: 23–27°C, L: 5 cm, pH: <7, D: 2–3

Moenkhausia sp. aff. *intermedia*   3/142
False spot-tailed tetra
H: SE Brazil, Paraguay.
♂: Longer A fin; pointed swimbladr.   S: +
B: Unknown.   F: C,O
T: 23–27°C, L: 4.5 cm, pH: <7, D: 2–3

119

CHARACINS

Moenkhausia lepidura ♂ 2/288
Half-mast flag tetra
H: Guianas, Amazon region.
♂: Anteriorly longer anal fin. S: +
B: Egg scatterer? F: C,O
T: 22–28°C, L: 8 cm, pH: 7, D: 1

Moenkhausia melogramma t.♀, b.♂
Golden-glass tetra 2/288
H: Colombia: upper Amazon.
♂: Pointed swimbladder. S: +
B: Plant thickets; peat filtration. F: C,O
T: 23–27°C, L: 4.5 cm, pH: <7, D: 2–3

Moenkhausia naponis 5/68
Blue-line or Napo moenkhausia
H: Ecuador: Rio Napo Basin.
♀: Fuller when ripe. S: +
B: Unknown. F: C,O
T: 25–28°C, L: 6 cm, pH: 7, D: 2

Moenkhausia phaenota 2/290
Black and gold moenkhausia
H: Brazil: Mato Grosso.
♀: Fuller and ca. 0.5 cm longer. S: +
B: Not described. F: C,O
T: 23–26°C, L: ♂4.5 cm, pH: ≪7, D: 2–3

Moenkhausia pittieri t.♂, b.♀ 1/302
Diamond tetra, Pittier's tetra
H: Venezuela: Lake Valencia.
♂: Flaglike dorsal fin. S: +
B: Perlon fibers; darkened tank. F: C,O
T: 24–28°C, L: 6 cm, pH: <7, D: 3

Moenkhausia sanctaefilomenae 1/302
Yellow-banded moenkhausia
H: E Ecuador, Peru, Bolivia, W Brazil, Para.
♀: Visibly fuller. S: +
B: Egg scatterer. F: O
T: 22–26°C, L: 7 cm, pH: 7, D: 1

CHARACINS

Moenkhausia simulata   2/290
Mimik moenkhausia
H: Upper Amazon.
♂: More concave anal fin.   S: +
B: Unknown.   F: C,O
T: 24–27°C, L: 6 cm, pH: 7, D: 2

Nematobrycon lacortei   1/304
Rainbow tetra
H: W Colombia.
♂: Elongated anal fin.   S: +
B: Scatterer; continuous setup.   F: C,O
T: 23–27°C, L: 5 cm, pH: <7, D: 2–3

Nematobrycon palmeri t.♂, b.♀   1/304
Emperor tetra
H: W Colombia.
SD: See photo.   S: +
B: Unprolific egg scatterer.   F: C,O
T: 23–27°C, L: 5 cm, pH: <7, D: 2

Nematocharax venustus ♂   5/70

H: Brazil: Bahía.
♂: 3 cm larger; long D, A, and V fins.   S: =
B: Paternal family.   F: O
T: 22–26°C, L: ♂ 8 cm, pH: <7, D: 2–3

Nematocharax venustus ♀   5/70

Paracheirodon axelrodi   1/260
Cardinal tetra
H: Venezuela, Colombia, W Brazil.
♀: Slightly fuller.   S: +
B: Eggs scattered; dark; <500 e.   F: C,O
T: 23–27°C, L: 5 cm, pH: ≪7, D: 2–3

CHARACINS

Paracheirodon innesi 1/307, (4/64)
Neon tetra
H: E Peru: Rio Putumayo.
♂: More slender; line straight. S: +
B: Eggs scattered; dark; <130 e. F: C,O
T: 20–26°C, L: 6 cm, pH: ≪7, D: 1–2

Paracheirodon innesi 1/307, 4/64
Diamond-head neon tetra

Paracheirodon innesi 1/307, 4/64
Veil-tail neon

Paracheirodon simulans 1/294
False neon tetra
H: Brazil: Rio Negro.
♀: Somewhat larger and fuller. S: +
B: Schoolwise. F: C,O
T: 23–27°C, L: <3.5 cm, pH: ≪7, D: 2–3

Petitella georgiae 1/308
False red-nose, false rummy-nose tetra
H: Brazil. Peru: Iquitos.
♂: Caudal fin more contrasting. S: +
B: Very soft water required. F: C,O
T: 22–26°C, L: 5 cm, pH: <7, D: 4

Paraphenacogaster calverti 4/112
H: Brazil: state of Maranhão.
♂: Much slimmer; slightly smaller. S: +
B: Egg scatterer. F: O
T: 23–27°C, L: 8 cm, pH: 7, D: 2–3

Piabarchus analis　3/144
Piaba glass tetra
H: Paraguay.
SD: Unknown.　S: =
B: Unknown.　F: C,O
T: 20–26°C, L: 4 cm, pH: 7, D: 3

Pristella maxillaris　1/308
X-ray fish
H: Venezuela, Guyana, Brazil.
♂: Slimmer; pointed swimbladder.　S: +
B: Harmonizing pair; <400 eggs.　F: C,O
T: 24–28°C, L: 4.5 cm, pH: 7, D: 1–2

Psellogrammus kennedyi　3/144
Kennedy's tetra
H: Paraguay.
SD: Unknown.　S: =
B: Unknown.　F: C
T: 22–28°C, L: 6.5 cm, pH: <7, D: 3

Pseudochalceus kyburzi　4/112
Kyburz's tetra
H: Colombia.
♂: Long D fin; more colorful C fin.　S: +
B: 30 adhesive eggs; brood care.　F:C,O
T: 23–26°C, L: 6 cm, pH: <7, D: 3

Pseudochalceus multifasciatus ♀ 2/292
Multi-lined tetra
H: SE Brazil.
♂: Slimmer; concave anal fin.　S: +,=
B: Egg scatterer.　F: C,O
T: 16–23°C, L: 12 cm, pH: 7, D: 2–3

Pseudopristella simulata　4/114
False x-ray fish
H: French Guiana.
♂: More colorful.　S: +
B: Unsuccessful.　F: C,O
T: 24–26°C, L: 5 cm, pH: <7, D: 2–3

CHARACINS

Tetragonopterus argenteus 1/310
Silver tetra
H: Venezuela? Brazil, Peru.
♂: More elongated dorsal fin? S: +
B: Egg scatterer. F: O
T: 22–27°C, L: 8 cm?, pH: 7, D: 1

Tetragonopterus chalceus 1/310
False silver tetra
H: Guianas, Brazil.
♂: More elongated dorsal fin. S: +,=
B: Eggs scattered among plants. F: C,O
T: 22–28°C, L: <12 cm, pH: <7, D: 2–3

Thayeria boehlkei 1/312
Boehlke's penguin
H: Brazil, Peru.
♀: Fuller when ripe. S: +
B: Among plants; 1000 eggs! F: C,O
T: 22–28°C, L: 6 cm, pH: <7, D: 2

Thayeria ifati 2/294
Half-striped penguin
H: French Guiana, Suriname.
♂: Anal fin anteriorly white. S: +
B: Not described. F: C,O
T: 23–28°C, L: 5 cm, pH: <7, D: 2–3

Thayeria obliqua 1/312
Penguin tetra
H: Brazil: Madeira Basin.
♀: Fuller when ripe. S: +
B: Unsuccessful. F: C,O
T: 22–28°C, L: 8 cm, pH: <7?, D: 3

Vesicatrus tegatus 4/114
Tegatus
H: Brazil/Paraguay border.
♀: Larger; fuller when ripe. S: +
B: Unknown. F: O
T: 23–27°C, L: 6–7 cm, pH: 7, D: 2–3

Family Chilodontidae

Some consider the Chilodontidae a subfamily (Chilodontinae) of the family Anostomidae (p. 66). At present, 2 genera and 5 species are recognized. *P. punctatus* maintains its attractiveness through adulthood. Although they are not schooling fishes in the full sense of the word, they are gregarious.

Chilodus punctatus   1/318
Spotted headstander
H: Guianas, Venezuela, Brazil.
♀: Only fuller when egg-laden.   S: +
B: Egg scatterer.   F: H,L
T: 24–28°C, L: 9 cm, pH: <7, D: 3

Caenotropus labyrinthicus   4/126
One-spot headstander
H: Venezuela, Columbia.
♀: Fuller when egg-laden.   S: +
B: Unknown.   F: O
T: 24–27°C, L: 18.5 cm, pH: <7, D: 3

CHARACINS

Ctenoluciidae   Pike Characins

Family Ctenoluciidae

This family contains 2 genera and 5 species. As can be deduced by their common name—pike characins—Ctenoluciidae are ambush predators which resemble pikes. Little is known about these uncommon aquarium guests.

Because of their large size and reluctance to accept frozen foods, much less dry foods, nutrition is problematic. Interested parties must have a good source of live foods.

Pike characins are surface-oriented, nervous fishes. A partial cover of floating plants and other shelters should be included in the decor.

Delicate and slow to heal, the snout frequently sustains injuries during transport. Animals with such traumas, especially those that refuse to eat, should not be purchased.

CHARACINS

Boulengerella lateristriga 2/299
Striped pike characin
H: Brazil: Rio Negro, Rio Urubu.
SD: Unknown. S: =
B: Unsuccessful. F: C!
T: 23–27°C, L: 40 cm, pH: ≪7, D: 3–4

Boulengerella lucia 2/300
Cuvier's pike characin
H: Guianas, Amazon region.
SD: Not described. S: =
B: Unsuccessful. F: C
T: 23–27°C, L: 60 cm, pH: <7, D: 3–4

Boulengerella maculata 1/316
Spotted pike characin
H: Amazon and its tributaries.
SD: Unknown. S: =
B: Unsuccessful. F: C!
T: 23–27°C, L: 35 cm, pH: <7, D: 3

Ctenolucius hujeta beani 4/125
Bean's pike characin
H: Venezuela: Rio Apure.
SD: Unknown. S: –
B: Unknown. F: C!
T: 23–28°C, L: >12 cm, pH: <7, D: 3–4

Ctenolucius hujeta beani 2/300
Bean's pike characin
H: Panama, Colombia.
SD: Unknown. S: =
B: Unsuccessful. F: C!
T: 23–26°C, L: 30 cm, pH: <7, D: 3

Ctenolucius hujeta hujeta 2/300
Hujeta pike characin, slant-nosed gar
H: Panama, Colombia, Venezuela.
♂: Larger, frayed-edged anal fin. S: –
B: Egg scatterer; 2000–3000 e. F: C!
T: 22–25°C, L: <70 cm, pH: 7, D: 4

Rio Aguarico (South America: eastern Ecuador); the home of many characins and catfishes.

Family Curimatidae

The family Prochilodontidae is often considered a subfamily of the family Curimatidae, e.g., NELSON, 1994. In the AQUARIUM ATLAS, they are treated as two independent but related families.

There is also a great deal of disagreement concerning the number of genera and species within the family. This incertitude is largely because all these fishes are so similar. At the present time, 8 genera and a total of 95 species are tentatively accepted figures.

Herbivorous and usually silver-colored, these fishes hold little appeal for the aquarium hobby, despite their moderate size. Because curimatas are significantly smaller than Prochilodontidae, they are uninteresting to aquaculturists as well.

To minimize their timidness and maximize their color, subdued illumination, artificial and floating plants, a dark sand substrate, and bogwood are recommended.

Curimatidae are robust, but like most South American fishes, they fare best in soft, slightly acid water. Aquarium reproduction has been very sporadic.

127

CHARACINS

Curimata cyprinoides 4/126
Carp curimata
H: Brazil: lower Amazon.
♀: Distinctly fuller. S: +
B: Flooded areas; 300 000 eggs. F: O
T: 23–27°C, L: 18 cm, pH: 7, D: 2

Curimata gillii 3/148
Gill's curimata
H: Paraguay.
SD: Unknown. S: +
B: Nature: rainy season. F: H,O
T: 20–28°C, L: 10 cm, pH: <7, D: 2

Curimata nasa 3/148
Nose curimata
H: Paraguay.
SD: Unknown. S: +
B: Nature: rainy season. F: H,O
T: 20–28°C, L: 10 cm, pH: <7, D: 2

Curimata spilura r. ♀ 2/304
Diamond-spot curimata
H: Broadly distributed.
♀: Much rounder. S: +
B: Flooded areas. F: H,O
T: 20–28°C, L: 9 cm, pH: 7, D: 2

Curimatopsis evelynae ♂ 4/130
Evelyn Axelrod's curimata
H: Colombia: upper Rio Meta.
♂: Slightly concave caudal fin. S: +
B: Unknown. F: O
T: 23–27°C, L: ♀ 5 cm, pH: 7, D: 2

Curimatopsis macrolepis 2/304
Shiny-scaled curimata
H: Colombia: upper Rio Meta.
♂: Usually brighter; laterally flatter. S: +
B: In plant thickets. F: H,O
T: 22–26°C, L: 6 cm, pH: 7, D: 2

Curimatopsis myersi 3/150
Myers's curimata
H: Paraguay.
SD: Unknown. S: +
B: Unsuccessful. F: H,O
T: 22–26°C, L: 5 cm, pH: <7, D: 2

Cyphocharax multilineatus 1/320
Many-lined curimata
H: Brazil: Rio Negro.
SD: Unknown. S: +
B: Unknown. F: H
T: 23–27°C, L: 12 cm, pH: <7, D: 2

Cyphocharax pantostictus 4/130

H: Ecuador, Peru.
♂: More slender. S: +
B: Unsuccessful. F: O
T: 24–28°C, L: 10 cm, pH: ≪7, D: 2–3

Pseudocurimata lineopunctata 4/128
Line-spotted curimata
H: Brazil, Colombia.
SD: Only during spawing season. S: +
B: Not described. F: O
T: 23–27°C, L: 12 cm, pH: <7, D: 3

Steindachnerina elegans 2/303
Elegant curimata
H: Central Brazil.
SD: Not described. S: +
B: Unsuccessful. F: H,O
T: 24–27°C, L: 10 cm, pH: <7, D: 2–3

Steindachnerina metae 4/128
Peridot curimata, Meta curimata
H: Colombia: Rio Meta. S Venezuela.
SD: None outside spaw. season. S: +
B: In flooded areas. F: H,O
T: 23–26°C, L: 10 cm, pH: <7, D: 2–3

CHARACINS

Family Erythrinidae

The family of trahiras contains 3 genera and at least 10 species. At 100 cm in length, *Hoplias macrophthalmus* is the largest member of the family. As a whole, the Erythrinidae are inapt for aquaria, as they are ferocious, awesome-toothed predators. Nevertheless, they will always find a home as a conversation piece in somebody's species tank despite their drab colors, especially since even piranhas respect these monsters.

In the aquarium, little energy is expended. They lie motionless on the substrate until passing prey arouses their interest. After a lightning fast capture and some chewing motions, the "active phase" enters remission once again.

Extremely robust, trahiras are among the last survivors in water remnants during the dry season. Some can breathe atmospheric oxygen and move from one water hole to another by snaking over land. The meat of *Hoplias malabaricus* is of inferior quality. Whether or not this is true of its confamilials is unknown.

Erythrinus erythrinus 1/322

H: N to S Brazil.
SD: Unknown.   S: !
B: Unknown.   F: C!
T: 22–26°C, L: 25 cm, pH: 7, D: 3

Hoplerythrinus unitaeniatus 1/322
Single-banded trahira

H: Venezuela, Trinidad, Paraguay.
SD: Unknown.   S: !
B: Not possible in an aquarium?   F: C!
T: 23–27°C, L: 40 cm, pH: 7, D: 4

Hoplias malabaricus ♂ 2/308
Common trahira, tiger tetra

H: Northern and southern South America.
♂: More slender.   S: !
B: Large show tank.   F: C!
T: 20–26°C, L: 50 cm, pH: 7, D: 4

Hoplias malabaricus ♀ 2/308
Common trahira, tiger tetra

Family Gasteropelecidae

Carnegiella strigata strigata bottom, *C.s. fasciata* top

The family of hatchetfishes consists of 3 genera with a total of 9 species. Although unremarkably colored, their unique body shape, peaceful nature, and small stature ensure them of a place in community aquaria, where they add a pleasant contrast. As evidenced by their superior mouth, hatchetfishes are adapted to living near the water surface. These are the only known fishes which actively fly through the air; i.e., they do not passively glide, but exert thrust during "flight." The pectoral fins beat like the wings of a hummingbird (NELSON, 1994). In nature, they escape danger by breaking through the water surface and flying several meters, leaving would-be predators in their wake.

It is unfortunate that at present there is no suitable technique to breed hatchetfishes methodically. Only *Carnegiella strigata* (p. 132) has been observed repeatedly depositing its eggs among fine-leaved plants.

Carnegiella marthae marthae   1/324
Black-winged hatchetfish
H: Venezuela, Brazil.
SD: None.   S: +
B: Unsuccessful.   F: C
T: 23–27°C, L: 3.5 cm, pH: ≪7, D: 4

Carnegiella myersi 1/324
Myers's hatchetfish
H: Peru, Bolivia.
SD: Unknown. S: +
B: Unsuccessful. F: C
T: 23–26°C, L: 2.5 cm, pH: <7, D: 3

Carnegiella strigata fasciata bottom 1/326
H: Guyana.
♀: Fuller. S: +
B: Among fine-leaved plants. F: C
T: 24–28°C, L: 4 cm, pH: <7, D: 3

Carnegiella strigata fasciata 1/326
Marbled hatchetfish
H: Guyana.
♀: Fuller. S: +
B: Among fine-leaved plants. F: C
T: 24–28°C, L: 4 cm, pH: <7, D: 3

Gasteropelecus maculatus 1/326
Spotted hatchetfish
H: Panama, Colombia, Venezuela, Suriname.
SD: Not discernible. S: +
B: Unsuccessful. F: C
T: 22–28°C, L: 9 cm, pH: <7, D: 3

Gasteropelecus sternicla 1/328
Common hatchetfish
H: Guyana, Suriname, Brazil.
♂: Slimmer from above. S: +
B: Unsuccessful. F: C
T: 23–27°C, L: 6.5 cm, pH: 7, D: 2

Thoracocharax securis 1/328
Pectorosus hatchetfish, silver hatchetfish
H: Central South America.
SD: Unknown. S: +
B: Unsuccessful. F: C
T: 23–30°C, L: 9 cm, pH: 7, D: 3

CHARACINS

Family Hemiodontidae

The family Hemiodontidae is comprised of 2 subfamilies (Hemiodontinae and Parodontinae—not taken into account in the alphabetic listing of species), 9 genera, and approximately 50 species.

With the exception of the bottom-oriented *Apareiodon, Parodon,* and *Saccodon* [= Parodontinae], hemiodontids are nimble, medium-sized, torpedolike fishes of open waters. Aufwuchs-feeders, herbivores, and omnivores are found among their ranks. Some wild-caught specimens are very sensitive to handling. During and after capture, they loose many of their scales and die shortly thereafter, despite careful treatment. Animals found in the trade are already somewhat adapted and therefore more robust.

As active schooling fishes, spacious aquaria are demanded. Unfortunately, attempts to breed them have met with little success. Other than a ventral fullness, evident in egg-laden females, there are no external characteristics to distinguish the genders.

Bivibranchia protractila   2/310
Silver sandsucker
H: Venezuela, Brazil.
SD: Unknown.   S: –
B: Unknown.   F: L
T: 22–28°C, L: 25 cm, pH: <7, D: 4

Hemiodopsis gracilis   2/310
Slender hemiodus
H: Guyana, Brazil.
SD: Unknown.   S: +
B: Unsuccessful.   F: L,O
T: 23–27°C, L: 16 cm, pH: <7, D: 2–3

Hemiodopsis microlepis   2/313

Hemiodopsis q. quadrimaculatus   1/330
Torpedo characin
H: Guyana.
SD: Unknown.   S: +
B: Unsuccessful.   F: O
T: 23–27°C, L: 10 cm, pH: 7, D: 2–3

133

CHARACINS

Hemiodopsis quadrimac. vorderwinkleri
Torpedo characin   3/154
H: Guyana, Suriname, upper Amazon.
SD: Unknown.   S: +
B: Unsuccessful.   F: O
T: 23–27°C, L: 10 cm, pH: 7, D: 2–3

Hemiodopsis sterni   2/312
Stern's hemiodus
H: Brazil: Mato Grosso.
SD: Unknown.   S: +
B: Unsuccessful.   F: H,O
T: 22–26°C, L: 12 cm, pH: <7, D: 3

Hemiodus orthonops   2/312
Paraguay hemiodus
H: Rio Paraguay.
SD: Unknown.   S: +
B: Unsuccessful.   F: L,O
T: 22–26°C, L: 16 cm, pH: 7, D: 2

Hemiodus unimaculatus

Argonectes longiceps

Pterohemiodus atranalis

Designs of *Hemiodopsis* and related genera. Additional sketches can be found on the opposite page.

(Sketches from BÖHLKE, 1955, modified from GÉRY, 1977.)

Hemiodus unimaculatus   2/314
Single-spot hemiodus
H: Venezuela, Guianas, Brazil.
SD: Unknown.   S: +
B: Unsuccessful.   F: L,O
T: 23–26°C, L: 18 cm, pH: 7, D: 3

CHARACINS

Hemiodopsis argenteus

Hemiodopsis fowleri

Hemiodopsis goeldii

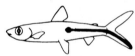

Hemiodopsis gracilis

Hemiodopsis huraulti

Hemiodopsis immaculatus

Hemiodopsis microlepis

Hemiodopsis parnaguae

Hemiodopsis q. quadrimaculatus

Hemiodopsis q. vorderwinkleri

Hemiodopsis rodolphoi

Hemiodopsis semitaeniatus

Hemiodopsis sterni

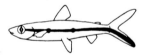

Hemiodopsis ternetzi

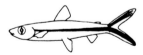

Hemiodopsis thayeria

Hemiodus orthonops

CHARACINS

Parodon affinis 2/318
Paraguay darter tetra
H: La Plata, Parana, Rio Paraguay.
SD: Unknown. S: +
B: Unsuccessful. F: L,H
T: 22–26°C, L: 6 cm, pH: <7, D: 2

Apareiodon gransabana 5/77
Mazuruni darter tetra
H: Guyana: Rio Caroni.
SD: Unknown. S: +
B: Unknown. F: H,O
T: 20–25°C, L: 10 cm, pH: <7, D: 2–3

Apareiodon piracicabae 1/330, 4/132
Brazilian darter tetra
H: SE Brazil: Paraná.
SD: Unknown. S: +
B: Unknown. F: H,O
T: 22–26°C, L: 8 cm, pH: 7, D: 2

Apareiodon sp. 1/330, 4/132

Parodon suborbitale 2/318
Green-banded or big-nose darter tetra
H: Venezuela, Colombia, Bolivia.
♀: Fuller when ripe. S: +
B: Unsuccessful. F: H,O
T: 23–26°C, L: 12 cm, pH: 7, D: 1

Parodon tortuosus tortuosus 3/154
Blue darter tetra
H: Brazil, Paraguay.
♀: Ventrally fuller. S: +
B: Unknown. F: H,O
T: 22–26°C, L: 10 cm, pH: <7, D: 2

Family Lebiasinidae

Many pencilfishes and pyrrhulinins make exceedingly interesting aquarium subjects. The family is comprised of 7 genera and 51 species. Two subfamilies are recognized (not taken into account in the alphabetic order of the species):

• Lebiasininae, small predators of the genera *Lebiasina* and *Piabucina* of limited interest for aquarists, and
• Pyrrhulininae, attractive community fishes of the genera *Nannostomus/ Nannobrycon* (pencilfishes) and *Copeina/Copella/Pyrrhulina* (pyrrhulinins).

The subfamily Lebiasininae is made up of robust species which inhabit small creeks with calcareous beds as well as oxygen-poor jungle pools with soft, acid waters. Consider their slight predatory tendencies when choosing tankmates; full-grown specimens are more difficult to associate. Their diet should include hardy live foods. These fishes frequent the middle and lower water strata. Aquarium breeding has not been accomplished.

Nannostomus trifasciatus (p. 142; see also 1/346). A jewel for the aquarium.

On the other hand, pencilfishes (*Nannostomus/Nannobrycon*) embody most of the optimal characteristics of an aquarium fish: they are exceedingly attractive, plant friendly, small, and absolutely peaceful. Their only shortcoming is their timidness and frailty. "Sophisticated" rain forest community aquaria are ideal for these mid- to upper-water fishes. When the aquarium is suitably decorated—e.g., ample bogwood and plants, a dark substrate, and subdued illumination (some floating plants)—their gorgeous coloration is displayed to the utmost.

Live foods or, at the very least, frozen foods should be included in the diet. Since their peak-feeding hours are at twilight, meals should be offered in the evening. Even live *Artemia* can be fed at that time, since they will be immediately eaten.

Maintain consistent low nitrate concentrations through frequent small water exchanges, thereby avoiding excessive variations in water chemistry which would come to pass if water exchanges were sporadic and large. Peat filtration will provide the desired pH of 5.5–7.0 and carbonate hardness of 4 °KH.

All pencilfishes in this book have been bred in the aquarium and found to be egg scatterers without exception. Perlon fibers and Java moss are the substrates of choice. Since the parents prey on their spawn, the use of a spawning grid is advised. Very soft, acid (pH 6.0) water is advantageous or, for the more particular species, even conditional for breeding (i.e., *Nannobrycon* spp.). During the first days, the fry require infusoria and rotifers; *Artemia* nauplii can be later added to the diet.

Additional details can be found on pages 337 ff. of the AQUARIUM ATLAS Volume 1.

In comparison to pencilfishes, the pyrrhulinins—genera *Copeina, Copella,* and *Pyrrhulina*—grow somewhat larger and are less sensitive overall. These fishes inhabit the middle water strata, some tending towards the surface and others towards the bottom.

In regard to aquarium decoration, it should follow the recommendations outlined for pencilfishes (see above). In relation to water conditions, the three genera are less demanding. Medium water hardness and a pH around neutral are perfectly suitable, especially for maintenance.

There are notable deviations from the typical characin mode of reproduction; for example:

- Generally, *Pyrrhulina* spp. spawn on broad, previously cleaned leaves, and males practice brood care.
- *Copella arnoldi* adheres its eggs to the underside of terrestrial plant leaves hanging above the water or, in captivity, the aquarium cover by jumping pairwise out of the water. By splashing water onto the eggs with his tail, the male keeps the spawn moist. After approximately 36 hours, the offspring hatch and fall into the water below and begin feeding two days later after the yolk sac has been absorbed.
- *Copeina guttata* cleans a depression in the sand or a rock and then lays its eggs there. The male guards the spawn.

All species can be maintained in community aquaria with peaceful tankmates.

Copeina guttata   1/332
Red-spotted characin
H: Amazon Basin.
♂: Brighter; upper C fin elongated.   S: +
B: Pit in sand; ♂ brood care.   F: C,O
T: 23–28°C, L: 7–15 cm, pH: 7, D: 2–3

Copella arnoldi t.♀, b.♂   1/332
Jumping characin, splash tetra
H: Guyana.
SD: See photo.   S: +
B: <200 e; ♂ tends; see p.138.   F: O,C
T: 22–29°C, L: 8 cm, pH: 7, D: 2

Copella metae   1/334
Brown-banded copella
H: Colombia, Peru.
♂: Longer dorsal fin.   S: +
B: Broad leaf; ♂ tends; <300 e.   F: C,O
T: 23–27°C, L: 6 cm, pH: <7, D: 2–3

Copella zigzag   1/334
Beautiful-scaled characin, plain copella
H: Lower Amazon to the Rio Negro.
♂: Brighter; longer caudal fin.   S: +
B: Broad leaf; ♂ tends; <300 e.   F: C,O
T: 23–27°C, L: 5 cm, pH: <7, D: 2–3

Copella nigrofasciata   1/334
Black banded pyrrhulina
H: Brazil: near Rio de Janeiro.
♂: Fins more colorful and pointed. S: +
B: On a broad leaf.   F: C,O
T: 21–25°C, L: 6 cm, pH: <7, D: 2–3

Copella vilmae ♂♂   2/320
Rainbow copella
H: Brazil: upper Amazon.
♂: Brighter; longer dorsal fin.   S: +
B: Unknown.   F: C,O
T: 23–25°C, L: 6.5 cm, pH: ≪7, D: 3–4

CHARACINS

Lebiasina astrigata　　　1/336
Non-striated lebiasina
H: W Colombia, W Ecuador.
♂: More colorful and slimmer.　　S: =
B: Unsuccessful.　　　　　　　F: C
T: 22–26°C, L: 8 cm, pH: 7, D: 2–3

Lebiasina boruca　　　4/133

H: Costa Rica.
♂: Brighter and more slender.　　S: –
B: Unknown.　　　　　　　　F: C,O
T: 22–26°C, L: 12 cm, pH: 7, D: 1–2

Nannobrycon eques　　　1/340
Three-striped or brown-tailed pencilfish
H: Colombia, Guyana, Brazil.
♂: Slimmer and more colorful.　　S: +
B: Eggs scatterer; Java moss.　　F: C
T: 23–28°C, L: 5 cm, pH: <7, D: 3

Lebiasina bimaculata　　　3/156
Two-spot lebiasina
H: W Ecuador, W Peru.
♂: More colorful and slimmer.　　S: =
B: Unknown.　　　　　　　　F: C
T: 22–26°C, L: 10 cm, pH: 7, D: 1

Lebiasina multimaculata　　　2/320
Multi-spotted lebiasina
H: NW Colombia.
♂: Brighter and more slender.　　S: =
B: Unsuccessful.　　　　　　F: C
T: 23–27°C, L: 7 cm, pH: 7, D: 3

Nannobrycon unifasciatus　　　1/340
One-lined pencilfish
H: Columbia, Guyana, Brazil.
♂: Black/red/white anal fin.　　S: +
B: Egg scatterer among Java moss.　F: C
T: 25–28°C, L: 6 cm, pH: <7, D: 3

CHARACINS

Nannostomus anduzei   4/134

H: Venezuela, Brazil.
♂: Slimmer and more colorful.   **S:** +
B: Unknown.   **F:** C
T: 24–28°C, **L:** 2 cm, **pH:** <7, **D:** 3

Nannostomus beckfordi   1/342
Golden pencilfish, Beckford's pencilfish

H: Guianas, Brazil.
♂: Slimmer; white-tipped fins.   **S:** +
B: Egg scatterer on Java moss.   **F:** C,O
T: 24–26°C, **L:** 6.5 cm, **pH:** <7, **D:** 1–2

Nannostomus bifasciatus   1/342
Two-lined pencilfish

H: Suriname, Guyana.
♂: Bluish-white ventral fins.   **S:** +
B: Egg scatterer on Java moss.   **F:** C,O
T: 23–27°C, **L:** 4 cm, **pH:** <7, **D:** 3

Nannostomus digrammus b.♂,t.♀   2/322
Twin-stripe pencilfish

H: Guyana. Brazil: Amazon.
♂: Broader anal fin.   **S:** +
B: Hard; egg scatterer; Java moss.   **F:** C
T: 24–26°C, **L:** 4 cm, **pH:** <7, **D:** 3

Nannostomus espei   1/344
Espe's pencilfish, barred pencilfish

H: SW Guyana.
♂: Slimmer, brighter; broader A fin.   **S:** +
B: Adhesive spawner; Java moss.   **F:** C,O
T: 22–26°C, **L:** 3.5 cm, **pH:** <7, **D:** 2–3

Nannostomus harrisoni   1/344
Harrison's pencilfish

H: Guyana.
♂: Broader anal fin.   **S:** +
B: Egg scattereron Java moss.   **F:** C
T: 24–28°C, **L:** 6 cm, **pH:** <7, **D:** 3–4

CHARACINS

Nannostomus marginatus　　　1/346
Dwarf pencilfish
H: Suriname, Guyana, Brazil (?).
♂: Slimmer.　　　　　　　　　　　S: +
B: Egg scatterer; Java moss.　　　F: C,O
T: 24–26°C, L: 3.5 cm, pH: <7, D: 2–3

Nannostomus marylinae　　　3/157
Marylin's pencilfish
H: Brazil.
♂: Slimmer.　　　　　　　　　　　S: +
B: Also continous; <30 eggs.　　　F: C,O
T: 24–26°C, L: 5 cm, pH: <7, D: 2–3

Nannostomus nitidus t.♂, b.♀　　5/78
Glittering pencilfish
H: Brazil: state of Parâ: Rio Capim.
♂: Slimmer; red A and C fins.　　　S: +
B: Floating plants; 200 eggs.　　　F: C,O
T: 24–28°C, L: ♂ 4.5 cm, pH: <7, D: 2

Nannostomus trifasciatus　　　1/346
Three-lined pencilfish
H: Brazil.
♂: Slimmer and more colorful.　　　S: +
B: Egg scatterer; Java moss.　　　F: C,O
T: 24–28°C, L: 5.5 cm, pH: <7, D: 2

Pyrrhulina brevis brevis　　　2/324
Short-lined pyrrhulina
H: Brazil: Manaus.
♂: Brighter, upper C fin longer.　　S: +
B: Pairwise substrate spawner.　　F: C,O
T: 24–28°C, L: 9 cm, pH: <7, D: 3

Pyrrhulina brevis melanistic form　2/324
P. b. australe: Paraguay: La Plata.
P. b. lugubris: Colombia: Rio Meta.

CHARACINS

Pyrrhulina eleanorae ♂♂ 5/78

H: Upper Amazon tributaries.
♀: Colorless fins. S: +
B: Adh. spawner; leaves; ♂ tends. F: C,O
T: 24–28°C, L: ♂ 8 cm, pH: 7, D: 2–3

Pyrrhulina filamentosa ♀♀♀ 1/348
Filamentous pyrrhulina

H: Venezuela, Guyana, Amazon.
♂: Slimmer; larger. S: −
B: Unknown. F: C,O
T: 23–28°C, L: 12 cm, pH: <7, D: 2–3

Pyrrhulina laeta ♂ 2/326
Half-lined pyrrhulina

H: Guianas? Amazon.
♂: Caudal fin superiorly longer. S: +
B: Unknown. F: C,O
T: 23–27°C, L: 8 cm, pH: <7, D: 2–3

Pyrrhulina laeta 4/134
Half-lined pyrrhulina

H: Peru: Jenaro Herrera.
♂: D fin and top of C fin longer. S: +
B: Adhesive spawner; 250 eggs. F: C,O
T: 25–28°C, L: 9 cm, pH: <7, D: 2–4

Pyrrhulina rachowiana 2/326
Eye-line pyrrhulina, red-spotted pyrrhulina

H: Argentina: Paraná, La Plata.
♂: Caudal fin superiorly longer. S: =
B: Adh. spa.; ♂ tends; 50–200 e. F: C,O
T: 15–22°C, L: 5 cm, pH: 7, D: 1–2

Pyrrhulina spilota 3/158
Blotched pyrrhulina

H: Nothing specific.
♂: Larger; slimmer; more colorful. S: +
B: Adhesive spawner. F: O
T: 23–26°C, L: 6 cm, pH: <7, D: 3

CHARACINS

Pyrrhulina stoli   3/158

H: Colombia, Suriname, Guyana.
♂: Larger; longer fins.   S: +
B: Adhesive spawner.   F: O
T: 20–24°C, L: 8 cm, pH: <7, D: 1–2

Pyrrhulina vittata   1/348
Striped pyrrhulina

H: Brazil: Amazon Basin, Madeira.
♂: Brighter at spawning time.   S: +
B: Adh. spawner; ♂ tends <300 e.   F: C
T: 23–27°C, L: 6 cm, pH: <7, D: 3

Prochilodontidae [= Curimatidae – Prochilodontinae]

Family Prochilodontidae

This family consists of 3 genera and up to 30 species. According to some, the Prochilodontidae is a subfamily within the family Curimatidae, the Prochilodontinae. All are herbivores and, to some degree, limnivores. The nutritional requirements of the latter are particularly difficult to meet in aquaria over the long term. Furthermore, since the great majority are large and silver in color, they are unappealing to aquarists.

Throughout their natural habitat, "bocachicos" [= small-mouthed ones] are appreciated food fishes, despite their many Y bones. They are hunted as they migrate upstream to spawn by any number of means: spear, net, "barbasco" (The active ingredient is rotenone, a fish poison extracted from a local plant.), and even dynamite. The ecological consequences of the latter two methods border on the unimaginable.

Modest success has been achieved with some Prochilodontidae in the realm of aquaculture. As migratory fishes, they require hormone injections to spawn in captivity, much like *Colossoma* spp. of the subfamily Serrasalminae. There is little interest in the Prochilodontidae because they have an inferior growth rate, are more difficult to feed, etc.

Prochilodus ortonianus juv.   3/150
Gray prochilodus
H: Amazon Basin.
SD: Unknown.   S: +
B: Unsuccessful.   F: H
T: 22–28°C, L: 25 cm, pH: <7, D: 3

Semaprochilodus insignis   3/152
Flag prochilodus
H: Guianas, Brazil.
SD: Unknown.   S: +
B: Unknown.   F: H,O
T: 22–26°C, L: 30 cm, pH: <7, D: 3

Semaprochilodus taeniurus juv.? 1/320
Plain-body prochilodus
H: Brazil, E Colombia.
SD: Unknown.   S: +
B: Unsuccessful.   F: H,L
T: 22–26°C, L: 30 cm, pH: <7, D: 3

Semaprochilodus taeniurus   3/153
Plain-body prochilodus
H: W Brazil, Colombia.
♀: Fuller when ripe.   S: +
B: In flooded areas.   F: H,L
T: 23–26°C, L: 30 cm, pH: 7, D: 2–4

Semaprochilodus theraponura   2/306
Flag-tailed prochilodus
H: Central and upper Amazon.
SD: Unknown.   S: +
B: Unsuccessful.   F: H,L
T: 23–26°C, L: 35 cm, pH: <7, D: 3

Potamorhina altamazonica   2/306

H: Amazon Basin, Rio Paraguay.
SD: Unknown.   S: +
B: Unsuccessful.   F: H,O
T: 22–26°C, L: 18 cm, pH: 7, D: 4

145

CARPLIKE F.

Barbus fasciatus; see p. 184.

Group 3

Origin/Taxonomy

At present, the taxonomy of FINK and FINK (1981) is the most widely accepted. It considers the Cypriniformes precursors of first the Characiformes (Group 2) and then the Siluriformes (Group 4). The "Weber's apparatus" (see p. 44) is common to all three orders.

Judging by species diversity, Southeast Asia seems to be the cradle of cyprinid development: their presence is particularly numerous there and all African genera are represented in Asia.

The goldfish, *Carassius auratus*, is probably the oldest decorative fish of all. Through the millennia, mankind has developed numerous linages through selective breeding. Which traits are decorative and which are degenerative abominations is a matter of personal opinion.

At the moment, there are 5 families, 279 genera, and about 2662 species within the Cypriniformes (NELSON, 1994). Listed below is the classification for Group 3; subfamilies were not taken into consideration when alphabetizing the genera within the families.

Geographic Distribution

Cyprinids are the predominant fishes of flowing waters in North America, Europe, and Asia. Species diversity is greatest in Southeast Asia. While their

147

distribution extends into Africa, they are not near as prevalent there. Interestingly, there are no cyprinids indigenous to either South America or Australia. Through introductions for aquaculture and aquaria, cyprinids enjoy a worldwide distribution, but not necessarily in natural waterways.

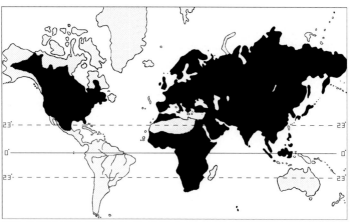

Area of distribution of the order Cypriniformes.

Behavior

The great majority of species is omnivorous, though there are aufwuchs feeders and herbivores as well. Cypriniformes are strictly nonpredatory. Nevertheless, live foods should be occasionally offered for optimal coloration.

Among the cyprinids, species which randomly scatter their eggs over the substrate far outnumber species which practice any form of brood care. Bitterlings are the most notorious among the latter, as they deposit their eggs between the branchial lamellae of bivalves of the family Unionidae. Some species deposit their eggs on stones or sand, whereas others produce copious quantities of planktonic eggs that generally drift downriver.

Particularities

Just through sheer number of species, cyprinids are a diverse assemblage. Generally speaking, most have a protrusile mouth void of teeth and, with the exception of a few loaches, lack an adipose fin. Their body shape is one of the most "typical" of fishes. The largest species (*Catlocarpio siamensis*) grows to a length of 2.5 m. Most are small schooling fishes.

Cyprinids touch many realms of our lives, from the various small species in our aquaria, to aquaculture of mirror carp and Chinese carps, and maintaining koi in garden ponds. According to Japanese culture, koi are bringers of good luck.

Family	Origin	Behavior	Diet	Reproduction	Remarks
Balitoridae Balitorinae	As	peaceful, bottom-oriented loners	H,O	few species successful; among plants, under stones, adhesive eggs	Affix themselves to hard substrates using pectoral and ventral fins to withstand current.
Nemacheilinae	Eu, As	territorial	C,O	flooded meadows	Some aggressive; cylindrical bodies.
Catostomidae	As, N Am	peaceful schooling fishes; prey on small fishes.	C,O	spawning migrations	Some species become very large.
Cobitidae	Eu, As, N Af	more or less bottom-oriented loners as well as schooling fishes	C,O	few successes; influenced by seasons; spawns in caves or among plants.	Some become restless when the barometric pressure falls (weather fish). Some burrow; accessory intestinal breathing by some species; some nocturnal and territorial.
Cyprinidae	Eu, As, Af, N Am	peaceful schooling fishes; some predators are loners as adults	C,O H	adhesive and nonadhesive eggs among plants; flooded meadows; nests w/ brood care; spawning migrations	Bitterling lay their eggs into the gill cavity of bivalves. Breeding of many species is still unsuccessful.
Gyrinocheilidae	SE As	territorial; juveniles are peaceful community fishes	H,O	in Asian ponds; perhaps stripped and artificially fertilized after hormone injections.	Suck themselves onto larger fishes, possibly sending the host into a panic.

CARPLIKE F.

Family Balitoridae

The family of the river/hillstream loaches includes species from the now dis-solved family Homalopteridae. Approximately 470 species are contained therein, whereby the number of genera is subject to a wide range of inter-pretations (between 37 and 59).

Just a few species have been bred in the aquarium. Since a certain de-gree of success has been registered in soft, neutral water, the fault does not seem to lie in the lack of proper water chemistry, but rather in the absence of stimulii which whould be physiologically interpreted as the onset of the rainy season, thereby triggering spawning. Wild populations have been observed numerous times spawning among plants of inundated areas during the rainy season. All the species bred in aquaria to date have produced adhesive eggs which were randomly scattered among clusters of plants, placed in gravel pits, or deposited under a rock. Some species practice brood care.

Most Balitoridae have an extremely elongated, wormlike, cylindrical body. At first glance, some hillstream loaches are mistaken for sucker-mouth catfishes (Loricariidae). A closer look reveals that they adhere onto the substrate by their ventral and pectoral fins, however, and not their mouth. By attaching themselves to the substrate in this manner, they are able to hold their position despite the force of the current.

Schistura notostigma; see page 159.

Acanthocobitis botia   2/348
Eye-spot loach
H: Asia: Sri Lanka, India, Thailand, China.
♂: Channel under eyes.   S: =
B: Plant thicket; 100–150 eggs.   F: O
T: 24–26°C, L: 8 cm, pH: >7, D: 1

Acanthocobitis botia   3/276
Ocellated loach
H: Asia: Burma, Bangladesh.
SD: Unknown.   S: +
B: Unknown.   F: O
T: 23–25°C, L: 6 cm, pH: 7, D: 1–2

Acanthocobitis zonalternans   5/84
Red-fin loach
H: Asia: Thailand to Indonesia.
♂: Dermal lobe under eyes.   S: +
B: Simulate rainy season?   F: C,O
T: 24–26°C, L: 6 cm, pH: 7, D: 2

Balitora burmanica   1/449
Burmese loach
H: SE Asia: Thailand, Burma.
SD: Unknown.   S: +
B: Unknown.   F: L,H
T: 22–24°C, L: 10 cm, pH: 7, D: 3–4

Nemacheilus mooreh   3/276
Ocellated loach

Homaloptera sp.   3/286
Chinese hillstream loach
H: Asia: China.
SD: Unknown.   S: +
B: Under stones.   F: O
T: 22–24°C, L: 12 cm, pH: 7, D: 2

Barbatula angorae   3/280
Angora loach
H: Asia: Turkey, CIS States.
♂: Pectoral rays 2,3,4 enlarged.   S: +
B: Unknown.   F: C
T: 14–22°C, L: 8.5 cm, pH: >7, D: 2–3

Barbatula barbatula   1/376
Common loach
H: Europe to Siberia.
♂: Longer; longer pectoral fins.   S: +
B: Adh. eggs; ♂ often tends spawn. F: C!
T: 16–18°C, L: 16 cm, pH: >7, D: 2–3

Barbatula barbatula ciscaucasica   5/86
Turkish loach
H: Europe: Turkey.
SD: Unknown.   S: +
B: Unsuccesful.   F: C
T: 10–20°C, L: 12 cm, pH: 7, D: 3

Barbatula barbatula toni   3/274
Toni's stone loach
H: Asia: CIS States.
♂: Thicker 2nd pectoral spine.   S: ?
B: Unsuccesful.   F: O
T: 18–22°C, L: <21 cm, pH: 7, D: 2–3

Barbatula brandti   3/282
Brandt's loach
H: Asia: CIS States.
SD: Unknown.   S: +
B: Unknown.   F: C
T: 10–20°C, L: 8.5 cm, pH: 7, D: 2

Barbatula angorae bureschi   5/84
Golden loach
H: Europe: Bulgaria.
♂: Larger; longer pectoral fins.   S: +
B: Adhesive eggs; ♂ often guards.   F: C
T: 10–20°C, L: 8.5 cm, pH: 7, D: 3

CARPLIKE F.

Barbatula cristata   5/86
Crystal loach
H: W Asia: Turkmenistan.
♂: More colorful and slimmer.   **S:** +
B: Unknown.   **F:** C
T: 10–20°C, **L:** 12 cm, **pH:** 7, **D:** 3

Barbatula insignis   3/282
H: W Asia: Syria, Jordan, Palestine.
♂: Longer fins; spawning eczema. **S:** +
B: Substrate spawner.   **F:** O
T: 7–24°C, **L:** 7 cm, **pH:** 7, **D:** 2

Barbatula labiata   3/280
Thick-lip loach
H: Asia: CIS States.
SD: Unknown.   **S:** ?
B: April/June; <60 000 eggs.   **F:** O
T: 14–20°C, **L:** 23 cm, **pH:** 7, **D:** 2–3

Barbatula namiri   3/284
H: Asia: Syria, Lebanon.
♂: Larger 2nd and 3rd P fin rays.   **S:** +
B: In dug depressions; brood care. **F:** O
T: 16–22°C, **L:** 11 cm, **pH:** 7, **D:** 2

Barbatula panthera   3/284
Panther loach
H: Asia: SW Syria.
♂: Longer pectoral fins.   **S:** +
B: Unknown.   **F:** O
T: 6–24°C, **L:** 10 cm, **pH:** 7, **D:** 2

Beaufortia leveretti   4/142
Leverett's hillstream loach
H: China: Hainan.
SD: Unknown.   **S:** +
B: Unknown.   **F:** H,O
T: 18–24°C, **L:** 12 cm, **pH:** 7, **D:** 2–3

CARPLIKE F.

Crossostoma tinkhami 2/426
Fukien hillstream loach
H: E Asia: China.
SD: Unknown. S: +
B: Unsuccesful. F: O
T: 22–24°C, L: 10 cm, pH: 7, D: 3–4

Gastromyzon ctenocephalus 5/88
Spiny-head hillstream loach
H: Borneo (Sarawak).
♂: Tubercles on head and P fins. S: +
B: Unknown. F: O
T: 19–23°C, L: 5 cm, pH: 7, D: 2–3

Gastromyzon punctulatus 2/426
Spotted hillstream loach
H: SE Asia: Indonesia, Kalimantan.
SD: Unknown. S: +
B: Unknown. F: O
T: 23–25°C, L: 5 cm, pH: 7, D: 2

Micronoemacheilus cf. *pulcher* ♂
(see right page)
H: Asia: China: Canton.
SD: Slight. S: =
B: Unsuccesful. F: H,O
T: 22–25°C, L: 10 cm, pH: 7, D: 2–3

Hemimyzon sinensis 5/88
Chinese hillstream loach
H: Asia: China: Szechwan Province.
SD: Unknown. S: +
B: Unsuccesful. F: H
T: 18–25°C, L: 8 cm, pH: >7, D: 2–3

Homaloptera orthogoniata 2/428
Saddled hillstream loach
H: SE Asia: Indonesia, Thailand.
♂: Unknown. S: +
B: Unknown. F: H,O
T: 20–24°C, L: 12 cm, pH: 7, D: 3

Homaloptera sp. 5/90
Green hillstream loach
H: SE Asia: Thailand.
SD: Unknown. S: +
B: Unknown. F: L,H,O
T: 18–22°C, L: 10 cm, pH: <7, D: 3

Homaloptera cf. *stephensoni* 5/90

H: SE Asia: Thailand.
SD: Unknown. S: +
B: Unknown. F: L,H,O
T: 20–24°C, L: 10 cm, pH: <7, D: 3

Lefua costata 2/344
Lefua
H: Asia: Russia, N China, Korea.
SD: Unknown. S: ?
B: Unknown. F: C
T: 18–22°C, L: 10 cm, pH: 7, D: 3

Lefua nikkonis 5/92
Nikkon loach
H: Asia: Japan
SD: Unknown. S: +
B: Unknown. F: C
T: 15–25°C, L: 8 cm, pH: 7, D: 2

Liniparhomaloptera disparis 2/430
Broken-band hillstream loach
H: Asia: China.
♀: Unknown. S: +
B: Unknown. F: O
T: 22–24°C, L: 5 cm, pH: 7, D: 2–3

Micronemacheilus pulcher ♂ 4/144
Beautiful hillstream loach
H: Asia: China: Canton.
SD: Slight. S: =
B: Unsuccessful. F: H,O
T: 22–25°C, L: 10 cm, pH: 7, D: 2–3

155

Micronemacheilus pulcher ♀   4/144
Beautiful hillstream loach

Nemacheilus abyssinicus ♂   4/144
Ethiopian loach
H: Africa: Ethiopia.
♀: Fuller during spawning season. **S:** +
B: Unknown.   **F:** C,O
T: 18–22°C, **L:** 9 cm, **pH:** 7, **D:** 3

Nemacheilus abyssinicus ♀   4/144
Ethiopian loach

Nemacheilus binotatus   3/274
Two-spot loach
H: Asia: N and W Thailand.
♂: Lobe under the eyes.   **S:** +
B: Unsuccessful.   **F:** O
T: 26–28°C, **L:** 6 cm, **pH:** 7, **D:** 2

Triplophysa dorsalis   2/350
Gray loach
H: Asia: CIS States.
SD: Unknown.   **S:** ?
B: Nature: April–June.   **F:** O
T: 18–22°C, **L:** 13 cm, **pH:** 7, **D:** 3

Nemacheilus fasciatus   2/350
Barred loach, spot-fin loach
H: Asia: Indonesia, Sumatra, Borneo, Java.
SD: Unknown.   **S:** –
B: Unsuccessful.   **F:** C!
T: 22–24°C, **L:** 9 cm, **pH:** <7, **D:** 2

Nemacheilus kangrae   5/92
Punjab loach
H: Asia: India: Punjab.
SD: None.   S: +
B: Unknown.   F: C,O
T: 10–22°C, L: 8 cm, pH: >7, D: 3

Nemacheilus merga ♀   5/94
Merga loach
H: E Europe: W Urals.
♀: Fuller during spawning season. S: +
B: Unknown.   F: C,O
T: 10–22°C, L: 9.5 cm, pH: 7, D: 2–3

Nemacheilus notostigma   2/352
Fighting loach
H: SE Asia: Sri Lanka.
♂: Upper caudal fin lobe longer.   S: –
B: In dense plants (20 young).   F: O
T: 22–24°C, L: 8 cm, pH: 7, D: 2–3

Nemacheilus oxianus   5/96

H: Asia: Uzbekistan: Amu-Darya.
♂: Larger dorsal fin; more contrast. S: +
B: Unknown.   F: C,O
T: 10–18°C, L: 6.5 cm, pH: 7, D: 2–3

Nemacheilus pardalis   5/96
Leopard loach
H: Asia: Uzbekistan: at Duschanbe.
♂: Longer; larger dorsal fin.   S: +
B: Nat.: May after snow melts.   F: C,O
T: 10–18°C, L: 9.5 cm, pH: 7, D: 3

Nemacheilus savona   4/147
Savona loach
H: India: Calcutta.
♂: Perhaps 1st D fin ray is thicker. S: +
B: Unknown.   F: C,O
T: 23–26°C, L: 10 cm, pH: 7, D: 2–3

Nemacheilus selangoricus 2/352
Kuiper's loach
H: Indonesia, Malaysia.
♂: Pointed P; upper C lobe longer. S: ?
B: Unsuccessful. F: C,O
T: 23–25°C, L: 7.5 cm, pH: <7, D: 2

Nemacheilus selangoricus 2/352
Kuiper's loach t.♂, b.♀

Tripophysa stoliczkae 2/354
Stoliczka's loach
H: Asia: CIS States, China.
♂: Thicker ventral fin rays. S: ?
B: Unsuccessful. F: C,O
T: 16–20°C, L: 15 cm, pH: 7, D: 3

Nemacheilus strauchi 2/354
Spotted thick-lipped loach
H: Asia: CIS States, China.
♂: Slimmer; shorter dorsal fin. S: ?
B: Nat.: April–June; <47000 e. F: C,O
T: 18–22°C, L: 25 cm, pH: 7, D: 3

Paracobitis malapterura longicauda 3/286
H: Asia: CIS States.
SD: Unknown. S: +
B: Unknown. F: C
T: 10–20°C, L: 20 cm, pH: >7, D: 2

Pseudogastromyzon cheni 2/430
Chinese hillstream loach
H: E Asia: S China.
♂: Carmine red dorsal fin? S: +
B: Unknown. F: O
T: 20–25°C, L: 5 cm, pH: 7, D: 2

158

Pseudogastromyzon fasciatus   5/98
Zebra hillstream loach
H: Asia: China.
SD: Only at spawning time.   S: +
B: Unsuccessful.   F: H,O
T: 18–23°C, L: 8 cm, pH: >7, D: 2–3

Schistura kessleri kessleri   3/278
Kessler's loach
H: Asia: Iran, Afg., Pak., India, CIS States.
♂: Canestrini scale; pointed P fins.   S: +
B: Unsuccessful.   F: O
T: 22–30°C, L: 8 cm, pH: >7, D: 2–3

Schistura magnifluvis   5/100
Mekong loach
H: Asia: Thailand: central Mekong River.
♂: Suborbital dermal appendage?   S: +
B: Egg Ø 1.5 mm; under stones?   F: C,H
T: 23–28°C, L: ♀ 40 cm, pH: <7, D: 2

Nemacheilus montanus   5/94
Mountain loach
H: Asia: N India.
♂: Brighter and slimmer (spawning). S: =
B: Unsuccessful.   F: C,O
T: 18–22°C, L: 6.5 cm, pH: 7, D: 2–3

Schistura notostigma ♂?   5/100

H: Asia: Sri Lanka.
♂: 2nd and 3rd P fin spines thick?   S: +
B: Egg Ø1.5 mm. Under stones? F: C,H
T: 23–28°C, L: ♀ 40 cm, pH: <7, D: 2

Additional similar species:

Schistura montana	12 bands
S. rupecola	14 bands
S. rupecola var.	13 bands
S. subfusca	10 bands
S. zonata	11 bands

159

Schistura sargadensis 5/102
Sarga loach
H: Asia: Turkmenistan.
♂: Longer; larger dorsal fin. S: +
B: Unknown. F: C,O
T: 15–22°C, L: 8.5 cm, pH: <7, D: 2–3

Schistura sp. aff. *spilota* 5/98
Kwai loach
H: Asia: W Thailand: Kwai River.
SD: Unknown. S: +
B: Unknown. F: C
T: 15–24°C, L: 7 cm, pH: 7, D: 2–3

Sinogastromyzon wui 4/142
Wui's hillstream loach
H: Asia: China: Quangsi.
SD: Unknown. S: +
B: Unknown. F: H,O
T: 18–26°C, L: 14 cm, pH: 7, D: 2–3

Triplophysa kuschakewitschi 3/278

H: Asia: CIS States.
♂: Broader head. S: +
B: Unknown. F: O
T: 10–20°C, L: 11 cm, pH: >7, D: 2–3

Vaillantella maasi 5/103

H: SE Asia: Sumatra, Borneo, Malaysia.
SD: Unknown. S: =?
B: Unknown. F: C,O
T: ca. 24°C, L: < 24 cm, pH: 7, D: 2–3

Yunnanilus brevis 3/276

H: SE Asia: Burma.
♂: Dermal lobe under eyes. S: +
B: Unknown. F: O
T: 22–24°C, L: 6 cm, pH: 7, D: 2

Family Catostomidae

All 13 genera and 68 species of this successful family are found in flowing waters of North America, where they are among to the most numerous of fishes. Although they inhabit Asia as well, they are not nearly as prevalent there.

Suckers easily adapt to life in aquaria. They are specialized substrate grazers in their natural biotopes. Typically, species hailing from stagnant waters have large, deep bodies. The wimple carp, *Myxocyprinus asiaticus*, belongs to this family, but it was classified as part of the Cyprinidae in the AQUARIUM ATLAS; hence, it is found on page 219 in the INDEX.

Their large size, drab brown/gray hues, and high oxygen requirement—characteristics of species from cool, flowing waters—translates into scant interest of aquarists in the Catostomidae.

CARPLIKE F.

Catostomus catostomus catostom. 4/148
Longnose sucker
H: N Am.:USA: E Rocky Mountns. to Maine.
♂: Almost black; pearllike knots.   S: –
B: Spring spawning migrations.   F: C
T: 0–15°C, L: 70 cm, pH: 7, D: 4

Catostomus catostomus rostratus   4/148
Siberian longnose sucker
H: Asia: Russia: Siberia.
♂: Much darker at spawning time.   S: –
B: Spring spawning migrations.   F: C
T: 4–18°C, L: 54 cm, pH: 7, D: 4

Catostomus commersonii   3/165
Commerson's sucker, white sucker
H: N Am.: Canada and United States.
♂: Usually smaller; colorful.   S: +
B: Nature: April–May; 20 000 e.   F: C,O
T: 4–20°C, L: 30 (45) cm, pH: 7, D: 2

Erimyzon sucetta   2/337
Lake chubsucker
H: N America: USA: NY to FL and TX.
♂: Slimmer.   S: +
B: Nature: March–April; <20 000 e. F: O
T: 4–20°C, L: 25 cm, pH: >7, D: 2–3

Family Cobitidae

There are 18 genera and about 110 species of loaches. Adapted to a bottom-oriented life, their body is round (*Pangio*) to triangular (*Botia*). The distribution extends throughout Europe and Asia as well as regions of northern and eastern Africa.

CARPLIKE F.

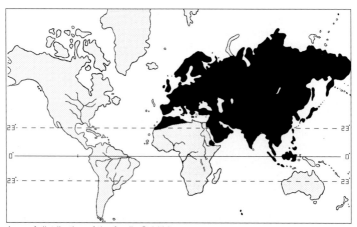

Area of distribution of the family Cobitidae.

In view of their shy demeanor, the aquarium should offer a multitude of hiding places. Some species even spend part of their time buried in the substrate; therefore, sharp-edged materials must not be employed as substrate. Compared to their confamilials, a few of the *Botia* spp. are gregarious, less timid, and not as bottom-oriented.

The reproductive biology of the Cobitidae has not been studied in much detail. At best, aquarium reproduction has been coincidental. There are genera that spawn in caves (e.g., *Acantopsis*) and some that scatter their eggs among plants (e.g., *Cobitis*); there is a paucity of information about the familiar genus *Botia*. The seasons—the rainy season in particular—seem to play a decisive role in reproduction.

Captive specimens rarely reach their full size. In its natural habitat, *Botia macracanthus* grows to a length of 30 cm, while its captive cognates, barely achieve 18 cm in length. Perhaps aquarium specimens never attain sexual maturity. The male's thick 2nd ray of the pectoral fins can be widely used to differentiate genders.

Some loaches are territorial, but their defense concentrates on conspecifics, not heterospecifics. Their diet is predominately omnivorous, but the carnivorous species among them frequently refuse dry commercial diets. Live and frozen foods must be offered in such cases.

Virtually all species are suitable for the community aquarium, but some species require cooler than average temperatures for maintenance. However, the wide distribution of this family implies that there are suitable species for almost all aquaria.

Acantopsis dialuzona   1/366
Long-nosed loach
H: SE Asia.
SD: Unknown.   S: +
B: In caves or under rocks.   F: C,O
T: 25–28°C, L: 22.5 cm, pH: <7, D: 2–3

CARPLIKE F.

Acantopsis sp.   5/104
Vietnam loach
H: SE Asia: Vietnam.
SD: Unknown.   S: +
B: In caves or under rocks.   F: C,O
T: 22–26°C, L: 18 cm, pH: 7, D: 2–3

Botia beauforti   2/342
Beaufort's loach
H: SE Asia: Thailand, Laos.
SD: Unknown.   S: =
B: Unknown.   F: O
T: 26–30°C, L: 25 cm, pH: <7, D: 2

Botia berdmorei   1/366

H: SE Asia: Burma, Thailand.
SD: Unknown.   S: =
B: Unknown.   F: C,O
T: 22–26°C, L: 25 cm, pH: 7, D: 2–3

Botia dario   3/166
Bengal loach
H: Asia: India.
♀: Ventrally fuller.   S: +
B: Unsuccessful.   F: C,O
T: 23–26°C, L: 6.5 cm, pH: 7, D: 3

Botia eos juv.   2/340, (5/105)
Sun loach
H: SE Asia: Laos, Thailand.
SD: Unknown.   **S:** +
B: In flooded regions.   **F:** C
T: 24–28°C, **L:** 6 cm, **pH:** <7, **D:** 2–3

Botia fasciata (= *Parabotia fasciata*)   4/152
Striped loach
H: Asia: China: Yangtze River.
SD: Unknown.   **S:** =
B: Unknown.   **F:** C
T: 20–26°C, **L:** >15 cm, **pH:** 7, **D:** 2–3

Botia helodes   1/368
Banded loach, tiger loach
H: SE Asia: Thailand, Laos, Cambodia.
SD: Unknown.   **S:** –
B: Unsuccessful.   **F:** C,O
T: 24–30°C, **L:** 22 cm, **pH:** <7, **D:** 2

Botia lecontei   2/342
Le Conte's loach, red-finned loach
H: SE Asia: E Thailand, Laos.
SD: Unknown.   **S:** +
B: Unknown.   **F:** C
T: 24–28°C, **L:** 15 cm, **pH:** <7, **D:** 2–3

Botia lecontei   2/342
Le Conte's loach, red-finned loach
See photo on p. 5/106.

Botia lohachata   1/370
Pakistani loach
H: Asia: NE India, Bangladesh.
SD: Unknown.   **S:** +
B: Unsuccessful.   **F:** O
T: 24–30°C, **L:** 7 cm, **pH:** <7, **D:** 2

Botia almorhae   5/105
Pakistani loach
H: SE Asia: China, Yangtse.
♂: Unknown.   S: =
B: Unknown.   F: C
T: 22–26°C, L: 15 cm, pH: 7, D: 2–3

Botia macracanthus   1/370
Clown loach, tiger loach
H: SE Asia: Indonesia: Sumatra, Borneo.
♂: Caudal fin more deeply forked.   S: –
B: Nat.: beginning of rainy season.   F: O
T: 25–30°C, L: <30 cm, pH: <7, D: 2–3

Botia macracanthus var.   1/370
Clown loach, tiger loach
(See photo on p. 5/108)

Botia morleti   1/368
Hora's loach
H: Asia: Thailand, Laos, Cambodia.
SD: Unknown.   S: –
B: Unsuccessful.   F: C,O
T: 24–30°C, L: 22 cm, pH: <7, D: 2

Botia morleti   1/368
Hora's loach
(See photo on p. 5/107)

Botia nigrolineata   5/109
Black-line loach
H: Asia: China.
SD: None.   S: +
B: Unsuccessful.   F: C,O
T: 15–25°C, L: 5 cm, pH: >7, D: 2–3

CARPLIKE F.

Botia robusta   4/154
Kansu loach
H: Asia: China.
SD: Unknown.   S: =
B: Unsuccessful.   F: C,O
T: 18–24°C, L: 18 cm, pH: >7, D: 3

Botia rostrata ♀   3/166
Ladder loach
H: Asia: Burma, India.
♀: Larger; few light blotches.   S: –
B: Unsuccessful.   F: C,O
T: 22–25°C, L: 6 cm, pH: <7, D: 1

Botia rubripinnis   1/372
Orange-finned loach
H: SE Asia: Thailand, Vietnam, Malay Pen.
♂: Smaller?   S: –
B: Unsuccessful.   F: C,O
T: 26–30°C, L: 24 cm, pH: <7, D: 2

Botia rubripinnis juvenile   1/372
Orange-finned loach
See photo on p. 5/107.

Botia sidthimunki   1/372
Dwarf loach
H: SE Asia: N Thailand.
SD: None.   S: +
B: Successful, but no data.   F: C,O
T: 26–28°C, L: 6 cm, pH: <7, D: 2

Botia sidthimunki   5/110
Dwarf loach
H: Asia: E India.
♀: Fuller and stouter.   S: +
B: Artificial insemination.   F: C,O
T: 22–27°C, L: 6 cm, pH: <7, D: 2–3

Botia striata   2/344
Zebra loach
H: Asia: S India.
SD: Unknown.   S: +
B: There are no breeding reports.   F: O
T: 23–26°C, L: <10 cm, pH: 7, D: 1–2

Botia superciliaris   4/152

H: Asia: China: Szeshwan.
SD: Not described.   S: =
B: Unknown.   F: C,O
T: 22–26°C, L: 15 cm, pH: <7, D: 3–4

Cobitis caspia   5/112
Caspian loach
H: Asia: Tributaries of the Caspian Sea.
♂: 2nd pectoral fin rays thicker.   S: +
B: Scatterer among plants & rocks.   F: C
T: 10–25°C, L: 7 cm, pH: >7, D: 2–3

Cobitis taenia   (4/163)
Spined loach

Cobitis taenia bilineata   (4/163)
Spined loach

Cobitis taenia taenia   1/374
Spined loach, spotted weather loach
H: Europe, W Asia.
♂: Smaller; 2nd P fin rays thicker.   S: +
B: Among plants.   F: C!
T: 14–18°C, L: 12 cm, pH: >7, D: 2–3

167

Kottelatlimia pristes   4/156

H: SE Asia: Malaysia.
SD: Unknown.   S: +
B: Unknown.   F: O
T: 22–25°C, L: 6 cm, pH: ≪7, D: 4

Lepidocephalus thermalis   2/346
Indian loach, lesser loach
H: Asia: India, Sri Lanka.
SD: Unknown.   S: (–)
B: Unknown.   F: O
T: 24–30°C, L: 8 cm, pH: <7, D: 2–3

Leptobotia elongata   4/156
Giant loach
H: Asia: China.
♂: Spine under eyes.   S: –
B: Nat.: spawning migrations.   F: C,O
T: 22–28°C, L: <50 cm, pH: <7, D: 4

Leptobotia guilinensis   4/158

H: Asia: China.
SD: Unknown.   S: +
B: Unknown.   F: C,O
T: 23–27°C, L: 12 cm, pH: 7, D: 2–3

Leptobotia mantschurica   2/346
Manchurian loach
H: Asia: Russia, China.
♂: Spine under eyes.   S: ?
B: Unsuccessful.   F: C,O
T: 16–20°C, L: 2 cm, pH: 7, D: 3

Leptobotia rubrilabris   4/158
Red-lipped loach
H: Asia: China.
♂: Red lips.   S: +
B: Unsuccessful.   F: C,O
T: 18–25°C, L: 12 cm, pH: 7, D: 2–3

Misgurnus anguillicaudatus   2/348
Chinese weatherfish
H: Asia: Siberia, China, Korea, Japan.
♂: 2nd pectoral fin rays thick.   S: +
B: Coincidentally successful.   F: O
T: 10–25°C, L: <50 cm, pH: 7, D: 1–2

Misgurnus bipartitus ♂   5/112
Russian weatherfish
H: Asia: N China, Mongolia.   Rare
♂: More colorful at spawning time.   S: –
B: There is no breeding report. F: C,O
T: 5–20°C, L: 15 cm, pH: 7, D: 3

CARPLIKE F.

Misgurnus fossilis   1/374
Weather loach, European weatherfish
H: Europe.
♂: Smaller; 2nd P fin rays thicker.   S: +
B: Coincidentally successful.   F: C
T: 4–25°C, L: 30 cm, pH: 7, D: 1–2

Misgurnus cf. *anguillicaudatus*   2/348
Chinese weatherfish
H: Asia: Siberia, China, Korea, Japan.
♂: 2nd pectoral fin rays thicker.   S: +
B: Coincidentally successful.   F: O
T: 10–25°C, L: <50 cm, pH: 7, D: 1–2

Schistura sp.   2/356

Pangio anguillaris Eel loach   2/338
(photo: *P. oblonga* or *P. piperata*)
H: SE Asia: Thailand, Borneo.
SD: Unknown.   S: +
B: Unknown.   F: O
T: 24–26°C, L: 6.5 cm, pH: 7, D: 1

CARPLIKE F.

Pangio kuhlii   4/160
Kuhli loach
H: E Asia: Vietnam (new site).
♀: Fuller during spawning season. S: +
B: There are no breeding reports. F: C,O
T: 20–26°C, L: 11 cm, pH: 7, D: 2

Pangio kuhlii   4/160
Albino kuhli loach
Bred form. Maintenance corresponds to
the wild form; however, albinos are more
sensitive and not as longevous.

Pangio kuhlii myersi   1/364
Kuhli loach, prickly eye
H: SE Asia.
SD: Unknown.   S: +
B: Among roots of floating plants. F: C,O
T: 24–30°C, L: 12 cm, pH: <7, D: 2

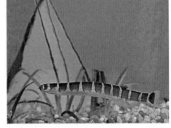

Pangio kuhlii sumatranus   1/364
Kuhli loach, prickly eye

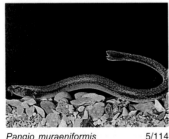

Pangio muraeniformis   5/114
Moray loach
H: SE Asia: Malay Peninsula.
♂: 2nd pectoral fin rays thickened. S: +
B: Unknown.   F: O
T: 24–28°C, L: 8 cm, pH: 7, D: 1

Pangio pangia   2/338
Cinnamon loach
H: Asia: India, Burma.
SD: Unknown.   S: +
B: Unknown.   F: O
T: 23–25°C, L: 6 cm, pH: 7, D: 1

Pangio semicinctus   2/340
Half-banded loach
H: SE Asia: Malay Peninsula.
♂: 2nd pectoral fin rays thicker.   S: +
B: Unsuccessful.   F: C!
T: 26–30°C, L: 8 cm, pH: <7, D: 2

Pangio shelfordii   1/364
Shelford's prickly eye
H: Malay Achipelago.
SD: Unknown.   S: +
B: Unknown.   F: C,O
T: 24–30°C, L: 8 cm, pH: <7, D: 2

CARPLIKE F.

Paramisgurnus dabryanus   5/114

H: Asia: China: Jangtse River.
SD: Unknown.   S: +
B: Unsuccessful.   F: C,O
T: 10–25°C, L: 9 cm, pH: 7, D: 2

Sabanejewia aurata bulgarica   4/162
Golden loach
H: Europe: central and upper Danube.
♂: Smaller. ♀: Fuller.   S: +
B: Unsuccessful.   F: C
T: 5–20°C, L: 12 cm, pH: 7, D: 2–3

Sabanejewia romanica   5/116
Romanian loach
H: Europe: Romania, Bulgaria.
SD: Unknown.   S: +
B: Nature: April–June.   F: C
T: 10–18°C, L: <12 cm, pH: 7, D: 4

Somileptes gongota   5/110
Cat-eye loach
H: Asia: India, Burma.
SD: Unknown.   S: =
B: Unsuccessful; under slate.   F: C!
T: 18–22°C, L: 14 cm, pH: 7, D: 4

Family Cyprinidae

With 210 genera and just over 2000 species, the Cyprinidae is the most species-rich family of freshwater fishes. Some grow to lengths in excess of 2 m, while others are diminutive. In fact, the smallest freshwater fish, *Danionella translucida* (12 mm long), is a Cyprinidae. The family is distributed throughout most of Europe and Asia (1270 species), Africa (475 species), and North America (about 270 species). The northernmost sections of Europe and Asia lack cyprinids.

Most people have been exposed to cyprinids through small, common aquarium fishes (especially of the genera *Barbus, Carassius, Danio,* and *Rasbora*), as laboratory animals in genetic research (e.g., *Brachydanio, Danio*), decorative fishes for the garden pond (e.g., koi—the bringers of good fortune in Japan), and/or bounty for the table. Certain large species, e.g., *Cyprinus carpio,* have been cultured for millennia in China and for centuries in Europe. *Ctenopharyngodon idellus* and some of the large *Barbus* species are now being cultured as well.

Carp pituitary extract is commonly used even today to induce migratory fishes to spawn in ponds, although synthetic analogues are progressively becoming more popular. Outside their natural habitat, Chinese carps such as the grass carp will not spawn without hormone injections. Large *Barbus,* and other tropical species are considerably easier to breed, since they do not require hormone injections.

Koi, beloved kings of garden ponds, are colorful linages of *Cyprinus carpio.* In Japan, award-winning specimens sell for tens of thousands of dollars.

Bred linages of *Barbus tetrazona*: top albino, bottom "moss barb" (p. 193).

Characteristically, males can readily be distinguished during the spawning season by their breeding coloration and so-called spawning eczema, or nuptial tubercles. The latter are white knots which appear chiefly on the cephalic region.

The Cyprinidae offer a rich selection of species suitable for aquaria:

- *Barbus*: These active schooling fishes come in all sizes. The aquarium must have a volume of at least 50 l, and larger species will require significantly more. A dark substrate and copious vegetation are of benefit, whereas an open swimming area is a necessity. Most species prefer the lower water column. Some have a tendency to pull on long, filamentous fins of their tankmates, e.g., the ventral fins of angelfishes and various gouramis. For breeding, soft, neutral, aged water is preferred by the majority of species. Aquarium reproduction is feasible for most, and even simplistic in some species. Place the aquarium so that it receives the morning sun. The scattered eggs adhere to fine-leaved plants or sink to the substrate. Avid spawn predators, barbs must be removed from the breeding tank after the spawning episode has concluded.

- *Epalzeorhynchus*: Although usually waspish among themselves, *Epalzeorhynchus* are peaceful towards heterospecifics. The aquarium's decor should provide numerous hiding places such that territories out of direct visual contact with their neighbors can be established. Their diet varies from live foods to algae. Reproduction—which is rarely successful because of pronounced intraspecific aggressions—is contingent on the presence of a cave and soft, slightly acid water. *E. bicolor* is pond-bred in tropical countries, mainly Asia.

- *Rasbora*: Most *Rasbora* are small schooling fishes which inhabit the central and upper water strata. Some species require very soft, acid water. Breeding has been successful with many species, whereby fine-leaved plants are generally preferred over broad-leaved species as a spawning substrate. Age and pair selection seem to play an important role. Despite their positive attributes as community fishes, some of the more delicate species should be housed in their own dedicated aquarium.

Abbottina elongata ♀   5/118

H: Asia: China: Amur Basin.
♂: Larger, convex dorsal fin.   S: +
B: June, July; brood care (♂).   F: C,O
T: 15–24°C, L: 8.5 cm, pH: 7, D: 2

Abbottina rivularis   3/168

H: Asia: CIS States, Korea, Japan, China.
♂: Larger; nuptial tubercles.   S: +
B: June, July; brood care (♂).   F: H,C
T: 18–23°C, L: 13.5 cm, pH: 7, D: 2–3

CARPLIKE F.

Abramis ballerus   4/164

H: Europe: Elbe to Newa; Scandinavia.
♂: Nuptial tubercles.   S: +
B: Migrates during early summer.   F: O
T: 5–25°C, L: 35 cm, pH: 7, D: 2–3

Abramis brama   3/169
Bream

H: Europe.
♂: Nuptial tubercles.   S: +
B: May, June; <300 000 eggs.   F: O
T: 10–24°C, L: 75 cm, pH: >7, D: 1–2

Abramis sapa bergi   5/118
Berg's bream

H: Asia: Azerbaijan, Georgia.
♂: Spawning eczema; slimmer.   S: +
B: May, June; <300 000 eggs.   F: O
T: 10–25°C, L: <39 cm, pH: 7, D: 4

Abramis vimba   3/272, 5/224
Vimba

H: Eu.: S Sweden, S Finland, Germany.
♂: Slimmer; no tubercles.   S:+
B: May/Aug.; shallow, rocky shores. F:C
T: 10–20°C, L: 40 cm, pH: >7, D: 2–4

Abramis vimba juv.   3/272, 5/224
Vimba

Acanthalburnus microlepis   3/170
Napotta

H: Asia: CIS States.
♀: Fuller during spawning season. S: +
B: Largely unknown.   F: C,O
T: 10–20°C, L: 25 cm, pH: >7, D: 2

Acanthorhodeus asmussi　　　2/358
Russian bitterling
H: Asia: CIS States, W South Korea.
♂: Breeding colors. ♀: Ovipositor. **S:** +
B: Nat.: mantle cavity of bivalve. **F:** H,O
T: 18–22°C, **L:** 16 cm, **pH:** 7, **D:** 2–3

CARPLIKE F.

Acanthorhodeus barbatulus　　　5/120
Chinese bitterling
H: Asia: China.
♂: Breeding colors. ♀: Ovipositor. **S:** +
B: Nat.: mantle cavity of bivalve.　**F:** O
T: 8–20°C, **L:** ♀ 7 cm, **pH:** 7, **D:** 2–3

Acanthorhodeus macropterus　　　5/120
Giant bitterling
H: Asia: China: Jangtse and Ningpo rivers.
♂: Spawning colors.　　　　　　**S:** +,=
B: Nat.: littoral zone among plants. **F:** O
T: 15–25°C, **L:** 27 cm, **pH:** 7, **D:** 1–4

Acheilognathus chankaensis　　　2/358

H: Asia: CIS States.
♂: Spawning colors. ♀: Ovipositor. **S:** +
B: Nat.: mantle cavity of bivalve. **F:** H,O
T: 18–22°C, **L:** 11 cm, **pH:** 7, **D:** 2–3

Acheilognathus tabira　　　5/122
Tabira bitterling
H: Asia: Japan.
♂: Spawning colors. ♀: Ovipositor.　**S:** =
B: Nat.: bivalve. Among stones? **F:** C,O
T: 10–25°C, **L:** 8.5 cm, **pH:** 7, **D:** 2

Acrossocheilus deauratus　　　5/122
Golden barb
H: Asia: China: Canton.
SD: Unknown.　　　　　　　　**S:** +
B: N.: e scattered among plants. **F:** O,H
T: 12–24°C, **L:** 12 cm, **pH:** 7, **D:** 2

CARPLIKE F.

Tor soro   2/360
Large-scaled barb
H: SE Asia: Sumatra, Thailand.
SD: Unknown.   S: –
B: There are no reports.   F: O,H
T: 22–26°C, L: <100 cm, pH: 7, D: 3

Alburnoides bipunctatus eichwaldi 5/124
Eichwald's chub ♀
H: Asia: surroundings of the Caspian Sea.
♂: Slimmer.   S: =
B: Spawning migrations.   F: C,O
T: 10–23°C, L: 4.5 cm, pH: >7, D: 2

Alburnoides oblongus   3/170
Tashkent tailorfish
H: Asia: CIS States.
♀: Fuller during spawning season. S: =
B: There are no reports.   F: C,O
T: 10–20°C, L: 14 cm, pH: >7, D: 2

Alburnoides bipunctatus   1/379
Chub, tailorfish
H: Europe.
♀: Stouter.   S: =
B: Rarely successful; on gravel. F: C,O
T: 10–18°C, L: 14 cm, pH: 7, D: 2

Alburnoides bipunctatus fasciatus 3/174
Striped tailorfish
H: Asia: CIS States.
♀: Stouter.   S: =
B: Unsuccessful.   F: C,O
T: 10–20°C, L: 12.5 cm, pH: 7, D: 2–3

Alburnoides taeniatus   2/360
Striped tailor
H: Asia: CIS States.
♀: Ventrally convex.   S: =
B: Nature: June–July.   F: C,O
T: 10–20°C, L: 9 cm, pH: >7, D: 2

Alburnus albidus   4/164
Mediterranean bleak, alborella
H: Europe: S Italy.
♂: Nuptial tubercles.   S: +
B: Substrate spawner; stones.   F: C,O
T: 12–28°C, L: 20 cm, pH: 7, D: 2–3

Alburnus alburnus   3/173
Bleak
H: Europe.
♂: Nuptial tubercles.   S: =
B: N.: April–June; also aquarium. F:C,O
T: 10–20°C, L: 25 cm, pH: 7, D: 2

Alburnus charusini hohenackeri 3/174
Transcaucasian bleak
H: Asia: CIS States.
♂: Nuptial tubercles.   S: =
B: Unknown.   F: C
T: 10–20°C, L: 12 cm, pH: 7, D: 2–3

Aspius aspius aspius   3/176
Asp
H: Central Europe, W Asia.
♂: Nuptial tubercles.   S: =,–
B: Nat.: April–June; <100 000 e.   F: C!
T: 4–20°C, L: <100 cm, pH: 7, D: 2

Aspius aspius taeniatus   3/176
Caspian asp
H: Asia: CIS States.
♂: Nuptial tubercles.   S: =,–
B: Nat.: March–April; <483 000 e.   F: C!
T: 10–20°C, L: 77 cm, pH: >7, D: 2–3

Balantiocheilus melanopterus   1/380
Silver shark, bala shark
H: SE Asia: Thai., Sum., Bor., Malay Pen.
♀: Fuller at spawning time.   S: +,–
B: Induced breeding?   F: O
T: 22–28°C, L: 35 cm, pH: <7, D: 2

177

Barbichthys nitidus   2/362
"Siam highfin shark," sucker barb
H: SE Asia.
SD: Unknown.   S: ?
B: Unsuccessful.   F: O
T: 23–26°C, L: 35 cm, pH: 7, D: 2–3

Barboides gracilis   4/166
Dwarf barb
H: Africa: Benin, Nigeria, SW Cameroon.
♀: Larger; fuller at spawning time. S: +
B: Unknown.   F: C,O
T: 24–26°C, L: 2.5 cm, pH: <7, D: 2

Barbus ablabes   2/362

H: W Africa.
♀: Clearly fuller.   S: +
B: Spawning grid; <500 eggs.   F: C,O
T: 23–25°C, L: 11 cm, pH: <7, D: 2–3

Barbus aboinensis   4/166
Aboina barb
H: Africa: S Nigeria.
♀: Much fuller.   S: +
B: Unknown.   F: C,O
T: 24–28°C, L: 8 cm, pH: 7, D: 2

Barbodes altus   3/179
Tall barb
H: Asia: Thailand, Laos.
♀: Fuller.   S: +
B: Unknown.   F: C,O
T: 22–27°C, L: 15 cm, pH: 7, D: 1–2

Barbus amphigramma   3/181

H: E Africa: Kenya, Uganda, Tanzania.
♂: Slimmer.   S: +
B: Unsuccessful.   F: C
T: 19–26°C, L: 7.5 cm, pH: 7, D: 2

Barbus apleurogramma   3/182

H: Africa: Uganda, Rwanda, Burundi, Tanz.
♂: Slimmer?   S: +
B: Unknown.   F: O
T: 23–26°C, L: 5 cm, pH: <7, D: 2

Puntius arulius   1/380
Arulius barb, longfin barb
H: S and SE India.
♂: Very elongated dorsal fin rays.   S: =
B: Plant thicket; <100 eggs.   F: O
T: 19–25°C, L: 12 cm, pH: <7, D: 2–3

Barbus atakorensis   3/184

H: Africa: Ghana, N Benin, Nigeria.
SD: Unknown.   S: +
B: There are no reports.   F: O
T: 22–25°C, L: 4 cm, pH: ≪7, D: 2–3

Barbus bandula ♀   3/197
Bandulla barb

Barbus bandula ♂   3/197
Bandulla barb

Barbus barbus   2/364
River barb, barbel
H: Europe: France to the Memel, England.
♂: Spawning eczema.   S: +,=
B: May–June; schoolwise; upriver.   F: O
T: 10–24°C, L: 90 cm, pH: 7, D: 2

Barbus barbus borystenicus   5/126
Lotus barb
H: Euro.: CIS States, Balkans, Switzerland.
♂: Nuptial tubercles.   S: +,=
B: Too large for aquarium breeding. F: O
T: 5–20°C, L: 85 cm, pH: 7, D: 4

Barbus barilioides   2/364
Blue-barred barb
H: Africa: Angola, Zimbab., Zambia, Zaïre.
♀: Fuller. Ink red when young?   S: +
B: Plant thicket.   F: O
T: 20–26°C, L: 5 cm, pH: <7, D: 1–2

Barbus baudoni   4/168
Baudoni barb
H: Africa: Nigeria.
♀: Fuller.   S: +
B: Unknown.   F: C,O
T: 24–26°C, L: 4 cm, pH: 7, D: 3–4

Puntius bimaculatus t.♀, b.♂   2/366
Two-spotted barb, red-striped barb
H: SE Asia: Sri Lanka.
♂: Slender; dark red longitu. band. S: +
B: Java moss; 400 e; spawn pred.   F: O
T: 22–24°C, L: 7 cm, pH: <7, D: 2

Puntius binotatus   2/366
Spotted barb
H: SE Asia: Malaysia, Indonesia, Philip.
♂: More slender.   S: +
B: Java moss; 400 e; spawn pred.   F: O
T: 24–26°C, L: <18 cm, pH: <7, D: 1–2

Puntius binotatus   3/196
Spotted barb

Barbus callipterus   1/382
Clipper barb
H: W Africa: Cameroon to Nigeria.
♀: Significantly fuller.   S: +
B: Unsuccessful.   F: O
T: 19–25°C, L: 9 cm, pH: 7, D: 1

Barbus camptacanthus   5/124
Black-spotted silver barb
H: Africa: Cameroon, Gabon, Niger Delta.
♀: Fuller at spawning time.   S: =
B: Eggs scattered over plants.   F: O
T: 22–28°C, L: 16 cm, pH: 7, D: 2

Barbus candens   3/184
Red three-spot barb
H: Africa: Zaïre.
♂: Slimmer, brighter, slightly larger.   S: +
B: Unsuccessful.   F: O
T: 24–26°C, L: 4 cm, pH: 7, D: 2–3

Puntius canius   4/170
Canine barb
H: India: Ganges River.
♂: Reddish dorsal and ventral fins.   S: =
B: Fine-leaved plants; spawn. grid.   F: O
T: 18–28°C, L: 10 cm, pH: 7, D: 2

Barbus graellsi   5/128
Ebro barb   Bw for older specimens
H: Europe: Spain: Ebro Basin.   E
♂: Nuptial tubercles; slimmer.   S: =
B: Spawning migrations.   F: C,O
T: 10–24°C, L: 50 cm, pH: 7, D: 4

Barbus caudovittatus   3/186
Striped tail barb
H: Africa: Zaïre Basin.
SD: Unknown.   S: =
B: Unsuccessful.   F: O
T: 24–27°C, L: 80 cm, pH: 7, D: 2

Barbus chlorotaenia   4/168

H: Africa: Ghana, Nigeria, Cameroon.
♂: Slightly smaller.   S: +
B: Unsuccessful.   F: O
T: 23–27°C, L: <8 cm, pH: 7, D: 2

Puntius chola   3/186
Cola barb

H: Asia: India, Bangladesh, Burma.
♂: Reddish fins when spawning.   S: +
B: Aquatic plants; spawning grid.   F: O
T: 20–25°C, L: 15 cm, pH: <7, D: 1–2

Barbus ciscaucasicus juv.   5/126
Caucasus barb

H: Asia: E rivers of the Caspian Sea.
♂: Nuptial tubercles; slimmer.   S: =
B: Spawning migrations.   F: C,O
T: 10–22°C, L: 39 cm, pH: 7, D: 4

Puntius conchonius l.♀, r.♂   1/382
Rosy barb

H: Asia: NW India.
SD: See photo.   S: =
B: Aquatic plants; preys on spawn.   F: O
T: 18–22°C, L: 15 cm, pH: <7, D: 1

Barbus congicus ♂   4/170
Congo barb

H: Af.: Zaire Basin. Malagarasi Basin?
♂: More colorful and slimmer.   S: =
B: Unsuccessful.   F: O
T: 22–26°C, L: 6 cm, pH: <7, D: 3

Barbus congicus ♀   4/170
Congo barb

Puntius cumingi   1/384
Cuming's barb
H: Sri Lanka.
♂: Slimmer; more colorful fins.   S: =
B: Difficult.   F: O
T: 22–27°C, L: 5 cm, pH: <7, D: 2–3

Barbodes pierrei front   2/368
(*Barbodes schwanenfeldi* back)   (2/369)
H: SE Asia: Thailand.
♂: Much more slender.   S: =
B: Unknown.   F: O
T: 22–25°C, L: 18 cm, pH: 7, D: 2

CARPLIKE F.

Barbus donaldsonsmithi   4/173

H: Africa: Niger Basin.
♂: Smaller and slimmer.   S: +
B: Unknown.   F: O
T: 23–27°C, L: <11 cm, pH: 7, D: 2–3

Barbus eburneensis   3/189

H: Africa: Guinea to W Ivory Coast.
SD: Unknown.   S: +
B: Unsuccessful.   F: O
T: 22–25°C, L: 9 cm, pH: ≪7, D: 2–3

Barbus eutaenia   4/174
Dusky black-striped barb
H: Central and southern Africa.
♂: Slightly brighter and slimmer.   S: =
B: Unknown.   F: O
T: 20–26°C, L: 8 cm, pH: 7, D: 2

Puntius everetti   1/386
Clown barb
H: SE Asia: Singapore, Borneo.
♂: Brighter and slimmer.   S: +
B: Among plants; morning sun.   F: O
T: 24–27°C, L: 10 cm, pH: <7, D: 2–3

CARPLIKE F.

Puntius fasciatus   1/386
Banded barb
H: SE Asia: Malay Peninsula, Indonesia.
♂: Slimmer and usually smaller.   S: +
B: Not easy.   F: O
T: 22–26°C, L: 15 cm, pH: <7, D: 2–3

Puntius filamentosus   1/388
Black-spot barb
H: Asia: India, Sri Lanka.
♂: Brighter; usually smaller.   S: +
B: Among fine-leaved plants.   F: O
T: 20–24°C, L: 15 cm, pH: <7, D: 2

Puntius foerschi   3/190
Foersch's barb
H: SE Asia: Indonesia (Borneo).
♂: Usually slimmer.   S: +
B: Unsuccessful.   F: O
T: 24–28°C, L: 6 cm, pH: <7, D: 2

Puntius gelius   1/388
Golden dwarf barb, golden barb
H: Africa: Zaïre Basin.
♂: Colorful lateral bands; slimmer. S: +
B: Underside of leaf; <100e; sp.pred. F: O
T: 18–23°C, L: 4 cm, pH: <7, D: 2

Barbus guirali   3/190

H: Africa: S Cameroon, Gabon.
SD: Unknown.   S: +
B: Unsuccessful?   F: O
T: 22–26°C, L: 17 cm, pH: ≪7, D: 2–3

Barbus holotaenia   1/390
African long-stripe barb
H: Africa: Cameroon to Zaïre and Angola.
SD: Unknown.   S: +
B: Unsuccessful.   F: O
T: 24–30°C, L: 12 cm, pH: <7, D: 2–3

Barbus hulstaerti   1/390
Butterfly barb
H: Africa: Angola, Zaïre.
♂: Anterior spot sickle-shaped.   S: +
B: Darkened aquarium; max. 22°C.   F: O
T: around 24°C, L: 3.5 cm, pH: ≪7, D: 3

Barbus jae ♂   2/368
Jae barb, puntius jae
H: Western central Africa.
♂: Much more colorful.   S: +
B: Preys on spawn.   F: O
T: 21–25°C, L: 4 cm, pH: ≪7, D: 2

Barbus jae ♀   2/368
Jae barb, puntius jae

Barbus cf. *jae*   5/130
Jae barb, puntius jae
H: W Africa: Gabon.
SD: No difference at 3 cm length.   S: +
B: There are no breeding reports.   F: C,O
T: 22–26°C, L: 4 cm, pH: 7, D: 2

Barbus janssensi ♂♂   2/370
Janssen's barb
H: Africa: Zaïre.
♂: Smaller; spots more contrasting. S: +
B: Unsuccessful.   F: O
T: 24–26°C, L: 10 cm, pH: <7, D: 2

Puntius johorensis   1/384
Johore barb, striped barb
H: Malay Pen., Malaysia, Sum., Borneo.
♂: Slimmer; more contrasting lines. S: +
B: On plants; very prolific.   F: O
T: 23–25°C, L: 12 cm, pH: ≪7, D: 2

185

Barbus kerstenii kerstenii 3/192
Kersten's barb
H: Af.: Kenya, Uganda, Tanzania, Ruanda.
♂: Slimmer. S: +
B: Unsuccessful. F: O
T: 23–26°C, L: 9 cm, pH: 7, D: 2

Puntius lateristriga 1/392
Spanner barb, T-barb
H: SE Asia.
♂: Brighter red and slimmer. S: +
B: Plant thicket; preys on spawn. F: O
T: 25–28°C, L: 18 cm, pH: <7, D: 2–3

Puntius lateristriga 5/144
Spanner barb, T-barb
H: Asia: India: Johore.
♂: More slender. S: +
B: Plant thicket; preys on spawn. F:O,H
T: 20–28°C, L: 7 cm, pH: >7, D: 1–2

Barbus leonensis 2/370
Sierra Leone barb
H: W Af.: Sierra L., Gambia, Niger, Chad.
SD: Unknown. S: +
B: Unsuccessful. F: O
T: 22–24°C, L: 3 cm, pH: ≪7, D: 2

Puntius lineatus t.♀, b.♂ 2/372
Striped barb, line barb
H: Africa: Zaïre Basin.
♂: Slimmer; more contrasting lines. S: +
B: Plants; very prolific. F: O
T: 21–24°C, L: 12 cm, pH: <7, D: 2

Barbus lineomaculatus 2/372
Dotted-line barb
H: Africa: Kenya, Tanzania, Zaïre.
♂: Slimmer? S: +?
B: Unsuccessful. F: C
T: 22–25°C, L: 8 cm, pH: <7, D: 2

Barbus macrops b.♂, t.♀   4/174
Slender black-striped barb
H: W Africa, Chad Basin.
♂: Smaller and slimmer.   S: +
B: Unsuccessful.   F: O
T: 22–28°C, L: 12 cm, pH: 7, D: 3–4

Barbus paludinosus t.♂, b.♀   5/132
Swamp barb
H: Africa: Ethiopia to Angola.
♂: Slimmer. Red fins?   S: +
B: Unsuccessful.   F: C,O
T: 20°C, L: 8–12 cm, pH: 7, D: 2

CARPLIKE F.

Barbus martorelli   4/178

H: Africa: Equatorial Guinea, Zaïre.
♂: Smaller and slimmer.   S: +
B: No reports known.   F: O
T: 22–26°C, L: <12 cm, pH: 7, D: 2–3

Barbus meridionalis   4/178
Trout barb
H: S Europe.
SD: None.   S: +
B: Nature: May/June.   F: O
T: 5–25°C, L: 30 cm, pH: 7, D: 2

Barbus miolepis miolepis   3/192
Reticulated barb
H: Africa: Zaïre Basin.
♂: 1st dorsal fin ray always dark?   S: +
B: Not a prolific species.   F: O
T: 24–28°C, L: 11 cm, pH: 7, D: 2

Barbus multilineatus   4/180
Many-lined barb
H: Africa: SE Zaïre.
♂: Slimmer.   S: +
B: Unsuccessful.   F: C,O
T: 22–26°C, L: <4.5 cm, pH: <7, D: 3

Barbus musumbi 4/182
Angola barb, Musumbi barb
H: Africa: Angola.
♂: Brighter and slimmer. S: +
B: Simple; plants; 500–600 eggs. F: C,O
T: 22–26°C, L: <6 cm, pH: 7, D: 1

Puntius narayani ♂ 2/374
H: S Asia: Sri Lanka.
♂: Slimmer. S: +
B: Unsuccessful. F: O
T: 22–26°C, L: 6 cm?, pH: <7, D: 2

Barbus neumayeri 3/194
Neumayer's barb
H: E Africa: Kenya, Uganda.
♂: Slimmer. S: +
B: Unsuccessful. F: O
T: 23–27°C, L: 12 cm, pH: <7, D: 2–3

Puntius nigrofasciatus front ♂ 1/392
Black ruby barb, purple-headed barb
H: Asia: S Sri Lanka.
SD: See photo. S: +
B: Fine-leaved plants. F: O
T: 22–26°C, L: 6.5 cm, pH: <7, D: 1

Barbus nyanzae 5/128
Nyanza barb
H: E Africa: Uganda, Kenya.
SD: Not described. S: +
B: Unsuccessful. F: C,O
T: 18–28°C, L: 6 cm, pH: 7, D: 2

Barbus oligogrammus 5/130
H: Africa: Burundi.
♂: Slimmer. S: +
B: Eggs scattered among plants. F: C,O
T: 22–27°C, L: 6 cm, pH: >7, D: 2

CARPLIKE F.

Puntius oligolepis t.♀, b.♂   1/394
Checkered barb, island barb
H: Indonesia: Sumatra.
♂: More colorful and slimmer.   S: +
B: Dense vegetation; <300 eggs.   F: O
T: 20–24°C, L: 5 cm, pH: <7, D: 1

Puntius orphoides adult   1/394
Red-cheek barb
H: SE Asia: Thai., Java, Madura, Borneo.
SD: Unknown.   S: +
B: Unsuccessful.   F: O,H
T: 22–25°C, L: 25 cm, pH: <7, D: 2

CARPLIKE F.

Puntius orphoides juvenile   1/394
Red-cheek barb

Barbus paludinosus t.♂, b.♀   5/132
Swamp barb
H: Africa: Ethiopia to Angola.
♂: Slimmer. Red fins?   S: +
B: Unsuccessful.   F: C,O
T: 20°C, L: 8–12 cm, pH: 7, D: 2

Barbus paludinosus Kenya   5/132
Swamp barb

Barbus paludinosus Tanzania   5/132
Swamp barb

Puntius partipentazona 3/194
Partially banded barb
H: Asia: Thailand, Laos, W Malaysia.
♂: Slimmer. S: =
B: Fine-leaved plants. F: O
T: 22–25°C, L: 4.5 cm, pH: 7, D: 1–2

Barbus pellegrini 4/177
Pellegrin's barb
H: Af.: lakes Kivu, Edward, Tanganyika.
SD: Very slight. S: +
B: Among plants; spawning grid. F:C,O
T: 22–28°C, L: 12 cm, pH: 7, D: 2

Puntius pentazona 1/396
Five-banded barb
H: SE Asia: Singapore, Malay Pen., Borneo.
♂: Brighter, smaller, slimmer. S: +
B: Harmonious pair; <200 eggs. F: C
T: 22–26°C, L: 5 cm, pH: <7, D: 2–3

Barbodes schwanenfeldi 1/398
Schwanenfeld's barb, tinfoil barb
H: SE Asia: Singapore, Malay P., Sum., Bor.
SD: Unknown. S: =
B: Unsuccessful. F: O,H
T: 22–25°C, L: 35 cm, pH: <7, D: 3–4

Barbus perince 4/184
H: Africa: Nile and tributaries, lakes Chad,
 Albert, Edward; Benue Basin.
♂: Smaller and slimmer. S: +
B: Unknown. F: O
T: 22–28°C, L: <12 cm, pH: 7, D: 2

Puntius phutunio 2/374
Dwarf barb
H: SE Asia: E India, Sri Lanka.
♂: Brighter and slimmer. S: +
B: Dense vegetation. F: O
T: 22–24°C, L: 5 cm, pH: <7, D: 1–2

190

Barbus plebejus tauricus 3/198
Crimea barb
H: Europe: Russia.
♂: Spawning eczema; slimmer. S: +
B: Nature: May–July. F: O
T: 10–22°C, L: 34 cm, pH: >7, D: 2

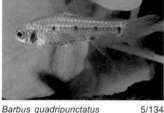

Barbus quadripunctatus 5/134
Four-spot barb
H: Africa: Tanzania.
♂: More golden. S: (–)
B: Unsuccessful? F: C,O
T: 23–27°C, L: 3.5 cm, pH: 7, D: 2

Puntius sahjadriensis 5/136
Khavli barb
H: Asia: India.
♂: Larger dorsal fin and slimmer. S: +
B: Among plants. F: O
T: 18–28°C, L: 7 cm, pH: >7, D: 2

Barbus punctitaeniatus 4/184
Spot-line barb
H: Africa: Senegal, Niger, Volta basins.
♂: Smaller and slimmer. S: +
B: Unsuccessful. F: O
T: 22–26°C, L: 4.5 cm, pH: 7, D: 2–3

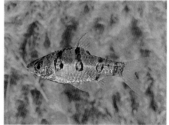

Puntius rhomboocellatus 1/396
Round-banded barb
H: Borneo?
♂: Redder, smaller, and slimmer. S: +
B: Unknown. F: O
T: 23–28°C, L: 5 cm, pH: 7, D: 2

Puntius semifasciolatus 1/398
Green barb, half-striped barb
H: Asia: SE China, Hong Kong.
♂: Brighter, slimmer, much smaller. S: +
B: Dense vegetation; <300 eggs. F: O
T: 18–24°C, L: 10 cm, pH: <7, D: 1

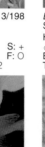

CARPLIKE F.

191

CARPLIKE F.

Puntius semifasciolatus   1/398
"*Barbus schuberti*"
Xanthic (yellow) form

Puntius semifasciolatus   5/140
Vietnamese half-striped barb
H: Asia: northern and central Vietnam.
♂: More colorful.   S: +
B: ♂♂ court intensely.   F: C,O
T: 16–25°C, L: 6–8 cm, pH: >7, D: 1–3

Barbus sp.   5/142

Barbus sp. "Ethiopia"   3/196

H: Africa: Zaïre.
♂: More slender.   S: +
B: Unknown.   F: O
T: 23–26°C, L: 8 cm, pH: 7, D: 2

Barbus stigmatopygus   5/136

H: Africa: Nile, Niger, Volta, Guinea-Bissau.
♂: Somewhat more slender.   S: (–)
B: Unknown.   F: C
T: 23–26°C, L: <2.5 cm, pH: <7, D: 3–4

Barbus sublineatus   5/138
Morse barb
H: Africa: Senegal, Niger, Gambia, Guinea.
♂: Notably slimmer.   S: +
B: Unsuccessful.   F: C,O
T: 22–27°C, L: 10 cm, pH: 7, D: 2

Barbus sylvaticus   4/186
Jungle barb
H: Africa: Benin, Nigeria.
♂: Slightly brighter and slimmer.   S: (–)
B: Unsuccessful.   F: C,O
T: 23–26°C, L: 2.5 cm, pH: ≪7, D: 3–4

Barbus taitensis   5/138
Taita barb
H: Africa: Kenya.
♂: Intensely yellow fins.   S: =
B: Unsuccessful.   F: O
T: 22–28°C, L: 14 cm, pH: 7, D: 2–3

Puntius terio   5/140
Gold-spot barb
H: Asia: India.
♂: Reddish fins; D fin w/ black.   S: +
B: Following a winter rest.   F: C,O
T: 18–22°C, L: 10 cm, pH: >7, D: 1

Puntius tetrazona   (1/363), 1/400
Tiger barb
H: Indonesia: Sumatra, Borneo.
♂: Brighter, smaller, and slimmer.   S: =
B: Harmonious pair needed.   F: O
T: 20–26°C, L: 7 cm, pH: <7, D: 1–2

Puntius ticto b.♂, t.♀   1/400
Two-spot barb, ticto barb
H: Asia: Sri Lanka to the Himalayas.
♂: Reddish and slimmer.   S: +
B: One ♂ with several ♀♀.   F: O
T: 14–22°C, L: 10 cm, pH: <7, D: 1

Puntius stoliczkanus   2/376
Stoliczka's barb
H: SE Asia: E Burma.
♂: More colorful and slimmer.   S: +
B: Plant thicket; preys on spawn.   F: O
T: 22–26°C, L: 6 cm, pH: <7, D: 1–2

CARPLIKE F.

193

Puntius titteya l.♀, r.♂   1/402
Cherry barb
H: Asia: Sri Lanka to the Himalayas.
♂: Red at spawning time; slimmer.   S: +
B: Plant thicket; preys on spawn.   F: O
T: 23–26°C, L: 5 cm, pH: 7, D: 1

Barbus trispilos   5/142
Black-spotted gold barb
H: Africa: Guinea, Ghana, Niger to Nigeria.
♂: Spawning color: ventrally red.   S: +
B: Typical for the genus.   F: C,O
T: 22–28°C, L: 10.5 cm, pH: <7, D: 1–2

Barbus trimaculatus   4/186
Three-spot barb
H: S Africa: broadly distributed.
SD: Unknown.   S: =
B: Unsuccessful.   F: O
T: 24–26°C, L: 12 cm, pH: 7, D: 3

Barbus toppini   2/376
Toppin's barb
H: Africa: South Africa to Malawi.
♂: Smaller, slimmer; knots on nose.   S: +
B: There are no reports.   F: O
T: 22–26°C, L: 4 cm, pH: <7, D: 2

Barbus venustus   4/188
Red Pangani barb
H: Africa: NE Tanzania, Kenya.
♂: Brighter and slimmer.   S: +
B: Spawning grid; color faded.   F: O
T: 20–26°C, L: 4 cm, pH: 7, D: 3

Puntius vittatus   2/378
Striped barb
H: Asia: India, Sri Lanka.
♂: Smaller and slimmer.   S: +
B: Spawning grid; <300 eggs.   F: O
T: 20–24°C, L: 6 cm, pH: <7, D: 1–2

Puntius viviparus   1/402
Suture barb, gold-striped barb
H: SE Africa.
SD: Unknown.   S: +
B: Unknown.   F: C,O
T: 22–24°C, L: 6.5 cm, pH: <7, D: 2

Barbus zanzibaricus   5/144
Zanzibar barb
H: Africa: Tanzania, Kenya, Somalia.
♂: Slimmer and pink.   S: +
B: Unknown.   F: C,O
T: 22–28°C, L: 10 cm, pH: >7, D: 2

Barilius barna   4/189
Ozola barb
H: Asia: India.
♂: More elongated.   S: +,=
B: Unsuccessful.   F: C,O
T: 20–26°C, L: >12 cm, pH: 7, D: 2

Barilius gatensis   5/146

H: Asia: India; up to 1700 m elevation.
♂: Nuptial tubercles; smaller.   S: =
B: Not described; among plants.   F: C,O
T: 16–24°C, L: 15 cm, pH: 7, D: 3

Blicca bjoerkna   3/201
Silver bream
H: Central Europe to W Asia.
♂: Nuptial tubercles.   S: +
B: Nature: May/June.   F: O
T: 4–20°C, L: <35 cm, pH: 7, D: 1

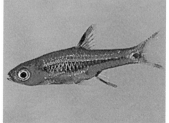

Boraras brigittae   1/440

H: Asia: Indonesia: Sumatra.
♂: Brighter, slimmer, and smaller.   S: +
B: Eggs on underside of leaves.   F: C,O
T: 23–25°C, L: 3.5 cm, pH: <7, D: 2–3

CARPLIKE F.

195

Boraras maculatus ♀ center   1/436
Dwarf or pygmy or spotted rasbora
H: SE Asia: W Malay., Singapore, W Sum.
♂: Brighter, slimmer, smaller.   S: +
B: Plant thickets; preys on spawn.   F: O
T: 22–25°C, L: 4.5 cm, pH: ≪7, D: 2–3

Brachydanio albolineatus b.♀, t.♂ 1/404
Pearl danio
H: SE Asia: Burma, Thailand, Malay Pen.
SD: See photo.   S: +
B: Plant thicket.   F: C,O
T: 20–25°C, L: 6 cm, pH: <7, D: 1

Brachydanio kerri   1/406
Kerr's danio
H: Asia: Thailand.
♂: Significantly slimmer.   S: +
B: Scattered above bottom; <400 e.   F: O
T: 23–25°C, L: 5 cm, pH: <7, D: 1–2

Brachydanio nigrofasciatus   1/406
Spotted danio
H: Asia: Burma.
♂: Gold-fringed anal fin; slimmer.   S: +
B: In plant thicket; <300 eggs.   F: C,O
T: 24–28°C, L: 4.5 cm, pH: <7, D: 1–2

Brachydanio rerio   1/408
Zebra danio
H: Asia: W India.
♂: Brighter and slimmer.   S: +
B: Fine-leaved plants; 400–500 e.   F: O
T: 18–24°C, L: 6 cm, pH: 7, D: 1

Brachydanio "frankei"   1/409
A morph of *B. rerio*?

Capoeta damascina   3/202

H: E Europe and W Asia.
SD: Unknown.   S: +
B: Unsuccessful.   F: O
T: 15–26°C, L: 40 cm, pH: 7, D: 3

Capoeta damascina sevrice   5/148
Damascus barb
H: W Asia: E Turkey: Hazar Gölü.
♂: Slimmer and smaller.   S: +
B: Among plants.   F: C,O
T: 16–23°C, L: 7 cm, pH: >7, D: 2

CARPLIKE F.

Capoetobrama kuschakewitschi 3/202
t. ♂, b. ♀

H: Asia: CIS States.
SD: See photo.   S: =
B: Apr.–June; 3000–4000 adh. eggs. F: O
T: 16–20°C, L: 21 cm, pH: 7, D: 2–3

Carassius auratus   1/410
Goldfish
H: Asia: China.
♂: Nuptial tubercles; slimmer.   S: +
B: There are many bred linages.   F: O
T: 10–20°C, L: 36 cm, pH: 7, D: 1

Carassius auratus gibelio   3/204
Prussian carp
H: E Asia to Siberia; today also Europe.
♂: Slimmer.   S: +
B: ♂♂ unnecessary?   F: O
T: 10–20°C, L: <45 cm, pH: >7, D: 1

Carassius carassius   1/410
Crucian, Prussian carp
H: Europe.
♀: Fuller during spawning season. S: +
B: Very large aquarium needed.   F: O
T: 14–22°C, L: 80 (20) cm, pH: 7, D: 1

197

CARPLIKE F.

Catla catla   4/190
Catla barb
H: Asia: India and Burma to Malaysia.
SD: None in juveniles.   S: −
B: In ponds.   F: O
T: 18–28°C, L: 180 cm, pH: 7, D: 1–4

Chalcalburnus chalcoides   4/190
H: Black Sea and Caspian Sea regions.
♂: Nuptial tubercles; slimmer.   S: +
B: Nature: on gravel.   F: C
T: 5–20°C, L: 10 cm, pH: 7, D: 2–3

Chela cachius b.♂, t.♀   4/192

H: Asia: India.
♀: Ventrally fuller (see photo).   S: +
B: At night; very small eggs.   F: O
T: 22–26°C, L: 10 cm, pH: 7, D: 2

Chela caeruleostigmata   2/378
Blue hatchetfish
H: SE Asia: central Thailand.
♂: Slimmer.   S: +
B: Small-leaved plants; nonpred.   F: O
T: 24–26°C, L: 6 cm, pH: <7, D: 2

Chela dadyburjori   2/380
Dadyburjor's or orange hatchetfish
H: SE Asia: Burma.
♂: Slimmer.   S: +
B: Fine-leaved plants.   F: C
T: 22–24°C, L: 4 cm, pH: <7, D: 3

Chela fasciata   2/380
Striped chela
H: SE Asia: S India.
♂: Slimmer?   S: +
B: Unknown.   F: O
T: 22–26°C, L: 6 cm, pH: 7, D: 2

CARPLIKE F.

Chela laubuca 1/412
Indian glassbarb, Indian hatchetfish
H: SE Asia.
♂: Slimmer.   S: +
B: Fine-leaved plants; not predatory. F: O
T: 24–26°C, L: 6 cm, pH: <7, D: 1–2

Chelaethiops bibie 4/192
H: Africa: Nile and Wadi Shebele.
SD: Difficult to discern.   S: +
B: Unknown.   F: C
T: 22–28°C, L: 5.5 cm, pH: >7, D: 2–3

Chelaethiops elongatus 5/148

H: Africa: Zaïre Basin.
SD: Unknown.   S: +
B: Undescribed.   F: C,O
T: 22–28°C, L: 6 cm, pH: 7, D: 2

Chelaethiops rukwaensis ♀ 3/205

H: Africa: Tanzania.
♀: Fuller at spawning time.   S: +
B: Unsuccessful.   F: C
T: 24–28°C, L: 8 cm, pH: >7, D: 2

Cirrhinus molitorella 3/250

H: Asia: China, Taiwan, Hong Kong.
SD: Unknown.   S: +
B: Unsuccessful.   F: C
T: 18–24°C, L: 15 cm?, pH: <7, D: 1–2

Couesius plumbeus ♀ 4/194
Lake chub
H: N America: Michigan, Alaska, Canada.
♂: Red spots at spawning time.   S: =
B: Unknown.   F: C,O
T: 4–25°C, L: 23 cm, pH: 7, D: 3

CARPLIKE F.

Crossocheilus reticulatus   2/384
Spotted flying fox, reticulated flying fox
H: SE Asia: Thailand.
SD: Unknown.   S: ?
B: Unsuccessful.   F: H,O
T: 23–25°C, L: 14 cm, pH: <7, D: 1

Crossocheilus (?) *denisonii*   5/150
Denison's flying fox
H: Asia: India.
♀: Fuller at spawning time.   S: +
B: After overwintering.   F: C,O
T: 15–25°C, L: 15 cm, pH: 7, D: 2–3

Crossocheilus cf. *reticulatus*   5/221
Reticulated flying fox
H: Unknown.
SD: Unknown.   S: +
B: Unknown.   F: L,H
T: 20–24°C, L: 8 cm, pH: 7, D: 2

Crossocheilus siamensis   1/418
Siamese flying fox, Siamese algae-eater
H: SE Asia: Thailand, Malay Peninsula.
SD: Unknown.   S: +
B: Unsuccessful.   F: H
T: 24–26°C, L: 14 cm, pH: <7, D: 1

Cyclocheilichthys apogon   1/412
Skin-head barb
H: SE Asia.
SD: Unknown.   S: +
B: Unsuccessful.   F: C
T: 24–28°C, L: 50 cm, pH: 7, D: 1

Cyclocheilichthys janthochir   3/206
Pretty-finned river barb
H: SE Asia: Indonesia, Kalimantan.
SD: Unknown.   S: +
B: Unsuccessful.   F: O
T: 24–26°C, L: >20 cm, pH: <7, D: 1

Ctenopharyngodon idella   1/414
Grass carp
H: Asia.   F: H
Used in aquaculture to control vegetation.
T: 10–20°C, L: 60 cm, pH: 7, D: 4

Cyprinus carpio   1/414
Common carp, koi (decorative carp)
H: Asia: Japan, China.
♂: Nuptial tubercles; slimmer.   S: +
B: Too large for normal aquarium.   F: O
T: 10–23°C, L: <120 cm, pH: >7, D: 1–2

Danio aequipinnatus   1/416
Giant danio, "Malabaricus"
H: Asia: W coast of India, Sri Lanka.
♂: Brighter and slimmer.   S: +
B: Egg scatterer; sun; <300 eggs.   F: O
T: 22–24°C, L: 10 cm, pH: <7, D: 1

Danio devario b.♀, t.♂   1/416
Bengal danio
H: Asia: Pakistan, N India, Bangladesh.
♂: Slimmer; see photo.   S: +
B: Egg scatterer; sunlight.   F: O
T: 15–26°C, L: 15 cm, pH: <7, D: 1

Danio pathirana   5/150

H: Asia: Sri Lanka.
♂: Slimmer.   S: +
B: Egg scatterer; sunlight.   F: O
T: 22–25°C, L: 6 cm, pH: 7, D: 1

Danio regina   2/382
Queen danio
H: SE Asia: S Thailand, N Malaysia.
♂: More colorful and slimmer.   S: +
B: Unsuccessful.   F: O
T: 23–25°C, L: 13 cm, pH: <7, D: 2

CARPLIKE F.

201

Dionda episcopa   4/194
Roundnose minnow
H: N America: USA, N Mexico.
♂: Smaller; more intensely colored.   S: +
B: Among gravel; nonadhesive e.   F: O
T: 23–25°C, L: 7 cm, pH: >7, D: 2–3

Discherodontus halei   3/200
Somphong barb
H: Asia: Thailand, Malay Peninsula.
♀: Fuller while ripe.   S: =
B: Unsuccessful.   F: O
T: 23–26°C, L: 10.5 cm, pH: 7, D: 2

Eirmotus octozona   2/382
Eight-banded false barb
H: SE Asia: Indonesia, Borneo.
♂: Reddish fins; slimmer.   S: +
B: Unsuccessful.   F: O
T: 24–26°C, L: 5 cm, pH: 7, D: 2

Elopichthys bambusa juv.   5/152

H: CIS States: Amur River.
SD: Unknown.   S: –
B: Early summer; pelagic eggs.   F: C!
T: 10–20°C, L: 200 cm, pH: >7, D: 4

Epalzeorhynchos bicolor 1/422, (5/152)
Red-tailed black shark, red-tailed labeo
H: SE Asia: Thailand.
♂: Posterior part of D fin pointed. S: =,–
B: Rarely accomplished.   F: C,O
T: 22–26°C, L: 12 cm, pH: 7, D: 2

Epalzeorhynchos frenatus   1/422
Red-finned shark, ruby shark
H: SE Asia: E Thailand.
♂: Brighter.   S: =,–
B: In ponds.   F: C,O
T: 22–26°C, L: 15 cm, pH: 7, D: 2

Epalzeorhynchos erythrurus   1/422
Rainbow shark
H: SE Asia: N Thailand.
♂: Black-fringed anal fin.   S: =,–
B: Rarely successful.   F: O
T: 22–26°C, L: 15 cm, pH: 7, D: 2

Epalzeorhynchos munensis   1/422,
2/388
H: SE Asia: N Thailand.
♂: Black-fringed anal fin.   S: =,–
B: Rarely successful.   F: O
T: 22–26°C, L: 15 cm, pH: 7, D: 2

Epalzeorhynchos kalopterus   1/418
Flying fox
H: SE Asia: Thailand, Sumatra, Borneo.
♂: Smaller and more slender.   S: =
B: Unsuccessful.   F: O
T: 24–26°C, L: 15 cm, pH: <7, D: 2

Epalzeorhynchos stigmaeus   1/420

H: SE Asia: northern and central Thailand.
SD: Unknown.   S: =
B: Unknown.   F: H,O
T: 18–22°C, L: 12.5 cm, pH: 7, D: 2

Erythroculter mongolicus   3/207

H: Asia: Mongolia, CIS States, China.
SD: Unknown.   S: =
B: Nature: June; pelagic eggs.   F: C
T: 10–20°C, L: 60 cm, pH: <7, D: 2–3

Esomus metallicus ♀   3/210
Silvery flying barb, metallic flying barb
H: Asia: Thailand, Laos.
♂: More slender.   S: +
B: Like other *Esomus*?   F: C
T: 22–26°C, L: 7.5 cm, pH: <7, D: 2

CARPLIKE F.

CARPLIKE F.

Esomus lineatus   3/208
Striped flying barb
H: Asia: India.
♂: Slimmer.   S: +
B: Probably has been successful.   F: O
T: 22–25°C, L: 6 cm, pH: 7, D: 1–2

Esomus malayensis? *(thermoicos)*   2/384
Malayan flying barb
H: SE Asia: Malay Peninsula, Thailand.
♂: Smaller and slimmer.   S: =
B: Fine-leaved plants; <700 eggs.   F: O
T: 21–25°C, L: 8 cm, pH: <7, D: 1–2

Esomus metallicus ♂ (♀ p. 203) 3/210
Silvery flying barb, metallic flying barb
H: Asia: Thailand, Laos.
♂: More slender.   S: +
B: Like other *Esomus*?   F: C
T: 22–26°C, L: 7.5 cm, pH: <7, D: 2

Garra barreimiae barreimiae   5/154

H: Asia: Oman: Wadi Sahtan.
SD: Unknown.   S: +
B: Biology unknown.   F: O,H
T: 18–24°C, L: 3–6.5 cm, pH: 7, D: 2–3

Garra barreimiae barreimiae   5/154
Cave form

Garra cambodgiensis   5/156
Cambodian log sucker
H: Asia: Thailand, Cambodia, Laos,...
SD: Unknown.   S: +
B: Unknown.   F: O
T: 20–25°C, L: 15 cm, pH: <7, D: 2–3

Garra ceylonensis ceylonensis   3/211
Ceylon log sucker
H: Asia: Sri Lanka.
SD: Unknown.   S: +
B: Unsuccessful.   F: O
T: 24–26°C, L: 15 cm, pH: 7, D: 2–3

Garra congoensis   3/212
Congo log sucker
H: Africa: Zaïre.
SD: Unknown.   S: ?
B: Unsuccessful.   F: O
T: 23–25°C, L: 10 cm, pH: <7, D: 2–3

CARPLIKE F.

Garra dembeensis   3/212
Cameroon log sucker
H: Africa: E Africa to Cameroon.
♂: Orange-tipped fins.   S: +
B: Unsuccessful.   F: H,O
T: 22–26°C, L: 11 cm, pH: 7, D: 2–3

Garra ghorensis   3/214
Jordanian log sucker
H: Asia: springs at the Dead Sea.
♂: Nup. tubercles; longer P fins.   S: +
B: Egg scatterer; preys on spawn. F: H,O
T: 25–28°C, L: 9 cm, pH: >7, D: 2

Garra hughi b.♀, t.♂   5/156
Hugh's log sucker
H: Asia: northern India.
♂: Smaller and slimmer.   S: +
B: There are no reports.   F: C,O
T: 15–25°C, L: 8 cm, pH: >7, D: 1–2

Garra gotyla   2/386

H: SE Asia: India, Pakistan, Nepal.
SD: Unknown.   S: ?
B: Unsuccessful.   F: O
T: 24–26°C, L: 20 cm, pH: 7, D: 2–3

CARPLIKE F.

Garra nasuta ♀   3/214
Nose log sucker
H: Asia: India, Burma, S China, Vietnam.
SD: Unknown.   S: +
B: Unsuccessful.   F: O
T: 20–25°C, L: 20 cm, pH: 7, D: 2–3

Garra ornata   4/196
Ornate log sucker
H: Africa: Niger and Zaïre basins.
SD: Unknown.   S: ?
B: Unsuccessful.   F: C,O
T: 22–26°C, L: 7.5 cm, pH: 7, D: 2–3

Garra pingi   4/196
Ping's log sucker
H: Asia: China, India.
SD: Unknown.   S: +
B: Unknown.   F: C,O
T: 15–25°C, L: 8 cm, pH: 7, D: 2–3

Garra rossica   5/158

H: Asia: Turkmenistan: Murga River.
♀: Fuller during spawning season.   S: +
B: Unsuccessful.   F: C,O
T: 8–20°C, L: 9.5 cm, pH: 7, D: 2–3

Garra rufa   3/216
Reddish log sucker
H: Asia: Levante and Mesopotamia.
♂: Tubercles; longer pectoral fins.   S: +
B: Egg scatterer; preys on spawn.   F: H,O
T: 15–28°C, L: 16 cm, pH: 7, D: 2

Garra cf. *pingi*

H: SE Asia: Thailand.
SD: Unknown.   S: ?
B: Unsuccessful.   F: O
T: 24–26°C, L: 15 cm, pH: 7, D: 2

Garra cambodgiensis   2/386
top adult ♂, bottom juvenile
Juveniles were described in 1935 as
Garra taeniatops (today a synonym).
See p. 204.

Gnathopogon biwae ♂   5/158
Lake Biwa barb
H: Asia: Japan: Lake Biwa.   E
♂: Slimmer; brighter at spawning. S: +
B: Unknown.   F: C,O
T: 10–24°C, L: 12 cm, pH: >7, D: 2–3

CARPLIKE F.

Gnathopogon tsianensis ♀   5/160

H: Asia: China.
♀: Fuller during spawning season. S: +
B: Unsuccessful.   F: H,O
T: 10–22°C, L: 10 cm, pH: 7, D: 1–2

Gobio albipinnatus belingi   5/160
Belingi gudgeon
H: Eurasia: CIS States.
♂: Nuptial tubercles; slimmer.   S: +
B: Nature: sand/stone bottoms.   F: O
T: 10–20°C, L: 13 cm, pH: 7, D: 2–3

Gobio benacensis   5/162
Po gudgeon
H: Europe: Italy.
♂: Nuptial tubercles?   S: +
B: Unknown.   F: O
T: 10–25°C, L: 12 cm, pH: >7, D: 2–3

Gobio ciscaucasicus   5/162
Caucasian gudgeon
H: Asia: Turkmenistan.
♂: Spawning eczema; slimmer.   S: +
B: N: shallow depressions in gravel.   F: O
T: 5–25°C, L: 15 cm, pH: >7, D: 2–3

Gobio gobio   1/420
Gudgeon
H: Europe.
♂: Nuptial tubercles   S: +
B: Occasionally successful.   F: C,O
T: 10–18°C, L: 20 cm, pH: >7, D: 2

Gobio gobio soldatovi   3/217
Soldatov's gudgeon
H: Asia: CIS States, China.
♂: Spawning tubercles.   S: +
B: N.: sand/stone substrate; <5300e. F:C
T: 4–18°C, L: 12 cm, pH: >7, D: 2

Gobio gobio tungussicus   3/218

H: Asia: CIS States.
♂: Nuptial tubercles.   S: +
B: Nature: sand substrates.   F: C
T: 10–18°C, L: 11 cm, pH: >7, D: 2–3

Gobio tenuicorpus   3/218
White-finned Amur gudgeon
H: Asia: CIS States, China.
♂: Nuptial tubercles.   S: +
B: Unknown.   F: C
T: 8–20°C, L: 12 cm, pH: >7, D: 2–3

Hampala macrolepidota   3/220
Silver and red barb
H: SE Asia: Sunda Is., Burma, Thailand.
SD: None.   S: ?
B: Too large for aquarium breeding.   F: O
T: 22–25°C, L: 70 cm, pH: 7, D: 2–4

Hemibarbus maculatus   3/220
Spotted Amur barb
H: Asia: CIS States, China.
♂: Slightly larger.   S: +
B: Nature: May/June.   F: C
T: 10–24°C, L: 36 cm, pH: 7, D: 3

Hemiculter leucisculus ♀   3/224

H: Asia: CIS States, China, Taiwan,...
♂: Slimmer.   **S: +**
B: Nature: spawns in the summer.   **F: O**
T: 18–22°C, L: 18 cm, pH: 7, D: 2

Hemigrammocapoeta sauvagei ♂   5/164
Tiberias barb

H: Asia: Turkey, Israel: Lake Tiberias.
SD: See photos.   **S: +**
B: Eggs scattered among plants?   **F: O**
T: 10–24°C, L: 18 cm, pH: >7, D: 2

CARPLIKE F.

Hemigrammocapoeta sauvagei ♀   5/164
Tiberias barb

Hemigrammocypris lini ♂   3/222
Garnet minnow

H: Asia: S China.
SD: See photos.   **S: +**
B: Spawning grid.   **F: O,C**
T: 18–22°C, L: 5 cm, pH: >7, D: 1–2

Hemigrammocypris lini ♀   3/222
Garnet minnow

Horadandia atukorali   3/224
Ceylon dwarf barb

H: SE Asia: Sri Lanka.
SD: Unknown.   **S: (–)**
B: Unknown.   **F: O**
T: 24–26°C, L: 2.8 cm, pH: <7, D: 3

CARPLIKE F.

Hypophthalmichthys molitrix   3/226
Silver carp
H: E Asia. Introduced into Europe.
♂: Much slimmer.   S: +
B: In flooded areas.   F: Plankton
T: 6–24°C, L: <100 cm, pH: 7, D: 2

Hypophthalmichthys nobilis   3/226
Bighead carp
H: Asia. Elsewhere for aquaculture.
SD: Difficult to distinguish.   S: +
B: In flooded areas.   F: O, H
T: 10–26°C, L: <100 cm, pH: 7, D: 2

Inlecypris auropurpureus ♂   5/164

H: Asia: Burma: Lake Inlé and affluents.
SD: Unknown.   S: +
B: Unsuccessful.   F: C
T: 22–24°C, L: 6 cm, pH: 7, D: 2

Rhinichthys erythrogaster   3/229

H: USA: Ohio, Michigan, Iowa, Alab., Miss.
♂: Red ventrum when spawning.   S: +
B: Nature: April to August.   F: O
T: 10–23°C, L: 9 cm, pH: 7, D: 2–3

Rhinichthys erythrogaster   3/229

Labeo chrysophekadion   1/426
Black labeo, black shark
H: SE Asia.
SD: Unknown.   S: –
B: Induced through hormones.   F: O
T: 24–27°C, L: 60 cm, pH: 7, D: 2

Labeo cylindricus   3/230
Cylindrical shark
H: Eastern and southern Africa.
SD: Unknown.   S: +
B: Unsuccessful.   F: O
T: 24–28°C, L: 40 cm, pH: 7, D: 3

Labeo forskalii   3/230, 2/388
Plain shark
H: Africa: Nile region.
♂: 1ˢᵗ and last D fin spines longer. S: =
B: Unsuccessful.   F: O
T: 18–25°C, L: 35 cm, pH: 7, D: 2

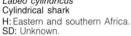

Labeo forskalii   2/388, 3/230
Plain shark

Labeo parvus   2/390
Small shark
H: Western Africa.
♂: Brighter and slimmer.   S: –
B: Unsuccessful.   F: O
T: 23–25°C, L: 45 cm, pH: 7, D: 3

Labeo rubropunctatus   5/168
Red-dotted shark
H: Africa: Zaïre.
♂: Smaller and slimmer.   S: –
B: Unsuccessful.   F: O
T: 22–26°C, L: <40 cm, pH: 7, D: 3

Labeo ruddi   3/232
Limpopo shark
H: Africa: South Afr., Mozamb., Zimbabwe.
♂: Spawning eczema?   S: =
B: Unsuccessful.   F: O
T: 23–27°C, L: 26 cm, pH: 7, D: 2–3

Labeo senegalensis   4/198
Senegal shark
H: Western Africa.
♂: Nuptial tubercles.   S: ?
B: Unsuccessful.   F: O
T: 22–26°C, L: 65 cm, pH: 7, D: 4

Labeo tibesti   4/198

H: Africa: Nigeria.
SD: Unknown.   S: ?
B: Unsuccessful.   F: O
T: 22–27°C, L: 13 cm, pH: 7, D: 3

Labeo variegatus   2/390
Variegated shark, harlequin shark
H: Africa: Zaïre.
SD: Unknown.   S: –
B: Unsuccessful.   F: O
T: 21–27°C, L: 30 cm, pH: 7, D: 2

Labiobarbus leptocheila   2/392

H: SE Asia: Burma, Thailand.
SD: Unknown.   S: +
B: Unsuccessful.   F: O
T: 24–26°C, L: 25 cm, pH: 7, D: 2–3

Labiobarbus festivus   2/392
Signal shark, festive apollo shark
H: SE Asia: Kalimantan.
♂: Brighter and slimmer?   S: +
B: Unsuccessful.   F: O
T: 22–24°C, L: 20 cm, pH: 7, D: 2–3

Labiobarbus leptocheilus   3/232

H: SE Asia: Thailand, Malaysia, Indonesia.
♂: Slimmer.   S: +
B: Unsuccessful.   F: O
T: 24–26°C, L: 25 cm, pH: 7, D: 2–3

Ladigesocypris ghigii ♂ (5/176), 5/168

H: Europe: Greece, Turkey.   Rare
SD: Unknown.   S: +
B: Not difficult.   F: C,O
T: 5–30°C, L: 10 cm, pH: >7, D: 2

Ladigesocypris ghigii   (5/176), 5/
168

CARPLIKE F.

Ladislavia taczanowskii   3/234

H: Asia: CIS States, China.
♂: Nuptial tubercles.   S: +
B: Nature: June/July.   F: O
T: 4–18°C, L: 8 cm, pH: >7, D: 2–3

Lagowskiella czekanowskii czerskii ♀
5/170

H: Eurasia: CIS States.
♂: Spawning coloration.   S: +
B: Unsuccessful.   F: C!
T: 10–20°C, L: 11.7 cm, pH: >7, D: 2

Lagowskiella czekanowskii suifunensis ♂
5/170

H: Eurasia: CIS States.
♂: Red fins during spawning time. S: +
B: Unsuccessful.   F: C
T: 10–20°C, L: 13.4 cm, pH: >7, D: 2–3

Leptobarbus hoevenii adult   2/394
Red-finned cigar shark
H: SE Asia: Thailand, Indonesia.
SD: Unknown.   S: +
B: Unsuccessful.   F: O
T: 23–26°C, L: 50 cm, pH: 7, D: 3

Leptobarbus hoevenii juv.   2/394
Red-finned cigar shark

Leptobarbus melanopterus   4/200
Tinfoil cigar shark
H: Asia: W Borneo.
SD: Unknown.   S: –
B: Unknown.   F: C,O
T: 22–30°C, L: 24 cm, pH: 7, D: 3

Leptobarbus melanotaenia juv.   2/394
Black-line cigar shark
H: SE Asia: Kalimantan.
SD: Unknown.   S: +
B: Unsuccessful.   F: O
T: 23–26°C, L: 25 cm, pH: 7, D: 2–3

Leptobarbus rubripinna   5/172
Red-tailed cigar shark
H: Asia: Indonesia.
SD: Unknown.   S: +
B: Unknown.   F: C,O
T: 20–26°C, L: 12 cm, pH: >7, D: 2–3

Leptocypris niloticus   3/234

H: Africa.
♂: Slimmer.   S: +
B: Unsuccessful.   F: O
T: 22–27°C, L: 9.5 cm, pH: >7, D: 2

Leucalburnus satunini ♂   3/237

H: Asia: CIS States.
♂: Nuptial tubercles.   S: +
B: Unsuccessful.   F: C
T: 10–20°C, L: 17.5 cm, pH: >7, D: 2–3

Leucalburnus satunini ♀   3/237

Leucaspius delineatus   1/424
Heckel's dace
H: Europe, W Asia.
♂: Smaller and slimmer.   S: +
B: On reeds; ♂ tends the spawn.   F: O
T: 10–20°C, L: 9 cm, pH: 7, D: 1–3

CARPLIKE F.

Leucaspius irideus ♂   5/174
Turkish dace
H: Asia: Turkey.   E
♂: Smaller and slimmer.   S: +
B: Unknown.   F: C,O
T: 10–24°C, L: 7 cm, pH: 7, D: 2

Leucaspius irideus ♀   5/174
Turkish dace

Leucaspius prosperoi   5/174
Greek dace
H: Europe: Greece: Rhodos.
♂: Smaller and slimmer.   S: +
B: In garden ponds?   F: C,O
T: 10–24°C, L: 8 cm, pH: 7, D: 2

Leuciscus cephalus cabeda   4/200
Italian chub
H: Europe: S France, Italy.
♂: Spawning eczema.   S: +
B: Unsuccessful.   F: O
T: 10–24°C, L: 40 cm, pH: 7, D: 2–4

CARPLIKE F.

Leuciscus cephalus cephalus   3/238
Chub
H: Europe.
♂: Spawning eczema; slimmer.   S: +,–
B: Nat.: April–June; 200 000 e.   F: C,O
T: 4–20°C, L: 80 cm, pH: 7, D: 1

Leuciscus cephalus orientalis   3/238
Oriental chub
H: Asia.
♂: Nuptial tubercles.   S: +,–
B: Unsuccessful.   F: O
T: 10–20°C, L: 45 cm, pH: 7, D: 1–2

Leuciscus idus   1/424
Ide, orfe
H: Europe.
♂: Nuptial tubercles; slimmer.   S: +,–
B: Nature: April–July.   F: C,O
T: 4–20°C, L: 80 cm, pH: >7, D: 1–2

Leuciscus idus adult   5/177
Ide, orfe
H: Europe.
♂: Nuptial tubercles.   S: +,–
B: Nature: early spring.   F: C,O
T: 10–22°C, L: 50 cm, pH: >7, D: 4

Leuciscus idus

There is white-golden, red-finned color sport of *L. idus*, the golden orfe. Due to its robustness, it is even more suitable for garden ponds than goldfish.

In nature, *L. idus* and *Aspius aspius* crossbreed, producing a hybrid which has been described as *Aspius hybridus*. This form has become rare in Germany. Because its meat is tasteless, it is not an appreciated game fish.

Leuciscus illyricus   4/202

H: Europe: Dalmatia.
♂: Nuptial tubercles; slimmer.   S: +,=
B: May/June; over gravel substrates. F: C
T: 5–25°C, L: 25 cm, pH: 7, D: 2

Leuciscus labiatus   5/178
Taiwan ide
H: Asia: Taiwan: Sin Chen River.
♂: Nuptial tubercles.   S: +,–
B: Unknown. Like barbs?   F: O,H
T: 15–25°C, L: >13 cm, pH: 7, D: 1–2

Leuciscus leuciscus   3/240

H: Europe: N of Alps and Pyrenees.
♂: Nuptial tubercles; slimmer.   S: +
B: Nature: March–June; plants.   F: C,O
T: 6–18°C, L: 30 cm, pH: 7, D: 2

CARPLIKE F.

Leuciscus souffia agassizi   3/240

H: Europe: Rhine and Danube systems.
♂: Colorful, esp. when spawning.   S: +
B: Nature: March–April; on gravel.   F: O
T: 10–20°C, L: 25 cm, pH: 7, D: 2

Leuciscus souffia souffia   5/178

H: Europe: France: Rhône and Var.
♂: Upper caudal fin lobe dark.   S: =
B: Nature: schoolwise.   F: C
T: 10–20°C, L: 25 cm, pH: 7, D: 3–4

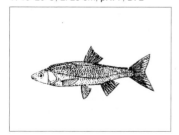

Leuciscus svallize   5/180

H: Europe: Yugoslavia, Albania.
SD: None.   S: +
B: Unknown.   F: C,O
T: 10–26°C, L: 25 cm, pH: 7, D: 2

Leuciscus waleckii   5/180

H: Asia: CIS States.
♂: Longer head; nuptial tubercles.   S: =
B: Nat.: schoolwise; adh. eggs.   F: O,C
T: 10–20°C, L: 37 cm, pH: 7, D: 4

217

Lobocheilus quadrilineatus   3/242

H: Asia: Thailand.
♂: Horny tubercles around mouth.   S: =
B: Unsuccessful.   F: O
T: 20–25°C, L: 26 cm, pH: 7, D: 1–2

Lobocheilus rhabdoura   5/182

H: Asia: Thailand.
♀: Fuller during spawning season. S: =
B: Spawning migration?   F: L,O
T: 18–26°C, L: 12 cm, pH: 7, D: 3

Luciosoma spilopleura   3/242

H: SE Asia: Thai., Malay Pen., Bor., Sum.
SD: Unknown.   S: =
B: Unsuccessful.   F: O
T: 24–27°C, L: 25 cm, pH: <7, D: 2

Luciosoma trinema   1/426

H: SE Asia.
♂: Elongated ventral fins.   S: =
B: Unsuccessful.   F: O
T: 24–27°C, L: 30 cm, pH: <7, D: 2

Megalobrama amblycephala   5/183

H: Asia: China: Yangtze River.
♂: Pronounced spawning eczema. S: –
B: Unknown.   F: C,O
T: 10–20°C, L: 200 cm, pH: 7, D: 4

Megalobrama terminalis   5/184

H: Asia: China: Canton: Amur River.
♂: Tubercles. ♀: Visible ovaries.   S:=
B: Unknown.   F: C,O
T: 10–24°C, L: 60 cm, pH: 7, D: 4

Mesobola spinifer   3/246

H: Africa: Tanzania.
SD: Unknown.   S: +
B: Unsuccessful.   F: O
T: 22–26°C, L: 4.5 cm, pH: 7, D: 2–3

Microphysiogobio tungtingensis amurensis
                                       3/244

H: Asia: Amur Drainage.
SD: Unknown.   S: +
B: Nature: June/July; pelagic eggs.   F: C
T: 14–22°C, L: 12 cm, pH: 7, D: 2–3

Microrasbora erythromicron   2/396
Cross-banded or emerald dwarf rasbora
H: S Asia: Burma.
♂: More colorful and slimmer.   S: +
B: On Java moss.   F: O
T: 21–25°C, L: 3 cm, pH: 7, D: 3

Microrasbora rubescens   2/396
Reddish dwarf rasbora, red-lined dwarf r.
H: S Asia: Burma.
♂: More colorful and slimmer.   S: +
B: On Java moss.   F: O
T: 21–25°C, L: 3 cm, pH: 7, D: 3

Mystacoleucus marginatus   3/244

H: SE Asia.
SD: Uncertain.   S: +
B: Unsuccessful.   F: O
T: 22–27°C, L: 20 cm, pH: <7, D: 1–2

Myxocyprinus asiaticus asiaticus 4/202
Wimple carp
H: Asia: N China.
SD: None in juveniles.   S: =
B: There are no breeding reports.   F: O
T: 15–28°C, L: 60 cm, pH: 7, D: 1–4

CARPLIKE F.

Notemigonus crysoleucas 5/185
Golden shiner
H: N America: Canada, USA to Florida.
♂: Distinct nuptial tubercles. S: +,=
B: Eggs scattered among plants. F: C,O
T: 5–24°C, L: 30 cm, pH: 7, D: 3

Notropis bifrenatus 2/398
Bridle shiner
H: N America: USA, E Canada.
♂: Larger fins. S: +
B: Unsuccessful? F: C,O
T: 6–20°C, L: 5 cm, pH: >7, D: 2

Notropis hudsonius 5/186
Spottail shiner
H: N America: Canada, USA.
♂: Brighter; spawning tubercles. S: +
B: Schools over gravel; June/July. F: C,O
T: 10–24°C, L: 15 cm, pH: 7, D: 2

Pteronotropis hypselopterus 2/398
Sailfin shiner
H: N America: USA.
♂: More colorful; black-tipped D fin. S: +
B: Unsuccessful? F: O
T: 6–20°C, L: 6 cm, pH: <7, D: 2

Notropis lutrensis 1/428
Red shiner
H: N America: USA.
♂: More colorful; black-tipped D fin. S: +
B: Unsuccessful. F: O
T: 15–25°C, L: 8 cm, pH: <7, D: 1

Notropis petersoni 5/186
Coastal shiner
H: N America: USA.
♂: Nuptial tubercles. S: +
B: May; in depressions. F: C,O
T: 5–25°C, L: 8 cm, pH: >7, D: 1–2

Notropis rubellus   5/188
Rosyface shiner
H: N America: Canada, USA.
♂: More colorful when spawning.   S: +
B: Several ♂♂ with few ♀♀.   F: C,O
T: 5–24°C, L: 10 cm, pH: 7, D: 2–3

Pteronotropis welaka ♂ front, ♀ back
Bluenose shiner   4/204
H: N America: USA.
♂: Larger fins; has more blue.   S: +
B: Coincidental: fine-leaved plants. F:C,O
T: 6–20°C, L: 6 cm, pH: <7, D: 2

CARPLIKE F.

Notropis welaka ♂   4/204
Bluenose shiner

Opsaridium chrystyi   1/404

H: Africa: N Ghana.
♂: Brighter and slimmer?   S: =
B: Unsuccessful.   F: C
T: 22–24°C, L: 15 cm, pH: <7, D: 2–3

Opsaridium zambezense   2/408
Zambezi barilius
H: Africa: upper Kasai Zambezi,...
SD: Unknown.   S: +
B: Unsuccessful.   F: C
T: 24–26°C, L: 16 cm, pH: <7, D: 2

Opsariichthys bidens   5/188
Korean predatory carp
H: Asia: Korea, N China.
♂: Striations; elongated fins.   S: –
B: Sexually mature from 16 cm.   F: C
T: 10–20°C, L: 30 cm, pH: 7, D: 2

Opsariichthys uncirostris amurensis
Amur predatory carp   3/246
H: Asia: CIS States, Korea, N China.
♂: Longer fins.   S: –
B: June–August; on sand/gravel.   F: C
T: 10–22°C, L: 32.5 cm, pH: 7, D: 2–3

Oreichthys cosuatis   3/198
H: Asia: Pakistan, India, Bangladesh,
   Burma, Thailand.
SD: Unknown.   S: +
B: Dense veg.; spawning grid.   F: O
T: 24–28°C, L: 7.5 cm, pH: <7, D: 1–2

Oreoleuciscus pewzowi ♀   5/190

Oreoleuciscus potanini   3/249

H: Asia: Mongolia.
♂: Brighter and slimmer.   S: =
B: Spawning migration?   F: C,O
T: 10–18°C, L: 43 cm, pH: >7, D: 4

H: Asia: CIS States.
♂: Spawning eczema.   S: =
B: June/July; <32 000 pelagic eggs. F: C
T: 10–20°C, L: 60 cm, pH: 7, D: 2–3

Osteobrama cotio   4/206
Gurda barb
H: Asia: India, Pakistan, Burma.
SD: Unknown.   S: +
B: Unknown.   F: O
T: 22–25°C, L: 9.5 cm, pH: 7, D: 2

Osteochilus hasselti   1/428
Hard-lipped barb
H: SE Asia.
♂: Slimmer?   S: +,–
B: Unsuccessfull; too large?   F: O
T: 22–25°C, L: 32 cm, pH: <7, D: 2

CARPLIKE F.

Osteochilus melanopleura   2/400

H: SE Asia: Indonesia, Malaysia, Thailand.
♂: Slimmer?   S: +
B: Unsuccessful.   F: O
T: 22–26°C, L: 40 cm, pH: <7, D: 3

Osteochilus microcephalus   3/250

H: SE Asia.
SD: Unknown.   S: −
B: Unsuccessful.   F: O,H
T: 22–26°C, L: 26 cm, pH: <7, D: 1–2

CARPLIKE F.

Osteochilus macrosemion   2/400

H: SE Asia: central Thailand.
SD: Unknown.   S: +
B: Unsuccessful.   F: O
T: 22–26°C, L: 22 cm, pH: <7, D: 2–3

Osteochilus triporos   4/206

H: Asia: Borneo.
♀: Fuller at spawning time.   S: =
B: Unsuccessful.   F: C,O
T: 22–28°C, L: 20 cm, pH: 7, D: 2–3

Oxygaster anomalura   5/190

H: Asia: Malay Peninsula.
♀: Fuller at spawning time.   S: =
B: Unknown.   F: C,O
T: 22–27°C, L: 9 cm, pH: 7, D: 2–3

Parabramis pekinensis   5/192
Beijing bream

H: Asia: China: Amur River.
♂: Nuptial tubercles.   S: +,=
B: In flooded areas.   F: C,O
T: 10–20°C, L: 55 cm, pH: 7, D: 4

Paracheilognathus himantegus   5/192
Taiwan bitterling
H: Asia: China, Taiwan.
♂: Brighter. ♀: Ovipositor.   S: +
B: Like tiger barb; e. not in bivalve.   F: O
T: 15–28°C, L: 7 cm, pH: 7, D: 1–2

Parachela maculicauda juv.   2/402
Glass barb
H: SE Asia: Thailand, Indonesia.
♀: Fuller during spawning season. S: +
B: There are no breeding reports.   F: C,O
T: 24–26°C, L: 20 cm, pH: <7, D: 2–3

Parachela maculicauda adult   2/402
Glass barb

Rasbora argyrotaenia   2/404
Black-edged rasbora
H: SE Asia.
♂: Smaller and slimmer.   S: +
B: Fine-leaved plants; 2000 eggs.   F: O
T: 20–26°C, L: 12 cm, pH: <7, D: 1

Rasbora cephalotaenia   2/412
Porthole rasbora
H: SE Asia.
♂: Much more slender.   S: +
B: Fine-leaved plants; 100 eggs.   F: O
T: 22–24°C, L: <14 cm, pH: <7, D: 2

Pelecus cultratus   3/252

H: Europe, Asia.
♀: Fuller during spawning season. S: =
B: May/June; 33 000 floating eggs. F: C
T: 10–20°C, L: 60 cm, pH: 7, D: 2

Phenacobius mirabilis   5/194
Suckermouth minnow
H: N America: N USA to Texas.
♂: Nuptial tubercles.   S: +
B: Unknown.   F: C,O
T: 5–25°C, L: 12 cm, pH: 7, D: 2–3

Phoxinellus adspersus   4/208

H: Europe: Yugoslavia.
SD: Unknown.   S: +
B: Unsuccessful.   F: O
T: 5–20°C, L: 10 cm, pH: 7, D: 2–3

CARPLIKE F.

Phoxinellus stymphalicus   4/208

H: Europe: Greece, Albania.
SD: Unknown.   S: +
B: Unknown.   F: C,O
T: 5–20°C, L: 12 cm, pH: 7, D: 2–3

Lagowskiella czekanowskii   2/404
Czekanowski's dace
H: Asia: CIS States.
♂: Smaller and slimmer.   S: +
B: There are no breeding reports.   F: C
T: 16–20°C, L: 9.5 cm, pH: >7, D: 2

Lagowskiella lagowskii   3/252
Amur dace
H: Asia: CIS States, Korea.
SD: Very slight.   S: +
B: Nature: June–August.   F: C
T: 16–20°C, L: 15 cm, pH: >7, D: 2

Eupallasella percnurus   4/214
Swamp dace
H: E Europe.
♂: Slimmer; no eczema.   S: +
B: June/July; on plant leaves.   F: C,O
T: 15–23°C, L: <12 cm, pH: >7, D: 1–2

Phoxinus phoxinus ♀   1/430
Eurasian dace
H: Europe, Asia.
♀: Plain; fuller while egg-laden.   S: +
B: On stones; <1000 eggs.   F: C
T: 12–20°C, L: 14 cm, pH: >7, D: 2

Phoxinus phoxinus l.♀, r.♂   1/430
Eurasian dace
See photo on p. 5/196

Phoxinus phoxinus 2♂♂, "³/₄" ♀ 1/430
Eurasian dace
See photo on p. 5/196.

Phoxinus phoxinus colchicus ♂   5/197
Eurasian dace
H: CIS States: Batumi, Gelendjik.
♂: Spawning eczema; more color.   S: +
B: On stones.   F: C
T: 10–22°C, L: 8.2 cm, pH: 7, D: 2–3

Phoxinus poljakowi ♀ center   5/198
Balkhash dace
H: CIS States: Lake Balkhash.   rare
♂: Nuptial tubercles; more spots. S: +
B: Unsuccessful.   F: C,O
T: 8–20°C, L: 10 cm, pH: 7, D: 2

Pimephales notatus   5/198
Bluntnose minnow
H: N America: S Canada, USA.
♂: Nuptial tubercles; brighter.   S: +
B: Under stones, roots; nuclear fam. F: O
T: 5–22°C, L: 11 cm, pH: 7, D: 2

Pimephales promelas promelas ♂ 3/254
Fathead minnow
H: N America: Can., USA, Mex.
♂: Nuptial tubercles; larger.   S: +
B: Under branches,stones; P fam.   F:O
T: 12–20°C, L: 9.5 cm, pH: 7, D: 2

Pimephales promelas promelas ♀ 3/254
Fathead minnow

CARPLIKE F.

Pseudoperilampus lighti   5/200
Light's bitterling
H: Asia: China, Taiwan.
♂: Slimmer; brighter when spawning. S: +
B: In mantle cavity of bivalves.   F: C,O
T: 10–25°C, L: 5.2 cm, pH: >7, D: 2

Pseudophoxinellus kervillei   5/200
Turkish dwarf minnow
H: Asia: E Turkey.   Rare
♂: Spawning eczema; brighter.   S: +
B: Unknown.   F: C,O
T: 10–20°C, L: 5 cm, pH: >7, D: 3

Pseudorasbora fowleri   5/202

H: Asia: China, Taiwan.
♂: Cephalic tubercles.   S: +
B: Cave spawner; paternal fam.   F: C,O
T: 12–22°C, L: 8 cm, pH: >7, D: 2

Pseudorasbora parva   2/406

H: Europe.
♂: Nuptial tubercles.   S: +
B: Eggs adhered to stones; P fam.   F:O
T: 14–22°C, L: 11 cm, pH: 7, D: 2

CARPLIKE F.

Pseudorasbora pumila   2/408

H: Asia: Japan.
♂: Slightly larger.   S: +
B: Unknown.   F: O
T: 15–20°C, L: 8 cm, pH: 7, D: 2

Psilorhynchus balitora ♀   4/222

H: Asia: India, Bangladesh, Burma.
SD: Unknown (♂ slimmer).   S: +
B: Unknown.   F: C,O
T: 22–27°C, L: 7 cm, pH: 7, D: 4

Psilorhynchus sucatio   5/226
Arrow barb

H: Asia: India, NE Bengal.
SD: Unknown.   S: +
B: Unknown.   F: C,O
T: 15–23°C, L: 8 cm, pH: 7, D: 2–3

Puntius asoka   3/182

H: Asia: Sri Lanka. S India?
SD: None.   S: =
B: Unsuccessful?   F: O
T: 25–30°C, L: 15 cm, pH: 7, D: 2–3

Puntius pleurotaenia   5/134

H: Sri Lanka.
♂: Slimmer.   S: +
B: Among plants.   F: C,O
T: 22–26°C, L: 8 cm, pH: 7, D: 1–2

Raiamas batesii   4/210

H: Africa: S Cameroon, Zaïre Basin.
SD: Unknown.   S: =
B: Unknown.   F: C,O
T: 20–26°C, L: 12 cm, pH: 7, D: 2–3

CARPLIKE F.

Raiamas batesii   5/146

Raiamas moori ♂   3/254

H: Africa: lakes Tanganyika, Rukwa, Kivu.
SD: Unknown.   S: =
B: Unknown.   F: O
T: 24–26°C, L: 19 cm, pH: 7, D: 2–3

Raiamas nigeriensis   4/210

H: Africa.
SD: Unknown.   S: =
B: Unknown.   F: C
T: 24–26°C, L: 13 cm, pH: 7, D: 2–3

Raiamas senegalensis   3/256

H: Africa: W Africa, Lake Chad Basin.
SD: Unknown.   S: =
B: Unknown.   F: O
T: 22–26°C, L: 25 cm, pH: 7, D: 2–3

Rastineobola argentea   3/273, 5/204

H: Africa: Lake Victoria.
SD: None.   S: +
B: Unsuccessful.   F: O
T: 22–26°C, L: 8 cm, pH: >7, D: 3

Rasbora axelrodi   2/410
Axelrod's rasbora
H: Indonesia: Sumatra.
♂: More colorful.   S: +
B: Unsuccessful.   F: O
T: 23–26°C, L: 3 cm, pH: <7, D: 2

Rasbora borapetensis   1/431
Red-tailed rasbora, magnificent rasbora
H: SE Asia: Thailand, W Malaysia.
♂: Slimmer.   S: +
B: Floating plants; spawn pred.   F: C,O
T: 22–26°C, L: 5 cm, pH: <7, D: 2

Boraras brigittae t.♂, b.♀   3/262
Mosquito rasbora
H: Asia: S Borneo.
♂: More intensely red; see photo.   S: (–)
B: Among dense vegetation.   F: C
T: 25–28°C, L: 2 cm, pH: <7, D: 2–3

Rasbora brittani ♀   2/410
Brittan's rasbora
H: SE Asia: Malaysia.
♂: Slimmer.   S: +
B: Unknown.   F: O
T: 23–26°C, L: 6 cm, pH: <7, D: 2

Rasbora caudimaculata   2/412
Greater scissortailed or spot-tailed rasbora
H: SE Asia: Indonesia, Malaysia, Thailand.
♂: Yellowish anal fin; slimmer.   S: +
B: Unknown.   F: O
T: 20–26°C, L: 12 cm, pH: <7, D: 2

Rasbora daniconius   2/414
Rasbora chrysotaenia (no photo)   3/256
H: SE Asia: Malay Peninsula, Sumatra.
♂: Slimmer.   S: +
B: Unknown.   F: O
T: 22–24°C, L: 3.5 cm, pH: <7, D: 2

Rasbora daniconius daniconius   2/414
Golden-striped rasbora
H: Asia: Thai., Burma, W India, Sri Lanka.
♂: Yellowish & reddish ventral area. S: +
B: In plant copses; large aquarium.   F: O
T: 24–26°C, L: 10 cm, pH: 7, D: 1

230

CARPLIKE F.

Rasbora dorsiocellata dorsiocellata   1/432
Hi-spot rasbora
H: SE Asia: Malay Peninsula, Sumatra.
♂: Reddish caudal fin; slimmer.   S: +
B: Plant thicket; preys on spawn.   F: O
T: 20–25°C, L: 6.5 cm, pH: ≪7, D: 1–2

Rasbora einthovenii   2/416
Long-band rasbora
H: SE Asia.
♀: Fuller during spawning season. S: +
B: Among dense aquatic plants.   F: O
T: 22–25°C, L: 8.5 cm, pH: <7, D: 1–2

Rasbora espei b.♀, t.♂   1/434
Espe's rasbora
H: Asia: Thailand.
♂: Brighter and slimmer.   S: +
B: On broad-leaved plants.   F: C,O
T: 23–28°C, L: 4.5 cm, pH: <7, D: 2

Rasbora dusonensis   1/438
Silver rasbora
H: SE Asia.
♂: Slimmer.   S: +
B: Unknown.   F: O
T: 23–26°C, L: 10 cm, pH: ≪7, D: 1–2

Rasbora elegans elegans   1/432
Elegant rasbora, two-spot rasbora
H: SE Asia: W Malay., Sing., Sum., Bor.
♂: Brighter and slimmer.   S: +
B: In clusters of plants; very prolific. F: O
T: 22–25°C, L: 20 cm, pH: <7, D: 2

Rasbora heteromorpha b.♂   1/434
Harlequin rasbora, red rasbora
H: SE Asia: W Malay, Sing., Sum., Thai.
♀: Fuller; ant. edge of spot straight. S: +
B: On broad-leaved plants.   F: O
T: 22–25°C, L: 4.5 cm, pH: ≪7, D: 2–3

CARPLIKE F.

Rasbora kalochroma   1/436
Clown rasbora, big-spot rasbora
H: SE Asia: W Malay.,Sum.,Bor.,Bangka.
♂: Dark anal fin; more slender.   S: =
B: Unknown.   F: O
T: 25–28°C, L: 10 cm, pH: 7, D: 2

Rasbora sp. cf. *meinkeni*   3/258
Meinken's rasbora
H: SE Asia: Indonesia, S Malaysia.
♂: More colorful and slimmer.   S: +
B: Unsuccessful.   F: O
T: 24–28°C, L: 5 cm, pH: <7, D: 1

Rasbora pauciperforata center ♀ 1/438
Redline rasbora, red-striped rasbora
H: SE Asia: W Malaysia, Sum., Belitung.
♂: Slimmer.   S: +
B: Among fine-leaved plants.   F: O
T: 23–25°C, L: 7 cm, pH: <7, D: 2–3

Rasbora gracilis   3/258
Slender rasbora
H: SE Asia: Malay Peninsula.
♂: Brighter, slimmer, and smaller.   S: +
B: Successful, but not reported.   F: O
T: 22–25°C, L: 12 cm, pH: <7, D: 2

Rasbora paviei   2/416
Line rasbora
H: SE Asia: Indo., Sunda I.,W Malay.,Thai.
♂: Slimmer.   S: +
B: Unsuccessful.   F: O
T: 22–24°C, L: 6 cm, pH: <7, D: 1–2

Rasbora rasbora   2/418
Ganges rasbora
H: Asia: India, Burma, Thailand.
♂: Slimmer.   S: +
B: Unsuccessful.   F: O
T: 20–25°C, L: 10 cm, pH: <7, D: 2

Rasbora reticulata   2/418
Net rasbora
H: SE Asia: Sumatra, Nias Island.
♂: Slimmer.   S: +
B: Among plants.   F: O
T: 22–26°C, L: 6 cm, pH: <7, D: 2

Rasbora somphongsi   3/260
Somphongs' rasbora
H: SE Asia: Thailand.
♂: Slimmer; slightly more colorful.   S: +
B: On plant leaves; 100 eggs.   F: C,O
T: 22–26°C, L: 3 cm, pH: <7, D: 2

Rasbora cf. *steineri*   3/260
Steiner's rasbora
H: E Asia: China, Hong Kong.
♂: Slimmer; difficult to distinguish.   S: +
B: Unsuccessful.   F: O
T: 22–24°C, L: 6 cm, pH: <7, D: 2

Rasbora sp.   2/421

L: 3.5 cm

Rasbora sumatrana   (2/417), 2/420
Sumatran rasbora
H: SE Asia: Malay Pen., Kali., Thailand.
♂: Slimmer.   S: +
B: Unsuccessful.   F: O
T: 23–25°C, L: 13 cm, pH: <7, D: 1

Rasbora taeniata (ph.: *R. gracilis*?)   2/420
Black-striped rasbora
H: SE Asia: W Malaysia, Suma., Belitung.
♂: C fin yellowish red; slimmer.   S: +
B: Among floating plants.   F: O
T: 22–24°C, L: 7 cm, pH: <7, D: 1–2

CARPLIKE F.

Rasbora trilineata   1/440
Scissortail rasbora, three-line rasbora
H: SE Asia: W Malaysia, Sumatra, Borneo.
♂: Smaller and slimmer.   S: +
B: Dense vegetation.   F: O
T: 23–26°C, L: 10 cm, pH: <7, D: 1–2

Rasbora tubbi   5/203
Tubb's rasbora
H: SE Asia: N Borneo.
♀: Fuller during spawning season.   S: +
B: Unknown.   F: C
T: 22–28°C, L: 13 cm, pH: 7, D: 3

Rasboroides vaterifloris var.   2/422
Singhalese fire barb, orange-finned barb
H: Asia: Sri Lanka.
♂: Slimmer; reddish fins.   S: +
B: In plant copses.   F: O
T: 25–29°C, L: 4 cm, pH: <7, D: 3

Rasboroides vaterifloris var.   3/262
Orange-finned barb
H: Asia: Sri Lanka.
♂: Slimmer and more colorful.   S: +
B: In plant clusters.   F: O
T: 25–27°C, L: 4 cm, pH: <7, D: 4

Rasbora vegae   2/422
Vega rasbora
H: SE Asia: Labuan Island at Kalimantan.
♂: Slimmer.   S: +
B: Unsuccessful.   F: O
T: 22–26°C, L: 6 cm, pH: <7, D: 2

Rastineobola argentea   5/204
Victoria sardine
H: Africa: Lake Victoria Basin.
♂: Brighter and slimmer.   S: +
B: Near shore.   F: C
T: 22–26°C, L: 8 cm, pH: 7, D: 3

Rhinichthys atratulus atratulus 3/264
Blacknose dace
H: N America: USA, Canada.
♂: Nuptial tubercles; brighter. S: =
B: Nature: May/June; on gravel. F: O
T: 12–20°C, L: 8 cm, pH: 7, D: 2

Rhinichthys cataractae 2/424
Longnose dace
H: N America: NE USA, E Canada.
SD: Unknown. S: +
B: Unsuccessful. F: C
T: 4–16°C, L: 10 cm, pH: 7, D: 3

CARPLIKE F.

Rhinichthys osculus 5/204
Speckled dace
H: N America: W USA.
♂: Nuptial tubercles; larger fins. S: +
B: Nat.: June; 1 ♀ w/ several ♂♂. F: C,O
T: 10–24°C, L: 11 cm, pH: 7, D: 2–3

Rhodeus amarus ♀ 1/442
Bitterling
H: Europe, W Asia.
♂: Nuptial tubercles. ♀: Ovipositor. S: +
B: Within freshwater mussels. F: O
T: 15–24°C, L: 10 cm, pH: >7, D: 2

Rhodeus amarus ♂ 1/442
Bitterling

Rhodeus atremius 5/206
Tabira bitterling
H: Asia: Japan.
♂: Slimmer. ♀: Short ovipositor. S: +
B: Within freshwater mussels. F: C,O
T: 10–25°C, L: 6 cm, pH: 7, D: 2–3

Rhodeus ocellatus l.♂, r.♀   2/406
Hong Kong bitterling
H: E Asia: China, Taiwan.
♂: More colorful at spawning time. **S:** +
B: Within freshwater mussels.   **F:** O
T: 18–24°C, **L:** 12 cm, **pH:** 7, **D:** 2–3

Rhodeus ocellatus smithii   5/206
Stripeshoulder bitterling
H: Asia: Japan.
♂: Spawning dress. ♀: Ovipositor. **S:** +
B: Freshwater mussels; <150 e.   **F:** O
T: 10–25°C, **L:** 7 cm, **pH:** 7, **D:** 1–2

Rhodeus sericeus   5/208
Amur bitterling, Eurasian bitterling
H: Asia: Russia: Amur region.
♂: Nuptial tubercles. ♀: Ovipositor. **S:** +
B: Within freshwater mussels.   **F:** C,O
T: 10–25°C, **L:** 9 cm, **pH:** 7, **D:** 2

Rhodeus suigensis juv.   5/208
Straw bitterling
H: Asia: N Korea.
♂: Nuptial tubercles. ♀: Ovipositor. **S:** +
B: Within freshwater mussels.   **F:** C,O
T: 10–25°C, **L:** 9 cm, **pH:** 7, **D:** 2–3

Rutilus atropatenus   4/212

H: Asia: Azerbaijan.
SD: Unknown.   **S:** +
B: Unknown.   **F:** C,O
T: 10–25°C, **L:** 10 cm, **pH:** >7, **D:** 2–3

Rutilus aula   4/212
Dalmatian roach
H: Europe: Italy.
♂: Brighter; nuptial tubercles.   **S:** +
B: Unsuccessful.   **F:** C,O
T: 8–24°C, **L:** 15 cm, **pH:** >7, **D:** 2–3

Rutilus erythrophthalmus   1/444
Pearl roach

H: Europe, Asia.
♂: Spawning eczema.   S: =
B: April/June; 100 000 eggs.   F: O
T: 10–24°C, L: 32 cm, pH: 7, D: 1–2

Rutilus erythrophthalmus   5/210
Pearl roach, east European form

H: Europe. CIS States, Bulgaria.
♂: Spawning eczema.   S: +
B: Hybridizes w/ *Alburnus alburnus*. F: O
T: 10–24°C, L: 32 cm, pH: 7, D: 1–2

Rutilus meidingeri   4/214
Pearlfish

H: Europe, Asia.
♂: More colorful; nuptial tubercles. S: =
B: Too large for aq. breeding.   F: C,O
T: 5–20°C, L: <70 cm, pH: >7, D: 4

Rutilus macedonicus   5/210
Macedonian roach

H: Europe: N Geece.   E
♂: Slimmer; nuptial tubercles.   S: +
B: Schoolwise among plants.   F: C,O
T: 5–25°C, L: 15 cm, pH: >7, D: 2

Rutilus pigus virgo   4/216

H: Europe: Danube system.
♂: More colorful; nuptial tubercles. S: +
B: April/May; along shorelines.   F: C,O
T: 5–20°C, L: 45 cm, pH: >7, D: 2–4

Rutilus rubilio rubilio   3/264
Southern European roach

H: Europe.
♂: Nuptial tubercles; slimmer.   S: +
B: Nature: March–June.   F: O
T: 10–27°C, L: 25 cm, pH: 7, D: 1–2

Rutilus rutilus   1/444
Roach
H: Europe, Asia.
♂: Nuptial tubercles.   S: +
B: Unsuccessful due to size.   F: O
T: 10–20°C, L: 40 cm, pH: >7, D: 1–2

Rutilus rutilus heckeli   4/216
Heckel's roach, taran
H: Black Sea, Sea of Asov.
♂: Nuptial tubercles.   S: +
B: April/May; over plants/gravel. F: C,O
T: 5–25°C, L: <50 cm, pH: >7, D: 2–4

Sarcocheilichthys nigripinnis czerskii ♀
                                     3/266
H: Asia: CIS States, China. Korea?
♀: Black caudal peduncle.   S: =
B: Within freshwater mussels?   F: C
T: 14–22°C, L: 12.5 cm, pH: 7, D: 2–3

Sarcocheilichthys sinensis   3/266
Amur sucker
H: Asia: CIS States, Korea, China.
♂: Nuptial tubercles. ♀: Ovipositor. S: +
B: May/July; pelagic eggs.   F: C
T: 16–22°C, L: 28 cm, pH: 7, D: 2–3

Sarcocheilichthys sinensis fukiensis l. ♀
Taiwan sucker   5/212
H: Asia: Taiwan.
♂: Nuptial tubercles. ♀: Ovipositor. S: +
B: Within mussels.   F: C
T: 15–28°C, L: 14 cm, pH: 7, D: 1

Saurogobio dabryi   3/268

H: Asia: Amur B., Korea, China, Vietnam.
SD: Unknown.   S: +
B: May/July; pelagic eggs.   F: C
T: 12–22°C, L: 28 cm, pH: 7, D: 2–3

Sawbwa resplendens t.♀, b.♂   2/424
Naked microrasbora
H: S Asia: Burma.
♂: Red head & caudal fin (photo).   S: +
B: Eggs laid on Java moss.   F: O
T: 21–25°C, L: 4 cm, pH: 7, D: 3

Schismatorhynchos heterorhynchos
Dolphin barb   5/212
H: Asia: China.
♂: Larger adipose hump.   S: =
B: Unknown.   F: O
T: 22–26°C, L: 20 cm, pH: 7, D: 2–3

CARPLIKE F.

Schizothorax intermedius   5/214
Salmon barb
H: Central Asia: highland rivers.
♂: Nuptial tubercles.   S: –
B: Similar to salmon (w/o sea).   F: C
T: 10–18 (25)°C, L: 50 cm, pH: 7, D: 4

Schizothorax pelzami   5/214
Pelzami's salmon barb
H: C Asia: Turkmenistan: Murgab River.
♂: Nuptial tubercles.   S: –
B: Similar to salmon (w/o sea).   F: C
T: 10–20°C, L: 36 cm, pH: 7, D: 4

Semotilus atromaculatus   5/216
Creek chub
H: N America: Canada, USA.
♂: 10 cm larger; brighter; tubercles. S: +
B: In a gravel depression.   F: C,O
T: 5–25°C, L: ♂ 30 cm, pH: 7, D: 3

Squalidus chankaensis chankaensis
                                     3/268
H: Asia: CIS States.
SD: Unknown.   S: +
B: June and July; on bottom/plants. F: C
T: 14–22°C, L: 10 cm, pH: 7, D: 2–3

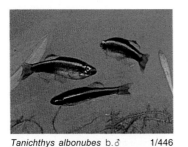

Tanichthys albonubes b. ♂   1/446
White Cloud Mountain minnow
H: Asia: S China.
♂: More intense colors; slimmer.   S: +
B: Among dense vegetation.   F: O
T: 18–22°C, L: 4 cm, pH: 7, D: 1

Tanichthys albonubes   1/446
Veil tail White Cloud Mountain minnow

Tanichthys albonubes   1/446
White Cloud Mountain minnow
Color variant. Presented by MEINKEN as
Aphyocypris pooni.

Tinca tinca   5/219
Tench
H: Throughout central Europe.
♂: Fins large, 2nd P fin spines thick.   S: +
B: N: 2♂♂ with 1♀; above plants.   F: O
T: 4–24°C, L: 40 cm, pH: 7, D: 2

Tinca tinca golden form   5/219
Tench

Tor khudree juv.   3/270
Giant barb
H: Asia: Sri Lanka.
SD: Unknown.   S: =
B: Unknown.   F: O
T: 20–30°C, L: <144 cm, pH: 7, D: 1–4

Tribolodon brandti   5/222
Mw,Bw,Fw
H: E Asia: Korea, China, Japan, Russia.
♂: Nuptial tubercles; brighter.   **S:** +,–
B: Enters rivers from the sea.   **F:** C,O
T: 10–24°C, **L:** 50 cm, **pH:** 7, **D:** 4

Varicorhinus capoeta capoeta   3/270
Common chramulja
H: Asia: CIS States.
♂: Nuptial tubercles.   **S:** +
B: May–July; stone/sand substrate.   **F:** H
T: 10–22°C, **L:** 41 cm, **pH:** >7, **D:** 2–3

Varicorhinus capoeta gracilis   5/222

H: CIS States: tributaries of Caspian Sea.
♂: Nuptial tubercles.   **S:** =
B: Unknown.   **F:** C, O
T: 8–24°C, **L:** 35 cm, **pH:** 7, **D:** 4

Zacco platypus   4/218
Odd-finned zacco
H: E Asia and Japan.
♂: Brighter and longer fins.   **S:** +,–
B: Egg scatterer; in ponds.   **F:** C,O
T: 10–22°C, **L:** 18 cm, **pH:** 7, **D:** 1

Zacco sp.   5/224

H: Asia: China, Taiwan.
♂: Long A fin; nuptial tubercles.   **S:** =
B: Unsuccessful. Like *Danio*?   **F:** C,O
T: 10–24°C, **L:** 12 cm, **pH:** >7, **D:** 2–3

Zacco temmincki   4/218
Taiwan zacco
H: Asia: Taiwan, S China.
♂: Long A fin; nuptial tubercles.   **S:** =
B: Unsuccessful.   **F:** C,O
T: 12–26°C, **L:** 15 cm, **pH:** 7, **D:** 2

CARPLIKE F.

Family Gyrinocheilidae

This very small family has but one genus and four species. The majority inhabits Southeast Asia, where the greatest concentration occurs in Thailand. Of the four species, *Gyrinocheilus aymonieri* is the most aquaristically significant. It was previously classified into the family Cobitidae.

The inferior mouth is eminently suited to rasping algae; hence their familiar nomen "algae-eaters." Rather than breathing water through their mouth like most fishes, the gill slit is divided into an inhalant and exhalant opening, allowing them to feed uninterrupted by their need to inhale. It is clearly their ability to control algae that endears them to aquarists, since their coloration is absolutely uninspiring.

The swimbladder is reduced and no longer lends bouyancy; these fishes must actively swim to maintain their position in the water column.

Unfortunately, algae-eaters grow quite large (although less so in the aquarium) and become aggressive with age.

Gyrinocheilus aymonieri   1/448
Chinese algae-eater, sucking loach
H: Asia: central Thailand.
♂: Thick spines at spawning time?   S: +,−
B: Unknown.   F: H
T: 25–28°C, L: 27 cm, pH: 7, D: 2

Gyrinocheilus aymonieri   4/220
Lemon algae-eater
H: Bred form from Asia.
♂: Spines around the eyes?   S: +,−
B: In ponds. Hormone induced? F: O,H
T: 20–20°C, L: 22 cm, pH: 7, D: 2–3

Gyrinocheilus kaznakowi   4/220   (= *Gyrinocheilus aymonieri*)
Russian algae-eater
H: Asia: China, CIS States.   B: Unknown.   F: O
SD: Unknown.   S: +,−   T: 15–25°C, L: 26 cm, pH: 7, D: 2–3

Peckoltia sp., clown peckoltia; see p. 344. This is one of the recent imports which has significantly contributed to the popularity of the Loricariidae.

Origin/Taxonomy

The Siluriformes consist of 34 families, 412 genera, and over 2400 species. Fossil records have shown the emergence of the order Siluriformes during the Eocene and Oligocene epochs, 54 and 38 million years ago, respectively (NELSON, 1994). It was previously considered a suborder of the Cypriniformes (Carplike Fishes—Group 3). Pointing to a common ancestor, cyprinids, characins, and catfishes all have a "Weber's apparatus," modified cervical vertebrae which transmit acoustic signals from the swimbladder to the inner ear.

The list of families below represents those addressed in Group 4. For reasons of simplicity, the alphabetic order of the species in this group does not take subfamilies into account.

Geographic Distribution

Siluriformes enjoy a worldwide distribution; fossils have even been found on Antarctica. At present, there are about 1440 species in America. Catfishes and characins are the two most specious orders of South American fishes. The Loricariidae are very prominent, representing one third of all catfishes there.

Catfishes abide in diverse ecological niches from oxygen-deficient lowland waters, where some families have adapted to their environs by developing the ability to breathe air (i.e., Callichthyidae, Clariidae, Loricariidae), to swiftly flowing, oxygen-rich mountain streams in which the fishes must attach themselves to the substrate by various means to prevent being swept downstream (suctorial mouth in Loricariidae and pectoral and ventral fin cup in Amphiliidae) as well as marine and brackish waters, although brackish water and even freshwater biotopes are sought, especially to spawn (Ariidae and Plotosidae).

Generalities

Catfishes include diurnal, crepuscular, and nocturnal species. The latter and inhabitants of turbid lowland rivers navigate their habitat with the help of long barbels, or antennae. Virtually every trophic level is represented. There

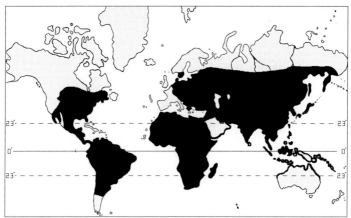

Area of distribution of the order Siluriformes.

are herbivores, algivores, omnivores, carnivores, predators, and even a few parasites (in the family Trichomycteridae).

Size is also highly variable in catfishes. Hundreds of small to medium-sized catfishes are appreciated guests in our aquaria, but true giants of more than 2 m have been reported throughout the distribution area of Siluriformes (confirmed for several species).

In the United States, the Ictaluridae (principally *Ictalurus punctatus*) are the foundation of the warmwater aquaculture industry. They are of great economic importance in the southern United States, especially the lower Mississippi Basin. Although there are numerous native South American catfish species of suitable size, none has been cultured with any commercial success. Clariidae and, to a lesser extent, Plotosidae and Siluridae are raised and marketed in Asia. The wels (*Silurus glanis*, p. 383) has a certain presence in European aquaculture.

Siluriformes lack scales—they are either naked or covered to some degree with bony plates. Since naked species are much more sensitive to malachite green, acriflavine, and other chemicals, medications should be administered carefully. A therapeutic dosage for scaled fishes can be deadly for a naked catfish!

The first ray of the dorsal and pectoral fins of many catfishes serve as a defense mechanism, as they can be locked in the splayed position. In some species, these spines are associated with poison glands. The toxin of *Plotosus lineatus*, a marine species which also enters rivers, may even prove fatal.

There are active schooling species (i.e., *Corydoras* and glass catfishes), loners (primarily large predators), and relatively lethargic species (e.g., Aspredinidae).

Although catfishes are not very colorful, there are numerous species with eye-catching contrasting designs.

Family	Common Name	Habitat/Water	Behavior	Active	Diet	Remarks
Ageneiosidae	Slopehead catfishes	S Am; Fw	predator;	night	C	Internal fertilization.
Amphiliidae	African hillstream cf.	Af; Fw	peaceful;	day,night	C	Adhere to substrate w/ their fins.
Ariidae	Sea/shark catfishes	World;Mw.,Fw	schooling;	day	O,C	Very active; mouthbrooder (♂).
Aspredinidae	Banjo catfishes	S Am; Fw,Bw	inactive;	night	O	Eggs adhered to ♀ or into a nest.
Auchenipteridae	Driftwood catfishes	C,S Am; Fw	schooling; also day	night	C,O	Internal fertilization.
Bagridae	Bagrid catfishes	Af., As; Fw	loners;	night	C,O	Somewhat predatory.
Callichthyidae	Armored catfishes	S Am; Fw	schooling;	day	O,C,L	Peaceful; suppl. air breather.
Cetopsidae	Whale catfishes	S Am; Fw	predator;	night	C	Pronounced predators.
Chacidae	Frogmouth catfishes	As; Fw	loner;	night	C	Preys on small fishes.
Clariidae	Labyrinth/walking cf.	Af., As; Fw	loners;	night	C,O	Suppl. air breather; food fishes.
Doradidae	Thorny/talking catf.	S Am; Fw	gregarious;	night	C,O	Some are very peaceful; bony plates.
Heiogenidae	Marbled catfishes	S AM; Fw	peaceful;	night	C,O	Extremely nocturnal.
Heteropneustidae	Airsack catfishes	As; Fw	aggressive;	night	C,O	Suppl. air breather; school; toxic spine.
Icaluridae	Bullhead catfishes	N,C Am; Fw	predator; day/night		O	Toxic spines; food fish.
Lcricariidae	Suckermouth catf.	S Am; Fw	peaceful; day/night		H,O	Some intraspecifically territorial.
Malapteruridae	Electric catfishes	Af; Fw	loner;	night	O	Electric organ; maintain alone.
Mochokidae	Upside-down catf.	Af; Fw	peaceful; day/night		C,O,H	Some species swim upside-down.
Olyridae	Bannertail catfishes	As; Fw	loner;	?	C	Very oxygen demanding.
Pangasiidae	Shark catfishes	As; Fw	schooling;	day	O	Slightly predatory; food fishes.
Pimelodidae	Antenna catfishes	C,S Am; Fw	predator;	night	C,O	Only preys on small fishes.
Plotosidae	Eeltail/tandan catf.	As; Mw-Fw	schooling;	night	O	Spines are very toxic.
Schilbeidae	Glass catfishes	Af, As; Fw	schooling;	day	C,O	Peaceful, transparent catfishes.
Siluridae	Sheath catfishes	As,Eu; Fw(Bw)	schooling;day/night		C,O	Glass catfishes are peaceful.
Sisoridae	Asian hillstream catf.	As; Fw	peaceful; day/night		C,O,H	Gregarious (Bagarius are predators).
Trichomycteridae	Parasitic catfishes	C,S Am; Fw	peaceful; day/night		C,P!	Two subfamilies are parasites.

CATFISHES

Family Ageneiosidae

Depending on the source, the family of slopehead catfishes is classified into 2 genera and 12 species or 3 genera and 28 species (NELSON, 1994 and BURGESS, 1989, respectively). Their relationship to the families Doradidae and, especially, Auchenipteridae is controversial.

Most are piscivores of open waters, inhabiting bodies of freshwater from Panama to Argentina. The largest species of slopehead catfishes grows to a length of up to 1 m. Due to the palatability of their flesh, they are desired and sought as food by local populations. Smaller species are candidates for the aquarium as long as their predatory livestyle is taken into consideration; i.e., tankmates must be too large to be considered prey.

During the spawning season, there is distinct sexual dimorphism: males have a larger dorsal fin spine, more prominent barbels, and an anteriorly elongated anal fin. However, the genders are virtually impossible to distinguish outside periods of sexual activity.

While juveniles have an appealing contrasting design, adults are plainly colored. They are mostly crepuscular and nocturnal.

These catfishes have probably not been bred in captivity, though it is known that the male inseminates the female with the help of the modified anterior anal fin rays. Oviposition occurs some days later on plants, independent of the male's presence. Since Auchenipteridae and this family are the only two families within the Siluriformes that practice internal fertilization, FERRARIS (1991) integrated the slopehead catfishes into the Auchenipteridae.

In view of their crepuscular and nocturnal lifestyle, the illumination should be attenuated with a partial cover of floating plants and a dark substrate. Bogwood and other shelters are also recommended to present these species in their "most favorable light."

CATFISHES

Ageneiosus brevifilis   2/433
Guyana slopehead catfish
H: S America: Suriname, Guyana, Amazon.
♂: D spine longer (when spawning). **S:** =
B: Nature: internal fertilization.   **F:** C
T: 22–24°C, **L:** 55 cm, **pH:** 7, **D:** 4

Ageneiosus marmoratus   4/224
Marbled slopehead catfish
H: S America: Guyana, Venezuela.
SD: Unknown.   **S:** =
B: Unsuccessful.   **F:** C
T: 23–26°C, **L:** 30 cm, **pH:** 7, **D:** 4

Amphiliidae   African Hillstream Catfishes, Loach Catfishes

Family Amphiliidae

A total of 7 genera and 47 species constitute the family Amphiliidae (NELSON, 1994). African hillstream catfishes are primarily inhabitants of mountain streams of the Congo Basin, where they occur at elevations of up to 1829 m (BURGESS, 1989). They are bottom-oriented fishes which live among rocks. Unlike Loricariidae which attach themselves to the substrate with their suctorial mouth, amphiliids use their broad pectoral and ventral fins in conjunction with their flattened ventral side to hold their position in current-rich waters. There are two subfamilies: Amphiliinae and Doumeinae. The former lack armor and fin spines, whereas the latter appear very similar to the Loricariidae, largely due to their partial armor. A closer look reveals the lack of a suctorial mouth.

With the exception of *Phractura ansorgii*, little is known about the reproductive biology of this family. It is the only species which has been successfully bred in an aquarium, even though the largest species grows to a length of just 18 cm. The frog-like spawn is released into the open water, and immediately sinks to the bottom. Rearing the young was problematic (FOERSCH, in FRANKE, 1985). According to some reports, the eggs are placed under stones in a manner similar to that of Loricariidae, their American cognates.

The diet of loach catfishes—as they are also called—is primarily based on insect larvae and other invertebrates.

Provided the water is oxygen-rich and not excessively warm, these fishes can be housed in community aquaria. Amphiliids are peaceful, diurnal catfishes that have an attractive shape and color.

Amphilius atesuensis   3/291
Golden African kuhli
H: W Africa: Ghana.
♂: More intense design?   **S:** +
B: Unsuccessful.   **F:** C,O
T: 18–22°C, **L:** 6 cm, **pH:** 7, **D:** 2

Amphilius jacksonii   4/225
Jackson's loach catfish
H: E and central Africa: highlands.
SD: Unknown.   **S:** +,–
B: Unknown.   **F:** O,C
T: 18–24°C, **L:** 15 cm, **pH:** 7, **D:** 2

Amphilius sp. nov.   3/292
East African loach catfish
H: E Africa: Tanzania.
SD: Unknown.   **S:** =
B: Unsuccessful.   **F:** O
T: 20–25°C, **L:** 21 cm, **pH:** 7, **D:** 2

Amphilius uranoscopus   3/292

H: Africa: Kenya.
SD: Unknown.   S: +
B: Unsuccessful.   F: C,O
T: 20–25°C, L: 7 cm, pH: 7, D: 2

Belonoglanis brieni   5/228

H: Africa: Zaïre Basin.
SD: Unknown.   S: +
B: Unsuccessful.   F: O,H
T: 20–25°C, L: 5 cm, pH: 7, D: 2–3

Belonoglanis tenuis   4/226

H: Africa: Zaïre Basin.
SD: Unknown.   S: +
B: Unsuccessful.   F: O
T: 24–28°C, L: 17 cm, pH: 7, D: 2–3

Leptoglanis brevis   5/228
Short loach catfish
H: Africa: upper Zaïre Basin.
SD: Unknown.   S: +
B: Unknown.   F: C!
T: 17–22°C, L: 4 cm, pH: 7, D: 2

Leptoglanis sp.aff. *rotundiceps*   3/316
Spotted mountain catfish
H: Africa: Tanzania.
SD: Unknown.   S: =
B: Unknown.   F: C
T: 22–25°C, L: 7 cm, pH: 7, D: 2

Phractura ansorgii ♂   3/294
African whiptailed catfish
H: W Africa: Nigeria, Zaïre.
♂: More red-brown; slimmer.   S: =
B: In plant thickets; <100 eggs.   F: O,C
T: 20–24°C, L: 9.5 cm, pH: 7, D: 2

CATFISHES

249

Phractura ansorgii ♀   3/294
African whiptailed catfish

Phractura brevicauda   5/230
African short-tailed catfish
H: W Africa: Gabon, Cameroon, Zaïre.
♂: More slender.   S: =
B: Unknown.   F: C,H
T: 22–26°C, L: 7 cm, pH: 7, D: 3

Phractura clauseni   4/226
Clausen's loach catfish
H: Africa: lower Niger, Cameroon.
♀: Fuller during spawning season. S: +
B: Unsuccessful.   F: C
T: 23–27°C, L: 8 cm, pH: 7, D: 2–3

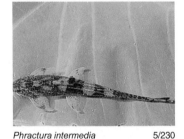

Phractura intermedia   5/230

H: W Africa: Cameroon: coastal rivers.
SD: Unknown.   S: ?
B: Unknown.   F: C
T: 22–26°C, L: 10 cm, pH: 7, D: 3

Phractura longicauda   5/232
African long-tailed catfish
H: Africa: S Cameroon, E Guinea, Zaïre.
SD: Unknown.   S: +
B: Unknown.   F: C
T: 23–28°C, L: 8 cm, pH: 7, D: 2–3

Zaïreichthys wamiensis   4/234
Wami loach catfish
H: Africa: Wami Drainage.
♂: Slimmer.   S: +
B: Unknown.   F: C
T: 23–26°C, L: <8 cm, pH: >7, D: 2

Family Ariidae

The family of sea catfishes consists of about 14 genera and almost 120 species, most of which are marine inhabitants. A few migrate upriver, or live exclusively in freshwater. It is the only catfish family with a worldwide distribution.

Unique among catfishes, ariids are paternal mouthbrooders. The eggs are large and correspondingly few in number.

Sea catfishes are omnivores with a carnivorous tendency; therefore, feeding in the aquarium is unproblematic.

Because they are so similar in appearance, species identification is difficult. They owe their popularity to a diurnal lifestyle and schooling behavior; colorwise they are rather uninspiring.

Large, edible species are little appreciated. To the contrary, they are considered a nuisance and a danger, since they become entangled in fishing nets and their dorsal and pectoral spines inflict slow-healing wounds.

Arius graeffei   3/297
Graeffe's salmon catfish
H: New Guinea, Australia.   Bw,Fw
♀: Longer, rounder ventral fins.   S: =
B: ♂·Mb; 2–4 w; 14 mm e; 25-70 y. F: O
T: 24–32°C, L: >40 cm, pH: >7, D: 1–4

Arius seemani   2/434
West American shark cat, Jordan's catf.
H: America: California to Colombia.   Bw
♀: Lighter fins.   S: =
B: Nature: ♂ mouthbrooder.   F: O
T: 22–26°C, L: 35 cm, pH: >7, D: 3

Hexanematichthys graeffei   2/434
Berney's shark cat
H: N Australia, New Guinea.   Bw, Fw   B: Nat: ♂ mouthbrooder (Nov/Dec).   F: C
SD: Not described.   S: =   T: 24–26°C, L: 25 cm, pH: >7, D: 2

Family Aspredinidae

At present, the family Aspredinidae contains 10 genera and 32 species, but a revision is in the works which will add additional genera and species (NELSON, 1994). The majority occur in freshwater (Bunocephalinae), but some species are found in brackish waters and even marine coastal areas (Aspredininae).

Because of their cryptic nocturnal lifestyle, banjo catfishes are not particularly popular aquarium fishes. Daylight hours are spent lying on the substrate, hidden among leaf litter or plants, or even buried. Colorwise they have little to recommend them, as brown hues dominate. Some aquarists are drawn by their unusual body shape and, especially, craggy skin. They are suitable additions for peaceful community aquaria.

Insect larvae and other invertebrates constitute the bulk of their diet in the wild. In the aquarium they are unfinicky omnivores.

Dysichthys coracoideus is the only species that has been successfully bred. After the male fans out a pit in the substrate, the female deposits her eggs therein. The male guards the spawn. It is a very prolific species, producing 4000–5000 young per spawn.

A very deviant mode of reproduction has been observed among the long-tailed banjos in their natural habitat. The eggs are attached to the ventrum of the female by a short peduncle. Capillaries connect each egg to the abdominal vein, thereby providing nourishment. This brood care seems to have evolved in response to the muddy substrates typical of the estuaries where they live; hard substrates suitable for oviposition are rare (FERRARIS, 1991).

Genders are difficult to distinguish.

Amaralia hypsiura   3/298
Two-rayed banjo catfish
H: S America: N Brazil.
SD: Unknown.   S: +
B: Unknown.   F: O
T: 22–24°C, L: 7 cm, pH: 7, D: 2–3

Bunocephalichthys verrucosus scabriceps
Large-head banjo catfish   3/298
H: S America: central Amazon.
SD: None.   S: +
B: Unknown.   F: C,O
T: 21–25°C, L: 10 cm, pH: 7, D: 2

Bunocephalichthys verrucosus verrucosus
Tall banjo catfish 2/436
H: S America: Amazon Basin.
♀: Sometimes much fuller. S: +
B: Unknown. F: C,O
T: 20–24°C, L: 8 cm, pH: 7, D: 1

Dysichthys coracoideus 1/454
Two-colored banjo catfish
H: S America: Amazon to La Plata.
SD: Unknown. S: +
B: On sand; 4000–5000 eggs. F: C
T: 20–27°C, L: 15 cm, pH: 7, D: 3

Dysichthys knerii 2/436
Kneri's banjo catfish
H: S America: Amazon and tributaries.
SD: Unknown. S: +
B: Sand pit; ♂ tends the spawn. F: C
T: 20–25°C, L: 8 cm, pH: <7, D: 1

Dysichthys quadriradiatus 5/233
Four-rayed banjo catfish
H: S America: Amazon region.
SD: Unknown. S: =
B: Unknown. F: C
T: 20–25°C, L: 12 cm, pH: <7, D: 2–3

Platystacus cotylephorus ♂ 2/438
Mottled whiptailed banjo catfish
H: S Am.: Suriname, Amazon estuaries.
♂: Narrower ventral fins. S: +
B: N.: eggs attached to ventrum. F: C,O
T: 22–25°C, L: 25 cm, pH: >7, D: 3

Platystacus cotylephorus ♀ 2/438
Mottled whiptailed banjo catfish

Family Astroblepidae (not presented in the AQUARIUM ATLAS)

Collected·by the author (G.F.), this fish could not be decisively placed in any family. Perhaps it is a Pimelodidae or even an Astroblepidae. However, the latter have a suctorial mouth and 2 pairs of barbels, whereas this specimen has 3 pairs of barbels and no suctorial mouth. Its body is very elongated and loachlike.

This rare catfish was found at an elevation of 600 m in the Rio Misahualli, a river of the eastern Andean foothills of Ecuador. It is a swift-flowing, stone bed river with a neutral pH and a temperature of ca. 22°C. The species is very sensitive to *Ichthyophtirius*, and its fast opercular movements in the aquarium emphasize its need of high oxygen concentrations. Sympatric catfishes include Loricariidae, a whale catfish (p. 297), and *Pimelodella* cf. *gracilis*.

Family Auchenipteridae

There are 21 genera and 60 species of driftwood catfishes, all of which inhabit bodies of freshwater from Panama to Argentina (NELSON, 1994).

FERRARIS (1991) places the genera *Centromochlus, Glanidium,* and *Tatia* into the family Centromochlidae. Unlike the rest of the family, these genera do not have a sexually dimorphic dorsal spine nor were they though to have internal fertilization. The INDEX, however, follows the classification of NELSON, especially since internal fertilization is now known to exist in *Tatia*.

The remainder of the family, along with the Ageneosidae (included within the Auchenipteridae by FERRARIS), is unique among the catfishes—they practice internal fertilization.

Because of their mode of reproduction, the sexual dimorphism in relation to the genitalia is pronounced. The first rays of the male's anal fin are modified into a copulatory organ, much like the andropodium or gonopodium of livebearing toothcarps (Group 6). During copulation, the spermatophore is transferred into the female's funnellike urogenital opening via the male's modified anal fin. The dorsal and pectoral fin spines thicken when the male is sexually active and revert to their normal state afterwards.

A few days or—in the case of *Tatia galaxias*—a few weeks after insemination, the female deposits the adhesive eggs on plants or in cryptic locals independent of the male's presence. Brood care has not been observed.

Community aquaria with subdued illumination and abundant shelter are appropriate for smaller species within the family. A small school should be maintained. Those species which are also active during the day and have an attractive contrasting design are generally popular among aquarists. Unfortunately, availability is rare and seasonal.

Auchenipterichthys longimanus ♂ 2/440
Spotted woodcat
H: S America: central and lower Amazon.
♂: A fin rays thicken (at spawning). S: =
B: ♀ stores sperm internally.   F: C,O
T: 20–23°C, L: 15 cm, pH: 7, D: 2

Auchenipterichthys longimanus ♀ 2/440
Spotted woodcat

Auchenipterichthys thoracatus   2/442
Midnight catfish, Zamora cat
H: S America: upper Amazon.
♂: Thickend D & P fin spines.   S: =
B: Nature: internal fertilization.   F: C,O
T: 20–24°C, L: 11 cm, pH: 7, D: 2

Auchenipterus nuchalis   2/442
Mustache woodcat, Demerara woodcat
H: S America: estuaries.
♂: Thicker maxillary barbels.   S: +
B: Internal fertilization.   F: C,O
T: 20–22°C, L: 15 cm, pH: 7, D: 2–3

Entomocorus benjamini ♂   4/228
Benjamin's catfish
H: S America: Bolivia.
♂: See photos; note V and A fins.   S: –
B: Unsuccessful.   F: C
T: 24–27°C, L: 7 cm, pH: 7, D: 3–4

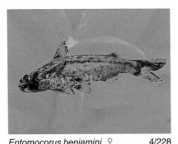

Entomocorus benjamini ♀   4/228
Benjamin's catfish

Parauchenipterus albicrux   5/234
White-cross woodcat
H: S America: N Argentina.
♂: Anal fin with copulatory organ.   **S:** =
B: Internal fertilization.   **F:** C,O
T: 18–24°C, **L:** 14 cm, **pH:** 7, **D:** 3

Parauchenipterus galeatus ♂ juv.   2/444
Starry woodcat
H: S America: northern region to Peru.
♂: Anal fin with copulatory organ.   **S:** =
B: Internal fertilization.   **F:** C,O
T: 20–24°C, **L:** 20 cm, **pH:** 7, **D:** 2–3

Entomocorus gameroi   3/300
Blue woodcat
H: S America: Suriname, Brazil.
♂: Anal fin with copulatory organ.   **S:** –
B: Nature: internal fertilization.   **F:** C,O
T: 20–24°C, **L:** 7 cm, **pH:** 7, **D:** 3

Parauchenipterus fisheri   5/234
Fisher's woodcat
H: S America: Guyana, Colombia.
♂: Anal fin with copulatory organ.   **S:** =
B: Internal fertilization.   **F:** C,O
T: 22–26°C, **L:** 28 cm, **pH:** 7, **D:** 3–4

Parauchenipterus galeatus adult   2/444
Starry woodcat

Parauchenipterus galeatus   5/236
Starry woodcat
H: S America: widely distributed.
♂: Anal fin with copulatory organ.   S: =
B: Internal fertilization.   F: C,O
T: 22–29°C, L: ca.15 cm, pH: 7, D: 2–3

Parauchenipterus insignis ♂   5/236
Flag woodcat
H: S America: Brazil, Colombia.
♂: Anal fin with copulatory organ.   S: –
B: Internal fertilization.   F: C,O
T: 23–28°C, L: 25 cm, pH: <7, D: 2–3

Parauchenipterus leopardinus   5/238
Leopard woodcat
H: S America: E Brazil.
♂: Anal fin with copulatory organ.   S: +
B: Internal fertilization; <400 e. F: C,O
T: 22–28°C, L: 18 cm, pH: 7, D: 2–3

Pseudauchenipterus nodosus juv.   2/446
Yellow woodcat, black tailband catfish
H: S Am.: Ven., Tri., Guianas; Amazon.
♂: Anal fin with copulatory organ.   S: =
B: Unsuccessful.   F: C,O
T: 20–25°C, L: 20 cm, pH: 7, D: 2–3

Tatia creutzbergi   3/300
Creutzberg's woodcat
H: S America: Suriname, Brazil.
♂: Anal fin with copulatory organ.   S: =
B: Internal fert.; eggs under wood. F: C
T: 21–24°C, L: 4 cm, pH: 7, D: 1

Tatia galaxias   4/228
Milky Way woodcat
H: S America: Venezuela: Orinoco Basin.
♂: Anal fin with copulatory organ.   S: +
B: Even 4 w after insemin.; 200 e. F:C,O
T: 22–26°C, L: 9 cm, pH: 7, D: 3

Tatia perugiae   5/238

H: S America: Colombia, Ecuador, Peru.
SD: Unknown.   S: +
B: Unknown.   F: C,L
T: 26–28°C, L: 6 cm, pH: <7, D: 3

Trachelyichthys exilis ♂   3/302

H: S America: Peru: Rio Mamón.
♂: Visible genital papilla.   S: +
B: Among Java moss and similar.   F: C
T: 22–24°C, L: 8 cm, pH: <7, D: 2–3

Trachelyopterus coriaceus ♂   5/240
Cheyenne woodcat
H: S America: French Guiana.
SD: Urogenital papilla.   S: =
B: Internal fertilization.   F: C,O
T: 24–29°C, L: 18 cm, pH: 7, D: 2–3

Trachelyichthys decaradiatus   5/242
Ten-rayed woodcat
H: S America: Guyana.
♂: Genital papilla prior to anal fin.   S: =
B: External fertilization.   F: C
T: 20–28°C, L: 12 cm, pH: 7, D: 2

Trachelyopterichthys taeniatus   2/446
Striped woodcat
H: S America: upper Amazon.
♂: Anal fin with copulatory organ.   S: =
B: Internal fertilization.   F: C
T: 20–25°C, L: 15 cm, pH: <7, D: 2–3

Trachelyopterus maculosos ♀   5/240
Spotted woodcat
H: S America: Brazil.
♂: Genital papilla prior to anal fin.   S: =
B: Internal fertilization.   F: C,O
T: 24–29°C, L: 18 cm, pH: 7, D: 2–3

Family Bagridae

The approximately 210 species of bagrid catfishes have been classified into 13 genera. Not everyone agrees on the systematics of the family. According to some opinions, the family Olyridae (containing just *Olyra*) is part of the Bagridae and some of the genera now considered part of the Bagridae are segregated from the family, creating two additional families—Claroteidae and Austroglanididae. Until this new classification gains broader acceptance, this book will maintain the "old" taxonomy (i.e., NELSON, 1994).

Bagrids are distributed in freshwater from Africa to Asia (Japan and Borneo). Chiefly medium to large in size (*Chrysichthys grandis* from Lake Tanganyika grows to a length of 2 m), they are important food fishes, but several species remain small enough for aquarium maintenance. They must be care for in a species tank or a community aquarium that does not contain small fishes.

Aquaculture of Bagridae as food fishes is still not very developed, but some medium-sized species have been studied in Africa for some time: *Auchenoglanis occidentalis, Bagrus docmac,* and various *Chrysichthys* species (BARDACH et. al., 1972). Because most bagrids are predators, an economically viable feeding regime for production is proving elusive. In aquarium maintenance, this consideration is less important, but their pronounced predatory activities have to be taken into account when choosing the tankmates; all must be too large to be considered prey.

In the aquarium, these catfishes are generally shy and crepuscular/nocturnal. Therefore, dim illumination and numerous hiding places among the decoration are recommended.

Water chemistry is usually of secondary importance for bagrids, but in such a widely distributed family, there are always exceptions.

Breeding success within this family has been rather modest. According to observations, members of the genera *Batasio, Mystus,* and *Pelteobagrus*

Hemibagrus wyckioides, the Asian red-tailed catfish. (Erroneously identified as *Mystus nemurus* in Volume 2, p. 454.)

deposit their adhesive eggs on fine-leaved plants or on roots. Some *Pelleobagrus* spp. are reportedly cave spawners with paternal brood care. Certain Asian species —i.e., *Aorichthys aor, A. seenghala,* and *Mystus gulio*—secrete a milky fluid from their spongy ventrum which is grazed by their offspring in a manner very similar to that found in the South American discus fishes (see Group 8—South America) (FERRARIS, 1991).

Auchenoglanis cf. *biscutatus*   3/303
Yellow bagrid
H: Africa: Nile. Lake Malawi?
SD: Not described.   S: =
B: Unknown.   F: O
T: 24–26°C, L: >35 cm?, pH: >7, D: 2

Auchenoglanis ngamensis   3/304
Largemouth bagrid
H: W Africa.
SD: Not described.   S: =
B: Unknown.   F: O
T: 22–26°C, L: 25 cm, pH: 7, D: 2

Auchenoglanis occidentalis   2/448
Giraffe-nosed catfish
H: Africa: tropics.
SD: Not described.   S: =
B: Unknown.   F: O
T: 21–25°C, L: 45 cm, pH: 7, D: 2

Auchenoglanis punctatus   4/231
Dotted bagrid
H: Africa: Zaïre Basin.
SD: Unknown.   S: =
B: Unknown.   F: C
T: 24–28°C, L: 8 cm, pH: 7, D: 2–3

Bagrichthys macracanthus   3/304
Humpbacked bagrid
H: SE Asia: Sum., Borneo, Thai., Burma.
SD: Unknown.   S: +
B: Unknown.   F: O
T: 20–25°C, L: 40 cm, pH: 7, D: 3

Bagrus bajad 4/232
Bajad bagrid
H: Africa.
SD: Unknown. S: –
B: Unknown. F: O
T: 22–28°C, L: 70 cm, pH: 7, D: 4

Bagrus docmac 2/448
Nile catfish, hog catfish
H: Africa: lakes Victoria, Stephan, Kainji.
SD: Not described. S: –
B: Unknown. F: C,O
T: 21–25°C, L: 60 cm, pH: 7, D: 3–4

Bagrus filamentosus 4/232
Hog catfish
H: Africa: Niger Basin.
♀: Ventrally fuller when ripe. S: =
B: Unknown. F: C
T: 20–27°C, L: 15 cm, pH: 7, D: 3

Pseudomystus poecilopterus 3/306

H: Asia: India, Bngl., Burma, Thai., Malay.
SD: Unknown. S: =
B: On plant leaves; <1000 eggs. F: C,O
T: 23–26°C, L: 20 cm, pH: 7, D: 2–3

Chrysichthys brevibarbis 3/306
Short-barbeled catfish
H: W Africa: Zaïre, Stanley Pool.
SD: Unknown. S: –
B: Unknown. F: C
T: 20–25°C, L: 44 cm, pH: 7, D: 3

Chrysichthys furcatus 4/234

H: W Africa.
SD: Unknown. S: –
B: Unknown. F: C,O
T: 22–28°C, L: 70 cm, pH: 7, D: 4

CATFISHES

Chrysichthys nigrodigitatus   3/290
Silver cat
H: W Africa: broadly distributed.
♂: Broader head as adult.   S: =
B: Nature: ♂ digs pit for spawning. F: O
T: 23–26°C, L: 65 cm, pH: 7, D: 3–4

Chrysichthys ornatus   3/308
Mottled catfish
H: W Africa: Zaïre, Congo, Ubangi.
SD: Unknown.   S: =
B: Unknown.   F: C
T: 20–25°C, L: 19 cm, pH: 7, D: 2

Chrysichthys walkeri   3/308
Walker's bagrid
H: W Africa: Gold Coast, Ghana.
SD: None.   S: =,–
B: Unknown.   F: C
T: 20–25°C, L: 24 cm, pH: 7, D: 2

Clarotes laticeps   3/310
Flathead bagrid
H: Africa: Egypt, Chad, Niger, Sen., Sud.
SD: Unknown.   S: –
B: Unknown.   F: C
T: 20–26°C, L: <80 cm, pH: 7, D: 2

Gephyroglanis longipinnis   3/310
Long-finned bagrid
H: Africa: Zaïre, Congo, Stanley Pool.
♂: More slender.   S: =
B: Unknown.   F: C
T: 20–25°C, L: 14 cm, pH: 7, D: 2

Gephyroglanis sp.   3/312

H: Africa: Zaïre.
♂: More slender.   S: –
B: Unknown.   F: C
T: 20–25°C, L: 48 cm, pH: 7, D: 3

Mystus bocourti   2/450
King bagrid
H: SE Asia: Thailand.
SD: Unknown.   S: =
B: Unknown.   F: C
T: 22–25°C, L: 18 cm, pH: 7, D: 3

Bagroides melapterus   1/455

H: SE Asia: Sumatra, Borneo.
SD: Unknown.   S: =
B: Unknown.   F: C,O
T: 18–28°C, L: 20 cm, pH: 7, D: 2–3

Leiocassis siamensis   2/450
Asian bumblebee cat
H: SE Asia: Thailand, Cambodia.
SD: Unknown.   S: =
B: Unknown.   F: C
T: 20–26°C, L: 20 cm, pH: 7, D: 2–3

Leiocassis stenomus   3/314

H: Asia: Sunda Arch.: Java, Sumatra, Bor.
SD: Unknown.   S: =
B: Unknown.   F: C
T: 20–26°C, L: 15 cm, pH: 7, D: 2

Liauchenoglanis maculatus   3/316
Leopard-spotted bagrid
H: Africa: Sierra Leone.   Rare
SD: Unknown.   S: +
B: Unknown.   F: C
T: 22–25°C, L: 8 cm, pH: <7, D: 2

Lophiobagrus cyclurus   2/452
Tanganyika bagrid, African bullhead
H: Africa: Lake Tanganyika.   E
SD: Unknown.   S: =
B: Cave spawner.   F: C
T: 23–26°C, L: 10 cm, pH: >7, D: 3

CATFISHES

263

Mystus argentivittatus   5/244
Silver-line bagrid
H: Asia: China.
SD: Unknown.   S: =
B: Unknown.   F: C,O
T: 20–25°C, L: 5 cm, pH: 7, D: 3

Mystus nigriceps   3/318
Black-head bagrid
H: Asia: India, Burma; perhaps all SE Asia.
♂: Larger and usually slimmer.   S: =
B: 1000 e; often only 50% hatch.   F: C,O
T: 22–25°C, L: 15 cm, pH: 7, D: 2–3

Mystus nigriceps   2/452
Blackhead bagrid
H: Asia: broadly distributed (India, Burma).
SD: Not described.   S: =
B: Unknown.   F: C,O
T: 22–25°C, L: 15 cm, pH: 7, D: 2–3

Mystus bimaculatus   1/456
Two-spot bagrid
H: Asia: Sumatra, Malaysia.
SD: Not described.   S: =
B: Unknown.   F: C,O
T: 20–26°C, L: 9 cm, pH: 7, D: 1

Mystus bleekeri (right)   3/318
Bleeker's bagrid
H: Asia: Pakistan, Nepal, Bngl., Burma.
SD: Unknown.   S: =
B: Unknown.   F: C
T: 18–26°C, L: <45 cm, pH: 7, D: 3

Mystus mica   3/320
Dwarf bagrid
H: Asia: CIS States.
♂: Genital papilla; anal fin smaller.   S: =
B: Nature: among bog plant roots.   F: C
T: 16–24°C, L: 6 cm, pH: 7, D: 2

CATFISHES

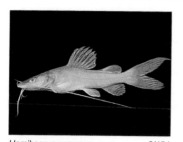

Hemibagrus nemurus   2/454
Asian red-tailed catfish
H: Asia: Malay., Thai., Sum., Sing., Java.
SD: Unknown.   S: –
B: Unknown.   F: C
T: 22–25°C, L: 60 cm, pH: >7, D: 4

Hemibagrus wyckii   3/320
H: SE Asia: Java, Sumatra, Borneo, Malay
Pen., Sri Lanka, Burma, Thailand.
SD: Unknown.   S: –
B: Unknown.   F: C
T: 22–25°C, L: <80 cm, pH: 7, D: 2

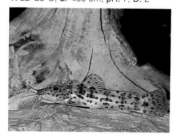

Parauchenoglanis macrostoma   1/456

H: Africa: Niger Delta, Burkina Faso.
SD: Unknown.   S: =,–
B: Unknown.   F: C,O
T: 23–27°C, L: 24 cm, pH: 7, D: 2

Mystus vittatus   1/456
Striped catfish, banded mystus
H: Asia: W India, Burma.
SD: Unknown.   S: =
B: Among roots and short plants.   F:C
T: 22–28°C, L: 20 cm, pH: 7, D: 1–2

Parauchenoglanis balayi   5/244

H: Africa: S Cameroon, Gabon, Zaïre.
SD: Unknown.   S: =
B: Unknown.   F: C,O
T: 22–28°C, L: 39 cm, pH: 7, D: 4

Pelteobagrus brashnikowi   3/312
Kosatok bagrid, Brashnikow's bagrid
H: Asia: CIS States.
♂: Smaller and probably slimmer.   S: =
B: Among roots of aquatic plants.   F: C
T: 12–25°C, L: <22 cm, pH: 7, D: 1

CATFISHES

Pelteobagrus crassilabris   5/246

H: Asia: China.
SD: Unknown.   S: =
B: Unknown.   F: C,O
T: 15–25°C, L: 16 cm, pH: 7, D: 2–3

Pelteobagrus fulvidraco   3/322
Tawny dragon catfish
H: Asia: Amur Basin.
♂: Larger.   S: –
B: ♂ brood care; <2000 eggs.   F: C
T: 16–25°C, L: <35 cm, pH: 7, D: 2

Pelteobagrus nudiceps   5/246
Honey bagrid
H: Asia: Japan.
SD: Unknown.   S: =
B: ♂ brood care; gravel pit.   F: C,O
T: 10–24°C, L: 30 cm, pH: >7, D: 2–3

Pelteobagrus ornatus   3/322
Ornate bagrid
H: Asia: Malaysia, Indonesia.
♂: Genital pap. ♀: Almost transpar.   S: +
B: Green eggs visible in body.   F: C
T: 21–25°C, L: 4 cm, pH: 7, D: 1

Pelteobagrus ussuriensis   3/314
Ussuri bagrid
H: Asia: CIS States.
♂: Smaller and usually slimmer.   S: =
B: Among roots of aquatic plants.   F:C
T: 12–25°C, L: 20 cm, pH: 7, D: 2

Rita rita   5/248
Rita catfish
H: Asia: India.
SD: Unknown.   S: =,–
B: Summer; eggs 7mm Ø.   F: C,O
T: 18–26°C, L: 120 cm, pH: 7, D: 4

Family Callichthyidae

There are about 7 genera and 130 species of armored catfishes. Callichthyids are native to freshwaters of Panama and South America as well as the island of Trinidad. Two subfamilies are recognized: the Callichthyinae and the Corydoradinae. The vast majority of Callichthyidae—122 species—are Corydoradinae, commonly known as corys. The remaining 8 species make up the Callichthyinae.

Typically, callichthyids have a strong body armor consisting of rows of bony plates that overlap like shingles on a roof. Since their sensitive barbels are used to scour the substrate in search of food, smooth-edged gravel or river sand is the substrate of choice.

Subfamily Callichthyinae

Callichthyid armored catfishes are primarily inhabitants of oxygen-deficient swamps and backwaters. By breathing atmospheric air, Callichthyinae are able to survive the low oxygen levels so commonly found in their habitat. The air is forced into the intestine, where the gases are exchanged. Spent air is released through the anus. When the ground is damp, these armored catfishes can wriggle over land from one water hole to another, an endeavor which is usually undertaken at night. As can be deduced from their success in inhospitable environments in the wild, they are extremely hardy aquarium fishes and longevous—even if subjected to a certain amount of neglect.

Sexually active males build a bubble nest and guard the site. All fishes—females included—are chased away from the territory. Following oviposition, it is advisable to remove all fishes save the male from the breeding tank. Between 200 and 800 offspring are produced.

Unfortunately, these species are not very colorful. One possible exception is a species described as *Hoplosternum magdalenae*; however, its existence is questionable.

They are absolutely peaceful and do not grow excessively large, so they are commonly maintained in aquaria despite their relatively inactive, bottom-oriented, cryptic lifestyle.

Subfamily Corydoradinae

This subfamily contains the genera *Aspidoras* (approximately 14 species), *Brochis* (3 species), and *Corydoras* (approximately 105 species, probably more).

All genera are capable of breathing atmospheric air, much like the Callichthyinae. Their presence is often divulged when they come to the surface to breathe. Apparently gulping air is not solely triggered by lack of oxygen in the water. *Corydoras* and *Brochis* commonly come up for air immediately following certain disturbances, for example, the throw of a cast net. Tranquility is quickly restored. One could deduce that corys gulp air to have a reserve in case danger arises.

As these catfishes are diurnal, capture is easier at night when their reactions are lethargic. They can be guided into a hand net or simply scooped out of shallow waters when they are blinded with a spot light.

Superficially, *Aspidoras* are small *Corydoras* that have a much smaller eye diameter. In comparison to *Corydoras*, this genus is much less common in the trade. Attempts to breed *Aspidoras* spp. in captivity have met with little success. A group consisting of four male and three female *A. poecilus* (Rio Xingú, Mato Grosso, Brazil) coincidentally bred in a densely planted 20 l species tank (FRANKE, 1985).

The genus *Brochis* came to the attention of American hobbyists a few years ago, when *B. britskii* was described and then commercially imported. All three species have similar coloration and body conformation; that is, they are metallic green and have a large, deep body. As inferred by its name, *B. multiradiatus* has numerous rays in the dorsal fin, although all *Brochis* spp. have more dorsal fin rays than *Corydoras*. *B. splendens*, the most readily available of the three, has already been bred. Although not always successful, breeding follows the accepted procedure for *Corydoras* (see below). Interestingly, the adult coloration is not attained until the offspring are 4–5 cm long.

The genus *Corydoras* is the most specious of the family Callichthyidae. Virtually every lowland creek and lagoon of tropical South America has at least one, but frequently three or four species. No community aquarium is complete without these small, social, lively, diurnal, peaceful catfishes. Because they are omnivorous "vacuum cleaners" that consume leftovers with gusto, they are invaluable towards maintaining a clean aquarium.

Corydoras are the most successfully bred catfishes in the hobby. Many imported species have already been aquarium bred. However, breeding for the most part continues to be on a hobby level. Since few species are being commercially bred, most purchased corys are wild-caught.

An expansive sand substrate, broad-leaved plants as spawning substrates, and a minimum volume of 50 l are required for reproduction. The water should be slightly acid (pH 6–7), soft (below 6 °dGH), and 24°–28°C. Place a pair or a group consisting of twice as many males as females into the breeding aquarium. Depending on species, up to 500 eggs are laid in multiple episodes, 2–25 at a time. The eggs are collected by the female in a cup formed by the ventral fins. They are then adhered to leaves or even the aquarium panes. After 5 or 6 days, the offspring hatch. The parents will prey on the newly laid eggs. Therefore, either the parents or the eggs should be transferred. In the latter case, scrape them from the glass with a razor blade or cut the egg-laden leaves and place them into a well-aerated rearing tank containing water from the breeding aquarium.

Aspidoras albater   2/455

H: S America: Brazil: Rio Tocantins.
SD: Not described.   S: +
B: Unknown.   F: C,O
T: 22–24°C, L: 4 cm, pH: 7, D: 2

Aspidoras fuscoguttatus   3/324
Spotted aspidoras
H: S America: Brazil, Peru.
♂: Slightly slimmer.   S: +
B: Unknown.   F: O
T: 22–25°C, L: 4 cm, pH: <7, D: 2

Aspidoras menezesi   2/456
H: S America: Brazil: Rio Salgado.
♂: More slender.   S: +
B: Unknown.   F: C,O
T: 21–24°C, L: 4.5 cm, pH: <7, D: 2–3

Aspidoras pauciradiatus   2/456
False corydoras, blotch-fin aspidoras
H: S America: Brazil: Rio Araguaia.
SD: Unknown.   S: +
B: Unsuccessful.   F: L,O
T: 22–25°C, L: 3.5 cm, pH: <7, D: 3

Aspidoras raimundi   5/250
Raimund's aspidoras
H: S America: NE Brazil.
♀: Fuller during spawning season. S: +
B: Recently successful.   F: C,O
T: 20–23°C, L: 4 cm, pH: <7, D: 3

Aspidoras rochai   3/324

H: S America: Brazil.
♀: Fuller during spawning season. S: +
B: Unknown.   F: C
T: 21–25°C, L: 4.5 cm, pH: 7, D: 2

Aspidoras spilotus   5/251
Spotted aspidoras
H: S America: Brazil: State of Ceará.
♀: Fuller during spawning season. S: +
B: ♂♂ are very active.   F: C
T: 22–25°C, L: 4.5 cm, pH: <7, D: 2

CATFISHES

Brochis britzkii   3/326
Giant brochis
H: S America: Brazil: Rio Paraguay.
SD: Not described.   S: +
B: Unknown.   F: C
T: 20–24°C, L: 8 cm, pH: 7, D: 2

Brochis multiradiatus   2/458
Hog-nosed brochis, long-finned brochis
H: S America: Ecuador: Rio Napo.
SD: Not described.   S: +
B: Successful; no reports.   F: L,O
T: 21–24°C, L: 8 cm, pH: <7, D: 2

Brochis splendens adult   1/458
Common brochis
H: S America: Ecuador, Peru, Brazil.
♀: Fuller during spawning season. S: +
B: Successful; like Corydoradinae. F: O
T: 22–28°C, L: 7 cm, pH: <7, D: 1

Brochis splendens juvenile   3/326
Common brochis
H: S America: Ecuador, Peru, Brazil.
SD: Unknown.   S: +
B: More than 1000 eggs.   F: O
T: 22–28°C, L: 7 cm, pH: <7, D: 1

Callichthys callichthys   1/458
Armoured catfish, slender armored catfish
H: S America: Ven., Brazil, Peru, Bol., Par.
♂: Brighter; P fin spines longer. S: +
B: Bubble nest; brood care; <120e. F: O
T: 18–28°C, L: <18 cm, pH: 7, D: 1

Corydoras acutus   1/460
Blacktop cory
H: S America: Peru: Rio Ampiyacu.
♂: Slimmer.   S: +
B: Unknown.   F: O
T: 22–26°C, L: 5.5 cm, pH: 7, D: 1–2

Corydoras adolfoi 3/328
Adolfo's cory
H: S America: Brazil: Rio Negro, Rio Uaupés.
SD: Unknown. S: +
B: Adhesive eggs. F: O
T: 22–26°C, L: 6 cm, pH: 7, D: 2

Corydoras aeneus 1/460, 5/252
Bronze corydoras
H: S Am.: Trinidad, Venezuela to La Plata.
♂: Slimmer. S: +
B: Typical for the subfamily. F: O
T: 22–26°C, L: <7 cm, pH: 7, D: 1–2

Corydoras aeneus 1/460, 5/252
Bronze corydoras
H: S America: Venezuela to Argentina.
♂: Slightly smaller and slimmer. S: +
B: On plant leaves. F: C,O
T: 22–26°C, L: 6–7 cm, pH: 7, D: 1–2

Corydoras aeneus 1/460, 5/252
Bronze corydoras
Artificially colored!

Corydoras cf. *aeneus* 5/253
Bronze corydoras
H: S America: Colombia.

Corydoras sp. aff. *aeneus* 5/253
Bronze corydoras
H: S America: N Venezuela.

CATFISHES

CATFISHES

Corydoras agassizii 1/460
Agassiz's corydoras
H: S America: Peru: Iquitos.
♂: Slimmer. S: +
B: Unknown. F: O
T: 22–26°C, L: 6.5 cm, pH: 7, D: 1–2

Corydoras amapaensis 3/328
Amapa cory
H: S America: Brazil, French Guiana.
♂: Slimmer. S: +
B: Typical for the subfamily. F: O
T: 22–26°C, L: 6.5 cm, pH: 7, D: 2

Corydoras amandajanea 5/254
Jane's cory
H: S America: Brazil: Rio Negro.
♂: Slightly slimmer. S: +
B: There are no reports. F: C,O
T: 20–25°C, L: 6.5 cm, pH: <7, D: 2

Corydoras amandajanea 5/254
Jane's cory
Spotted form.

Corydoras ambiacus 2/458
Half-masked cory
H: S America: Peru: Rio Ampiyacu.
♂: More slender. S: +
B: There are no reports. F: O
T: 21–24°C, L: 6 cm, pH: <7, D: 2

Corydoras araguaiaensis (3/289),
Araguaia cory 4/236, 5/257
H: S America: Brazil: Rio Araguaia.
♂: Slightly smaller and slimmer. S: +
B: On plant leaves; <100 eggs. F: O
T: 23–26°C, L: <6 cm, pH: <7, D: 2

Corydoras arcuatus   1/460
Arched corydoras, skunk cory
H: S America: Brazil: Tefe.
♂: Slimmer.   S: +
B: Unknown.   F: O
T: 22–26°C, L: <5 cm, pH: 7, D: 1–2

Corydoras armatus   1/460

H: S America: E Bolivia.
♂: Slimmer.   S: +
B: Unknown.   F: O
T: 22–26°C, L: 4.5 cm, pH: 7, D: 1–2

Corydoras atropersonatus   2/460
Masked cory
H: S America: Ecuador.
♀: Fuller during spawning season. S: +
B: Unknown.   F: O
T: 21–24°C, L: 4.5 cm, pH: <7, D: 3

Corydoras axelrodi   1/460
Axelrod's cory
H: S America: Colombia: Rio Meta.
♂: Slimmer?   S: +
B: Unknown.   F: O
T: 22–26°C, L: 5 cm, pH: 7, D: 1–2

Corydoras baderi   1/470

H: S America: Brazil.
SD: Unknown.   S: +
B: Unknown.   F: O
T: 22–26°C, L: <4 cm, pH: 7, D: 1–2

Corydoras barbatus ♀   1/460
Banded corydoras, filigree cory
H: S America: Brazil: Rio to São Paulo.
SD: See photos   S: +
B: Unknown.   F: O
T: 22–26°C, L: 12 cm, pH: 7, D: 1–2

CATFISHES

273

Corydoras barbatus ♂   1/460
Banded corydoras, filigree cory

Corydoras blochi blochi   1/462
Bloch's cory
H: S America: Guyana.
♂: Slimmer?   S: +
B: Unknown.   F: O
T: 22–26°C, L: <6 cm, pH: 7, D: 1–2

Corydoras blochi vittatus   1/462
Bloch's striped cory
H: S America: Amazonia: Rio Itapecuru.
♂: Slimmer?   S: +
B: Unknown.   F: O
T: 22–26°C, L: <6 cm, pH: 7, D: 1–2

Corydoras bolivianus ♀   4/238
Bolivian giant cory, C 5
H: S America: Bolivia: Rio Mamoré.
SD: See photos.   S: +
B: Unknown.   F: C,O
T: 22–25°C, L: 8 cm, pH: 7, D: 3

Corydoras bolivianus ♂   4/238
Bolivian giant cory, C 5

Corydoras bondi bondi   1/462
Bond's cory
H: S America: Guyana, Suriname.
♂: Slimmer?   S: +
B: Unknown.   F: O
T: 22–26°C, L: <5.5 cm, pH: 7, D: 1–2

Corydoras bondi coppenamensis   3/330
Coppename cory
H: S Am.: Suriname: Coppename River.
SD: Not described.   S: +
B: Successful.   F: C,O
T: 20–24°C, L: 5 cm, pH: 7, D: 1–2

Corydoras breei ♀   (3/341), 4/236
Bree's cory
H: S America: Suriname.
♂: Smaller and slimmer.   S: +
B: Darkened aq.; strong current. F: C,O
T: 24–26°C, L: 5 cm, pH: 7, D: 2–4

Corydoras breei ♂   (3/341), 4/
236
Bree's cory

Corydoras burgessi   4/240
Burgess' cory
H: S America: Brazil: Amazonia.
♂: Slimmer and slightly smaller.   S: +
B: Adhesive eggs.   F: O
T: 23–26°C, L: 6 cm, pH: 7, D: 2–4

Corydoras caudimaculatus   2/460
Tail-spot cory, big-blotch cory
H: S America: Brazil/Bolivia
SD: Unknown.   S: +
B: Rarely bred.   F: O
T: 22–26°C, L: 6 cm, pH: 7, D: 2

Corydoras cervinus   5/258

H: S America: Brazil: Rio Guaporé.
SD: Unknown.   S: +
B: There are no specific reports. F: C,O
T: 21–24°C, L: 5 cm, pH: 7, D: 3

Corydoras concolor   1/462
Color cory
H: S America: W Venezuela.
♂: Slimmer?   S: +
B: Unknown.   F: O
T: 22–26°C, L: <6 cm, pH: 7, D: 1–2

Corydoras condiscipulus   5/258
Comrade cory
H: S America: French Guiana.
SD: Unknown.   S: +
B: Unsuccessful.   F: C,O
T: 20–25°C, L: 6.5 cm, pH: <7, D: 2–3

Corydoras copei   3/330
Cope's cory
H: S America: Peru: Rio Huytoyacu.
SD: Unknown.   S: +
B: Unknown.   F: O
T: 22–25°C, L: 5 cm, pH: 7, D: 2

Corydoras cortesi   4/240
Cortez' cory
H: S America: Colombia: Rio Arauca.
♂: Smaller and slimmer.   S: +
B: >100 eggs on *Anubias* leaves.   F: C,O
T: 23–26°C, L: 5.5 cm, pH: 7, D: 2–3

Corydoras crypticus   4/242
Cryptic cory
H: S America: Brazil: upper Rio Negro.
SD: Unknown.   S: +
B: Unknown.   F: C,O
T: 22–28°C, L: 6 cm, pH: 7, D: 2

Corydoras davidsandsi   3/332
Sands' cory
H: S America: Brazil: Amazonia.
♂: Slimmer.   S: +
B: Typical for the genus.   F: C,O
T: 20–25°C, L: 6.5 cm, pH: 7, D: 2

Corydoras delphax   2/462
Delphax cory
H: S America: Colombia: Rio Inirida.
♂: Slimmer.   S: +
B: Typical for the genus.   F: O
T: 21–24°C, L: 6 cm, pH: 7, D: 1

Corydoras delphax   3/332
Delphax cory
Color morph?

Corydoras duplicareus   5/260
Duplicate cory
H: S America: Brazil: upper Rio Negro.
♀: Fuller during spawning season. S: +
B: Typical for the genus; <30 e. F: C,O
T: 20–24°C, L: 5 cm, pH: 7, D: 2–3

Corydoras duplicareus left   5/260
Corydoras serratus right   5/276

Corydoras ehrhardti   2/462
Ehrhardt's cory
H: S America: S Brazil.
♂: Slimmer and more elongated. S: +
B: No reports are available.   F: C,O
T: 19–22°C, L: 7 cm, pH: 7, D: 2–3

Corydoras elegans   1/464
Elegant cory
H: S America: Brazil: Amazon region.
♂: Slimmer?   S: +
B: Unknown.   F: O
T: 22–26°C, L: <6 cm, pH: 7, D: 1–2

Corydoras ellisae   1/464, 5/260

H: S America: Paraguay.
♂: Slimmer and 1 cm smaller.   S: +
B: 250–300 eggs.   F: O
T: 20–26°C, L: ♀ 6 cm, pH: 7, D: 1–2

Corydoras ephippifer   4/242

H: S America: Brazil: Rio Amapari.
SD: Unknown.   S: +
B: Unknown.   F: C,O
T: 22–25°C, L: 6 cm, pH: 7, D: 3

Corydoras eques   1/464
Golden-eared cory

H: S America: Brazil: central Amazon.
♂: Slimmer?   S: +
B: Unknown.   F: O
T: 22–26°C, L: <5.5 cm, pH: 7, D: 1–2

Corydoras evelynae   1/464
Evelyn's cory

H: S America: Brazil: Rio Purus region.
♂: Slimmer?   S: +
B: Unknown.   F: O
T: 22–26°C, L: 4 cm, pH: 7, D: 1–2

Corydoras flaveolus   4/244

H: S America: Brazil: Rio Piracicaba.
♂: Slimmer; ventral fins pointed.   S: +
B: Unsuccessful.   F: O
T: 20–23°C, L: 5 cm, pH: 7, D: 2–3

Corydoras fowleri   3/334
Fowler's cory

H: S America: Peru: Pebas region.
♂: Slimmer.   S: +
B: Unknown.   F: C,O
T: 21–23°C, L: 8 cm, pH: 7, D: 2

Corydoras garbei   1/464
Garbe's cory
H: S America: Brazil: Rio Xingú.
♂: Slimmer?   S: +
B: Unknown.   F: O
T: 22–26°C, L: 4 cm, pH: 7, D: 1–2

Corydoras gomezi   4/246
Gómez's cory
H: S America: Colombia: Leticia.
SD: Unknown.   S: +
B: Unknown.   F: C,O
T: 22–26°C, L: 5 cm, pH: 7, D: 3

Corydoras gossei   5/263
Gosse's cory   Endangered
H: S America: Brazil: Rio Mamoré.
♀: Fuller during spawning season. S: +
B: Unsuccessful.   F: C,O
T: 22–26°C, L: 2.5 cm, pH: 7, D: 2

Corydoras gracilis   1/466
Pretty dwarf cory
H: S America: Brazil: Rio Madiera.
♂: Slimmer?   S: +
B: Unknown.   F: O
T: 22–26°C, L: 2.5 cm, pH: 7, D: 1–2

Corydoras griseus   1/466
Gray cory
H: S Am.: Amazon: southern tributaries.
♂: Slimmer?   S: +
B: Unknown.   F: O
T: 22–26°C, L: <3 cm, pH: 7, D: 1–2

Corydoras guapore   2/464
Guapore cory
H: S America: Brazil: Rio Guaporé.
SD: Unknown.   S: +
B: Unknown.   F: C,O
T: 21–24°C, L: 5 cm, pH: 7, D: 2–3

CATFISHES

279

Corydoras habrosus 1/466
Rio Salinas cory
H: S America: Venezuela: Rio Salinas.
♂: Slimmer? S: +
B: Unknown. F: O
T: 22–26°C, L: <3.5 cm, pH: 7, D: 1–2

Corydoras haraldschultzi 2/464
Harald Schulz's cory
H: S America: central Brazil.
♂: Slimmer. S: +
B: Typical for the genus. F: C,O
T: 24–26°C, L: 7 cm, pH: <7, D: 2

Corydoras hastatus 1/466
Spotlight mini cory, dwarf corydoras
H: S America: Brazil: Rio Guaporé.
♂: Slimmer? S: +
B: Unknown. F: O
T: 22–26°C, L: <3 cm, pH: 7, D: 1–2

Corydoras imitator 3/334
Imitator cory
H: S America: Brazil.
♂: Smaller and slimmer. S: +
B: About 20 eggs are adhered. F: O
T: 21–23°C, L: 8 cm, pH: 7, D: 2

Corydoras incolicana 4/246
Icana cory, C 1
H: S America: Brazil: upper Rio Negro.
♂: Slimmer. S: +
B: Unknown. F: C,O
T: 23–26°C, L: 6 cm, pH: 7, D: 3

Corydoras julii 2/466
Juli corycat
H: S America: Brazil: lower Amazon.
SD: None. S: +
B: Unknown. F: O
T: 23–26°C, L: 5 cm, pH: 7, D: 1

Corydoras lacerdai ♂   5/264
Lacerda's cory, C 15
H: S America: Brazil: SE Bahia.
♂: Smaller, slimmer; pigmented fins. S: +
B: Unsuccessful; pairwise?   F: C,O
T: 20–25°C, L: 4.5 cm, pH: ≪7, D: 3–4

Corydoras lacerdai ♀♀   5/264
Lacerda's cory, C 15

Corydoras latus subadult ♀   5/267
Iridescent cory
H: S America: Bolivia.
♂: Slimmer.   S: +?
B: Unsuccessful.   F: O
T: 23–27°C, L: 6 cm, pH: 7, D: 2

Corydoras leopardus   2/466
Leopard cory
H: S America: Brazil. Peru?
♂: Slimmer.   S: +
B: Unknown.   F: C,O
T: 20–25°C, L: 7 cm, pH: 7, D: 1–2

Corydoras leucomelas   2/468
Blackfin cory, false spotted cory
H: S America: Colombia, Peru.
♂: Ventral fins are more pointed. S: +
B: Unknown.   F: L,O
T: 22–26°C, L: 4.5 cm, pH: 7, D: 1–2

Corydoras loretoensis   3/336
Loreto cory
H: S America: Peru.
SD: Unknown.   S: +
B: Unknown.   F: O
T: 22–25°C, L: 5 cm, pH: 7, D: 2

CATFISHES

281

Corydoras loxozonus   (1/462), 3/336
Slant-bar cory
H: S America: Colombia: Rio Meta.
SD: None.   S: +
B: Unknown.   F: O
T: 21–24°C, L: 6 cm, pH: 7, D: 1–2

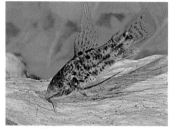

Corydoras macropterus ♂   2/468
Sail-fin cory, long-finned cory
H: S America: Brazil: São Paulo.
♂: Larger bristles; D & P fins larger.   S: +
B: So far unsuccessful.   F: O
T: 18–21°C, L: 10 cm, pH: 7, D: 1–2

Corydoras maculifer   4/248

H: S America: Brazil: Mato Grosso.
SD: Difficult to distinguish.   S: +
B: On vallisneria leaves; 100 eggs.   F: O
T: 25–27°C, L: 7 cm, pH: 7, D: 2–3

Corydoras melanistius brevirostris
Spotted corycat, black sail cory   2/470
H: S America: Venezuela: Orinoco.
♀: Fuller during spawning season.   S: +
B: Repeatedly successful.   F: C,O
T: 20–24°C, L: 6 cm, pH: 7, D: 1

Corydoras melanistius melanistius   1/468
Black-spotted corydoras, black sail cory
H: S America: Guyana.
♂: Slimmer?   S: +
B: Unknown.   F: O
T: 22–26°C, L: <6 cm, pH: 7, D: 1–2

Corydoras melanotaenia   2/470
Blackband cory
H: S America: Colombia: Rio Meta.   rare
♂: Slimmer.   S: –
B: On broad plant leaves; <180 e.   F: C,O
T: 20–23°C, L: 6.5 cm, pH: 7, D: 2

Corydoras melini   1/468
Diagonal stripe cory
H: S America: Colombia.
♂: Slimmer?   S: +
B: Unknown.   F: O
T: 22–26°C, L: <6 cm, pH: 7, D: 1–2

Corydoras metae   1/468
Bandit cory
H: S America: Colombia: Rio Meta.
♂: Slimmer?   S: +
B: Unknown.   F: O
T: 22–26°C, L: <5.5 cm, pH: 7, D: 1–2

Corydoras sp.aff. *multimaculatus*   4/248
Many-spot cory
H: S America: Brazil: Rio Preto.
SD: Not described.   S: +
B: Unknown.   F: C,O
T: 23–26°C, L: ca. 5 cm, pH: 7, D: 2–3

Corydoras napoensis   (1/474), 3/338
Napo cory
H: S America: Ecuador, Peru.
♂: More intense design.   S: +
B: Unknown.   F: O
T: 22–26°C, L: 5 cm, pH: 7, D: 2

Corydoras narcissus   4/250
Narcissus cory
H: S America: Brazil, Colombia.
♂: Slightly slimmer.   S: +
B: Unsuccessful.   F: O
T: 24–26°C, L: 12 cm, pH: 7, D: 2–4

Corydoras nattereri   4/250
Blue cory
H: S America: Brazil.
♂: Slimmer and smaller.   S: +
B: 30–60 eggs.   F: C,O
T: 20–23°C, L: 6.5 cm, pH: 7, D: 2–3

CATFISHES

Corydoras nijsseni ♀   4/253
Nijssen's cory
H: S America: Brazil: Rio Negro.
♂: Slimmer.   S: +
B: 30–160 eggs.   F: C,O
T: 22–26°C, L: 5 cm, pH: <7, D: 3

Corydoras nijsseni   4/252
Nijssen's cory

Corydoras oiapoquensis   5/269
Oiapoque cory
H: S America: French Guiana.
SD: Unknown.   S: +
B: Not described.   F: C,O
T: 23–28°C, L: 5 cm, pH: <7, D: 2–3

Corydoras oiapoquensis right   5/269
Corydoras condiscipulus left   5/258

Corydoras ornatus   (1/470), 2/472
Ornate cory
H: S America: Brazil: Rio Tapajos.
SD: None.   S: +
B: It has been bred.   F: O
T: 23–26°C, L: 6 cm, pH: <7, D: 2

Corydoras orphnopterus   2/472
Spotfin cory   (few dots)
H: S Am.: Ecuador/Peru: Rio Pastaza.
SD: Unknown.   S: +
B: Unknown.   F: C,O
T: 20–24°C, L: 5.5 cm, pH: <7, D: 1–2

CATFISHES

Corydoras orphnopterus   3/338
Spotfin cory   (many dots)
H: S Am.: Ecuador/Peru: Rio Pastaza.
♀: Paler; smaller dots.   S: +
B: Unknown.   F: C,O
T: 20–24°C, L: 5.5 cm, pH: <7, D: 1–2

Corydoras osteocarus juv.   3/340
Pepper-spot cory
H: S America: Venezuela, Suriname.
♂: Smaller and slimmer.   S: +
B: <300 eggs adhered on plants.   F: O
T: 22–25°C, L: 5 cm, pH: 7, D: 2

Corydoras ourastigma   4/254

H: S America: Brazil: Rio Iquiri.
♂: Pointed ventral fins.   S: +
B: Up to 30 eggs.   F: C,O
T: 24–26°C, L: 7 cm, pH: 7, D: 3

Corydoras paleatus   1/470
Peppered cory
H: S America: SE Brazil: La Plata.
♂: Slimmer?   S: +
B: Typical for the genus.   F: O
T: 20–24°C, L: <7 cm, pH: 7, D: 1–2

Corydoras paleatus albino   1/470
Peppered cory

Corydoras panda   2/474
Panda cory
H: S America: Peru: Ucayali Basin.
♂: Slightly smaller and slimmer.   S: +
B: Among Java moss.   F: L,O
T: 20–25°C, L: 4.5 cm, pH: 7, D: 2–3

CATFISHES

Corydoras parallelus　　　(1/474), 4/254
Parallel-line cory
H: S America: Peru/Bolivia: Amazonia.
♂: Slightly smaller and slimmer.　　S: +
B: Unsuccessful.　　　　　　　　　F: O
T: 24–27°C, L: <7.5 cm, pH: 7, D: 2–4

Corydoras pastazensis　　　　　3/342
Pastaza cory
H: S America: Ecuador/Peru: Rio Tigre.
♂: Slimmer.　　　　　　　　　　　S: +
B: Unknown.　　　　　　　　　　F: C,O
T: 20–24°C, L: 6.5 cm, pH: 7, D: 2

Corydoras pinheiroi　　　　　　5/271
C 25, Pinheiro's cory
H: S America: Brazil: Rondônia.
♀: Larger and fuller.　　　　　　　S: +
B: Unsuccessful (difficult).　　　　F: O
T: 25–28°C, L: 7 cm, pH: 7, D: 2–3

Corydoras polystictus　　　　　2/474
Many-spotted cory
H: S America: Brazil: Mato Grosso.
♂: Slimmer; flat ventral area.　　　S: +
B: More ♂♂ than ♀♀.　　　　　　F: O
T: 22–28°C, L: 4 cm, pH: 7, D: 1–2

Corydoras polystictus　　　　　3/342 ˙
Many-spotted cory
Older specimen with aberrant coloration.

Corydoras prionotus　　　　　　3/348
H: S America: S Brazil.
♀: Fuller during spaawning season.　S: +
B: Unknown.　　　　　　　　　　F: O
T: 22–26°C, L: 8 cm, pH: 7, D: 3

CATFISHES

Corydoras pulcher   3/344
White-fin cory
H: S America: W Brazil: Rio Purus.
SD: Not described.   S: +
B: Unknown.   F: O
T: 21–24°C, L: 6 cm, pH: <7, D: 1

Corydoras cf. *punctatus*   1/470
Dotted cory
H: S Am.: Suriname, S Amazon tributaries.
♂: Slimmer?   S: +
B: Unknown.   F: O
T: 20–24°C, L: <6 cm, pH: <7, D: 1–2

Corydoras pygmaeus   1/472
Pygmy cory
H: S America: Brazil: Rio Madeira.
♂: Slimmer.   S: +
B: Unknown.   F: C,O
T: 22–26°C, L: <2.5 cm, pH: <7, D: 1–2

Corydoras rabauti juv.   (1/472), 4/256
Rabaut's cory
H: S America: Peru, Brazil.
♂: Slimmer.   S: +
B: Difficult; >100e on fine-leaved plants.
                                      F: C,O

Corydoras rabauti   (1/472), 4/256
Rabaut's cory
Subadult after changing from juvenile
coloration; adult ♀ below.
T: 23–25°C, L: 5.5 cm, pH: <7, D: 2–4

Corydoras rabauti   (1/472), 4/256
Rabaut's cory
10 day old young.

CATFISHES

287

Corydoras reticulatus   1/472
Net cory
H: S America: Peru: Iquitos.
♂: Slimmer.   S: +
B: Unknown.   F: O
T: 22–26°C, L: <7 cm, pH: <7, D: 1–2

Corydoras robineae   2/477
Flagtail corycat
H: S America: Brazil: upper Rio Negro.
SD: Unknown.   S: +
B: Details have not been reported.   F: C,L
T: 23–26°C, L: 4 cm, pH: <7, D: 2–3

Corydoras robustus   5/272
Robust cory, heavy cory
H: S America: E Brazil: Rio Purus.
SD: Unknown.   S: +
B: Unsuccessful.   F: C,O
T: 22–26°C, L: 8.5 cm, pH: <7, D: 3

Corydoras robustus   5/272, (5/ 292)
Robust cory, heavy cory

Corydoras cf. *sanchesi*   4/258
Sanchez's cory
H: S America: Suriname.
♂: Slimmer?   S: +
B: Not described.   F: C,O
T: 23–26°C, L: 4–5 cm, pH: 7, D: 3

Corydoras cf. *saramaccensis*   4/258
Saramacca cory
H: S America: Suriname.
♂: Slimmer?   S: +
B: Unknown.   F: C,O
T: 23–26°C, L: 6–7 cm, pH: 7, D: 3

Corydoras sarareensis ♂   5/272
C 23
H: S America: Brazil: Rio Sarare.
♂: Brown pectoral spine w/ bristles. S: +
B: Up to 80 eggs.   F: O
T: 25–28°C, L: 6 cm, pH: 7, D: 2–3

Corydoras semiaquilus ♀   5/274
Sharp-nosed cory
H: S America: Peru: Rio Ucayali.
♂: Orange V fins; large D fin.   S: +
B: There are no reports.   F: C,O
T: 22–26°C, L: 6 cm, pH: <7, D: 3

Corydoras semiaquilus ♂   5/274
Sharp-nosed cory

Corydoras septentrionalis   (1/474), 2/478
Southern green cory
H: S America: Colombia: Rio Meta.
SD: No obvious differences.   S: +
B: There are no reports.   F: O,L
T: 20–23°C, L: 5.5 cm, pH: 7, D: 2

Corydoras serratus   5/276
Serrated cory
H: S America: Brazil: upper Rio Negro.
SD: Not described.   S: +
B: There are no reports.   F: C,O
T: 22–26°C, L: 6 cm, pH: ≪7, D: 2

Corydoras seussi   5/278
Seuss' cory, C 27
H: S America: Brazil: at Guajara-Mirim.
SD: Not described.   S: +
B: Unsuccessful.   F: C,O
T: 20–25°C, L: <7 cm, pH: <7, D: 2–3

Corydoras similis 4/260
Similis cory
H: S America: Brazil: Amazonia.
♂: Longer dorsal fin spine?   S: +
B: Typical for the genus.   F: O
T: 22–26°C, L: 5 cm, pH: 7, D: 2

Corydoras simulatus 2/478
Masquerade cory
H: S America: Colombia: Amazonia.
♂: Probably slimmer.   S: +
B: So far unsuccessful.   F: O
T: 20–25°C, L: 5.5 cm, pH: 7, D: 1–2

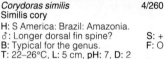

Corydoras sodalis (1/474), 3/344
Netted cory
H: S America: Peru, Brazil.
SD: Unknown.   S: +
B: Unknown.   F: O
T: 22–27°C, L: 5 cm, pH: <7, D: 2

Corydoras sp. 5/268
C 5
H: S America: Brazil: Pantanal.
♂: Slimmer; darker design; smaller.   S: +
B: Unsuccessful.   F: O
T: 24–28°C, L: <9 cm, pH: 7, D: 2–3

Corydoras sp. subadult 5/268
C 5

Corydoras sp. 5/284
C 6
H: S America: Brazil: Rio Guamá.
♂: Slimmer?   S: +
B: Unknown.   F: O

CATFISHES

Corydoras sp. 5/284
C 7
H: S America: Peru.
♂: Long dorsal and pectoral fins. S: +
B: Continuous setup. F: O

Corydoras sp. 5/284
C 9
H: S America: Peru.
♂: Slimmer? S: +
B: Unknown. F: O

Corydoras sp. 5/256
C 10

Corydoras sp. 4/244, (5/286)
C 11
H: S America: Bolivia.
♂: Dots less intense; smaller. S: +
B: Occasionally successful. F: C,O
T: 23–26°C, L: 4.5 cm, pH: 7, D: 3

Corydoras sp. 5/256
C 12

Corydoras sp. 5/286
C 16
H: S America: Colombia.
♂: Slimmer? S: +
B: Unknown. F: O
D: 3–4

Corydoras sp.   5/286
C 17
H: S America: Peru.
♂: Slimmer?   S: +
B: Unknown.   F: O

Corydoras sp.   5/292
C 18, white fin cory
H: S America: Brazil.
SD: Unknown.   S: +
B: Unsuccessful.   F: O
L: 6 cm

Corydoras sp.   5/270
C 19
H: S America: Peru, W Brazil.
♂: Dots less intense.   S: +
B: Unsuccessful (difficult).   F: O
T: 24–28°C, L: 6 cm, pH: 7, D: 2–3

Corydoras sp.   5/288
C 21
H: S America: Brazil: Rio Xingú.
♂: Slimmer?   S: +
B: Possible?   F: O

Corydoras sp. l.♀, r.♂   5/288
C 22
H: S America: Brazil: Rio Xingú.
♂: Slimmer?   S: +
B: Spawns spontaneously.   F: O
L: ♀ 3 cm, ♂ 2.5 cm

Corydoras sp.   5/288
C 24
H: S America: Brazil: Rio Guamá.
♂: Slimmer?   S: +
B: Unknown.   F: O
L: 6–7 cm

Corydoras sp.   5/290
C 26
H: S America: Bolivia/Brazil?
♂: Slimmer?   S: +
B: Unknown.   F: O
L: 5 cm

Corydoras sp.   5/290
C 28
H: S America: Brazil: Rondônia.
♂: Slimmer?   S: +
B: Unproblematic; about 30 eggs.   F: O
L: 7 cm

Corydoras sp.   5/290
C 29
H: S America: Brazil: State of Amapá.
SD: Unknown.   S: +
B: Unknown.   F: O

Corydoras sp.   5/292
C 30
H: S America: Brazil: State of Amapá.
♂: Slimmer?   S: +
B: Unknown.   F: O

Corydoras steindachneri   2/480
Steindachner's cory
H: S America: S Brazil: Paranagua.
♂: Longer dorsal fin; slimmer.   S: +
B: Typical for the genus.   F: C,O
T: 22–26°C, L: 6 cm, pH: <7, D: 1–2

Corydoras stenocephalus   5/276

H: S America: Peru: Rio Ucayali Basin.
♂: Smaller; V fins more pointed.   S: +
B: Unsuccessful.   F: C,L
T: 25–27°C, L: 6 cm, pH: 7, D: 3

CATFISHES

293

Corydoras sterbai   2/480
Sterba's cory
H: S America: Brazil: Rio Guaporé.
♂: Slightly slimmer.   S: +
B: Unknown.   F: O
T: 21–25°C, L: 8 cm, pH: <7, D: 1–2

Corydoras surinamensis   3/346
Suriname cory
H: S America: Suriname.
SD: Unknown.   S: +
B: Typical for the genus?   F: C,O
T: 22–25°C, L: 6 cm, pH: 7, D: 1–2

Corydoras sychri   1/474
Sichri cory
H: S America.
♂: Slimmer.   S: +
B: Unknown.   F: O
T: 22–26°C, L: <4.5 cm, pH: <7, D: 1–2

Corydoras treitlii   3/346
Long-nosed cory
H: S America: Brazil: Rio Parnaiba.
SD: Unknown.   S: +
B: Successfully bred in Scotland.   F: O
T: 20–25°C, L: 7 cm, pH: <7, D: 2

Corydoras treitlii Colombia   5/278
Long-nosed cory
H: S America: Brazil, Colombia.
♀: Triangle only to body's center?   S: +
B: <70 very small eggs.   F: C,O
T: 20–24°C, L: 7 cm, pH: <7, D: 2–3

Corydoras trilineatus   1/466
Three-line cory
H: S America: Peru: Rio Ampiyacu,...
♂: Dorsal spot larger; darker design. S: +
B: Unknown.   F: O
T: 22–26°C, L: 5 cm, pH: <7, D: 2

CATFISHES

Corydoras undulatus   5/280
Wavy-line cory
H: S America: Argentina.
♂: Black; slimmer.   S: +
B: Almost all the eggs hatch.   F: O
T: 23–27°C, L: 4.5 cm, pH: 7, D: 2

Corydoras virginiae   4/260
Miguelito cory, C 4
H: S America: Peru: Rio Ucayali.
SD: Unknown.   S: +
B: Unsuccessful.   F: C,O
T: 23–26°C, L: 6 cm, pH: 7, D: 2–3

Corydoras xinguensis   5/280
Xingú cory
H: S America: Brazil: upper Rio Xingú.
♀: Slightly fuller and larger.   S: +
B: 30–50 eggs.   F: C,O
T: 23–27°C, L: 5 cm, pH: <7, D: 2

Corydoras zygatus   3/348, 5/282
Zygatus cory
H: S America: Peru: Loreto region.
♂: Smaller and slimmer.   S: +
B: Typical for the genus.   F: C,O
T: 22–25°C, L: 5.5 cm, pH: <7, D: 1

Corydoras zygatus   3/348, 5/282
Zygatus cory
21 days old. Compare with *Corydoras rabauti*.

Corydoras zygatus bottom   3/348, 5/282
Zygatus cory
Corydoras rabauti top.

CATFISHES

Dianema longibarbis   1/476
Porthole catfish
H: S America: Peru: Rio Ampiyacu.
SD: Only at spawning time (♀ fuller). S: +
B: Rare; bubble nest.   F: O
T: 22–26°C, L: 9 cm, pH: 7, D: 1–2

Dianema urostriata ♂   1/476
Flagtail porthole catfish
H: S America: Brazil: Rio Negro.
♂: Pectoral plates w/o gaps.   S: +
B: Successful but no reports.   F: C,O
T: 22–26°C, L: 12 cm, pH: <7, D: 1–2

Hoplosternum littorale   2/480
Clay hoplo, cascudo
H: S America: broadly distributed.
♂: P fin spine curved upward.   S: +
B: Bubble nest.   F: O
T: 18–26°C, L: 23 cm, pH: 7, D: 1–3

Leptoplosternum pectorale   2/482
Pepper and salt hoplo, spotted hoplo
H: S America: Brazil: Rio Magdalena.
♂: P fin spine curved upward.   S: =
B: Bubble nest.   F: O
T: 20–22°C, L: 12 cm, pH: 7, D: 1–2

Megalechis thoracatum   1/478
Port hoplo
H: S America: broadly distributed.
♂: Bluish ventrally (spawning time). S: =
B: Bubble nest; paternal family.   F: L,O
T: 18–28°C, L: 18 cm, pH: 7, D: 1

Megalechis thoracatum var. *niger*
Black port hoplo   3/351
H: S America: near human settlements.
♂: P fin spine thicker and spiny.   S: =
B: Bubble nest; paternal family.   F: O
T: 18–28°C, L: 16 cm, pH: 7, D: 1

CATFISHES

A whale catfish, possibly *Pseudocetopsis ventralis* from the Misahualli River, north-eastern Ecuador.

Family Cetopsidae

The family of whale catfishes consists of 12 medium-sized species in 4 genera. There is a paucity of information concerning this rarely imported family. Due to their highly pronounced predatory nature, a species tank is demanded. Coloration is plain and they are inactive, often lying motionless for hours on the substrate. Other than their status as a novelty, whale catfishes contribute little to an aquarium.

Both the barbels and the eyes are vestigial. Compensating for their lack of sight and tactility, their sense of smell seems highly developed. The feeding habits of some—most notably *Cetopsis* and *Hemicetopsis* species—are comparable to those of the most vicious piranhas; fishes and even warm-blooded animals are savagely attacked.

Nothing is known about their reproductive biology. Water composition seems to be of secondary importance for maintenance, but presumably species hailing from mountain streams will require high oxygen concentrations.

Cetopsis coecutiens   4/269
Whale catfish
H: S America: Brazil, Peru.
SD: Unknown.   S: –
B: Unsuccessful.   F: C
T: 22–28°C, L: <15 cm, pH: 7, D: 4

Family Chacidae

The small family of frogmouth catfishes contains just one genus and
three species (NELSON, 1994), all of
which are easily distinguished from
other Siluriformes.

As can be deduced by their dis-
proportionately large mouth, smaller
tankmates are in emminent danger
of becoming prey. Larger fishes are
not molested. *Chaca* can be trained
to accept pelleted foods.

Despite their rather unattractive
coloration and nocturnal, unsociable
lifestyle, frogmouth catfishes still find
favor among aquarists because of
their unorthodox appearance. They
are poor swimmers which spend the
majority of their time among the
mulm and litter of their home waters.
Even a light touch elicits little response. This can have painful consequences, since a careless step
onto their erected dorsal spine un-
doubtedly belongs to the unforget-
table experiences of a touristic fishing expedition.

Reproduction is unknown, but
maturity is attained at sizes easily
accommodated in normal aquaria.

Chaca bankanensis   3/352
Chocolate frogmouth catfish
H: Asia: Indonesia, S Malay Peninsula.
SD: Unknown.   S: –
B: Unknown.   F: C
T: 24–28°C, L: 15 cm, pH: 7, D: 3–4

Chaca chaca   1/479, 3/352
Frogmouth catfish
H: Asia: Kalimantan, Burma, India, Sumatra.
SD: Unknown.   S: –
B: Unknown.   F: C
T: 22–24°C, L: 20 cm, pH: 7, D: 3

Chaca chaca, a frogmouth catfish; see 1/479 and 3/352.

Family Clariidae

Thirteen genera and around 100 species are presently considered part of the labyrinth or walking catfishes. Although this family is distributed through Africa, Syria, and Southeast Asia, it is most prevalent in Africa: 12 genera and 74 species hail from that continent (NELSON, 1994).

The family is easily recognized by its many-rayed, fringelike anal fin and spineless dorsal fin. Most walking catfishes are large to extremely large in size. Even the few medium-sized species are largely inapt for aquaria because of their distinct predatory tendencies—even as juveniles. In the aquarium they are voracious omnivores which devour everything in sight until their stomach is grossly distended.

They frequently occur in muddy water holes. If their habitat falls dry—as it tends to do in the dry season—the catfishes retreat into mud tunnels during the day, emerging at night to search for food. Naturally, Clariidae are capable of breathing atmospheric air. This ability is so developed in some species, it has become obligatory instead of facultative. A branched organ behind the branchial arches which extends into a breathing sac allows for gas exchange; hence the occasionally employed nomen airsack catfishes—today the independent family Heteropneustidae.

During nocturnal expeditions and when searching for a new habitat, these catfishes move effortlessly over land with the help of their well-developed pectoral fin spines (walking catfishes). This ability has made them *persona non grata* in Florida (United States). The import of Clariidae into the United States is now forbidden. Even those who wish merely to maintain a specimen in an aquarium must apply for a special permit.

The Clariidae are gaining popularity in aquaculture as food fishes, particularly in Africa and Asia. Their suitability as aquaculture subjects is greatly enhanced by their omnivorous diet and ability to thrive under virtually all water conditions. Although the meat of *Clarias macrocephalus* is rated somewhat superior to that of *C. batrachus,* the latter grows faster and is therefore cultured in larger quantities. Pond breeding is successful. To breed, pairs excavate horizontal holes with a diameter of 25–35 cm into the pond banks. Each nest yields 2000–5500 offspring. Inducing spawning through hormone injections has proven successful as well. Because of the incredible density at which these fish can be stocked, the production per hectare is enormous, i.e., up to 100 tons per year. Of course, a small fence around the pond must not be forgotten (BARDACH et al., 1972).

Although these fishes are very robust, aquarium care is discouraged. A large exhibition aquarium is demanded, and all tankmates must be similar-sized and capable of defending themselves. Colorwise, the Clariidae leave much to be desired; only the albino form of *Clarias batrachus* can be considered to have an aesthetically pleasing color. For those who care to attempt maintenance, the aquarium should be as large as possible with shelters commensurate to the fish's size. If the illumination is subdued and the decor dark, they will emerge during the day, though they are usually nocturnal.

Channallabes apus   2/484
Eel catfish
H: Africa: Zaïre, Angola.
SD: Unknown.   S: –
B: Never attempted?   F: C
T: 22–25°C, L: 30 cm, pH: 7, D: 3

Clariallabes longicauda   5/294
Long-fin labyrinth catfish
H: Africa: central Zaïre Basin.
SD: Unknown.   S: =
B: Unknown.   F: C
T: 22–28°C, L: <28 cm, pH: 7, D: 3

Clarias angolensis   2/484
Angola walking catfish
H: W and central Africa.
♂: More slender.   S: –
B: Unknown.   F: C
T: 23–28°C, L: 35 cm, pH: >7, D: 3–4

Clarias anguillaris
Eellike walking catfish

Clarias batrachus   1/480
Frog catfish, walking catfish
H: Asia: Sri Lanka, E India to Malaysia.
♂: Dotted dorsal fin.   S: –
B: Ponds in Florida.   F: O
T: 20–25°C, L: 50 cm, pH: 7, D: 2–3

Clarias buettikoferi   5/294

H: W Africa: Guinea-Bissau to Ivory Coast.
SD: Unknown.   S: =
B: In flooded areas.   F: C
T: 20–27°C, L: 19 cm, pH: 7, D: 3

Clarias buthupogon   4/262

H: Africa: Benin to Zaïre (coastal rivers).
SD: Unknown.   S: –
B: Unknown.   F: C
T: 22–28°C, L: 30 cm, pH: 7, D: 4

Clarias camerunensis   4/263
H: Africa: Togo, Benin, Nigeria, Came-
roon, Gabon, Zaïre.
SD: Unknown.   S: –
B: There are no reports.   F: C,O
T: 23–28°C, L: 45 cm, pH: 7, D: 4

Clarias cavernicola   2/486
Blind cave walking catfish
H: Africa: Namibia: Aigumas Cave.
SD: Unknown.   S: –
B: There are no reports.   F: C,O
T: 15–25°C, L: 25 cm, pH: 7, D: 3

Clarias gabonensis   4/264
Gabonese walking catfish
H: Africa: central and lower Zaïre.
SD: Unknown.   S: –
B: There are no reports.   F: C,O
T: 22–28°C, L: 35 cm, pH: 7, D: 4

Clarias gariepinus   2/486, 4/265
African walking catfish
H: Africa: tropics.
♂: More pointed genital papilla.   S: –
B: Possible w/ hormone injections.   F: C,O
T: 22–28°C, L: <150 cm, pH: 7, D: 4

Clarias gariepinus   2/486, 4/265
African walking catfish

CATFISHES

301

Clarias liocephalus   4/266

H: Africa: lakes in Uganda.
SD: Unknown.   S: –

B: There are no reports.   F: C,O
T: 22–28°C, L: 35 cm, pH: 7, D: 4

Clarias salae   5/296

H: W Africa: Guinea to Ivory Coast.
SD: Unknown.   S: =
B: Unknown.   F: C
T: 22–28°C, L: 50 cm, pH: 7, D: 4

Heterobranchus bidorsalis   4/268

H: Afr.: Nile, Niger, Benue, Senegal, Gambia.
♀: Fuller while egg-laden.   S: –
B: Only possible with hormones?   F: C
T: 22–28°C, L: <150 cm, pH: 7, D: 4

Heterobranchus isopterus   4/266

H: Africa: Nigeria to Guinea (coastal rivers).
SD: Unknown.   S: –
B: Only possible with hormones?   F: O
T: 22–28°C, L: <50 cm, pH: 7, D: 4

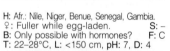

Heterobranchus longifilis   3/354
Long-fin walking catfish

H: Africa: Nigeria to Guinea (coastal rivers).
SD: W/ age? Difficult to distinguish.   S: –
B: Unknown   F: C
T: 22–23°C, L: >70 cm, pH: 7, D: 4

Family Doradidae

Much has changed in the last 10 years in the classification of the Doradidae. While FRANKE in 1985 acknowledged 20 genera and approximately 80 species, today the thorny catfishes contain 35 genera and approximately 90 species (NELSON, 1994). They and the families Auchenipteridae and Ageneiosidae form a group in a constant state of flux: genera and species are subject to repeated reassignments. The talking catfishes, as they are also called, inhabit freshwaters of tropical South America, especially the Amazon Basin and the Guianas.

A row of bony plates running along the length of their otherwise naked body clearly distinguishes them from fellow catfishes. Most of the plates, particularly those on the posterior half of the body, have a posteriorly curved hook. Their dorsal and pectoral spines are always well-developed.

While most species are small- to moderate-sized, a few genera are known for their giant constituents, i.e., *Megalodoras* spp., *Pseudodoras* spp., *Perodoras* spp., none are of any economic importance because of their rarity.

Little is known about doradids. The species most familiar to aquarists is the commonly imported species *Platydoras costatus*, or raphael. Few other species are even offered. Doradids can be maintained in community aquaria. Although the majority are carnivores, they are not predators. The substrate is scoured for worms, insects, and other invertebrates. Therefore, sand or small-grained, smooth-edged gravel is necessary. Alimentation in the

Juvenile *Liosomadoras oncinus* (see p. 306). Unfortunately, the contrast diminishes with age.

aquarium is greatly facilitated by their willingness to accept flake foods and other dry commercial diets from the substrate.

Various specimens of the same or different genera can be kept together. Even though they are not schooling fishes, diurnal hiding places are shared without incident.

Doradids adapt to most types of waters. As they are nocturnal or crepuscular, the illumination should be subdued. Dark hiding places where they can retreat during the day are required.

There is a paucity of information on the reproductive biology of this family. In its natural habitat, *Amblydoras hancocki* has been observed depositing its egg mass into a nest of leaves; both parents cared for the spawn. *Agamyxis flavopictus, Amblydoras hancocki,* and *Platydoras costatus* have been induced to spawn through hormone injections (GRUNDMANN in FRANKE, 1985). For breeding, the water should always be soft and slightly acid.

Several species produce sounds when they are lifted out of the water, hence the common name "talking catfishes."

Acanthodoras cataphractus   1/481
Painted talking catfish
H: S America: Amazon River estuary.
SD: Unknown.   S: +
B: Unknown.   F: O
T: 22–26°C, L: 10 cm, pH: 7, D: 1

Agamyxis pectinifrons   1/482
White-spotted doradid
H: S America: Peru: Pebas.
SD: Unknown.   S: +
B: Unknown.   F: O
T: 20–26°C, L: 16 cm, pH: <7, D: 1–2

Amblydoras hancockii   1/482
Hancock's doradid
H: S America: Guyana to Colombia.
♂: Brown speckled ventrum.   S: +
B: Nat: bubble nest among plants.   F: O
T: 23–28°C, L: <15 cm, pH: 7, D: 1

Anadoras grypus   2/489
Dusky doradid
H: S America: Amazon Basin.
SD: Unknown.   S: =
B: Unknown.   F: C,O
T: 22–26°C, L: 15 cm, pH: <7, D: 2

CATFISHES

Astrodoras asterifrons   2/490
Helmet doradid
H: S America: Brazil, Bolivia.
♂: Longer dorsal fin spine.   S: +
B: Unknown.   F: O
T: 20–25°C, L: 10–12 cm, pH: 7, D: 1

Doras eigenmanni   5/297
Eigenmann's doradid
H: S America: Brazil, Bolivia, Paraguay.
SD: Unknown.   S: +
B: Unsuccessful.   F: C
T: 24–28°C, L: 11 cm, pH: 7, D: 2–4

Hassar affinis   5/298
Rio Poto hassar
H: S America: NE Brazil: Rio Poto.
♂: Longer dorsal fin spine.   S: =
B: Unknown.   F: C,O
T: 22–28°C, L: 25 cm, pH: 7, D: 3

Hassar notospilus   2/490
Black-finned doradid
H: S America: Guianas.
♂: Longer dorsal fin spine.   S: +
B: Unsuccessful.   F: C,O
T: 21–25°C, L: 7.5 cm, pH: <7, D: 2–3

Hassar ucayalensis   5/298
Rio Ucayali hassar
H: S America: Peru: Rio Ucayali.
♂: Longer dorsal fin spine; slimmer. S: +
B: Unsuccessful.   F: C,O
T: 23–27°C, L: 25 cm?, pH: 7, D: 3

Hassar wilderi   3/355

H: S America: Brazil: Rio Tocantins.
SD: Unknown.   S: +
B: Unsuccessful.   F: O,C
T: 22–25°C, L: 20 cm, pH: <7, D: 3–4

CATFISHES

305

Leptodoras linnelli juv.   2/492

H: S America: Colombia, Brazil.   rare
♂: Longer dorsal fin spine?   S: =
B: Unknown.   F: L,C
T: 18–22°C, L: 21 cm, pH: <7, D: 2–3

Liosomadoras oncinus juv.   2/494
Jaguar catfish

H: S America: Peru, Brazil.
♂: Urogenital papilla at the anterior edge
   of the anal fin; coloration more intense.

Liosomadoras oncinus   2/494
Jaguar catfish

                                       S: =
B: Nature: internal fertilization.   F: C
T: 20–24°C, L: 25 cm, pH: ≪7, D: 2–3

Megalodoras irwini   3/356

H: S America: Guyana, Brazil.
SD: Unknown.   S: =
B: Unknown.   F: O
T: 22–25°C, L: 60 cm, pH: 7, D: 4

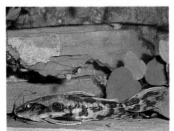

Megalodoras irwini Iquitos   5/300

H: S America: Peru, W Brazil, Guyana.
SD: Unknown.   S: =
B: Rainy season spawning migra.   F: O
T: 23–28°C, L: 70 cm, pH: 7, D: 3–4

Megalodoras paucisquamatus   5/300
Giant doradid

H: S America: Brazil: upper Amazon.
SD: Unknown.   S: =
B: Unknown.   F: O
T: 23–28°C, L: <60 cm, pH: 7, D: 3–4

CATFISHES

Opsodoras humeralis   5/302
Shoulder-spot doradid
H: S America: Brazil: Rio Negro.
♂: Longer dorsal fin spine?   S: +
B: Unknown.   F: C,O
T: 23–28°C, L: 12 cm, pH: <7, D: 3–4

Opsodoras leporhinus   2/492

H: S America: Brazil, Bolivia, Peru.
SD: Unknown.   S: =
B: Unknown.   F: C
T: 22–25°C, L: 8 cm, pH: <7, D: 3

Opsodoras stubeli   2/496

H: S America: Brazil: Rio Marañón.
SD: Not described.   S: +
B: Unknown.   F: O
T: 22–25°C, L: 12 cm, pH: <7, D: 1–2

Physopyxis lyra   5/302
Lyra doradid
H: S America: Brazil: Rio Ampiyacu.
SD: Unknown.   S: +
B: Unknown.   F: C
T: 23–26°C, L: 4 cm, pH: <7, D: 4

Platydoras costatus   1/484
Chocolate doradid
H: S America: Peru: Amazon region.
SD: Not pronounced.   S: +
B: Unknown.   F: O
T: 24–30°C, L: 22 cm, pH: 7, D: 1–2

Platydoras dentatus   3/356

H: S America: Suriname.
SD: Unknown.   S: =
B: Unknown.   F: O,C
T: 22–25°C, L: 13 cm, pH: 7, D: 3

CATFISHES

Pseudodoras holdeni   5/304
Holden's doradid
H: S America: Venezuela: Rio Apure.
SD: Unknown.   S: =
B: Spawning migrations?   F: C,O
T: 23–28°C, L: 150 cm, pH: <7, D: 4

Pseudodoras niger   2/496
Black doradid
H: S America: Brazil, Peru.
SD: Not described.   S: +,=
B: Unknown.   F: O
T: 21–24°C, L: 80 cm, pH: 7, D: 2–4

Pterodoras granulosus   2/498
Common bacu
H: S America: almost all large rivers.
SD: Unknown.   S: =
B: Unknown.   F: O
T: 20–24°C, L: 90 cm, pH: 7, D: 4

Pterodoras lentiginosus   5/304
Freckled doradid
H: S America: Brazil: Amazon.
SD: Unknown.   S: =
B: In flooded areas?   F: O
T: 22–28°C, L: 60 cm, pH: 7, D: 4

Rhinodoras dorbignyi   2/498
Fog doradid
H: S America: S Brazil, Paraguay.
SD: Unknown.   S: +,=
B: Unknown.   F: C,O
T: 20–25°C, L: 17 cm, pH: <7, D: 2

Trachydoras paraguayensis   5/306
Paraguay doradid
H: S America: Brazil, Paraguay.
♂: Larger D and P fin spines.   S: +
B: Unknown.   F: C,O
T: 20–26°C, L: 10 cm, pH: <7, D: 2–3

Family Helogenidae

This small family consists of just one genus with four species. Occasionally the family name is written Helogeneidae.

A dimly illuminated aquarium rich in hiding places is recommended for these small, nocturnal fishes. During the day, they are often observed lying on their side, alarming hobbyists; however, this seems to be a natural resting position. At night they swim in the open water.

The reproductive biology is unknown.

Helogenes marmoratus   3/358
Marbled catfish
H: S America: Peru, Brazil, Guyana.
SD: Unknown.   S: =
B: Unknown.   F: O
T: 22–26°C, L: 12 cm, pH: <7, D: 2–3

CATFISHES

Family Heteropneustidae

Airsack catfishes are closely related to walking catfishes (Clariidae). The family consists of only one genus and the two species presented below. Like the Clariidae, this family breathes atmospheric air with the aid of an accessory breathing organ (see Clariidae, p. 299). Because the pectoral spines are associated with a poison gland, they present a danger to people wading.

When choosing the decor and tankmates, the nocturnal and predacious nature of these catfishes must be taken into account. Breeding reports are contradictory: some claim that the eggs are deposited among fine-leaved plants and others say there is a paternal family.

Heteropneustes fossilis   2/500
Asian stinging catfish
H: Asia: India, Sri Lanka, Thailand, Burma.
♂: Slimmer.   S: –
B: Egg ball in gravel pit; nuclear fam.   F:O
T: 21–25°C, L: 50 cm, pH: 7, D: 4

Heteropneustes microps   2/500
Small Asian stinging catfish
H: Asia: Sri Lanka.   Fw, Bw
♂: Slimmer.   S: –
B: Egg ball in gravel pit; N fam.   F: C,O
T: 22–26°C, L: 25 cm, pH: 7, D: 3

Family Ictaluridae (Ameiuridae)

The family of bullhead catfishes consists of 7 genera and 45 species. The family is distributed from North America to Central America (i.e., Canada to Guatemala). Within the Ictaluridae, there exist both small species—*Noturus* spp.—and large species—*Ameiurus* spp., *Ictalurus* spp., and *Pylodictis olivares*.

By merit of their relatively small size, *Noturus* species are the only members of this family apt for aquarium maintenance. With a length of 30 cm, *N. flavus* is significantly larger than its congeners; all of which are 6 to 12 cm long. Beware!—the dorsal and pectoral fin spines are toxic. The effect of the toxin is species-specific, but it is comparable to that of a wasp sting. Pain will last from a few minutes to as long as an hour. However, as with any poison, those persons allergic to the substance will be more acutely affected.

Bullhead catfishes are nocturnal and spend the day hidden or buried in the substrate. At night, they emerge to search for food, swimming just above the substrate. They are omnivorous in the aquarium. Most species prefer clear, oxygen-rich flowing water and a rock or sand substrate.

The diameter of the eggs varies from 1.5 to 4.5 mm, depending on the number of eggs produced; that is, the more eggs, the smaller the size of each individual egg and vice versa. Smaller species normally lay between 45 and 300 eggs. In clumps or as strings, they are deposited in secluded areas and then guarded by the male. He often helps the young emerge from the eggs.

Of the large species, especially the albino *Ictalurus punctatus* (channel catfish) is especially popular among aquarists, but just like their normal pigmented brothers, they quickly outgrow the limited confines of the aquarium. Large catfishes are mostly raised to grace the dinner table. *Ictalurus* has poison glands connected to the fins spines. However, the pores close with age, unlike those of *Noturus*. Always handle these fishes carefully to avoid incidental injuries.

The commercial production of catfish—especially *Ictalurus punctatus*—is of great economic importance in the United States, comparable only to trout culture. Other species cultured for food are *I. furcatus,* and *I. catus* and—to a lesser degree—the carnivorous *Pylodictis olivaris* and the smaller—*I. melas, I. natalis,* and *I. nebulosus.*

In step with its commercial production, *I. punctatus* is bred on a commercial scale. Sexual maturity is attained at 2 years of age, but breeders 3 years old and over yield more eggs per unit body weight (up to 6.000 eggs per kg) than younger specimens. Males are darker and have a shorter, broader head. Females have a slitlike genital papilla, whereas in males it is tubular.

Spawning occurs in a cave or cavelike structure (e.g., 45 l milk can or wooden box) placed in a breeding pond. After oviposition, the male guards the gelatinous egg mass. Aquarium breeding of larger species is only possible through hormone injections.

There are three species of blind, unpigmented cave dwellers: *Satan eurystomus, Trogloglanis pattersoni,* and *Prietella phreatophila. S. eurystomus* surely takes the price; it was discovered in an artesian well in San Antonio, Texas at a depth of 380 m!

Ameiurus melas   3/359
Black bullhead
H: N America: USA.
♀: Fuller during spawning season.   S: –
B: Pond: pit in the embankment.   F: O
T: 8–30°C, L: 60 cm, pH: 7, D: 1–4

Ameiurus natalis   5/308
Yellow bullhead
H: N America: USA: S and E rivers.
♀: Fuller during spawning season.   S: –
B: 500 eggs; ♂ tends the spawn.   F: O
T: 5–25°C, L: 45 cm, pH: 7, D: 4

Ameiurus nebulosus   3/360
Brown bullhead
H: N America: E and central region.
♀: Fuller at spawning time.   S: –
B: 500 eggs; ♂ tends the spawn.   F: C,O
T: 4–30°C, L: 40 cm, pH: 7, D: 1–4

Ameiurus punctatus albino   1/485
Channel catfish
H: N America: S and W USA.
♀: Fuller at spawning time.   S: –
B: Pond: pit in sand; ♂ tends spawn. F:O
T: 12–24°C, L: <70 cm, pH: 7, D: 2–3

Ameiurus punctatus normal   1/485
Channel catfish

Noturus flavus   5/308
Stonecat
H: N America: Canada, USA.
♀: Fuller at spawning time.   S: –
B: 500 eggs; ♂ tends the spawn.   F: C,O
T: 5–23°C, L: 31 cm, pH: 7, D: 2–3

CATFISHES

Family Loricariidae

With approximately 80 genera and more than 550 species, the suckermouth catfishes are the most species-rich family within the Siluriformes. As the rain forests of South America become progressively more accessible, new species are constantly being discovered. Loricariidae are distributed from Panama through the entire tropical region of South America to Uruguay. In elevation, suckermouth catfishes occur from the lowlands of the Amazon Basin to Andean mountain creeks at an elevation of 3000 m. A few species even enter estuaries for brief periods of time. From the diminutive 4–7 cm *Otocinclus* spp. to the gigantic *Liposarcus* spp. and *Pterygoplichthys* spp., this family is represented by a broad range of sizes.

Bone plates typically cover their body, but some genera, e.g., *Ancistrus, Hypostomus,* and *Panaque,* have a "naked" ventral region. The inferior, suctorial mouth is often void of barbels. It allows loricariids to attach themselves onto smooth substrates, an especially useful ability for inhabitants of swift-flowing waters, such as *Ancistrus* and *Chaetostoma.*

When choosing a loricariid for the community aquarium, size is virtually the only criterium that needs to be considered, as all species are intrinsically peaceful fishes. They are awkward swimmers which spend the vast majority of their time adhered to a substrate, e.g., stones, wood, broad plant leaves, or aquarium panes. Usually they transverse just a few meters before affixing themselves to a new substrate.

Loricariidae are not schooling fishes, but they do not seem to mind sharing precious substrates during the dry season. When submersed logs and branches in lagoons are examined at night with a spotlight, hundreds of ruby red eyes can be seen peering back. Even with so many to choose from, collectors have their work cut out for them. As the net nears, the fishes skitter onto the back side of the wood and then flee into the darkness.

The eye of suckermouth cats has an unique mechanism to regulate the amount of light entering the pupil. Under bright light a superior dermal appendage enlarges, partially covering the pupil. Most animals contract and expand the pupil to control the quantity of light reaching the retina.

As suggested by their long intestine, the Loricariidae are herbivores, known and desired for their ability to curtail or eliminate algae in the aquarium. Many species, however, have a superior growth rate when fed a high protein, animal-based diet. Fiber-rich foods must always be available to prevent intestinal problems. Small but numerous meals—e.g., tablet foods—should be offered. Because most of theses catfishes are crepuscular and/or nocturnal, evening meals are especially important. Some genera such as the *Panaque* seem to require wood in their diet. They constantly rasp away at any wood included in the decor.

In view of their crepuscular and nocturnal tendencies, the aquarium should be dimly illuminated and have a dark substrate. Pieces of wood are beneficial (see above).

It is important to know from what type of biotope the fish originated to best ascertain its requirements. Ignoring the few species which enter estuaries, suckermouth catfishes principally hail from two biotopes: stone/sand bed rivers and muddy lowland waters. Inhabitants from the former biotope depend on cool (20°–24°C), flowing, oxygen-rich water. They are typically intolerant of metabolites, necessitating frequent water exchanges. As long as extremes are avoided, pH and hardness are of secondary importance. Species from the lowlands, on the other hand, are tolerant of low oxygen concentrations and frequently have the ability to breathe atmospheric air. *Hypostomus* and *Pterygoplichthys* absorb atmospheric oxygen through their stomach, whereas *Otocinclus* use part of their intestine. Warm, tropical temperatures are appropriate (24°–27°C), and water movement is not very important. While they are not very sensitive to dissolved metabolites, pH and hardness should tend towards typical Amazon values, i.e., slightly acid and soft. Optimal values, of course, are particularly relevant when breeding.

Sexual differences among suckermouth catfishes are common, but often only apparent during the spawning season. Long odontodes (spines; see glossary) covering their body or in patches on the head (the "beard" of the *Rineloricaria* group), large and soft tentaclelike appendages in the cephalic region ("horns" on *Ancistrus* and others), or an enlarged lower lip (*Loricaria*) are all characteristics of sexually active males. With a bit of practice, the genders can often be distinguished by the genital papilla (see below).

A paternal family structure—i.e., males caring for the spawn—is the norm among the loricariids. Nuclear families or a lack of family structure are rare. The following reproductive strategies are displayed:

- *Ancistrus* and other genera of rivers with stone beds: under stones.
- *Hypostomus* and other genera of waters with clay banks: the fish dig a tunnel commensurate to their size (up to 20 cm in diameter and 70 cm long) just below the high water mark. The eggs are deposited therein and fanned and guarded by the male until they hatch. Smaller species of this and the previous type can often be bred in the aquarium using PVC pipes.
- *Loricaria*: the lump of eggs is brooded on the male's lower lip. During this period, total tranquility must reign around the aquarium, lest the eggs become dislodged by an abrupt movement of the male.
- *Otocinclus, Sturisoma*, etc.: substrate spawners w/ or w/o brood care.

Incidently, there are those who consider the eggs a high quality caviar.

Pseudorinelepis genibarbis ♀   5/410
L 95
A short, recessed genital papilla can be distinguished. This papilla transforms into a tubular ovipositor when spawning.

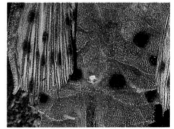

Pseudorinelepis genibarbis ♂   5/410
L 95
The anal opening is thick, bulgelike, and not recessed.

Chaetostoma sp.   5/326

Ventral view. See page 323.

Chaetostoma sp.   5/328
L 146
Ventral view. See page 323.

Cochliodon sp.   5/331
L 60?
Ventral view. See page 324.

Corymbophanes bahianus ♂   5/334
LDA 17
Ventral view. See page 325.

Loricaria nickeriensis   3/374
Nickerie suckermouth
Ventral view.

Pseudorinelepis genibarbis   5/410
L 95
Suctorial mouth. See page 347.

The beautiful markings and contrasting colors of species such as the recently discovered *Hypancistrus zebra* (p. 329) and *Acanthicus adonis* (pp. 316 f.) have awakened aquarists to the beauty found within this group.

Loricariidae sp. L 4/L 5   5/366
L 4, L 5, L 28, L 73
H: S America: Brazil: Rio Tocantins.
♂: Head broader; thicker odontodes. S: +
B: L 28 in clay cave; ca. 45 eggs. F: O
T: 26–29°C, L: <14 cm, pH: 7, D: 2–3

Loricariidae sp.   5/366
L 73

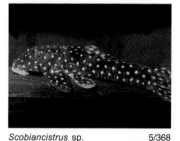

Scobiancistrus sp.   5/368
L 82
H: S America: Brazil: Rio Xingú.
SD: Unknown.   S: +
B: Breeders rarely available.   F: C
T: 27–30°C, L: 12 cm, pH: 7, D: 3

Loricariidae sp.   5/370
L 106, L 122
H: S America: Venezuela.
SD: Unknown.   S: +
B: Unsuccessful.   F: O
T: 27–30°C, L: >15 cm, pH: 7, D: 3

Loricariidae sp. L 136b   5/314
LDA5, LDA6, L136a, L136b, L136c, L158
H: S America: Brazil: Rio Negro.
SD: Unknown.   S: +
B: L 136b successful; <35 eggs.   F: O
T: 24–27°C, L: 13 cm, pH: <7, D: 3

315

CATFISHES

Loricariidae sp. L 136a   5/314
L136a, LDA 5

Loricariidae sp.   5/370
L 163
H: S America: Brazil: Rio do Pará.
SD: Unknown.   S:+
B: Breeders rarely available.   F: O
T: 26–29°C, L: 20 cm, pH: 7, D: 3

Loricariidae sp.   5/374
L 174
H: S America: Brazil: Rio Xingú.
♂: Odontodes on caudal peduncle. S:+
B: Unknown.   F: H,L
T: 27–30°C, L: 5–7 cm, pH: 7, D: 3

Ancistrinae sp.   5/352
Una hypostomus, L 127
H: S America: Brazil: Rio Iara.
♂: Pectoral fin rays spinier.   S: +
B: Unknown.   F: H,O
T: 22–24°C, L: 20 cm, pH: 7, D: 2

Hypostominae sp.   5/372
Pitbull suckercat, LDA 25
H: S America: Brazil: Rio Xingú.
SD: Unknown.   S:+
B: Simulation of rainy season.   F: H,O
T: 22–27°C, L: 5 cm, pH: 7, D: 3

Acanthicus adonis   2/502, 3/361

H: S America: Brazil, Peru.
♂: Larger.   S: =
B: Unknown.   F: H,O
T: 22–27°C, L: <100 cm, pH: <7, D: 3–4

Acanthicus adonis   2/502, 3/361

Ventral view.

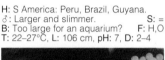

Acanthicus hystrix   3/363

H: S America: Peru, Brazil, Guyana.
♂: Larger and slimmer.   S: =
B: Too large for an aquarium?   F: H,O
T: 22–27°C, L: 106 cm, pH: 7, D: 2–4

Ancistrus dolichopterus   1/486, 3/365
Big-fin bristlenose
H: S America: Amazon tributaries.
♂: Tentacles.   S: +
B: Caves and pits; ♂ tends spawn.   F: H
T: 23–27°C, L: <13 cm, pH: <7, D: 1–2

Ancistrus dolichopterus   1/486, 3/365
Big-fin bristlenose
Spawn (seen through the bottom pane
of the aquarium).

Ancistrus hoplogenys?   1/486
Snowflake bristlenose
H: S America: Amazon headwaters.
♂: Larger; tentacles.   S: +
B: Caves and pits; ♂ tends spawn.   F: H
T: 22–26°C, L: 8 cm, pH: <7, D: 2–3

Ancistrus cf. *hoplogenys*   5/310
Snowflake bristlenose, L 4, L 5, L 73
H: S America: Brazil.
♂: Odontodes.   S: +
B: Adh. spawner; ♂ tends spawn.   F: H
T: 23–26°C, L: 16 cm, pH: <7, D: 2–3

CATFISHES

317

Ancistrus cf. *hoplogenys* juv.   5/310
Snowflake bristlenose, L 4, L 5, L 73

Ancistrus cf. *hoplogenys*   5/310
Snowflake bristlenose, L 4, L 5, L 73

Ancistrus cf. *leucostictus*   5/324
Yellow-spot bristlenose
H: S America: Guyana, Peru.
♂: More tentacles.   S: +
B: About 70 yellow eggs.   F: H,O
T: 25–28°C, L: <16 cm, pH: 7, D: 2

Ancistrus cf. *leucostictus*   5/324
Yellow-spot bristlenose

Ancistrus sp. aff. *leucostictus* ♂   3/
                                            364
Yellow-spot bristlenose

Ancistrus ranunculus   5/316
Frog bristlenose, L 34
H: S America: Brazil: Xingú, Tocantins.
♂: More tentacles.   S: +
B: Unsuccessful.   F: H,O
T: 25–28°C, L: 20 cm, pH: 7, D: 3–4

Ancistrus sp.   5/313

(*Ancistrus hoplogenys* group)
H: S America: Brazil: Rio Negro.

Ancistrus sp.   5/320

H: S America: Venezuela: S of Caicara.
SD: Unknown.   S: +
B: Unsuccessful.   F: H
T: 20–25°C, L: 10 cm, pH: 7, D: 2–3

Ancistrus sp.   5/322

H: S America: Venezuela: Puerto Ayacucho.

Ancistrus sp.   5/320

H: S America: Venezuela: S of Caicara.
SD: Unknown.   S: +
B: Unsuccessful.   F: H
T: 20–25°C, L: 15 cm, pH: 7, D: 2–3

Ancistrus sp.   5/324

H: S America: Brazil: Rio Negro.

Ancistrus sp. cf. *ranunculus*   4/272
L 88

H: S America: Brazil.
♂: Longer tentacles.   S: +
B: Not described.   F: H
T: 24–28°C, L: 10 cm, pH: 7, D: 2

CATFISHES

319

Ancistrus sp.   5/312
L 107, L 184

Ancistrus sp.   5/313
L 107, L 184

Ancistrus sp.   5/318
L 110, L 157
H: S America: Brazil: Rio Negro.
♂: Larger tentacles.   S: +
B: Unsuccessful.   F: H,O
T: 25–27°C, L: 15 cm, pH: <7, D: 3

Ancistrus sp.   4/272
L 156
H: S America: Brazil: Rio Tocantins.
♂: Longer tentacles on mouth.   S: +
B: Typical for the genus.   F: H
T: 23–28°C, L: 12 cm, pH: 7, D: 2–3

Ancistrus sp. "black"   5/316
L 183

Ancistrus sp.   4/271
LDA 3
H: S America: Brazil.
♂: Longer tentacles on mouth.   S: +
B: Unsuccessful.   F: H
T: 23–26°C, L: 10 cm, pH: 7, D: 2–3

Ancistrus sp.   5/318
LDA 8
H: S America: Brazil: Mato Grosso.
♂: More tentacles; 1–2 cm smaller. S: +
B: Cs, 40 e; ♂ tends spawn.   F: H,C,L
T: 26–29°C, L: ♀ 9 cm, pH: 7, D: 2–3

Ancistrus sp. "Barcelos"   5/323
L 183

Ancistrus sp. "São Gabriel" ♂   5/323
L 182

Ancistrus sp. "São Gabriel"   5/322

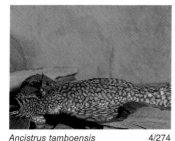

Ancistrus tamboensis   4/274
L 89, mosaic bristlenose
H: S America: Peru. Brazil?
♂: Larger tentacles.   S: +
B: In the ♂'s cave.   F: H
T: 23–26°C, L: 10 cm, pH: 7, D: 2–3

Ancistrus temminckii   2/502
Temminck's bristlenose
H: S Am.: Fr.Gu., Suriname, Brazil. Peru?
♂: Longer cephalic bristles.   S: +
B: Under wood; ♂ cares for spawn. F: H
T: 21–24°C, L: 12 cm, pH: 7, D: 1

CATFISHES

Ancistrus cf. *temminckii* ♂   3/366
Temminck's bristlenose
H: S America: Guyana.
♂: Long, branched tentacles.   S: +
B: Under wood; ♂ tends the spawn. F: O
T: 22–25°C, L: 12 cm, pH: 7, D: 1

Ancistrus triradiatus   4/274
Three-ray bristlenose
H: S America: Colombia. Brazil?
♂: Larger tentacles.   S: +
B: Unsuccessful.   F: H
T: 24–28°C, L: 10 cm, pH: 7, D: 2

Aphanotorulus frankei ♂   4/276
Leopard suckercat
H: S America: Peru: Ucayali tributaries.
SD: Note upper C fin and peduncle. S: +
B: Unknown.   F: H,C,O
T: 25–28°C, L: <15 cm, pH: 7, D: 3–4

Aphanotorulus frankei ♀   4/276
Leopard suckercat

Aposturisoma myriodon   4/278

H: S America: Peru: Ucayali tributaries.
SD: Unknown.   S: +
B: Unknown.   F: ?
T: 24–28°C, L: <20 cm, pH: 7, D: 3–4

Baryancistrus sp.   4/280
L 81
H: S America: Brazil: Rio Xingú and Iriri.
SD: Unknown.   S: +
B: Unknown.   F: H,O
T: 23–26°C, L: >15 cm, pH: 7, D: 3–4

Baryancistrus sp.   4/280
L 18, L 177
H: S America: Brazil: Rio Xingú and Iriri.
SD: Unknown.   S: +
B: Unknown.   F: H,O
T: 23–26°C, L: >15 cm, pH: 7, D: 3–4

Chaetostoma sp.   2/506
Bulldog catfish
H: S America: upper Amazon.
SD: Unknown   S: +
B: Unknown.   F: O
T: 20–24°C, L: 25 cm, pH: 7, D: 2–3

Chaetostoma sp.   5/326
Bulldog catfish
H: N South America: foothills of Andes.
♂: Slimmer.   S: +
B: Unknown.   F: O
T: 18–24°C, L: 8 cm, pH: 7, D: 2–3

Chaetostoma sp.   5/328
Rio Meta bulldog catfish, L 146
H: S America: Colombia: upper Rio Meta.
♂: Larger; broader head.   S: +
B: Under stone plates; <60 eggs.   F: O
T: 24–26°C, L: <11 cm, pH: 7, D: 2–3

Chaetostoma sp.   5/328
Spotted bulldog catfish, L 148
H: S America: Venezuela.
♂: Larger; broader head.   S: +
B: Unsuccessful.   F: O
T: 22–26°C, L: <15 cm, pH: 7, D: 3–4

Chaetostoma sp.   2/504

H: S America: Colombia: mountain creeks.
♂: Tentacles?   S: +
B: Nature: under stones.   F: H,O
T: 20–22°C, L: 10 cm, pH: 7, D: 2–3

CATFISHES

Cochliodon cochliodon   2/504
Cochliodon catfish
H: S America: Paraguay.
SD: Unknown.   S: +
B: Unsuccessful.   F: H
T: 21–24°C, L: 15 cm, pH: <7, D: 2–3

Cochliodon cf. *cochliodon*   5/332
Chocolate cochliodon
H: S America: Paraguay.
SD: Unknown.   S: +
B: Unsuccessful.   F: H,O
T: 18–23°C, L: 25 cm, pH: <7, D: 3

Cochliodon oculeus   5/332

H: S America: Colombia, Brazil.
SD: Position of genital papilla. S: +
B: Simulate rainy season?   F: C,O
T: 18–24°C, L: 20 cm, pH: <7, D: 2–3

Cochliodon sp.   4/282
Giant cochliodon, L 50
H: S America: Brazil.
SD: Unknown.   S: +
B: Unsuccessful.   F: O
T: 23–27°C, L: >15 cm, pH: 7, D: 3

Cochliodon sp.   5/331
L 60?
H: S America: habitat unknown.
SD: Unknown.   S: +
B: Unsuccessful.   F: O
T: 23–27°C, L: >15 cm, pH: 7, D: 2–3

Cochliodon sp.   4/282
Rusty pleco
H: S America: Paraguay.
SD: Unknown.   S: +
B: Unsuccessful.   F: O
T: 20–26°C, L: >15 cm, pH: 7, D: 2

Corymbophanes bahianus ♂   5/334
LDA 17
H: S America: Brazil: Bahia.
♂: Head fringed with bristles.   S: +
B: Unsuccessful.   F: H,O
T: 23–25°C, L: 12 cm, pH: 7, D: 2–3

Crossoloricaria rhami   4/284

H: S America: Peru: Rio Ucayali Basin.
SD: Unknown.   S: +
B: Unknown.   F: O,H
T: 25–28°C, L: 13 cm?, pH: 7, D: 3–4

Crossoloricaria venezuelae   4/284
Photo is *Pseudohemiodon lamina* (similar)
H: S America: Venezuela: Rio Palmar.
SD: Unknown.   S: +
B: Unknown.   F: H
T: 22–26°C, L: <18 cm, pH: 7, D: 2–3

Dekeyseria scaphirhyncha   3/367
Flathead suckermouth
H: S America: Brazil, Amazonia.
SD: None.   S: +
B: Unknown.   F: H,O
T: 22–26°C, L: 20 cm, pH: <7, D: 2–3

Dekeyseria scaphirhyncha   3/367
Flathead suckermouth
See photo on page 3/373.

Exastilithoxus cf. *fimbriatus*   5/336

H: S America: Venezuela.
SD: Unknown.   S: +
B: 40-60 eggs; ♂ guards spawn. F: H,O
T: 25–28°C, L: 7 cm, pH: 7, D: 2–3

CATFISHES

Farlowella acus   1/488
Common twig catfish
H: S America: Brazil, S Amazonia.
♂: "Nose" broader and bristled.   S: +
B: 40-60 eggs; ♂ guards spawn.   F: H
T: 24–26°C, L: 15 cm, pH: <7, D: 3–4

Farlowella curtirostra   5/336
H: S Am.: Venezuela: Maracaibo basin.
♂: Side of nose has odontodes.   S: +
B: Unknown.   F: H,O
T: 23–25°C, L: 15 cm, pH: 7, D: 3

Farlowella gracilis   1/488
Mottled twig catfish
H: S America: Colombia.
SD: Unknown.   S: +
B: Unknown.   F: H,L
T: 22–26°C, L: <19 cm, pH: <7, D: 3–4

Farlowella knerii   4/286
Kner's twig catfish
H: S America: Ecuador: Canelos.
SD: Unknown.   S: +
B: Not described.   F: H
T: 24–27°C, L: >12 cm, pH: <7, D: 3–4

Glyptoperichthys gibbiceps   1/496
Spotted sailfin pleco
H: S America: Peru: Rio Pacaya.
SD: Unknown.   S: +
B: Unknown.   F: H,O
T: 23–27°C, L: 50 cm, pH: 7, D: 1

Glyptoperichthys joselimaianus   4/286
L 1, L 22   (nocturnal or fright coloration)
H: S America: Brazil: Rio Aruana.
SD: Unknown.   S: +
B: Unknown.   F: O
T: 24–29°C, L: >15 cm, pH: 7, D: 2

CATFISHES

Glyptoperichthys cf. *lituratus*   3/384
Metal sailfin pleco
H: S America: Peru: Rio Ucayali.
SD: Unknown.   S: +
B: Unknown.   F: O
T: 24–28°C, L: >40 cm, pH: <7, D: 3–4

Glyptoperichthys punctatus   2/516
Spotted sailfin pleco
H: S America: Venezuela: Amazonia.
SD: Unknown.   S: +
B: Unknown.   F: H,L
T: 22–26°C, L: 18 cm, pH: 7, D: 1–2

Harttia kronei   5/338

H: S America: Brazil: São Paulo.
♂: Unknown.   S: +
B: Unknown.   F: C,H
T: 22–24°C, L: 12 cm, pH: 7, D: 3–4

Harttia loricariformis   5/338

H: S America: Brazil: Rio Itabapoana.
♂: P fin spines longer and thicker.   S: +
B: Unsuccessful.   F: O
T: 24–27°C, L: 20 cm, pH: 7, D: 2–3

Hemiancistrus annectens   3/368

H: S America: NW Ecuador.
SD: None.   S: +
B: Unknown.   F: H,O
T: 22–28°C, L: 18 cm, pH: 7, D: 2

Hemiancistrus landoni   3/369

H: S America: W Ecuador: Rio Guayas.
SD: Unknown.   S: +
B: Unknown.   F: H,O
T: 24–28°C, L: >25 cm, pH: 7, D: 2

CATFISHES

Hemiancistrus sp.   5/368
L 20
H: S America: Brazil: Rio Xingú.
SD: Unknown.   S: +
B: Unsuccessful.   F: O
T: 27–30°C, L: >15 cm, pH: 7, D: 3

Hemiodontichthys acipenserius ♂   5/340
Knobnose whiptail catfish
H: S America: Peru, Brazil, Bolivia.
♂: Oral lobes; blunt teeth.   S: +
B: ♂ carries eggs w/ oral lobes.   F: C
T: 24–28°C, L: <14 cm, pH: 7, D: 3–4

Hopliancistrus sp.   5/342
L 17
H: S America: Brazil: Rio Xingú.
SD: Unknown.   S: +
B: Unknown.   F: H,O
T: 20–24°C, L: 25 cm, pH: <7, D: 2–3

Hopliancistrus sp.   5/342
L 17

Hopliancistrus sp.   5/343
L 67, LDA 15

Hopliancistrus cf. *tricornis*   4/308
Flathead pleco, L 17
H: S America: Brazil: Rio Xingú.
♂: Larger odontodes.   S: +
B: Unknown.   F: H,O
T: 20–24°C, L: 25 cm, pH: <7, D: 2–3

Hypancistrus zebra ♂   4/288
Zebra suckermouth, L 46
H: S America: Brazil: Rio Xingú.
♂: Longer odontodes; differing design
  (see photos).
B: Pond-bred in Florida (USA).

Hypancistrus zebra ♀   4/288
Zebra suckermouth, L 46

S: +, larger specimens bite!
F: H, later also C
T: 23–26°C, L: 15 cm, pH: 7, D: 2–4

CATFISHES

Hypoptopoma carinatum   3/370

H: S America: Peru/Brazil region.
♂: Smaller and more slender.   S: +
B: In a corner of the aquarium.   F: H
T: 20–25°C, L: 5 cm, pH: <7, D: 3

Hypoptopoma gulare   5/344
Flatnose dwarf suckercat
H: S America: Peru, Brazil.
♂: Smaller and more slender?   S: +
B: Unknown.   F: H,L
T: 23–26°C, L: 8 cm, pH: 7, D: 2–4

Hypoptopoma sp.   5/344

H: S America: Venezuela: Llanos.
SD: Virtually indistinguishable.   S: +
B: Unknown.   F: H,L
T: 26–28°C, L: 8 cm, pH: 7, D: 3

Hypoptopoma sp.   5/346

H: S America.
SD: Virtually indistinguishable.   S: +
B: Very difficult.   F: H,O
T: 26–28°C, L: 8 cm, pH: 7, D: 3

329

Hypoptopoma thoracatum   1/490

H: S America: Brazil and Amazonia.
SD: Unknown.   S: +
B: Unknown.   F: H
T: 23–27°C, L: 8 cm, pH: 7, D: 2–3

Hypostomus emarginatus   4/290

H: S America: Brazil.
SD: Unknown.   S: +
B: Unknown.   F: O
T: 24–27°C, L: >15 cm, pH: 7, D: 2

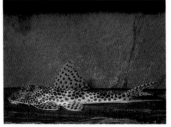

Hypostomus cf. *emarginatus*   5/346
L 108, L 116, L 133, L 153, L 166

H: S America: Ecuador, Peru, Brazil, Ven.
SD: Unknown.   S: +
B: Unknown.   F: O
T: 25–28°C, L: 50 cm, pH: 7, D: 4

Hypostomus jaguribensis   4/290
Jaguribé pleco

H: S America: Brazil: Rio Jaguribé.
SD: Unknown.   S: +
B: Unknown.   F: O
T: 24–27°C, L: >12 cm, pH: 7, D: 2

Hypostomus margaritifer   4/292

H: S America: Brazil: Rio Piracicaba.
SD: Unknown.   S: +
B: Unknown.   F: O
T: 24–27°C, L: >15 cm, pH: 7, D: 2–3

Hypostomus plecostomus   2/506
Pleco

H: S America: northern region.
SD: Unknown.   S: +
B: In ponds: caves in steep banks. F: H,O
T: 20–28°C, L: 28 cm, pH: 7, D: 1–2

Hypostomus punctatus   1/490
Spotted suckercat
H: S America: S and SE Brazil.
SD: Unknown.   S: +
B: Unsuccessful.   F: H
T: 22–28°C, L: <30 cm, pH: 7, D: 1

Hypostomus regani   3/370
Regan's hypostomus
H: S America: Brazil: Rio Piracicaba.
SD: Unknown.   S: +
B: Unknown.   F: H,O
T: 22–25°C, L: >30 cm?, pH: <7, D: 4

Hypostomus boulengeri   5/348

H: S America: W Brazil.
SD: Position of genital papilla.   S: +
B: Unsuccessful.   F: O
T: 22–25°C, L: 20 cm, pH: 7, D: 2

Hypostomus sp.   5/349

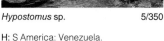

Hypostomus sp.   5/350

H: S America: Venezuela.
SD: Unknown.   S: +
B: Unsuccessful.   F: H,O
T: 25–28°C, L: <30 cm, pH: 7, D: 3

Hypostomus sp.   5/351

H: S America: Venezuela.

Hypostomus sp.   5/351

H: S America: Brazil: São Paulo.

Hypostomus unicolor   5/352
Clay pleco
H: S America: Brazil: Rio Purus.
SD: Location of genital papilla.   S: +
B: Unknown.   F: H,O
T: 22–26°C, L: 15 cm, pH: 7, D: 2–3

Hypostomus cf. *watwata*   5/354
L 192
H: S America: Guianas, Venezuela.
SD: Unknown.   S: +
B: Unknown.   F: H,O
T: 26–29°C, L: >20 cm, pH: 7, D: 3

Isorineloricaria spinosissima   3/372
Spiny suckermouth catfish
H: S America: W Ecuador: Guayas Basin.
♂: Long thornlike spines.   S: +
B: Unknown.   F: H,O
T: 24–30°C, L: <60 cm, pH: 7, D: 2–3

Kronichthys subteres   5/354

H: S America: Brazil: state of São Paulo.
SD: Unknown.   S: +
B: Unknown.   F: C,O
T: 20–24°C, L: 12 cm, pH: 7, D: 3–4

Lamontichthys filamentosus   5/356
Filamentous suckercat
H: S America: Brazil, Ecuador, Peru, Bol.
SD: Location of genital papilla.   S: +
B: Unknown.   F: O
T: 24–27°C, L: 16 cm, pH: 7, D: 2–3

Lamontichthys filamentosus   5/356
Filamentous suckercat

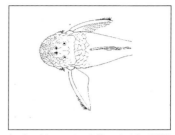

Lasiancistrus carnegiei (no photo)   3/372
Carnegie's suckermouth
H: S America: Colombia: Rio Magdalena.
♂: Longer pectoral spines.   S: +
B: Unknown.   F: O
T: 22–26°C, L: 14 cm, pH: <7, D: 2–3

Lasiancistrus scolymus   5/358
Reticulated suckercat
H: S America: Brazil: Rio Guamá.
♂: Odontodes; rounded ventral fins. S:+
B: Under stone plates; <200 e.   F: H,O
T: 25–27°C, L: <15 cm, pH: 7, D: 2–3

Lasiancistrus sp.   5/358
Ichthyo suckercat, L 194
H: S America: Venezuela: Llanos.
SD: Unknown.   S:+
B: Unsuccessful.   F: O,H
T: 26–28°C, L: 15–20 cm, pH: 7, D: 3

Lasiancistrus sp.   5/360

H: S America: E Peru.
♂: Stouter odontodes.   S: +
B: Unsuccessful.   F: C,H
T: 27–30°C, L: 17–20 cm, pH: 7, D: 3

Leporacanthicus galaxias   3/386, (4/280)
Galactical suckermouth
H: S America: Brazil: Amazonia.
SD: Unknown.   S: +
B: Unknown.   F: H
T: 22–25°C, L: 40 cm?, pH: <7, D: 3

CATFISHES

Leporacanthicus galaxias juv. (4/280)
Galactical suckermouth
See 3/386 for text.

Liposarcus anisitsi 2/514
Snow king sailfin pleco
H: S America: Brazil, Paraguay.
SD: Unknown. S: +
B: Pond-bred in Florida (USA). F: H
T: 21–24°C, L: 42 cm, pH: 7, D: 2

Liposarcus multiradiatus 1/496
Many-rayed sailfin suckercat
H: S America: Peru, Bolivia, Paraguay.
SD: Unknown. S: +
B: Unknown. F: H,O
T: 23–27°C, L: >50 cm, pH: 7, D: 1

Liposarcus pardalis 5/360
Leopard sailfin pleco
H: S America: Peru: central Rio Ucayali.
SD: Unknown. S: +
B: Unknown. F: H,O
T: 23–28°C, L: >40 cm, pH: 7, D: 3–4

Lithoxancistrus orinoco 5/362
Orinoco suckercat, L 126
H: S America: Venezuela: Rio Orinoco.
♂: Stouter odontodes. S: +
B: Unsuccessful. F: H,O
T: 25–27°C, L: 10 cm, pH: 7, D: 3

Lithoxancistrus orinoco 5/362
Orinoco suckercat, L 126

Lithoxancistrus sp.   4/292
L 127
H: S America: Venezuela.
SD: Unknown.   **S:** +
B: Unknown.   **F:** H
T: 23–27°C, **L:** 10 cm, **pH:** 7, **D:** 2

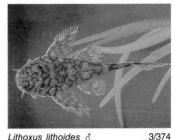

Lithoxus lithoides ♂   3/374
Rock suckermouth
H: S America: Suriname, Guyana.
SD: See photos (pectoral spines). **S:** +
B: Unknown.   **F:** H,O
T: 18–22°C, **L:** 9 cm, **pH:** 7, **D:** 2–3

Lithoxus lithoides ♀   3/374
Rock suckermouth

Loricaria nickeriensis   3/374
Nickerie suckermouth
H: S America: Suriname.
♂: Lobe of suctorial mouth larger. **S:** +
B: Unsuccessful.   **F:** O
T: 20–24°C, **L:** 15 cm, **pH:** <7, **D:** 2

Loricaria simillima   5/365

H: S America: Ecuador: Canelos.
SD: Only in sexually active fish.   **S:** +
B: ♂ carries eggs in "lip pouch."   **F:** O
T: 24–28°C, **L:** 25 cm, **pH:** 7, **D:** 3–4

Loricariichthys platymetopon   4/294

H: S America: S Brazil, Par., Uru., Arg.
♂: "Lip pouch" when spawning.   **S:** +
B: ♂ carries <1000 eggs in pouch.   **F:** O
T: 23–26°C, **L:** 30 cm, **pH:** 7, **D:** 2

CATFISHES

335

Loricariichthys ucayalensis   4/294
Ucayali suckercat
H: S America: Peru: Rio Ucayali.
♂: Lip pouch when spawning.   S: +
B: Unsuccessful.   F: O
T: 24–28°C, L: 25 cm, pH: 7, D: 2

Hisonotus leucofrenatus   5/376

H: S America: Brazil: Rio de Janeiro.
♂: Smaller and more slender.   S: +
B: Unknown.   F: O
T: 22–26°C, L: 6 cm, pH: 7, D: 3

Hisonotus notatus   5/376

H: S America: SE Brazil.
♂: Smaller and slimmer.   S: +
B: Unknown.   F: O,H
T: 22–26°C, L: 5 cm, pH: 7, D: 2

Pseudorinelepis genibarbis   3/376
Black suckercat, carachama
H: S America: E Peru.
SD: Unknown.   S: +
B: Unknown.   F: H,O
T: 20–24°C, L: 11 cm, pH: 7, D: 1–2

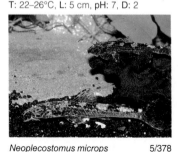

Neoplecostomus microps   5/378

H: S America: Brazil: Rio de Janeiro.
♂: Smaller and slimmer.   S: +
B: Unsuccessful.   F: H,O
T: 20–25°C, L: 8 cm, pH: 7, D: 3–4

Otocinclus affinis   1/492
Dwarf otocinclus, golden otocinclus
H: S America: SE Brazil.
♂: Slimmer and smaller.   S: +
B: Eggs adhered to plant leaves. F: L,H
T: 20–26°C, L: 4 cm, pH: <7, D: 2

Macrotocinclus flexilis   2/508
Imitator suckercat
H: S America: Brazil: Rio Grande do Sul.
♂: Slimmer.   S: +
B: Eggs adhered to the aquarium.   F: H,L
T: 20–25°C, L: 6 cm, pH: 7, D: 1

Lampiella gibbosa   5/378
Humpback otocinclus
H: S America: Brazil: state of São Paulo.
♀: Larger; fuller when spawning.   S: +
B: Unknown.   F: O
T: 22–25°C, L: 5 cm, pH: 7, D: 3

Hisonotus leucofrenatus   3/376

H: S America: Brazil.
♂: More slender and smaller.   S: +
B: Unknown.   F: H
T: 20–25°C, L: 7 cm, pH: <7, D: 3

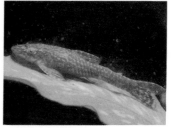

Hisonotus notatus   2/508
Marked otocinclus
H: S America: SE Brazil.
SD: Unknown.   S: +
B: Unknown.   F: H,L
T: 22–24°C, L: 4 cm, pH: 7, D: 2

Otocinclus vittatus   3/378
Striped otocinclus
H: S America: Peru, Bolivia, Brazil.
♂: Slimmer.   S: +
B: Eggs adhered to leaves, etc.   F: H,O
T: 20–25°C, L: 5.5 cm, pH: 7, D: 2

Otothyris lophophanes   2/510
Brown otocinclus
H: S America: SE Brazil.
SD: Only present when spawning. S: +
B: Eggs adhered to leaves, etc.   F: H,O
T: 20–24°C, L: 4 cm, pH: <7, D: 2

CATFISHES

337

Otothyris (?) sp.   5/380

H: S America: SE Brazil: mountain creeks.
SD: Urogenital papilla.   S: +
B: Unknown.   F: H,O
T: 22–26°C, L: 5 cm, pH: 7, D: 2–3

Panaque nigrolineatus   1/492
Royal panaque
H: S America: S Colombia.
SD: Unknown.   S: +
B: Unknown.   F: H
T: 22–26°C, L: 25 cm , pH: 7, D: 3

Panaque sp.   5/381
Hairy tiger catfish, L 2, L 74
H: S America: Brazil: Rio Tocantins.
♂: Odontodes on caudal peduncle.   S: =
B: There are no reports.   F: C,O,H
T: 26–29°C, L: 12 cm, pH: 7, D: 4

Panaque sp. adult   4/296
L 90
H: S America: Peru.
♂: Odontodes on P fin spines?   S: +
B: Unknown.   F: H,O
T: 23–27°C, L: >30 cm, pH: <7, D: 3

Panaque sp. juvenil   4/296
L 90

Panaque suttonorum   2/510
Blue-eyed panaque
H: S America: Guianas, Colombia.
SD: Unknown.   S: +
B: Unknown.   F: H,O
T: 20–24°C, L: 18 cm, pH: 7, D: 3

CATFISHES

Parancistrus aurantiacus   3/378
Gold-fin suckermouth
H: S America: Peru: Rio Ucayali.
SD: Unknown.   S: +
B: Unknown.   F: H,O
T: 22–27°C, L: 18 cm, pH: 7, D: 2–3

Parancistrus aurantiacus   5/382
L 30, L 31   spotted
H: Brazil: Tocantins (L 30), Xingú (L 31).
♂: Broader head; stouter odontodes. S: +
B: Unknown.   F: O
T: 26–30°C, L: 15 cm, pH: 7, D: 2–3

Parancistrus aurantiacus   5/382
L 30, L 31   variegated
There is also a solid yellow morph.

Parancistrus niveatus = Baryancistrus niv.
Snowflake bristlenose   3/380
H: S America: Brazil: Rio Araguaia.
SD: Unknown.   S: +
B: Unknown.   F: H
T: 22–24°C, L: 20 cm, pH: <7, D: 2–3

Parancistrus sp.   4/302
L 47
H: S America: Brazil: Rio Xingú.
♂: Stouter fin rays; odontodes.   S: +
B: Unknown.   F: H,O
T: 24–30°C, L: >25 cm, pH: <7, D: 3

Parancistrus sp.   5/315
LDA 4
Probably *P. niveatus*.

CATFISHES

Parancistrus sp.   5/383

Parancistrus sp.   5/383

Pareiorhina rudolphi   5/385

H: S America: Brazil: São Paulo.
♂: Slightly smaller and slimmer.   S: +
B: Unknown.   F: O
T: 21–25°C, L: 4.5 cm, pH: 7, D: 3

Otocinclus cf. *affinis*
Midget suckercat
See page 336[6].

Parotocinclus cf. *britskii*   5/386
Alligator otocinclus
H: S America: Suriname.
SD: Unknown.   S: +
B: Unknown.   F: H
T: 22–27°C, L: 6 cm, pH: 7, D: 2–3

Parotocinclus cesarpintoi   5/386
Cesar Pinto's otocinclus
H: S Am.: Brazil: Rio Paraiba do Norte.
♀: Fuller during spawning season.   S: +
B: Unsuccessful.   F: H,O
T: 25–30°C, L: 4 cm, pH: 7, D: 2–3

Parotocinclus cristatus   5/388
Yellow-spot otocinclus
H: S America: Brazil: state of Bahia.
♂: Smaller and more delicate.   S: +
B: 20 e throughout the aquarium.   F: H,O
T: 22–25°C, L: 4 cm, pH: 7, D: 2–3

Parotocinclus jimi   5/388
H: S America: Brazil: state of Bahia.
♀: Larger and more robust.   S: +
B: They mature, but don't spawn.   F: H,O
T: 22–25°C, L: 4 cm, pH: 7, D: 2–3

Parotocinclus maculicauda ♂   5/390
Redfin otocinclus
H: S America: Brazil.
♂: 1st ray of D and V fins red.   S: +
B: Underside of leaves; no care.   F: H,O
T: 20–24°C, L: 6 cm, pH: 7, D: 2–3

Parotocinclus maculicauda   5/390
Redfin otocinclus

Parotocinclus spilosoma   5/392
Spotted otocinclus, cascudo
H: S America: Brazil: Paraiba.
SD: Not described.   S: +
B: Unknown.   F: H
T: 22–28°C, L: 6 cm, pH: 7, D: 2–3

Parotocinclus cf. *spilosoma*   5/392
Spotted otocinclus, cascudo

Parotocinclus sp. "Rio Cristalino"   5/394

H: S America: Brazil: Araguaia Basin.
♂: Slightly smaller and graceful.   S: +
B: Unsuccessful.   F: O
T: 24–27°C, L: 2 cm, pH: 7, D: 3–4

Peckoltia cf. *arenaria*   5/398

H: S America: Peru: Rio Huallaga.
♂: Unknown.   S: +
B: Unsuccessful.   F: O
T: 22–26°C, L: 10 cm, pH: <7, D: 2–3

Peckoltia brevis   2/512
Spotted peckoltia

H: S America: W Brazil: Rio Purus.
♂: Odontodes on D and P fins.   S: +
B: Cave spawner; nuclear family.   F: H,L
T: 22–26°C, L: 9 cm, pH: 7, D: 2–3

Peckoltia cf. *brevis*   5/394
Spotted peckoltia

H: S America: Peru: Rio Purus tributary.
♂: Odontodes on D and P fins.   S: +
B: Cave spawner; nuclear family.   F: H,L
T: 22–26°C, L: 9 cm, pH: 7, D: 2–3

Peckoltia oligospila   5/396
L 6

H: S America: Brazil: Rio Guamá, Capin.
SD: Unknown.   S: +
B: Unknown.   F: O
T: 23–27°C, L: >12 cm, pH: 7, D: 2–3

Peckoltia platyrhynchus   5/396
Flat-faced peckoltia, L 121?, L 135?

H: S Am.: Colombia. Guyana? Brazil?
SD: Unknown.   S: +
B: Unknown.   F: O
T: 23–27°C, L: >12 cm, pH: 7, D: 2–3

Zonancistrus pulcher   1/494
Pretty peckoltia
H: S America: Brazil: Rio Negro.
SD: Unknown.   S: +
B: Unsuccessful.   F: L,O
T: 24–28°C, L: 6 cm, pH: 7, D: 1–2

Peckoltia sp.   5/404
H: S America: Brazil: Rio Negro.
♂: W/ odontodes; more slender.   S: +
B: Cave spawner (♂); pH ≪7.   F: O
T: 22–29°C, L: <15 cm, pH: <7, D: 2–4

Peckoltia sp.   5/405
L 2?
H: S America: Brazil.

Peckoltia sp.   5/398
L 2, L 169
H: S America: Brazil: Amazonia.
♂: Odontodes; more slender.   S: +
B: Unknown.   F: O
T: 24–27°C, L: 12 cm, pH: 7, D: 2–3

Peckoltia sp.   adult ♂   5/400
L 66
H: Brazil: Rio Xingú/Tocantins.
♂: With odontodes; darker.   S: +
B: Unsuccessful.   F: C,O
T: 26–28°C, L: <16 cm, pH: 7, D: 2–3

Peckoltia sp.   juvenile   5/400
L 66

Peckoltia sp.　　　　　　　　4/300
L 102, snowball peckoltia
H: S America: Brazil: Rio Negro.
♂: Odontodes.　　　　　　　　S: +
B: Unsuccessful.　　　　　　　F: O
T: 23–26°C, L: 15 cm, pH: <7, D: 3

Peckoltia sp.　　　　　　　　5/402
L 102
H: S America: Venezuela.

Peckoltia sp.　　　　　　　　4/300
L 122
H: S America: Venezuela.
SD: Unknown.　　　　　　　　S: +
B: Unsuccessful.　　　　　　　F: O
T: 23–28°C, L: 10 cm, pH: 7, D: 2–3

Peckoltia sp.　　　　　　　　5/403
L 129

Peckoltia (?) sp.　　　　　　5/402
Mega clown, LDA 19
H: S America: Venezuela.
SD: Unknown.　　　　　　　　S: +
B: Unsuccessful.　　　　　　　F: H,O
T: 20–25°C, L: 10 cm, pH: 7, D: 2–3

"Peckoltia" sp.　　　　　　　5/400
LDA 2
Similar to L 75 and L 124.

CATFISHES

Peckoltia vermiculata   4/298
Vermiculated peckoltia
H: S America: Brazil: Pará.
SD: Unknown.   S: +
B: Unsuccessful.   F: O
T: 23–27°C, L: 10 cm, pH: 7, D: 2–3

Peckoltia vermiculata   4/298
Vermiculated peckoltia

CATFISHES

Peckoltia cf. *vermiculata*   4/298
LDA 1, vermiculated peckoltia
See photo on p. 5/399.

Peckoltia vittata   1/494
Striped peckoltia
H: S America: Brazil: Amazonia.
SD: Unknown.   S: +
B: Unknown.   F: H
T: 23–26°C, L: <14 cm, pH: <7, D: 2

Planiloricaria cryptodon   5/407
Cryptic whiptail suckercat
H: S America: Peru: Rio Ucayali.
SD: Not described.   S: +
B: Unknown.   F: H,O
T: 22–28°C, L: 15 cm, pH: <7, D: 3–4

Planiloricaria cryptodon   5/407
Cryptic whiptail suckercat
H: Peru: Rio Nanay.

Planiloricaria cryptodon   5/407
Cryptic whiptail suckercat

Pseudacanthicus leopardus   4/304
Xingu cactus suckercat, L 25
H: S America: Brazil: Rio Xingú.
♂: Longer odontodes.   S: +
B: Unsuccessful.   F: O
T: 24–27°C, L: >30 cm, pH: 7, D: 4

Pseudacanthicus serratus   4/304
Red-fin cactus suckercat, L 24
H: S America: Brazil: Rio Tocantins.
♂: Longer odontodes.   S: +
B: Unsuccessful.   F: O
T: 24–27°C, L: >30 cm, pH: 7, D: 4

Pseudacanthicus spinosus   3/380
Spiny cactus suckercat
H: S America: Venezuela: Orinoco Basin.
♂: Stouter odontodes.   S: +
B: Coincidentally successful.   F: H,O
T: 20–24°C, L: 12 cm, pH: 7, D: 3–4

Pseudohemiodon laticeps   5/408
Flathead suckercat
H: S America: Paraguay.
SD: Unknown.   S: +
B: There are no reports.   F: H,O?
T: 24–28°C, L: >22 cm, pH: 7, D: 2–3

Pseudohemiodon laticeps   5/408
Flathead suckercat

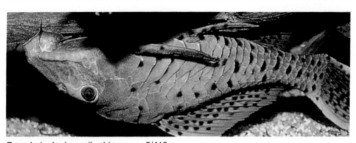

Pseudorinelepis genibarbis   5/410
L 95
H: S America: Peru: upper Amazon.   B: There are no reports.   F: H,O
SD: Genital papilla; see p. 313.   S: +   T: 23–27°C, L: >40 cm, pH: 7, D: 2–4

Pseudorinelepis genibarbis   5/410
L 95

Pterosturisoma microps   5/414

H: S America: Peru: Amazonia.
SD: Unknown.   S: +
B: Unknown.   F: H,O
T: 24–28°C, L: >15 cm, pH: 7, D: 3–4

Pterosturisoma microps   5/414

Pterosturisoma sp.   4/296

Similar in coloration to L 90.

CATFISHES

Pterygoplichthys duodecimalis   2/516
Twelve-ray sailfin pleco
H: S America: Brazil: Rio São Francisco.
SD: Unknown.   S: +
B: Unknown.   F: O
T: 22–30°C, L: 50 cm, pH: 7, D: 1

Pterygoplichthys etentaculatus   3/384
H: S America: Brazil: Rio São Francisco.
SD: Unknown.   S: +
B: Unknown.   F: H
T: 22–25°C, L: 40 cm, pH: 7, D: 2–3

Pterygoplichthys sp.   2/514

H: S America: Peru.

Ricola macrops   3/386

H: S America: Uruguay, Argentina.
♂: P fin spines slightly thicker.   S: +
B: Substrate spawner.   F: O
T: 20–24°C, L: 27 cm, pH: <7, D: 2–3

Rineloricaria castroi   3/388 (5/420)
Castro's whiptail catfish
H: S America.
♂: With "beard."   S: +
B: Cave spawner; nuclear family. F: H,O
T: 20–24°C, L: 14 cm, pH: <7, D: 2

Rineloricaria eigenmanni   5/416
Eigenmann's whiptail catfish
H: S America: Venezuela.
♂: With "beard."   S: +
B: Cs; ♂ tends spawn; fry sensitive. F: O
T: 25–29°C, L: 12 cm, pH: 7, D: 2–3

Rineloricaria fallax   1/498
Delicate whiptail catfish
H: S Am: Paraguay: La Plata region.
♂: With "beard."   S: +
B: Cs; ♂ carries eggs on oral disc.   F: H
T: 15–25°C, L: 12 cm, pH: 7, D: 2

Rineloricaria formosa   5/416

H: S Am.: Colombia: at Puerto Inirida.
♂: With "beard;" larger dorsal fin.   S: +
B: Cs; ♂ tends 20–120 eggs.   F: H,O
T: 22–26°C, L: 10 cm, pH: <7, D: 3

Rineloricaria hasemani   5/418
Haseman's whiptail catfish
H: S America: Brazil: Rio Guama.
♂: With odontodes?   S: =
B: Unsuccessful.   F: H,O
T: 24–27°C, L: >17 cm, pH: 7, D: 2–4

Leliella heteroptera   3/388

H: S America: Brazil: near Manaus.
♂: With "beard."   S: =
B: Unknown.   F: H,O
T: 20–25°C, L: 26 cm, pH: 7, D: 2–3

Rineloricaria lanceolata   2/518
Laceolate whiptail catfish
H: S America: Rio Paraguay.
♂: With "beard."   S: +
B: Cave spawner.   F: C,O
T: 20–24°C, L: 13 cm, pH: 7, D: 2–3

Rineloricaria latirostris   5/418

H: Brazil: highlands around São Paulo.
♂: With odontodes.   S: +
B: Unknown.   F: O
T: 22–25°C, L: 20 cm, pH: 7, D: 2

CATFISHES

Rineloricaria sp. aff. *latirostris* ♂ 5/420

Rineloricaria sp. aff. *latirostris* ♀ 5/420

H: Brazil: near Rio de Janeiro.
♂: With odontodes. ♀: Green-gray.   S: +
B: Cs; ♂ tends the orange eggs.   F: O
T: 22–25°C, L: 20 cm, pH: <7, D: 2–3

Rineloricaria microlepidogaster   1/498
Small-scaled whiptail catfish
H: S America: central and SE Brazil.
♂: With "beard."   S: +
B: Cs; ♂ carries eggs in "lip pouch." F: H
T: 22–26°C, L: 20 cm, pH: <7, D: 2–3

Rineloricaria morrowi   3/390
Yellow suckermouth catfish
H: S America: Peru.
♂: With "beard"?   S: +
B: Unknown.   F: H
T: 20–24°C, L: 12 cm, pH: 7, D: 2–3

Rineloricaria nigricauda   5/422
Black-tail whiptail catfish
H: S Am.: Brazil: Province Rio de Janeiro.
♂: Snout more blunt.   S: +
B: Cs; ♂ tends the 50–200 eggs.   F: H,O
T: 23–27°C, L: 15 cm, pH: 7, D: 2

Rineloricaria sp. "Red"   4/306
Red whiptail catfish
H: S America: Brazil, Rio Tocantins,...
♂: With odontodes.   S: +
B: In tubes; remove ♀.   F: O,H
T: 22–27°C, L: 14 cm, pH: 7, D: 2–4

CATFISHES

Rineloricaria teffeana   3/390
Tefe whiptail catfish
H: S America: Peru, Brazil.
♂: Broader head; slight difference. S: +
B: Unknown.   F: H,O
T: 20–25°C, L: 16 cm, pH: <7, D: 3

Schizolecis guentheri   5/422
H: SE Brazil: coastal rainforest.
♂: Slimmer.   S: +
B: Unknown.   F: H,O
T: 21–25°C, L: 4.5 cm, pH: 7, D: 3–4

Scobinancistrus aureatus   4/308
Sun suckercat, L 14
H: S America: Brazil: Rio Xingú.
♂: Odontodes on pectoral fins.   S: +
B: Unknown.   F: O
T: 24–30°C, L: 30 cm, pH: 7, D: 4

Scobinancistrus pariolispos   4/302
Golden cloud pleco, L 48
H: S America: Brazil: Rio Tocantins,...
♂: Odontodes on pectoral fins.   S: +
B: Unknown.   F: O
T: 24–30°C, L: >15 cm, pH: 7, D: 3

Spatuloricaria cf. *caquetae*   4/306
H: S America: Colombia, Ecuador.
♂: With odontodes.   S: +
B: Unsuccessful.   F: O,H
T: 22–25°C, L: 25 cm, pH: 7, D: 2–3

Sturisoma aureum ♀   2/518
Giant whiptail, golden whiptail
H: S America: Brazil: Amazonia.
♂: With odontodes: see photos.   S: +
B: Open spawner; <100 eggs.   F: H,O
T: 22–26°C, L: 22 cm, pH: 7, D: 2–3

CATFISHES

351

Sturisoma aureum   2/518
Golden whiptail ♂ guarding the spawn.

Sturisoma barbatum   2/523
Long-nosed whiptail
H: S America: Paraguay: Rio Cajuba.
♂: With "beard."   S: +
B: Not described.   F: H,L
T: 20–22°C, L: 25 cm, pH: 7, D: 2–3

Sturisoma nigrirostrum juv.   2/524
Black-nosed sturisoma
H: S America: Brazil, central Amazon.
♂: With "beard."   S: +
B: Substrate spawner; ♂ fans eggs.   F: H
T: 25–30°C, L: 24 cm, pH: <7, D: 2

Sturisoma panamense ♂   2/524
Panama sturisoma
H: C America: Panama.
♂: With "beard."   S: +
B: Substrate sp.; ♂ guards spawn.   F: H
T: 20–22°C, L: 17 cm, pH: 7, D: 2

Sturisomatichthys leightoni   3/393
Leighton's sturisoma ♂ w/ spawn
H: S America: Colombia.
♂: 1st D fin ray very elongated.   S: +
B: Substrate sp.; ♂ tends spawn.   F: H
T: 20–24°C, L: 15 cm, pH: 7, D: 2

Sturisomatichthys leightoni ♀   3/393
Leighton's sturisoma

Family Malapteruridae

The family of electric catfishes consists of only one genus and the two species presented below. They inhabit tropical Africa and the Nile. Looking at them, their most obvious characteristic is their lack of a dorsal fin.

These are the only Siluriformes which produce electrical impulses. In reality, the discharges are a series of short bursts (up to 500 per second) of more than 350 Volt, which can be sustained for approximately one second (FERRARIS, 1991). The strength of the discharge is proportional to the length of the fish. The mentioned rating is typically produced by adults and is sufficient to stun some people. Always handle large specimens with extreme caution. While tame malapterurids normally do not discharge electricity, do not take a chance.

The electricity they generate is only used to stun prey and as a defense mechanism; it does not play a role in orientation, as is the case with knifefishes (Gymnotiformes—Group 10).

The genders can be distinguished on the basis of the genital papilla and the depth of the body; i.e., males are more slender. However, so far, they have not been bred in an aquarium. In a manner reminiscent of loricariids, they spawn in caves which they excavate in clay banks. Some suspect it its a mouthbrooder (BURGESS, 1989).

As their ability to produce electricity presents a danger to any tankmate, solitary maintenance is demanded. Malapterurids' nocturnal nature must be considered when choosing the decor. Water chemistry is of secondary importance; average values are preferred. Feed in moderation, since these fishes are prone to obesity. With a correct diet, they are longevous charges which can become tame.

CATFISHES

Malapterus electricus   1/500
Electric catfish
H: Central Africa: N of the Zambezi River.
SD: Unknown.   S: –
B: Unknown.   F: C
T: 23–30°C, L: 100 cm, pH: >7, D: 4

Malapterus microstoma   3/394
Small electric catfish
H: Tropical Africa: Zaïre Basin.
SD: None.   S: –
B: Unknown.   F: C
T: 23–28°C, L: 70 cm, pH: 7, D: 3

353

Family Mochokidae

There are 10 genera and 167 species of upside-down catfishes. They are distributed only in freshwaters of Africa.

As suggested by their common name, mochokids have a reputation for swimming upside-down; however, very few species of this family actually spend much time swimming in such a manner. Most swim normally, only inverting for brief periods of time, e.g., to feed from the surface. The "true" upside-down catfishes are *Synodontis nigriventris* (p. 363) and the less familiar *Brachysynodontis batensoda* (p. 355) and *S. nigrita* (p. 362). Unlike most other fishes, they have a light dorsum and a dark ventrum and rest vertically (i.e., with the head up or down) or laying on their back.

Virtually all species hide during the day if, contrary to their nocturnal lifestyle, the aquarium is intensely illuminated and the decoration and substrate are too bright.

Brachysynodontis and *Hemisynodontis* are two very similar monotypical genera. They as well as the two dwarf synodontis species (*Microsynodontis*) should be cared for as outlined below for *Synodontis*.

Chiloglanis has 7 species. They cling to substrates with their suctorial mouth, thereby maintaining their position in the swift waters they inhabit. Accordingly, clear, oxygen-rich water is required in their captive environment. They are small and peaceful fishes which are suitable for peaceful community aquaria. Breeding has proven unsuccessful.

Euchilichthys with its four species, like *Chiloglanis*, has a suctorial mouth. As can be deduced by the fast-flowing waters of their habitat, they require high oxygen concentrations. Other maintenance needs and their reproductive biology are unknown.

Synodontis is the only genus brought to mind when the family Mochokidae is mentioned among hobbyists. It eclipses all the other genera of Mochokidae in sheer number of species (>100). These catfishes are basically peaceful, though small tankmates may be considered prey by the large species.

Although *Synodontis* spp. are adaptive and hardy fishes, those species from the Rift Valley lakes prefer hard, alkaline water (see Group 8), while inhabitants of African rivers such as the Zaïre are most content in soft and neutral to slightly acid environments.

In the case of the cave spawning *S. nigriventris*, breeding is occasionally successful. Some species spawn among plants. Apparently neither group practices brood care (FERRARIS, 1991). *S. multipunctatus* (p. 362) has a very unusual spawning method. This catfish from Lake Tanganyika "participates" in the spawning sequence of mouth-brooding cichlids, depositing its eggs among those of the cichlid. The cichlid, ignorant of the presence of the foreign eggs, picks up both groups of eggs and mouthbroods them. They are often compared to cuckoos which also plant their eggs s in the nests of others.

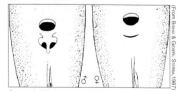

Sexual differences of *Synodontis* spp.

(From BISHAI & GIDEIRI, STERBA, 1987)

CATFISHES

Brachysynodontis batensoda   4/310

H: Africa: Nile, Chad, Niger, Sen., Gam.
♂: Slimmer.   S: +,=
B: Unsuccessful.   F: O,C
T: 23–27°C, L: 21 cm, pH: >7, D: 2–4

Chiloglanis batesii   4/316

H: Africa: Cameroon.
SD: Unknown.   S: +
B: Unsuccessful.   F: H,O
T: 20–24°C, L: <10 cm?, pH: 7, D: 2–3

Chiloglanis cameronensis   (3/395), 4/312

H: Africa: Cameroon, Gabon, Eq. Guinea.
SD: Unknown.   S: =
B: Unknown.   F: O
T: 23–27°C, L: 6 cm, pH: 7, D: 2–3

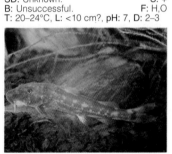

Chiloglanis deckenii   3/396

H: Africa: Kenya, Tanzania.
SD: Unknown.   S: +
B: Unknown.   F: H,O
T: 20–26°C, L: 7 cm, pH: 7, D: 2–3

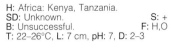

Chiloglanis cf. *deckenii*   4/312

H: Africa: Kenya, Tanzania.
SD: Unknown.   S: +
B: Unsuccessful.   F: H,O
T: 22–26°C, L: 7 cm, pH: 7, D: 2–3

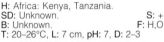

Chiloglanis cf. *neumanni*   3/396

H: Africa: Zaïre.
♂: Slimmer.   S: +
B: Unknown.   F: H,O
T: 20–26°C, L: 5 cm, pH: 7, D: 2–3

CATFISHES

355

Chiloglanis paratus   2/527

H: Africa: from the Nile to Cameroon.
♂: Slimmer.   S: +
B: Unknown.   F: H,O
T: 20–24°C, L: 8 cm, pH: 7, D: 2–3

Chiloglanis somereni   4/314

H: Africa: W Kenya: Migori River.
SD: Unknown.   S: +
B: Unknown.   F: H,O
T: 20–24°C, L: <10 cm?, pH: 7, D: 2–3

Chiloglanis sp. "Kisangani"   4/314

H: Africa: Zaïre: Kisangani.
SD: Unknown.   S: +
B: Unknown.   F: O
T: 22–26°C, L: 7 cm, pH: 7, D: 2–3

Euchilichthys cf. *boulengeri*   4/318

H: Africa: Zaïre: Kasai District.
SD: None.   S: +
B: Unsuccessful.   F: O
T: 23–26°C, L: 13 cm, pH: 7, D: 3–4

Euchilichthys guentheri   4/318

H: Africa: throughout the Zaïre Basin.
SD: None.   S: +
B: Unsuccessful.   F: H,O
T: 23–26°C, L: 7.5 cm, pH: 7, D: 3

Synodontis membranaceus   2/528
Membrane synodontis

H: Africa: Nile Basin, Chad, Senegal,...
SD: Unknown.   S: =
B: Unknown.   F: C,O
T: 22–25°C, L: 30 cm, pH: 7, D: 2–3

Microsynodontis batesii   5/424
Dwarf synodontis
H: Africa: Cameroon, Zaïre Basin.
SD: Unknown.   S: +
B: Unsucceful.   F: C
T: 22–26°C, L: 12 cm, pH: 7, D: 2–3

Microsynodontis cf. *polli*   5/424
Pretty woman dwarf synodontis
H: Africa: Nigeria.   Rare
SD: Unknown.   S: =
B: Unsuccessful.   F: C
T: 22–25°C, L: 6 cm, pH: 7, D: 2–3

Mochokus brevis   5/426
Dwarf synodontis
H: Africa: White Nile, Chad Basin, Lake No.
SD: Unknown.   S: +
B: Unknown.   F: C,O
T: 22–28°C, L: 3–4 cm, pH: 7, D: 2–3

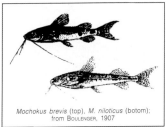

Mochokus brevis (top), *M. niloticus* (botom);
from BOULENGER, 1907

Mochokus niloticus   5/426
Nile dwarf synodontis
H: Africa: Nile and Niger Basin.
SD: Unknown.   S: +
B: Unknown.   F: C,O
T: 18–28°C, L: 6.5 cm, pH: 7, D: 3

Mochokiella paynei   2/528
Payne's synodontis
H: Africa: Sierra Leone.
♀: Fuller during spawning season. S: +
B: Unknown.   F: C
T: 22–24°C, L: 7 cm, pH: 7, D: 1

Synodontis acanthomias   2/530
Black-spotted dusky synodontis
H: Africa: Zaïre Basin.
SD: Unknown.   S: =
B: Unknown.   F: O
T: 22–24°C, L: 40 cm, pH: 7, D: 2–3

Synodontis afrofisheri   2/530

H: Africa: Nile and Zaïre Basin.
SD: Unknown.   S: +
B: Unknown.   F: C
T: 22–26°C, L: 12 cm, pH: 7, D: 1–2

Synodontis alberti   1/502

H: Africa: Zaïre Basin.
SD: Unknown.   S: =
B: Unknown.   F: O
T: 23–27°C, L: 16 cm, pH: 7, D: 2

Synodontis angelicus   1/502
Polka-dot synodontis, angel catfish
H: Africa: Zaïre, Cameroon.
SD: Unknown.   S: =
B: Unknown.   F: O
T: 20–25°C, L: 55 cm, pH: 7, D: 4

Synodontis brichardi juv.   2/532
Brichard's synodontis
H: Africa: lower Zaïre River.
SD: Unknown.   S: =
B: Unsuccessful.   F: C,O
T: 22–25°C, L: 15 cm, pH: 7, D: 2

Synodontis brichardi adult   2/532
Brichard's synodontis

Synodontis budgetti   4/320
Brown synodontis
H: Africa: Niger, Dahomey, Cameroon.
SD: Unknown.   S: –
B: Unknown.   F: C,O
T: 22–27°C, L: 40 cm, pH: 7, D: 4

CATFISHES

Synodontis camelopardalis 2/534
Panther synodontis
H: Africa: Congo Basin, Lake Victoria.
SD: Unknown.   S: +
B: Unknown.   F: C,O
T: 22–26°C, L: 15 cm, pH: 7, D: 1–2

Synodontis caudovittatus 3/398
White-finned synodontis
H: Africa: upper Nile, Sudan, Uganda.
SD: Unknown.   S: =
B: Unknown.   F: C,O
T: 21–24°C, L: 25 cm, pH: 7, D: 2

Synodontis clarias 2/534
Red-tailed synodontis
H: Africa: Nile, Chad B., Sen., Gam. Niger.
SD: Unknown.   S: =
B: Unknown.   F: O
T: 21–24°C, L: 20 cm, pH: 7, D: 2

Synodontis congicus 2/536
Congo synodontis, domino synodontis
H: Africa: Zaïre Basin.
SD: Unknown.   S: +,=
B: Unknown.   F: C,O
T: 22–25°C, L: 22 cm, pH: 7, D: 2–3

Synodontis contractus 2/536
Big-nosed upside-down catfish
H: Africa: Zaïre: Stanley Pool.
SD: Unknown.   S: +
B: Unknown.   F: C,O
T: 22–25°C, L: 7 cm, pH: 7, D: 1–2

Synodontis courteti 2/538
Dotted synodontis
H: Africa: Niger Basin, Lake Chad.
SD: Unknown.   S: =
B: Unknown.   F: C,O
T: 22–26°C, L: >25 cm, pH: 7, D: 3

CATFISHES

Synodontis decorus juv.   1/501
Decorated synodontis
H: Africa: upper Zaïre, Cameroon.
SD: Unknown.   S: +,–
B: Unknown.   F: O
T: 23–27°C, L: <24 cm, pH: 7, D: 2–3

Synodontis decorus   1/501
Decorated synodontis
Subadult.

Synodontis eburneensis   2/538
Ivory synodontis
H: Africa: Ivory Coast.
SD: Unknown.   S: =
B: Unknown.   F: O
T: 22–25°C, L: 16 cm, pH: 7, D: 2

Synodontis eupterus juv.   1/508
Feather-fin synodontis
H: Africa: White Nile, Chad Basin, Niger.
SD: Unknown.   S: =
B: Unknown.   F: O
T: 22–26°C, L: 15 cm, pH: <7, D: 2

Synodontis eupterus adult   1/508
Feather-fin synodontis

Synodontis filamentosus   2/540
Filamentous synodontis
H: Africa: Nile Basin, Chad, Niger, Volta.
♂: Very elongated fins?   S: –
B: Unknown.   F: O
T: 21–24°C, L: 17 cm, pH: 7, D: 2–3

CATFISHES

Synodontis flavitaeniatus   1/504
Yellow-stripe synodontis
H: Africa: Zaïre: Stanley Pool.
SD: Unknown.   S: +
B: Unknown.   F: O
T: 23–28°C, L: 20 cm, pH: 7, D: 1

Synodontis sp. aff. *fuelleborni*   4/320
H: Africa: Tanzania.
SD: Unknown.   S: =
B: Unknown.   F: C,O
T: 20–25°C, L: 23 cm, pH: 7, D: 3

Synodontis gambiensis   4/322
Gambia synodontis
H: Africa: Niger, Chad, Gambia.
SD: Unknown.   S: =
B: Unknown.   F: C,O
T: 22–28°C, L: 35 cm, pH: 7, D: 4

Synodontis granulosus   3/398
Granular synodontis
H: Africa: Lake Tanganyika.   E
SD: Unknown.   S: =
B: Unknown.   F: O
T: 22–26°C, L: 27 cm, pH: >7, D: 3

Synodontis greshoffi   5/428
Greshoff's synodontis
H: Africa: Congo Basin.
♂: Slimmer.   S: =
B: Successful, but no reports.   F: C, O
T: 23–27°C, L: 27 cm, pH: >7, D: 2–3

Synodontis cf. *khartoumensis* juv. 3/400
Khartoum synodontis
H: Africa: White Nile.
SD: Unknown.   S: =
B: Unknown.   F: O
T: 23–26°C, L: 30 cm, pH: 7, D: 2

CATFISHES

Synodontis cf. *koensis*   3/400

H: Africa: Guinea, Ivory Coast.
SD: Unknown.   S: =
B: Unknown.   F: C,O
T: 22–25°C, L: 15 cm, pH: 7, D: 2

Synodontis longirostris   2/540
Long-nosed synodontis
H: Africa: Zaïre River.
SD: Unknown.   S: =
B: Unknown.   F: C,O
T: 21–24°C, L: 45 cm, pH: 7, D: 2–4

Synodontis macrops   3/402
Large-eyed synodontis
H: Africa: Uganda: upper Nile Basin.
SD: Unknown.   S: =
B: Unknown.   F: C,O
T: 20–24°C, L: 18 cm, pH: 7, D: 2

Synodontis marmoratus   3/402
Marble synodontis
H: Africa: Cameroon.
SD: Unknown.   S: +
B: Unknown.   F: C,O
T: 22–25°C, L: 6 cm, pH: 7, D: 2–3

Synodontis multipunctatus   2/542
Cuckoo synodontis, multi-spot synodontis
H: Africa: Tanzania, Lake Tanganyika.
SD: Unknown.   S: =
B: Cuckoo method.   F: C,O
T: 21–25°C, L: 12 cm, pH: >7, D: 2–3

Synodontis nigrita   2/542
Black synodontis
H: Africa: Nile B., Niger, Sen., Gam., Ghana.
SD: Unknown.   S: +,=
B: Unknown, probably successful.   F: O
T: 21–26°C, L: 16 cm, pH: 7, D: 2

CATFISHES

Synodontis nigriventris   1/506
Upside-down catfish
H: Africa: Zaïre Basin: Kinshasa–Basonga.
♂: Slightly more colorful; slimmer.   S: +
B: Cave spawner; brood care.   F: C,O
T: 22–26°C, L: <10 cm, pH: 7, D: 1

Synodontis nigromaculatus juv.   3/404
Leopard synodontis
H: Africa: Zaïre, Zambezi, Lake Tanganyika,...
SD: Unknown.   S: =
B: Unknown.   F: C,O
T: 22–26°C, L: 40 cm, pH: 7, D: 2

Synodontis njassae   2/544
Njassa synodontis
H: Africa: Lake Malawi.
SD: Unknown.   S: =
B: Unknown.   F: O
T: 20–23°C, L: 12 cm, pH: >7, D: 2

Synodontis notatus   1/506
Spotted synodontis
H: Africa: Zaïre: Stanley Pool–Mousembe.
SD: Unknown.   S: +
B: Unknown.   F: O
T: 22–26°C, L: 14 cm, pH: 7, D: 2–3

Synodontis nummifer   2/544
Penny synodontis
H: Africa: lower Zaïre River, Stanley Pool.
SD: Unknown.   S: =
B: Unknown.   F: C,O
T: 22–25°C, L: 20 cm, pH: 7, D: 2–3

Synodontis obesus   3/404
Obese synodontis
H: W Africa: Guinea: coastal waters.
SD: Unknown.   S: =
B: Unknown.   F: C,O
T: 24–28°C, L: 40 cm, pH: 7, D: 2

CATFISHES

Synodontis ocellifer   4/322
Ocellated synodontis
H: Africa: Senegal to Chad.
SD: Unknown.   S: +,?
B: Unknown.   F: C,O
T: 23–27°C, L: 26 cm, pH: 7, D: 2–3

Synodontis ornatipinnis   2/546
White-barred synodontis
H: Africa: Zaïre River.
SD: Unknown.   S: –
B: Unknown.   F: C,O
T: 22–25°C, L: 22 cm, pH: 7, D: 2–3

Synodontis petricola   2/546, 3/406
Even-spotted synodontis
H: Africa: N Lake Tanganyika.   E
SD: Unknown.   S: =
B: Free-spawning.   F: C,O
T: 22–25°C, L: 11 cm, pH: 7, D: 2

Synodontis pleurops   2/548
Big-eyed synodontis, forked-tail synodontis
H: Africa: upper Zaïre River.
SD: Unknown.   S: +
B: Unknown.   F: C,O
T: 22–26°C, L: 20 cm, pH: <7, D: 1–2

Synodontis polli   3/406
Poll's upside-down catfish
H: Africa: Lake Tanganyika.   E
SD: Unknown.   S: +
B: Cuckoo method.   F: O
T: 22–26°C, L: 23 cm, pH: >7, D: 1–2

Synodontis polli   3/406
Poll's upside-down catfish
Photographed in its natural habitat.

Synodontis sp. aff. *pulcher*   5/428

Synodontis sp. aff. *pulcher*   5/428

H: Africa: lower Zaïre.
SD: Anal opening differs.   S: =
B: Unknown.   F: C,O
T: 22–28°C, L: 3–4 cm, pH: 7, D: 2–3

Synodontis rebeli   3/410
Cameroon synodontis
H: Africa: Cameroon, Sanaga River.
♂: Slimmer.   S: =
B: Unknown.   F: C,O
T: 22–25°C, L: 27 cm, pH: 7, D: 2–3

Synodontis robbianus   2/548
Spotfin synodontis, red-brown synodontis
H: Africa: Gold Coast, Niger Delta.
SD: Unknown.   S: +
B: Unknown.   F: C,O
T: 21–24°C, L: 13 cm, pH: 7, D: 1

Synodontis robertsi   5/430
Large-blotched synodontis
H: Africa: central Zaïre.
♀: Fuller while egg-laden.   S: =
B: Unsuccessful.   F: C,O
T: 23–27°C, L: 16 cm, pH: 7, D: 3

Synodontis schall   2/550
Schall's synodontis
H: Africa: widely distributed.
SD: Unknown.   S: –
B: Unknown.   F: C,O
T: 22–26°C, L: <41 cm, pH: 7, D: 3

CATFISHES

Synodontis schoutedeni   1/504, 2/550
Vermiculated synodontis
H: Africa: central Zaïre Basin.
SD: Unknown.   S: =   B: Unknown.   F: O
T: 22–26°C, L: 14 cm, pH: 7, D: 2–3

Synodontis soloni   3/409
Scissortail synodontis
H: Africa: Zaïre Basin.
SD: Unknown. S: =   B: Unknown. F: C,O
T: 23–25°C, L: 16 cm, pH: <7, D: 3

Synodontis smiti   5/432
Smit's synodontis
H: Africa: Zaïre: Ubangi and Malaba rivers.
SD: Unknown.   S: =
B: Unknown.   F: C,O
T: 23–25°C, L: 22 cm, pH: <7, D: 3

Synodontis sp.   4/311
O: Africa (ex Zaire).
H: Africa: Zaïre.

Synodontis victoriae   5/432
Victoria synodontis
H: Af.: lakes Victoria & Malagarasi, Nile.
SD: Unknown.   S: ?
B: Cuckoo method?   F: C,O
T: 23–27°C, L: 30 cm, pH: >7, D: 3–4

Synodontis waterloti   3/410
Waterlot's synodontis
H: Africa: Ghana, Ivory Coast, Liberia,...
SD: Unknown.   S: =
B: Unknown.   F: C,O
T: 22–25°C, L: 18 cm, pH: 7, D: 2–3

Family Olyridae

The family of bannertail catfishes consists of just 1 genus and 4 species. Some experts consider it part of the Bagridae. They are distributed in freshwaters of Asian from India to Burma and western Thailand.

Bannertail catfishes are rare in their natural habitat and, correspondingly, almost unknown in the aquarium hobby. The dorsal fin does not have a spine. Although they live among rocks in fast-flowing waters, they do not posses a suctorial mouth.

Olyra longicaudatus   5/434
Long-tail bannertail catfish
H: Asia: India, Burma.
SD: Unknown.   S: =
B: Unknown.   F: C!
T: 16–22°C, L: 10–13 cm, pH: 7, D: 3–4

CATFISHES

Family Pangasiidae

A certain degree of discrepancy exists concerning the number of genera and species within this family: 2 genera and 19 species (NELSON, 1994), 6 genera (BURGESS, 1991), and 8 genera with approximately 25 species (FRANKE, 1985). Shark catfishes are inhabitants of freshwaters of southern Asia. At a length of 2.5 m, *Pangasius gigas* is one of the largest Siluriformes.

Only juveniles are suitable for aquaria, and all tankmates must be of similar size. *Pangasius hypophthalmus* (syn.: *P. sutchi*) is a diurnal, lively schooling fish. Because of its activity level and size, a spacious aquarium is needed. In Asia this species, like others from the family, is cultured as a food fish.

Pangasius hypophthalmus   1/509
Siamese shark
H: Asia: Thailand: Bangkok.
SD: Unknown.   S: =
B: Artificially?   F: O
T: 22–26°C, L: <100 cm?, pH: 7, D: 3

Pangasius pangasius   3/412
Black-finned shark
H: Asia: Pakistan to Indonesia.
SD: Unknown.   S: =
B: Unknown.   F: O
T: 23–28°C, L: <130 cm, pH: 7, D: 4

Family Pimelodidae

With its 56 genera and approximately 300 species, the antenna catfishes are one of the largest families of the Siluriformes. They are widely distributed in freshwater biotopes from southern Mexico to tropical Argentina, where they inhabit small creeks, large rivers, calm lagoons, etc. Their oxygen requirement varies accordingly.

Many of the catfishes of this family are large and therefore spatially demanding, but some are an apt size for community aquaria. When considering purchasing juveniles, remember that the majority of species are rapid-growing predators. Small fishes will inevitably be devoured. Breeding successes have been elusive, which is perfectly understandable for the large species, but inexplicable for the small species (FERRARIS, 1991). GRUNDMAN and JOB induced *Microglanis iheringi* to spawn through hormone injections. About 1000 eggs were deposited. The water was slightly acid with a hardness of 8°–12°dGH, values typical for this family (FRANKE, 1985). This success appears to have been an exception.

Even though the large Pimelodidae, *Colossoma* spp., *Cichla* spp., and *Arapaima gigas* constitute the group of most important food fishes of Amazonia, the problematic breeding of this family removes them from consideration as culture subjects. *Rhamdia*, a genus that has been experimentally cultured in southern South America, must also be induced to spawn with hormones.

Antenna catfishes are twilight and night active, which should be reflected in the aquarium's decor, i.e., a dark substrate, hiding places, subdued illumination, etc. The aquarium must be sufficiently wide that the long barbels (antennas) cannot bridge the width, lest panic ensues. Open swimming space is just as important to this family as hiding places. Recently, juveniles of several large species have appeared in pet stores. Whether they are the result of successful breeding endeavors or wild captures could not be determined. Do not be lured by beautiful markings and spry behavior—they quickly grow to mammoth proportions with an appetite to match.

Aguarunichthys torosus   5/435
Bull antenna catfish
H: S America: Peru: Dept. Amazonas.
SD: Not described.   S: =
B: Unknown.   F: C
T: 22–27°C, L: 25 cm?, pH: <7, D: 3

Brachyplatystoma juruense adult   4/324
Gold-zebra antenna catfish
H: S America: Peru, Brazil.
SD: Unknown.   S: –
B: Unknown.   F: C
T: 22–27°C, L: <200 cm, pH: 7, D: 4

Brachyplatystoma juruense juv.   4/324
Gold-zebra antenna catfish

Brachyrhamdia imitator   2/552
False cory
H: S America: Venezuela. Colombia?
SD: Unknown.   S: =
B: Unknown.   F: C,O
T: 21–25°C, L: 7.5 cm, pH: 7, D: 1–2

Brachyrhamdia marthae   3/413, 5/436
Blue imitator catfish
H: S America: Peru: upper Amazon.
SD: Unknown.   S: =
B: Unknown.   F: C,O
T: 24–26°C, L: 9 cm, pH: <7, D: 2

Brachyrhamdia meesi   3/414
Mees' pimelodid
H: S America: Brazil: Belém?
SD: Unknown.   S: =
B: Unknown.   F: C,O
T: 24–26°C, L: 8 cm, pH: <7, D: 2

Brachyrhamdia sp.   5/441

Undescribed species.

Duopalatinus malarmo   3/414
Malarmo catfish
H: S America: Venezuela.
SD: Unknown.   S: =
B: Unknown.   F: C
T: 24–28°C, L: <65 cm, pH: <7, D: 2–3

CATFISHES

Hemisorubim platyrhynchos   2/552
Spotted shovelnose catfish
H: S America: Ven., Sur., Brazil, Paraguay.
SD: Unknown.   S: =
B: Unknown.   F: C
T: 20–22°C, L: 35 cm, pH: 7, D: 3–4

Heptapterus mustelinus   5/436
Slinky rockcat
H: S America: SE Brazil. Suriname?
SD: Unknown.   S: +
B: Unknown.   F: C
T: 18–24°C, L: 9 cm, pH: ≪7, D: 3

Imparfinis longicauda   3/416
Long-tailed antenna catfish
H: S America: Ecuador, Peru.
SD: Unknown.   S: =
B: Unknown.   F: C,O
T: 20–24°C, L: 15 cm, pH: <7, D: 2

Imparfinis minutus   3/416

H: S America: Guianas, W Brazil.
SD: Unknown.   S: =
B: Unknown.   F: C,O
T: 24–28°C, L: 12 cm, pH: <7, D: 2

Leiarius marmoratus ♂   4/326
Marble antenna catfish
H: S America: Peru, Brazil.
♂: Slimmer.   S: =
B: Unknown.   F: C
T: 24–26°C, L: <60 cm, pH: <7, D: 3–4

Lophiosilurus alexandri   5/438

H: S America: Brazil: Amazonia.
SD: Unknown.   S: –
B: Unknown.   F: C!
T: 22–27°C, L: >20 cm, pH: <7, D: 4

Lophiosilurus alexandri   5/438

Head

Merodontotus tigrinus   4/326
Tiger-striped catfish
H: S America: Brazil: Rio Madeira.
SD: Unknown.   **S:** =
B: Unknown.   **F:** C
T: 22–26°C, **L:** >50 cm, **pH:** 7, **D:** 4

Microglanis iheringi   2/554
South American bumblebee catfish
H: S America: Venezuela, Colombia.
SD: Not described.   **S:** +
B: Unknown.   **F:** C,O
T: 21–25°C, **L:** 6 cm, **pH:** 7, **D:** 1–2

Microglanis parahybae   3/418

H: S Am.: SE Brazil, Argentina, Paraguay.
SD: Unknown.   **S:** =
B: Unknown.   **F:** C,O
T: 21–26°C, **L:** 9 cm, **pH:** 7, **D:** 1–2

Perrunichthys perruno   2/556
Reticulated pimelodid
H: S America: Venezuela, Brazil.
SD: Unknown.   **S:** =
B: Undescribed.   **F:** C
T: 21–25°C, **L:** 60 cm, **pH:** <7, **D:** 3–4

Phractocephalus hemioliopterus   2/556
Redtail catfish
H: S America: Venezuela, Guyana, Brazil.
SD: Unknown.   **S:** =
B: Impossible in an aquarium.   **F:** O
T: 20–26°C, **L:** <60 cm, **pH:** <7, **D:** 4

CATFISHES

371

Pimelodella chagresi   5/440

H: C America: Costa Rica, Panama.
SD: Unknown.   S: =
B: Unsuccessful.   F: C,O
T: 23–26°C, L: >10 cm, pH: 7, D: 2–3

Pimelodella gracilis   2/558
Slender pimelodella
H: S America: Venezuela, Brazil.
SD: Unknown.   S: =
B: Unsuccessful.   F: C,O
T: 20–24°C, L: 30 cm, pH: 7, D: 2–3

Pimelodella lateristriga   2/558
Striped pimelodellla
H: S America: E Amazon Basin.
SD: Unknown.   S: =
B: Unknown.   F: C,O
T: 20–24°C, L: 20 cm, pH: 7, D: 2–3

Pimelodella rambarrani   3/418
Masked imitator catfish
H: S America: Brazil: Rio Unini.
♂: Slimmer.   S: =
B: Unknown.   F: C,O
T: 24–26°C, L: 7 cm, pH: <7, D: 2

Pimelodella sp.   5/440

Pimelodella steindachneri (?)   5/442
Steindachner's antenna catfish
H: S America: Brazil: Rio Madeira.
SD: Unknown.   S: =
B: Unknown.   F: C
T: 20–26°C, L: 15 cm, pH: 7, D: 3

Pimelodus albofasciatus 2/560
White striped pimelodus
H: S America: Suriname, Guyana.
SD: Unknown. S: =
B: Unknown. F: C
T: 22–25°C, L: 25 cm, pH: <7, D: 3

Pimelodus blochii 1/510
Dusky pimelodus
H: S America: Panama to Brazil.
SD: Unknown. S: =
B: Unknown. F: C,O
T: 20–26°C, L: <30 cm, pH: 7, D: 1–2

Pimelodus cf. *blochii* 5/442
Dusky pimelodus
H: Northern S America.
SD: Unknown. S: =
B: Unknown. F: C,O
T: 18–26°C, L: 15–30 cm, pH: 7, D: 3

Pimelodus maculatus 2/560
Spotted pimelodus
H: S America: Brazil, Paraguay.
SD: Unknown. S: =
B: Unknown. F: C
T: 20–24°C, L: 26 cm, pH: 7, D: 2–3

Pimelodus ornatus 2/562
Ornate pimelodus
H: S America: widely distributed.
SD: Unknown. S: =
B: Unknown. F: C,O
T: 24–25°C, L: 28 cm, pH: 7, D: 3

Pimelodus pictus 2/562
Angelicus pimelodus
H: S America: Colombia.
SD: Unknown. S: +
B: Unknown. F: O
T: 22–25°C, L: >11 cm, pH: <7, D: 2

CATFISHES

373

Pimelodus sp. "green"   5/445
Green antenna catfish
H: S America: Peru: Requena District.
SD: Unknown.   S: ?
B: Unknown.   F: C
T: 23–28°C, L: 20–25 cm, pH: 7, D: 3–4

Pinirampus pirinampu   3/420
Long-finned catfish
H: S America: Venezuela to Paraguay.
SD: Unknown.   S: =
B: Unknown.   F: C
T: 22–28°C, L: <120 cm, pH: 7, D: 4

Platystomatichthys sturio   2/564
Sturgeon catfish
H: S America: entire Amazon Basin.
SD: Unknown.   S: =
B: Unknown.   F: C
T: 21–25°C, L: 40 cm, pH: 7, D: 3–4

Pseudopimelodus nigricaudus   4/328
Mottled marbled catfish
H: S America: Suriname: Sipaliwini region.
SD: Unknown.   S: –
B: Unknown.   F: C!
T: 20–25°C, L: 35 cm, pH: 7, D: 4

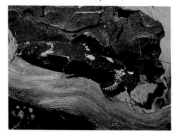

Pseudopimelodus raninus raninus   2/564
Frog marbled catfish
H: S America: widely distributed.
SD: Not described.   S: =
B: Unsuccessful.   F: C
T: 21–25°C, L: 10 cm, pH: <7, D: 1–2

Pseudopimelodus zungaro bufonius   2/566
Black-banded marbled catfish
H: S America: Col., Ven., Guy., Sur., Brazil.
SD: Unknown.   S: =
B: Unknown.   F: C
T: 20–24°C, L: 18 cm, pH: 7, D: 2–3

CATFISHES

Pseudoplatystoma fasciatum   1/510
Tiger-striped shovelnose catfish
H: S America: Venezuela, Peru, Paraguay.
SD: Unknown.   S: –
B: Unknown.   F: C
T: 24–28°C, L: <100 cm, pH: 7, D: 3

Pseudoplatystoma tigrinum   4/328
Tiger shovelnose
H: S America: Amazon Basin.
SD: Unknown.   S: =
B: Unknown.   F: O
T: 22–26°C, L: 60 cm, pH: 7, D: 4

Rhamdia guatemalensis   2/566
Guatemala rhamdid
H: C&S America: S Mexiko to Colombia.
SD: Unknown.   S: =
B: Unknown.   F: O
T: 22–28°C, L: 28 cm, pH: 7, D: 2

Rhamdia laticauda laticauda   3/420
Long-tailed rhamdid
H: Central and South America.
SD: Unknown.   S: +
B: Unknown.   F: O
T: 24–28°C, L: 12 cm, pH: >7, D: 1

Sciades pictus   2/554
Sailfin pimelodid
H: S America: Amazon region.
SD: Unknown.   S: =
B: Unknown.   F: C
T: 22–26°C, L: 60 cm, pH: 7, D: 4

Sorubim lima   1/512
Shovelnose catfish
H: S America: Amazon region.
SD: Unknown.   S: =
B: Unknown.   F: C
T: 23–30°C, L: <60 cm, pH: 7, D: 4

CATFISHES

375

Family Plotosidae

There are 9 genera and 32 species of eeltail catfishes. Their area of distribution includes marine, brackish, and fresh waters of the Indian Ocean and the western Pacific from Japan to Australia and Fiji. According to NELSON (1994), about half the species occur in freshwaters of Australia and New Guinea.

Characteristically, the many-rayed anal fin is fused with the caudal fin, creating one fringelike fin, which in some species extends far onto the dorsum.

The genus *Plotosus,* among others, has poison glands associated with the dorsal and pectoral spines. Caution!—the poison is extremely toxic; human mortality has been reported!

Marine species are cave spawners. As a form of defense, juveniles congregate into dense clusters. With age, they loose their gregariousness, becoming progressively more solitary-natured. Freshwater species excavate a nest in a gravel substrate, deposit their eggs therein, and practice brood care.

All larger species are considered food fishes, but they are not specifically bred for this purpose. *Plotosus anguillaris* and *P. canius* are marine species which are often part of the harvest of *Chanos chanos* ponds in Indonesia. Of the freshwater species, *Tandanus tandanus* is the main focus of aquaculture of plotosids in Australia. It has been experimentally bred and raised in ponds and has demonstrated potential. According to BURGESS (1989), *Anodontoglanis dahli,* a species endemic to Australia, has exceptionally palatable pink flesh. The future of this family in the field of aquaculture seems bright.

The most difficult part of aquarium maintenance is obtaining the fish, since they are rarely offered in the trade. They are unselective omnivores. A dark aquarium with numerous hiding places and average water chemistry is generally suitable. Always maintain a small group.

Neosilurus argenteus   2/568
Silver eeltail catfish
H: Australia: inner territories.   B: Unknown.   F: C,O
SD: Unknown.   S: =   T: 5–30°C, L: 20 cm, pH: >7, D: 2–3

Neosilurus ater juvenile   2/568
Black tandan
H: New Guinea, N Australia: in rivers.
SD: Unknown.   S: +,=
B: Unknown.   F: C,O
T: 22–30°C, L: 50 cm, pH: 7, D: 2

Neosilurus glencoensis   2/570
Yellow-fin tandanus
H: NW to NE Australia.   Fw
SD: Unknown.   S: =
B: Unknown.   F: C,O
T: 22–28°C, L: 20 cm, pH: 7, D: 1–2

Neosilurus glencoensis juvenile   2/570
Yellow-fin tandanus
The yellow fringe on the fins disappears
with age.

Plotosus bostocki   5/446
Cobbler
H: Australia. 1 teaspoon salt/10 l water.
♀: Fuller during spawning season.   S: =?
B: Unknown.   F: C,O
T: 24–26°C, L: >12 cm?, pH: 7, D: 2–3

Porochilus rendahli   5/446
Rendahl's tandan
H: New Guinea, Australia.
♀: Fuller at spawning time.   S: =?
B: Unknown.   F: C
T: 18–20°C, L: >12 cm, pH: >7, D: 1–4

Tandanus tandanus   2/570
Dewfish
H: Australia: Tweed River, Murray-Darling.
♂: Triangular urogenital papilla.   S: =
B: Nonadhesive eggs in gravel pit. F:C,O
T: 5–25°C, L: 90 cm, pH: 7, D: 4

CATFISHES

Parailia pellucida, Nile glass catfish; see p. 379.

Family Schilbeidae

The family of glass catfishes is comprised of 18 genera and approximately 45 species (NELSON, 1994). In 1985, FRANKE acknowledged 40 species within the family. Their area of distribution is Africa and southern Asia, with about $^3/_4$ of the species in Africa.

As suggested by the common name, the vitreous members of Schilbeidae have brought fame to the family. The genus *Kryptopterus* is very similar in appearance to the transparent Schilbeidae, but as a Siluridae, there are certain anatomical differences, e.g., one pair of barbels versus the four pairs of glass catfishes.

Smaller members of the family are eminently suitable for the aquarium. Their active diurnal lifestyle, acceptance of commercial dry diets, and peaceful behavior in front of other small species practically assures their popularity. Even though their coloration cannot be described as stunning, the contrasting linear markings of some species are rather attractive. Of course, it is exactly the total lack of coloration—that is, their crystalline transparency—that makes them so popular. Their gregarious nature must be respected; a small school of 4–6 animals is strongly advised.

Eutropiellus buffei is practically the only species which has been aquarium bred without hormone injections. The approximately 100 eggs are scattered among fine-leaved plants. The parents should be transferred thereafter to curtail spawn predation.

Since the majority of glass catfishes are omnivores with carnivorous tendencies, feeding is straightforward. Quality flake foods are readily accepted after a short acclimation. The diet, however, must not consist solely of flake foods: the aquarist should bear the inconvenience a couple of times each week and offer live foods.

Eutropiellus buffei 1/513, 2/572
Swallow-tail glass catfish
H: Africa: Nigeria, Cameroon. Gabon? Zaïre?
♂: Slimmer. S: +
B: Among plants; <100 eggs. F: C,O
T: 22–27°C, L: 8 cm, pH: 7, D: 2–3

Horabagrus brachysoma 5/448

H: Asia: S India: state of Kerala.
SD: Not described. S: =
B: Unknown. F: C,O
T: 23–25°C, L: 13 cm, pH: 7, D: 2

Parailia congica 2/572
African glass catfish
H: Africa: Zaïre: Stanley Pool.
SD: Unknown. S: +
B: Unsuccessful. F: C,O
T: 23–26°C, L: 9 cm, pH: 7, D: 2

Parailia pellucida 2/574
Nile glass catfish, African glass catfish
H: Africa: headwaters of the Nile.
SD: Unknown. S: +
B: Unknown. F: C
T: 25–28°C, L: 15 cm, pH: 7, D: 3

Pareutropius longifilis 4/330

H: Africa: Tanzania.
♂: Very slender; somewhat smaller. S: ?
B: Unknown. F: O
T: 23–27°C, L: 10 cm, pH: 7, D: 2–3

CATFISHES

Platytropius siamensis   2/574
False siamese shark
H: Asia: Thailand.
♂: Fleshy appendage prior to anus.   S: =
B: Unknown.   F: O
T: 21–25°C, L: 20 cm, pH: 7, D: 2

Schilbe brevianalis   4/331
H: Af.: coastal rivers of Nigeria, Cameroon.
♂: Slimmer.   S: +
B: With hormones; 3000 eggs.   F: C
T: 24–27°C, L: <13 cm, pH: 7, D: 2–3

Schilbe grenfelli   4/332
H: Africa: Zaïre Basin.
SD: Unknown.   S: ?
B: Unknown.   F: C,O
T: 23–26°C, L: 50 cm, pH: 7, D: 3

Schilbe intermedius   1/514
Striped glass catfish
H: W Af.: Nile, Niger, lakes Victoria & Chad.
SD: Unknown.   S: =
B: Successful (w/ hormones?).   F: O
T: 23–27°C, L: 35 cm, pH: 7, D: 2

Schilbe marmoratus   3/422
African shoulder-spot catfish
H: Africa: Zaïre.
♀: Fuller at spawning time.   S: =
B: Unknown.   F: C,O
T: 24–26°C, L: >15 cm, pH: 7, D: 2–3

Silonia silondia   5/449
H: Asia: India: lower Ganges.
SD: Unknown.   S: ?
B: Migrates into headwaters.   F: C,O
T: 23–26°C, L: 180 cm, pH: 7, D: 4

Kryptopterus bicirrhis. Drawing from C. & V., 1839, Volume 14, p. 272.

Family Siluridae

There are approximately 12 genera and 100 species of sheath catfishes. The family is widely distributed in Asia, but only 2 species (genus *Silurus*) occur in Europe. One of the two, *Siluris glanis*, is the largest of all Siluriformes with a confirmed record weight of 330 kg and a length of 5 m (NELSON, 1994). Sheath catfishes are predominantly freshwater inhabitants; a few enter brackish waters.

Aquaristically speaking, species of the genera *Kryptopterus* and *Ompok*, are the most popular members of the family. These are the glass catfishes, not to be confused with the glass catfishes of the Schilbeidae. Unlike the Schilbeidae, Siluridae lack an adipose fin as well as nasal barbels.

When kept individually or in small groups, they are timid and adopt a cryptic, bottom-oriented lifestyle. Properly maintained animals are mid-water, diurnal schooling fishes. Large species are inapt for the aquarium—a group of 80 cm fish just cannot be accomodated in a home aquarium.

They accept dry commercial diets, which facilitates care; however, the diet should be supplemented with insect larvae and frozen foods.

With the notable exception of *Kryptopterus minor*, few species have been bred. Even in the case of *K. minor*, success seems to be coincidental. The simulation of annual cycles seems to play a significant role.

381

The larger members of the family are typically less sociable and more bottom-oriented. Since they are also comparably more predatory, they are more difficult to associate with other fishes.

Some Siluridae are cultured as food fishes; for example, *Ompok bimaculatus* in Asia and *Silurus glanis* in eastern Europe. The former must be induced to spawn through hormone injections.

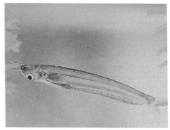

Kryptopterus cryptopterus   2/576

H: SE Asia: Thailand, Sumatra, Borneo.
SD: Unknown.   S: =
B: Nature: June/July.   F: C
T: 22–25°C, L: 20 cm, pH: 7, D: 3

Kryptopterus macrocephalus   2/576
Striped glass catfish
H: SE Asia: Borneo, Sumatra.
SD: Unknown.   S: =
B: Unknown.   F: C,O
T: 22–26°C, L: 11 cm, pH: 7, D: 1–2

Kryptopterus minor   1/515
Ghost catfish, erroneously *K. bicirrhis*
H: SE Asia: Thailand, Malaysia, Indonesia.
SD: Unknown.   S: +
B: Among fine-leaved plants.   F: C,O
T: 21–26°C, L: 8 cm, pH: 7, D: 3

Ompok bimaculatus   1/516
Two-spot glass catfish
H: SE Asia: Nepal, Thailand, Indonesia,...
SD: Unknown.   S: =
B: In ponds.   F: O
T: 20–26°C, L: <45 cm, pH: 7, D: 2

Ompok eugeneiatus   2/578
Borneo glass catfish
H: SE Asia: Sumatra, Borneo.
♂: Longer dorsal fin?   S: =
B: Unknown.   F: C
T: 20–24°C, L: 18 cm, pH: <7, D: 3

CATFISHES

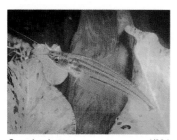

Ompok sabanus   4/334
Tawny glass catfish
H: SE Asia: Indonesia, Malaysia, Borneo.
♂: Hooklets on P fin spines?   S: =
B: Unknown.   F: C,O
T: 23–27°C, L: 18 cm, pH: 7, D: 3–4

Parasilurus asotus   5/450
Amur catfish
H: Asia: Amur Basin.
SD: Unknown.   S: –
B: Pit among roots; brood care ♂.   F: C,O
T: 5–25°C, L: 100 cm, pH: 7, D: 4

Silurus glanis   3/423
Wels
H: Europe, Asia.
♀: Ventrally fuller at spawning time.   S: –
B: Nat: May to July; pit as nest.   F: C
T: 4–20°C, L: <250 cm, pH: 7, D: 4

Silurus soldatovi   5/450
Russian wels
H: Asia: Amur from Siberia to China.
SD: Unknown.   S: –
B: Artificially bred for aquaculture.   F:C,O
T: 5–25°C, L: <400 cm, pH: 7, D: 4

Wallago attu   2/578
Helicopter catfish
H: Asia: Java, Sum., Thai., India, Bur.,...
SD: Unknown.   S: =
B: Unknown.   F: O
T: 22–25°C, L: 90 cm, pH: 7, D: 4

Wallago leeri

H: Asia: Borneo, Sumatra.
SD: Unknown.   S: –
B: Unknown.   F: C
T: 22–27°C, L: >50 cm, pH: 7, D: 4

CATFISHES

Family Sisoridae

The family of the Asian hillstream catfishes is comprised of about 20 genera and around 85 species. They are inhabitants of freshwaters of southern Asia. With the exception of *Bagarius* spp., which comprises large to very large species (in excess of 2 meters), Sisoridae are small- to medium-sized fishes.

As indicated by their common name, these fishes are adapted to life in swiftly flowing waters. The majority of species has a ventrally positioned mouth; in some it is even suctorial. The inferior mouth allows the fish to rasp algae from stony substrates. Once again the *Bagarius* are exceptional, as they are predators, not algivores. To better withstand the strong current of their habitat, sisorids have a flattened head and folds of skin in their pectoral region that act as an adhesive organ.

There is little information concerning care in the aquarium, largely because of the lack of imports. As can be deduced from its natural habitat—i.e., swift, oxygen-rich waters—a current and optimal oxygen concentrations are essential to successful husbandry. Water hardness and pH are of secondary importance. Those that originate from higher elevations—sisorids occur up to 1500 m above sea level—demand cool temperatures.

All smaller species have proven to be peaceful fishes which can be kept in community with fishes of like nature. Large tankmates are contraindicated. The rest of their habits are rather diverse—there are loners as well as schooling fishes and diurnal as well as nocturnal species. Their reproductive biology is presently unknown.

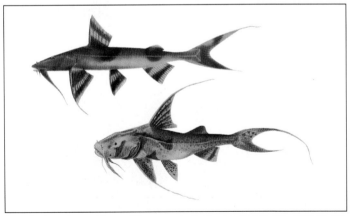

Bagarius bagarius and *B. yarellii* (one species?). Drawing from C. & V., 1840, pl. 433.

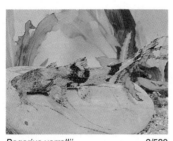

Bagarius yarrellii   2/580
Devil catfish
H: Asia: India, Bur., Thai., Viet., Sum., Bor.
SD: Unknown.   S: –
B: Unknown.   F: C
T: 18–25°C, L: <200 cm, pH: 7, D: 3–4

Conta conta ♂   3/424

H: Asia: India, Bangladesh.
♂: Upper C fin ray longer; w/ spots. S: =
B: Unknown.   F: O
T: 18–28°C, L: 12 cm, pH: 7, D: 2

Erethistes pusillus   4/336

H: Asia: India: Assam.
SD: Unknown.   S: +
B: Unknown.   F: C
T: 22–24°C, L: 6 cm, pH: 7, D: 2

Gagata cenia   3/426

H: Asia: Pak., India, Bngl., Burma, Nepal.
SD: Unknown.   S: =
B: Unknown.   F: C
T: 20–24°C, L: 30 cm, pH: <7, D: 2–3

Gagata schmidti (= *G. cenia*)   2/580
Clown catfish
H: Asia: Sumatra.
SD: Unknown.   S: +
B: Unknown.   F: C
T: 20–22°C, L: 7 cm, pH: 7, D: 1–2

Glyptosternum reticulatum   3/426

H: Asia: Afg., Pakistan, China, S CIS States.
SD: Unknown.   S: +
B: Unknown.   F: O
T: 12–24°C, L: 15 cm, pH: 7, D: 3

CATFISHES

385

Glyptothorax cf. *lampris*   5/452

H: Asia: Thailand.
SD: Unknown.   S: =
B: Unknown.   F: C,O
T: 20–24°C, L: 15 cm, pH: 7, D: 3

Glyptothorax cf. *laosensis*   5/452
Laos hillstream catfish
H: Asia: Thailand, Laos: Mekong.
SD: Unknown.   S: +
B: Unsuccessful.   F: H,O
T: 18–23°C, L: 15 cm, pH: 7, D: 3

Glyptothorax platypogon   3/428
Brown hillstream catfish
H: Asia: Java, Sumatra, Borneo, Malaysia.
SD: Unknown.   S: +
B: Unknown.   F: O
T: 18–22°C, L: 10 cm, pH: <7, D: 2–3

Glyptothorax trilineatus   3/428
Three-striped hillstream catfish
H: Asia: Thai., Burma, India, Pak., Bngl.
SD: Unknown.   S: ?
B: Unknown.   F: ?
T: 10–20°C, L: <30 cm, pH: <7, D: 4

Hara hara   3/430

H: Asia: India, Nepal, Bangladesh.
SD: Unknown.   S: +
B: Unknown.   F: O
T: 12–28°C, L: 7 cm, pH: 7, D: 2–3

Hara jerdoni   4/335

H: Asia: Bangladesh.
♂: Smaller and slimmer.   S: +
B: Unsuccessful.   F: O
T: 18–24°C, L: <3.5 cm, pH: 7, D: 3–4

CATFISHES

Family Trichomycteridae

The family of parasitic catfishes contains 8 subfamilies, 36 genera, and 155 species (NELSON, 1994). Two of these subfamilies—Stegophilinae and Vandelliinae—contain parasitic species. Much like the piranhas of the Characidae, these parasitic species have brought notoriety to their family. Trichomycterids are distributed in freshwaters of Costa Rica, Panama, and expansive areas of South America.

The approximately 30 species of the subfamily Stegophilinae feed on the mucus and scales of other fishes, whereas the roughly 18 species of the subfamily Vandelliinae feed on the blood of other fishes. Some species even enter the branchial chamber of large fishes to feed therein on the blood of the branchial lamellae. It is these latter species—locally known as "candiru" or "canero"—which are so famous. Conditioned by their mode of feeding, they swim towards nitrogenous excretions and against localized currents in the hope of reaching a branchial chamber. Once inside, they splay their ocular spines to anchor themselves against the respiratory current. Trichomycteridae have no fin spines.

Occasionally, these catfishes mistakenly enter the urinary tract of mammals, thereby posing a threat to humans as well. Just as if they had entered a branchial cavity, they instinctively spread their ocular spines and lock themselves in place. They quickly die and cannot be pushed or worked out of the urinary tract. This extremely painful situation must be rectified through surgery posthaste. Snug-fitting swim trunks and refraining from urinating in waters suspected of containing such parasitic fishes is probably sufficient to circumvent any problems. Because of their dietary requirements they are absolutely inadequate as aquarium residents.

The vast majority of species in this family are well suited for aquaria. As small- to moderate-sized "normal" fishes that feed on aquatic insects and their larvae as well as worms and crustacea, their requirements are not very unusual and easily satisfied in captivity. The aquarium's substrate should consist of sand, since many of these catfishes bury themselves from time to time. Some species are also diurnal and appreciate warm temperatures, while those species from higher elevations require oxygen-rich, cool water (refer to "T:" of the individual species descriptions).

note: The "parasitic status" of each species is indicated below the AQUARIUM ATLAS page number (refer also to F:).

Bullockia maldonadoi   3/431
Chilenian parasitic catfish   Non-p
H: S America: central Chile.
SD: Unknown.   S: +
B: Unknown.   F: O

387

Eremophilus mutisii   4/337
                                         Non-p

H: S America: Colombia.
♂: Probably slimmer.   S: +
B: Unknown.   F: C
T: 22–28°C, L: 15 cm, pH: 7, D: 3

Ochmacanthus orinoco   4/338
Orinoco catfish   Unknown

H: S America: Venezuela: Orinoco.
SD: Unknown.   S: ?
B: Unknown.   F: C
T: 23–26°C, L: 5 cm, pH: 7, D: 3–4

Pygidium cf. *stellatum*   3/432
                                         Non-p

H: S America: Brazil: Puerto Barrios.
SD: Unknown.   S: +
B: Unknown.   F: C,O
T: 22–24°C, L: 4 cm, pH: 7, D: 2–3

Ochmacanthus alternus   5/454
Quiribana parasitic catfish   P

H: S America: Colombia, Venezuela.
SD: Unknown.   S: –
B: Unknown.   F: C,P
T: 22–26°C, L: 7 cm, pH: <7, D: 3–4

Pseudostegophilus nemurus   4/338
Blue-yellow parasitic catfish   P

H: S America: Brazil: Rio Mamoré.
SD: Unknown.   S: –
B: Unknown.   F: P!
T: 26–28°C, L: 15 cm, pH: <7, D: 4

Trichogenes longipinnis   5/454
Long-fin catfish   Non-p

H: Am.: Brazil: Rio de Janeiro, São Paulo.
♀: Somewhat fuller and paler.   S: =
B: Unsuccessful.   F: C
T: 20–24°C, L: <12 cm, pH: 7, D: 2–3

CATFISHES

Trichomycterus banneaui maracaiboensis
5/456
H: S America: Venezuela: Rio San Juan.
SD: Unknown.   S: +
B: Unknown.   F: C,O
T: 22–25°C, L: 6 cm, pH: 7, D: 3

Trichomycterus sp. cf. *zonatus*   5/456
H: S America: Colombia, Peru.
♂: Slimmer.   S: ?
B: Unknown.   F: C,(P?)
T: 22–26°C, L: 10 cm, pH: <7, D: 2–3

Trichomycterus cf. *vermiculatus*   5/458
Vermiculated parasitic catfish   Non-p
H: S Am.: Rio Paraguay and tributaries.
♂: Slimmer.   S: +
B: Unknown.   F: O
T: 20–24°C, L: 10 cm, pH: 7, D: 2–3

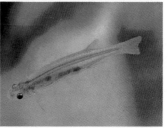

Tridensimilis brevis   1/517
                                        Unknown
H: S America: Amazon region.
SD: Unknown.   S: +
B: Unknown.   F: C,L (P?)
T: 20–30°C, L: 3 cm, pH: <7, D: 2

Tridensimilis venezuelae   5/458
Venezuelan parasitic catfish   P
H: S America: Venezuela, Brazil.
SD: Unknown.   S: +
B: Unknown.   F: P!
T: 22–28°C, L: 2.5 cm, pH: <7, D: 3–4

Vandellia (?) sp.   5/460
                                           P
H: S America: Brazil.
SD: Unknown.   S: +
B: Unknown.   F: P!
T: 23–28°C, L: 4 cm, pH: <7, D: 3–4

CATFISHES

KILLIFISHES

Nothobranchius melanospilus (see p. 434) diving into the substrate to spawn (♂ red).

Origin/Taxonomy

The taxonomic classification within the order Cyprinodontiformes is constantly exposed to new discoveries and interpretations. According to NELSON (1994), there are 8 families, 88 genera, and approximately 807 species within this order.

In the course of publishing the AQUARIUM ATLAS series, the systematics of this group changed significantly. Pages 583 and 434 of Volume 2 and Volume 3, respectively, show outlines of the classification prevalent at the time of publication. For the INDEX we have decided to follow NELSON. The work by COSTA (1996) could not be considered here. It will be presented in Volume 6 of the AQUARIUM ATLAS.

To correlate the various volumes of the AQUARIUM ATLAS, the INDEX alphabetizes the subfamilies of Group 5 under their respective families. The fact that the families Anablepidae, Goodeidae, and Poeciliidae are now found in both groups of Cyprinodontiformes (Groups 5 and 6) could be somewhat confusing aquaristically; however, the characteristic of being an egg-layer or a livebearer is divided systematically at the level of subfamily at the current time. The ricefishes—now classified as the subfamily Oryziinae within the family Adrianichthyidae of the order Beloniformes—are found in Group 10 (pp. 866 ff.).

Below is the classification of all Cyprinodontiformes (including livebearing toothcarps—Group 6):

KILLIFISHES

KILLIFISHES

Geographic Distribution

Egg-laying toothcarps are primarily inhabitants of freshwaters, but they are also found in brackish waters and even coastal marine areas. Since the majority are tiny in stature, small bodies of water and shore areas are their biotopes of choice. Killifishes are famous for the way they have adapted to ensure the survival of the species through the brutal dry seasons of their natural habitat, when the bodies of water they inhabit so frequently fall dry. While all the fish die, their eggs resist desiccation and hatch the following rainy season.

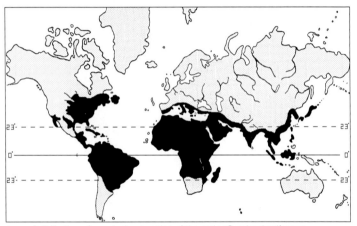

Area of ditribution of egg-laying species of the order Cyprinodontiformes.

Generalities

With few exceptions, killifishes are small fishes of less than 10 cm length. The stunning coloration possessed by the males of so many of the species largely compensates for the idiosyncracies involved in maintenance and reproduction. Males are often extremely aggressive towards conspecific males and those of similar species. In general, only one male and a group of females can be housed in a medium-sized aquarium rich in hiding places. (More detailed information on social behavior and maintenance can be found in the family/subfamily descriptions.) Take heed: when transporting the fish home, each male must be individually packed. Few killifishes school. One exception are the lampeyes. Most can be associated with peaceful fishes of similar size. As long as the prospective tankmate is dissimilar in form and color, it is normally ignored.

Species from coastal areas fare best in brackish water or hard water with 1%–3% sea salt added. Unfortunately, the selection of tankmates and decorations is severely limited in such an environment. Generally speaking, killifishes from inland waters require soft, slightly acid water; some are extreme in this regard. The appropriate pH for maintenance is listed on the data line.

The diet should be based on live and frozen foods. For most species, flake foods should only be offered temporarily as a stopgap measure. Algae and blanched lettuce are accepted by the occasional species, but the grand majority are carnivores.

Conditions in the natural biotope determine the reproductive strategy of the species. Whether or not the biotope maintains water during the dry season is also a key factor determining the duration (from a few weeks to several months) and required temperature of egg storage in moist peat. Species hailing from permanent bodies of water lay "normal" eggs.

Annual fishes—species which endure the dry season as eggs in the upper layers of the substrate of their dried-up biotope—deposit their eggs in peat fibers covering the substrate of the breeding aquarium. So-called "substrate divers" (e.g., *Cynolebias* spp.) disappear totally in the peat to lay their eggs deep in the substrate (included with the subtrate spawners in the species descriptions under **B:**). The peat is removed after oviposition has concluded, blotted, and allowed to dry slightly. It is then stored humid in a labeled plastic bag for a species-specific period of time in the dark. (The recommended incubation time is indicated for the various species as "weeks storage"—ws.) Once that time has lapsed, the peat is hydrated using clean water and the young are "harvested." If it is suspected that many young still have not hatched, the peat should be dried and stored (as before) for an additional two weeks and then rehydrated. This procedure can be repeated several times until a satisfactory hatching rate has been achieved.

The rate of development of the eggs is not uniform. As a consequence of low oxygen concentrations, the eggs enter diapauses, or periods of minimal metabolic activity. The metabolic rate increases and egg development continues up to a prehatching state once the oxygen level rises. Actual hatching is triggered by the presence of water. African species can have a second diapause prior to hatching, which is not environmentally induced. Unlike most other fishes, killies hatch as juveniles or alevins, i.e., without a yolk sac and free-swimming. They must be immediately fed (*Artemia,* etc.). The young quickly become sexually mature, as perpetuation of the species rests on completing their entire lifecycle before the onset of the dry season. Hence, most annuals are short-lived, but the stable environmental conditions present in aquaria allow them a longer life span.

Nonannual species, i.e., those that inhabit permanent bodies of water, normally lay their eggs on Java moss bunches or artificial spawning mops (adhesive spawners) in the aquarium. The eggs can be collected, the young skimmed from the aquarium as they hatch or, once the spawning phase has concluded, the parents or the egg-laden spawning medium can be transferred to another aquarium. A low dosage of acriflavine can be added to the water as a prophylaxis against fungal attack on the eggs. After one to two weeks, the fry hatch. They are fully developed and immediately begin searching for food. No true brood care has so far been observed among the killies.

Some Cyprinodontiformes—both egg-laying and livebearing—are used in the tropics as a control measure against mosquitoes.

Family / Subfamily	Habitat	Water	Diet	Reproduction	Remarks
Anablepidae / Oxyzygonectinae	C. America;	Bw	C	spawning mop	Monotypic.
Aplocheilidae / Aplocheilinae	Af., S Asia;	Fw, (Bw)	C	annual fishes & nonannual species	♂♂ very colorful and often aggressive among themselves and towards ♀♀.
Rivulinae	S America;	Fw, (Bw)	C	annual & nonannual species	Only ♂ and hermaphrodite *Rivulus ocellatus* have been found (no ♀♀!).
Cyprinodontidae / Cubanichthyinae	Caribbean	Fw	C,O	non-annual species	Only 2 species.
Cyprinodontinae	Eu. & N, C, S Am.	Fw, Bw, (Mw)	O,C	store *Orestias* eggs 4 weeks	Live at highest temperature (43.8°C) of any fish. Some species endangered.
Fundulidae	N & C Am., Caribbean;	Fw, Bw, (Mw)	C,O	nonannual species, adhesive spawner	Breeding over several generations is problematic; overwinter at cool temps.
Goodeidae / Empetrichthynae	N Am (S Nevada);	Fw	O,C	adhesive spawner and among gravel	Small area of distribution. One species extinct. Mineral-rich water.
Poeciliidae / Aplocheilichthyinae	Africa;	Fw	C	substrate and crevice spawner	♂♂ very colorful. Several species are continuous spawners. Gregarious.
Fluviphylacinae	S America;	Fw	C	nonannual; no other information	Monotypic. Small sensitive species.
Profundulidae	C America;	Fw	C,O	nonannual species	Spawning colors. 1 genus w/ 5 species.
Valenciidae	Europe;	Fw	C,O	nonannual species	Only 2 species. Garden pond in summer.

Anablepidae (Oxyzygonectinae)

Subfamily Oxyzygonectinae

The Oxyzygonectinae only consist of the single species presented below. Numerous persons consider it part of the Fundulidae.

O. dovii is one of the large species within the Cyprinodontiformes. Although a schooling fish in its natural habitat, this behavior is not exhibited in the aquarium. The addition of marine salt eases maintenance and breeding, which has no annual character.

Oxyzygonectes dovii ♂   3/435

Oxyzygonectes dovii ♀   3/435

H: C America: Pacific coast. Bw,(Fw,Mw)
♂: Longer fins; more yellowish.   S: =
B: Spawning mop; 40 eggs.   F: C
T: 22–28°C, L: <35 cm, pH: >7, D: 2–3

Aplocheilidae (Aplocheilinae)   Old World Rivulines

Subfamily Aplocheilinae

The subfamily of Old World rivulines contains 8 genera and close to 185 species. They inhabit Africa and southern Asia (NELSON, 1994).

Selected genera can be classified by their reproductive biology (SEEGERS, 1980):

Adamas: nonannual. *Aphyosemion*: mostly nonannual species, but also some annual species and some which can be bred both ways. *Aplocheilus*: nonannual. *Diapteron*: nonannual. *Epiplatys*: nonannual. *Nothobranchius*: annual. *Pachypanchax*: annual.

Because of their small stature, sensitivity, and timid nature, a species aquarium is recommended for the majority of species. Males tend to be very aggressive among themselves, but absolutely amiable to unrelated tankmates, making them from that point of view good candidates for community aquaria.

An additional advantage of a species tank becomes apparent at feeding time, since these shy fishes often fare poorly when forced to compete for food. Most species depend on a diet of small live foods. In community arrangements, most of this special, expensive food would be "wasted" on the tankmates.

Adamas formosus ♂　　　　2/584

H: W Africa: Congo.
♂: Much more colorful.　　　　　　　S: =
B: Spawns on peat or perlon fibers.　F: C
T: 22–24°C, L: <3 cm, pH: <7, D: 4

Aphyoplatys duboisi ♂　　　　3/456
Congo killie

H: Africa: E Congo, W Zaïre.
♂: Much more colorful; longer fins. S: +
B: Spawning mop or peat fibers.　　F: C
T: 22–26°C, L: 3.5 cm, pH: <7, D: 4

Aphyoplatys duboisi ♂　　　　3/456
Congo killie

Aphyosemion ahli ♂　　　　4/364
Ahl's lyretail

H: W Africa: Cameroon to Eq. Guinea.
♂: Much more colorful; longer fins. S: +
B: Substrate or adhesive spawner. F: C
T: 22–26°C, L: 5 cm, pH: 7, D: 2

Aphyosemion amieti ♂　　　　3/458
Amiet's killie

H: Africa: W Cameroon.
SD: See photos.　　　　　　　　　S: +
B: Substrate spawner.　　　　　　　F: C
T: 22–28°C, L: 7 cm, pH: 7, D: 2–3

Aphyosemion amieti ♀　　　　3/458
Amiet's killie

KILLIFISHES

Aphyosemion amoenum ♂　　　3/460

H: W Africa: Cameroon.
♂: Much more colorful; longer fins. **S:** +
B: Adhesive spawner.　　　　　　**F:** C
T: 20–24°C, L: 5 cm, pH: <7, D: 3–4

Aphyosemion arnoldi ♂　　　2/588
Arnold's killie
H: W Africa: Nigeria.
♂: Much more colorful; longer fins. **S:** +
B: Substrate spawner: 8–13 ws.　**F:** C
T: 22–25°C, L: 5 cm, pH: <7, D: 3–4

Aphyosemion aureum ♂　　　2/588
Gold killie
H: W Africa: S Gabon.
♂: Much more colorful; longer fins. **S:** +
B: Substrate or adhesive spawner.　**F:** C
T: 18–22°C, L: 5 cm, pH: <7, D: 2–3

Aphyosemion australe t.♂, b.♀　1/524
Cape Lopez lyretail
H: W Africa.
♂: Much more colorful; longer fins. **S:** +
B: Plants or perlon fibers.　　　**F:** C,O
T: 21–24°C, L: 6 cm, pH: <7, D: 2

KILLIFISHES

Aphyosemion bamilekorum ♂　　2/590
Bamileke killie
H: W Africa: W Cameroon.
♂: More colorful; elongated fins.　**S:** +
B: Substrate spawner: 3–4 ws.　**F:** C
T: 18–22°C, L: 4 cm, pH: <7, D: 2–3

Aphyosemion banforense ♂　　3/460

H: W Africa: Guinea, Mali, Ivory Coast.
♂: Much more colorful; longer fins. **S:** +
B: Substrate or adhesive spawner.　**F:** C
T: 22–26°C, L: 5 cm, pH: 7, D: 3

Aphyosemion banforense ♂   3/460

Aphyosemion batesii ♂   3/462
Bates' killie, Z 86/9
H: W Africa: SE Cameroon, N Gabon, N Zaïre.
♂: Much more colorful; longer fins. S: +
B: Substrate spawner: 6 ws.   F: C
T: 22–26°C, L: 7.5 cm, pH: <7, D: 3

Aphyosemion bertholdi ♂   1/580
Berthold's killie
H: W Africa: Sierra Leone, Guinea, Liberia.
♂: Much more colorful; longer fins. S: +
B: Pseudo substrate spawn.; <30 e. F: C
T: 22–24°C, L: 5 cm, pH: <7, D: 3

Aphyosemion bitaeniatum ♂   2/610
Multicolored lyretail   (1/525)
H: W Africa: Togo, Benin, Nigeria.
♂: Much more colorful; longer fins. S: +
B: Adhesive spawner.   F: C
T: 22–24°C, L: 5 cm, pH: <7, D: 2–3

Aphyosemion bitaeniatum ♂   2/610
Multicolored lyretail   (1/525)

Aphyosemion bivittatum ♂   1/524
Red aphyosemion (large photo)
H: W Africa: SE Nigeria/SW Cameroon.
♂: Much more colorful; longer fins. S: +
B: On Java moss or perlon fibers. F: C!
T: 22–24°C, L: 5 cm, pH: <7, D: 2

Aphyosemion bualanum kekemense ♂
3/462

H: Africa: W Cameroon.
♂: Much more colorful; longer fins. S: +
B: Adh. or substrate spawner: 3 ws. F: C
T: 20–24°C, L: 5 cm, pH: <7, D: 3–4

Aphyosemion buytaerti ♂   3/464
Buytaert's killie

H: Africa: SW Congo.
♂: More colorful.   S: +
B: Very difficult.   F: C
T: 17–21°C, L: 5 cm, pH: 7, D: 4

Aphyosemion calliurum ♂   2/590
Red-seam killie

H: W Africa: S Benin, S Nigeria, SW Cam.
♂: Much more colorful; longer fins. S: +
B: Substrate (4ws) or adh. spawner. F: C
T: 24–26°C, L: 5 cm, pH: <7, D: 2

Aphyosemion cameronense ♂   2/592
Cameroon killie, powder-blue killie

H: W Africa: Cameroon, Eq. Guinea.
♂: Much more colorful; longer fins. S: +
B: Adhesive spawner.   F: C
T: 18–22°C, L: 5 cm, pH: <7, D: 4

Aphyosemion cameronense "SAM" ♂
Cameroon killie, powder-blue killie
4/401

Aphyosemion cameronense haasi 4/364
Haas' killie

H: W Africa: N Gabon.
♂: Very colorful; longer fins.   S: +
B: Substrate or adhesive spawner. F: C
T: 20–23°C, L: 6.5 cm, pH: 7, D: 3–4

KILLIFISHES

399

Aphyosemion cameronense halleri   4/366
Haller's killie ♂
H: W Africa: S Cameroon/Gabon.
♂: Much more colorful; longer fins. **S**: =
B: Adhesive spawner: 2 ws.   **F**: C
T: 23–25°C, L: ♂ 5 cm, pH: <7, D: 3

Aphyosemion cameronense halleri   4/366
Haller's killie ♂

Aphyosemion cameronense halleri   4/366
Haller's killie ♂

Aphyosemion cameronense obscurum
Spotted Cameroon killie ♂   4/366
H: W Africa: SW central Cameroon.
♂: Very colorful; longer fins.   **S**: (–)
B: Adhesive spawner.   **F**: C
T: 22–26°C, L: 4.5 cm, pH: <7, D: 3–4

Aphyosemion cameronense obscurum
Spotted Cameroon killie ♂   4/366

Aphyosemion caudofasciatum ♂   2/592
Tail stripe killie
H: W Africa: S Congo.
♂: Much more colorful.   **S**: +
B: Adhesive spawner.   **F**: C
T: 18–22°C, L: 5 cm, pH: <7, D: 2–3

Aphyosemion celiae ♂   3/464
Margined killie Loc. 26
H: Africa: W Cameroon.
♂: Much more colorful; longer fins. S: +
B: Substrate spawner.   F: C
T: 22–26°C, L: 4.5 cm, pH: <7, D: 3

Aphyosemion chauchei ♂   4/370
Chauche's killie
H: Africa: N Congo, Zaïre.
♂: Much more colorful; longer fins. S: +
B: Substrate (4 ws) or adh. spawner. F: C
T: 22–26°C, L: 4.5 cm, pH: <7, D: 3

Aphyosemion chaytori ♂   1/582
Chaytor's killie
H: Africa: Sierra Leone.
♂: Much more colorful.   S: +
B: Adhesive spawner.   F: C
T: 22–24°C, L: 5 cm, pH: <7, D: 2

Aphyosemion christyi ♂   2/594
Christy's lyretail, spotfin killie
H: Africa: entire Congo Basin.
♂: Much more colorful; longer fins. S: +
B: Substrate (3 ws) or adh. spawner. F: C
T: 20–24°C, L: 5 cm, pH: <7, D: 3

Aphyosemion cinnamomeum ♂   2/594
Cinnamon killie
H: W Africa: W Cameroon.
♂: More colorful.   S: =
B: Substrate or adhesive spawner. F: C
T: 22–24°C, L: 5 cm, pH: <7, D: 2–3

Aphyosemion citrineipinnis ♂   3/466
Lemon-fin killie
H: W Africa: central Gabon.
♂: Much more colorful.   S: +
B: Substrate or adhesive spawner. F: C
T: 18–22°C, L: 5 cm, pH: <7, D: 4

KILLIFISHES

Aphyosemion coeleste ♂   2/596
Sky blue killie
H: W Africa: SE Gabon, Congo.
♂: Much more colorful; longer fins. S: =
B: Substrate (4 ws) or adh. spawner. F: C
T: 18–22°C, L: 5 cm, pH: <7, D: 3

Aphyosemion cognatum ♂   1/526
Red-spotted lyretail
H: W Africa: Zaïre: Stanley Pool.
♂: Much more colorful; longer fins. S: +
B: Adhesive spawner; <250 eggs.   F: C
T: 22–24°C, L: 5.5 cm, pH: <7, D: 2

Aphyosemion cognatum ♂   2/596
Red-spotted lyretail
H: W Africa: SW Zaïre: Kinshasa.
♂: Much more colorful; longer fins. S: +
B: Substrate (3 ws) or adh. spawner. F: C
T: 20–24°C, L: 5 cm, pH: <7, D: 3

Aphyosemion congicum ♂   2/598
Black-tail killie
H: W Africa: SW Zaïre.
♂: Much more colorful; longer fins. S: +
B: Substrate or adhesive spawner. F: C
T: 20–24°C, L: 4.5 cm, pH: <7, D: 2–3

Aphyosemion dargei ♂   4/370
Mbam lyretail
H: Africa: central S Cameroon.
♂: Much more colorful; longer fins. S: +
B: Substrate (4 ws) or adh. spawner. F: C
T: 20–24°C, L: 4.5 cm, pH: <7, D: 2

Aphyosemion deltaense ♂   1/528
Delta lyretail
H: W Africa: Nigeria: W Niger Delta.
♂: Much more colorful; longer fins. S: +
B: Substrate spawner: 13 ws.   F: C
T: 22–26°C, L: 10 cm, pH: <7, D: 2

Aphyosemion edeanum ♂   4/372
Edea lyretail
H: W Africa: Cameroon: coastal region.
♂: Much more colorful; longer fins. **S:** +
B: Substrate (4 ws) or adh.spawner. **F:** C
T: 22–26°C, **L:** 5 cm, **pH:** 7, **D:** 2

Aphyosemion elberti ♂   1/526
H: Afr.: Cameroon (W=t., E=b.), C. Af. Rep.
♂: Much more colorful; longer fins. **S:** +
B: Adhesive spawner.   **F:** C
T: 21–25°C, **L:** 5 cm, **pH:** <7, **D:** 1–2

Aphyosemion elegans ♂   2/598
Elegant lyretail
H: W Africa: Zaïre, Congo.
♂: Much more colorful; longer fins. **S:** =
B: Dense spawning mop.   **F:** C
T: 20–24°C, **L:** 4.5 cm, **pH:** <7, **D:** 4

KILLIFISHES

Aphyosemion escherichi ♂   2/608
H: W Africa: N Gabon to Congo.
♂: More colorful; longer fins.   **S:** +
B: Substrate (3 ws) or adh.spawner. **F:** C
T: 22–24°C, **L:** 5 cm, **pH:** <7, **D:** 2–3

Aphyosemion etzeli ♂   2/692
Etzel's killie
H: W Africa: Sierra Leone.
♂: Much more colorful; longer fins. **S:** +
B: Substrate spawner.   **F:** C
T: 22–28°C, **L:** 5 cm, **pH:** <7, **D:** 2–3

Aphyosemion exigoideum ♂   1/528
H: Africa: Gabon.
♂: Much more colorful.   **S:** ?
B: Adhesive spawner.   **F:** C
T: 22–24°C, **L:** 3.5 cm, **pH:** >7, **D:** 2–3

Aphyosemion exiguum ♂   1/530
Jewel killie
H: W Africa: E Cameroon, N Gabon.
♂: More colorful; pointed dorsal fin. S: +
B: Adhesive spawner.   F: C
T: 21–24°C, L: 4 cm, pH: 7, D: 2

Aphyosemion fallax ♂   2/602, 3/466
Kribi lyretail, swallow-tail killie
H: Africa: SW Cameroon.
♂: Much more colorful; longer fins. S: +
B: Substrate spawner.   F: C
T: 22–26°C, L: 9 cm, pH: <7, D: 3–4

Aphyosemion fallax ♂   2/602, 3/466
Kribi lyretail, swallow-tail killie
H: Africa: W Cameroon: coastal basin.

Aphyosemion fallax ♀   2/602, 3/466
Kribi lyretail, swallow-tail killie
H: Africa: Cameroon: Malende.

Aphyosemion fallax ♂   2/602, 3/466
Kribi lyretail, swallow-tail killie
H: Africa: Cameroon: Movanke.

Aphyosemion filamentosum t.♂, b.♀
Plumed lyretail, togo lyretail   1/530
H: W Africa: W Nigeria, Togo.
♂: More colorful; longer fins.   S: =
B: Substrate spawner: 4–12 ws. F: C,O
T: 21–23°C, L: 5.5 cm, pH: <7, D: 3

KILLIFISHES

Aphyosemion fredrodi t.♂, b.♀   5/468

H: W Africa: Sierra Leone.
♂: Much more colorful; longer fins. **S:** =
B: Adhesive spawner.   **F:** C
T: 23–27°C, **L:** 4 cm, **pH:** 7, **D:** 2

Aphyosemion franzwerneri ♂   3/469
Werner's roundtail killie

H: W Africa: Cameroon.
♂: Somewhat brighter; longer fins. **S:** +
B: Adhesive spawner.   **F:** C
T: 22–26°C, **L:** 5 cm, **pH:** ≪7, **D:** 4

Aphyosemion gabunense boehmi ♂
Böhm's killie   2/600

H: W Africa: NW Gabon.
♂: Much more colorful; longer fins. **S:** +
B: Substrate or adhesive spawner. **F:** C
T: 22–25°C, **L:** 4.5 cm, **pH:** 7, **D:** 2

Aphyosemion gabunense gabunense t.♂
Gabon killie   2/600

H: W Africa: NW Gabon.
♂: Much more colorful; longer fins. **S:** +
B: Substrate or adhesive spawner. **F:** C
T: 22–25°C, **L:** 5 cm, **pH:** 7, **D:** 2–3

Aphyosemion gabunense marginatum ♂
                                    2/600

H: W Africa: NW Gabon.
♂: Much more colorful; longer fins. **S:** +
B: Substrate or adhesive spawner. **F:** C
T: 22–25°C, **L:** 4.5 cm, **pH:** 7, **D:** 2

Aphyosemion gardneri gardneri ♂ 3/470
Steel-blue killie

H: W Africa: Nigeria.
♂: Much more colorful.   **S:** +
B: Substrate (3 ws) or adh.spawner. **F:** C
T: 22–26°C, **L:** 6 cm, **pH:** 7, **D:** 2

KILLIFISHES

405

Aphyosemion gardneri lacustre ♂ 3/472

Aphyosemion gardneri lacustre ♂ 3/472

H: W Africa: Nigeria, W Cameroon.
♂: Much more colorful.　　　　　　S: +
B: Substrate spawner.　　　　　　　F: C
T: 22–26°C, L: 6 cm, pH: 7, D: 2–3

Aphyosemion gardneri mamfense ♂
Mamfe killie　　　　　　　　　　3/472
H: W Africa: W Cameroon.
♂: Much more colorful; longer fins. S: +
B: Better as an adhesive spawner.　F: C
T: 22–24°C, L: 6 cm, pH: 7, D: 2–3

Aphyosemion gardneri nigerianum ♂
Steel-blue lyretail　　　　　　　　1/532
H: W Africa: Nigeria, W Cameroon.
♂: Much more colorful; longer fins. S: =
B: Adhesive spawner.　　　　　　　F: C
T: 22–26°C, L: 6 cm, pH: <7, D: 2

Aphyosemion gardneri nigerianum ♂
Nigeria killie　　　　　　　　　　3/472
H: W Africa: Nigeria, W Cameroon.
♂: Much more colorful; longer fins. S: +
B: Substrate spawner.　　　　　　　F: C
T: 22–26°C, L: 6 cm, pH: 7, D: 2

Aphyosemion geryi t.♂, b.♀　　2/692
Gery's killie
H: W Africa: Gambia to Sierra Leone.
♂: Much more colorful; longer fins. S: +
B: Substrate or adhesive spawner.　F: C
T: 22–26°C, L: 5 cm, pH: <7, D: 2–3

KILLIFISHES

Aphyosemion guignardi ♂　　4/372
Guignard's killie
H: Africa: Guinea. Burkina Faso?
♂: Much more colorful; longer fins. S: +
B: Substrate (4 ws) or adh. spawner. F: C
T: 22–26°C, L: 5 cm, pH: 7, D: 2

Aphyosemion guignardi ♀　　4/372
Guignard's killie

Aphyosemion guineensis ♂　　2/694
Guinea roundfin killie
H: W Africa: Guinea, S.Leone, Mali, Ivory C.,...
♂: Much more colorful; longer fins. S: +
B: Adhesive spawner.　　　　F: C
T: 18–23°C, L: 9 cm, pH: <7, D: 3

Aphyosemion gulare ♂　　1/532
Red-spotted gularis
H: W Africa: S Nigeria.
♂: Much more colorful; longer fins. S: –
B: Substrate spawner: 13 ws.　　F: C
T: 20–22°C, L: 8 cm, pH: 7, D: 2

KILLIFISHES

Aphyosemion hanneloreae ♀　　3/474
Hannelore's killie
H: W Africa: Gabon. Congo?
♂: Much more colorful; longer fins. S: +
B: Like *A. punctatum*?　　　F: C
T: 19–21°C, L: 4 cm, pH: <7, D: 4

Aphyosemion heinemanni ♂　　4/374
Heinemann's killie
H: W Africa: W Cameroon.
♂: Much more colorful; longer fins. S: +
B: Substrate or adhesive spawner. F: C
T: 22–26°C, L: 4.5 cm, pH: 7, D: 2

Aphyosemion herzogi bochtleri ♂   2/602
Herzog's killie
H: W Africa: N Gabon.
♂: Much more colorful; longer fins. **S:** +
B: Adhesive spawner.   **F:** C
T: 18–22°C, **L:** 5 cm, **pH:** <7, **D:** 4

Aphyosemion herzogi herzogi ♂   5/472
Herzog's killie
See text on 2/602.

Aphyosemion hofmanni ♂   3/474
Hofmann's killie
H: Africa: SW Gabon.
♂: Much more colorful; longer fins. **S:** ?
B: Unknown   **F:** C
T: 19–22°C, **L:** 4 cm, **pH:** <7, **D:** 3–4?

Aphyosemion jeanpoli ♂   2/694
H: W Africa: N Liberia.
♂: More colorful; longer fins.   **S:** (–)
B: Spawns among plants.   **F:** C
T: 22–28°C, **L:** 5 cm, **pH:** <7, **D:** 3

Aphyosemion joergenscheeli ♂   3/476
H: Africa: Gabon.
♂: Much more colorful.   **S:** +
B: Unsuccessful.   **F:** C
T: 18–20°C, **L:** 5 cm, **pH:** <7, **D:** 4

Aphyosemion labarrei ♂   2/604
Red-streaked killie, Labarre's killie
H: W Africa: SW Congo, Zaïre.
♂: Much more colorful; longer fins. **S:** +
B: Adhesive or substrate spawner. **F:** C
T: 22–24°C, **L:** 5 cm, **pH:** <7, **D:** 2–3

KILLIFISHES

Aphyosemion lamberti ♂   2/604
Lambert's lyretail
H: W Africa: central Gabon.
♂: Much more colorful; longer fins. S: +
B: Adhesive or substrate spawner. F: C
T: 18–22°C, L: 5 cm, pH: <7, D: 2–3

Aphyosemion lefiniense ♂   3/476
Lefini killie
H: W Africa: S Congo.
♂: Much more colorful; longer fins. S: +
B: Substrate (3 ws) or adh. spawner. F: C
T: 22–26°C, L: 4.5 cm, pH: <7, D: 3

Aphyosemion liberiensis ♂   1/582
Liberian killie
H: W Africa: W Liberia. Nigeria?
♂: Much more colorful; longer fins. S: +
B: Substrate or adhesive spawner. F: C
T: 22–24°C, L: 6 cm, pH: <7, D: 1–2

Aphyosemion loennbergii ♂   3/478
Lönnberg's killie, "CCMP 85/12"
H: W Africa: SW Cameroon.
♂: Much more colorful; longer fins. S: +
B: Adh. or substrate spawner: 3 ws. F: C
T: 22–26°C, L: 7 cm, pH: 7, D: 3

Aphyosemion louessense ♂   2/606
Louesse's killie, "RPC 24"
H: W Africa: S Congo.
♂: Much more colorful; longer fins. S: +
B: Adhesive or substrate spawner. F: C
T: 18–22°C, L: 5 cm, pH: <7, D: 2–3

Aphyosemion louessense ♂   2/606
Louesse's killie, "RPC 31"

KILLIFISHES

409

Aphyosemion maculatum ♂   2/608
Spotted killie
H: W Africa: N Gabon.
♂: Much more colorful; longer fins. S: =
B: Adhesive or substrate spawner. F: C
T: 18–22°C, L: 5 cm, pH: <7, D: 4

Aphyosemion maeseni ♂   2/696
Maesen's killie
H: W Af.: W Ivory C., NW Lib., SE Guinea.
♂: Much more colorful.   S: +
B: Substrate or adhesive spawner. F: C
T: 20–24°C, L: 5 cm, pH: 7, D: 2–3

Aphyosemion marmoratum ♂   1/532
Green-spangled chocolate killie
H: W Africa: Cameroon.
♂: Much more colorful.   S: +
B: Adhesive spawner; 30 eggs.   F: C
T: 20–22°C, L: 8 cm, pH: <7, D: 2

Aphyosemion mimbon ♂   2/610

H: W Africa: N Gabon.
♂: Much more colorful; longer fins. S: –
B: Difficult; adhesive spawner.   F: C
T: 18–22°C, L: 5 cm, pH: <7, D: 4

Aphyosemion mirabile ♂   1/536
Azure killie
H: W Africa: W Cameroon.
♂: Much more colorful; longer fins. S: +
B: Java moss or perlon fibers.   F: C
T: 22–25°C, L: 7 cm, pH: <7, D: 2

Aphyosemion mirabile intermittens ♂
Half-band azure killie   4/374
H: W Africa: Cameroon.
♂: Much more colorful; longer fins. S: +
B: Substrate spawner: 4 ws.   F: C
T: 20–24°C, L: 6.5 cm, pH: 7, D: 2

Aphyosemion mirabile intermittens ♂
Half-band azure killie   4/374

Aphyosemion mirabile moense ♀ 4/376

H: Africa: W Cameroon.
♂: Much more colorful; longer fins. S: +
B: Substrate spawner: 4 ws.   F: C
T: 22–26°C, L: 6.5 cm, pH: 7, D: 2

Aphyosemion mirabile traudeae ♂ 3/478
Traude's azure killie
H: W Africa: W Cameroon.
♂: Much more colorful; longer fins. S: +
B: Substrate spawner: 3 ws.   F: C
T: 22–26°C, L: 5 cm, pH: <7, D: 2–3

Aphyosemion ndianum ♂   3/482
Red-tail killie
H: W Africa: SE Nigeria/SW Cameroon.
♂: Much more colorful; longer fins. S: +
B: Substrate (8 ws) or adh. spawner. F: C
T: 22–25°C, L: 7 cm, pH: 7, D: 3–4

Aphyosemion ocellatum ♂   2/612
Shoulder-spot killie
H: W Africa: S Gabon.
♂: Much more colorful; longer fins. S: +
B: Substrate spawner: 8–12 ws.   F: C
T: 18–22°C, L: 5 cm, pH: <7, D: 3–4

Aphyosemion oeseri ♂   3/482
Oeser's killie
H: W Africa: Equatorial Guinea.
♂: Much more colorful; longer fins. S: +
B: Adhesive spawner: 4 ws.   F: C
T: 22–26°C, L: 7 cm, pH: 7, D: 3

KILLIFISHES

411

Aphyosemion ogoense ogoense ♂　2/612
Broken-striped killie "Malinga"
H: W Africa: S Gabon, S Congo.
♂: Much more colorful; longer fins. S: +
B: Adhesive spawner.　　　　　　　F: C
T: 18–22°C, L: 5 cm, pH: <7, D: 2–3

Aphyosemion ogoense ogoense ♂　2/612
Broken-striped killie

Aphyosemion ogoense ottogartneri ♂
Gartner's killie　　　　　　　　　4/376
H: W Africa: S Congo.
♂: Much more colorful; longer fins. S: +
B: Adhesive spawner.　　　　　　　F: C
T: 18–24°C, L: 4.5 cm, pH: <7, D: 2

Aphyosemion ogoense pyrophore t.♂
"RPC 18"　　　　　　　　　　　　2/614
H: W Africa: S Gabon, S Congo.
♂: Much more colorful; longer fins. S: +
B: Adhesive spawner.　　　　　　　F: C
T: 18–22°C, L: 5 cm, pH: <7, D: 2–3

Aphyosemion ogoense pyrophore ♂
"GHP 23/80"　　　　　　　　　　2/614
H: W Africa: S Gabon, S Congo.
♂: Much more colorful; longer fins. S: +
B: Adhesive spawner.　　　　　　　F: C
T: 18–22°C, L: 5 cm, pH: <7, D: 2–3

Aphyosemion pascheni ♂　　　2/616
Gray killie
H: W Africa: S Cameroon.
♂: Much more colorful; longer fins. S: +
B: Substrate spawner: 3–4 ws.　　F: C
T: 22–25°C, L: 5 cm, pH: <7, D: 3

Aphyosemion petersii ♂   2/696, 4/378
Peter's killie
H: W Africa: SW Ghana, S Ivory Coast.
♂: Much more colorful; longer fins. S: =
B: Adhesive spawner.   F: C
T: 22–26°C, L: <5.5 cm, pH: <7, D: 2–3

Aphyosemion poliaki ♂   4/380
Poliak's killie
H: Africa: Cameroon.
♂: Much more colorful; longer fins. S: +
B: Substrate (3 ws) or adh. spawner. F: C
T: 20–24°C, L: 5.5 cm, pH: 7, D: 2

Aphyosemion primigenium ♂   2/616

H: W Africa: SW Gabon.
♂: Much more colorful; longer fins. S: +
B: Adhesive or substrate spawner. F: C
T: 18–22°C, L: 5 cm, pH: <7, D: 2–3

Aphyosemion puerzli b. ♀, t. ♂   1/536

H: W Africa: W Cameroon.
♂: Much more colorful; longer fins. S: +
B: Substrate (8 ws) or adh. spawner. F: C
T: 21–24°C, L: 6 cm, pH: 7, D: 2

Aphyosemion punctatum ♂   3/484
Spotted killie
H: Africa: NE Gabon to Congo.
♂: Much more colorful; longer fins. S: +
B: Substrate (3 ws) or adh. spawner. F: C
T: 20–22°C, L: 4.5 cm, pH: <7, D: 3–4

Aphyosemion raddai ♂   3/484
Radda's killie
H: Africa: S Cameroon.
♂: Much more colorful; longer fins. S: +
B: Adhesive spawner; not fecund. F: C
T: 22–26°C, L: 5 cm, pH: <7, D: 3–4

KILLIFISHES

413

Aphyosemion rectogoense b.♀, t.♂ 2/618
Silver-yellow killie
H: W Africa: SE Gabon.
♂: Much more colorful; longer fins. **S:** +
B: Better as adhesive spawner.   **F:** C
T: 23–26°C, **L:** 5 cm, **pH:** <7, **D:** 2–3

Aphyosemion riggenbachi ♂   1/538
Red-spotted purple killie
H: W Africa: SW Cameroon.
♂: Much more colorful; longer fins. **S:** +
B: On Java moss.   **F:** C
T: 20–23°C, **L:** 10 cm, **pH:** ≪7, **D:** 2

Aphyosemion robertsoni ♂   2/618
Robertson's killie
H: W Africa: W Cameroon.
♂: Much more colorful; longer fins. **S:** +
B: Substrate spawner: 8–10 ws. **F:** C
T: 21–24°C, **L:** 6 cm, **pH:** <7, **D:** 2–3

Aphyosemion roloffi ♂   1/580, 5/468
Roloff's killie
H: W Africa: Sierra Leone.
♂: Much more colorful.   **S:** +
B: Substrate spawner.   **F:** C
T: 22–24°C, **L:** 5 cm, **pH:** <7, **D:** 2–3

Aphyosemion roloffi ♂   1/580, 5/468
Roloff's killie
"Brama Junction"

Aphyosemion rubrolabiale ♂   2/620
Red-lipped killie
H: W Africa: SW Cameroon.
♂: Much more colorful; longer fins. **S:** +
B: Substrate spawner: 8–10 ws. **F:** C
T: 21–24°C, **L:** 6 cm, **pH:** <7, **D:** 2–3

Aphyosemion scheeli ♂ 3/486
Orange-fringed killie
H: Africa: SE Nigeria.
♂: Much more colorful; longer fins. S: +
B: Substrate (4 ws) or adh. spawner. F: C
T: 22–26°C, L: 5 cm, pH: 7, D: 2–3

Aphyosemion schioetzi ♂ 4/380
Schioetz's killie
H: Africa: central and E Congo, W Zaïre.
♂: Much more colorful; longer fins. S: +
B: Better as adhesive spawner. F: C
T: 22–26°C, L: 4.5 cm, pH: <7, D: 2

Aphyosemion schluppi ♂ 2/620
Schlupp's killie
H: W Africa: Congo.
♂: Slightly more colorful; longer fins. S: +
B: Substrate or adhesive spawner. F: C
T: 18–22°C, L: 4 cm, pH: <7, D: 2

Aphyosemion schmitti ♂ 2/698
Schmitt's killie
H: W Africa: E Liberia.
♂: Much more colorful; longer fins. S: +
B: Substrate or adhesive spawner. F: C
T: 22–24°C, L: 6 cm, pH: <7, D: 2–3

Aphyosemion sjoestedti ♂ 1/538
Blue gularis, golden pheasant
H: W Africa: S Nigeria, W Cam. to Ghana.
♂: Much more colorful; longer fins. S: +
B: Substrate spawner: 4–6 ws. F: C
T: 23–26°C, L: 12 cm, pH: <7, D: 3

Aphyosemion splendopleure ♂ 3/486
Slendid killie
H: Africa: SE Nig., Cam., Eq.Guinea, Gab.
♂: Much more colorful; longer fins. S: +
B: Adhesive spawner: 3 ws! F: C
T: 22–26°C, L: 6 cm, pH: 7, D: 3

KILLIFISHES

KILLIFISHES

Aphyosemion spoorenbergi ♂   2/622
Spoorenberg's killie
H: W Africa: SE Nigeria/W Cameroon?
♂: Much more colorful; longer fins. **S**: +
B: Substrate or adhesive spawner. **F**: C
T: 20–24°C, **L**: 8 cm, **pH**: 7, **D**: 2–3

Aphyosemion striatum ♂   1/540
Red striped killie
H: Africa: N Gabon.
♂: Much more colorful.   **S**: +
B: On Java moss; about 30 eggs.   **F**: C
T: about 22°C, **L**: 5 cm, **pH**: <7, **D**: 2–3

Aphyosemion thysi ♂   2/622
Thys' lyretail, "RPC 20"
H: W Africa: Congo.
♂: Much more colorful; longer fins. **S**: +
B: Adhesive spawner: or < 3 ws.   **F**: C
T: 18–22°C, **L**: 4 cm, **pH**: <7, **D**: 3

Aphyosemion thysi ♂   2/622
Thys' lyretail, "RPC 9"

Aphyosemion viridis ♂   2/698
Green killie
H: W Africa: SE Guinea, NW Liberia.
♂: Much more colorful; longer fins. **S**: –
B: Substrate spawner.   **F**: C
T: 20–24°C, **L**: 6 cm, **pH**: 7, **D**: 3–4

Aphyosemion volcanum ♂   1/534
Volcano killie
H: W Africa: W Cameroon.
♂: Much more colorful; longer fins. **S**: +
B: Adhesive spawner: or 2–3 ws.   **F**: C
T: 23–26°C, **L**: 4.5 cm, **pH**: <7, **D**: 2–3

Aphyosemion wachtersi mikeae ♂ 2/624
Wachters' killie, "RPC 19"
H: W Africa: Congo.
♂: Much more colorful; longer fins. **S:** +
B: Adhesive spawner: or 3 ws.   **F:** C
T: 18–22°C, L: 4 cm, pH: <7, D: 3

Aphyosemion wachtersi wachtersi ♂ 3/488
Wachters' killie, "RPC 78/30"
H: W Africa: S Congo.
♂: Much more colorful; longer fins. **S:** +
B: Adhesive spawner.   **F:** C
T: 17–22°C, L: 5 cm, pH: ≪7, D: 3–4

Aphyosemion walkeri ♂   1/542
Walker's killie
H: W Africa: SW Ghana, SE Ivory Coast.
♂: Much more colorful; longer fins. **S:** +
B: Substrate (5 ws) or adh. spawner. **F:** C
T: 20–23°C, L: 6.5 cm, pH: <7, D: 2

Aphyosemion wildekampi ♂   3/488
Wildekamp's killie
H: W Africa: SE Cameroon, Cen.Af.Rep.
♂: Much more colorful; longer fins. **S:** +
B: Peat fibers: 3 ws.   **F:** C
T: 20–24°C, L: 4.5 cm, pH: <7, D: 3–4

Aphyosemion zygaima ♂   3/490
Mindouli killie
H: W Africa: Congo.
♂: Much more colorful; longer fins. **S:** +
B: Peat fibers: 3 ws.   **F:** C
T: 18–22°C, L: 5 cm, pH: <7, D: 3–4

Aplocheilus blockii t.♀, b.♂   1/546
Green panchax
H: Asia: S India. Sri Lanka?
♂: Much more colorful; larger.   **S:** +
B: Adhesive spawner.   **F:** C,O
T: 22–26°C, L: 5 cm, pH: <7, D: 2

Aplocheilus dayi ♂   1/546
Ceylon killifish, Day's panchax
H: Asia: S India, Sri Lanka.
♂: Slightly more colorful; longer fins. **S:** =
B: Moss lawn or fine-leaved plants. **F:** C
T: 20–25°C, **L:** 10 cm, **pH:** <7, **D:** 2

Aplocheilus dayi werneri ♂   3/492
Werner's panchax
H: Asia: S Sri Lanka.
♂: Slightly more colorful; longer fins. **S:** +
B: Continuous adhesive spawner. **F:** C
T: 22–26°C, **L:** 9 cm, **pH:** <7, **D:** 2

Aplocheilus dayi werneri ♀   3/492
Werner's panchax

Aplocheilus dayi werneri ♂   3/492
Werner's panchax

Aplocheilus lineatus t.♂, b.♀   1/548,
Sparkling panchax, striped panchax   5/472
H: Asia: W India.
♂: Much more colorful; longer fins. **S:** –
B: Adhesive spawner. **F:** C,O
T: 22–25°C, **L:** 10 cm, **pH:** <7, **D:** 2

Aplocheilus lineatus gold ♂   1/548,
Sparkling panchax, striped panchax   5/472

Aplocheilus lineatus India ♂   1/548,
Sparkling panchax, striped panchax 5/472

Aplocheilus panchax   1/548
Blue panchax
H: Asia: India, Burma, Thailand,...
SD: Differences are slight.   S: =
B: On moss lawn, fine-leaved plants. F: C
T: 20–25°C, L: 8 cm, pH: <7, D: 1–2

Callopanchax monroviae ♂   3/480
Monrovia killie "blue"
H: W Africa: S Liberia.
♂: Much more colorful; longer fins. S: +
B: Substrate spawner: 6–8 ws.   F: C
T: 22–26°C, L: 9 cm, pH: <7, D: 3

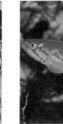

Callopanchax monroviae ♂   3/480
Monrovia killie "red"

Callopanchax occidentalis l.♂,r.♂ 1/584
Golden pheasant
H: W Africa: Sierra Leone.
♂: Much more colorful; longer fins. S: +
B: Substr. spawner: months storage. F: C
T: 20–24°C, L: 9 cm, pH: <7, D: 2–3

Callopanchax toddi ♂   1/540
Blue-throat pheasant
H: W Africa: Sierra Leone.
♂: Much more colorful; longer fins. S: +
B: Substrate spawner: 21 ws.   F: C
T: 22–24°C, L: 8 cm, pH: <7, D: 3

Diapteron abacinum ♂　　　2/640

H: Africa: E Gabon, Peo. Rep. Congo.
♂: Much more colorful; longer fins. **S:** (–)
B: Adhesive spawner.　　　　**F:** C!
T: 18–22°C, **L:** 4 cm, **pH:** <7, **D:** 3–4

Diapteron cyanostictum ♂　　1/556

H: Africa: Gabon.
♂: Much more colorful; longer fins. **S:** +
B: Adhesive spawner.　　　　**F:** C
T: 25–35°C, **L:** 6.5 cm, **pH:** <7, **D:** 3

Diapteron fulgens ♂　　　3/496

H: Africa: NE Gabon.
♂: Much more colorful; longer fins. **S:** +
B: Adhesive spawner.　　　　**F:** C!
T: 18–22°C, **L:** 3.5 cm, **pH:** <7, **D:** 4

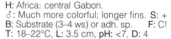

Diapteron georgiae ♂　　　3/496

H: Africa: central Gabon.
♂: Much more colorful; longer fins. **S:** +
B: Substrate (3–4 ws) or adh. sp.　**F:** C!
T: 18–22°C, **L:** 3.5 cm, **pH:** <7, **D:** 4

Epiplatys ansorgii ♀　　　5/474
Ansorge's panchax
H: W Africa: Gabon.
♂: Much more colorful; longer fins. **S:** +
B: Moderately difficult; adh. spawn.　**F:** C
T: 22–24°C, **L:** 7.5 cm, **pH:** <7, **D:** 3

Epiplatys ansorgii ♂　　　5/474
Ansorge's panchax

Epiplatys ansorgii ♂   5/474
Ansorge's panchax
H: W Africa: SW Gabon: Gamba.

Epiplatys ansorgii ♂   5/474
Ansorge's panchax
H: W Africa: Gabon: Sindara.

Epiplatys ansorgii ♂   5/474
Ansorge's panchax
H: W Africa: Gabon: Lambarene.

Epiplatys barmoiensis ♂   2/642
Barmoi panchax
H: Africa: Sierra Leone, Liberia, Nigeria.
♂: Slightly more colorful; longer fins. S: +
B: Adhesive spawner.   F: C
T: 24–27°C, L: 7 cm, pH: <7, D: 3

Epiplatys berkenkampi ♂   2/642
Berkenkamp's panchax
H: W Africa: central Gabon.
♂: More colorful; longer fins.   S: +
B: Not simple: adhesive spawner.   F: C
T: 20–24°C, L: 6 cm, pH: <7, D: 3–4

Epiplatys biafranus ♂   4/384
Biafra panchax
H: Africa: SE Nigeria.
♂: More colorful; longer fins.   S: (–)
B: Adhesive spawner.   F: C!
T: 21–25°C, L: 5 cm, pH: <7, D: 3

KILLIFISHES

Epiplatys biafranus ♀ 4/384
Biafra panchax

Epiplatys bifasciatus ♂ 2/644
Two-striped panchax
H: W and central Africa.
♂: Slightly more colorful; longer fins. S:(−)
B: Adhesive spawner. F: C!
T: 23–27°C, L: 5 cm, pH: 7, D: 2–3

Epiplatys boulengeri ♂ 4/384
Boulenger's panchax, "CHP 82/16"
H: Africa: W Zaïre, SE Gabon.
♂: More colorful; longer fins. S: +
B: Adhesive spawner. F: C!
T: 24–28°C, L: 5.5 cm, pH: <7, D: 3

Epiplatys sp. aff. *boulengeri* ♂ 4/384
Boulenger's panchax
See photo on page 4/382.

Epiplatys chaperi chaperi ♂ 4/386
Gold Coast panchax
H: Africa: Ivory Coast, Togo, Ghana.
♂: More colorful; longer fins. S: +
B: Not difficult; adhesive spawner. F: C!
T: 24–28°C, L: 6.5 cm, pH: <7, D: 2

Epiplatys chaperi spillmanni ♂ 2/644
Spillmann's panchax
H: W Africa: Ivory Coast.
♂: More colorful; longer fins. S: +
B: Not difficult; adhesive spawner. F: C!
T: 23–27°C, L: 7 cm, pH: <7, D: 2–3

KILLIFISHES

Epiplatys chevalieri ♂   1/558
Chevalier's panchax
H: Africa: Zaïre: near Stanley Pool.
♂: Much more colorful; longer fins. **S:** +
B: Adhesive spawner.   **F:** C
T: 24–26°C, L: 6 cm, pH: <7, D: 2

Epiplatys coccinatus ♂   3/498
"RL 46"
H: Africa: central Liberia.
♂: More colorful; longer fins.   **S:** +
B: Adhesive spawner.   **F:** C!
T: 22–26°C, L: 5 cm, pH: <7, D: 2–3

Epiplatys dageti b. ♀, t. ♂   1/560
Black-lipped panchax
H: Africa: Sierra L., Lib., Ivory C., Ghana.
♂: More colorful; longer fins.   **S:** =
B: V. easy; adh. spawner; <300 e. **F:** C,O
T: 21–23°C, L: 7 cm, pH: <7, D: 2

Epiplatys esekanus ♂   3/498
Eseka panchax
H: Africa: Cameroon.
♂: Much more colorful; longer fins.   **S:** (–)
B: Not simple; adhesive spawner. **F:** C!
T: 22–26°C, L: 7 cm, pH: <7, D: 4

Epiplatys etzeli ♂   2/646
Etzel's panchax
H: W Africa: S Ivory Coast.
♂: More colorful; longer fins.   **S:** =
B: Adh. or substrate spawner: 3 ws. **F:** C!
T: 23–27°C, L: 5 cm, pH: <7, D: 3

Epiplatys fasciolatus fasciolatus ♂ 4/386
Orange panchax
H: Africa: Guinea-Bissau to S Liberia.
♂: Much more colorful; longer fins. **S:** +
B: Adhesive spawner.   **F:** C!
T: 24–28°C, L: 9.5 cm, pH: <7, D: 2

KILLIFISHES

423

Epiplatys fasciolatus puetzi ♂　　3/500

H: Africa: Liberia: 20 km N of Buchanan.
♂: Much more colorful; longer fins. **S:** +
B: Adhesive spawner.　　　　　　**F:** C!
T: 22–28°C, L: 8 cm, pH: ≪7, D: 2–3

Epiplatys fasciolatus tototaensis ♂　3/500
Totota panchax

H: Africa: SW Liberia.
♂: Much more colorful; longer fins. **S:** +
B: Adhesive spawner.　　　　　　**F:** C!
T: 22–28°C, L: 8 cm, pH: <7, D: 2–3

Epiplatys fasciolatus zimiensis ♂　4/388
Zimi panchax

H: Africa: SE Sierra Leone.
♂: Much more colorful; longer fins. **S:** +
B: Adhesive spawner.　　　　　　**F:** C!
T: 24–28°C, L: 7 cm, pH: <7, D: 2

Epiplatys grahami ♂　　　　　　2/646
Graham's panchax

H: Africa: S Benin, Nigeria, Cameroon.
♂: More colorful; longer fins.　　**S:** +
B: Uncomplicated adh. spawner. **F:** C,O
T: 23–28°C, L: 6 cm, pH: 7, D: 2–3

Epiplatys guineensis ♂　　　　　5/477
Guinea panchax
H: Africa: Guinea.
♂: More colorful fins.　　　　　　**S:** +
B: Easy; adhesive spawner.　　**F:** C,O
T: 22–26°C, L: 6 cm, pH: 7, D: 2

Epiplatys guineensis ♀　　　　　5/477
Guinea panchax

Epiplatys hildegardae ♂   4/388
Hildegard's panchax
H: Africa: SE Guinea/NE Liberia.
♂: Much more colorful; longer fins. S: +
B: Slightly difficult; adh. spawner.   F: C
T: 22–26°C, L: 9 cm, pH: <7, D: 3

Epiplatys huberi ♂   2/648
Green-bellied panchax
H: Africa: S Gabon, S Peo. Rep. Congo.
♂: Much more colorful; longer fins. S: +
B: Adh. or substrate sp: peat, 3 ws. F: C!
T: 18–22°C, L: 5.5 cm, pH: <7, D: 2–3

Epiplatys lamottei ♂   1/560

H: Africa: Liberia, Guinea.
♂: Much more colorful; longer V fins. S: +
B: Adhesive spawner; 70 eggs.   F: C
T: 21–23°C, L: 5.5 cm, pH: 7, D: 4

Epiplatys longiventralis ♂   4/390

H: Africa: Nigeria, E Togo.
♂: More colorful; longer fins.   S: (–)
B: Adhesive spawner.   F: C!
T: 22–28°C, L: 6 cm, pH: <7, D: 3

Epiplatys mesogramma ♂   2/648

H: Africa: Central African Republic.
♂: Much more colorful; longer fins. S: +
B: Adhesive spawner.   F: C!
T: 20–24°C, L: 5.5 cm, pH: <7, D: 3–4

Epiplatys multifasciatus ♂   4/390
Striped panchax
H: Africa: central Zaïre.
♂: More colorful; longer fins.   S: (–)
B: Adhesive spawner.   F: C
T: 22–26°C, L: 5 cm, pH: <7, D: 2–3

KILLIFISHES

Epiplatys neumanni ♂ 5/479
Neumann's panchax
H: W Africa: NE Gabon.
♂: More colorful; longer fins. S: +
B: Easy; adhesive spawner. F: C
T: 22–24°C, L: 7 cm, pH: <7, D: 2

Epiplatys neumanni ♀ 5/479
Neumann's panchax

Epiplatys cf. *nigricans* ♂ 3/502
Black panchax
H: Africa: entire Congo Basin?
♂: Little more colorful; longer fins. S: +
B: Adhesive spawner. F: C!
T: 20–26°C, L: 5.5 cm, pH: <7, D: 3

Epiplatys njalaensis ♂ 3/502
Red-spotted panchax
H: Africa: SW Sierra Leone/Guinea.
♂: Much more colorful; longer fins. S: +
B: Adhesive spawner. F: C!
T: 22–28°C, L: 6 cm, pH: <7, D: 3

Epiplatys olbrechti azureus ♂ 4/392
Blue Olbrecht's panchax, "RL 56"
H: Africa: central Liberia.
♂: More colorful; longer fins. S: +
B: Adhesive spawner. F: C
T: 22–28°C, L: 8 cm, pH: <7, D: 2

Epiplatys olbrechti kassiapleuensis ♂
Kassiapleu panchax 4/394
H: Africa: central Liberia.
♂: More colorful; longer fins. S: =
B: Adhesive spawner. F: C!
T: 22–25°C, L: 8 cm, pH: <7, D: 2

Epiplatys olbrechtsi olbrechtsi ♂   4/392
Olbrecht's panchax
H: Af.: central and E Liberia, Ivory Coast.
♂: More colorful; longer fins.   S: +
B: Adhesive spawner.   F: C!
T: 22–28°C, L: 8 cm, pH: <7, D: 2

Epiplatys phoeniceps ♂   4/394
Phoenix panchax
H: Africa: E Congo.
♂: More colorful; longer fins.   S: (–)
B: Adhesive spawner.   F: C!
T: 22–28°C, L: 6 cm, pH: <7, D: 2–3

Epiplatys phoeniceps ♀   4/394
Phoenix panchax

Epiplatys roloffi ♂   2/650
Roloff's panchax
H: W Africa: Liberia: St. Paul River.
♂: Little more colorful; longer fins. S: +
B: Adh. spawner (direct or 3 ws).   F: C!
T: 22–25°C, L: 7 cm, pH: 7, D: 2–3

Epiplatys ruhkopfi ♂   2/650
Ruhkopf's panchax
H: Africa: Liberia: town of Kaningali.
♂: More colorful; longer fins.   S: +
B: Adhesive spawner.   F: C
T: 22–26°C, L: 8 cm, pH: 7, D: 2–3

Epiplatys sangmelinensis ♂   2/652
Sangmelina panchax
H: Africa: S Cameroon, N Gabon.
♂: More colorful; longer fins.   S: =
B: V. difficult; adhesive spawner.   F: C!
T: 20–24°C, L: 5 cm, pH: <7, D: 4

KILLIFISHES

427

Epiplatys sexfasciatus baroi ♂　　3/504
Red six-barred panchax
H: W Africa: SW Cameroon.
♂: More colorful; longer fins.　　　　S: +
B: Adhesive spawner.　　　　　　　F: C,O
T: 22–26°C, L: 7 cm, pH: 7, D: 2–3

Epiplatys sexfasciatus rathkei ♂　3/504
Rathke's six-barred panchax
H: W Africa: W Cameroon.
♂: More colorful; longer fins.　　　　S: =
B: Adhesive spawner.　　　　　　　F: C,O
T: 22–26°C, L: 8 cm, pH: 7, D: 2–3

Epiplatys sexfasciatus sexfasciatus
Six-barred panchax t.♀,b.♂ 1/562, 2/652
H: W Africa: from S Togo to NW Gabon.
♂: More colorful; longer fins.　　　　S: +
B: Simple adhesive spawner.　　　F: C,O
T: 22–26°C, L: 8 cm, pH: 7, D: 2–3

Epiplatys sexfasciatus togolensis ♂ 4/396
Togo six-barred panchax
H: W Africa: from Togo to S Nigeria.
♂: More colorful; longer fins.　　　　S: +
B: Adhesive spawner.　　　　　　　F: C!
T: 22–28°C, L: 8 cm, pH: 7, D: 2

Epiplatys sheljuzhkoi ♂　　　　4/396
Sheljuzhko's panchax
H: Africa: central and E Congo.
♂: Much more colorful; longer fins. S: =
B: Adhesive spawner.　　　　　　　F: C!
T: 24–28°C, L: 6 cm, pH: <7, D: 2

Epiplatys singa ♂　　　　　　1/562
One-bar panchax, spotted epiplatys
H: Africa: lower Zaïre.
♂: More colorful; longer fins.　　　　S: –
B: Adh. spawner; 80–100 eggs.　　F: C!
T: 23–25°C, L: 5.5 cm, pH: <7, D: 4

KILLIFISHES

Epiplatys sp. "Lac Fwa" ♂   4/398
Fwa panchax
H: Africa: Zaïre: Lac Fwa Basin.
♂: Much more colorful; longer fins. S: (–)
B: Not difficult; adhesive spawner. F: C
T: 22–28°C, L: 5 cm, pH: <7, D: 2

Epiplatys spilargyreius ♂   4/398
Green panchax
H: Senegal to Nile and Zaïre Basin.
♂: Slightly more colorful; longer fins. S: +
B: Adhesive spawner.   F: C!
T: 24–30°C, L: 5 cm, pH: 7, D: 2

Epiplatys spilargyreius ♀   4/398
Green panchax

Epiplatys spilargyreius ♂   4/398
Green panchax
H: E Nigeria.

Episemion callipteron ♂   4/402

Episemion callipteron ♀   4/402

H: Africa: N Gabon. Equatorial Guinea?
♂: More colorful; longer fins.   S: (–)
B: Difficult; adhesive spawner.   F: C!
T: 20–24°C, L: 4 cm, pH: ≪7, D: 3

KILLIFISHES

429

Foerschichthys flavipinnis b.♂, t.♀   4/404
Yellow-finned killie

H: Africa: SE Ghana to the Niger Delta.
♂: More colorful fins.   S: +
B: Not easy; adhesive spawner.   F: C
T: 23–28°C, L: 3.5 cm, pH: <7, D: 3

Foerschichthys flavipinnis ♂   4/404
Yellow-finned killie

Fundulopanchax huwaldi ♂   5/542

H: Africa: Sierra Leone.
♂: Much more colorful; longer fins. S: +
B: Not simple; substrate sp.: 20 ws.   F:C
T: 24–30°C, L: 12 cm, pH: 7, D: 3

Fundulopanchax huwaldi ♂   5/542

H: Africa: Sierra Leone: Fullaba.

Fundulopanchax sp. "Lago" ♂   5/542

Fundulosoma thierryi ♂   1/564

H: Africa: Guinea to SW Niger.
♂: Much more colorful.   S: –
B: Easy; substrate spawner: 16 ws.   F:C
T: ca. 22°C, L: 3.5 cm, pH: 7, D: 1–2

Nothobranchius cyaneus ♂　　2/662
Blue notho
H: E Africa: S Somalia, NE Kenya.
♂: Much more colorful; longer fins. **S:** –
B: Substrate spawner: 12 ws.　　**F:** C
T: 24–26°C, **L:** 5 cm, **pH:** 7, **D:** 2–3

Nothobranchius eggersi ♂　　3/506
Eggers' notho "blue"
H: Africa: E Tanzania.
♂: Much more colorful; longer fins. **S:** =
B: Substrate spawner: 6 ws.　　**F:** C
T: 24–28°C, **L:** 5 cm, **pH:** <7, **D:** 3

Nothobranchius eggersi ♂　　3/506
Eggers' notho
Red × blue cross.

Nothobranchius eggersi ♂　　3/506
Eggers' notho
Wild form; red.

Nothobranchius elongatus ♂　　3/510
Slender notho
H: Africa: SE Kenya.
♂: Much more colorful; longer fins. **S:** =
B: Substrate spawner: 6 ws.　　**F:** C
T: 24–28°C, **L:** 6 cm, **pH:** <7, **D:** 3

Nothobranchius elongatus ♂　　3/510
Slender notho
Wild form, Kenya.

KILLIFISHES

431

Nothobranchius fasciatus ♂   4/406
Striped notho
H: Africa: S Somalia.
♂: Posterior body has dark stripes.   S: =
B: Substrate spawner: 6–8 ws.   F: C
T: 24–30°C, L: 7 cm, pH: >7, D: 3

Nothobranchius foerschi ♂   3/512
Foersch's notho
H: Africa: E Tanzania.
♂: Much more colorful.   S: =
B: Substrate spawner: 6 ws.   F: C!
T: 22–26°C, L: 5 cm, pH: 7, D: 3

Nothobranchius furzeri ♂   2/662
Furzer's notho
H: Africa: E Zimbabwe/Mozambique.
♂: Much more colorful.   S: =
B: Substrate spawner: 12 ws.   F: C,O
T: 22–26°C, L: 8 cm, pH: <7, D: 2–3

Nothobranchius guentheri ♂   1/568
Günther's notho
H: Africa: Zanzibar Island.
♂: Much more colorful; longer fins. S: (–)
B: Substrate spawner: 12–16 ws.   F: C
T: 22–25°C, L: 4.5 cm, pH: <7, D: 3

Nothobranchius interruptus ♂   3/512
Kikambala notho
H: Africa: SE Kenya.
♂: Much more colorful; longer fins. S: =
B: Substrate spawner: 6 ws.   F: C
T: 22–26°C, L: 6.5 cm, pH: <7, D: 3

Nothobranchius janpapi ♂ WC   2/664
Topwater fire killie, Jan Pap's notho
H: Africa: Tanzania.
♂: Much more colorful; longer fins. S: (–)
B: Substrate spawner: 8–12 ws.   F: C
T: 23–30°C, L: 3.5 cm, pH: 7, D: 3–4

Nothobranchius jubbi ♂　　2/664
Jubb's notho
H: E Africa: S Kenya/Somalia.
♂: Much more colorful; longer fins. **S:** +
B: Substrate spawner.　　　**F:** C
T: 24–26°C, **L:** 5 cm, **pH:** <7, **D:** 2–3

Nothobranchius kafuensis b.♀, t.♂　3/522
WC
H: Africa: Zambia.
♂: Much more colorful; longer fins. **S:** +
B: Substrate spawner: 6 ws.　　**F:** C
T: 22–28°C, **L:** 5 cm, **pH:** <7, **D:** 3

Nothobranchius kirki ♂　　1/568
Kirk's notho
H: E Africa: Malawi: Lake Chilwa.
♂: Much more colorful; longer fins. **S:** –
B: Substrate spawner.　　　**F:** C
T: 20–23°C, **L:** 5 cm, **pH:** <7, **D:** 3

Nothobranchius korthausae t.♂　1/568
Korthaus' notho
H: Africa: Tanzania (Mafia Island).
♂: Much more colorful; longer fins. **S:** (–)
B: Substrate spawner.　　　**F:** C
T: 23–26°C, **L:** 6 cm, **pH:** <7, **D:** 3

Nothobranchius kuhntae ♂　　4/406
Kuhnt's notho
H: Africa: Mozambique, Malawi.
♂: More colorful; longer fins.　**S:** (–)
B: Continuous substr. spa.: 6–8 ws. **F:** C
T: 24–28°C, **L:** 6.5 cm, **pH:** 7, **D:** 2

Nothobranchius lourensi ♂　　3/514
Green notho
H: Africa: Tanzania.
♂: More colorful.　　　　　**S:** +
B: Substrate spawner: 6 ws.　**F:** C!
T: 24–28°C, **L:** 5 cm, **pH:** <7, **D:** 3

KILLIFISHES

433

Nothobranchius luekei ♂   3/514
Lüke's notho
H: Africa: E Tanzania: coastal lowlands.
♂: More colorful.   S: (–)
B: Substrate spawner: 6 ws.   F: C!
T: 24–30°C, L: 4 cm, pH: 7, D: 4

Nothobranchius melanospilus ♂   3/516
Beira notho
H: Africa: SE Kenya, E Tanzania.
♂: Much more colorful.   S: +
B: Substrate spawner: 6 ws.   F: C
T: 22–28°C, L: 7 cm, pH: <7, D: 2–3

Nothobranchius microlepis ♂   2/666
Small-scaled notho
H: Africa: E Kenya, SE Somalia.
♂: Bullish; colorful fins.   S: –
B: Substrate spawner: 12 ws.   F: C
T: 23–30°C, L: 6 cm, pH: <7, D: 3

Nothobranchius neumanni ♂ WC   3/516
Neumann's notho
H: Africa: central Tanzania.
♂: Much more colorful.   S: =
B: Substrate spawner.   F: C!
T: 24–28°C, L: 6 cm, pH: <7, D: 3

Nothobranchius ocellatus ♂   4/408
Ocellated notho
H: Africa: E Tanzania.
♂: Much more color.   S: –
B: Brief; substr. sp.; white peat; 12 ws. F: C!
T: 24–30°C, L: <10 cm, pH: <7, D: 2–3

Nothobranchius orthonotus ♂   2/666
Dusky notho
H: Af.: South Africa, Mozambique, Malawi.
♂: More colorful.   S: (–)
B: Brief; substrate spawner: 12 ws.   F: C
T: 23–30°C, L: 9 cm, pH: 7, D: 2–3

Nothobranchius palmqvisti ♂   1/570
Palmqvist's notho
H: Africa: S Kenya, Tanzania.
♂: Much more colorful; longer fins. **S:** –
B: Continuous sub. sp.:12 ws; 200 e. **F:** C
T: 18–22°C, **L:** 5 cm, **pH:** <7, **D:** 3

Nothobranchius patrizii b.♀, t.♂ 2/668
Red-tailed turquoise notho, Patrizi's notho
H: Africa: E Kenya/SE Somalia.
♂: Much more colorful; longer fins. **S:** =
B: Substrate spawner: 8–12 ws.   **F:** C!
T: 23–30°C, **L:** 5 cm, **pH:** <7, **D:** 2–3

Nothobranchius polli ♂ ♂   3/518
Poll's notho
H: Africa: SE Zaïre/Zambia.
♂: Much more colorful; longer fins. **S:** =
B: Substrate spawner: 6 ws.   **F:** C!
T: 22–28°C, **L:** 5 cm, **pH:** <7, **D:** 3

Nothobranchius rachovii b.♀, t.♂ 1/570
Rachow's notho
H: Africa: Mozambique to South Africa.
♂: Much more colorful; longer fins. **S:** (–)
B: Substrate spawner.   **F:** C
T: 20–24°C, **L:** 5 cm, **pH:** <7, **D:** 3

Nothobranchius robustus ♂   3/518
Robust notho, C 86/13
H: Africa: Lake Victoria Basin.
♂: Much more colorful; longer fins. **S:** (–)
B: Substrate spawner: 6 ws.   **F:** C
T: 24–28°C, **L:** 5.5 cm, **pH:** <7, **D:** 3

Nothobranchius rubripinnis ♂   3/520
Red-finned notho, KTZ85/28
H: Tanzania: Mbemkuru River.
♂: Much more colorful; longer fins. **S:** (–)
B: Substrate spawner: 6 ws.   **F:** C!
T: 22–28°C, **L:** 5 cm, **pH:** <7, **D:** 3–4

KILLIFISHES

435

Nothobranchius rubripinnis　　3/520
Red-finned notho, Tz 83/5　b.♀, t.♂
H: Africa: Tanzania: Mbezi River.

Nothobranchius sp. "C 86/9" ♂　5/482

H: Africa: Kenya: "Lake Victoria."

Nothobranchius sp. "Lake Victoria" ♂
Victoria notho　　　　　　　　　4/410
H: Africa: Kenya, Tanzania.
♂: Much more colorful; longer fins.　S: (–)
B: Substrate spawner.　　　　　　F: C!
T: 24–28°C, L: 4 cm, pH: 7, D: 2–3

Nothobranchius sp. "Ruvuma" t.♂　5/480
Ruvuma notho
H: Africa: Tanzania. Mozambique?
♂: Much more colorul; longer fins.　S: (–)
B: Substrate spawner: 6 ws.　　　F: C
T: 22–28°C, L: 5 cm, pH: 7, D: 2

Nothobranchius sp. "Uganda" ♂ 4/412
Uganda notho
H: Africa: Uganda.
♂: Much more colorful; longer fins. S: =
B: Substrate spawner.　　　　　　F: C
T: 24–28°C, L: 5 cm, pH: 7, D: 2

Nothobranchius steinforti ♂　　4/408
Steinfort's notho
H: Africa: Tanzania.
♂: Much more colorful; longer fins.　S: (–)
B: Substrate spawner: 6–8 ws.　　F: C!
T: 24–28°C, L: 5 cm, pH: 7, D: 2–3

Nothobranchius steinforti ♀　　4/408
Steinfort's notho

Nothobranchius symoensi ♂　　4/412
Symoen's notho
H: Africa: Zaïre.
♂: More colorful; longer fins.　　　　S: =
B: Substrate spawner.　　　　　　　　F: C
T: 24–28°C, L: 4.5 cm, pH: 7, D: 2

Nothobranchius taeniopygus ♂　　3/522
Stripe-finned notho, KTZ 85/9
H: Africa: central Tanzania.
♂: More colorful; longer fins.　　　　S: =
B: Substrate spawner: 6 ws.　　　　　F: C
T: 18–24°C, L: 6 cm, pH: >7, D: 3

Nothobranchius ugandensis ♂　　5/480
Uganda notho
H: Africa: Uganda.
♂: Much more colorful; longer fins.　S: (–)
B: Substr. spawner: after 2 w, 8 ws. F: C!
T: 24–30°C, L: ♂ 5 cm, pH: 7, D: 2

Nothobranchius vosseleri ♂　　5/482
Vosseler's notho
H: Africa: Tanzania.
♂: Much more colorful; longer fins.　S: (–)
B: Substr. spawner; after 2 w, 8 ws. F: C!
T: 24–28°C, L: ♂ 4.5 cm, pH: 7, D: 2

Nothobranchius vosseleri ♀　　5/482
Vosseler's notho

KILLIFISHES

Nothobranchius willerti ♂　　　　4/410
Mnanzini notho
H: Africa: Kenya.
♂: Much more colorful; longer fins.　S: (–)
B: Substrate spawner; 6–8 ws.　　F: C!
T: 24–28°C, L: 4 cm, pH: <7, D: 3

Pachypanchax omalonotus l.♀, r.♂　3/524
Powder-blue panchax
H: W and N Madagascar.
♂: Pointed fins; slimmer.　　　　S: +
B: Adhesive spawner.　　　　　　F: C
T: 22–28°C, L: 8 cm, pH: 7, D: 2

Pachypanchax playfairii t.♂, b.♀　1/574
Playfair's panchax
H: Seychelles, Zanzibar, Madagascar.
♂: More colorful fins; slimmer.　S: –
B: Adhesive spawner; <200 e.　F: C
T: 22–24°C, L: 10 cm, pH: <7, D: 1

Paranothobranchius ocellatus ♀　3/524
WC
H: Africa: E Tanzania.
♂: More colorful. 2 ocelli?　　S: ?
B: Unknown.　　　　　　　　F: C
T: 22–26°C, L: 6 cm, pH: <7, D: 3?

Pronothobranchius kiyawensis b.♀, t.♂
3/526
H: Africa: Gambia, Ghana, N Nigeria.
♂: More colorful; longer fins.　S: =
B: Difficult; substrate spawner: 6 ws. F: C
T: 22–26°C, L: 6 cm, pH: <7, D: 4

Pseudepiplatys annulatus t.♂, b.♀　1/558
Rocket panchax, clown killie
H: Africa: from Guinea to Niger.
♂: More colorful; longer fins.　　S: +
B: Very difficult; adhesive spawner.　F: C
T: 23–25°C, L: 4 cm, pH: <7, D: 4

KILLIFISHES

Subfamily Rivulinae

The subfamily Rivulinae is sometimes classified as a family—Rivulidae—within the order Cyprinodontiformes. To ease the search for species, they have been alphabetically listed under their respective subfamilies throughout Group 5.

The subfamily of New World rivulines consists of 12 genera and at least 125 species. They inhabit North America from southern Florida, through Central America, to Uruguay in South America. The vast majority inhabit freshwater; some species, however, can be found in highly saline brackish biotopes. About 100 of the species belong to either *Rivulus* or *Cynolebias*.

All the reproductive strategies known for killifishes are represented within the subfamily Rivulinae. The most specious genera can be summarized as follows: *Austrofundulus*: annual fishes. *Campellolebias*: see below. *Cynolebias*: bottom-diving annual fishes. *Leptolebias*: annual fishes and nonannual species. *Pterolebias* and *Rachovia*: annual fishes, some of which have an extremely long storage (incubation) period. *Rivulus*: adhesive spawners and substrate spawners, some of which have a short storage period. *Trigonectes*: annual fishes that typically have a long storage period.

Rivulus ocellatus (syn.: *R. marmoratus*), p. 464, is rather unique. As yet, a female *R. ocellatus* has not been found, only males and hermaphrodites. The eggs of this egg-laying species are sometimes self-fertilized internally. The males of *Campellolebias brucei* and *C. dorsimaculatus* (p. 440) have a gonopodium. Like livebearing toothcarps, the eggs are internally fertilized, but then deposited in the normal manner of a substrate spawner. These species are considered links to the livebearing toothcarps of Group 6.

Most species in this subfamily require a closely fitting cover on the aquarium. *Rivulus* are accomplished jumpers, commonly leaping from the water and sticking to the glass above the water surface. Whether in a bag coming

Rivulus sp. WC ♂ (5 cm length) from the Rio Payamino/Rio Napo drainage, Ecuador, South America.

home from the pet store or in a collectors bucket at their natural habitat, they readily display their dexterity. Just a moment of forgetfulness or an ill-fitting lid can result in an aquarium empty of *Rivulus*.

Rivulines are inhabitants of small and extremely small streams and shallow shores of floodplains in the shade of the rain forest, where jump from one puddle to the other. Correspondingly, there are many species and subspecies with localized areas of distribution.

Austrofundulus limnaeus t.♀, b.♂ 2/630
Venezuelan killie
H: S Am.: Guyana, Venezuela, Colombia.
♂: More colorful; larger fins.   S: +
B: Substrate spawner: 12–26 ws. F: C!
T: 22–26°C, L: 8 cm, pH: <7, D: 3

Austrofundulus limnaeus ♂   2/630
Venezuelan killie "myersi type"

Campellolebias brucei ♂   5/504
Turner's gaucho
H: S America: SE Brazil: Santa Catarina.
♂: Longer fins; colorful; gonopodium. S:–
B: Internal fert.; substrate sp; 8 ws. F: C!
T: 20–24°C, L: 4.5 cm, pH: <7, D: 3–4

Campellolebias dorsimaculatus ♂   5/504

Cynolebias adloffi ♂   2/634
Adolf's pealfish, banded pearlfish
H: S America: N Uruguay/SE Brazil.
♂: More colorful; longer fins.   S: (–)
B: Substrate spawner: 6–8 ws.   F: C
T: 20–28°C, L: 4 cm, pH: 7, D: 2–3

H: S America: SE Brazil: São Paulo.
♂: Longer fins; colorful; gonopodium.   S:–
B: Internal fert.; substrate sp.: 8 ws. F: C!
T: 22–28°C, L: 3.5 cm, pH: <7, D: 4

KILLIFISHES

Cynolebias affinis ♂   5/506
Pearlfish
H: S America: Uruguay.
♂: More colorful; larger fins.   S: =
B: Substrate spawner.   F: C
T: 18–24°C, L: 5 cm, pH: <7, D: 2–3

Cynolebias albipunctatus   5/506
White-dot pearlfish   blue wild form
H: S America: Brazil: Pernambuco.
♂: 3 cm larger; longer fins.   S: (–)
B: Substr. sp.: 16–24ws; 20% hatch.   F:C
T: 26–30°C, L: ♂ 12 cm, pH: 7, D: 3

Cynolebias bellottii l.♂, r.♀♀   1/550
Argentine pearlfish
H: S America: Rio de la Plata Basin.
♂: More colorful; larger.   S: (–)
B: Substrate spawner: 12–16 ws. F: C,O
T: 18–22°C, L: 7 cm, pH: <7, D: 3

Cynolebias boitonei ♂   2/636
Brazilian pearlfish
H: S America: Brazil: at Brasilia.
♂: Much more colorful; longer fins. S: (–)
B: Substrate spawner: 8 ws.   F: C!
T: 20–24°C, L: 4 cm, pH: 7, D: 3

Cynolebias bokermanni ♂   5/508
Bahia pearlfish
H: S America: Brazil: Bahia.
♂: Much more colorful; longer fins. S: (–)
B: Substrate spawner: 12–20 ws.   F: C
T: 22–28°C, L: 5 cm, pH: <7, D: 2

Cynolebias bokermanni ♀   5/508
Bahia pearlfish

KILLIFISHES

441

Cynolebias chacoensis ♂　　5/510
Chaco pearlfish
H: S America: Paraguay: La Serena.
♂: More colorful; 1 cm larger.　　S: +
B: Substrate spawner: 8 ws.　　F: C
T: 22–28°C, L: ♂ 5 cm, pH: 7, D: 2

Cynolebias chacoensis ♂　　5/510
Chaco pearlfish
H: S America: Paraguay: San Juan.

Cynolebias cheradophilus t.♂, b.♀　2/636
Fine-scaled pearlfish
H: S America: E Uruguay.
♂: Slightly more colorful; larger.　　S: +
B: Substrate spawner: 12 ws.　　F: C
T: 18–25°C, L: 8 cm, pH: >7, D: 3

Cynolebias cinereus ♂　　5/508
Green pearlfish
H: S America: Uruguay: Colonia.
♂: Greenish; longer fins.　　S: +
B: Substrate spawner: 12–16 ws.　　F: C
T: 18–24°C, L: 6 cm, pH: <7, D: 2–3

Cynolebias constanciae ♂　　5/512
Feather-fin pearlfish
H: S America: SE Brazil.
♂: More colorful; elongated fins.　　S: =
B: Substrate spawner: 12–16 ws.　　F: C
T: 22–25°C, L: 5 cm, pH: 7, D: 2–3

Cynolebias costai ♂　　5/512
Costa's pearlfish
H: S America: Brazil: Goias.
♂: Much more colorful.　　S: (–)
B: Substrate spawner: 12–20 ws.　　F: C!
T: 24–30°C, L: 4 cm, pH: <7, D: 4

KILLIFISHES

Cynolebias costai ♀   5/512
Costa's pearlfish

Cynolebias cyaneus ♂   5/515
Cyan pearlfish
H: S America: Brazil: Rio Grande do Sul.
♂: More colorful.   S: (–)
B: Substrate spawner: 12–20 ws.   F: C
T: 22–28°C, L: 4 cm, pH: <7, D: 2–3

Cynolebias elongatus ♂   3/491
Elongated pearlfish
H: S America: S Uruguay, Argentina.
♂: Little more colorful; broader fins. S: =
B: Substrate spawner: 12–16 ws.   F: C!
T: 16–25°C, L: 14 cm, pH: 7, D: 3

Cynolebias flammeus ♂   5/516
Flame pearlfish
H: S America: Brazil: Rio Paraná.
♂: Much more colorful; longer fins. S: (–)
B: Easy; substr. spawn.: 12–16 ws. F: C!
T: 22–26°C, L: 3.5 cm, pH: <7, D: 2

Cynolebias flavicaudatus ♂   5/516
Yellow-finned pearlfish
H: S America: Brazil: Pernambuco.
♂: More colorful; larger fins.   S: +
B: Substrate spawner.   F: C
T: 22–26°C, L: 5.5 cm, pH: >7, D: 2

Cynolebias flavicaudatus ♀   5/516
Yellow-finned pearlfish

KILLIFISHES

Cynolebias sp. aff. *flavicaudatus* ♂   5/528
Yellow-finned pearlfish
H: S America: Brazil: Minas Gerais.

Cynolebias fulminantis ♂   5/518
Jewel pearlfish
H: S America: Brazil: Minas Gerais.
♂: Much more colorful.   S: +
B: Easy substrate spawner.   F: C
T: 18–24°C, L: 4 cm, pH: <7, D: 2

Cynolebias griseus ♀   5/518

H: S America: Brazil: N Goiás.
♂: Slightly lighter.   S: =
B: Substrate spawner: 12 ws.   F: C
T: 22–26°C, L: 7.5 cm, pH: 7, D: 3

Cynolebias hellneri ♂   5/520
Hellner's pearlfish
H: S America: Brazil: Minas Gerais.
♂: Much more colorful; longer fins. S: =
B: Substr. spawner; sand/clay/peat. F: C
T: 22–26°C, L: ♂ 5.5 cm, pH: >7, D: 2

Cynolebias hellneri ♀   5/520
Hellner's pearlfish

Cynolebias heloplites ♂   2/638

H: S America: E Brazil.
♂: More colorful; longer fins.   S: +
B: Substr. spawner: 12 ws at 30°C.   F: C
T: 25–30°C, L: 5 cm, pH: 7, D: 3

Cynolebias leptocephalus ♂   5/522
Small-head pearlfish
H: S America: Brazil: Minas Gerais.
♂: More colorful; longer fins.   S: –
B: Substrate spawner.   F: C
T: 15–25°C, L: ♂ 15 cm, pH: <7, D: 3

Cynolebias magnificus ♂   5/522
Magnificent pearlfish
H: Brazil: central Rio São Francisco.
♂: Much more colorful; longer fins. S: (–)
B: Substrate spawner.   F: C!
T: 22–26°C, L: 4 cm, pH: >7, D: 2

Cynolebias monstrosus ♂   5/524
Monster pearlfish
H: S America: Paraguay: La Serena.
♂: Larger, stouter; ♂♀ color similar. S: –
B: Substrate spawner.   F: C!
T: 25–30°C, L: >13 cm, pH: 7, D: 4

Cynolebias monstrosus ♂   5/524
Monster pearlfish
H: S America: Paraguay: Faro Maro.

Cynolebias myersi ♂   5/526
Myers's pearlfish
H: S America: Brazil: Espirito Santo.
♂: Much more colorful; longer fins. S: (–)
B: Substrate spawner: 12–20 ws. F: C!
T: 23–28°C, L: ♂ 5.5 cm, pH: <7, D: 3

Cynolebias myersi ♀   5/526
Myers's pearlfish

KILLIFISHES

Cynolebias nigripinnis alexandri ♂   1/550
Alexander's black-finned pearlfish
H: S America: Argentina: Entre Rios.
♂: More colorful.   S: +
B: Substrate spawner: 12 ws.   F: C!
T: 22–28°C, L: 9 cm, pH: <7, D: 3

Cynolebias nigripinnis nigripinnis   1/552
Black-finned pearlfish t.♂, b.♀
H: S America: Argentina: Paraná.
♂: More colorful.   S: –
B: Substrate spawner: ≥12 ws.   F: C
T: 20–22°C, L: 4.5 cm, pH: <7, D: 3

Cynolebias nonoiuliensis ♂ WC   3/494
Giant pearl fish
H: S Am.: Argentina: prov. of Buenos Aires.
♂: Larger fins.   S: =
B: Substrate spawner: 16–20 ws.   F: C!
T: 15–25°C, L: 10 cm, pH: <7, D: 3–4

Cynolebias notatus ♂   5/529
Spotted pearlfish
H: S America: Brazil: Goias.
♂: More colorful; longer fins.   S: (–)
B: Substr. spawner; sand/clay/peat.   F: C
T: 22–26°C, L: 4 cm, pH: >7, D: 2

Cynolebias notatus ♀   5/529
Spotted pearlfish

Cynolebias perforatus ♂   5/531

H: S America: Brazil: Minas Gerais.
♂: More colorful; longer fins.   S: –
B: Substrate spawner: 16 ws.   F: C
T: 22–26°C, L: ♂ >18 cm, pH: 7, D: 4

Cynolebias perforatus ♂   5/531

H: S America: Brazil: Itacarambi.

Cynolebias perforatus ♀   5/531

H: Brazil: Minas Gerais.

Cynolebias porosus ♂   5/532
Pernambuco pearlfish
H: S America: NE Brazil: Pernambuco.
♂: More colorful; longer fins.   S: –
B: Substrate spawner.   F: C!
T: 22–26°C, L: >16 cm, pH: 7, D: 4

Cynolebias prognathus ♂   5/532

H: S America: Uruguay.
♂: D 17–18, A 23–25 rays. ♀: Fewer. S: –
B: Substrate spawner: 12 ws.   F: C!
T: 22–26°C, L: >18 cm, pH: 7, D: 4

Cynolebias prognathus ♀   5/532

Cynolebias stellatus ♂   5/535
Starred pearlfish
H: S America: Brazil: Minas Gerais.
♂: More colorful; longer fins.   S: +
B: Substr. spawner; sand/clay/peat. F: C
T: 22–26°C, L: 4 cm, pH: >7, D: 3

KILLIFISHES

447

Cynolebias vandenbergi ♂   5/537
Vandenberg's pearlfish
H: S America: Paraguay.
♂: Larger; more colorful.   **S:** +
B: Substrate spawner: 8–12 ws.   **F:** C
T: 25–30°C, **L:** 7 cm, **pH:** 7, **D:** 3

Cynolebias vandenbergi ♂   5/537
Vandenberg's pearlfish
H: S America: Paraguay: Caracol.

Cynolebias vandenbergi ♂   5/537
Vandenberg's pearlfish
H: S America: Paraguay: Faro Moro.

Cynolebias vazferreirai ♂   5/538
Vazferreira's pearlfish
H: S America: Uruguay: Cerro Largo.
♀: Dark spots; smaller fins.   **S:** –
B: Easy; substr. spawner: 12–16 ws. **F:** C
T: 15–25°C, **L:** ♂ 10 cm, **pH:** 7, **D:** 3

Cynolebias vazferreirai ♀   5/538
Vazferreira's pearlfish

Cynolebias viarius l.♂, r.♀   2/638
Blue-banded pearlfish
H: S America: Uruguay: coastal plain.
♂: Stripes. ♀: Dots.   **S:** +
B: Substrate spawner: 12 ws.   **F:** C!
T: 18–23°C, **L:** 6 cm, **pH:** 7, **D:** 2–3

Cynolebias withei ♂   1/552
White's pearlfish
H: S America: Brazil: at Rio de Janeiro.
♂: More colorful; longer fins.   S: (–)
B: Substrate spawner: 12–16 ws.   F: C!
T: 20–23°C, L: ♂ 8 cm, pH: <7, D: 3

Cynolebias wolterstorffi ♂   5/540
Wolterstorff's pearlfish
H: S America: S Brazil/N Uruguay.
♂: More colorful; longer fins.   S: –
B: Substrate spawner: 12–32 ws.   F: C
T: 20–25°C, L: ♂ 10 cm, pH: 7, D: 2

Cynolebias wolterstorffi ♀   5/540
Wolterstorff's pearlfish

Cynolebias zonatus ♂   5/540
Striped pearlfish
H: S America: Brazil: Minas Gerais.
♂: More colorful.   S: –
B: Substr. spawner: 6 ws at >30°C. F: C
T: 20–24°C, L: 4.5 cm, pH: 7, D: 3

Cynopoecilus ladigesi ♂   1/554
Ladiges's pearlfish
H: S-Am.: Brazil: near Rio de Janeiro.
♂: Much more colorful; longer fins. S: +
B: Substrate spawner: 8–12 ws.   F: C
T: 20–22°C, L: 4 cm, pH: <7, D: 3

Cynopoecilus melanotaenia ♂   3/494
Black-banded pearlfish
H: S America: SE Brazil, N Uruguay.
♂: More colorful; longer fins.   S: =
B: Substrate spawner: 8–12 ws.   F: C!
T: 18–24°C, L: 5.5 cm, pH: <7, D: 3–4

KILLIFISHES

449

KILLIFISHES

Leptolebias aureoguttatus ♂   5/544
Gold-dot dwarf pearlfish
H: S America: Brazil: Santos lowlands.
♂: Much more colorful.   S: –
B: Substrate spawner: 34–42 ws.   F: C
T: 23–26°C, L: 4 cm, pH: 7, D: 4

Leptolebias fluminensis ♂   5/544

H: S America: Brazil: Rio de Janeiro.
♂: Much more colorful.   S: –
B: Substrate spawner: 8 ws.   F: C
T: 22–27°C, L: 3 cm, pH: ≪7, D: 1

Leptolebias leitaoi ♂   5/546
Leitao's dwarf pearlfish
H: S America: Brazil: Bahia.
♂: Much more colorful.   S: +
B: Substrate spawner: 8 ws.   F: C
T: 22–26°C, L: 3.5 cm, pH: ≪7, D: 3

Leptolebias minimus ♂   5/546
Dwarf pearlfish
H: S America: Brazil: Rio de Janeiro.
♂: Much more colorful.   S: =
B: Substrate or adhesive spawner. F: C
T: 22–26°C, L: 3 cm, pH: ≪7, D: 1

Leptolebias minimus ♂   5/546
Dwarf pearlfish

Leptolebias minimus ♂   5/546
Dwarf pearlfish

Maratecoara lacortei ♂   5/549

H: S America: Brazil: Goias.
♂: Much more colorful; longer fins. **S:** +
B: Substrate spawner: 11–17 ws.   **F:** C
T: 22–26°C, **L:** ♂ 4 cm, **pH:** <7, **D:** 4

Moema piriana ♂   5/552

H: S America: Brazil: Pará.
♂: More colorful; larger fins.   **S:** (–)
B: Substr. spawner: 6 ws at <30°C.   **F:** C
T: 24–32°C, **L:** 16 cm, **pH:** <7, **D:** 3

Moema piriana ♀   5/552

Neofundulus ornatipinnis ♂   5/554

H: S America: Brazil.
♂: Much more colorful; longer fins. **S:** =
B: Substrate spawner: 4–6 ws.   **F:** C
T: 24–30°C, **L:** 7 cm, **pH:** 7, **D:** 3

Neofundulus paraguayensis ♂   5/554

H: S America: Brazil, Paraguay.
♂: More colorful; 1.5 cm larger.   **S:** =
B: Substrate spawner: 4–8 ws.   **F:** C
T: 22–26°C, **L:** ♂ 7 cm, **pH:** 7, **D:** 2

Neofundulus parvipinnis ♂   5/556

H: S America: Brazil: Mato Grosso.
♂: More colorful.   **S:** –
B: Substrate spawner: 4–8 ws.   **F:** C
T: 22–26°C, **L:** 6 cm, **pH:** 7, **D:** 3

KILLIFISHES

451

Pituna poranga ♂   5/556

Pituna poranga ♀   5/556

H: S America: Brazil: Goiás.
♂: More colorful.   S: +
B: Substrate spawner: 6–20 ws.   F: C
T: 24–30°C, L: 6 cm, pH: <7, D: 2

Plesiolebias aruana ♂   5/558
Aruana pearlfish
H: S America: Brazil: Goiás.
♂: Little more colorful; longer fins.   S: (–)
B: Substrate spawner: 21 ws.   F: C!
T: 24–26°C, L: 3 cm, pH: 7, D: 3–4

Plesiolebias bitteri ♂   5/558
Bitter's pearlfish
H: S America: Paraguay?
♂: Much more colorful; longer fins.   S: +
B: Substrate spawner: 12–21 ws.   F: C!
T: 22–26°C, L: 4.5 cm, pH: 7, D: 2–3

Plesiolebias bitteri ♀   5/558
Bitter's pearlfish

Plesiolebias glaucopterus ♂   5/560
Pantanal pearlfish
H: S America: Brazil: Mato Grosso.
♂: Little more colorful; longer fins.   S: (–)
B: Substrate spawner: 21 ws.   F: C!
T: 22–26°C, L: 3 cm, pH: 7, D: 3–4

KILLIFISHES

Pterolebias hoignei ♂   5/562

H: S America: Venezuela: Orinoco Llanos.
♂: Brighter; longer fins; 6 cm larger. S: =
B: Substr. spawner: 10 ws at 35°C! F: C
T: 19–30°C, L: ♂ 15 cm, pH: <7, D: 4

Pterolebias longipinnis ♂ 1/576, 5/562
Longfin killifish

H: S America: Brazil, Par., Bol., Arg.
♂: Brighter; longer fins; 6 cm larger. S: –
B: Substrate spawner: 10–12 ws. F: C
T: 24–30°C, L: ♂ 15 cm, pH: <7, D: 2

Pterolebias longipinnis ♂ 1/576, 5/562
Longfin killifish

Pterolebias phasianus ♂   5/564
Pheasant longfin killie

H: S America: Brazil: Mato Grosso.
♂: More colorful; longer fins.   S: +
B: Substrate spawner: 10–12 ws. F: C
T: 22–28°C, L: ♂ 8 cm, pH: 7, D: 3

Pterolebias phasianus ♀   5/564
Pheasant longfin killie

Pterolebias peruensis t.♀, b.♂   5/566
Peruvian longfin killie

H: S America: Peru: Loreto Province.
♂: Much more colorful; longer fins. S: =
B: Substrate spawner: 21 ws.   F: C
T: 22–26°C, L: 7 cm, pH: 7, D: 2

KILLIFISHES

Pterolebias staecki ♂ WC　　　3/527
Staeck's longfin killie
H: S America: Brazil: Lago Janauacá.
♂: Much more colorful; longer fins. S: (–)
B: Substrate spawner: 26 ws.　　F: C!
T: 24–28°C, L: 10 cm, pH: 7, D: 4

Pterolebias wischmanni ♂　　　3/528
Spangled longfin killie
H: S Am.: Peru: 120 km S of Pucallpa.
♂: Much more colorful; longer fins. S: =
B: Substrate spawner: 26 ws.　　F: C
T: 24–26°C, L: ♂ 14 cm, pH: 7, D: 3–4

Pterolebias xiphophorus ♂　　　5/566
Swordtail longfin killie
H: S Am.: Venezuela: Puerto Ayacucho.
♂: Much more colorful; longer fins. S: (–)
B: Substrate spawner: 34–52 ws!　F: C
T: 24–28°C, L: ♂ 5 cm, pH: <7, D: 4

Pterolebias xiphophorus ♀　　　5/566
Swordtail longfin killie

Pterolebias zonatus ♂　　　1/576
Lace-finned killie
H: S America: Venezuela.
♂: Larger; longer fins.　　　　　S: –
B: Difficult; substrate sp.: 12–16 ws. F: C
T: 18–23°C, L: 9 cm, pH: <7, D: 3–4

Rachovia brevis front ♂　　　2/672
Magdalena stop-finned killie
H: S Am.: N Colombia, NW Venezuela.
♂: More colorful; longer fins.　　S: =
B: Substrate spawner: 23 ws.　　F: C!
T: 22–26°C, L: ♂ 8 cm, pH: <7, D: 3–4

Rachovia hummelincki ♂   3/528
Coastal spot-finned killie
H: S America: Colombia, Venezuela.
♂: Much more colorful; longer fins. S: (–)
B: Substrate spawner: 26 ws.   F: C!
T: 22–26°C, L: 6 cm, pH: 7, D: 3–4

Rachovia maculipinnis ♂   2/672
Venezuelan spot-finned killie
H: S Am.: Venezuela: Rio Apure Basin.
♂: More colorful; longer fins.   S: =
B: Substrate spawner: 26–30 ws. F: C
T: 22–27°C, L: <8 cm, pH: 7, D: 3–4

Rachovia pyropunctata ♂   3/530
Red-spotted spot-finned killie
H: Venezuela: Lake Maracaibo Basin.
♂: More colorful; longer fins. S: (–)
B: Substrate spawner: 26 ws.   F: C!
T: 22–28°C, L: 6 cm, pH: <7, D: 4

Rachovia stellifer l.♂, r.♀   2/674

H: S America: Venezuela: Cojedes.
♂: Larger; longer fins.   S: –
B: Substr. spawner; brief storage. F: C!
T: 22–27°C, L: <7 cm, pH: 7, D: 4

KILLIFISHES

Rachovia transilis ♂   5/568
Orinoco spot-finned killie
H: S Am.: Venezuela: Orinoco Llanos.
♂: More colorful.   S: (–)
B: Problematic; substrate spawner. F: C
T: 24–32°C, L: 5 cm, pH: <7, D: 2–3

Rivulus agilae ♂   2/674
Agila rivulus
H: S America: Guianas.
♂: More colorful. ♀: Rounded fins. S: =
B: Difficult; adh. spa. or 3–4 ws. F: C!
T: 22–27°C, L: 5 cm, pH: <7, D: 3–4

Rivulus agilae ♂   2/674
Agila rivulus
See photo on p. 5/574.

Rivulus amphoreus ♂   2/676
Guianas rivulus
H: S America: Suriname: to 1000 m elev.
♂: More colorful. ♀: Caudal spot.   S: =
B: Difficult; adhesive spawner.   F: C!
T: 20–26°C, L: 7 cm, pH: 7, D: 3–4

Rivulus atratus ♂ WC   3/530
Butterfly rivulus
H: S America: Peru: Rio Ucayali.
♂: Longer caudal fin.   S: +
B: Very difficult; adhesive spawner. F: C
T: 22–26°C, L: <5 cm, pH: <7, D: 4

Rivulus bondi ♂   5/570
Bond's rivulus
H: S Am.: Venezuela: Caracas due east.
♂: More colorful. ♀: Caudal spot.   S: +
B: Simple; adhesive spawner.   F: C!
T: 22–26°C, L: 11.5 cm, pH: 7, D: 2

Rivulus bondi ♀   5/570
Bond's rivulus
H: S America: Venezuela: Guatire.

Rivulus cf. *bondi* ♂   5/570
Bond's rivulus
H: S America: Venezuela: Caracas.

Rivulus brasiliensis ♂　　　　2/676
Half-banded rivulus
H: S Am.: SE Brazil: Rio de Janeiro.
♂: More colorful. ♀: No caudal spot. **S:** =
B: Very difficult adh. sp.: 3–4 ws.　**F:** C
T: 20–24°C, **L:** 6 cm, **pH:** 7, **D:** 4

Rivulus breviceps ♂　　　　5/572
Short-headed rivulus
H: S America: Guyana. Venezuela?
♂: More colorful. ♀: No C spot.　**S:** (–)
B: Adhesive spawner.　　　　**F:** C!
T: 24–28°C, **L:** 5.5 cm, **pH:** <7, **D:** 3–4

Rivulus breviceps ♀　　　　5/572
Short-headed rivulus

Rivulus cf. *brunneus* ♂　　　　3/532

H: C America: Panama, Costa Rica.
♂: More colorful. ♀: Transparent fins. **S:** =
B: Adhesive spawner.　　　　**F:** C!
T: 20–26°C, **L:** <7 cm, **pH:** 7, **D:** 3

Rivulus caudomarginatus t.♂, b.♀　2/679
Band-tail rivulus
H: S Am.: SE Brazil: Rio de Janeiro.
♀: Caudal fin lacks a border.　**S:** (–)
B: Adhesive spawner: 3–4 ws.　**F:** C!
T: 20–24°C, **L:** 6 cm, **pH:** <7, **D:** 4

Rivulus christinae ♂　　　　5/572
Christina's rivulus
H: S America: Peru: Puerto Maldonado.
♂: More colorful.　　　　　　**S:** =
B: Adhesive spawner.　　　　**F:** C
T: 22–26°C, **L:** 6 cm, **pH:** 7, **D:** 2

Rivulus chucunaque ♂　3/532, (5/574)

Rivulus chucunaque ♂　3/532, (5/574)

H: C America: Panama.
♂: More colorful. ♀: Caudal spot.　S: (–)
B: Adhesive spawner.　　　　　　　　F: C
T: 22–26°C, L: 7 cm, pH: 7, D: 3

Rivulus cladophorus　　　　5/575

H: S America: French Guiana.
♂: Slightly slimmer & more colorful. S: (–)
B: Not easy; adhesive spawner.　F: C!
T: 22–26°C, L: 5 cm, pH: <7, D: 3

Rivulus cryptocallus ♂　　　　2/680
Iridescent rivulus, Martinique rivulus
H: C America: Lesser Antilles.
♂: More color. ♀: *Rivulus* spot(s). S: (–)
B: Very difficult; adhesive spawner. F: C!
T: 24–28°C, L: 5 cm, pH: <7, D: 4

Rivulus cylindraceus ♂　　　　1/578
Cuban rivulus, green rivulus, brown rivulus
H: C America: Cuba.
♂: More colorful. ♀: Caudal spot.　S: =
B: Adh. spawner; e hatch in 2 w. F: C,O
T: 22–24°C, L: 5.5 cm, pH: 7, D: 1–2

Rivulus deltaphilus ♂　　　　5/576
Orinoco rivulus
H: S America: E and SE Venezuela.
♂: Little more color. ♀: Caudal spot. S: (–)
B: Not simple; adhesive spawner.　F: C!
T: 22–26°C, L: 6 cm, pH: 7, D: 3

KILLIFISHES

Rivulus derhami ♂   3/534

H: S America: Peru: at Tingo María.
♂: More colorful. ♀: Caudal spot.   S: =
B: Easy; adhesive spawner.   F: C!
T: 22–26°C, L: 5 cm, pH: 7, D: 3

Rivulus dibaphus ♂   3/534

H: S America: NE Brazil.
♂: More colorful and larger.   S: =
B: Adhesive spawner.   F: C!
T: 24–28°C, L: 5 cm, pH: <7, D: 4

Rivulus elegans ♂   5/576
Elegant rivulus

H: S America: NW Colombia.
♀: Transparent fins.   S: +
B: Hard; adhesive spawner: 2 w.   F: C!
T: 22–26°C, L: 6 cm, pH: 7, D: 3

Rivulus elongatus ♂   5/578
Elongated rivulus

H: S America: Peru, Ecuador, Brazil.
♂: More colorful. ♀: Caudal spot.   S: =
B: Adh. sp.; eggs hatch after 2½ w. F: C
T: 22–26°C, L: 7.5 cm, pH: 7, D: 3

Rivulus erberi ♂   5/578
Coca rivulus

H: S America: E Ecuador: Coca.
♂: More colorful. ♀: Caudal spot.   S: +
B: Simple; adhesive spawner.   F: C
T: 22–26°C, L: 6 cm, pH: 7, D: 2–3

Rivulus frenatus ♂   5/580
Red-tailed rivulus

H: S America: Guyana.
♂: More color. ♀: Transparent fins. S:(–)
B: Not difficult; adhesive spawner. F: C!
T: 22–26°C, L: 4.5 cm, pH: <7, D: 4

KILLIFISHES

Rivulus fuscolineatus b.♀, t.♂   3/536

H: C America: Costa Rica.
♂: Little more color. ♀: Caudal spot. S: =
B: Adh. spawner; e hatch in 2–3 w. F:C!
T: 20–26°C, L: 7 cm, pH: 7, D: 2–3

Rivulus geayi ♂   2/680
Chevron rivulus
H: S Am.: Sur., Fr. Gui., Amazon mouth.
♂: More colorful.   S: (–)
B: Very difficult; adh. spawner.   F: C!
T: 24–28°C, L: 5 cm, pH: 7, D: 4

Rivulus gransabanae ♂   5/580
Gran Sabana rivulus
H: S America: SE Venezuela. Guyana?
♂: More colorful; blue caudal fin. S: (–)
B: Adh. spawner; e hatch in 2 w.   F: C!
T: 22–25°C, L: 4.5 cm, pH: <7, D: 3

Rivulus haraldsiolii ♂   5/582
Harald Sioli's rivulus
H: S America: SE Brazil: coastal basin.
♂: More colorful. ♀: Caudal spot. S: =
B: Extremely difficult; adh. spawner. F: C!
T: 20–24°C, L: 4.5 cm, pH: <7, D: 3

Rivulus haraldsiolii ♂   5/582
Harald Sioli's rivulus

Rivulus hartii ♂   3/536
Giant rivulus
H: S Am.: Trinidad, Tobago. Venezuela?
♂: More colorful.   S: (–)
B: Adh. or substrate spawner: 3ws. F: C!
T: 22–26°C, L: 9 cm, pH: 7, D: 3

KILLIFISHES

Rivulus hildebrandi ♂　　　　3/538
Panama rivulus
H: C America: W Panama.
♂: Little more color. ♀: Caudal spot.　S: (–)
B: Adhesive spawner; not fecund.　F: C
T: 20–22°C, L: 8 cm, pH: 7, D: 3

Rivulus sp. aff. *holmiae* ♂　　　　2/685
Golden-tailed rivulus

Rivulus igneus ♂　　　　5/584
Fire rivulus
H: S America: French Guiana.
♂: More colorful; 2 cm smaller.　S: (–)
B: Mature 2nd year; substr. sp.: 4 ws.　F: C
T: 22–28°C, L: ♀16 cm, pH: 7, D: 2

Rivulus igneus ♀　　　　5/584
Fire rivulus

Rivulus immaculatus ♂　　　　5/586
Black-fringe rivulus
H: S America: Venezuela: Rio Essequibo.
♂: More colorful. ♀: Spots on body. S: (–)
B: Adh. spa.: 3 ws in humid peat.　F: C
T: 20–24°C, L: 7 cm, pH: <7, D: 3

Rivulus immaculatus ♀　　　　5/586
Black-fringe rivulus

KILLIFISHES

461

Rivulus iridescens ♂   3/538
Iridescent rivulus
H: S America: Peru: at Jenaro Herrera.
♂: More colorful. ♀: Caudal spot. S: =
B: Adh. spawner: e hatch in 2–3 w. F: C
T: 22–26°C, L: 7 cm, pH: <7, D: 3

Rivulus janeiroensis ♂   5/588
Janeiro rivulus
H: S America: Brazil: Rio de Janeiro.
♂: More colorful. ♀: Caudal spot. S: =
B: Adhesive spawner.   F: C
T: 22–26°C, L: 6.5 cm, pH: 7, D: 2–3

Rivulus sp. aff. *jucundus* ♂   5/588
Puyo rivulus
H: S Am.: Ecuador: Puyo, Rio Upano.
♂: More color. ♀: No fringes on fins. S: =
B: Not difficult: adhesive spawner. F: C
T: 22–24°C, L: 4.5 cm, pH: 7, D: 2

Rivulus limoncochae t.♂, b.♀   5/590
Limoncocha rivulus, Napo rivulus
H: S America: Ecuador: Napo River
♂: More colorful. ♀: Caudal spot. S: +
B: Adhesive spawner.   F: C!
T: 24–28°C, L: 6 cm, pH: <7, D: 3

Rivulus luelingi ♂ WC   3/540
Lüling's rivulus
H: S America: S Brazil: at Joinville.
♂: More colorful. ♀: Caudal spot. S: (–)
B: Difficult; adhesive spawner.   F: C!
T: 18–24°C, L: 4.5 cm, pH: <7, D: 4

Rivulus luelingi ♀ WC   3/540
Lüling's rivulus

Rivulus lyricauda ♂   5/590
Lyre-tail rivulus
H: S America.
♂: More colorful. ♀: Rounded fins. S: –
B: Adh. spawner; brief set-up.   F: C
T: 20–24°C, L: ♂ 5 cm, pH: <7, D: 3

Rivulus lyricauda ♀   5/590
Lyre-tail rivulus

Rivulus magdalenae ♂   5/592
Magdalena rivulus
H: S Am: Colombia: upper Magdalena B.
♂: More colorful. ♀: Caudal spot. S: +
B: Adh. or substrate spawner: 3 ws. F: C
T: 20–26°C, L: 8 cm, pH: 7, D: 2–3

Rivulus micropus ♂   5/594
Small-finned rivulus
H: S America: Brazil: Manaus.
♂: More colorful. ♀: Usually C spot. S:(–)
B: Adhesive spawner; not prolific. F: C!
T: 24–28°C, L: 7 cm, pH: 7, D: 3–4

Rivulus micropus ♂   5/594
Small-finned rivulus

Rivulus micropus ♀   5/594
Small-finned rivulus

KILLIFISHES

463

Rivulus modestus ♂   5/595

H: S America: Brazil: Mato Grosso.
♂: More colorful.   S: (–)
B: Extremely difficult; adh. spawner. F: C
T: 25–28°C, L: 5 cm, pH: <7, D: 4

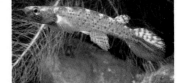

Rivulus obscurus ♂   5/596

H: S America: Brazil: Amazon, Rio Negro.
♂: More colorful. ♀: Transp. C fin. S: (–)
B: Adh. sp.; 3 ws; 75% e fungus. F: C!
T: 24–30°C, L: 4 cm, pH: <7, D: 3–4

Rivulus obscurus ♀   5/596

Rivulus ocellatus   2/682
Marbled rivulus
H: America: Florida to Brazil: coasts.
SD: Only hermaphrodites and ♂♂. S: =
B: Adhesive spawner. F: C,O
T: 18–24°C, L: 5 cm, pH: 7, D: 3–4

Rivulus ornatus ♂   2/682
Ornate rivulus
H: Brazil, Peru: Amazon Basin.
♂: More colorful.   S: (–)
B: Slightly difficult; adh. spawner. F: C,O
T: 24–28°C, L: 3 cm, pH: 7, D: 2–3

Rivulus peruanus ♂ WC   3/542
Perimparoo rivulus
H: S America: Peru: Ucayali.
♂: More colorful. ♀: Also no C spot. S: =
B: Adhesive spawner; belligerent. F: C!
T: 22–26°C, L: 7 cm, pH: 7, D: 3

KILLIFISHES

Rivulus pictus   5/596
Painted rivulus
H: S America: S Brazil: Rio Santana.
SD: None pronounced.   S: (–)
B: Diff. depends on pop.; adh. sp.   F:C
T: 22–26°C, L: 4.5 cm, pH: <7, D: 2–4

Rivulus pictus   5/596
Painted rivulus
H: S America: S Brazil: Bataguassu.

Rivulus pictus   5/596
Painted rivulus
H: S America: S Brazil: Goias.

Rivulus punctatus ♂   2/684, 3/542
Spotted rivulus
H: S Am.: N Argentina, Par., Bolivia.
♂: More color. ♀: Often caudal spot. S: =
B: Brazilian pop. difficult; adh. sp.   F: C
T: 22–26°C, L: 6 cm, pH: 7, D: 3–4

Rivulus punctatus ♂ WC   2/684, 3/542
Spotted rivulus

Rivulus rectocaudatus t.♂, b.♀   3/544
Straight-tail rivulus
H: S America: Peru: vicinity of Iquitos.
♂: More colorful. ♀: Rounded fins.   S: (–)
B: Adhesive spawner.   F: C!
T: 22–25°C, L: 8 cm, pH: <7, D: 3–4

465

Rivulus roloffi ♂   2/686
Roloff's rivulus
H: C America: Hispaniola.
♂: More colorful. ♀: Also no C spot. S:(–)
B: Adh. spawner; not very prolific.   F: C
T: 20–26°C, L: 5 cm, pH: 7, D: 3–4

Rivulus rubrolineatus ♂   3/544
Red-line rivulus
H: S America: Peru: lower Ucayali.
♂: More colorful. ♀: Caudal spot.   S: =
B: Substrate (3 ws) or adhesive sp.   F: C
T: 22–28°C, L: 7 cm, pH: 7, D: 3

Rivulus santensis t.♂, b.♀   2/686
Santos rivulus
H: S America: SE Brazil.
♂: More colorful. ♀: Usually C spot. S: =
B: Sometimes diff.; adhesive spawn. F: C
T: 20–26°C, L: 5 cm, pH: 7, D: 3–4

Rivulus sp. ♂   5/599

H: S America: Colombia.

Rivulus speciosus   5/602

Rivulus tenuis ♂   2/688
Mexico rivulus
H: C Am.: S Mex., Belize, Gua., Honduras.
♂: More colorful. ♀: Caudal spot.   S: =
B: Adhesive spawner.   F: C!
T: 22–28°C, L: ♂ 6 cm, pH: <7, D: 2–3

Rivulus uroflammeus uroflammeus ♂
Flame-tail rivulus　　　　　　2/690
H: C America: SW Costa Rica.
♂: More colorful. ♀: Caudal spot.　S: =
B: Adhesive spawner: 3–4 ws.　　F: !
T: 22–26°C, L: 6 cm, pH: <7, D: 2–3

Rivulus urophthalmus ♂ WC　　3/546
Golden rivulus
H: S America: E Guyana to Brazil.
♂: More color. ♀: Often caudal spot. S:(–)
B: Adh. or substr. spawner: 3–4 ws.　F:C!
T: 22–26°C, L: 6 cm, pH: <7, D: 3

Rivulus violaceus ♂　　　　　5/600
Violet rivulus
H: S Am.: Brazil: Mato Grosso, Goias.
♂: More color. ♀: Transparent fins.　S: (–)
B: Adh. spawner; collect eggs daily. F: C!
T: 24–28°C, L: 4.5 cm, pH: 7, D: 3

Rivulus waimacui ♂　　　　　5/600

H: S America: Guyana: Potaro River.
♂: More colorful. ♀: Fins smaller.　S: (–)
B: Largely unknown; adh. spawner.　F: C
T: 24–28°C, L: 9 cm, pH: <7, D: 3

Rivulus waimacui ♂ in front　　5/600

Rivulus weberi ♂　　　　　　5/603
Weber's rivulus, ladder rivulus
H: C America: Panama: Pacific coast.
♂: More colorful. ♀: Colorless fins. S: =
B: Simple; adhesive spawner.　　F: C
T: 20–24°C, L: 9 cm, pH: 7, D: 2

KILLIFISHES

Rivulus xanthonotus t.♂, b.♀   1/578
Yellowback rivulus
H: S America: Amazon?
♂: More colorful. ♀: Caudal spot.   S: =
B: Not difficult; adhesive spawner. F: C
T: 22–25°C, L: 7 cm, pH: <7, D: 2

Rivulus xiphidius ♂   2/690
Band-tailed rivulus, blue-stripe rivulus
H: S Am.: Suriname and Fr.Guiana: coast.
♂: More colorful. ♀: Smaller.   S: (–)
B: Continuous adh. sp. or 3 ws.   F: C!
T: 22–25°C, L: ♂ 4 cm, pH: <7, D: 4

Terranatos dolichopterus ♂   1/584
Sabre fin, sicklefin killie
H: S America: Venezuela.
♂: More color; very elongated fins. S: (–)
B: Substrate spawner: 21–26 ws.   F: C!
T: 20–25°C, L: ♂ 5 cm, pH: <7, D: 3

Trigonectes balzanii ♂   5/604
Paraguay killie, rivulichthys
H: S Am.: Brazil, Paraguay, Argentina.
♂: More colorful; longer fins.   S: (–)
B: Substrate spawner: 26 ws.   F: C
T: 22–28°C, L: 10 cm, pH: 7, D: 3

Trigonectes balzanii ♀   5/604
Paraguay killie, rivulichthys

Trigonectes rubromarginatus ♂   5/606
Red-fringe killie
H: S America: Central Brazil: Goias.
♂: More colorful; C fin w/ red fringe. S: (–)
B: Substrate spawner: 26 ws.   F: C
T: 23–27°C, L: 11 cm, pH: 7, D: 3

Subfamily Cubanichthinae

The subfamily of Cuban pupfishes presently contains only the two species presented below. According to some opinions, both belong to the genus *Cubanichthys*.

Despite being distributed in the Caribbean, saline water is not required. The water must be at least medium-hard, however. These small, peaceful fishes should only be associated with like-natured species of similar size, lest they adopt a cryptic lifestyle. In a species aquarium, they freely exhibit their natural behavior. Their coloration is most intense in brightly illuminated environments.

Provided there is sufficient vegetation, some of the young will survive predation without intervention by the hobbyist.

Cubanichthys pengelleyi ♂   2/633
Jamaican large-scaled killie
H: C America: Jamaica.
♂: Larger and more colorful.   S: (–)
B: Adh. spawner (plants, stones). F: C,O
T: 23–25°C, L: 6 cm, pH: >7, D: 2

Cubanichthys cubensis l.♂, r.♀ 2/634
Cuban minnow
H: C America: W Cuba.
♂: More colorful.   S: (–)
B: Adhesive spawner.   F: C,O
T: 23–28°C, L: 4 cm, pH: 7, D: 2–3

Subfamily Cyprinodontinae

The subfamily of pupfishes consists of 8 genera and 89 species which inhabit freshwater, brackish water, and coastal marine waters. Geographically, the various genera are widely distributed (NELSON, 1994):

- *Aphanius*: about 10 species in brackish waters and freshwaters of the Mediterranean region.
- *Cyprinodon*: about 36 species in the deserts of the southern United States (California, Arizona, Nevada, Oklahoma, Texas) and Mexico.

Lake Titicaca, Peru/Bolivia. Fisherman in a typical reed canoe.

KILLIFISHES

- *Kosswigichthys*: about 4 species in freshwater lakes of Turkey.
- *Orestias*: 43 species in highland lakes of the Andes of Peru, Bolivia, and northern Chile (mainly Lake Titicaca).

The genus *Cyprinodon* (desert pupfishes) contains many species with extremely localized distributions, e.g., a single spring in the desert. Consequently, these populations are extremely vulnerable and many are threatened or endangered. Several of these interesting species are protected. *C. pachycephalus* (p. 479) lives and breeds in water that can have a temperature of 43.8°C. This is the warmest temperature in which a teleost (bony fish) lives. (Some tilapias tolerate higher temperatures, but not on a continuous basis.)

The majority are rarely sold commercially—with little change expected in the near future—due in part to their humble coloration as well as their remote, limited distribution and frequently difficult maintenance (they often inhabit very hard saline). *Jordanella floridae* (p. 481), the American flagfish from Florida, is a notable exception. It is rather attractive, easily maintained, and regularly sold in pet stores.

Virtually all species of this subfamily have been bred in an aquarium. While annuals do not rank among their numbers, the embryonal development of members of the genus *Orestias* requires four weeks. Attempts to speed the process through elevated temperatures have failed. Young that hatch prematurely do not survive. The genus is an important source of protein for the people living in its Andean distribution area.

Most Cyprinodontinae lay their eggs onto a spawning mop or Java moss. Many require saline water to breed, although not necessarily for maintenance.

Jordanella floridae lays its eggs either on fine-leaved plants or in pits. The male guards the eggs, and the female should be removed shortly after oviposition has concluded.

Aphanius anatoliae ♂ WC   3/547
Anatolian killifish
H: Europe: central Asia Minor.
♀: Larger; transparent fins.   S: +
B: Spawns on plants.   F: O
T: 10–25°C, L: <5 cm, pH: >7, D: 3

Aphanius anatoliae ♂   3/547
Anatolian killifish

Aphanius splendens ♂   4/414
Shiny Anatolian killifish
H: Asia: SW Turkey.
♂: Dark vertical stripes.   S: +
B: Difficult; spawns on plants.   F: O
T: 15–24°C, L: 5.5 cm, pH: 7, D: 4

KILLIFISHES

Aphanius sureyanus ♂   4/414
Burdur killifish
H: Asia: SW Turkey: Lake Burdur.
♂: Dark vertical stripes.   S: +
B: Spawns among plants.   F: O
T: 16–24°C, L: 5.5 cm, pH: 7, D: 4

Aphanius sureyanus ♀   4/414
Burdur killifish

Aphanius transgrediens ♂   4/416
Acigöl killie
H: Asia: SW Turkey: Lake Aci. Endangered
♂: Dark vertical stripes.   S: +
B: Spawns on plants.   F: O
T: 16–24°C, L: 5 cm, pH: >7, D: 4

Aphanius transgrediens ♂   4/416
Acigöl killie

Aphanius apodus   3/549, (4/420)

Aphanius apodus ♂   3/549, (4/420)

H: N Africa: NW Algeria.
♂: More colorful; colorful fins.   S: (–)
B: Adh. spawner; hatch after 2 w.   F: O
T: 18–28°C, L: 4.5 cm, pH: >7, D: 4

Aphanius asquamatus ♂   2/585
Naked Turkish killifish
H: Asia: Turkey: E Anatolia: Lake Hazer.
♂: More colorful; slightly slimmer.   S: (–)
B: Simple; adhesive spawner.   F: C,O
T: 10–25°C, L: 4 cm, pH: ≫7, D: 2–3

Aphanius chantrei ♂   4/418
Chantre's killifish
H: Asia: Turkey: central Anatolia.
♂: Vertical bands.   S: =
B: Very feasible; adhesive spawner. F: O
T: 16–24°C, L: 6.5 cm, pH: >7, D: 2

KILLIFISHES

Aphanius chantrei ♀   4/418
Chantre's killifish

Aphanius dispar ♂   2/586
Mother-of-pearl killie
H: Coasts Ind.Oc., Red & Dead Seas, E Sah.
♂: Larger fins; more colorful.   S: +
B: Adhesive sp. Even in seawater. F: O
T: 16–26°C, L: 7 cm, pH: >7, D: 3–4

Aphanius dispar richardsoni ♂   4/418
Jordan mother-of-pearl killie
H: Middle East: Israel, Jordan.
♂: More pronounced design.   S: –
B: Adhesive spawner.   F: O
T: 15–24°C, L: 6 cm, pH: >7, D: 3

Aphanius dispar richardsoni ♀   4/418
Jordan mother-of-pearl killie

Aphanius fasciatus ♂   1/522
Mediterranean killie
H: Europe, Asia, Africa: Mediterranean.
♂: Colorful fins; crossbands.   S: +
B: Adh. spawner. Brackish water. F: C
T: 10–24°C, L: 7 cm, pH: >7, D: 1–2

Aphanius iberus ♂   1/522
Spanish pupfish
H: Europe, Africa: Spain, Morocco, Algeria.
♂: More colorful.   S: +
B: Adhesive spawner.   F: C
T: 10–32°C, L: 5 cm, pH: 7, D: 1–2

KILLIFISHES

Aphanius iberus ♀   1/522
Spanish pupfish

Aphanius mento ♂   2/586
Orient killie
H: Middle E: S Turkey, Israel, Persian Gulf.
♀: Dark spots on light-colored body. S: =
B: Adhesive spawner.   F: O
T: 10–25°C, L: 5 cm, pH: >7, D: 2–3

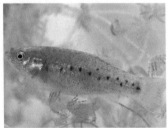

Aphanius sirhani ♂   3/550
Sirhanian killie
H: Asia: Jordan: Azraq Oasis.
♂: Dark crossbands. ♀: Spotted.   S: +
B: Adhesive spawner.   F: O
T: 20–25°C, L: 4.5 cm, pH: >7, D: 3

Aphanius sirhani ♀   3/550
Sirhanian killie

Aphanius sophiae ♂   5/484
Persian killie
H: Middle East: W Iran, SW Iraq.   Bw
♂: More colorful.   S: –
B: Not simple; adhesive spawner. F: O
T: 20–30°C, L: 4 cm, pH: >7, D: 3

Cualac tessellatus ♂ WC   3/554
Checkered pupfish
H: C America: Mexico: Rio Verde.
♂: More colorful.   S: +
B: Eggs died during development. F: O
T: 28–30°C, L: 5.5 cm, pH: ≫7, D: 4

KILLIFISHES

Cualac tessellatus ♀ WC   3/554
Checkered pupfish

Cyprinodon alvarezi ♂   4/422
El Potosi pupfish
H: C Am.: Mexico: El Potosí. Protected
♂: More colorful. ♀: Dorsal fin spot.   **S:** –
B: Wool mop in saline water.   **F:** O
T: 18–22°C, **L:** 6.5 cm, **pH:** >7, **D:** 3

Cyprinodon atrorus t.♂, b.♀   3/556

H: C America: Mexico: Cuatro Cienegas.
♂: More colorful. ♀: Dorsal fin spot.   **S:**+
B: In pits in saline water.   **F:** H
T: 25–35°C, **L:** 5 cm, **pH:** >7, **D:** 3

Cyprinodon beltrani ♂   4/422
Chichancanab pupfish   Protected
H: C Am.: Mexico: Laguna Chichancanb. E
♂: More colorful. ♀: Dark spots.   **S:** –
B: Unknown.   **F:** O
T: 27–32°C, **L:** 4.5 cm, **pH:** >7, **D:** 3

Cyprinodon bondi ♂   4/424
Bond's pupfish
H: Caribbean: West Indies: Haiti.
♂: More colorful. ♀: Dorsal fin spot.   **S:** –
B: Wool mop in saline water.   **F:** O
T: 20–28°C, **L:** 8 cm, **pH:** >7, **D:** 3

Cyprinodon bondi ♀   4/424
Bond's pupfish

KILLIFISHES

475

Cyprinodon bovinus ♂   4/424
Leon Springs pupfish
H: N America: USA: Texas: Rio Pecos.
♂: More colorful. ♀: More spots.   S: –
B: Wool mop in saline water.   F: O
T: 10–28°C, L: 5 cm, pH: >7, D: 3

Cyprinodon elegans ♂   5/486
Comanche Springs pupfish
H: N America: USA: W Texas.
♂: Spots. ♀: Band of spots.   S: –
B: Wool mop in saline water.   F: O,H
T: 18–26°C, L: 5 cm, pH: >7, D: 3

Cyprinodon elegans ♀   5/486
Comanche Springs pupfish

Cyprinodon eximius ♂   4/428
Conchos pupfish
H: N America: N Mexico, USA: Texas.
♂: More colorful. ♀: Dorsal fin spot. S: –
B: Wool mop in saline water.   F: O
T: 15–25°C, L: 4.5 cm, pH: >7, D: 3

Cyprinodon eximius ♀   4/428
Conchos pupfish

Cyprinodon fontinalis ♂   4/428
Guzmán pupfish
H: C America: Mexico: Chihuahua.
♂: More color. ♀: Dorsal fin spot. S: –
B: Wool mop in saline water.   F: O
T: 24–28°C, L: 5.5 cm, pH: >7, D: 2–3

KILLIFISHES

Cyprinodon labiosus ♂   5/488
Thick-lip pupfish
H: C Am.: Mexico: Lake Chichancanab.
♂: More colorful. ♀: Dorsal fin spot. S: =
B: Not simple; wool mop.   F: C
T: 22–26°C, L: 4 cm, pH: 7, D: 3

Cyprinodon labiosus ♀   5/488
Thick-lip pupfish

Cyprinodon macrolepis ♂   3/556
Dolores pupfish   Endangered
H: C America: Mexico: Chihuahua.
♂: More colorful fins.   S: =
B: Simple; wool mop w/ salt.   F: H,O
T: 26–32°C, L: 5 cm, pH: >7, D: 3

Cyprinodon macrolepis ♀   3/556
Dolores pupfish

KILLIFISHES

Cyprinodon macularius ♂   1/554
Desert pupfish
H: N and C America: S USA, N Mexico.
♂: More colorful. ♀: Spotted.   S: =
B: Simple; wool mop w/ salt in water. F:C
T: 25–35°C, L: 6.5 cm, pH: >7, D: 3

Cyprinodon macularius eremus ♂ 4/430
Quitobaquito desert pupfish
H: N America: USA: Arizona.
♂: More colorful. ♀: Spotted.   S: =
B: Wool mop in saline water.   F: O
T: 18–24°C, L: 5.5 cm, pH: >7, D: 2–3

Cyprinodon maya ♂   5/490
Maya pupfish

Cyprinodon maya ♀   5/490
Maya pupfish

H: C Am.: Mexico: Lake Chichancanab.
♂: More colorful. ♀: Dorsal fin spot.   S: –
B: Unsuccessful.   F: C
T: 22–26°C, L: 8 cm, pH: 7, D: 4

Cyprinodon nevadensis amargosae ♂
Amargosa pupfish   4/430

Cyprinodon nevadensis mionectes ♂
Ash Meadows pupfish   (1/556), 4/432

H: N America: USA: California.
♂: Blue sheen. ♀: Spotted.   S: =
B: In wool mop.   F: O
T: 10–26°C, L: 4.5 cm, pH: >7, D: 2–3

H: N America: USA: Nevada.
♂: More colorful. ♀: Dorsal fin spot. S: –
B: Wool mop in saline water.   F: O
T: 24–30°C, L: 5.5 cm, pH: >7, D: 2–3

Cyprinodon nevadensis pectoralis ♂
Warm Springs pupfish   4/432

Cyprinodon nevadensis shoshone l.♂, r.♀
Shoshone pupfish   5/484

H: N America: USA: Nevada: Nye County.
♂: More colorful; ♀: Dorsal fin spot. S: –
B: Wool mop in saline water.   F: O
T: 25–30°C, L: 5.5 cm, pH: >7, D: 2–3

H: N Am.: USA: California: Inyo County.
♂: More colorful; ♀: Dorsal fin spot. S: –
B: Wool mop in saline water.   F: O
T: 18–24°C, L: 5.5 cm, pH: >7, D: 2–3

KILLIFISHES

Cyprinodon pachycephalus ♂   4/435
San Diego pupfish

Cyprinodon pachycephalus ♂   4/435
San Diego pupfish

H: C America: N Mexico: Chihuahua.
♂: More colorful. ♀: Dorsal fin spot.   S: –
B: Wool mop in saline water.   F: O
T: 24–28 °C, L: 5.5 cm, pH: >7, D: 2–3

Cyprinodon pecosensis ♂   4/436
Pecos pupfish

Cyprinodon pecosensis ♀   4/436
Pecos pupfish

H: N America: USA: Texas, New Mexico.
♂: More colorful. ♀: Dorsal fin spot.   S: –
B: Wool mop.   F: O
T: 10–28°C, L: 5.5 cm, pH: >7, D: 2–3

Cyprinodon radiosus ♂   5/492
Owens pupfish

Cyprinodon radiosus ♀   5/492
Owens pupfish

H: N Am.: USA: California.   ·Protected
♂: More colorful. ♀: Spotted.   S: –
B: Rolled artificial turf.   F: O
T: 22–30°C, L: 4 cm, pH: >7, D: 4

KILLIFISHES

479

KILLIFISHES

Cyprinodon rubrofluviatilis ♂   4/436
Red River pupfish
H: N Am.: USA: Oklahoma, Texas.
♂: Bluish brown. ♀: Dorsal fin spot.   S: –
B: Wool mop in saline water.   F: O
T: 10–30°C, L: 5 cm, pH: >7, D: 2–3

Cyprinodon salinus salinus ♂   4/438
Salt Creek pupfish
H: N America: USA: California.
♂: More color. ♀: Spotted.   S: –
B: Wool mop in saline water.   F: C
T: 15–30°C, L: 4.5 cm, pH: >7, D: 2–3

Cyprinodon tularosa ♂   5/494
White Sands pupfish   Protected
H: USA: New Mexico: Tularosa Basin.   E
♂: More colorful. ♀: Dorsal fin spot.   S: –
B: Rolled artificial turf.   F: O
T: 26–30°C, L: 5 cm, pH: >7, D: 3

Cyprinodon variegatus dearborni ♂
                              3/558

H: S Am.: Curaçao, Aruba, Bonaire, Venez.
♂: More colorful. ♀: Dorsal fin spot.   S: –
B: Wool mop in saline water.   F: O
T: 20–27°C, L: 4.5 cm, pH: >7, D: 3

Cyprinodon variegatus ovinus ♂ 4/438
Sheepshead minnow
H: N America: USA: east coast.
♂: More colorful. ♀: Dorsal fin spot.   S: –
B: Wool mop in saline water.   F: O
T: 10–22°C, L: 6 cm, pH: >7, D: 2–3

Cyprinodon variegatus ovinus ♀ 4/438
Sheepshead minnow

Cyprinodon variegatus variegatus ♂
Sheepshead minnow   3/558
H: E coast USA (Carolina) to N Mexico.
♂: More colorful. ♀: Dorsal fin spot.   S: –
B: Wool mop in saline water.   F: O
T: 15–25°C, L: 6 cm, pH: >7, D: 3

Floridichthys polyommus ♂   3/574
H: C Am.: Mexico: Yucatan.   Bw,(Mw)
♂: Brighter. ♀: Round, colorless fins. S: =
B: Wool mop in saline water.   F: O
T: 22–28°C, L: 9 cm, pH: >7, D: 4

Jordanella pulchra l.♀, r.♂   2/660
Yucatan pupfish
H: C Am.: Mexico: Yucatan.   Fw–Mw
♂: More color.♀: Round, transp. fins. S: =
B: Wool mop in saline water.   F: O
T: 22–28°C, L: 5–6 cm, pH: >7, D: 3

Jordanella floridae t.♂, b.♀   1/564
American flagfish
H: N America: Florida to Yucatan.
♂: More colorful. ♀: Dorsal fin spot. S: –
B: Plants/pits; 70 e; paternal family. F: O
T: around 20°C, L: 6 cm, pH: 7, D: 1–2

Megupsilon aporus ♂ WC   3/576
Black-blotch pupfish
H: N America: Mexico: Nuevo León.
♂: More colorful. ♀: Gray/brown.   S: =
B: In a wool mop?   F: O
T: 18–22°C, L: 4.5 cm, pH: >7, D: 3–4

Orestias agassii agassii ♂   5/495
Large Andes pupfish
H: S Am.: Peru, Bol., Chile, Lake Titicaca.
♂: Yellowish. ♀: Insemination pouch. S:+
B: 4 w embryonal development.   F: C
T: 10–15°C, L: <15 cm, pH: >7, D: 4

KILLIFISHES

Orestias agassii tschudii ♂　　　5/498
Tschud's Andes pupfish
H: S Am.: Peru, Bol.: Lake Titicaca; Chile.
♂: Yellowish. ♀: Insemination pouch. S:+
B: 4 w embryonal development.　　F: C
T: 10–15°C, L: 15 cm, pH: >7, D: 4

Orestias agassii tschudii ♀　　　5/498
Tschud's Andes pupfish

Orestias agassii agassii × *T. a. tschudii*
Natural hybrid　　　　　　　　　(5/498)
H: S America: Peru/Bolivia: Lake Titicaca.

Orestias luteus ♂　　　5/500
Yellow Andes pupfish
H: S Am.: Peru, Bol.: Lake Titicaca; Chile.
♂: Yellowish. ♀: Insemination pouch. S:+
B: 4 w embryonal development.　　F: C
T: 5–15°C, L: <15 cm, pH: >7, D: 4

Orestias luteus ♀　　　5/500
Yellow Andes pupfish

Orestias muelleri ♂　　　5/503
Mueller's Andes pupfish
H: S Am.: Peru, Bol.: Lake Titicaca; Chile.
♂: Yellowish. ♀: Insemination pouch. S:+
B: 4 w embryonal development.　　F: C
T: 10–15°C, L: 6–8 cm, pH: >7, D: 4

KILLIFISHES

Family Fundulidae

This family contains 5 genera (4 according to some sources) and a total of 48 species. More than half of all the species of fundulids (29) belong to the genus *Fundulus*. The family is distributed from southeastern Canada to the Yucatan Peninsula, including Bermuda and Cuba (NELSON, 1994). Several species are very adaptive, capable of living both in marine waters of coastal biotopes and freshwaters.

Since Fundulidae inhabit permanent bodies of water, none are annuals. Most are adhesive spawners, laying their eggs on fine-leaved plants or a spawning mop. The amount of salt—if any—needed for the breeding aquarium depends on the species. Remember, plants are intolerant of saline water. Although the majority of species has been successfully bred in an aquarium, continued reproduction over several generations has proven problematic. Overwintering at cool temperatures seems to be of benefit, particularly for species from northern latitudes. An unheated basement is appropriate.

KILLIFISHES

Adinia multifasciata ♂   1/521
Diamond killifish
H: N Am.: S USA: Texas to W Florida.
♂: Pearl-colored bands.   S: =
B: Adhesive spawner; Bw.   F: O
T: 20–23°C, L: 5 cm, pH: >7, D: 2

Fundulus catenatus ♂   3/560
Chain topminnow, northern studfish
H: N America: USA: Mississippi Basin.
♂: Much more colorful.   S: +
B: Spawning mop; overwinter cool. F: C!
T: 15–25°C, L: <20 cm, pH: 7, D: 3–4

Fundulus chrysotus ♂ WC   2/654
Golden topminnow, golden ear
H: N America: SE USA.
♂: More colorful.   S: (–)
B: Continuous; fine-leaved plants. F: C,O
T: 18–25°C, L: 7 cm, pH: 7, D: 3

Fundulus cingulatus t. ♂, b. ♀   2/654
Banded topminnow
H: N America: SE USA.
♂: Much more colorful; longer fins. S: (–)
B: Continuous; fine-leaved plants. F: C,O
T: 20–25°C, L: 7 cm, pH: <7, D: 3

KILLIFISHES

Fundulus confluentus ♂　　　3/560
Marsh killifish
H: N America: SE USA: coastal areas.
♂: Much more colorful; longer fins. S: +
B: Substrate spawner; salt add.　F: C
T: 15–26°C, L: 6 cm, pH: 7, D: 3

Fundulus diaphanus t.♂, b.♀　　2/656
Banded killie
H: N America: S Canada to Carolina.
♂: Broader stripes; olive–blue/gray. S: (–)
B: Dense veg. or garden pond.　F: C,O
T: 10–25°C, L: 10 cm, pH: 7, D: 4

Fundulus dispar　　　　　3/562
Northern starhead topminnow, thin-stripe t.
H: N America: USA: central west.
♀: Striations fade with age.　　S: +
B: Adhesive spawner.　　　　F: C
T: 15–25°C, L: 7 cm, pH: 7, D: 3–4

Fundulus dispar WC, Ohio River 3/562
Northern starhead topminnow, thin-stripe t.

Fundulus escambiae t.♂, b.♀　4/440
Eastern starhead topminnow
H: N America: southern USA.
♂: Vertical bands posteriorly.　S: +?
B: Unknown.　　　　　　　　F: C
T: 15–25°C, L: 6 cm, pH: 7, D: 3

Fundulus grandis l.♂, r.♀　　2/656
Gulf Killifish
H: N & C Am.: USA, Mexico, Cuba. Bw,Fw
♂: Metallic spots.　　　　　　S: +
B: On peat fibers or wool mop.　F: C,O
T: 22–26°C, L: <15 cm, pH: >7, D: 2

Fundulus grandissimus   4/440
Large Yucatan topminnow
H: C Am.: Mexico: Yucatán Peninsula.
♂: Intense iridescent dots; smaller. **S:** –?
B: Unsuccessful.   **F:** C
T: 25–35°C, **L:** 18 cm, **pH:** >7, **D:** 3–4

Fundulus heteroclitus ♂   4/442
Mummichog
H: N America: Canada, USA.
♂: More colorful. ♀: Dorsal fin spot. **S:** =
B: Wool mop; preys on spawn. **F:** C,O
T: 10–24°C, **L:** 13 cm, **pH:** >7, **D:** 3

Fundulus jenkinsi ♂   3/564
Jenkins' topminnow
H: N America: SE USA.
♂: More colorful.   **S:** +
B: Adhesive spawner.   **F:** C
T: 18–25°C, **L:** 7 cm, **pH:** >7, **D:** 4

Fundulus julisiae ♂   3/564
Barrens topminnow   Threatened
H: N Am: USA: Tennessee: Coffee County.
♂: Much more colorful. **S:** (–)
B: Not easy; adh. spawner; 25 e. **F:** O
T: 10–25°C, **L:** 9 cm, **pH:** 7, **D:** 4

Fundulus lineolatus ♂   2/658
Lined topminnow
H: N Am.: USA: North Carolina to Florida.
♂: Intense crossbands. **S:** (–)
B: Plant sp.; light-sensitive eggs. **F:** C,O
T: 18–24°C, **L:** 7 cm, **pH:** 7, **D:** 3–4

Fundulus luciae   3/566

H: USA: Long Island to Georgia. Fw,Bw
♂: More colorful and smaller. **S:** (–)
B: Unsuccessful.   **F:** C
T: 10–25°C, **L:** 4.5 cm, **pH:** >7, **D:** 4

KILLIFISHES

485

Fundulus majalis t.♂, b.♀   3/566

H: N Am.: east coast to NE Mexico. Bw
♂: Crossbands; smaller.   S: (–)
B: Very difficult; garden pond.   F: C
T: 10–25°C, L: 14 cm, pH: >7, D: 4

Fundulus notatus ♂ WC   3/568
Blackstripe topminnow

H: N America: USA: Mississippi Basin.
♂: W/ horizontal band; longer fins. S: +
B: Adh. spawner; overwinter cool.   F: C
T: 15–26°C, L: 7.5 cm, pH: 7, D: 3–4

Fundulus olivaceus ♂   3/568
Olive topminnow, blackspotted topminnow

H: N America: USA: Mississippi Basin.
♂: Longer fins; slimmer.   S: +
B: Adh. spawner; overwinter cool. F: C!
T: 15–25°C, L: 8 cm, pH: 7, D: 3–4

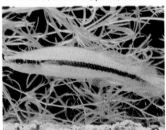

Fundulus olivaceus ♀   3/568
Olive topminnow, blackspotted topminnow

Fundulus pulvereus ♂   3/571
Powder topminnow

H: N America: Alabama to Texas. Fw,Bw
♂: Light dots; crossbands.   S: +
B: Adh. spawner; overwinter cool.   F: C
T: 15–26°C, L: 7 cm, pH: 7, D: 3

Fundulus sciadicus ♂   4/442
Plains topminnow

H: N Am.: USA: Nebraska, S Missouri.
♂: More color, particularly the fins. S: =
B: Adhesive spawner; add no salt.   F: C!
T: 5–22°C, L: 7 cm, pH: 7, D: 2–3

KILLIFISHES

Fundulus seminolis t.♂, b.♀   4/444
Seminole killifish
H: N America: USA: Florida.
♂: More colorful.   S: +
B: Nature: mainly April/May.   F: C!
T: 5–24°C, L: 15 cm, pH: 7, D: 3

Fundulus zebrinus ♂   2/658
Zebra topminnow, plains killifish
H: N America: SE USA.
♂: Crossbands and colorful fins.   S: +
B: Simple; adhesive spawner.   F: C,O
T: 20–25°C, L: 6 cm, pH: >7, D: 2–3

Leptolucania ommata ♂ WC   3/572
Pygmy killifish
H: N Am.: USA: S Georgia, N Florida.
♂: Larger; elongated fins.   S: (–)
B: Adhesive spawner.   F: C!
T: 18–24°C, L: 4 cm, pH: <7, D: 4

Leptolucania ommata ♀   3/572
Pygmy killifish

Lucania goodei t.♂, b.♀   1/566
Blue-fin topminnow
H: N America: USA: S Georgia, Florida.
♂: More colorful; slightly larger fins. S: =
B: On fine-leaved plants; 200 eggs. F: C
T: 16–22°C, L: 6 cm, pH: <7, D: 1–2

Lucania parva ♂   3/574
Rainwater killifish
H: N America: USA: E Coast and drainage.
♀: Paler; transparent fins.   S: =
B: Fine-leaved plants; some salt. F: C,O
T: 10–25°C, L: 5 cm, pH: >7, D: 2–3

KILLIFISHES

487

Family Goodeidae – Subfamily Empetrichthyinae

Both the livebearing goodeids of the subfamily Goodeinae (presented in Group 6—see pp. 505 ff.) and the egg-laying springfishes and poolfishes of the subfamily Empetrichthyinae are contained within this family. The latter subfamily consists of two genera and four species, one of which probably became extinct just recently. Their distribution is limited to southern Nevada (United States).

    Empetrichthyinae are seldom sought as aquarium fishes, largely because of their uninspiring coloration and pronounced aggressiveness. In species tanks, they breed with relative ease. The eggs hatch in approximately 10 days at a temperature of 25°C. Like most Cyprinodontiformes, the young are fully developed upon hatching and immediately begin searching for food (*Artemia salina* nauplii).

Crenichthys baileyi albivallis l.♀, r.♂ **3/552**

H: N America: USA: Nevada.   B: Substrate spawner.   F: O
♂: More colorful, smaller, and slimmer.S: –   T: 20–25°C, L: 5.5 cm, pH: 7, D: 3

Crenichthys baileyi baileyi ♂   **4/444**
White River springfish
H: N America: USA: Nevada.   B: Wool mop or among gravel.   F: O
♂: More colorful fins; golden band.   S: –   T: 26–30°C, L: 5.5 cm, pH: >7, D: 2–3

Crenichthys baileyi baileyi ♀   4/444
White River springfish
See photo on p. 4/426.

Crenichthys baileyi grandis   4/446
Large springfish
H: N America: USA: Nevada.
♂: More colorful fins; golden band.   S: –
B: Wool mop or among gravel.   F: O
T: 26–30°C, L: 7.5 cm, pH: >7, D: 2–3

Crenichthys baileyi moapae ♂   4/446
Moapa springfish
H: N America: USA: Nevada.
♂: More colorful fins; golden band.   S: –
B: Wool mop or among gravel.   F: O
T: 26–30°C, L: 5.5 cm, pH: >7, D: 2–3

Crenichthys baileyi thermophilus 4/448
Mormon springfish
H: N America: USA: Nevada.
♂: More colorful fins; golden band.   S: –
B: Wool mop or among gravel.   F: O
T: 26–30°C, L: 5.5 cm, pH: >7, D: 2–3

Crenichthys nevadae ♂   4/448
Railroad Valley springfish
H: N America: USA: Nevada.
♂: Darker fins.   S: –
B: Wool mop or among gravel.   F: O
T: 26–30°C, L: 6 cm, pH: >7, D: 2–3

Empetrichthys latos latos   4/462
Pahrump killifish
H: N America: USA: Nevada.
♂: Darker & slimmer when spawning. S: (–)
B: Pairwise on dense algae mats. F: C!
T: 20–25°C, L: <3.5 cm, pH: >7, D: 2

KILLIFISHES

Family Poeciliidae

The family Poeciliidae includes both the livebearing toothcarps of the subfamily Poeciliinae (presented in Group 6; see pp. 514 ff.) and the egg-laying lampeyes of the subfamilies Aplocheilichthyinae and Fluviphylacinae introduced below.

Although they are often found in groups, they are not true schooling fishes, since each fish maintains its individual space.

Subfamily Aplocheilichthyinae

The subfamily of African lampeyes presently contains 7 genera and at least 100 species. Their natural habitat is located in central and eastern Africa and includes the Rift Valley lakes and Madagascar.

The reproductive biology of the genera can be summarized as follows:
* *Aplocheilichthys* and *Hypsopanchax*: Most are adhesive spawners which deposit their eggs among fine-leaved plants. *A. schioetzi* can be bred as a substrate spawner, in which case the peat should be stored for 14 days.
* *Lamprichthys*: *L. tanganicanus*, the largest African killifish, is endemic to the rocky littoral of Lake Tanganyika. It is a substrate spawner.
* *Plataplochilus* and *Procatopus*: these are crevice spawners; i.e., adhesive spawners which press their eggs into cracks and crevices of the aquarium's decor (e.g., roots and rocks) and the aquarium's equipment (e.g., sponges and filter inlet mesh). Several species are continuous spawners.

The majority of the species within this subfamily are peaceful, gregarious fishes. Even though they swim in groups, however, each fish maintains its individual space. Many are small and therefore should only be associated with especially amiable, tranquil fishes. Finding suitable tankmates for the larger species is easier.

Subfamily Fluviphylacinae

The subfamily Fluviphylacinae is monotypic, containing just *Fluviphylax pygmaeus* (see p. 499). This species hails from the Amazon basin of Brazil. To date, attempts to breed it have failed, and it has not been offered for sale.

Extremely small, delicate, and modestly colored, *F. pygmaeus* should only be maintained by specialists. In view of its rarity, a species aquarium is required.

Aplocheilichthys antinorii   2/626
Black lampeye
H: NE Africa: Ethiopia.
♂: Slightly slimmer and smaller.   S: +
B: Among Java moss.   F: C
T: 18–22°C, L: 4 cm, pH: 7, D: 4

Aplocheilichthys camerunensis ♂   3/436
Cameroon lampeye
H: W Africa: S Cameroon, N Gabon.
♂: More colorful; longer fins.   S: +
B: Wool mop.   F: C
T: 20–24°C, L: 3 cm, pH: <7, D: 4

Aplocheilichthys hutereaui ♂   4/346
Hutereau's lampeye
H: Africa: SW Sudan, Chad, Zaïre,...
♂: Much more colorful; reticulated. S: +
B: Dense spawning substrate.   F: C
T: 22–30°C, L: 4 cm, pH: 7, D: 3

Aplocheilichthys hutereaui ♂   4/346
Hutereau's lampeye
Southern population: Zambia: Mansa.

Aplocheilichthys johnstoni ♂   2/626
Johnston's lampeye
H: S Af.: Malawi, Tanzania to South Africa.
♂: More colorful; larger fins.   S: +
B: Perlon fibers.   F: C
T: 18–26°C, L: 5.5 cm, pH: 7, D: 2–3

Aplocheilichthys kassenjiensis ♂ 4/346
Lake Albert lampeye   5/470
H: Africa: Lake Albert.
♂: Much more colorful.   S: +
B: Continuous, schooling; Java moss. F:C
T: 22–26°C, L: 4.5 cm, pH: 7, D: 3

Aplocheilichthys kassenjiensis ♂ 4/346
Lake Albert lampeye   5/470
H: Africa: Uganda: Paraa.

KILLIFISHES

Aplocheilichthys kassenjiensis ♀ 4/346
Lake Albert lampeye   5/470
H: Africa: Uganda: Paraa.

Aplocheilichthys katangae ♂   2/628
Katanga lampeye
H: Africa: S central to S Africa.
♂: More colorful; yellow fins.   S: +
B: Adh. spawner; spawning mop.   F: C
T: 20–28°C, L: 4 cm, pH: 7, D: 3–4

Aplocheilichthys congoranensis   3/436
WC
H: Africa: E Tanzania: rivers Rufiji, Ruvu.
♂: More colorful; slightly longer fins. S: +
B: Adhesive spawner on Java moss. F: C
T: 22–26°C, L: 4 cm, pH: <7, D: 3–4

Aplocheilichthys lacustris ♂   3/438
WC
H: Africa: Tanzanian coastal basin.
♂: Larger; colorful fins.   S: +
B: Adhesive spawner on Java moss. F: C
T: 22–26°C, L: 3.5 cm, pH: <7, D: 2–3

Aplocheilichthys lamberti ♂   4/350
Lambert's lampeye
H: Af.: upper Guinea, Senegal, Gambia.
♂: Much more colorful; longer fins. S: +
B: On wool mop.   F: C
T: 22–28°C, L: 4.5 cm, pH: 7, D: 2–3

Aplocheilichthys sp.aff. *lamberti* ♂ 4/350
Lambert's lampeye

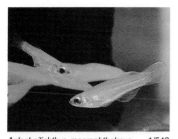

Aplocheilichthys macrophthalmus   1/542
Lampeye panchax, iridescent lampeye
H: W Africa: S Dahomey to Niger Delta.
♂: Much more colorful; longer fins. S: +
B: Adhesive eggs among plants.   F: C
T: 22–26°C, L: 4 cm, pH: >7, D: 3

Aplocheilichthys macrophthalmus hannerzi
Orange-fringe lampeye ♀   4/350
H: W Africa: Nigeria.
♂: More colorful; lanceolate tail fin. S: +
B: Dense spawning substrate.   F: C
T: 23–28°C, L: 3.5 cm, pH: <7, D: 3–4

Aplocheilichthys macrophthalmus hannerzi
Orange-fringe lampeye ♂   4/350

Aplocheilichthys maculatus   3/438
Spotted lampeye
H: Africa: Tanzania, Kenya (Lake Baringo).
♂: Much more colorful; longer fins. S: +
B: Adhesive spawner.   F: C
T: 22–26°C, L: 3.5 cm, pH: 7, D: 2–3

Aplocheilichthys meyburgi ♂   2/628
Meyburg's lampeye
H: Africa: around Lake Victoria.
♂: Slightly more colorful; larger fins. S: +
B: Plant/adhesive spawner.   F: C
T: 22–26°C, L: 3 cm, pH: 7, D: 3–4

Aplocheilichthys moeruensis   3/440
Moeru lampeye
H: Africa: S Zaïre, N Zambia.
♂: More colorful; smaller.   S: +
B: On fine-leaved plants.   F: C
T: 20–26°C, L: 4 cm, pH: <7, D: 3

KILLIFISHES

Aplocheilichthys myaposae   3/440

H: S Africa: Angola, Zambia, Zimbabwe,...
♂: Much more colorful; longer fins. **S:** +
B: Adhesive spawner.   **F:** C
T: 20–26°C, **L:** 4 cm, **pH:** <7, **D:** 3

Aplocheilichthys myersi ♂   4/352
Myers's lampeye

H: Africa: W Zaïre, S Congo.
♂: Much more colorful; longer fins. **S:** +
B: Spawning mop; slow growth.   **F:** C
T: 21–24°C, **L:** 2.5 cm, **pH:** <7, **D:** 3

Aplocheilichthys nimbaensis ♂   4/352
Nimba lampeye

H: Africa: SE upper Guinea, NE Liberia.
♂: Reticulate design; longer fins.   **S:** +
B: Dense spawning substrate.   **F:** C
T: 21–24°C, **L:** 4.5 cm, **pH:** >7, **D:** 3

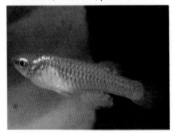

Aplocheilichthys nimbaensis ♀   4/352
Nimba lampeye

Aplocheilichthys normani ♂ WC   3/442
Norman's lampeye

H: Afr.: Senegal, Chad, Sudan, Nigeria.
♂: More colorful; longer fins.   **S:** +
B: Fine-leaved plants.   **F:** C
T: 22–26°C, **L:** 4 cm, **pH:** 7, **D:** 3

Aplocheilichthys omoculatus ♂   3/444
WC

H: Africa: Tanzania.
♂: More colorful; slightly larger.   **S:** +
B: Adhesive spawner.   **F:** C
T: 16–22°C, **L:** 3.5 cm, **pH:** <7, **D:** 3

Aplocheilichthys pfaffi 　　　3/444
Pfaff's lampeye
H: Africa: south of the Sahel.
♂: Slightly more colorful; longer fins. **S:** +
B: Unsuccessful. 　　　　　　　**F:** C
T: 22–26°C, **L:** 3 cm, **pH:** <7, **D:** 3–4

Aplocheilichthys pumilus ♀, ♂♂ 1/544
H: E Africa: crater lakes.
♂: Fins more colorful; (see photo). **S:** +
B: Adh. spawner; fine-leaved plants. **F:** C
T: 24–26°C, **L:** 5.5 cm, **pH:** 7, **D:** 2–3

Aplocheilichthys rancureli ♂ 　3/446
Filamentous lampeye
H: Africa: SW Ghana, S Ivory Coast.
♂: Slightly more colorful; longer fins. **S:** +
B: Adhesive spawner; not prolific. **F:** C
T: 24–26°C, **L:** 3.5 cm, **pH:** <7, **D:** 4

Aplocheilichthys scheeli ♂ 　　4/354
Scheel's lampeye
H: Africa: SE Nigeria to Equatorial Guinea.
♂: Ventral longer fins. 　　　　　**S:** –
B: Unsuccessful. 　　　　　　　**F:** C
T: 24–28°C, **L:** 3.5 cm, **pH:** ≪7, **D:** 3–4

Aplocheilichthys scheeli ♀ 　　4/354
Scheel's lampeye

Aplocheilichthys schioetzi 　　4/354
Schioetz's lampeye
H: Af.: E Lib., SE Guinea, Ivory C., Ghana.
♂: Larger; more colorful; longer fins. **S:** +
B: Peat fibers or substr. sp. (2 ws). **F:** C
T: 24–28°C, **L:** 4 cm, **pH:** 7, **D:** 3

KILLIFISHES

495

Aplocheilichthys sp. "Uvinza"   4/358
Uvinza lampeye
H: Africa: Tanzania.
♂: More colorful; longer fins.   S: +
B: Adhesive spawner.   F: C
T: 22–28°C, L: 4.5 cm, pH: 7, D: 2–3

Aplocheilichthys spilauchen   1/544
Banded lampeye
H: W Africa: Senegal to the lowerZaïre.
♂: Larger; deeper-bodied; colorful fins. S: +
B: Adhesive spawner; <15% Mw.   F: C
T: 24–32°C, L: 7 cm, pH: >7, D: 2

Aplocheilichthys usanguensis ♂ 3/446
Usangu lampeye
H: Africa: SW Tanzania.
♂: Yellow fins.   S: +
B: Java moss.   F: C
T: 17–22°C, L: 3 cm, pH: <7, D: 3–4

Aplocheilichthys vitschumbaensis 4/358
Vitschumba lampeye ♀
H: Africa: NE Zaïre, W Uganda.
♂: Much more colorful; larger.   S: +
B: Dense spawning substrate.   F: C
T: 24–30°C, L: 6 cm, pH: ≫7, D: 3

Aplocheilichthys vitschumbaensis 4/358
Vitschumba lampeye ♂

Hypsopanchax stictopleuron ♂　　2/660

H: W Africa: Gabon, Congo, Zaïre.
♂: Much more colorful.　　　　　　　　S: +
B: Unsuccessful.　　　　　　　　　　　F: C
T: 20–24°C, L: 3.5 cm, pH: ≪7, D: 4

Hypsopanchax modestus t.♀, b.♂　　4/360
Ruwenzori lampeye

H: Af.: upper Nile, NE Zaïre, W Uganda.
♂: More colorful; deeper-bodied.　　S: +
B: Adh. spawner; spawning mop.　　F: C
T: 18–24°C, L: 5.5 cm, pH: 7, D: 3

Hypsopanchax platysternus ♀　　4/360

Hypsopanchax catenatus ♂ WC　3/448
Chain lampeye

H: Africa: SE Gabon.
♂: More colorful; longer fins.　　　　S: +
B: Unsuccessful.　　　　　　　　　　　F: C
T: 22–26°C, L: 6 cm, pH: 7, D: 4

Hypsopanchax platysternus ♂　　4/360

H: Africa: Zaïre.
♂: More colorful; see photos.　　　　S: +
B: Adh. spawner; spawning mop.　　F: C
T: 22–25°C, L: 6 cm, pH: 7, D: 3–4

Hypsopanchax zebra　　　　　　　4/362
Zebra lampeye

H: Africa: Gabon and Congo.
♂: More colorful; deeper-bodied.　　S: +
B: Adhesive spawner.　　　　　　　　F: C
T: 20–22°C, L: 5.5 cm, pH: >7, D: 3

497

Lamprichthys tanganicanus ♂   1/566
Tanganyika lampeye
H: Africa: Lake Tanganyika.   E
♂: With blue dots; larger.   S: +
B: Substrate spawner.   F: C
T: 23–25°C, L: <15 cm, pH: ≫7, D: 3

Pantanodon podoxys ♂ WC   3/450
H: Africa: Kenya to Tanzania: coast.
♂: Much more colorful; longer fins. S: +
B: Unsuccessful.   F: C
T: 24–28°C, L: 5 cm, pH: 7, D: 4

Plataplochilus cabindae ♂   4/362
Cabinda lampeye
H: Af.: SW Gabon,Congo, Cabinda, Zaïre.
♀: Rounded and transparent fins. S: =
B: Adhesive spawner.   F: C
T: 22–25°C, L: 4.5 cm, pH: 7, D: 3–4

Plataplochilus chalcopyrus ♂   3/450
H: W Africa: Gabon.
♀: Smaller; duller colors.   S: +
B: On Java moss or in crevices.   F: C
T: 22–26°C, L: 5 cm, pH: 7, D: 3

Plataplochilus loemensis   3/452

Plataplochilus miltotaenia ♂   3/452

H: Af.: Zaïre, Angola, Congo, SW Gabon.
♂: Slightly brighter; A fin right-angled. S: +
B: Adh. spawner; on plants, mop.   F: C
T: 22–24°C, L: 6 cm, pH: <7, D: 3–4

H: W Africa: Gabon.
♂: More colorful; longer fins.   S: +
B: On Java moss and in crevices.   F: C
T: 22–26°C, L: 5 cm, pH: 7, D: 3

Poeciliidae (Aplocheilichthyinae[1–4])
(Fluviphylacinae[5, 6])

African Lampeyes
South American Lampeyes

Plataplochilus ngaensis ♂ WC   3/454

H: Af.: NW Gabon, SW Equatorial Guinea.
♂: More colorful; elongated fins.   S: +
B: On Java moss and in crevices   F: C
T: 20–26°C, L: 5 cm, pH: 7, D: 3

Procatopus aberrans t.♂, b.♀   2/668

H: W Africa: Nigeria, W Cameroon.
♂: More colorful; elongated fins.   S: =
B: Continuous crevice spawner.   F: C
T: 24–26°C, L: 6 cm, pH: 7, D: 2–3

Procatopus nototaenia t.♂, b.♀   1/574
Red-finned lampeye.
H: W Africa: S Cameroon.
SD: See photo.   S: +
B: Crevice spawner.   F: C
T: 20–25°C, L: 5 cm, pH: <7, D: 2–3

Procatopus similis t.♂, b.♀   2/670
Nigerian lampeye
H: W Africa: SE Nigeria, W Cameroon.
SD: See photo.   S: =
B: Continous crevice spawner.   F: C
T: 24–26°C, L: 7 cm, pH: 7, D: 3

KILLIFISHES

Fluviphylax pygmaeus ♂   3/448
South American lampeye, pygmy lampeye
H: S America: Amazonia.
♂: Elongated and yellowish fins.   S: (–)
B: Unknown.   F: C
T: 24–26°C, L: 2 cm, pH: <7, D: 4

Fluviphylax pygmaeus ♀   3/448
South American lampeye, pygmy lampeye

499

Family Profundulidae

This family has but one genus—*Profundulus*—and five species. They are found in the Central American countries of Mexico, Guatemala, and Honduras (NELSON, 1994).

Profundulus labialis ♂   3/577

H: C America: SE Mexico, W Guatemala.
♂: More colorful; yellow fin fringes.   **S:** +
B: Unknown.   **F:** C,O
T: 18–26°C, **L:** <10 cm, **pH:** >7, **D:** 2

Profundulus punctatus ♂   2/670

H: C America: SE Mexico, S Guatemala.
♂: More color; yellow (spawing time).   **S:**+
B: Java moss; preys on spawn. **F:** C,O
T: 22–26°C, **L:** 8 cm, **pH:** >7, **D:** 2

Valenciidae

Family Valenciidae

The family Valenciidae only contains the two species listed below. They inhabit freshwaters of southeastern Spain, Italy, and western Greece. Most are peaceful, gregarious fishes, although males are sometimes belligerent among themselves.

Valencia hispanica ♂   3/578
Valencia minnow
H: Europe: E Spain: Mediterranean coast.
♂: More colorful, including fins.   **S:** =
B: On fine-leaved plants; in pond. **F:** C,O
T: 10–28°C, **L:** 8 cm, **pH:** 7, **D:** 2–3

Valencia letourneuxi ♂   2/700
Corfu minnow
H: SE Europe: Corsica, Albania, Greece.
♂: More colorful, including fins.   **S:** +
B: On fine-leaved plants; in pond. **F:** C,O
T: 15–24°C, **L:** 6 cm, **pH:** >7, **D:** 2

Xiphophorus variatus ♂, the Hawaii brush-tail highfin (see pp. 563/564), a bred form.

Group 6

Origin/Taxonomy

Because the egg-laying toothcarps (Group 5; see pp. 392 ff.) and the live-bearing toothcarps are treated separately, three families of Cyprinodontiformes which contain both—that is, Anablepidae, Goodeidae, and Poeciliidae—are found in Group 5 as well as Group 6. Additional livebearing fishes can be found in Group 1 (Class Chondrichthys—Cartilaginous Fishes), pp. 33 ff., and in Group 10 (Beloniformes—Hemiramphidae—Halfbeaks), pp. 870 ff.

Geographic Distribution

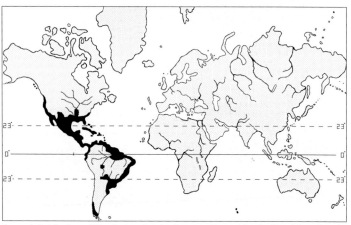

Area of distribution of the livebearing toothcarps. The subfamily Goodeinae is only found in the highlands of Mexico (northern Central America). Anablepinae colonize coastal drainage basins from southern Mexico to Honduras (Atlantic side) and to northern South America (Pacific side) as well as the lowlands of Brazil, Paraguay, Uruguay, and Argentina (*Jenynsia*).

LIVEBEARERS

Group 6

While some species originate from brackish waters and a few live in the littoral zone of the sea, livebearing toothcarps are primarily inhabitants of freshwater habitats. The world map shows the distribution of Group 6. The attractive, colorful bred linages commonly sold today in the trade mostly hail from Southeast Asia (e.g., Singapore) and the United States (Florida).

Generalities

The most notable characteristic of this group is the presence of a copulatory organ in males, i.e., the andropodium or gonopodium. This organ is formed by the anterior rays of the anal fin. The morphology of the gonopodium and its associated features is distinctive to the genus level and, by and large, even to species.

In Poeciliinae and Anablepinae, the copulatory organ is called a gonopodium and it is introduced approximately 1 mm into the female's genital papilla. The Goodeinae have a much simpler copulatory organ, the andropodium. It is merely pressed to the papilla.

Livebearing toothcarps can be generalized as peaceful fishes. As long as the water chemistry is consistent to their requirements, most community aquaria are ideal environments for these fishes. Only the delicate or rare—several species are endangered—need a species aquarium. Typically, the highly inbred, colorful strains of guppies, platies, and swordtails require higher temperatures and are less hardy than their wild counterparts.

Depending on the species involved, there is a danger of hybridization when goodeids or poeciliids are maintained together. Try to keep the species and races pure.

The precocious sexual maturity of this group is both a course and a blessing for breeding. Females must be selected and removed from their male cohorts at an early age, lest they become inseminated by inferior males. Sperm storage occurs on the part of the females of some species, but not within the subfamily Goodeinae. In extreme cases, the females need only be inseminated once to bear offspring their whole life, rendering a fortuitously inseminated female worthless as a breeder. At just 4 weeks of age, the females of many species can be recognized by a black pregnancy spot—called such even though in reality it is a localized concentration of pigment.

These fishes are surface-oriented. Various species are used in tropical regions to control mosquito populations, thereby moderating outbreaks of malaria and yellow fever. Like their egg-laying relatives in Group 5, livebearers characteristically live along shallow shores of all types of aquatic biotopes. Smaller species are found in "mosquito paradises": puddles and slow-flowing, tiny creeks.

LIVEBEARERS

There are a few peculiarities in the species-specific information of this group.
- Indications about the maximum length of a species always refers to the larger gender, but without the sword, where applicable.
- Under breeding, the following specific abbreviations are used:
  dg = days of gestation,
  wg = weeks of gestation,
  y = number of young,
  mm = length (in mm) of young when born.

Subfamily Anablepinae

There are only two genera within the subfamily of four-eyes: *Anableps* and *Jenynsia*. The former has three species, whereas the latter contains approximately five species.

Anableps are unusual in that the male's gonopodium can solely be moved either to the left or to the right and female's genital opening is left or right of the center of the body. Complimentary pairs—e.g., a left-handed male and a right-handed female— are apparently needed for successful insemination. In nature, the ratio of left- and right-handed animals is about 1:1.

Because the well-being of these fishes is dependent on saline water, plants must be waived. Likewise, only brackish or salt-tolerant species can be associated with four-eyes.

The genus *Anableps* inhabits Central America and northern South America. Their unusual eyes immediately set them apart from other fishes (common name): a horizontal conjunctiva divides each eye into a superior (emersed) and inferior (submersed) half, allowing the fish to simultaneously observe their environment above and below the water. Since they are adept at jumping, a tightly-fitting cover is required. Breeding is contingent on seawater.

Jenynsia species occur in southeastern South America. Compared to *Anableps*, they are typically less dependent on a saline environment. However, *J. lineata* (lower right) is frail and disease-prone when maintained in freshwater.

Anableps anableps   1/820
Four-eye
H: C and N S America.   Bw, Fw
♂: Anal fin with gonopodium.   S: =
B: Marine water; 3–4 cm.   F: C
T: 24–28°C, L: ♀ 30 cm, pH: >7, D: 3

Anableps dowi ♂   3/583
Dow's four-eye
H: C America: western coast.   Bw, Mw
♂: A fin w/ gonopodium; smaller.   S: =
B: 20 wg; young are 5–6 cm.   F: C
T: 24–28°C, L: ♀ 34 cm, pH: >7, D: 3

Jenynsia lineata l. ♀, r. ♂   2/702
Broken stripe livebearer   0.1% salt
H: S America: SE Brazil, N Arg.; coast.
♂: A fin w/ gonopodium; smaller.   S: –
B: 42 dg; 10–40 young, 10 mm.   F: O
T: 18–23°C, L: ♀ 10 cm, pH: 7, D: 3

Rio Colima system, highlands of Mexico.

LIVEBEARERS

Subfamily Goodeinae

The goodeinae, also called splitfins because of the shape of their anal fin, have 17 genera and approximately 36 species. Their area of distribution is very reduced; i.e., they only occur in the central high plains (Mesa Central) of Mexico, with the preponderance of species found in the basin of the Rio Lerma.

In comparison to the other two subfamilies, goodeids have a primitive copulatory organ called an andropodium. It is formed by the entire anterior section of the anal fin and is separated from the remainder of the fin by a notch, hence the common name splitfins. The andropodium does not penetrate the female's genital papilla and the female is incapable of storing sperm, unlike Poeciliinae. Although some species live for up to ten years in the aquarium, they are only fertile for about one half of their lifespan. While dense vegetation in the breeding aquarium is advised, the parents' tendency to prey on their offspring is not very pronounced.

Many of the species in this subfamily must be overwintered at cool temperatures (18°–20°C) to retain vigor and size over several generations.

With few exceptions, these fishes are suitable for community aquaria. Some, however, are very aggressive, even attacking tankmates *en masse*.

Those threatened or endangered should always be cared for in a species aquarium to foment reproduction.

Because their natural habitat is very reduced and their colors are rather humble, few species are offered to aquarists. That is a pity, since aquarists could play a major role towards the conservation of goodeids.

Allodontichthys hubbsi ♂　　　4/452
Hubb's splitfin
H: C America: Mexico: Rio Tuxpan.
♂: Andropodium; more colorful.　　S: –
B: 60 dg; 10 young, 20 mm.　　F: O,C
T: 21–25°C, L: 6 cm, pH: >7, D: 3

Allodontichthys polylepis ♂　　　4/452
Many-scale goodeid
H: C America: Mexico: Rio Ameca.
♂: Andropodium; more colorful.　　S: –
B: 60 dg; 10 young, 20 mm.　　F: O,C
T: 21–25°C, L: 7 cm, pH: >7, D: 3

Allodontichthys polylepis ♀　　　4/452
Many-scale goodeid

Allodontichthys zonistius ♂　　　4/454
Colima goodeid
H: C America: Mexico: Rio Colima.
♂: Andropodium; more colorful.　　S: –
B: 60 dg; 15 young, 20 mm.　　F: C,O
T: 21–25°C, L: 7 cm, pH: >7, D: 2

Allodontichthys zonistius ♀　　　4/454,
Colima goodeid　　　　　　　　　　(4/474)

Alloophorus regalis ♂　　　　　4/456
Dwarf goodeid
H: C America: Mexico.　　　Endangered
♂: Andropodium; more colorful.　　S: =
B: Unsuccessful.　　　　　　　F: O,C
T: 21–25°C, L: 8 cm, pH: >7, D: 2

Alloophorus robustus ♀　　　　4/456
Bulldog goodeid
H: C America: Mexico.　　　Very rare
♂: Andropodium; more colorful.　　S: =
B: 60 dg; <25 young, <20 mm.　F: O,C
T: 21–25°C, L: 12 cm, pH: >7, D: 2

Allotoca diazi ♀　　　　　　4/458
Diaz's goodeid
H: C America: Mexico: Michoacán.
♂: Andropodium; more colorful.　S: +
B: 55 dg; 20 young, 10 mm.　　F: O
T: 23–27°C, L: 10 cm, pH: 7, D: 3

Allotoca goslinei ♂　　　　　4/458
Gosline's goodeid
H: C America: Mexico.　　　Endangered
♂: Andropodium; more colorful.　S: (–)
B: 55 dg; 20 young, 10 mm.　　F: C,O
T: 24–28°C, L: 6 cm, pH: >7, D: 3

Allotoca maculata ♂　　　　4/460
Magdalena goodeid
H: C America: Mexico.　　　Endangered
♂: Andropodium; larger dorsal fin.　S: =
B: 55 dg; 25 young, 10 mm.　　F: O,C
T: 22–26°C, L: 4 cm, pH: >7, D: 3

Allotoca maculata ♀　　　　4/460
Magdalena goodeid

LIVEBEARERS

Ameca splendens t.♀, b.♂   2/703
Butterfly goodeid
H: C America: Mexico: Jalisco.
♂: Andropodium; C fin w/ band.   S: =
B: <60 dg; 5–30 young, 20 mm. F: H,O
T: 26–32°C, L: ♀12 cm, pH: 7, D: 1

Ataeniobius toweri ♂   3/584
Tower's goodeid
H: C America: Mexico: Rio Verde.
♂: Andropodium; smaller.   S: +
B: 10–15 young, 10–15 mm.   F: C,O
T: 22–30°C, L: ♀10 cm, pH: >7, D: 3

Ataeniobius toweri ♀   3/584
Tower's goodeid

Chapalichthys encaustus ♂   2/704
Side-spot goodeid
H: C America: Mexico: Jalisco.
♂: Andropod.; slightly more colorful. S: –
B: 10 young, 15 mm.   F: C,O
T: 20–28°C, L: ♀8 cm, pH: >7, D: 2

Chapalichthys pardalis ♂   3/587
Panther goodeid
H: C America: Mexico: Tocumbo.
♂: Andropodium; yellow fin edges.   S: =
B: 12 young, 15 mm.   F: C,O
T: 18–24°C, L: ♀7 cm, pH: >7, D: 3

Characodon lateralis ♂   2/706
Rainbow goodeid
H: C America: Mexico: Durango.
♂: Andropodium; more colorful.   S: +
B: 55 dg; 5–20 young, 10 mm.   F: H,O
T: 18–27°C, L: ♀5 cm, pH: 7, D: 3

Girardinichthys multiradiatus   2/706
Large-finned goodeid
H: C America: Mexico: Rio Lerma.
♂: Small andropodium; smaller.   S: ?
B: 55 dg; 10–30 young, 10 mm.   F: C
T: 12–20°C, L: ♀5 cm, pH: 7, D: 3

Goodea atripinnis atripinnis ♂   3/588
Black-finned goodeid
H: C America: Mexico.
♂: Andropodium; smaller.   S: =
B: 55 dg; 15–50 young, 20 mm.   F: O
T: 18–24°C, L: ♀12 cm, pH: >7, D: 2

Goodea atripinnis atripinnis ♀   3/588
Black-finned goodeid

Goodea atripinnis martini ♂   5/608

H: C America: Mexico: Michoacán.
♂: Andropodium; 2 cm smaller.   S: =
B: 55 dg; 15–50 y, 15–18 mm.   F: C,O
T: 21–27°C, L: ♀9 cm, pH: 7, D: 1–2

Goodea atripinnis luitpoldi ♀   5/608

H: C America: C Mexico: Pacific side.
♂: Andropodium; 2 cm smaller.   S: +
B: 42 dg; <60 young, 12–18 mm.   F: O
T: 21–27°C, L: ♀9 cm, pH: 7, D: 1–2

Goodea gracilis ♂   4/464
Slender goodeid
H: C America: Mexico.
♂: Andropodium; smaller.   S: +
B: 55 dg; <50 young, 15 mm.   F: O
T: 21–27°C, L: ♀12 cm, pH: >7, D: 1–2

Goodea gracilis   4/464, (4/475)
Slender goodeid

Hubbsina turneri ♀   4/464
Turner's goodeid
H: C America: Mexico.   Endangered
♂: Andropodium; darker.   S: (–)
B: 55 dg; 15 young, 7 mm.   F: O
T: 23–26°C, L: 6 cm, pH: >7, D: 3

Ilyodon furcidens ♂   3/590

H: C America: Mexico: coastal areas.
♂: Andropodium; smaller.   S: –
B: 60 dg; 15–40 young, 10 mm.   F: O
T: 24–27°C, L: ♀9 cm, pH: >7, D: 2

Ilyodon furcidens ♀   3/590

Ilyodon furcidens "amecae" ♂   4/466

H: C America: Mexico: Ameca Basin.
♂: Andropodium; more colorful.   S: =
B: 55 dg; <50 young, 10 mm.   F: O
T: 24–28°C, L: ♀10 cm, pH: >7, D: 1

Ilyodon furcidens "amecae" ♀   4/466

LIVEBEARERS

Ilyodon lennoni ♂   2/708
Lennon's goodeid
H: C America: Mexico.   Endangered
♂: Andropodium; more colorful.   S: (–)
B: 60 dg; 15–40 young, 10 mm.   F: H,O
T: 24–30°C, L: ♀8 cm, pH: >7, D: 2–3

Ilyodon whitei ♂   2/708
Balsas goodeid
H: C America: Mexico: Rio Balsas.
♂: Andropodium; more colorful.   S: –
B: 60 dg; 15–40 young, 10 mm.   F: O
T: 20–26°C, L: ♀7 cm, pH: >7, D: 2

Skiffia bilineata ♂   3/592

Skiffia bilineata ♀   3/592

H: C America: Mexico.
♂: Andropodium; dark A and D fins. S: =
B: 55 dg; 7–20 young, 10 mm.   F: O
T: 22–28°C, L: ♀6 cm, pH: >7, D: 2

Skiffia francesae t.♀, b.♂   4/468
Frances' goodeid
H: C America: Mexico.   Endangered
♂: Andropodium; larger dorsal fin.   S: –
B: 40–55 dg; <25 young, 10 mm.   F: O
T: 21–27°C, L: 6 cm, pH: >7, D: 3

Skiffia lermae r.♀, l.♂   4/468
Lerma goodeid
H: C America: Mexico: Michoacán.
♂: Andropodium; yellowish fins.   S: –
B: 50–60 dg; 25 young, 10 mm.   F: O
T: 21–28°C, L: 5 cm, pH: >7, D: 3

Skiffia lermae ♂   4/468
Lerma goodeid
Unspotted

Skiffia multipunctata ♂   3/594, 4/470

H: C America: Mexico.   Endangered
♂: Andropodium; smaller.   S: –
B: 50–55 dg; 30 young, 12 mm.   F: O
T: 21–28°C, L: ♀6 cm, pH: 7, D: 2–3

Skiffia multipunctata ♂   3/594, 4/470

Unspotted

Skiffia multipunctata ♂   3/594, 4/470

Spotted

Xenoophorus captivus t.♀, b.♂   2/710
Green goodeid
H: C America: Mexico.   Endangered
♂: Andropodium; larger A & D fins.   S: +
B: 55 dg; 10–30 young, 18 mm.   F: H,O
T: 18–26°C, L: ♀6 cm, pH: >7, D: 2

Xenotaenia resolanae   2/710
Resolana goodeid
H: C America: Mexico: Rio Resolana.
♂: Andropodium; brighter yellow.   S: =
B: 60 dg; 10–30 young, 12 mm.   F: H,O
T: 22–25°C, L: ♀5 cm, pH: >7, D: 2

Xenotoca eiseni ♂   2/712
Red-tailed goodeid
H: C America: Mexico.
♂: Slimmer; orange C peduncle.   S: +
B: 60 dg; 10–50 young, 15 mm.   F: O
T: 15–32°C, L: ♀7 cm, pH: >7, D: 1–2

Xenotoca variata t.♂, b.♀   2/712

H: C America: Mexico: Rio Lerma Basin.
♂: Andropodium; more colorful C fin. S: +
B: 60 dg; 20–40 young, 15 mm.   F: H,O
T: 20–27°C, L: ♀7 cm, pH: 7, D: 2–3

Zoogoneticus quitzeoensis ♀   2/714
Gold-edged goodeid
H: C America: Mexico: Michoacán.
♂: Gold-fringed D and A fins.   S: +
B: 55 dg; 15 young, 10 mm.   F: C,O
T: 25–28°C, L: ♀4.5 cm, pH: 7, D: 3

Zoogoneticus quitzeoensis ♂   4/472
Gold-edged goodeid
Nominate form (see p. 2/714 for text).

Zoogoneticus tequila ♂   4/472
White-edged goodeid
H: Mexico: Lago Chapala.   Endangered?
♂: White-edged D and A fins.   S: +
B: 55–60 dg; 25 young, 10 mm.   F: O
T: 25–28°C, L: 6 cm, pH: 7, D: 2

Zoogoneticus tequila ♀   4/472
Gold-edged goodeid

Rio de la Palma, Mexico. The type locality of *Priapella olmecae*.

Subfamily Poeciliinae

The subfamily of livebearing toothcarps consists of about 22 genera and at least 192 species (NELSON, 1994). Their natural habitat extends from North America (eastern United States) and the Caribbean to South America (northeastern Argentina and Uruguay). At 4–8 cm length, the vast majority of species are an ideal size for aquaria; very few attain 20 cm length. Species which live in brackish waters or enter littoral regions of marine environments are exceptions. In the Caribbean, poeciliids are a significant part of the piscine freshwater fauna of the islands.

Guppies, platies, and swordtails are the foundation of the aquarium hobby. Massive numbers are reproduced in ponds, cement tanks, and aquaria in Singapore and the United States (Florida). Hardly any aquarist can claim that he/she has never kept at least one of these species in one of its seemingly endless number of linages at one time or another.

Although Poeciliinae are often collectively considered to be "beginners fishes," candidates of interest for the advanced hobbyist and specialist rank among their numbers. There is fertile ground within this group for those who wish to study genetics: startling colors and forms are the successful result of the art and science of the serious breeder. Just think of the large fan-shaped caudal fin of guppies or the lyre factor in swordtails—both the result of constant human selection. With their beckoning colors and large-finned sluggishness, they would have little chance of survival in nature.

There are robust community species as well as frail, exacting charges which demand a species aquarium. Not only do these livebearers grace our aquaria, they are also of grand importance in tropical and subtropical countries where they help control mosquito-borne diseases by feeding on the mosquitoes' larvae: *Gambusia affinis* and *G. holbrooki* are the species most commonly employed for this purpose (hence, "mosquitofishes"). With a diet centered around insects and their larvae, a superior mouth, a surface-oriented lifestyle, and aquatic habitats which include the smallest, most obscure corners, they are eminently suited to the task.

Two genera among the Poeciliinae are distinct misfits:
- The monotypic genus *Tomeurus* with its sole member, *T. gracilis* (p. 550), is not a livebearing. The eggs are adhered to fine-leaved plants a few days after internal fertilization. Aquarium maintenance and reproduction of this delicate species are difficult.
- Another monotypic genus, *Xenodexia*, consists of *X. ctenolepis* (p. 550). Its right pectoral fin has been modified into a hand-shaped appendage which probably plays a role during copulation.

Although livebearing toothcarps are mostly robust charges—highly inbred forms less so—this should not seduce us to neglect aquarium maintenance. They prefer sunny, well-established aquaria with dense vegetation. The upper water strata should offer open swimming space, but a modest amount of floating plants provides welcome refuge for timid species.

Water chemistry is not of paramount importance, but hard, slightly alkaline water is preferred over soft, acid water. Fishes that originate from marine coastal areas fare better when a small quantity of marine salt is added to the water.

When born, the offspring are fully developed. They quickly swim to the water surface, fill their swimbladder with air and then begin searching for food. *Artemia* nauplii and ground flake foods are appropriate initial foods. Provided the aquarium has ample vegetation, numerous hiding places, and a sparse population, some of the young will escape predation. However, for those who wish to maximize the yield of their breeding endeavors, either place the pregnant female into a separate birthing aquarium until the offspring are born, at which point the female should be removed, or place the gestating female into a spawning box hanging in a breeding tank. Caution!—not all species tolerate such handling during gestation. Stillbirths may result. As soon as possible, the offspring should be separated by sex. Rigorously evaluate the young for vigor, body conformation, and color, thereby selecting the next generation of breeders.

Unfortunately, Poeciliinae with a similar gonopodium tend to hybridize when they are maintained in a single aquarium. The offspring of such unions are not only viable, but frequently fertile. The integrity of the species is adulterated and ultimately eliminated. Hence, a species aquarium is strongly suggested for those aquarists fortunate enough to have endangered species in their care. Make a positive difference towards species protection!

LIVEBEARERS

Acanthophacelus bifurca ♂   4/510
Small Amazon livebearer
H: S America: Brazil: Para.   Rare
♂: Smaller; more colorful; w/ gonop. S: –
B: Every 3–4 d; 1–3 young.   F: O
T: 24–29°C, L: ♀ 4 cm, pH: >7, D: 3

Acanthophacelus bifurca ♀   4/510
Small Amazon livebearer

Acanthophacelus bifurca ♂   4/510
Small Amazon livebearer

Acanthophacelus bifurca ♀   4/510
Small Amazon livebearer

Alfaro cultratus ♂   2/715
Knife-edged livebearer
H: C America: Nicaragua to W Panama.
♂: Gonopodium; longer ventral fins. S: =
B: 24 dg; 10–30 young, 8 mm.   F: C
T: 24–28°C, L: ♀ 8 cm, pH: 7, D: 2–3

Alfaro huberi   2/716
H: C Am.: S Gua., Hon., Nic: Atlantic side.
♂: Gonopodium; ♀ & ♂ same color. S: =
B: Unsuccessful.   F: C
T: 26–32°C, L: ♀ 20 cm, pH: >7, D: 3

LIVEBEARERS

Belonesox belizanus   1/590
Pike topminnow
H: C America: S Mexico to Honduras.
♂: Much smaller.   S: =,–
B: 100 young, 20–30 mm.   F: C
T: 26–32°C, L: ♀ 20 cm, pH: >7, D: 3

Belonesox belizanus maxillosus   4/476
Yellow pike topminnow t. ♀, b. ♂
H: C America: S Mexico to Honduras.
♂: Gonop.; yellow chest (courtship). S: =
B: 60 dg; 20–100 young, 30 mm.   F: C
T: 24–28°C, L: ♀ 20 cm, pH: >7, D: 2–3

Brachyrhaphis cascajalensis ♂   4/476
Cascajal livebearer
H: C America: S Costa Rica to Panama.
♂: Gonopodium; more colorful.   S: =
B: 28 dg; 15–40 young, 7 mm.   F: O,C
T: 24–28°C, L: ♀ 7 cm, pH: 7, D: 2

Brachyrhaphis parismina ♀   4/476
Cascajal livebearer

Brachyrhaphis episcopi t. ♂, b. ♀ 2/716
Bishop
H: C America: Panama: Canal Zone.
♂: Gonopodium; more colorful.   S: =
B: 28 dg; 10–20 young.   F: C
T: 25–30°C, L: ♀ 5 cm, pH: >7, D: 3–4

Brachyrhaphis cf. *episcopi* ♂   4/478
False bishop
H: C Am.: Panama: Altantic & Pacific side.
♂: Gonopodium; much smaller.   S: =
B: Disease-prone: sterile tank.   F:C,O
T: 23–27°C, L: ♀ 7 cm, pH: >7, D: 2

Brachyrhaphis cf. *episcopi* ♀   4/478
False bishop

Brachyrhaphis hartwegi t.♀, b.♂ 2/718
Hartweg's bishop
H: C America: Mexico, S Guatemala.
♂: Gonopodium; smaller.   S: –
B: 28 dg; 10–20 young.   F: C
T: 25–28°C, L: ♀5 cm, pH: >7, D: 3–4

Brachyrhaphis parismina ♂   3/595
Parismina bishop
H: C America: Costa Rica: Atlantic side.
♂: Gonopodium; smaller.   S: +
B: 42 dg; 10–20 young, 6–7 mm.   F: C
T: 25–28°C, L: ♀5 cm, pH: >7, D: 3–4

Brachyrhaphis parismina ♀   3/595
Parismina bishop

Brachyrhaphis rhabdophora ♂   2/718
Regan's bishop
H: C America: Costa Rica.
♂: Gonopodium. ♀: Stouter.   S: –
B: 28 dg; 10–30 young, 7 mm.   F: C,O
T: 25–28°C, L: ♀6 cm, pH: ≫7, D: 2

Brachyrhaphis roseni ♂   3/596
Rosen's bishop
H: C America: S Costa Rica: Pacific side.
♂: Gonopodium; more slender.   S: –
B: 42 days gestation.   F: C,O
T: 25–28°C, L: ♀6 cm, pH: >7, D: 2

LIVEBEARERS

Brachyrhaphis roseni ♀ 3/596
Rosen's bishop

Brachyrhaphis terrabensis ♂ 3/598
Térraba mosquitofish
H: C America: S Costa Rica, W Panama.
♂: Gonopodium; smaller. S: (–)
B: 42 dg; 10–30 young, 8–9 mm. F: C
T: 23–26°C, L: ♀6 cm, pH: >7, D: 3

Carlhubbsia kidderi ♂ 2/720
Straw widow
H: C America: Mexico, Guatemala.
♂: Long gonopodium; color like ♀. S: +
B: 24 dg; 15–60 young. F: C
T: 27–30°C, L: ♀5 cm, pH: >7, D: 3

Carlhubbsia stuarti t.♀, b.♂ 4/480
Banded widow
H: C America: Guatemala.
♂: Long gonopodium. S: +
B: 28 dg; 10–50 young, 6–8 mm. F: O
T: 23–27°C, L: ♀5 cm, pH: 7, D: 2

Cnesterodon raddai t.♂, b.♀ 2/720
Carnegie's millionsfish
H: S America: Brazil, Uruguay, Argentina.
♂: Gonopodium; smaller. S: +
B: 24 dg; 5–15 young, 2.5 mm. F: O
T: 18–26°C, L: ♀3.5 cm, pH: 7, D: 1–2

Cnesterodon decemmaculatus ♀ 5/610
Carnegie's millionsfish
H: S America: S Brazil, Uruguay.
♂: Gonopodium; smaller. S: (–)
B: Young 3–4 mm long. F: C
T: 20–26°C, L: ♀5 cm, pH: 7, D: 1–2

LIVEBEARERS

Cnesterodon decemmaculatus ♀　5/610

H: S Am.: S Brazil, Bolivia, Arg., Uruguay.
♂: Gonopodium; smaller; darker.　S: (–)
B: Young 3–4 mm long.　　　　　　　F: C
T: 17–21°C, L: ♀4.5 cm, pH: >7, D: 1–2

Gambusia vittata l.♀, r.♂　　　　　2/722
One-band mosquitofish

H: C America: Mexico: Rio Panuco Basin.
♂: Gonopodium; more colorful.　　S: +
B: 28 dg; 10–30 young, 10 mm.　F: C,O
T: 24–28°C, L: ♀6 cm, pH: 7, D: 2

Gambusia affinis affinis b.♀, t.♂ 2/722
Mosquitofish

H: N America: USA: Texas.
♂: Gonopodium; smaller.　　　　　　S: +
B: 24 dg; 10–60 young.　　　　　F: C,O
T: 18–24°C, L: ♀6.5 cm, pH: 7, D: 1

Gambusia alvarezi ♂　　　　　　　4/480
Alvarez's mosquitofish

H: C America: Mexico.　　　Endangered
♂: Gonopodium; slimmer.　　　　　S: =
B: 38 dg; 20–25 young.　　　　　　F: O,C
T: 24–28°C, L: ♀4 cm, pH: >7, D: 3

Gambusia alvarezi ♀　　　　　　　4/480
Alvarez's mosquitofish

Gambusia atrora t.♀, b.♂　　　　　3/598
Blackfin mosquitofish

H: C America: Mexico.
♂: Gonopod.; smaller; more colorful.　S: –
B: 35 dg; 10–20 young.　　　　　　F: O
T: 24–28°C, L: ♀4 cm, pH: >7, D: 3–4

Gambusia aurata ♂   4/482
Golden mosquitofish
H: C America: Mexico.   Endangered
♂: Gonopodium; smaller.   S: –
B: 28–35 dg; 15–30 y, 6–8 mm. F: O,C
T: 24–28°C, L: ♀ 4 cm, pH: 7, D: 3

Gambusia aurata ♀   4/482
Golden mosquitofish

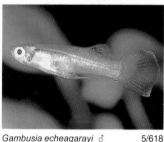

Gambusia echeagarayi ♂   5/618

H: C America: Mexico: Chiapas.
♂: Gonopodium; ca.1 cm smaller. S: (–)
B: 27 dg; 4–20 young, 6 mm.   F: C,O
T: 27–29°C, L: ♀ 4.5 cm, pH: >7, D: 1–2

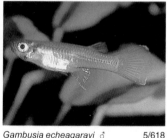

Gambusia echeagarayi ♂   5/618

Gambusia eurystoma ♂   4/482

H: C America: Mexico.   Endangered
♂: Gonopodium; slimmer.   S: (–)
B: 35 dg; 4 young, 8 mm.   F: O,C
T: 24–29°C, L: ♀ 3.5 cm, pH: >7, D: 3

Gambusia hispaniolae ♂   4/484
Hispaniola mosquitofish
H: Caribbean: Haiti, Dominican Republic.
♂: Gonopopium; red unpaired fins. S: –
B: 35 dg; 10–40 y, 7–10 mm.   F: C,O
T: 23–27°C, L: ♀ 6 cm, pH: >7, D: 2

LIVEBEARERS

521

Gambusia hispaniolae ♀   4/484
Hispaniola mosquitofish

Gambusia holbrooki l. ♀, r. ♂   1/590
Holbrook's mosquitofish
H: N and C America: S USA, N Mexico.
♂: Gonopodium; more colorful.   S: =
B: 35–56 dg; 40–60 young.   F: C,O
T: 15–35°C, L: ♀ 8 cm, pH: 7, D: 1

Gambusia hurtadoi ♂   4/486
Dolores mosquitofish
H: C America: Mexico.   Endangered
♂: Gonopodium; smaller.   S: –
B: 38 dg; 20 young, 6–8 mm.   F: O,C
T: 24–28°C, L: ♀ 3.5 cm, pH: >7, D: 3

Gambusia hurtadoi ♀   4/486
Dolores mosquitofish

Gambusia krumholzi ♂   5/612

Gambusia krumholzi ♀   5/612

H: S America: Mexico: Coahuila.   Rare
♂: Gonopod.; more color, esp. C fin. S: –
B: 48 dg; 30 young, 7–8 mm.   F: C
T: 26–29°C, L: ♀ 6 cm, pH: >7, D: 2–3

LIVEBEARERS

Gambusia lemaitrei ♂   3/600
Totuma mosquitofish

H: S America: Colombia: Lake Totuma.
♂: Gonopodium; more colorful.   S: –
B: 25–28 days of gestation.   F: O
T: 24–28°C, L: ♀ 4 cm, pH: >7, D: 3

Gambusia lemaitrei ♀   3/600
Totuma mosquitofish

Gambusia longispinis ♂   4/486
Cuatro Cienegas mosquitofish

H: C America: Mexico.   Endangered
♂: Gonopodium; smaller.   S: –
B: 35 dg; 10–30 young, 7 mm.   F: O,C
T: 23–28°C, L: ♀ 4 cm, pH: >7, D: 2

Gambusia longispinis ♀   4/486
Cuatro Cienegas mosquitofish

Gambusia luma ♂   4/490

Gambusia luma ♀   4/490

H: C America: Belize, Honduras, Guatemala.
♂: Gonopodium; spawning colors. S: =
B: 34 dg; 10–25 young, 6–8 mm.   F: O,C
T: 22–27°C, L: ♀ 6 cm, pH: >7, D: 3

Gambusia marshi ♂   2/724
Pelucid mosquitofish, Salado mosquitofish
H: C America: NE Mexico.
♂: Gonopodium; more slender.   S: +
B: 28 dg; 5–60 young, 6–7 mm.   F: O
T: 22–26°C, L: ♀6 cm, pH: 7, D: 2

Gambusia nobilis ♂   5/614
Pecos gambusia
H: N America: USA: Texas, New Mexico.
♂: Gonopodium; more slender.   S: –
B: 40 dg; ca. 25 young, 8 mm.   F: C
T: 24–28°C, L: ♀6 cm, pH: >7, D: 2–3

Gambusia nobilis ♀   5/614
Pecos gambusia

Gambusia panuco ♂   3/602
Rio Panuco mosquitofish
H: C America: Mexico: Panuco Basin.
♂: Gonopodium; much smaller.   S: –
B: 35–42 dg; 10–40 y, 6–7 mm.   F: O
T: 22–28°C, L: ♀5.5 cm, pH: 7, D: 3

Gambusia punctata ♂   5/616
Dotted gambusia
H: C America: Cuba, Isle of Pines.
♂: Gonopodium; more slender.   S: =
B: 28 days of gestation.   F: C
T: 24–28°C, L: ♀8 cm, pH: >7, D: 1–2

Gambusia punctata ♀   5/616
Dotted gambusia

Gambusia puncticulata ♂   2/724
Yucatan spotted mosquitofish
H: C America: Mexico to Panama.
♂: Gonopodium; smaller.   S: –
B: 24 dg; 10–30 young, 10 mm.   F: C,O
T: 22–28°C, L: ♀8 cm, pH: >7, D: 3

Gambusia puncticulata yucatana ♀ 2/724
Yucatan spotted mosquitofish

Gambusia rachowi ♂   3/608
Rachow's mosquitofish
H: C America: Mexico: Veracruz.
♂: Gonopodium; slightly smaller.   S: +
B: 35 dg; 5–20 young, 6–7 mm.   F: C,O
T: 22–26°C, L: ♀3.5 cm, pH: 7, D: 2

Gambusia regani ♂   2/726
Regan's mosquitofish
H: C America: Mexico.
♂: Gonopodium; ♀ & ♂ equal color. S: +
B: 24 dg; 10–20 young.   F: L,O
T: 21–28°C, L: ♀4 cm, pH: 7, D: 3

Gambusia rhizophorae ♂   3/602
Mangrove mosquitofish
H: Caribbean, N Am.: Cuba, S Florida.
♂: Gonopodium; smaller.   S: –
B: 42 dg; 30 young; Bw.   F: O
T: 22–28°C, L: ♀5 cm, pH: >7, D: 3

Gambusia senilis ♂   4/492
Blotched gambusia
H: C and N America: Mexico, Texas.
♂: Gonop.; yellowish D and C fins. S: –
B: 38 dg; 10–30 young, 7 mm.   F: O,C
T: 21–25°C, L: ♀5.5 cm, pH: >7, D: 2

LIVEBEARERS

Gambusia senilis ♀　　　4/492
Blotched gambusia

Gambusia sexradiata ♀　　　2/726
Tropical mosquitofish
H: C America: Mexico, Guatemala, Belize.
♂: Gonopodium; smaller.　　　S: +
B: 28 dg; 10–35 young, 5 mm.　　　F: O
T: 22–26°C, L: ♀6.5 cm, pH: 7, D: 2

Gambusia speciosa ♂　　　4/492

Gambusia speciosa ♀　　　4/492

H: C and N America: N Mexico, S Texas.
♂: Gonopodium; slimmer.　　　S: =
B: 28–35 dg; 10–50 young, 7 mm. F: C,O
T: 23–28°C, L: ♀5 cm, pH: 7, D: 1

Gambusia wrayi t.♀, b.♂　　　4/494
Jamaica mosquitofish
H: Caribbean: Jamaica.
♂: Gonopodium; smaller.　　　S: =
B: 35 dg; 10–40 young, 6–9 mm. F: O,C
T: 23–28°C, L: ♀6 cm, pH: >7, D: 2

Girardinus creolus ♀　　　3/604
Creole mosquitofish
H: Caribbean: Cuba.　　　Rare
♂: Gonopodium; smaller.　　　S: +
B: 30 days of gestation.　　　F: C,O
T: 22–26°C, L: ♀7 cm, pH: >7, D: 2

Girardinus creolus ♂   3/604
Creole mosquitofish

Girardinus denticulatus ♂   4/496

H: Caribbean: Cuba.
♂: Gonopodium; smaller.   S: +
B: 28 dg; 12–30 young, 8 mm.   F: O
T: 22–28°C, L: ♀6 cm, pH: 7, D: 2

Girardinus falcatus ♂   2/728
Sickle girardinus
H: Caribbean: Cuba.
♂: Gonopodium; smaller.   S: +
B: 25 dg; 10–40 young, 8 mm.   F: O
T: 24–30°C, L: ♀7 cm, pH: 7, D: 2

Girardinus metallicus t. ♀, b. ♂   1/592
Metallic girardinus
H: Caribbean: Cuba.   E
♂: Gonopod.; smaller; more colorful. S: +
B: 28–30 dg; 10–100 y, 6–7 mm.   F: C,O
T: 22–25°C, L: ♀9 cm, pH: 7, D: 1–2

Girardinus microdactylus ♂   3/606
Finger girardinus
H: Caribbean: Cuba, Isle of Pines.
♂: Gonopodium; smaller.   S: +
B: 28 dg; 10–50 young, 6–9 mm.   F: O
T: 22–26°C, L: ♀6 cm, pH: 7, D: 3

Girardinus uninotatus l. ♀, r. ♂   3/606
Single-spot girardinus
H: Caribbean: Cuba.   Rare
♂: Gonopodium; smaller.   S: +
B: 28 dg; 10–40 young, 8 mm.   F: O
T: 24–28°C, L: ♀8 cm, pH: >7, D: 2

LIVEBEARERS

Pseudoxiphophorus anzuetoi ♀   4/496
Variable heterandria
H: C America: Guatemala, Honduras.
♂: Gonopodium; smaller.   S: =
B: 42 dg? <20 young, 10 mm.   F: O,C
T: 21–26°C, L: ♀7 cm, pH: >7, D: 2

Pseudoxipho. bimaculata t.♀, b.♂ 2/728
Spotted-tail mosquitofish
H: C & N America: Gulf of Mex. to Hon.
♂: Long gonopodium.   S: =
B: 42–56 dg; 20–110 y, 15 mm.   F: C
T: 20–28°C, L: ♀ 15 cm, pH: 7, D: 3–4

Heterandria formosa t.♂, b.♀   1/592
Dwarf topminnow, least killifish
H: N Am.: USA: South Carolina, Florida.
♂: Gonopodium; much smaller.   S: +
B: 10–77 day of gestation.   F: C,O
T: 22–26°C, L: ♀4.5 cm, pH: 7, D: 1

Pseudoxiphophorus jonesi ♂   3/608
Puebla mosquitofish
H: C America: Mexico.
♂: Gonopodium; slightly smaller. S: +
B: 60 dg; 20–50 y, 11–14 mm.   F: C
T: 20–28°C, L: ♀9 cm, pH: 7, D: 2

Heterophallus milleri ♂   4/498
Miller's livebearer
H: C America: Mexico.
♂: Gonopodium; smaller.   S: +
B: 19–21 dg; 4–25 y, 6 mm.   F: O,C
T: 23–28°C, L: ♀5 cm, pH: >7, D: 3

Heterophallus milleri ♀   4/498
Miller's livebearer

Poecilia reticulata ♀　　　1/598
Guppy, millionsfish
H: C America to S America (Brazil).
♂: Gonopod.; more colorful; smaller. **S:** +
B: 20–40 young.　　　　　**F:** O
T: 18–28°C, **L:** ♀ 6 cm, **pH:** 7, **D:** 1

Poecilia reticulata ♂　　　2/742
Wild guppy Mexican population
H: C America: Mexico.
♂: Gonopod.; more colorful; smaller. **S:** +
B: 20–40 young.　　　　　**F:** O
T: 22–28°C, **L:** ♀ 6 cm, **pH:** 7, **D:** 2

Poecilia reticulata ♂　　　1/598
Guppy, millionsfish
Fantail guppy
Today most are bred in Asia, e.g., Singapore.

Poecilia reticulata ♂　　　2/742
Wild guppy Peruvian population
H: S America: Peru.

T: 22–28°C, **L:** ♀ 5–6 cm, **pH:** >7, **D:** 2

Poecilia reticulata ♂　　　1/598
Guppy, millionsfish
Fantail guppy.
Today most are bred in Asia (e.g., Singapore).

Poecilia reticulata ♂　　　2/742
Wild giant guppy
H: C America: Mexico.

T: 22–28°C, **L:** ♀ 6–8 cm, **pH:** 7, **D:** 2

LIVEBEARERS

529

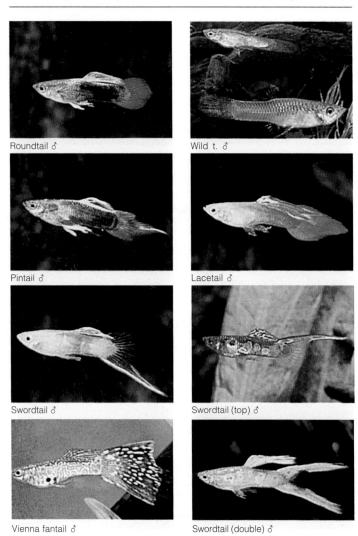

Roundtail ♂

Wild t. ♂

Pintail ♂

Lacetail ♂

LIVEBEARERS

Swordtail ♂

Swordtail (top) ♂

Vienna fantail ♂

Swordtail (double) ♂

Limia dominicensis   2/730, (4/500)
Domonican limia l.♂, r.♀
H: Caribbean: Hispaniola.
♂: Gonopodium; longer V fins.   S: +
B: 24 dg; 15–50 young, 6 mm.   F: O
T: 22–26°C, L: ♀4.5 cm, pH: 7, D: 1–2

Limia dominicensis ♂   (2/730), 4/500
Haitian limia
H: Caribbean: Haiti.
♂: Gonopopium; more colorful.   S: +
B: 42 dg; 15–40 young, 8 mm.   F: O
T: 24–29°C, L: ♀5 cm, pH: 7, D: 2

Limia dominicensis ♀   (2/730), 4/500
Haitian limia

Limia grossidens ♂   4/500
Broad-tooth limia
H: Caribbean: Haiti.
♂: Gonopodium; more colorful.   S: +
B: 42 dg; 10–40 young, 10 mm.   F: O
T: 24–29°C, L: ♀6 cm, pH: >7, D: 2

Limia melanogaster t.♂, b.♀   1/596
Black-bellied limia
H: Caribbean: Jamaica, Haiti.
♂: Gonopodium; more colorful.   S: +
B: Rarely successful.   F: H,O
T: 22–28°C, L: ♀6.5 cm, pH: ≫7, D: 2

LIVEBEARERS

Limia nigrofasciata ♂   4/502
Humpbacked limia, black-barred limia
H: Caribbean: Haiti.   Fw,Bw
♂: Gonopodium; humpback.   S: +
B: 42 dg; 10–60 young, 8 mm.   F: O
T: 24–29°C, L: ♀8 cm, pH: >7, D: 2

Limia nigrofasciata ♂   4/502
Humpbacked limia, black-barred limia

Limia nigrofasciata × *L. dominicensis*
Humpbacked limia t.♂, b.♀   1/596

Limia pauciradiata ♂   4/504
Puerto Plata Limia
H: Caribbean: Hispaniola.
♂: Gonopodium; smaller.   S: +
B: 42 dg; 10–60 young, 8 mm.   F: O
T: 23–28°C, L: ♀6 cm, pH: >7, D: 2

Limia pauciradiata ♀   4/504
Puerto Plata Limia

Limia perugiae ♂   2/730
Perugia's limia
H: Caribbean: Hispaniola.
♂: Gonopodium; orange chest.   S: +
B: 24 dg; 10–100 young, 7 mm.   F: O
T: 24–28°C, L: 7 cm, pH: 7, D: 1–2

LIVEBEARERS

Limia sulphurophila ♂　　　　　　　　4/506
Sulphur-spring limia
H: Caribbean: Dominican Republic.
♂: Gonopodium; smaller.　　　　　　S: +
B: 42 dg; 10–30 young, 8 mm.　　　　F: O
T: 23–28°C, L: ♀ 5 cm, pH: >7, D: 2

Limia tridens b. ♂, t. ♀　　　　　　4/506
Tiburon limia
H: C America: Haiti.
♂: Gonopodium; more colorful.　　　S: +
B: 42 days of gestation.　　　　　　F: O
T: 24–29°C, L: ♀ 4 cm, pH: 7, D: 2

Limia cf. *versicolor* ♂　　　　　　4/508

H: Caribbean: Dominican Republic.
♂: Gonopodium; smaller.　　　　　　S: +
B: 42 dg; 10–35 young, 8 mm.　　　　F: O
T: 22–27°C, L: ♀ 5 cm, pH: >7, D: 2

Limia cf. *versicolor* ♀　　　　　　4/508

Limia vittata ♂ (spotted form)　　1/604
Cuban limia
H: Caribbean: Cuba.
♂: Gonopodium; more colorful.　　　S: +
B: 21–35 dg; 20–50 young.　　　　　F: H,O
T: 18–24°C, L: ♀ 12 cm, pH: >7, D: 2

Limia vittata ♂ (normal form)　　4/508
Cuban limia
H: Caribbean: Cuba.
♂: Gonopodium; smaller.　　　　　　S: +
B: 42 dg; 10–60 young, 8 mm.　　　　F: O
T: 22–28°C, L: ♀ 10 cm, pH: >7, D: 1

LIVEBEARERS

Limia vittata ♀ (normal form)   4/508
Cuban limia

Limia zonata ♂   2/732

H: Caribbean: Dominican Republic.
♂: Gonopodium; smaller.   S: +
B: 30–40 dg; 12–30 young, 7 mm.   F: O
T: 22–25°C, L: ♀ 4.5 cm, pH: 7, D: 2

Pamphorichthys minor t. ♀, b. ♂   4/530
Mini molly

H: S America: Brazil: Amazon Basin.
♂: Gonopodium; smaller.   S: –
B: Only to the 2nd generation.   F: O
T: 23–28°C, L: ♀ 2.5 cm, pH: 7, D: 3

Micropoecilia parae ♂   3/618, 4/530
Para molly

H: S America: Guyana to Brazil.
♂: Gonopodium; smaller.   S: +
B: 5–16 y, 7mm; over 2nd gen. difficult. F: O
T: 24–28°C, L: ♀ 5 cm, pH: 7, D: 3

Micropoecilia parae ♀   3/618, 4/530
Para molly

Micropoecilia picta l. ♀, r. ♂ 2/740, 5/620
Variegated molly (wild coloration)
H: S America: Guyana, Trinidad, Brazil.
♂: Gonopodium; more colorful.   S: +
B: 25 dg; 15–30 young, 7 mm.   F: C
T: 25–29°C, L: ♀ 4 cm, pH: >7, D: 2

LIVEBEARERS

Micropoecilia picta ♂   2/740, 5/620
Variegated molly (aquarium strain)

Micropoecilia picta ♂   2/740, 5/620
Variegated molly

Micropoecilia picta ♂   2/740, 5/620
Red picta

Micropoecilia picta ♂   2/740, 5/620
Black picta

LIVEBEARERS

Neoheterandria elegans t.♂, b.♀ 4/514
Elegant poeciliid
H: S America: Colombia.   Very rare
♂: Gonopod.; smaller, more colorful. **S:** –
B: Every 3–4 d; 1–4 y, 2–3 mm. **F:** O,C
T: 22–26°C, **L:** ♀3.5 cm, pH: >7, **D:** 2

Phallichthys amates amates b.♀, t.♂
Merry widow   1/594
H: C Am.: Guatemala, Panama to Hond.
♂: Gonopodium; smaller.   **S:** +
B: 28 dg; 10–80 young.   **F:** O,H
T: 22–28°C, **L:** ♀6 cm, pH: 7, **D:** 2

535

Phallichthys amates pittieri t.♀, b.♂
Iridescent widow   2/732
H: C America: Costa Rica, N Panama.
♂: Gonopodium; slimmer.   S: +
B: 28 dg; 10–50 young.   F: O,H
T: 20–24°C, L: ♀8 cm, pH: 7, D: 2

Phallichthys fairweatheri ♂   2/734
Fairweather widow
H: C America: Mexico.
♂: Gonopodium; smaller.   S: +
B: 24 dg; 15–30 young, 5 mm.   F: O
T: 22–29°C, L: ♀4 cm, pH: >7, D: 2

Phallichthys quadripunctatus ♂   2/734
Four-spot widow
H: C America: E Costa Rica.
♂: Gonopodium; smaller.   S: +
B: Easy.   F: O
T: 20–20°C, L: ♀3.5 cm, pH: 7, D: 2

Phallichthys tico ♂   4/514
H: C America: Costa Rica.
♂: Gonopodium; smaller, slimmer. S: +
B: 28 dg; 10–25 young, 6 mm.   F: O
T: 24–29°C, L: ♀4 cm, pH: >7, D: 3

Phallichthys tico ♀   4/514

Phallocerus caudimaculatus ♂   3/610
Unspotted caudo
H: C America: S Brazil, Par., Uruguay.
♂: Gonopodium; smaller.   S: +
B: 24 dg; 10–50 young, 5–6 mm.   F: O
T: 18–24°C, L: ♀4.5 cm, pH: >7, D: 1

Phallocerus caudimaculatus ♀   3/610
Spotted caudi

Phallocerus caudimaculatus b. ♀   1/594
Spotted caudi (golden form)
H: S Am.: S Brazil, Paraguay, Uruguay.
♂: Gonopodium; smaller.   S: +
B: 10–40 young, 7 mm.   F: C,O
T: 20–24°C, L: ♀4.5 cm, pH: >7, D: 1

Phalloptychus januarius t.♂, b.♀ 2/736
Barred millionsfish
H: S America: Brazil, Arg., Par., Uru.
♂: Gonopodium; slimmer.   S: +
B: 24 dg; 10–30 young.   F: O
T: 20–25°C, L: ♀4.5 cm, pH: >7, D: 1

Phallotorynus jucundus t.♂, b.♀ 4/516
Paraná millionsfish
H: S America: Brazil, Paraguay.
♂: Gonopodium; slimmer.   S: +
B: 30 dg; 6–10 young, 8 mm.   F: C
T: 20–25°C, L: ♀3 cm, pH: >7, D: 2

Poecilia branneri ♂   3/612
Ocellated micromolly
H: S America: Brazil: Pará.
♂: Caudal fin w/ design (see photo). S: –
B: 3–5 young every few days.   F: C
T: 26–28°C, L: ♀4 cm, pH: <7, D: 3

Poecilia butleri ♂   3/612
Pacific Mexican molly
H: C America: W Mexico to W Panama.
♂: Gonopodium; slightly smaller.   S: +
B: 28 dg; 20–60 young, 8 mm.   F: H
T: 23–27°C, L: ♀8 cm, pH: >7, D: 2

537

Poecilia catemaconis ♂   3/614
Lemon molly

H: C Am.: Mexico: Lake Catemaco.   E
♂: Gonopodium; smaller.   S: –
B: 200 l tank; rearing is easy.   F: H,O
T: 24–28°C, L: ♀ 10.5 cm, pH: >7, D: 2–3

Poecilia catemaconis ♀   3/614
Lemon molly

Poecilia caucana ♂   3/614
Cauca molly

H: C and S America: Panama, Col., Ven.
♂: Gonopodium; more colorful.   S: +
B: 28 dg; 8–25 young, 7 mm.   F: H,O
T: 26–30°C, L: ♀ 6 cm, pH: >7, D: 2

Poecilia chica t.♂, b.♀   2/736
Dwarf molly

H: C America: Mexico.
♂: Gonopod.; dark to almost black. S: +
B: 30 dg; 30–50 young, 6 mm.   F: H,O
T: 23–26°C, L: ♀ 5 cm, pH: 7, D: 1–2

Poecilia elegans ♂   4/520
Elegant molly

H: Caribbean: Dominican Republic.
♂: Gonopodium; smaller.   S: –
B: Rare; 45 dg; 10 y, 10 mm.   F: O,C
T: 21–24°C, L: ♀ 6 cm, pH: >7, D: 3

Poecilia gillii ♂   4/520
Costa Rica molly, Gill's molly

H: C and S Am.: Guatemala to Colombia.
♂: Gonopod.; colors more intense. S: +
B: 24 dg; 10–40 young, 8 mm.   F: O,H
T: 22–26°C, L: ♀ 5 cm, pH: >7, D: 2–3

Poecilia gillii ♀　　　　　4/520
Costa Rica molly, Gill's molly

Poecilia heterandria ♂　　　　4/522
Venezuela molly
H: S America: central Venezuela: coast.
♂: Gonop.; smaller; more colorful.　S: +
B: 28–35 dg; 15–40 young, 7 mm.　F: O
T: 23–27°C, L: ♀4 cm, pH: 7, D: 2

Poecilia heterandria ♀　　　　4/522
Venezuela molly

Poecilia hispaniolana ♂　　　4/524
Hispaniola molly
H: Caribbean: central Hispaniola.
♂: Gonopodium; more colorful.　S: +
B: 35 dg; 10–30 young, 8 mm.　F: O
T: 22–25°C, L: ♀6.5 cm, pH: >7, D: 3

Poecilia hollandi　t.♂, b.♀　5/622
Holland's molly
H: S America: Brazil: Rio São Francisco.
♂: Gon.; more color; 1.5 cm smaller. S: =
B: Young are sensitive.　　　F: C,O
T: 23–28°C, L: ♀4 cm, pH: >7, D: 2

Poecilia latipinna ♂　　　　2/738
Sailfin molly
H: USA: S Virginia, Carolina, Florida, Texas.
♂: Gonopodium; larger dorsal fin.　S: +
B: 60–70 dg; 10–60 y, 12 mm.　F: H,O
T: 20–28°C, L: ♀12 cm, pH: >7, D: 2

Poecilia latipinna ♂   1/602, (2/738)
Sailfin molly
Black form.

Poecilia latipinna × *P. sphenops* ♂ 2/740

Lyretail

Poecilia latipunctata 2 ♂♂ WC   3/617
Porthole molly
H: C America: Mexico.
♂: Gonopodium; more colorful.   S: =
B: 28 dg; 10–30 young, 7 mm.   F: H,O
T: 25–29°C, L: ♀6 cm, pH: 7, D: 3

Poecilia latipunctata ♀   3/617
Porthole molly
Population from Mante, Mexico.

Poecilia maylandi ♂   4/524
Mayland's molly
H: C America: Mexico: Rio Balsas Basin.
♂: Gonopodium; more colorful.   S: +
B: 42 dg; 25–60 young, 8–10 mm.   F: O
T: 24–29°C, L: ♀12 cm, pH: >7, D: 2

Poecilia maylandi ♀   4/524
Mayland's molly

Poecilia cf. *mexicana* ♂   4/526
Cave molly
H: C America: Mexico: Tapijulapa Cavern.
♂: Gonopodium; smaller.   S: –
B: 35 dg; 10–25 young, 8 mm.   F: O
T: 22–28°C, L: ♀ 5 cm, pH: >7, D: 2

Poecilia cf. *mexicana* ♀   4/526
Cave molly

Poecilia mexicana mexicana ♂   2/738
Mexico molly, shortfin molly
H: C and S Am.: Caribbean, Colombia.
♂: Gonopodium; more colorful.   S: +
B: 28 dg; 30–80 y, 8 mm; add salt.   F: H
T: 23–28°C, L: ♀ 8.5 cm, pH: >7, D: 1–2

Poecilia dominicensis ♂   4/518
Dominica molly
H: Caribbean: Hispaniola.
♂: Gonopodium; smaller.   S: –
B: 35dg; 10–40y, 8mm; 2nd gen. diff.   F: O
T: 21–25°C, L: ♀ 5 cm, pH: >7, D: 3

Poecilia petenensis ♂   3/618
Petén molly, swordtail molly
H: C America: Mexico, Guatemala, Belize.
♂: Gonopodium; prettier fins.   S: +
B: 45–60 dg; 10–60 y, 8–12 mm.   F: H,O
T: 22–28°C, L: ♀ 12 cm, pH: >7, D: 2

Poecilia scalpridens ♀   4/542
Chiseltooth molly
H: S America: Brazil: Amazon.
♂: Gonopodium; smaller.   S: +
B: 28–35 dg; 5–12 young, 6–7 mm.   F: O
T: 23–28°C, L: ♀ 3 cm, pH: 7, D: 3

LIVEBEARERS

Poecilia sphenops ♂   1/602
Pointed-mouth molly, short-finned molly
H: C and S America: Mexico to Colombia?
♂: Gonopodium; smaller.   S: =
B: Very prolific.   F: H
T: 18–28°C, L: ♀ 6 cm, pH: >7, D: 1–2

Poecilia sphenops l. ♀, r. ♂   1/602
Black molly

Poecilia sulphuraria ♂   4/534
Sulphur molly
H: C America: Mexico: Baños del Azufre.
♂: Gonopodium; smaller.   S: +
B: 28–35 dg; 10–25 young, 7 mm.   F: O
T: 24–28°C, L: ♀ 3.5 cm, pH: >7, D: 3

Poecilia vandepolli ♂   5/624
Variegated
H: Col., Ven., Aruba, Curaçao, Bonaire.
♂: Gonopodium; more colorful.   S: +
B: 28 dg; 30 young.   F: O
T: 26–29°C, L: ♀ 6 cm, pH: >7, D: 1–2

Poecilia vandepolli ♂   5/624
normal coloration

Poecilia velifera ♂   1/604
Mexican sailfin molly, green sailfin molly
H: C America: Mexico: Yucatán.
♂: Gonopodium; high dorsal fin.   S: +
B: Difficult.   F: H,O
T: 25–28°C, L: ♀ 18 cm, pH: >7, D: 2–3

Poecilia velifera ♂   1/604
Mexican sailfin molly, green sailfin molly
Albino

Poecilia vivipara l.♂, r.♀   2/744

H: S America: W Venezuela to Argentina.
♂: Gonopodium; smaller.   S: +
B: 28 dg; 100 young, 6 mm.   F: C,O
T: 26–28°C, L: ♀ 7 cm, pH: >7, D: 1

Poecilia cf. *vivipara* ♂   4/534

H: S America: Venezuela: coastal waters.
♂: Gonopodium; D fin more colorful. S: +
B: 35 dg; 5–10 young, 7 mm.   F: O
T: 23–27°C, L: ♀ 6 cm, pH: 7, D: 2

Poecilia cf. *vivipara* ♀   4/534

Poeciliopsis baenschi ♂   2/744
Baensch's mosquitofish
H: C America: Mexico.
♂: Gonopodium; smaller.   S: +
B: 28 dg; 8–25 young.   F: C,O
T: 18–24°C, L: ♀ 3 cm, pH: <7, D: 3

Poeciliopsis baenschi t.♀, b.♂   2/744
Baensch's mosquitofish

Poeciliopsis balsas ♂   4/536
Balsas mosquitofish

H: C America: Mexico: Rio Balsas Basin.
♂: Gonopodium; more colorful.   S: +
B: 5 y; rarely for several generations. F: O
T: 23–27°C, L: ♀ 6 cm, pH: >7, D: 3

Poeciliopsis balsas ♀   4/536
Balsas mosquitofish

Poeciliopsis catemaco ♀   3/620
Catemaco poeciliid

H: C Am.: Mexico: Lake Catemaco.   E
♂: Gonopodium; much smaller.   S: +
B: Rarely for several generations.   F: O
T: 24–28°C, L: ♀ 8 cm, pH: >7, D: 2

Poeciliopsis elongata ♂   4/538
Green poeciliid

H: C America: Costa Rica to S Panama.
♂: Gonopodium; smaller.   S: +
B: Only possible for 1st generation. F: O
T: 24–28°C, L: ♀ 8 cm, pH: >7, D: 3

Poeciliopsis fasciata ♀   3/620
Cross-striped poeciliid

H: C America: Mexico.
♂: Gonopodium; smaller.   S: +
B: 30 dg; 15–30 young, 8 mm.   F: O
T: 24–28°C, L: ♀ 5 cm, pH: >7, D: 3

Poeciliopsis gracilis t. ♂, b. ♀   2/746
Porthole livebearer (see also 4/538)

H: C America: S Mex., Gua., Honduras.
♂: Gonopodium; smaller.   S: +
B: 30 dg; 10–50 young, 7–8 mm.   F: O
T: 24–28°C, L: ♀ 6 cm, pH: 7, D: 1–2

LIVEBEARERS

Poeciliopsis hnilickai ♂ 　　　2/746
Chiapas mosquitofish
H: C America: Mexico: Chiapas.
♂: Gonopodium; smaller.　　　S: +
B: 28–35 days of gestation.　　F: O
T: 24–28°C, L: ♀5 cm, pH: 7, D: 2

Poeciliopsis infans ♂ 　　　4/540
Highland mosquitofish
H: C America: Mexico.
♂: Gonop.; black during courtship.　S: +
B: 28 dg; 10–25 young, 7 mm.　　F: O
T: 20–27°C, L: ♀5 cm, pH: 7, D: 1–2

Poeciliopsis infans ♀ 　　　4/540
Highland mosquitofish

Poeciliopsis latidens t.♂, b.♀ 　　2/749

H: C America: Mexico.
♂: Gonopodium; smaller.　　　S: –
B: Rare; 28 dg; 8–25 young.　　F: H,O
T: 23–26°C, L: ♀5 cm, pH: >7, D: 3

Poeciliopsis lutzi ♂ 　　　4/542
Lutz's poeciliid
H: C America: Mexico.
♂: Gonopodium; smaller.　　　S: +
B: 13 dg; 4–14 young, 7 mm.　　F: O
T: 24–28°C, L: ♀6 cm, pH: >7, D: 2

Poeciliopsis lutzi ♀ 　　　4/542
Lutz's poeciliid

Poeciliopsis occidentalis sonoriensis
Arizona poeciliid l. ♀, r. ♂　　　3/622
H: N America: USA: Arizona.
♂: Gonopodium; smaller.　　　　S: +
B: Unknown.　　　　　　　　　　F: C,O
T: 25–28°C, L: ♀ 5 cm, pH: 7, D: 3

Poeciliopsis paucimaculata ♂　　4/542
H: C America: Costa Rica.
♂: Gonopodium; smaller.　　　　S: +
B: Difficult; 4 young.　　　　　　F: O
T: 24–27°C, L: ♀ 7 cm, pH: 7, D: 3

Poeciliopsis paucimaculata ♀　　4/542

Poeciliopsis prolifica t.♂, b.♀　　3/622
H: C America: Mexico.
♂: Gonopodium; smaller.　　　　S: +
B: Not beyond the 4th generation.　F: H,O
T: 24–28°C, L: ♀ 3.5 cm, pH: >7, D: 2

Poeciliopsis retropinna ♂　　　3/624
H: C America: Costa Rica, W Panama.
♂: Gonopodium; smaller.　　　　S: +
B: 35 dg; 5–15 young, 7 mm.　　F: O
T: 25–28°C, L: ♀ 8 cm, pH: >7, D: 3

Poeciliopsis scarlli ♂　　　　3/624
Scarll's poeciliid
H: C America: Mexico.
♂: Gonopodium; smaller.　　　　S: +
B: Difficult; 28–42 dg; 10 young.　F: O,C
T: 23–30°C, L: ♀ 4 cm, pH: 7, D: 2–3

LIVEBEARERS

Poeciliopsis turneri ♀   4/544
Turner's poeciliid
H: C America: Mexico: Jalisco.
♂: Gonopodium; smaller.   S: +
B: 2–3y, 15mm; only 1st generation. F: O
T: 24–28°C, L: ♀6 cm, pH: >7, D: 3

Poeciliopsis turrubarensis ♂   3/626
Turrubarés poeciliid
H: C Am.: Mex., Costa Rica, Guatemala.
♂: Gonopodium; smaller.   S: +
B: Difficult; 30 dg; 10–60 y, 8 mm. F: H,O
T: 23–28°C, L: ♀8 cm, pH: >7, D: 3

Poeciliopsis turrubarensis ♀   3/626
Turrubarés poeciliid

Poeciliopsis viriosa ♂   2/750
Viriosa livebearer
H: C America: Mexico.
♂: Long gonopodium; smaller.   S: =
B: 10 dg; 6–15 young, 7 mm.   F: C,O
T: 24–26°C, L: ♀6 cm, pH: 7, D: 2–3

LIVEBEARERS

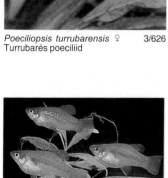

Priapella compressa t.♂, b.♀♀   2/750
Slab-sided blue-eye
H: C America: Mexico.
♂: Gonopodium; smaller.   S: +
B: Only when well-fed.   F: C
T: 24–28°C, L: ♀5 cm, pH: 7, D: 3

Priapella intermedia l.♂, r.♀   1/606
Blue-eyed livebearer
H: C America: Mexico.
♂: Gonopodium develops 5th month. S: +
B: 28–42 dg; 6–20 y, 10 mm.   F: C,O
T: 24–26°C, L: ♀7 cm, pH: >7, D: 3

Priapella olmecae ♂   4/546
Olmeca poeciliid
H: C America: Mexico.   Rare
♂: Gonopodium; smaller.   S: –
B: 35–42dg; 8–25young, 8mm.   F: O,C
T: 21–26°C, L: ♀6 cm, pH: 7, D: 3

Priapella olmecae ♀   4/546
Olmeca poeciliid

Priapichthys annectens ♂   5/624

H: C America: Costa Rica, Panama.
♂: Gonopodium; smaller; slimmer. S: –
B: Difficult; disease-prone.   F: C
T: 23–26°C, L: ♀7 cm, pH: 7, D: 2–3

Priapichthys austrocolumbiana ♂   4/548
Nariño poeciliid
H: S America: Colombia: Nariño.
♂: Gonopod.; smaller, more colorful. S: +
B: 12–15 dg; 2–6 young, 6 mm.   F: O
T: 23–27°C, L: ♀3.5 cm, pH: >7, D: 2

Priapichthys chocoensis ♂   3/628
Colombian diamond-scale
H: S America: Colombia.
♀: Yellow anal fin.   S: +
B: 14 dg; 3–15 young, 5–7 mm.   F: C
T: 23–28°C, L: ♀4.5 cm, pH: >7, D: 3

Priapichthys chocoensis ♀   3/628
Colombian diamond-scale

Priapichthys dariensis ♂   4/548
Darien poeciliid
H: C America: E Panama.
♂: Gonopod.; smaller; more colorful. **S:** +
B: To 1ˢᵗ generation.   **F:** O
T: 24–28°C, **L:** ♀ 4 cm, **pH:** >7, **D:** 3

Priapichthys festae ♂   2/752
Festa livebearer
H: S America: Ecuador.
♂: Gonopod.; smaller; more colorful. **S:** +
B: 28 dg; 3–7 young, 5 mm.   **F:** C
T: 21–30°C, **L:** ♀ 4.5 cm, **pH:** >7, **D:** 1–2

Pseudopoecilia nigroventralis ♂   3/630
Black-finned poeciliid
H: S America: Colombia.
♂: Gonopodium; smaller.   **S:** +
B: 14 dg; 3–15 young, 5–7 mm.   **F:** C
T: 23–28°C, **L:** ♀ 3 cm, **pH:** >7, **D:** 2–3

Pseudopoecilia nigroventralis ♀   3/630
Black-finned poeciliid

Quintana atrizona t. ♀, b. ♂   2/752
Black-barred livebearer
H: Caribbean: Cuba.   E
♂: Gonopodium; smaller.   **S:** +
B: 28–45 dg; <35 y; later difficult. **F:** O
T: 24–28°C, **L:** ♀ 4 cm, **pH:** <7, **D:** 4

Scolichthys greenwayi t. ♂, b. ♀   2/754
Big-spot mosquitofish
H: C America: Guatemala.
♂: Gonopod.; smaller; more colorful. **S:** +
B: 30 dg; 10–30 young.   **F:** O
T: 22–26°C, **L:** ♀ 5 cm, **pH:** >7, **D:** 2

LIVEBEARERS

549

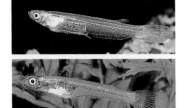

Tomeurus gracilis t.♂, b.♀   5/626

H: S Am.: E Ven., Guyana, Sur., Brazil.
♂: Gonopodium. ♀: Large anal fin.   S: (–)
B: Adh. e laid 3 d after fertilization.   F: C
T: 26–29°C, L: ♀ 4 cm, pH: >7, D: 3

Xenodexia ctenolepis ♂   4/550, 5/628

Note the right, handlike pectoral fin.

Xenodexia ctenolepis ♂   4/550, 5/628

H: C America: Guatemala.
♂: Gonopod.; right P fin handlike.   S:(–)
B: Only to 2nd gen.; 1–6 y, 15 mm.   F:C,O
T: 15–22°C, L: ♀ 4.5 cm, pH: 7, D: 2–3

Xenophallus umbratilis ♂   2/754
Shade livebearer

H: C America: Costa Rica.
♂: Gonopodium; larger dorsal fin.   S: +
B: 30 dg; 10–50 young, 8 mm.   F: C,O
T: 22–26°C, L: ♀ 6 cm, pH: 7, D: 2–3

Xiphophorus alvarezi t.♀, b.♂   2/756
Blue swordtail

H: C America: S Mexico.
♂: Gonopodium; sword.   S: +
B: 20–50 young.   F: O
T: 25–28°C, L: ♀ 8 cm, pH: >7, D: 2

Xiphophorus alvarezi t.♀, b.♂   4/550
Blue swordtail

H: C America: Mexico, Guatemala.
♂: Gonopodium; sword.   S: +
B: 28 dg; 10–20 young, 8 mm.   F: O
T: 23–27°C, L: ♀ 10 cm, pH: >7, D: 2

LIVEBEARERS

Xiphophorus andersi l. ♂, r. ♀   2/756
Atoyac platy

H: C America: Mexico: Rio Atoyac.   E
♂: Gonopodium; short sickle-sword. S: +
B: Difficult; 10–40 young.   F: H,O
T: 24–28°C, L: 4.5 cm, pH: >7, D: 3

Xiphophorus birchmanni ♂   3/633
Swordless swordtail

H: C America: Mexico.
♂: Gonopodium; large dorsal fin.   S: +
B: 28 dg; 15–25 young.   F: C,O
T: 24–28°C, L: ♀7 cm, pH: >7, D: 2–3

Xiphophorus birchmanni ♀   3/633
Swordless swordtail

Xiphophorus clemenciae ♂   2/758
Gilded swordtail

H: C Am.: Mexico: Coatzacoalcos Basin.
♂: Gonopodium; sword.   S: +
B: Very diffic.; 24–28 dg; 10–25 y. F:C,O
T: 22–26°C, L: ♀5 cm, pH: >7, D: 4

Xiphophorus continens ♂   4/552
El Quince swordtail

H: C America: Mexico.
♂: Gonopodium; 1 mm appendage. S: +
B: Difficult; 28 days gestation.   F: O
T: 22–26°C, L: ♀5 cm, pH: >7, D: 3

Xiphophorus cortezi ♂   2/758
Cortez swordtail (short sword)

H: C America: Mexico.
♂: Gonopodium; sword.   S: +
B: 28–35 dg; 10–30 young.   F: O
T: 24–28°C, L: ♀6 cm, pH: >7, D: 2

Xiphophorus cortezi ♂   2/758
Cortez swordtail
Long sword.

Xiphophorus couchianus t.♂, b.♀ 2/760
Monterrey platy
H: C America: Mexico: Rio Grande Basin.
♂: Gonopodium; same color as ♀. S: +
B: Very difficult.   F: C,O
T: 27–30°C, L: ♀6 cm, pH: >7, D: 4

Xiphophorus couchianus t.♂, b.♀ 2/761
Monterrey platy "Apodoca"

Xiphophorus evelynae ♂   2/762
Puebla platy
H: C America: Mexico.
♂: Gonopodium; more colorful.   S: +
B: Not difficult.   F: O
T: 22–27°C, L: ♀6 cm, pH: >7, D: 2

Xiphophorus gordoni ♂   2/762
Gordon's platy
H: C America: Mexico.   Endangered
♂: Gonopodium; more colorful.   S: –
B: 5–25 young, 6 mm.   F: O
T: 28–32°C, L: ♀4 cm, pH: >7, D: 4

Xiphophorus helleri   1/606
Swordtail (t. neon, b. red)
H: C America: between 12° and 26° N.
♂: Gonopodium; sword.   S: +
B: <80 young.   F: C,O
T: 18–28°C, L: ♀12 cm, pH: >7, D: 1

LIVEBEARERS

Xiphophorus helleri   1/606
Red Simpson swordtail

Xiphophorus helleri   1/606
Red lyretail swordtail

Xiphophorus helleri t.♂, b.♀   1/609
Spotted swordtail
H: C America: S Mexico to Guatemala.
♂: Gonopodium; sword.   **S:** +
B: <80 young.   **F:** C,O
T: 20–28°C, **L:** ♀ 10 cm, **pH:** >7, **D:** 1–2

Xiphophorus helleri ♂   2/765, 3/631
Catemaco swordtail, brass swordtail
H: C America: Mexico: Lake Catemaco.
♂: Gonopodium; sword.   **S:** +
B: 25–28 dg; 20–60 young, 8 mm.   **F:** O
T: 24–28°C, **L:** <12 cm, **pH:** >7, **D:** 3

Xiphophorus helleri r.♂, l.♀   2/768
Green swordtail
H: C America: Mexico, Belize, Honduras.
♂: Gonopodium; sword.   **S:** –
B: Easy to difficult; 20–100 young.   **F:** O
T: 22–28°C, **L:** ♀ <14 cm, **pH:** >7, **D:** 1–4

Xiphophorus helleri ♂ red albino   5/632
Wild and bred forms
H: C Am.: Central Mexico to Honduras.
♂: Gonopodium; sword.   **S:** +
B: Easy to difficult; 20–100 young.   **F:** O
T: 22–27°C, **L:** ♀ <8 cm, **pH:** 7, **D:** 1–2

LIVEBEARERS

553

Xiphophorus helleri ♂   5/632
Red-stripe swordtail
H: C America: S Mexico: Veracruz: Jala-
pa.

Xiphophorus helleri ♀   5/632

H: C America: S Mexico: Veracruz: Jala-
pa.

Xiphophorus helleri ♂   5/632
Golden swordtail

Xiphophorus helleri ♂   5/632
Black albino swordtail

Xiphophorus helleri ♂   5/632
Blue-black albino

Xiphophorus helleri ♂   5/632
Black swordtail

LIVEBEARERS

Xiphophorus helleri ♂   2/764
Belize swordtail (1)
H: C America: Belize: Rio Belize.
♂: Gonopodium; sword.   S: +
B: Relatively unproblematic.   F: O
T: 24–28°C, L: <5 cm, pH: >7, D: 3

Xiphophorus helleri ♂   2/764
Atoyac swordtail (2, 3, 4)
H: C America: Mexico: Rio Atoyac.
♂: Gonopodium; sword.   S: +
B: Not problematic.   F: O
T: 24–28°C, L: ♀8–10 cm, pH: >7, SG:1–2

Xiphophorus helleri ♂　　　　2/764
Five-striped swordtail (1)
H: C America: Mexico: Rio Sontecomapan.
♂: Gonopodium; sword.　　　　S: +
B: Not difficult.　　　　　　　F: O
T: 24–28°C, L: ♀ 12 cm, pH: >7, D: 2

Xiphophorus helleri ♂　　　　2/765
Yucatan swordtail (2)
H: C America: Mexico: Yucatan, Campeche.
♂: Gonopodium; sword.　　　　S: +
B: Occasionally difficult.　　　F: O
T: 24–28°C, L: ♀ 9 cm, pH: >7, D: 4

Xiphophorus helleri ♂　　　　2/765
Oaxaca swordtail (3)
H: C America: Mexico: Rio del Reyon.
♂: Gonopodium; sword.　　　　S: +
B: Unproblematic.　　　　　　F: O
T: 24–28°C, L: 5–7 cm, pH: >7, D: 1–2

Xiphophorus helleri t. ♀, b. ♂　2/765
Catemaco swordtail, brass swordtail (4)
H: C Am.: Mexico: Lake Catemaco.　　E
♂: Gonopodium; sword.　　　　S: =
B: Difficult; 15 months to mature.　F: O
T: 24–28°C, L: 8–10 cm, pH: >7, D: 3

Biotope of several *Xiphophorus* species: Lake Catemaco, Mexico.

Xiphophorus maculatus t.♂, b.♀   1/610
Coral platy, red platy
H: C Am.: Mexico, Guatemala, N Honduras.
♂: Gonop.; more colorful (wild form). S:+
B: Mature at 3–4 months.   F: O
T: 18–25°C, L: ♀ <6 cm, pH: >7, D: 1

Xiphophorus maculatus ♂   1/610
Blue mirror platy

557

Xiphophorus maculatus 2 ♂♂   1/610
Wagtail platy

Xiphophorus maculatus   1/610
Golden moon platy

Xiphophorus maculatus   1/610
Simpson tuxedo platy

Xiphophorus maculatus   1/610
Simpson coral platy

Xiphophorus maculatus l. ♀, r. ♂   2/770
Gray platy
H: C America: Mexico: Rio San Juan.
♂: Gonopod.; distinct black spots.   S: +
B: Mature after 3–4 months.   F: O
T: 24–28°C, L: ♀ <6 cm, pH: >7, D: 1

Xiphophorus maculatus t. ♀, b. ♂   2/770
Jamapa platy, variegated platy
H: C America: Mexico: Veracruz.
♂: Gonopodium.   S: +
B: Like nominate form.   F: O
T: 24–28°C, L: ♀ <6 cm, pH: >7, D: 2

Xiphophorus maculatus t.♂, b.♀   2/772
Black platy
H: C America: Mexico: Veracruz.
♂: Gonopodium: smaller.   S: +
B: Prone to fungal infections.   F: O
T: 24–30°C, L: ♀ 5 cm, pH: >7, D: 3

Xiphophorus maculatus l.♀, r.♂   2/772
Belize platy
H: C America: Belize: Rio Belize.
♂: Gonopodium; smaller.   S: +
B: Easy.   F: O
T: 24–30°C, L: ♀ 6 cm, pH: >7, D: 1

Xiphophorus maculatus ♂   2/772
Red-eyed platy (photo p. 4/556)
H: C America: Belize: Rio Belize estuary.
♂: Gonopodium.   S: +
B: Soft, nitrate-free water.   F: H,O
T: 24–30°C, L: ♀ 4 cm, pH: 7, D: 4

Xiphophorus maculatus ♂   4/554
Platy (Rio Jamapa, Mexico)
H: C America: Mex., Gua., Belize, Hon.
♂: Gonopodium.   S: +
B: 24 dg; 10–80 young, 7 mm.   F: O
T: 24–28°C, L: ♀ 5 cm, pH: 7, D: 1

Xiphophorus maculatus ♀   4/554
Platy
H: C America: Mexico: Rio Jamapa.

Xiphophorus maculatus ♂   4/554
Platy
H: C America: Mexico: Rio Papaloapán.

Xiphophorus maculatus ♂ WC　　4/554
Platy
H: C America: Belize.

Xiphophorus malinche ♂　　　　5/634

H: C America: Mexico: Hidalgo.
♂: Gonopodium; short sword.　　S: =
B: <15 young.　　　　　　　　　　F: C,O
T: 15–21°C, L: ♀6 cm, pH: 7, D: 2–3

Xiphophorus meyeri b.♀, t.♂　　4/557
Muzquiz platy
H: C America: Mexico: Coahuila.
♂: Gonopodium; smaller.　　　　S: +
B: 24 dg; 10–35 young, 7 mm.　　F: O
T: 23–28°C, L: ♀4 cm, pH: >7, D: 2

Xiphophorus milleri l.♀, r.♂　　2/774
Catemaco platy
H: C Am.: Mexico: Lake Catemaco.　　E
♂: Gonopodium; smaller.　　　　S: +
B: Very difficult; 3–10 young.　　F: O
T: 24–28°C, L: ♀4.5 cm, pH: >7, D: 4

Xiphophorus montezumae ♂　　1/612
Montezuma swordtail, Mexican swordtail
H: C America: E central Mexico.
♂: Gonopodium; sword.　　　　　S: +
B: Hybridizes with *X. helleri*.　　F: O
T: 20–26°C, L: ♀6.5 cm, pH: >7, D: 2

Xiphophorus montezumae ♂　　2/774
Tail-spot Montezuma swordtail
H: C America: Mexico: Rio Panuco.
♂: Gonopodium; sword.　　　　　S: +
B: 28–35 dg; 15–30 young, 8 mm.　F: O
T: 22–26°C, L: ♀7 cm, pH: >7, D: 3

Xiphophorus multilineatus ♀   4/558
Striped swordtail
H: C America: Mexico.
♂: Gonopod.; sword; crossbands. S: =
B: Not simple; 28 dg; <15 young.   F: O
T: 22–26°C, L: ♀6 cm, pH: 7, D: 3

Xiphophorus multilineatus ♂   4/558
Striped swordtail
Long sword, blue.

Xiphophorus multilineatus ♂   4/558
Striped swordtail
Short sword, yellow.

Xiphophorus nezahualcoyotl t.♂, b.♀
Neza swordtail   3/634
H: C America: Mexico.
♂: Gonopodium; sword.   S: +
B: 28 dg; 15–35 young.   F: O
T: 24–28°C, L: 6 cm, pH: 7, D: 2–3

Xiphophorus nezahualcoyotl ♂   4/560
Neza swordtail
H: C America: Mexico.
♂: Gonopodium; sword.   S: +
B: 28 dg; 10–40 young, 7 mm.   F: O
T: 21–26°C, L: ♀7 cm, pH: >7, D: 2

Xiphophorus nezahualcoyotl ♀   4/560
Neza swordtail

LIVEBEARERS

Xiphophorus nigrensis t.♀, b.♂　　2/776
Black swordtail
H: C America: Mexico.
♂: Gonopodium; sword; bluish.　　S: +
B: 28 dg; 15 young.　　　　　　F: C,O
T: 24–25°C, L: ♀5.5 cm, pH: >7, D: 3

Xiphophorus nigrensis ♂　　2/776
Black swordtail

Xiphophorus nigrensis ♀　　2/776
Black swordtail

Xiphophorus pygmaeus　　1/612
Pigmy swordtail, dwarf swordtail
H: C America: Mexico.
♂: Gonopodium; slimmer.　　S: +
B: Spawning box; not prolific.　F: C,O
T: 24–28°C, L: 4 cm, pH: >7, D: 2

Xiphophorus pygmaeus　　2/778
Pigmy swordtail (top: yellow variety ♂)
H: C America: Mexico.
♂: Gonopodium; slimmer.　　S: +
B: Dense vegetation.　　　　F: C
T: 24–26°C, L: 4 cm, pH: >7, D: 3–4

Xiphophorus pygmaeus l.♀, r.♂　　2/778
Pigmy swordtail
Normal color.

LIVEBEARERS

Xiphophorus signum t. ♀, b. ♂　　2/780
Comma swordtail
H: C America: Guatemala.
♂: Gonopodium; slimmer.　　　　　　S: =
B: Difficult; 28–35 dg; 20–40 y.　　F: C,O
T: 24–28°C, L: 8 cm, pH: >7, D: 4

Xiphophorus variatus t. ♂, b. ♀　　2/782
Platy variatus
H: C America: Mexico: Rio Nautla.
♂: Gonopod. ♀: Pregnancy spot.　S: +
B: Spawning box.　　　　　　　　　　F: O
T: 22–28°C, L: ♀ <7 cm, pH: >7, D: 1–2

Xiphophorus variatus t. ♂, b. ♀　　2/782
Platy variatus
Rio Axtla

Xiphophorus variatus ♂　　2/782
Platy variatus
Rio Axtla

Xiphophorus variatus　　1/614
Variegated platy, variatus platy
H: C America: S Mexico.
♂: Gonopod. ♀: Pregnancy spot.　S: +
B: Spawning box.　　　　　　　　　　F: H,O
T: 15–25°C, L: ♀ 7 cm, pH: >7, D: 1

Xiphophorus variatus ♂　　4/562
Hawaii highfin variatus
H: Bred linage.
♂: Gonopodium; tall dorsal fin.　S: +
B: <10 young.　　　　　　　　　　　F: O
T: 21–28°C, L: 6 cm, pH: 7, D: 2

LIVEBEARERS

Xiphophorus variatus ♂   4/562
Hawaii brush-tail highfin platy

Xiphophorus variatus ♂   4/560
Marigold brush-tail platy
See text on p. 4/562.

Xiphophorus variatus × *couchianus*
Yellow hybrid platy   2/780
H: C America: Mexico: Nuevo León.
♂: Gonopodium.   S: +
B: Not difficult; 20–40 young.   F: C,O
T: 24–30°C, L: ♀5 cm, pH: >7, D: 1

Xiphophorus xiphidium   1/615
Swordtail platy (Rio Purificación)
H: C America: Mexico.
♂: Gonopodium; short sword.   S: +
B: 24 young; not very prolific.   F: C,O
T: 18–25°C, L: ♀5 cm, pH: >7, D: 2–3

Xiphophorus xiphidium t. ♀, b. ♂   2/785
Sword platy (Rio Purificación)
H: C America: Mexico.
♂: Gonopodium; short sword.
B: Soft water: <10° hardness.   F: C
T: 22–26°C, L: ♀5 cm, pH: >7, D: 3

Xiphophorus xiphidium × *variatus* 2/784
A natural hybrid from Rio Soto la Marina.
It has been described as *Xiphophorus kosszanderi*.

Betta coccina spawning (see p. 578).

Origin/Taxonomy

From a developmental point of view, the labyrinth fishes are relatively young. Their age is estimated at 50–60 million years; i.e., they originate during the Tertiary Era.

Technically the Anabantoidei are part of the order Perciformes (see Group 9), but since aquarists recognize them as a distinct "type of fish," we have placed them into their own group. According to NELSON (1994), the suborder Anabantoidei contains 5 families with 81 species classified into 18 genera. Controversy surrounds the classification of the families Luciocephalidae (1 species) and Channidae (approximately 21 species). The group has been divided as follows:

All fishes of Group 7 possess an accessory breathing organ in their branchial cavity called a labyrinth. While snakeheads (Channidae) also have such a suprabranchial organ, they have been classified into their own suborder, the Channoidei, instead of into Anabantoidei. They are thought to have less in common with the labyrinth fishes than the pikeheads (Luciocephalidae), even though both deviate markedly in appearance and demeanor from "standard labyrinth fishes."

Geographic Distribution

With the exception of the easternmost section and the great deserts, labyrinth fishes colonize Africa as well as Southeast Asia. The familiar, small, colorful community fishes of this group are found in Asia.

The labyrinth is an adaptation to the oxygen-poor waters the Anabantoidei and Channoidei typically inhabit, allowing the fishes to breathe atmospheric air. For the most part, water chemistry is of secondary importance, although the few species within this group that live in flowing waters are customarily more exacting in this regard. Rice fields, roadside ditches, turbid water remnants, and weed-choked canals are all biotopes in which many of these species commonly occur. Some can even displace themselves for long distances

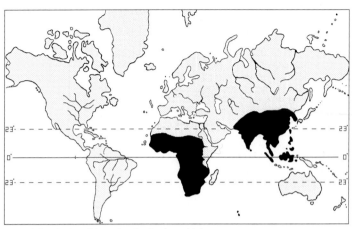

Area of distribution of the suborder Anabantoidei.

over land to reach the next water hole. It is even said that *Anabas testudinus* is capable of climbing onto trees, hence the common name "climbing perch."

Generalities

The suborder Anabantoidei predominantly contains small, colorful fishes ideal for the aquarium, but the giant gourami, an appreciated food fish which grows to 70 cm in length, is found within this suborder as well.

Since all are air-breathers, it is important—especially for fry and juveniles—that the air above the water is humid and just as warm as the water. The labyrinth is so developed in most species that breathing air is obligatory and not facultative; that is, almost all of the fishes within this suborder would drown if they were prevented from reaching the water surface, regardless of the oxygen concentration of the water.

Bubble nests are often an intrinsic part of the reproductive strategy of Asian species. They vary from small to large, stable to fragile, and free-floating to anchored among plants. The sinking or floating eggs are spit into the bubble nest and the male attends to all custodial duties. Aside from bubble nest builders, there are also mouthbrooders and cave spawners (with a bubble nest inside). Whatever the reproductive strategy, it is the male that cares for the spawn.

Some African species (i.e., those in the newly established genus *Microctenopoma*) build bubble nests and practice brood care, while others scatter their numerous floating eggs.

Most species are intolerant of saline water.

LABYRINTH F.

567

Family Anabantidae

The family of climbing gouramis contains 30 species within 4 genera, including *Microctenopoma,* a newly established genus for species that build bubble nests. Anabantids are found in freshwaters and brackish waters of Africa and Asia (from India to the Philippines). A few species are capable of surviving the dry season in muddy substrates, but they die if the water hole falls completely dry. Thanks to the spiny opercula and fins, they move with surprising speed over dry land. This ability is utilized to travel from one water hole to the next and, reputedly, to scale trees.

Despite the colorful attributes of some of the species, anabantids are the least popular members of the suborder. Most are predacious and quick to seek cover, and large species are typically aggressive bullies. Some of the smaller members of the family—especially those of the genus *Microctenopoma*—are behaviorally similar to their Asian gourami cousins.

There is sexual dimorphism. Mature males have more intense coloration, more elongated fins, and spiny patches (see below). The spiny patches are not always visible under casual observation, but when males are captured with a net, they have a greater tendency to become entangled.

Ctenopoma multispinis ♂. Note the spiny patches behind the eye and on the operculum.

LABYRINTH F.

Anabas oligolepis   3/637

H: Asia: NE India, Bangladesh.
♂: Longer anal fin.   S: =
B: Unsuccessful.   F: O
T: 22–28°C, L: <18 cm, pH: 7, D: 1

Anabas testudineus   1/619
Climbing perch
H: India, S China, Indonesia, Malay Pen.
♂: Elongated anal fin.   S: –
B: Floating eggs.   F: O
T: 22–30°C, L: 10–23 cm, pH: 7, D: 1

Ctenopoma acutirostre   1/619
Leopard ctenopoma, spotted climbing perch
H: Africa: Zaïre.
♂: Spiny patches on the body.   S: =
B: Difficult; no brood care.   F: C
T: 20–25°C, L: 12–18 cm, pH: 7, D: 3

Ctenopoma kingsleyae   1/622
Kingsley's ctenopoma
H: W Africa: Zaïre to Gambia.
♂: Pronounced spiny patches.   S: =
B: <20 000 floating eggs.   F: C,O
T: 25–28°C, L: 19 cm, pH: 7, D: 3

Ctenopoma maculatum   1/622
Single-spot ctenopoma
H: Africa: S Cameroon, upper Zaïre.
♂: Spiny patches.   S: =
B: No brood care.   F: C,O
T: 22–28°C, L: 20 cm, pH: 7, D: 3

Ctenopoma multispinis   2/790
Many-spined ctenopoma
H: Africa: SE Congo region.
♂: Spiny patches.   S: =
B: Floating eggs.   F: C,O
T: 24–27°C, L: 16 cm, pH: 7, D: 2–3

LABYRINTH F.

Ctenopoma multispinis ♂　　　3/638
Many-spined ctenopoma

Ctenopoma muriei　　　　　　　1/623
Nile ctenopoma
H: Af.: Nile, lakes Albert & Edward; Chad B.
♂: Spiny scales.　　　　　　　　　S: =
B: Egg scatterer, no brood care.　F: C,O
T: 23–28°C, L: 8.5 cm, pH: 7, D: 2

Ctenopoma nebulosum　　　　　5/636

H: W Africa: Niger and other rivers.
♂: Smaller and slimmer.　　　　　S: =
B: Egg scatterer; no brood care.　F: C
T: 24°C, L: 20 cm, pH: 7, D: 3

Ctenopoma nigropannosum　　2/790
Two-spotted ctenopoma
H: Central Africa.
♂: Spiny patches.　　　　　　　　S: –
B: Unsuccessful.　　　　　　　　　F: C,O
T: 24–27°C, L: 17 cm, pH: 7, D: 4

Ctenopoma ocellatum　　　　　1/624
Bullseye ctenopoma
H: Africa: Zaïre.
♂: Spiny patches.　　　　　　　　S: =
B: Preys on spawn.　　　　　　　　F: C
T: 24–28°C, L: 15 cm, pH: 7, D: 2

Ctenopoma maculatum　　　　　1/624
Mottled ctenopoma
H: Africa: Zaïre.
♂: More intense coloration.　　　S: =
B: Egg scatterer.　　　　　　　　　F: C
T: 24–28°C, L: 10 cm, pH: 7, D: 2–3

LABYRINTH F.

Ctenopoma pellegrini   3/640
Pellegrin's ctenopoma
H: Tropical Africa.
♂: Spiny patches.   S: =
B: Egg scatterer.   F: C,O
T: 22–27°C, L: 15 cm, pH: 7, D: 3

Ctenopoma petherici   3/640
Blunt-headed ctenopoma
H: Central Africa.
♂: Spiny patches.   S: =
B: Unsuccessful; egg scatterer.   F: C
T: 22–26°C, L: 16 cm, pH: <7, D: 3

Microctenopoma ansorgii   1/620
Ornate ctenopoma
H: Africa: Zaïre.
♂: Slightly more colorful.   S: =
B: Bubble nest; ♂ tends spawn.   F: C
T: 26–28°C, L: 8 cm, pH: 7, D: 2–3

Microctenopoma argentoventer   1/620
Dusky ctenopoma
H: W Africa: Niger.
♂: 2 yellowish bands.   S: =
B: Bubble nest; ♂ tends spawn.   F: C
T: 22–27°C, L: <15 cm, pH: <7, D: 3

Microctenopoma congicum   2/788
Congo ctenopoma
H: Africa: lower Zaïre.
♂: Pointed and elongated fins.   S: =
B: Bubble nest; ♂ tends spawn. F: C,O
T: 23–27°C, L: 8.5 cm, pH: 7, D: 2

Microctenopoma congicum   5/638
Congo ctenopoma
H: W Africa: Congo: Stanley Pool.
♂: Larger fins; more colorful.   S: =
B: Bubble nest; ♂ tends spawn.   F: C
T: 22°C, L: 8 cm, pH: <7, D: 2–3

Microctenopoma damasi   2/788
Pearlscale ctenopoma
H: Africa: E Uganda.
♂: Elongated ventral fins; larger.   S: (–)
B: Bubble nest; ♂ tends spawn.   F: C
T: 26–30°C, L: 7 cm, pH: 7, D: 3

Microctenopoma fasciolatum ♂ juv.   1/621
Banded ctenopoma
H: Africa: Zaïre.
♂: Elongated dorsal and anal fins. S: =
B: Unknown.   F: O
T: 24–28°C, L: 8 cm, pH: <7, D: 2

Microctenopoma intermedium   5/638

H: W Africa.
♂: Larger fins; more colorful.   S: =
B: Bubble nest; ♂ tends spawn.   F: C
T: 24°C, L: 8 cm, pH: <7, D: 2

Microctenopoma nanum   1/623
Dwarf climbing perch
H: Africa: Cameroon to Zaïre.
♂: Longer A & D fins; more colorful. S: =
B: Bubble nest; ♂ tends the spawn. F: C
T: 18–24°C, L: 7.5 cm, pH: 7, D: 2–3

Sandelia bainsii   2/792
Bain's perch
H: South Africa.   Protected
SD: Unknown.   S: –
B: Nature: egg scatterer.   F: C
T: 18–22°C, L: 25 cm, pH: 7, D: 2–3

Sandelia capensis   2/792
Cape perch
H: South Africa.
SD: Unknown.   S: –
B: Egg scatterer; ♂ guards.   F: C,O
T: 18–22°C, L: <22 cm, pH: 7, D: 2–3

LABYRINTH F.

Family Belontiidae

The family of gouramis consists of 12 genera and about 46 species. They inhabit freshwater from India to the Malay Peninsula and Korea.

Three subfamilies are recognized: Belontiinae (combtail gouramis), Macropodinae (fighting fishes and paradise fishes), and Trichogastrinae (gouramis).

Subfamily Belontiinae

This subfamily only contains one genus and the two species, which are presented on page 575. The markings on the unpaired fins of *Belontia hasselti* distinguish it from its congener, *B. signata*. In their natural habitat, the two cannot be confused, since their areas of distribution do not overlap.

Juveniles are peaceful, but adults can only be associated with fishes capable of defending themselves. The air above the water surface must be warm and humid.

The breeding tank should not be less than 100 cm in length, a considerable size for gouramis. According to LINKE (1990), *B. signata* has a nuclear family, a very unusual trait among labyrinth fishes.

Subfamily Macropodinae

The subfamily of fighting fishes and paradise fishes contains 7 genera and approximately 32 species (NELSON, 1994). At least 30 species belong to the genus *Betta* alone. The paradise fish (*Macropodus opercularis*, p. 586) was the first tropical aquarium fish imported into Germany (1876).

LABYRINTH F.

Betta splendens (see p. 584). Two adult males together spells trouble. Immediately following the photograph, the fish were separated!

Betta splendens, commonly known as the Siamese fighting fish, is the most familiar representative of the Anabantoidei. It is part of the Macropodinae. Various strains of *B. splendens* have been developed, manifest in the wide array of color combinations and finnages. Double-tail bettas with their many-rayed dorsal fin and split caudal fin are particularly attractive. When breeding bettas, it is important to strive for full but symmetrical fins with appropriate conformation, i.e., elongated teardrop for the dorsal fin, square for the anal fin, and round for the caudal fin. Metallic green, steel blue, black, yellow, and red as well as solid colors, bicolors, and multicolors are all available to those who wish to try their hand at this satisfying field.

Within the Macropodinae there are mouthbrooders as well as those that build bubble nests. Brood care is always performed by the male. Since males are often brutal towards females unwilling to spawn, the breeding aquarium should contain shelters, permitting the female to escape and hide from the male. Remove the female from the breeding aquarium immediately following the conclusion of oviposition. Some species depend on extremely acid and soft water to reproduce.

- Bubble nesting members of this subfamily, depending on species, built a loose or dense nest openly on the water surface or anchored among plants (e.g., *Betta* and *Trichopsis*). Others build it underwater in caves or underneath broad plant leaves (e.g., *Parosphromenus*). Some species are very prolific, laying up to 500 eggs. Because those that construct their nests underwater are generally smaller species, they are less fecund (approximately 50 eggs).
- Mouthbrooders are found in the genus *Betta*. After the eggs are fertilized, the female spits them towards the male. He, in turn, takes the approximately 20 eggs into his mouth and incubates them for a period of 10 to 14 days. *B. macrophthalma* is somewhat of an exception—it lays up to 70 eggs which are buccally incubated for 28 days.

Bettas are famous for their intraspecific male aggressiveness. In Thailand, the predisposition of *B. splendens* and *B. smaragdina* males to engage in combat is exploited (LINKE, 1990). Much like the cock fight of Mexico, betta fights are public spectacles which commonly culminate in the death of the exhausted loser. Hostilities are rarely, if ever, directed towards heterospecifics. A male alone or a pair is a suitable addition for well-appointed community aquaria.

In comparison to its congeners, *B. imbellis* is uncommonly peaceful. As long as a wary eye is kept during periods of sexual activity, even several pairs can be kept in a spacious aquarium.

Subfamily Trichogastrinae
The subfamily of the gouramis consists of 4 genera and about 12 species. All are peaceful community aquarium fishes which are known and appreciated for their undemanding care.

Colisa: These small fishes are noted for their beautiful colors, especially the males. Several color strains have been developed.

Trichogaster: The threadlike ventral fins detect chemical stimuli, much like the barbels of the Siluriformes. Ensure that tankmates do not pull on the filaments (e.g., *Barbus* spp.). *Trichogaster* spp. construct bubble nests. Some are extremely prolific, producing from 600 to 1000 eggs; other species lay a scant 50 eggs. In Asia, larger species are also appreciated as food fishes.

Sphaerichthys: The chocolate gouramis are mouthbrooders. They are the delicate members of the Trichogasterinae and are therefore not recommended for novice aquarists.

Belontia hasselti   1/626
Java combtail
H: Java, Sum., Borneo, Sing., Malacca.
♂: Stouter fins. ♀: Paler.   S: +,–
B: Loose bubble nest; <700 e.   F: C,O
T: 25–30°C, L: 19 cm, pH: 7, D: 3

Belontia signata   1/626
Combtail, comb-tailed paradise fish
H: Sri Lanka.
♂: Slightly longer dorsal fin.   S: +,=
B: Under plant leaves.   F: O
T: 24–28°C, L: 13 cm, pH: 7, D: 2

Betta akarensis   5/640
Sarawak betta
H: SE Asia: W and N Borneo.
♂: Longer fins; more colorful.   S: =
B: ♂ mouthbroods 13–15 days.   F: C
T: 22–25°C, L: 14 cm, pH: <7, D: 2–3

Betta akarensis juv.   5/640
Sarawak betta

Betta anabatoides   2/794
Pearly betta
H: SE Borneo.
♂: Longer fins; more colorful.   S: =
B: ♂ mouthbroods 10 days.   F: C,O
T: 27–30°C, L: 12 cm, pH: ≪7, D: 3

LABYRINTH F.

Betta balunga ♂　　　　5/642
Balung betta
H: SE Asia: N Borneo: Balung River.
♂: Larger fins; more colorful.　　S: =
B: ♂ mouthbroods 12–14 days.　　F: C
T: 21–27°C, L: 14 cm, pH: <7, D: 2–3

Betta balunga ♀　　　　5/642
Balung betta

Betta bellica ♂　　　1/628, 3/642
Slender betta, striped fighting betta
H: SE Asia: Thailand, Malaysia, Sumatra.
♂: Longer fins; more colorful.　　S: =
B: Bubble nest.　　F: C
T: 24–30°C, L: ♂ 13 cm, pH: <7, D: 2

Betta bellica ♂　　　1/628, 3/642
Slender betta, striped fighting betta

Betta bellica ♀　　　1/628, 3/642
Slender betta, striped fighting betta

Betta brederi　　　　3/644
Breder's betta
H: SE Asia: W and N Borneo.
♂: Larger fins.　　S: =
B: ♂ mouthbroods 12–14 d; 7 mm.　　F: C
T: 23–28°C, L: 11 cm, pH: <7, D: 2–3

Betta brownorum   4/566

H: SE Asia: Sarawak, Borneo.
♂: Spot on side more pronounced. S: =
B: Bubble nest.   F: C
T: 22–26°C, L: 5 cm, pH: <7, D: 3

Betta burdigala ♂   5/644
Burgundy fighting fish
H: SE Asia: NW Borneo, Sumatra.
♂: Larger fins; more colorful.   S: +
B: Bubble nest, ♂ tends spawn. F: C,O
T: 24°C, L: 5 cm, pH: ≪7, D: 2–3

Betta akarensis   3/644
Ladder-finned betta
H: SE Asia: W and N Borneo.
♂: Larger; larger fins.   S: =
B: ♂ Mb; rearing unsuccessful.   F: C
T: 21–27°C, L: 14 cm, pH: <7, D: 3

Betta akarensis "Matang"   3/644
Ladder-finned betta

Betta akarensis "pointed head" 3/644
Ladder-finned betta

Betta akarensis "pointed head" 3/644
Ladder-finned betta

LABYRINTH F.

Betta coccina ♂ 1/628, 3/646, (5/645)
Wine-red betta
H: SE Asia.
♂: Larger fins; pointed caudal fin. **S:** =
B: Small bubble nest. **F:** C
T: 22–28°C, L: 6 cm, **pH:** ≪7, D: 3

Betta coccina ♂ 1/628, 3/646, (5/645)
Wine-red betta

Betta coccina ♀ 1/628, 3/646, (5/645)
Wine-red betta

Betta coccina   1/628, 3/646, (5/645)
Wine-red betta

LABYRINTH F.

Betta edithae   2/794
Edith's betta
H: SE Asia: S Borneo.
♂: Iridescent dots; slightly larger. **S:** =
B: ♂ mouthbroods for 10 days. **F:** C,O
T: 24–28°C, L: 7.5 cm, **pH:** 7, D: 3

Betta enisae ♂   5/648
Long-finned betta
H: SE Asia: NW Borneo.
SD: Unknown; larger fins? **S:** +
B: Paternal mouthbrooder. **F:** C
T: 24°C, L: 11 cm, **pH:** <7, D: 3

Betta enisae juv.   5/648
Long-finned betta

Betta foerschi ♂   2/796
Foersch's betta
H: SE Asia: S Borneo.
♂: D and A fins broader & pointed.   S: =
B: ♂ mouthbroods for 10 days.   F: C
T: 24–26°C, L: 6.5 cm, pH: <7, D: 3–4

Betta foerschi "Nataisedawak" ♂   4/570

Betta foerschi "Tarantag" ♀   4/570

H: SW central Kalimantan.
♂: More colorful. ♀: Crossbands.   S: =
B: ♂ mouthbroods for 6–12 days.   F: C
T: 22–26°C, L: 6 cm, pH: ≪7, D: 3

H: SW central Kalimantan.
♂: More colorful?   S: =
B: ♂ mouthbrooder?   F: C
T: 22–26°C, L: 6 cm, pH: ≪7, D: 4

Betta fusca ♂   3/648
Dark betta
H: SE Asia: Sumatra, S Malay Peninsula.
♂: Larger fins.   S: =
B: Mouthbrooder.   F: C
T: 22–26°C, L: 8 cm, pH: <7, D: 3

Betta fusca   3/648
Dark betta
H: Sumatra

Betta fusca ♀   3/648
Dark betta
Sumatra

Betta fusca ♂   3/648
Dark betta
See photo on p. 5/646.

Betta imbellis ♀, Penang   3/650
Peaceful betta
H: SE Asia: Penang Island.
♂: Larger fins; more colorful.   S: =
B: Bubble nest.   F: C
T: 22–26°C, L: 5 cm, pH: <7, D: 2

Betta imbellis ♂, Phuket   3/650
Peaceful betta
H: SE Asia: Phuket Island.
♂: Larger fins; more colorful.   S: =
B: Bubble nest.   F: C
T: 25–30°C, L: 5 cm, pH: <7, D: 3

Betta macrophthalma   3/653
Giant betta
H: SE Asia.
♂: Larger fins; not easily distinguish. S: +
B: ♂ mouthbrooder, 28 d, 70 eggs. F: C
T: 20–26°C, L: 14 cm, pH: 7, D: 2–3

Betta macrophthalma   3/653
Giant betta
See photo on p. 5/647.

Betta macrophthalma   3/653
Giant betta
See photo on p. 5/647.

Betta macrostoma ♂   2/796
Brunei beauty
H: SW Borneo.
♀: Plain.   S: (–)
B: Paternal mouthbrooder.   F: C,O
T: 24–26°C, L: 11 cm, pH: 7, D: 3–4

Betta patoti w/ ventral fins, ♂   3/654
Black betta
H: SE Asia.
♂: More intense colors.   S: =
B: Mouthbrooder?   F: C
T: 23–28°C, L: 9 cm, pH: <7, D: 2

Betta patoti w/o ventral fins   3/654
Black betta

Betta persephone ♂   3/656
Dwarf betta
H: SE Asia: S Malaysia.
♂: Slightly larger fins.   S: –
B: Bubble nest.   F: C,O
T: 23–28°C, L: 3.2 cm, pH: <7, D: 3

Betta persephone ♂   3/656
Dwarf betta
Breeding coloration.

Betta persephone ♂ 3/656
Dwarf betta
Normal coloration.

Betta persephone 3/656
Dwarf betta
H: Riau Archipelago.
See photo on p. 5/645.

Betta picta 2/798
Painted betta
H: Indonesia.
♂: Broader anal fin fringe. S: +
B: ♂ mouthbroods for 10–14 d. F: C,O
T: 22–24°C, L: 5.5 cm, pH: 7, D: 1

Betta prima 5/651
H: SE Asia: Thailand/Vietnam?
♂: Larger fins; more colorful. S: +
B: ♂ mouthbroods for 10–16 d. F: C,O
T: 24°C, L: 6 cm, pH: 7, D: 2

Betta pugnax 1/630
H: SE Asia: Malaysia.
♂: Larger fins; more colorful. S: =
B: Bubble nest. F: C,O
T: 22–28°C, L: 12 cm, pH: 7, D: 3

Betta pugnax 1/630
See photo on p. 5/648.

LABYRINTH F.

Betta rubra ♂♂   1/630
Peaceful betta
H: Asia: S Malaysia: Kuala Lumpur.
♂: Larger fins; more colorful.   S: +
B: Bubble nest.   F: C,O
T: 24–28°C , L: 5.5 cm, pH: 7, D: 2

Betta rutilans   4/566

H: Asia:W Kalimantan, Borneo: Anjungan.
♀: Fuller during spawning season. S: =
B: Bubble nest.   F: C
T: 22–26°C, L: 5 cm, pH: ≪7, D: 3

Betta simplex ♂   4/568

H: SE Asia: S Thailand.
♂: More colorful; larger head.   S: =
B: ♂ mouthbroods for ca. 12 d.   F: C
T: 22–26°C, L: 6 cm, pH: 7, D: 2

Betta simplex ♂   4/568

Betta simplex ♀   4/568

Betta smaragdina ♂   1/632
Emerald betta
H: SE Asia: NE Thailand.
♂: Longer ventral fins.   S: +
B: Bubble nest, also in caves.   F: C
T: 24–27°C, L: 7 cm, pH: 7, D: 2–3

LABYRINTH F.

Betta splendens ♂♂　　　　　1/632
Siamese fighting fish
H: Thailand, Cambodia. Laos?
♂: More colorful; larger fins.　　S: =
B: Bubble nest.　　　　　　　　F: C
T: 24–30°C, L: 6–7 cm, pH: 7, D: 2

Betta splendens ♂　　　　　1/632
Siamese fighting fish
Wild form.
See photo on p. 4/565.

Betta splendens ♂　　　　　1/632
Siamese fighting fish
Bred form.
See photo on p. 4/565.

Betta splendens ♂　　　　　1/632
Siamese fighting fish
Bred form.
See photo on p. 4/565.

Betta splendens ♂　　　　　1/632
Siamese fighting fish
Bred form.
See photo on p. 4/565.

Betta splendens ♂　　　　　1/632
Siamese fighting fish
Bred form.
See photo on p. 4/565.

LABYRINTH F.

Betta taeniata   2/798
Banded betta
H: SE Asia: NW Borneo.
♂: Elongated fin rays.   S: =
B: Paternal mouthbrooder.   F: C,O
T: 23–26°C, L: 8 cm, pH: 7, D: 3–4

Betta tussyae ♂ ♂   3/658
Tussy's betta
H: SE Asia: Malaysia.
♂: Larger fins.   S: (–)
B: Small bubble nest.   F: C,O
T: 21–24°C , L: 5.5 cm, pH: ≪7, D: 3

Betta tussyae ♀   3/658
Tussy's betta

Betta unimaculata   2/800
One-spot betta
H: SE Asia: N Borneo.
♂: More colorful; single shiny scale. S: =
B: ♂ mouthbroods for 9 d (25°C).   F: C,O
T: 21–25°C, L: 12 cm, pH: 7, D: 2–3

Ctenops nobilis ♂   3/660

Ctenops nobilis ♀   3/660

H: India: Bramaputra and Bangladesh.
♂: Red fringe on A and C fins.   S: –
B: Paternal mouthbrooder.   F: C
T: 20–24°C, L: 10 cm, pH: <7, D: 2–4

LABYRINTH F.

585

Macropodus chinensis × M. opercularis
Red macropodus   3/636
H: N/A. Hybrid.
♂: More colorful; longer fins.   S: +
B: Rarely successful.   F: O
T: 18–28°C, L: 10 cm, pH: 7, D: 1

Macropodus concolor   1/638
Black paradise fish
H: Asia: S China, Vietnam.
♂: Pointed dorsal and anal fins.   S: +
B: Bubble nest.   F: C,O
T: 20–26°C, L: 12 cm, pH: 7, D: 1

Macropodus ocellatus ♀ light   2/803
Ocellated paradise fish
H: Asia: Korea, E China, Vietnam.
♂: More colorful; slightly larger.   S: =
B: Bubble nest.   F: C,O
T: 15–22°C, L: 8 cm, pH: 7, D: 2–3

Macropodus opercularis ♂♂   1/638
Paradise fish
H: E Asia: China, Korea, Taiwan.
♂: More colorful; longer fins.   S: +,–
B: Bubble nest; <500 eggs.   F: O
T: 16–26°C, L: 10 cm, pH: 7, D: 1

Macropodus opercularis ♂   1/638
Albino paradise fish
Albino strain. See photo on p. 3/638.

Malpulutta kretseri   1/640
Malpulutta
H: SE Asia: Sri Lanka.
♂: Larger; colorful; long C & D fins. S: =
B: Cave spawner.   F: C
T: 24–28°C, L: 9 (♀4) cm, pH: 7, D: 4

LABYRINTH F.

Parosphromenus alleni   3/662
Allen's gourami
H: SE Asia: W Borneo, Sarawak.
♂: Courtship coloration.   S: –
B: Cave spawner?   F: C
T: 20–24°C, L: 3.5 cm, pH: ≪7, D: 4

Parosphromenus anjunganensis ♂
          4/572
H: Asia: W Kalimantan, Borneo.
♂: More colorful. ♀: Plain.   S: =
B: Bubble nest w/ plant fragments.   F: C
T: 20–24°C, L: 4 cm, pH: ≪7, D: 3–4

Parosphromenus dayi   1/642
Brown spike-tailed or Day's paradise fish
H: Asia: W India.
♂: Longer caudal fin rays.   S: +
B: Bubble nest, sometimes caves.   F: O
T: 25–28°C, L: 7.5 cm, pH: 7, D: 2

Parosphromenus deissneri   1/640
Licorice gourami   (5/652)
H: SE Asia: Malaysia (photo), Singapore.
♂: More colorful.   S: (–)
B: Cave spawner; ♂ tends spawn.   F: C
T: 24–28°C, L: 3.5 cm, pH: <7, D: 4

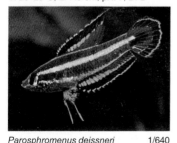

Parosphromenus deissneri   1/640
Licorice gourami
H: SE Asia: Borneo.
See photo on p. 5/652.

Parosphromenus sp.aff. *deissneri*   1/640
Licorice gourami   (5/652)
H: SE Asia: Sumatra.
See photo on p. 5/652.

LABYRINTH F.

587

Parosphromenus filamentosus   2/807
Spike-tailed licorice gourami
H: Asia: SE Borneo.
♂: Longer caudal and dorsal fins.   S: =
B: Cave spawner; 50 eggs.   F: C,O
T: 21–28°C, L: 4 cm, pH: 7, D: 3

Parosphromenus harveyi ♂   3/664
Harvey's gourami
H: SE Asia: Malay Peninsula.
♂: More colorful.   S: =
B: Cave spawner.   F: C
T: 20–24°C, L: 3.5 cm, pH: ≪7, D: 4

Parosphromenus harveyi ♀   3/664
Harvey's gourami

Parosphromenus linkei ♂   4/572
Linke's licorice gourami
H: SE Asia: SW central Kalimantan, Borneo.
♂: Darker; more colorful fins.   S: =
B: Bubble nest; 40–50 young.   F: C
T: 20–24°C, L: 4 cm, pH: ≪7, D: 3–4

Parosphromenus nagyi ♂   3/666
Nagy's licorice gourami
H: SE Asia: E Malaysia.
♂: More colorful.   S: (–)
B: Cave spawner; 10–40 eggs.   F: C
T: 20–24°C, L: 4 cm, pH: ≪7, D: 3–4

Parosphromenus nagyi ♀   3/666
Nagy's licorice gourami

Parosphromenus ornaticauda   4/574
Ornate-tail licorice gourami
H: SE Asia: W Kalimantan, Borneo.
♂: Slightly more colorful.   S: =
B: Cave spawner; 20–40 eggs.   F: C!
T: 20–25°C, L: 2.5 cm, pH: ≪7, D: 4

Parosphromenus paludicola   2/808
Pallid licorice gourami
H: SE Asia: Malay Peninsula, S Thailand.
♂: Slightly longer ventral fins.   S: (–)
B: Cave spawner.   F: C,O
T: 25–27°C, L: 3.7 cm, pH: ≪7, D: 4

Parosphromenus parvulus   2/808
Pygmy licorice gourami
H: SE Asia: S Borneo.
♀: Colorless fins.   S: (–)
B: Unsuccessful.   F: C,O
T: 23–26°C, L: 2.7 cm, pH: ≪7, D: 4

Pseudophromenus cupanus   1/642
"Black" spike-tailed paradise fish
H: SE Asia: S India, Sri Lanka.
♂: Pointed dorsal fin; diff. slight.   S: +
B: Bubble nest.   F: C
T: 24–27°C, L: 6 cm, pH: 7, D: 1–2

Trichopsis pumila   1/650
Dwarf croaking gourami
H: SE Asia: Vietnam, Thailand, Sumatra.
♂: More pointed dorsal fin.   S: +
B: Loose bubble nest;<170eggs.   F:C,O
T: 25–28°C, L: 3.5 cm, pH: <7, D: 2

Trichopsis schalleri   3/668
Three-striped croaking gourami
H: SE Asia: Thailand.
♂: Longer fins.   S: +
B: Bubble nest; <300 eggs.   F: C,O
T: 22–28°C, L: 6 cm, pH: <7, D: 2–3

LABYRINTH F.

Trichopsis vittata 1/650
Croaking gourami
H: Asia: E India, Thai., S Viet., Malay., Indo.
♂: Red-fringed, pointed anal fin. S: +
B: Bubble nest. F: O
T: 22–28°C, L: 6.5 cm, pH: 7, D: 2–3

Colisa chuna t.♂, b.♀ 1/634
Honey gourami
H: Asia: NE India & Assam, Bangladesh.
♂: Honey-colored. S: +
B: Loose bubble nest. F: C,O
T: 22–28°C, L: 5 cm, pH: 7, D: 2–3

Colisa fasciata t.♂, b.♀ 1/634
Banded gourami
H: Asia: India, Bengal, Assam, Burma.
♂: Darker; pointed dorsal fin. S: +
B: Large bubble nest; 20–50 e. F: O
T: 22–28°C, L: 10 cm, pH: <7, D: 2

Colisa labiosa t.♂, b.♀ 1/636
Thick-lipped gourami
H: Asia: India.
♂: More colorful, pointed dorsal fin. S: +
B: Dense bubble nest; <600 eggs. F: O
T: 22–28°C, L: 9 cm, pH: 7, D: 1

Colisa lalia t.♀, b.♂ 1/636
Dwarf gourami
H: Asia: India, Borneo.
♂: More colorful. S: +
B: Tall, dense bubble nest; 600 e. F: O
T: 22–28°C, L: 5 cm, pH: <7, D: 2

Colisa lalia 2/800
Red dwarf gourami, sunset gourami
H: N/A. Bred strain.
♂: More colorful. S: +
B: Loose bubble nest; 500 eggs. F: C,O
T: 25–28°C, L: 5 cm, pH: <7, D: 2

LABYRINTH F.

590

Parasphaerichthys ocellatus   3/662
Burmese chocolate gourami
H: SE Asia: Burma.
SD: Unknown.   S: =
B: Unknown.   F: C
T: 24–26°C, L: 4 cm, pH: <7, D: 3–4

Sphaerichthys acrostoma ♂   2/804
Black-tailed chocolate gourami
H: SE Asia: S central Borneo.
♂: Lighter.   S: +
B: Unknown. Mouthbrooder?   F: C
T: 24–26°C, L: 9 cm, pH: 7, D: 3–4

Sphaerichthys acrostoma ♂   2/804
Black-tailed chocolate gourami
Melanistic coloration.

Sphaerichthys os. osphromenoides   1/644
Chocolate gourami
H: Asia: Malacca, Malaysia, Sum., Borneo.
♂: A and C fins w/ yellow fringe.   S: +
B: ♀ mouthbrooder; 20–40 eggs.   F: C
T: 25–30°C, L: 5 cm, pH: <7, D: 3–4

Sphaerichthys os. selatanensis   2/806
Thin-barred chocolate gourami
H: SE Asia: SE Borneo.
♂: White-fringed anal fin.   S: +
B: Maternal mouthbrooder.   F: C
T: 25–30°C, L: 5 cm, pH: <7, D: 3–4

Sphaerichthys vaillanti   5/653

H: SE Asia: Borneo.
♂: More colorful; longer fins.   S: ?
B: Unsuccessful; mouthbrooder.   F: C
T: 22–28°C, L: 8 cm, pH: ≪7, D: 2–3

LABYRINTH F.

Trichogaster leeri back ♀, front ♂ 1/644
Pearl gourami

H: SE Asia: Malaysia, Borneo, Sumatra.
♂: Redder; longer D and A fins. **S:** +
B: Bubble nest; ♂ guards spawn. **F:** O,C
T: 24–28°C, L: 12 cm, pH: 7, D: 1

Trichogaster microlepis   1/646
Moonlight gourami

H: SE Asia: Thailand, Cambodia.
♂:V threads orange/red. ♀: Yellow. **S:** +
B: Bubble nest; 500–1000 eggs.   **F:** O
T: 26–30°C, L: 15 cm, pH: <7, D: 2

Trichogaster pectoralis   1/646
Snakeskin gourami

H: SE Asia: Thai., Cambodia, Malay Pen.
♂:V threads orange/red, ♀: Yellow. **S:** +
B: Bubble nest.   **F:** O
T: 23–28°C, L: 20 cm, pH: 7, D: 1

Trichogaster trichopterus   1/648
Blue gourami

H: Malay., Thai., Bur., Viet., Indo-Aust. Arch.
♂: Pointed, elongated anal fin.   **S:** +
B: Bubble nest.   **F:** O
T: 26–28°C, L: 10 cm, pH: 7, D: 1

Trichogaster trichopterus   1/648
Blue gourami
Albino form

Trichogaster trichopterus sumatranus
Blue gourami   3/668

H: SE Asia: Sumatra.
♂: Pointed, longer D and A fins.   **S:** +
B: Bubble nest.   **F:** O
T: 22–28°C, L: 12 cm, pH: <7, D: 1

LABYRINTH F.

Family Helostomidae

The family of kissing gouramis is monotypic; i.e., the presented species is its sole member. There is a greenish wild form, but the pink bred strain is much more common in the trade.

At a length of 20 cm and an age of 12–18 months, sexual maturity is attained. Lettuce leaves are a good spawning substrate, since they are covered with bacteria and infusoria which provide the best initial source of food for the fry.

It is bred and raised in Asia as a food fish, despite rather modest annual production levels of just 500 kg/ha.

H. temminckii feeds on plant fare as well as plankton. The latter is sieved from the water with its dense gill rakers. Since it is fond of grazing algae lawns, the back pane of the aquarium should not be cleaned.

"Kissing" is interpreted as a method of establishing dominance over a rival male.

Helostoma temminckii   1/652
Kissing gourami
H: SE Asia: Thailand, Java.
♀: Fuller.   S: +
B: No bubble nest; floating eggs.   F: O,H
T: 22–28°C, L: 15–30 cm, pH: 7, D: 3

Helostoma temminckii   5/654
Kissing gourami   marbled

Family Luciocephalidae

The only representative of the monotypic family Luciocephalidae is *Luciocephalus pulcher*, the pikehead.

Of all the teleosts, the mouth of pikeheads is the most protrusive, extending up to 33% of the length of the head. The fish lunges forward and simply encompasses the prey with its open, flared mouth (NELSON, 1994). All fishes too large to be considered prey are ignored. Live food is a prerequisite for successful maintenance.

Luciocephalus pulcher   1/845
Pikehead
H: SE Asia: Malay Peninsula, Indonesia.
♀: Fuller.   S: =
B: ♂Mb, 28 d, <90 y; 12–13 mm.   F: C!
T: 22–26°C, L: 18 cm, pH: <7, D: 4

LABYRINTH F.

Family Osphronemidae

The family of the giant gouramis consists of one genus and 3 species (ROBERTS, 1992; in NELSON, 1994). Among these, *Osphronemus gorami* is by far the most familiar. Largely because of its size—*O. gorami* is the largest species in the suborder Anabantoidei—this species is cultured as a food fish virtually circumtropically, but principally in Asia.

With age, the aggressive juveniles become peaceful, but by that time they are too large for home aquaria (up to 70 cm!). They require dense vegetation and strong filtration. Water chemistry is of secondary importance; average values are suitable. Juveniles and chocolate gouramis (p. 591) are so similar in appearance that the two are sometimes confused.

While *O. gorami* has little to recommend it as an aquarium fish, it is highly appreciated in Asia for its meat. As a labyrinth fish, its accessory organ allows it to breathe the air, thereby tolerating suboptimal water conditions. Its hardiness increases its appeal to aquaculturists.

The edible gourami is bred in ponds. The thick lips of the males and the full ventral area and reddish fins of the females distinguish the genders. Using plant material, a spherical subaquatic nest is constructed among plants. Between 3000 and 4000 eggs are laid therein. These have a diameter of 2.8 mm and the same specific gravity as water (some claim the eggs are buoyant). Until the fry leave the nest at approximately $2^1/_2$ weeks postspawning, the nest and the spawn are guarded. Although it is suspected that this species becomes sexually mature at an age of $1^1/_2$ years, 4–8 year old breeders are preferred.

In 3 months the young are about 3 cm long but frail. At an age of 5 months (and a length of 5–8 cm), they are more robust and better survival during transport can be expected.

Growth is slower than what is normally achieved with tropical fishes. In exchange for the lengthy growout (18 months), a handsome price is fetched at market, since the meat is considered a delicacy.

LABYRINTH F.

Osphronemus gorami adult   3/670
Giant gourami, edible gourami
H: SE Asia: China, Malaysia, Java, India.
♂: Pointed D and A fins, not easy.   S: –,=
B: Bubble nest.   F: O
T: 20–30°C, L: 70 cm, pH: 7, D: 4

Osphronemus gorami juvenile   1/652
Giant gourami, edible gourami

Haplochromis sp. "Thick Skin Like" (p. 680), Lake Victoria; an endangered species.

Teniacara candidi, one of the dwarf cichlids from Amazonia (p. 778).

CICHLIDS

Group 8

Origin/Taxonomy

The family Cichlidae—cichlids—is part of the order Perciformes, suborder Labroidei (previously of the Percoidei); i.e., according to latest taxonomy, cichlids are close relatives of the marine wrasses, damselfishes, and parrot-fishes.

Based on merit of popularity and sheer numbers, the cichlids have been placed in their own group. From a taxonomic point of view, however, they and the labyrinth fishes (Group 7) should actually be part of Group 9—Various Perches.

The oldest fossil records date from the Eocene Era about 55 million years ago. Estimates as to the present number of genera and species are highly variable, but 105 genera and 1300 species are accepted ball park numbers (NELSON, 1994).

The taxonomy within the Cichlidae is subject to numerous interpretations. For example, the problems with speciation in the Great African Rift Lakes (Malawi, Tanganyika, and Victoria), where hundreds of endemic species live together in species flocks or—depending on interpretation—groups consisting of many independent species. The collective genus *Haplochromis* was partially renamed *Cyrtocara* and then splintered into numerous other genera. In America the situation with *Cichlasoma* and *Heros* is similar.

Nevertheless, the name changes suffered by individual species leave their trail in the Comprehensive Index as synonyms (pp. 965–1196). The reader is hereby assured continued access to any fish in question through its present scientific name, its common name, or one of its synonyms.

Geographic Distribution

Cichlids primarily inhabit freshwater, but some species enter brackish waters. Throughout their range, cichlids have adapted to highly diverse condi-

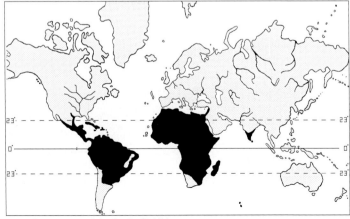

Area of distribution of the family Cichlidae.

CICHLIDS

tions, efficiently occupying almost all aquatic niches. For example, *Oreochromis alcalicus grahami* of Lake Magadi endures temperatures of more than 40°C and a pH of 10.5! The vertical distribution of cichlids is rather limited, since it is largely dictated by the presence of slow-moving waters. At the western edge of the Amazon Basin in South America, the cichlid population becomes sparse at 700 m elevation, but at 1100 m above sea level in Africa within Lake Victoria—a static biotope—there is a thriving specious cichlid population.

Sexual Differences

The surest method to determine the sex of a cichlid (and many other groups of fishes) is by recognizing the morphological differences of the genital papilla (see drawing at right). Even juveniles can be reliably sexed thusly. The dark line of females can be highlighted in small individuals with the help of a small brush and diluted India ink. The disadvantage of this method lies in the necessary capture and stressful handling of the animal.

The evaluation of more obvious characteristics (see table) is "fish friendlier," but restricted to certain groups of cichlids and often based on relative factors, i.e., size or color. Oftentimes females, subdominant males, and juveniles have the same coloration.

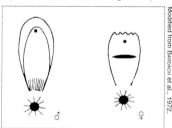

Modified from BARDACH et al., 1972.

Typical differences in the sex-dependent morphology of the urogenital papilla in cichlids. In smaller specimens, India ink and even a magnifying glass can help. Similar differences are sometimes found in other fish groups.

Exteriorly Recognizable Sexual Differences in Cichlids		
Characteristic	Sex	Fish Group
(More pronounced) frontal hump	♂	America, also Africa
Dark spot on the dorsal fin	♀	Tilapines
Elongated fins (dorsal, anal, and other fins)	♂	America
Egglike design (egg spots) on the anal fin	♂	African lakes
More color	♂	Dwarf cichlids, "*Haplochromis*,"...
More color	♀	*Pelvicachromis, Crenicichila*,...
Extreme (dichromatism)	♀♂	*Melanochromis*,...

CICHLIDS

Generalities

Cichlids come in all sizes, ranging from a length of 5 cm for dwarf cichlids to 80 cm in the case of *Boulengerochromis microlepis* from Lake Tanganyika.

There are schooling species and loners; inhabitants of torrential rivers and pacific lakes, limnivores and scale-eaters, green-gray "mice" and colorful "peacocks;" and deep-bodied discoidal fishes and cigar-shaped individuals. With the notable exception of accessory breathing organs that allow respiration of atmospheric air, electrical generating abilities, and poisonous spines, virtually everything can be found among this group.

To better organize this very large family and present similar species together, the INDEX subdivides Group 8 according to geographic criteria as follows:

- AFRICA—LAKE MALAWI: Endemic species of Lake Malawi.
- AFRICA—LAKE TANGANYIKA: Endemic species of Lake Tanganyika.
- AFRICA—VARIOUS LAKES: The cichlids of other large African lakes (Victoria, Edward, etc.), including non-endemic species of lakes Malawi and Tanganyika.
- AFRICA—FLOWING WATERS: Riverine inhabitants and those whose habitat is centered in flowing waters. Madagascar endemics are found in the subgroup "Remaining World."
- NORTH AND CENTRAL AMERICA: Cichlids with an area of distribution limited to, or predominantly in, North and/or Central America.
- SOUTH AMERICA: Cichlids with an area of distribution limited to, or predominantly in, South America.
- REMAINING WORLD: All other areas not addressed in the previous categories. At present, these are species hailing from the Caribbean, Madagascar, and India.

It is difficult and not altogether recommendable to house cichlids originating from different geographic regions in one aquarium, particularly American cichlids and African cichlids. Not only do their water chemistry requirements rarely conform, but more importantly, they do not "speak" the same language; i.e., the social structures and forms of communication of one are unrecognized by the other. The aquarist must be quite skillful to overcome such impediments. It is preferable to keep cichlids among themselves in the geographic sense. In sight of the seemingly endless choices of beautiful, interesting species within any of the geographic regions, surely this will not prove too much of a sacrifice.

CICHLIDS

Abbreviations Used in Group 8 Under Breeding (explanations see glossary):	
ESM: Egg spot method	M fam: Maternal family
LMb: Larvophile mouthbrooder	N fam: Nuclear family
Mb: Mouthbrooder (ovophile)	P fam: Paternal family
d: Days mouthbrooding	Os: Open spawner
Cs: Cave spawner	P-M fam: Paternal-maternal family
e: Eggs	Pch-M fam: Patriarch-maternal family

For example:
B: ♀ Mb, 21 d; <30 e; ESM; agamic; M fam.
Breeding: Female mouthbroods for about 21 days; up to 30 eggs; fertilization of the eggs follows the egg spot method; the fish is agamic (lack of a lasting bond between the sexes); maternal family.

Physical Characteristics (PITCHER and HART, 1995; KONINGS, 1988)

With a length of 550 km, a width of up to 80 km, and a surface area of 30 800 km², Lake Malawi is the third largest African lake and the ninth largest lake in the world. Situated at an elevation of 474 m above sea level, it is part of the African Rift Valley system with an estimated age between 1 and 2 million years (other estimates place the age at between 3 and 20 million years). Over the course of its evolution, the lake has been subject to extreme fluctuations in water level. For example, 25000 years ago the water level was 400 m below today's level. At its deepest point, the lake has a depth of 756 m; or almost 300 m below sea level.

Additional parameters:

pH:	7.7–8.6
Conductivity:	200–260 µS
Temperature:	23°–28°C

Bordering States:

Lake Malawi is bordered by Malawi in the west and south, Mozambique in the center and southeast, and Tanzania in the north and northeast.

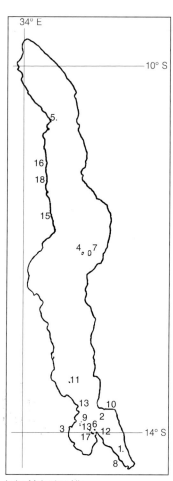

Points of Reference

Boadzulu	1
Chinyamwezi	2
Chipoka	3
Chisumulu Island	4
Chitendi Island	5
Domwe Islands	6
Likoma Island	7
Makakola	8
Maleri	9
Mankanjila	10
Mbenji Island	11
Monkey Bay	12
Mumbo	13
Namalenji Island	14
Nhkata Bay	15
Ruarwe	16
Thumbi Island	17
Usisya	18

Lake Malawi or Njassa.

Ichthyological Characteristics

Eleven fish families with a total of 545 species in 42 genera can be found in Lake Malawi (PITCHER and HART, 1995).

- Non-cichlids: 19 genera (1 endemic) and 45 species (28 endemic).
- Cichlids: 23 genera (20 endemic) and 500 species (495 endemic).

The classification of the fish fauna is constantly changing. The taxonomic splitting of collective genera such as *Haplochromis* and then *Cyrtocara* as well as the ongoing discovery of new species as permitted by the political situation of the bordering countries will further contribute to the flux. About 200 additional species are expected (KONINGS, 1989).

By far, cichlids are the most successful group of fishes in Lake Malawi. The lake community as a whole undergoes little genetic exchange with fishes of surrounding aquatic systems. Today, there is a chemical barrier between the mineral-rich waters of the lake and the mineral-poor waters of its affluent rivers: no species from one biotope breeds in the other.

Based on general behavior, the majority of cichlid species are classified as one of two types, mbuna or utaka. (It is interesting to note that in the language of some natives of the east Andean rain forests of Ecuador, South America, the denomination "mbuni" is used locally for several cichlids.)

- **Mbuna:** This denomination is primarily in reference to the genera *Labidochromis, Pseudotropheus,* and *Melanochromis.* These species typically grow larger in captivity than in their natural habitat. Some species (e.g., *Melanochromis* spp.) undergo dramatic color changes as they achieve sexual maturity: the male's colors basically become opposite of those of the females and juveniles.

  Mbuna lead a strongly rock-bound life, grazing the aufwuchs from sun-bathed surfaces. Conditions in the aquarium should approximate the natural biotope, i.e., numerous rock caves and niches and intense illumination to foment algae growth. Not only are aquatic plants an innecessary part of the decor—there are none in their natural biotope either—they are frequently eaten when included. Ample fiber in the diet is required. Occasionally, small quantities of rich foods such as Enchytraeidae or even *Tubifex* can be offered, but this practice is not recommended. Animals which do not receive sufficient fiber are susceptible to commonly fatal intestinal disorders (infections) and bloated stomachs (Malawi bloat). However, among the mbuna there are also a few predators and parasites (scale-eaters). They cannot be associated with fishes incapable of defending themselves. Caution!—several species will hybridize and produce fertile offspring.

- **Utaka:** The fishes in the genera *Aulonocara, Haplochromis, Cyrtocara,* and their derivative genera constitute the second group. The females of the various species are all very similar, and many will hybridize. When several species are kept in the same aquarium, steps must be taken to avoid such an occurrence.

Utaka have a rather pelagic life style, i.e., they are often found in the open water, where they feed on plankton. In the aquarium, the majority are unparticular omnivores. Since they do not nibble on plants, vegetation can be included in the decor. Normally, examination of the genital papilla is the only reliable method to distinguish the virtually identical females, juveniles, and subordinate males.

Several other cichlids are predators; some even strategically pretend to be dead to lure their prey closer, e.g., *Nimbochromis livingstoni*, p. 623.

Most, if not all, cichlids of Lake Malawi are agamic maternal mouthbrooders. To prevent the male's aggressions from becoming focused, a small group of 3–5 females for each male is recommended. Associating several species of mbuna and utaka also helps distribute hostilities, but opens up the possibility of crossbreeding.

Always strive to keep a small group of each species. The pellmell of these bright, beautiful fishes is strongly reminiscent of marine coral reef fishes, explaining the popularity of Lake Malawian cichlids. Furthermore, they are hardy and easily acclimated to aquarium life.

When associating Lake Malawian cichlids with cichlids from other habitats, great care must be taken. These lively fishes can quickly terrorize unsuitable tankmates to death. Even cichlids of Lake Tanganyika are not always appropriate companions. American cichlids, especially those from South America, are largely unsuitable because of divergent water chemistry requirements and their incompatible "social language."

Aristochromis christyi ♂   2/834, 5/728

H: Northern section.
♂: Blue when courting.   S: –
B: Mb? Maternal family?   F: C
T: 24–26°C, L: 25 cm, pH: >7, D: 3

Aristochromis christyi ♀   5/728

H: Monkey Bay, SW section.
♂: Blue when courting.   S: –
B: Mb? Maternal family?   F: C
T: 23–27°C, L: 20 cm, pH: >7, D: 2–3

Aulonocara baenschi ♂   2/836
Yellow regal cichlid, Baensch's peacock
H: Endemic.
♂: Blue/yellow.   S: =
B: Egg spot method.   F: C,O
T: 22–26°C, L: 10 cm, pH: >7, D: 1–2

CICHLIDS

601

Aulonocara baenschi ♀   2/836
Yellow regal cichlid, Baensch's peacock

Aulonocara baenschi ♂   2/836
Yellow regal cichlid, Baensch's peacock
Maleri strain.

Aulonocara baenschi ♂   2/836
Yellow regal cichlid, Baensch's peacock
Blue-yellow strain, Chipoka.

Aulonocara baenschi ♂   2/836
Yellow regal cichlid, Baensch's peacock
Usisya strain (photo p. 2/847).

Aulonocara baenschi ♀   2/836
Yellow regal cichlid, Baensch's peacock
Usisya strain (photo p. 2/847).

Aulonocara ethelwynnae ♂   3/698
Northern aulonocara
H: Chitendi Island; >3 m depth.
♂: Blue-black unpaired fins.   S: =
B: ♀ Mb, 21 d; 10 mm.   F: C,O
T: 22–26°C, L: 8 cm, pH: >7, D: 3

CICHLIDS

Aulonocara gertrudae ♂   5/734
Gertrude's peacock
H: E coast; lakewide (?).
♂: Much more colorful; larger.   S: =
B: ♀ Mb; ESM; agamic.   F: C,O
T: 24–27°C, L: 13 cm, pH: >7, D: 2–3

Aulonocara hansbaenschi ♂   1/682
African peacock
H: Rock/sand transition zone.
♂: Much more colorful.   S: =
B: ♀ Mb, <60 e; ESM.   F: C,O
T: 24–26°C, L: 20 cm, pH: >7, D: 2–3

Aulonocara hansbaenschi ♂   3/700
Red flush aulonocara
H: E coast: Masinje.
♂: Much more colorful.   S: =
B: ♀ mouthbrooder, 21 days.   F: C,O
T: 23–27°C, L: 10 cm, pH: >7, D: 2–3

Aulonocara hansbaenschi ♀   1/682
African peacock

Aulonocara hansbaenschi ♂   3/700
Red flush aulonocara
Makanjila Point.

Aulonocara hansbaenschi ♀   3/700
Red flush aulonocara

Aulonocara hueseri ♂   2/845, 3/702
White top peacock
H: Likoma Island: from 12 m depth.
♂: Much more colorful.   S: =
B: ♀ Mb, 21 days; 10 mm.   F: C,O
T: 24–26°C, L: 9.5 cm, pH: >7, D: 2–3

Aulonocara hueseri ♂   3/702
White top peacock

Aulonocara jacobfreibergi ♂   1/780
Freiberg's peacock
H: Rocky littoral: cave dweller.
♀: Red-fringed dorsal fin.   S: =
B: ♀ mouthbrooder, <50 eggs.   F: C
T: 24–26°C, L: 15 cm, pH: >7, D: 2

Aulonocara korneliae ♂   2/845, 3/704
Blue-gold aulonocara
H: Chisumulu Island: at 9–12 m.
♂: Much more colorful.   S: =
B: ♀ Mb, 21 days; 10 mm.   F: C,O
T: 23–27°C, L: 9 cm, pH: >7, D: 2–3

Aulonocara maylandi ♂   2/838
Mayland's peacock, sulphurhead peacock
H: Mankanjila Point.
♂: Much more colorful; egg spots. S: =
B: ♀ Mb, <50 e; ESM.   F: C,O
T: 22–26°C, L: 12 cm, pH: >7, D: 1–2

Aulonocara maylandi (?) ♀   2/838
Mayland's peacock, sulphurhead peacock

Aulonocara maylandi kandeensis ♂ 4/578
Blue orchid peacock
H: Kande Island: littoral zone.
♂: Much more colorful. **S:** =
B: ♀ Mb, 21d; <40 y;10 mm; ESM. **F:** C,O
T: 24–26°C, **L:** <15 cm, **pH:** >7, **D:** 3

Aulonocara maylandi kandeensis ♂ 4/578
Blue orchid peacock
See photo on p. 2/839.

Aulonocara rostratum ♂ 4/580
Sand peacock
H: Broadly distr.; sand, sand/rock biotopes.
♂: Much more colorful. **S:** =
B: ♀ Mb, 21 d; >100 y; 10 mm. **F:** C,O
T: 24–26°C, **L:** <25 cm, **pH:** >7, **D:** 3–4

Aulonocara rostratum ♀ 4/580
Sand peacock

Aulonocara saulosi ♂ 3/704

H: E coast: Masinje: at 6–15 m depth.
♂: Much more colorful. **S:** =
B: ♀ Mb; <60 young; ESM. **F:** C,O
T: 22–26°C, **L:** 11 cm, **pH:** >7, **D:** 2–3

Fishing in the African lakes.

Aulonocara sp. "walteri" ♂   5/736

Aulonocara sp. "walteri" ♀   5/736

H: Likoma Island: at 3–5 (10) m depth.
♂: Much more colorful; larger.   S: =
B: ♀ Mb, 20–25 days; ESM.   F: O,L
T: 24–26°C, L: <15 cm, pH: >7, D: 2–3

Aulonocara stuartgranti ♂   2/842
Grant's peacock, blue regal peacock

H: Endemic.
♂: Much more colorful.   S: =
B: ♀ Mb; egg spot method.   F: C,O
T: 22–26°C, L: 10 cm, pH: >7, D: 1–2

Aulonocara stuartgranti ♂   2/842
Grant's peacock, blue regal peacock
Mbenji Island.

Aulonocara stuartgranti ♀   2/842
Grant's peacock, blue regal peacock

Buccochromis heterotaenia ♂   4/582

H: Lakewide: rocky substrates.
♂: Much more colorful.   S: –
B: ♀ Mb, 21 d; 100 y; 10–12 mm.   F: C,O
T: 24–27°C, L: <35 cm, pH: >7, D: 4

Buccochromis heterotaenia ♀   4/582

Buccochromis lepturus ♂   3/772
Slender-tail hap, green lepturus
H: Widely distributed on sandy substrates.
♂: Much more colorful.   S: =
B: ♀ Mb; egg spot method.   F: O
T: 24–26°C, L: <40 cm, pH: >7, D: 2–3

Buccochromis rhoadesii ♂   5/740
Yellow lepturus
H: Lakewide: sandy biotopes.
♂: Much more colorful. ♀: Yellow.   S: –
B: Maternal mouthbrooder.   F: C
T: 23–27°C, L: 35 cm, pH: >7, D: 3

Champsochromis caeruleus ♂   5/742
Trout cichlid
H: Thoughout the lake.
♂: More colorful; see photos.   S: –
B: ♀ Mb, 21 d; >100 y; agamic.   F: C
T: 24–26°C, L: <30 cm, pH: >7, D: 3–4

Champsochromis caeruleus ♀   5/742
Trout cichlid

Champsochromis spilorhynchus ♂ 2/904

H: Various biotopes.
♂: See photos.   S: –
B: Nat.: ♀ Mb; 100 y; agamic.   F: C!
T: 24–26°C, L: 30 cm, pH: >7, D: 4

CICHLIDS

Champsochromis spilorhynchus ♀ 2/904

Cheilochromis euchilus ♀   1/712
Big-lipped cichlid
H: Rocky littoral zone.
♂: Much more colorful.   S: =
B: ♀ Mb; 150 eggs; ESM.   F: L,O
T: 24–26°C, L: <35 cm, pH: ≫7, D: 3

Chilotilapia rhoadesii ♂   2/854

H: Primarily above sand.
♂: Much more colorful.   S: =
B: ♀ mouthbrooder, 21 days.   F: C,O
T: 23–28°C, L: 23 cm, pH: >7, D: 3

Copadichromis sp. aff. *azureus* ♂   3/778

H: Mbenji Island: at ca. 20 m depth.
♂: Much more colorful.   S: =
B: Spawns on sand; ♀ Mb.   F: C,O
T: 22–28°C, L: 16 cm, pH: ≫7, D: 2

Copadichromis borleyi t.♀, b.♂   2/894

H: Rocky littoral zone.
♂: Much more colorful; egg spots. S: =
B: ♀ Mb, 20 days; <60 e; ESM.   F: C
T: 24–26°C, L: 15 cm, pH: ≫7, D: 2–3

Fishing: "Our" aquarium fishes are the most important protein source of the local population.

CICHLIDS

Copadichromis chrysonotus   1/710
(no photo)
H: Nkata Bay and Monkey Bay.
♂: Much more colorful; egg spots. **S:** =
B: ♀ Mb; pit in the sand.   **F:** C,O
T: 23–26°C, **L:** 15 cm, **pH:** ≫7, **D:** 2–3

Copadichromis cyaneus ♂   5/756

H: Throughout the south.
♂: Much more colorful.   **S:** =
B: ♀ Mb, 21–28 days.   **F:** C
T: 23–27°C, **L:** 17 cm, **pH:** >7, **D:** 2

Copadichromis cyaneus ♀   5/756

Copadichromis jacksoni ♂   4/592
Jackson's nkata
H: Primarily Nkhata Bay and Monkey Bay.
♀: Silver with two spots.   **S:** =
B: ♀ Mb, 21 d; ca. 100 young.   **F:** C
T: 23–27°C, **L:** 21 cm, **pH:** >7, **D:** 2

Copadichromis "Kadango" ♂   3/770

Copadichromis "Kadango" ♀   3/770

H: SE coast (Kadango): at 2–10 m.
SD: See photos.   **S:** =
B: ♀Mb, 21d; 20–60y; ESM, agamic.   **F:** O
T: 24–26°C, **L:** <15 cm, **pH:** >7, **D:** 2–3

CICHLIDS

Copadichromis mbenjii ♂ 4/592

H: Mbenji Islands.
♂: Much more colorful. **S:** =
B: ♀ Mb, 21 d; pit in the sand. **F:** C,O
T: 24–27°C, L: 15 cm, pH: >7, D: 2–3

Copadichromis pleurostigma 5/758

H: Chilumba: rock/sand transition zone.
♂: Blue body and D fin. ♀: Spot. **S:** =
B: Unknown. **F:** C
T: 23–27°C, L: 21 cm, pH: >7, D: 2

Copadichromis sp. ♂ 1/711

Copadichromis trimaculatus ♂ 5/758
Three-spot hap

H: Likoma Island: Nkhata Bay.
♂: More colorful. ♀: 3 spots. **S:** =
B: ♀ Mb; egg spot method; agamic. **F:** C
T: 23–27°C, L: 21 cm, pH: >7, D: 2

Copadichromis trimaculatus ♀ 5/758
Three-spot hap

Copadichromis verduyni ♂ 4/594

H: E coast: Makanjila.
SD: See photos. **S:** =
B: ♀ Mb, 21 d; ESM; agamic. **F:** C,O
T: 24–27°C, L: 15 cm, pH: >7, D: 2–3

Copadichromis verduyni ♀   4/594

Corematodus taeniatus ♂   5/760
Striped corematodus
H: Widely distributed; relatively rare.
♂: Green; pointed D and A fins.   S: =
B: ♀ Mb, 21 d; on a rock plate.   F: P,C
T: 24–26°C, L: <20 cm, pH: >7, D: 4

Corematodus taeniatus ♀   5/760
Striped corematodus

Ctenopharynx pictus   2/902

H: Rock substrate: 2–30 m depth.
♂: More colorful.   S: =
B: Unsuccessful.   F: C,O
T: 24–26°C, L: 13 cm, pH: >7, D: 2–3

Cynotilapia afra ♂   2/890
Dogtooth cichlid
H: Rocky coast.
♂: Light blue to turquoise; 7 crossb. S: =
B: ♀ Mb, 20 days; agamic.   F: C
T: 23–27°C, L: 12 cm, pH: ≫7, D: 2

Cyrtocara moorii ♂   1/718
Blue lumphead
H: Sandy coastal areas.
♂: Unclear: often larger & brighter. S: =
B: ♀ Mb; 20–90 young.   F: C
T: 24–26°C, L: 25 cm, pH: >7, D: 3

611

Dimidiochromis compressiceps ♂   1/710
Malawi eye-biter
H: Rock/sand transition zone.
♂: Much more colorful; egg spots. **S:** –
B: ♀ Mb; egg spot method.   **F:** C,O
T: 22–28°C, **L:** <25 cm, **pH:** >7, **D:** 3

Docimodus evelynae ♂   4/616
Evelyn's cichlid
H: Probably widely distributed.
♀: Lacks crossbands.   **S:** –
B: Unknown   **F:** C!
T: 23–27°C, **L:** 30 cm, **pH:** >7, **D:** 4

Eclectochromis ornatus ♂   5/812
Ornate pouting hap
H: Seemingly lakewide.
♂: Much more colorful.   **S:** =
B: ♀ Mb, 21–28 d; 30–70 e; ESM   **F:** C
T: 23–27°C, **L:** 20 cm, **pH:** >7, **D:** 2

Eclectochromis ornatus ♀   5/812
Ornate pouting hap

Exochochromis anagenys ♂   4/616
Malawi pike cichlid
H: Widely distributed: rock/sand transition.
♀: Silver-yellow.   **S:** –
B: Maternal mouthbrooder?   **F:** C
T: 23–27°C, **L:** 30 cm, **pH:** >7, **D:** 3–4

Fossorochromis rostratus ♂   1/720
Rostratus
H: Sandy littoral.
♂: More intensely colored.   **S:** –
B: ♀ Mb; egg spot method?   **F:** C,O
T: 24–28°C, **L:** 25 cm, **pH:** >7, **D:** 2–3

Fossorochromis rostratus ♂ 3/778
Rostratus
H: Sand bottom. Rocks to spawn.
♀: A row of 5 black dots.　　　　　S: =
B: ♀ Mb, 21 d; 50–100 y.　　　　　F: O
T: 24–28°C, L: <25 cm, pH: >7, D: 2

Genyochromis mento ♂ 4/618
Malawian scale-eater
H: Lakewide on rock coasts & rubble zones.
♂: Slightly more intensely colored.　S: –
B: ♀Mb; agamic. Unsuccessful.　　F: P
T: 24–28°C, L: 12 cm, pH: >7, D: 3–4

Gephyrochromis sp. aff. *lawsi* 4/620
Violet cichlid
H: Transition sand/rubble sections.
♂: Slightly more colorful.　　　　　S: =
B: ♀ Mb, 21 d; agamic.　　　　　F: C,O
T: 24–28°C, L: 12 cm, pH: >7, D: 2

Gephyrochromis moorii t.♀, b.♂ 2/908
Black-tailed violet cichlid
H: Northern section: over sand bottoms.
♂: Egg spots?　　　　　　　　　　S: ?
B: ♀ Mb? Egg spot method?　　　F: C,O
T: 24–26°C, L: 12 cm, pH: >7, D: 2

Tanzania: Mmamba Bay in Lake Malawi.

"Haplochromis" cf. *lobochilus* ♂ 3/772
(2/950)
H: Sand/stone bottom: 2–10 m depth.
♀: Silvery; dark crossbands.　　　S: =
B: ♀Mb, 21d, 20–60y, ESM, agamic. F: O
T: 24–26°C, L: 17 cm, pH: >7, D: 2–3

CICHLIDS

613

"Haplochromis" sp. ♂   2/950

Haplochromis sp., Jaro, ♂   2/846

"Haplochromis steveni eastern"♂ 3/784

"Haplochromis steveni Maleri" ♂ 3/784

H: E coast: Makanjila.
♂: More intensely blue.   S: =
B: ♀ Mb, 21 days; 20–40 eggs.   F: O
T: 24–26°C, L: 15 cm, pH: >7, D: 3

Hemitaeniochromis urotaenia ♂ 5/838

Hemitilapia oxyrhynchus ♂   2/918

H: Lakewide: transition to sand bottom.
♂: More colorful. ♀: Silver.   S: =
B: ♀ Mb, 21 d; ESM; pits.   F: C,O
T: 23–27°C, L: 23 cm, pH: >7, D: 2–3

H: Sandy littoral with vallisneria.
♂: Very colorful.   S: =
B: ♀ Mb, 18–21 days; agamic.   F: C
T: 24–26°C, L: 20 cm, pH: >7, D: 3

Hemitilapia oxyrhynchus ♀ 2/918

Iodotropheus sprengerae ♂ 2/918
Rusty cichlid
H: Boadzulu & Mumbo islands: rocky littoral.
♂: More colorful. S: =
B: ♀ Mb; egg spot method; agamic. F: O
T: 24–26°C, L: 10 cm, pH: >7, D: 2

Labeotropheus fuelleborni ♂ 1/730
Fuelleborn's cichlid
H: Rubble and rocky littoral.
♂: Egg spots. S: –
B: ♀ Mb; egg spot method. F: C,O
T: 22–25°C, L: 15 cm, pH: >7, D: 2

Labeotropheus fuelleborni ♀ 1/730
Fuelleborn's cichlid
♀♀ appear in several color morphs. The normal form is very similar to ♂♂. Otherwise, they are usually checkered (photo).

Labeotropheus trewavasae ♂ 1/730
Trewavas' cichlid
H: Rubble and rock littoral.
♂: Egg spots more intense. S: –
B: ♀ Mb;<40 e; egg spot method. F: C,O
T: 21–24°C, L: 12 cm, pH: >7, D: 2

Labidochromis caeruleus 2/920
Blue-white labido, caeruleus
H: Nhkata Bay: rocks, vallisneria; 2–40 m.
♂: More colorful; somewhat larger. S: =
B: ♀ Mb, 25–40 days. F: O
T: 23–26°C, L: 8 cm, pH: >7, D: 2–3

CICHLIDS

615

Labidochromis chisumulae ♂   5/848

Labidochromis chisumulae ♀   5/848

H: Chisumulu Island.
♂: Blue design. ♀: All white.   S: +
B: ♀ Mb, 21 d; egg spot method. F: C,O
T: 24–26°C, L: 8 cm, pH: >7, D: 1–2

Labidochromis flavigulis ♂   5/850

Labidochromis flavigulis ♀   5/850

H: Likoma and Chisumulu islands.
♂: Defined egg spots. ♀: Yellowish. S: =
B: ♀ Mb, 21 d; 15–25 e; ESM.   F: O
T: 24–26°C, L: 6–7 cm, pH: >7, D: 1–2

Labidochromis freibergi ♂   4/628
Freiberg's mbuna
H: Likoma Island.
♀: Gray, can turn blue w/ age.   S: –
B: ♀Mb, 21d; 20–30y; ESM; agamic. F: C,O
T: 24–26°C, L: 8 cm, pH: >7, D: 1–2

Labidochromis gigas ♂   5/852

H: Likoma & Chisumulu islands: littoral.
♂: More colorful. ♀: Brownish.   S: =
B: ♀Mb, 21d, 20–30e, ESM; agamic. F: O
T: 24–26°C, L: 8–9 cm, pH: >7, D: 2

Labidochromis gigas ♀   5/852

Labidochromis ianthinus ♂   2/920

H: Mbenji Island: rocks in shallow water.
♂: More colorful and darker.   S: =
B: There are no reports.   F: O
T: 23–26°C, L: 9 cm, pH: >7, D: 2–3

Labidochromis lividus ♂   1/714

H: Likoma Island: N+W rock littoral: <6 m.
♂: Much more colorful.   S: =
B: ♀ Mb, 21 days; agamic.   F: L,O
T: 24–26°C, L: 7 cm, pH: >7, D: 2

Labidochromis maculicauda   5/854

H: Nkhata Bay: Chirombo Point.
♂: More blue; distinct egg spots.   S: =
B: ♀Mb, 21d; 20–30 e; ESM; agamic. F:O
T: 24–26°C, L: 8 cm, pH: >7, D: 1–2

Labidochromis mbenjii ♂   5/856

H: Mbenji Islands.
♂: Bluish; distinct egg spots.   S: =
B: ♀Mb, 21d; 20–30e, ESM; agamic.   F:O
T: 24–26°C, L: <10 cm, pH: >7, D: 1–2

Labidochromis mbenjii ♀   5/856

CICHLIDS

617

Labidochromis pallidus ♂   3/794

H: Maleri Islands: rock littoral: at <25 m.
♂: Unclear; distinct egg spots.   S: –
B: ♀ Mb, 21 days; agamic.   F: O
T: 24–26°C, L: 8 cm, pH: ≫7, D: 2

Labidochromis sp. "yellow"   3/792

H: Between Charo and Mbowe Island.
♀: Slightly paler.   S: =
B: ♀ Mb, 18 days; agamic.   F: C,O
T: 23–28°C, L: 10 cm, pH: >7, D: 1–2

Labidochromis sp. "Hongi" ♂   5/858
also *Labidochromis* sp. "Puulu"

H: NE coast: Hongi and Puulu islands.
♂: Bluish; egg spots more defined. S: =
B: ♀ Mb, 21d; 20–30e; ESM; aga. F: C,O
T: 24–26°C, L: 8–9 cm, pH: >7, D: 2

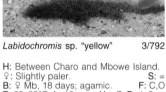

Labidochromis sp. "Hongi" ♀   5/858
also *Labidochromis* sp. "Puulu"

Labidochromis vellicans ♂   2/922
Vellicans

H: Rock littoral.
♂: Metallic blue and orange-yellow. S: =
B: ♀ Mb, <21 days; 30 e; agamic. F: O
T: 23–26°C, L: 10 cm, pH: >7, D: 2–3

Labidochromis zebroides ♂   5/860
Ice blue labidochromis

H: S of Likoma: Masimbwe Island.
♂: Blue w/ black crossbands.   S: =
B: ♀ Mb; agamic; egg spot method. F: C
T: 24–26°C, L: 8–9 cm, pH: >7, D: 2?

Lethrinops sp. "yellow collar" ♂ 5/864

Lethrinops sp. "yellow collar" ♀ 5/864

H: Monkey Bay, Likoma, NE coast.
♂: Much more colorful.   S: +
B: ♀ Mb, 21 d; ESM; agamic.   F: C,O
T: 24–27°C, L: 11 cm, pH: >7, D: 2–3

Maravichromis epichorialis ♂   1/712

Maravichromis formosus ♂   3/777

H: Endemic.
♂: Much more colorful; egg spots. S: ?
B: Maternal mouthbrooder?   F: C,O
T: 24–26°C, L: 20 cm, pH: >7, D: 2

H: Rocky littoral.   Rare
♂: Golden. ♀: Silver.   S: ?
B: Maternal mouthbrooder?   F: C,O
T: 24–26°C, L: 12.5 cm, pH: >7, D: 2

Maravichromis formosus ♀   3/777

Maravichromis mola ♂   3/774

CICHLIDS

H: Widely distributed: sand, mixed bottoms.
♂: Much more colorful; egg spots. S: =
B: Maternal mouthbrooder?   F: O
T: 24–26°C, L: 17 cm, pH: >7, D: 2–3

Maravichromis mola ♀   3/774

Melanochromis auratus t.♂, b.♀ 1/738
Malawi golden cichlid, auratus
H: Rocky shores.
♂: Less yellow: colors opposite of ♀. S: –
B: ♀Mb, 30 e; egg spot method. F: L,O
T: 22–26°C, L: ♂ 11 cm, pH: >7, D: 2–3

Melanochromis chipokae ♂   2/951
Chipokae mbuna
H: Close to Chipoka: rock littoral.
♂: Egg spots. ♀: Negative (yellow). S: –
B: ♀Mb 20d; 20–40e; ESM; agamic. F: C
T: 24–26°C, L: 15 cm, pH: >7, D: 2–3

Melanochromis joanjohnsonae ♀ 1/740
Pearl of Likoma, banner cichlid
H: Likoma Island: rubble littoral.
♂: Egg spots; D fin w/ black band. S: –
B: ♀ Mb, 30 e; egg spot method. F: L,O
T: 24–26°C, L: 10 cm, pH: >7, D: 2

Melanochromis joanjohnsonae ♂ 1/740
Pearl of Likoma, banner cichlid

Melanochromis johannii ♂   1/740
Cobalt cichlid
H: Rocky littoral zone.
♂: Egg spots; usually larger. S: –
B: ♀Mb, <35 e; egg spot method. F: L,O
T: 22–25°C, L: 12 cm, pH: >7, D: 2

Melanochromis labrosus ♂   1/714
black morph
H: Rock littoral.
♂: More intense egg spots.   S: ?
B: ♀ Mb; ca. 35 eggs; ESM.   F: O
T: 23–26°C, L: 13 cm, pH: >7, D: 2

Melanochromis "lepidophage" ♂ 3/800
H: E coast: Makanjila Point: rock zone.
♂: Egg spots. ♀: Silver.   S: =
B: ♀ Mb, <25 d; ESM; agamic.   F: O
T: 24–26°C, L: 12 cm, pH: >7, D: 2–3

Melanochromis "lepidophage" ♀ 3/800

Melanochromis melanopterus ♂ 2/952
Black mbuna
H: SW section: rubble and rock zone.
♂: Egg spots. ♀: The negative.   S: –
B: ♀ Mb, 21 d; <60 e; ESM; agamic. F: C
T: 24–26°C, L: 13 cm, pH: >7, D: 2–3

Melanochromis parallelus ♂   2/952
Parallel-striped mbuna
H: Nkata Bay: upper rocky littoral.
♂: Egg spots. ♀: The negative.   S: –
B: ♀ Mb, 21 d; <30 e; ESM; agamic. F: O
T: 24–26°C, L: 12 cm, pH: >7, D: 2–3

Melanochromis parallelus ♀   2/952
Parallel-striped mbuna

Melanochromis simulans ♂   5/868
Longsnout mbuna
H: E coast: at Makanjila/Fort Maguire.
♂: Egg spots. ♀: The negative.   S: –
B: ♀ Mb, 21d; 20–40 e; ESM; agamic. F: O
T: 24–26°C, L: 12 cm, pH: >7, D: 3

Melanochromis simulans ♀   5/868
Longsnout mbuna

Melanochromis vermivorus   1/742
Purple mbuna
H: Likoma Island: rubble littoral.
♂: Egg spots.   S: =
B: ♀ Mb; 30 e; egg spot method.   F: C,O
T: 22–26°C, L: 15 cm, pH: >7, D: 2

Mylochromis anaphyrmus ♂   4/640
Deep nkata
H: Southern section: sand bottom.
♂: Significantly more colorful.   S: –
B: ♀ Mb; egg spot method.   F: C
T: 23–27°C, L: 23 cm, pH: >7, D: 2–3

Mylochromis lateristriga ♂   5/872
Flame oxyrhynchus, basket hap
H: Monkey and Senga Bay, Maleri Island.
♂: Significantly more colorful.   S: =
B: ♀ Mb, 21 d; <60 young; ESM.   F: C
T: 23–27°C, L: 23 cm, pH: >7, D: 2–3

Mylochromis lateristriga ♀   5/872
Flame oxyrhynchus, basket hap

Naevochromis chrysogaster ♂♂ 5/874

H: Widely distributed, but rare.
♀: Like the ♂, but w/o egg spots. S: =
B: ♀ mouthbrooder? Unknown. F: O
T: 24–26°C, L: <25 cm, pH: >7, D: 3

Nimbochromis fuscotaeniatus ♂ 2/898
Fuscotaeniatus

H: South: rubble and rock littoral, sand.
♂: Much more colorful. S: –
B: ♀ Mb; agamic. No reports. F: C
T: 24–26°C, L: 25 cm, pH: >7, D: 3

Nimbochromis linni ♂ 1/716
Elephant-nose cichlid

H: Rock littoral.
♂: D fin red/yellow/white; egg spots. S: –
B: ♀ mouthbrooder; <20 e; ESM. F: C,O
T: 23–25°C, L: 25 cm, pH: >7, D: 2

Nimbochromis linni ♀ 1/716
Elephant-nose cichlid

Nimbochromis livingstonii 1/716
Livingstoni

H: Shores w/ sand and vallisneria.
♂: More colorful; egg spots. S: –
B: ♀ Mb; <100 e; egg spot meth. F: C,O
T: 24–26°C, L: 20 cm, pH: >7, D: 2

Nimbochromis polystigma ♂ 1/718
Polystigma

H: Rocky littoral.
♂: Egg spots. S: =
B: ♀ Mb; <20 e; egg spot method. F: C
T: 23–25°C, L: <23 cm, pH: >7, D: 2–3

CICHLIDS

623

Nimbochromis polystigma ♂   1/718
Polystigma

Nyassachromis eucinostomus ♂   5/896
Thin-mouth utaka
H: Chilumba, Mwaya, Vua, Malawi.
♂: Much more colorful.   S: =
B: ♀Mb, 21d; 15–30 eggs; ESM.   F:C
T: 23–27°C, L: 12 cm, pH: >7, D: 2

Nyassachromis microcephalus ♂ 5/896
Green utaka
H: N and S parts of the lake.
♂: Much more color.   S: =
B: ♀ Mb; 21–28 d; 25–40 e; ESM.   F: C
T: 23–27°C, L: 16 cm, pH: >7, D: 2

Nimbochromis venustus ♂   1/720
Venustus
H: Sandy littoral zones.
♂: More colorful; slightly larger.   S: –
B: ♀ mouthbrooder; 120 eggs.   F: C,O
T: 25–27°C, L: <25 cm, pH: >7, D: 3

Otopharynx heterodon ♂   5/898

Otopharynx heterodon ♀   5/898

H: Monkey, Nkhata Bay, Chilumba, Likomals.
♂: Much more colorful.   S: =
B: Egg spot method; else unknown.   F: C
T: 23–27°C, L: 13 cm, pH: >7, D: 2–3

CICHLIDS

Otopharynx lithobates ♂   4/662
Sulphurhead hap
H: South: Cape Maclear, Chinyamwezi Is.
♂: Blue color.   S: =
B: ♀ Mb, 21 d; 30–60 y; agamic.   F: C
T: 24–27°C, L: 15 cm, pH: >7, D: 2

Otopharynx lithobates ♀   4/662
Sulphurhead hap

Otopharynx ovatus ♂   2/902, 5/900

H: South: medium depths near shore.
♂: Blue.   S: =
B: Unsuccessful.   F: C
T: 23–27°C, L: 20 cm, pH: >7, D: 2–3

Otopharynx tetraspilus   5/900
Four-spot otopharynx
H: Nkhudzi, Monkey Bay, Malombe, Malawi.
♂: Yellow blue; egg spots.   S: ?
B: Unsuccessful.   F: C
T: 23–27°C, L: 15 cm, pH: >7, D: 2

Petrotilapia genalutea ♂   4/672
Yellow-brown petrotilapia
H: W: Chinyamwezi to Ruarwe; E: Makanjila.
♂: More colorful; see photos.   S: –
B: ♀Mb, <28 d; 50 e; ESM in cave. F: C
T: 23–27°C, L: 16 cm, pH: >7, D: 3

Petrotilapia genalutea ♀   4/672
Yellow-brown petrotilapia

CICHLIDS

625

Petrotilapia cf. *genalutea* ♀   4/657
Yellow-brown petrotilapia
Brooding coloration.

Petrotilapia tridentiger ♂   (1/752), 5/908
Lavender mbuna
H: Rock zone.
♂: More pronounced egg spots.   S: –
B: ♀ Mb; 35 e; egg spot method.   F: L,O
T: 24–26°C, L: <25 cm, pH: >7, D: 3–4

Petrotilapia tridentiger ♀   (1/752), 5/
                                             908
Lavender mbuna

Placidochromis electra ♂   2/896
Deepwater hap
H: Likoma Island: sand substrate.
♂: More colorful; larger.   S: =
B: ♀ Mb, 18 d; 50 eggs; agamic.   F: O
T: 24–26°C, L: ♂ 16 cm, pH: >7, D: 2

Placidochromis electra ♀   2/896
Deepwater hap

Placidochromis johnstonii ♂   2/900
Johnston's hap
H: Sand littoral w/ vallisneria stands.
♂: More colorful; egg spots.   S: =
B: ♀ Mb, 18 days; 120 eggs.   F: O
T: 24–26°C, L: <17 cm, pH: >7, D: 2–3

Placidochromis milomo ♂ 2/900
Big-lip hap, super VC 10
H: Mbenji Islands: rocky littoral.
♂: More colorful. S: =
B: ♀ mouthbrooder, 20 days. F: O
T: 23–26°C, L: 15 cm, pH: ≫7, D: 2

Placidochromis milomo juv. 2/900
Big-lip hap, super VC 10

Platygnathochromis melanonotus ♂
Black-line hap 3/774
H: Widely distributed.
♂: More colorful. S: =
B: Unknown F: C
T: 24–26°C, L: 26 cm, pH: >7, D: 3

Platygnathochromis melanonotus ♀
Black-line hap 3/774

Protomelas annectens ♂ 2/892
Chunky hap
H: Moderate depths close to shore. Rare
♂: More colorful; elongated fins. S: =
B: Nature: ♀ Mb; agamic. F: L,O
T: 24–26°C, L: 20 cm, pH: >7, D: 2

Protomelas fenestratus t.♂, b.♀ 2/898
Fenestratus
H: Maleri Islands: rock littoral: at 3–6 m.
♂: More colorful. S: =
B: ♀ Mb, 20 days; agamic. F: C
T: 22–26°C, L: 14 cm, pH: >7, D: 2

Protomelas similis ♂   3/780
Gorgeous hap
H: Widely distributed: sand littoral: at 10 m.
♀: Silver.   S: =
B: ♀ Mb; egg spot method; agamic. F: O
T: 24–26°C, L: 12 cm, pH: >7, D: 2–3

Protomelas spilopterus ♂   5/910

H: Lakewide distribution.
♂: More colorful.   S: =
B: ♀ Mb; egg spot method; agamic. F:O
T: 24–26°C, L: <25 cm, pH: >7, D: 3–4

Protomelas spilopterus ♀   5/910

Protomelas taeniolatus ♂   3/782,
Spindle hap   (2/895)
H: Widely distributed: rock substrates.
♂: More colorful.   S: =
B: ♀ Mb, 21 d; 20–40 y; agamic.   F: O
T: 24–26°C, L: 12 cm, pH: >7, D: 2–3

Protomelas taeniolatus ♀   3/782,
Spindle hap   (2/895)

Protomelas taeniolatus var. ♂   3/782,
Spindle hap   (2/895)

Pseudotropheus aurora ♂   1/756
Aurora mbuna

H: Likoma Island: sand/rock transition zone.
♂: More colorful; egg spots.   S: –
B: ♀ Mb, <21 d; <70 e; ESM.   F: C,O
T: 24–26°C, L: 11 cm, pH: >7, D: 1–2

Pseudotropheus aurora ♀   1/756
Aurora mbuna

Pseudotropheus barlowi ♂   4/676

H: S part: Mbenji Islands, Maleri Islands,...
♀: Monotone gray-brown.   S: –
B: ♀ Mb <28 d; 20–40y; ESM; aga.   F:C,O
T: 24–26°C, L: 15 cm, pH: >7, D: 3

Pseudotropheus callainos ♂   5/914
Cobalt blue

H: NW coast: broadly distributed.
♂: More pronounced egg spots.   S: =
B: ♀ Mb, 21d; 20–40y; ESM; agamic. F:O
T: 24–26°C, L: 10 cm, pH: >7, D: 2

Pseudotropheus callainos ♂   5/914
Cobalt blue
White morph.

Pseudotropheus crabro ♀?   3/852
Pseudotropheus "chameleo"

H: Mbenji Islands: rock and mixed bottoms.
♂: More egg spots; black.   S: –
B: ♀ Mb, <24 d; 20–60y; ESM; aga.   F:O
T: 24–26°C, L: 15 cm, pH: >7, D: 2–3

CICHLIDS

629

Pseudotropheus elegans ♂   5/916
Elegans
H: Lakewide distribution: also over sand.
♂: Adults have longer D and A fins.   S: =
B: ♀ Mb, 21d; 20–40y; ESM; agamic. F:O
T: 24–26°C, L: 10–15 cm, pH: >7, D: 2

Pseudotropheus elegans ♀   5/916
Elegans

Pseudotropheus elongatus   1/756
Slender mbuna
H: Rock zone.
♂: Egg spots; larger.   S: –
B: ♀ Mb, <37 e; ESM.   F: L,O
T: 22–25°C, L: 13 cm, pH: ≫7, D: 2–3

Pseudotropheus estherae t.♂   (1/763)
Red zebra   5/918
H: Mozambique coast: Metangula.
♂: Blue. ♀: Brownish.   S: =
B: ♀ Mb, 21 days; 20–40 y; ESM.   F: O
T: 24–27°C, L: <14 cm, pH: >7, D: 2–3

Pseudotropheus estherae ♂   (1/763)
Red zebra   5/918

Pseudotropheus estherae ♀   (1/763)
Red zebra   5/918

Pseudotropheus estherae ♂ (1/763)
Red zebra 5/918

Pseudotropheus estherae ♂ 1/763

Pseudotropheus estherae ♀ 1/763

Pseudotropheus fainzilberi ♂ 1/758

H: NE coast: town of Makonde.
♂: More colorful; egg spots. S: –
B: ♀ Mb, <60 eggs; ESM. F: C,O
T: 22–26°C, L: 13 cm, pH: >7, D: 2

Pseudotropheus flavus ♂ 4/676

H: Chinyankwazi Island: rock zone.
♂: More intensely color. S: =
B: ♀ Mb; 20–30 y; agamic; ESM. F: C
T: 23–27°C, L: 9 cm, pH: >7, D: 2

Pseudotropheus greshakei ♂ 3/855
Red top ice blue

H: Makokola (S arm of the lake).
♀: Monochrome red-brown. S: –
B: ♀ Mb; agamic; ESM. F: C,O
T: 24–26°C, L: >10 cm, pH: >7, D: 2

CICHLIDS

Pseudotropheus hajomaylandi ♂ 3/856

H: Chisumulu Island: sand at 10–30 m.
♀: Gray-blue; dark crossbands.   S: –
B: ♀ Mb, <25 days; agamic.   F: O
T: 24–26°C, L: <15 cm, pH: >7, D: 2–3

Pseudotropheus heteropictus ♂
(2/972) 5/921

H: Chisumulu Island. Not Tumbi Island.
♀: Yellow-orange.   S: –
B: ♀ Mb, 14 days; 25–30 eggs.   F: O
T: 24–27°C, L: 10 cm, pH: >7, D: 2–3

Pseudotropheus lanisticola ♀   1/758
Snail-shell mbuna

H: Sandy bottoms.
♂: Egg spots.   S: =
B: ♀ Mb; <60e; egg spot method. F: O
T: 23–25°C, L: 7 cm, pH: ≫7, D: 2

Pseudotropheus livingstonii ♂   2/972
Livingston's mbuna

H: Sandy coastal regions.
♂: More colorful; egg spots.   S: =
B: ♀Mb <21d; <60 e; ESM; agamic. F: O
T: 22–26°C, L: 15 cm, pH: ≫7, D: 2

Pseudotropheus lombardoi ♂   2/974
Kennyi mbuna

H: Mbenji Islands: rubble & rock littoral.
♂: Egg spots; see photos.   S: –
B: ♀ Mb, <24d; <50e; ESM; agamic. F: O
T: 24–26°C, L: 15 cm, pH: >7, D: 2–3

Pseudotropheus lombardoi ♀   2/974
Kennyi mbuna

Pseudotropheus macrophthalmus 1/760
Large-eyed mbuna
H: Rocky littoral.
♂: More pronounced egg spots.   S: =
B: ♀ Mb; 40–70 e; ESM.   F: L,O
T: 23–25°C, L: 15 cm, pH: ≫7, D: 2

Pseudotropheus microstoma ♂   2/974
Small-mouthed tropheops
H: Rubble and rock littoral.
♂: More colorful; egg spots.   S: –
B: ♀ Mb; <20 d; ESM; agamic.   F: O
T: 24–26°C, L: 13 cm, pH: ≫7, D: 2

Pseudotropheus saulosi ♂   4/678

Pseudotropheus saulosi ♀   4/678

H: Chisumulu Island.
SD: See photos.   S: –
B: ♀ Mb; 30 y; agamic; ESM.   F: C
T: 23–27°C, L: <10 cm, pH: >7, D: 2

Pseudotropheus socolofi ♂   2/976
Eduard's mbuna
H: E coast: upper rubble & rock littoral.
♂: Egg spots; longer ventral fins. S: =
B: ♀ Mb, 21 d; 20–50 e; ESM.   F: C,O
T: 24–26°C, L: 12 cm, pH: >7, D: 2–3

Pseudotropheus sp. "tropheops Chilumba"
♂   5/922

CICHLIDS

633

Pseudotropheus sp. "tropheops Chilumba"
♀
5/922

Pseudotropheus tropheops ♂ (1/760)
Tropheops 5/924
H: South: rock littoral.
♂: Blue/yellow. ♂: Gray/brown. S: =
B: ♀ Mb, 40 y; egg spot method. F: O
T: 24–27°C, L: 13 cm, pH: >7, D: 2–3

Pseudotropheus "tropheops lilac Mumbo"
(1/760) 5/924

Pseudotropheus "tropheops Mauve"
(1/760) 5/924

Pseudotropheus "tropheops red fin"
(1/760) 5/924

Pseudotropheus tropheops gracilior ♂
5/923
H: Thumbi West and Domwe Island.
♀: Shiny yellow-orange. S: =
B: Not easy; ♀ Mb; ESM. F: C
T: 23–27°C, L: 10 cm, pH: >7, D: 2

Pseudotropheus williamsi ♂ 3/856
William's mbuna
H: Rocky littoral.
♀: Plain gray. S: =
B: ♀ Mb; ESM; agamic. F: C,O
T: 24–26°C, L: 11 cm, pH: >7, D: 2–3

Pseudotropheus xanstomachus ♂ 5/926
Zebra yellow throat Maleri
H: W coast: Maleri Islands.
♂: Blue. ♀: Brownish. S: =
B: ♀ Mb, 21 d; 20–40 y; ESM. F: L,O
T: 24–26°C, L: 13 cm, pH: >7, D: 2

Pseudotropheus xanstomachus 5/926
Yellow chin

Pseudotropheus xanstomachus 5/926
Zebra yellow throat Maleri b.♂, f.♀

Pseudotropheus zebra ♂ 1/762
False zebra mbuna, Nyassa blue cichlid
H: Rocky littoral.
♂: Egg spots. S: –
B: ♀ Mb; <60 eggs; ESM. F: L,O
T: 23–25°C, L: 13 cm, pH: ≫7, D: 1–2

Rhamphochromis esox 5/934
Lake Malawi pike cichlid
H: Throughout the lake.
SD: Unknown. S: =
B: ♀ Mb; unsuccessful. F: C
T: 24–27°C, L: 30–40 cm, pH: >7, D: 4

CICHLIDS

635

Rhamphochromis leptosoma juv. 5/936
Slender Lake Malawi pike cichlid
H: Throughout the lake.
♂: Bluish. ♂: Silver-gray.   S: –
B: Unsuccessful; ♀ Mb.   F: C!
T: 23–27°C, L: 40 cm, pH: >7, D: 4

Rhamphochromis macrophthalmus
Malawi torpedo   5/936
H: Southern section of the lake.
♂: Slightly more colorful?   S: –
B: Unsuccessful; ♀ Mb.   F: C
T: 20–25°C, L: 27 cm, pH: >7, D: 4

Sciaenochromis ahli ♂   3/768
Electric blue hap
H: Various rocky coasts.
♂: Bright blue when sexually active. S: =
B: Maternal mouthbrooder.   F: C
T: 24–26°C, L: 20 cm, pH: >7, D: 3

Sciaenochromis fryeri ♂   5/944

H: Likoma Island: at 5–10 m depth.
♂: Bright blue when sexually active. S: =
B: ♀ Mb, 21 d; 20–50 y; ESM.   F: O
T: 24–26°C, L: <15 cm, pH: >7, D: 2–3

Sciaenochromis gracilis ♂   5/946

Sciaenochromis gracilis ♀   5/946

H: Southern section.
♂: Iridescent blue; egg spots.   S: =
B: Unsuccessful. ♀Mb? Agamic.   F: C
T: 24–26°C, L: 20 cm, pH: >7, D: 3

CICHLIDS

Sciaenochromis psammophilis ♂ 5/946
Electric blue Kande Island
H: NW coast and Kande Island.
♂: Bright blue; egg spots.　　　　S: =
B: ♀ Mb; 21 d; 20–50 y; agamic.　F: O
T: 24–26°C, L: 15 cm, pH: >7, D: 3

Stigmatochromis modestus ♂　　5/950

H: Widely distributed.
♂: More colorful.　　　　　　　S: =
B: ♀Mb, 21d; 30–60y; ESM; agamic.　F:C
T: 24–26°C, L: 16 cm, pH: >7, D: 2–3

Stigmatochromis modestus ♀　　5/950

Stigmatochromis pholidophorus　5/952
Candle hap
H: Widely distributed.
♂: More color; ♀ also w/ egg spots.　S:=
B: ♀Mb, 21d; 30–60y; ESM; agamic.　F:C
T: 24–26°C, L: 17 cm, pH: >7, D: 3

Stigmatochromis pholidophorus ♂ 5/952
Candle hap

Trematocranus placodon ♂　　2/904
Snail-crusher hap
H: Sand bottoms and vallisneria stands.
♂: More colorful; slightly larger.　　S: =
B: ♀ Mb, <100 young; agamic.　　F: O
T: 24–26°C, L: 25 cm, pH: >7, D: 2

CICHLIDS

Trematocromis microstoma ♂   5/970
Small-mouth hap
H: South: Namalenji Island.
♂: More colorful; egg spots.   S: =
B: ♀ Mb; agamic. No reports.   F: C
T: 24–26°C, L: 20–25 cm, pH: >7, D: 3

Tyrannochromis macrostoma ♂   4/700
Big-mouth hap
H: Widely distrib.: Monkey Bay: rock zone.
♂: Much more colorful; see photos.   S: =
B: ♀ Mb; long care after release.   F: C
T: 23–27°C, L: 30 cm, pH: >7, D: 3

Tyrannochromis macrostoma ♀   4/700
Big-mouth hap

Tyrannochromis nigriventer ♂   5/972

H: Widely distr.: among, rocks, vallisneria.
♂: Blue; egg spots; see photos.   S: =
B: ♀ Mb, 21 days; >100 young.   F: C
T: 24–26°C, L: <30 cm, pH: >7, D: 3–4

Tyrannochromis nigriventer ♂   5/972

Tyrannochromis nigriventer ♀   5/972

CICHLIDS

638

Physical Characteristics

Lake Tanganyika is 650 km long, up to 80 km wide in parts, and located 773 m above sea level. With a surface area of 33000 km², it is the second largest lake of Africa and the sixth largest lake in the world. It is part of the African Rift Valley system and has an estimated age of 2 to 4 million years (PITCHER and HART, 1995), although some place its age at 11 to 30 million years (KONINGS, 1988). Like Lake Malawi, Lake Tanganyika was also exposed to extreme variations in water level over the course of its evolution. For example, there was a time when the lake was subdivided into three smaller lakes. Today it has a depth of 1470 m at its deepest point—about 700 m below sea level—and an average depth of 570 m. Visibility under water can exceed 20 m, making this one of the clearest freshwater habitats of the world.

Additional parameters:
pH: 8.6–9.2
Conductivity: 550–600 µS
Temperature: 23.5°–27°C

Bordering States:

Lake Tanganyika is bordered by Zaïre in the west, Zambia in the south, Tanzania in the east, and Burundi in the northeast.

Points of Reference

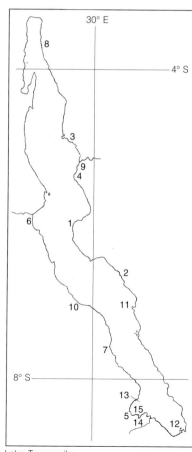

Lake Tanganyika.

Ichthyological Characteristics

Fourteen fish families with a total of 240 species in 79 genera can be found in Lake Tanganyika (PITCHER and HART, 1995).

- Non-cichlids: 42 genera (8 endemic) and 75 species (28 endemic).
- Cichlids: 37 genera (33 endemic) and 165 species (164 endemic).

As in Lake Malawi, these numbers convey the dominance of cichlids in Lake Tanganyika. The high mineral concentration of the lake indirectly favors secondary freshwater fishes like cichlids, since these are most likely to have a high tolerance for salts. At the same time, an ecological barrier to the relatively mineral-poor biotopes outside the lake is present, restricting the populations from interchanging genetic information. The result is a high number of endemic species and genera.

Below 200 depth begins the hypolimnion, the anaerobic zone of the lake. It has a relatively constant temperature of 23.3°C, but since the water is void of oxygen, no fishes inhabit the zone. Due to the proximity of the lake to the equatorial line, seasonal temperature fluctuations are minimal and there is no turnover as is found in temperate lakes.

Most species in the lake belong to the genera *Lamprologus* and *Neolamprologus*. *Tropheus moorii* has the most color morphs of any given species of the lake (see pp. 667 ff.).

Secondary sexual differences are slight; frequently only a detailed study of the genital papilla identifies the sex. The reproductive strategies are numerous:

- Mouthbrooders: Most of the mouthbrooders of Lake Tanganyika are maternal mouthbrooders, but there are several species in which both parents brood the spawn, e.g., *Xenotilapia* spp. The presence of egg spots is not nearly as prevalent among cichlids of Lake Tanganyika as it is among those of Lake Malawi. Species among the genera *Cyathopharynx* and *Ophthalmotilapia* practice a modified egg spot method: Males have extremely elongated ventral fins with tips the shape and color of eggs. Their function is analogous to that of the egg spots on the anal fin. The female snaps at the decoys close to the male's genital papilla thinking they are eggs. By doing so, sperm enters her mouth and fertilizes the eggs within.
- Cave spawners: Among the species spawning in hiding places, we find "normal" cave spawners and several species that have specialized into shell spawners, using gastropod shells as their spawning substrates. Only the female fits in the shell to lay her eggs. The male releases his sperm at the shell's entrance. As the female emerges from the shell, the water replacing her rushes in, carrying the spermatozoa to the eggs adhered inside.
- Open spawners: This form of reproduction is the least common of the three. Its best-known representative is the largest cichlid in the world, *Boulengerochromis microlepis*.

Lake Tanganyikan cichlids leave no food niche unexploited. *Altolamprologus* species are especially deep-bodied and narrow to gain better access to rock crevices.

Altolamprologus calvus   2/926
Pearly lamprologus, pearly compressiceps
H: Sumbu Natl. Park: rubble/rock littoral.
♂: Pointed V, D, and A fins.   S: =
B: Cave spawner; >200 e; P-M fam.   F: C
T: 23–25°C, L: 15 cm, pH: 7, D: 3

Altolamprologus calvus juv.   2/926
Pearly lamprologus, pearly compressiceps

Altolamprologus compressiceps   1/732
Compressiceps
H: Stony/rocky substrate.
SD: Unknown.   S: =
B: Cave sp.; <300 e; Pch-M fam?   F: C
T: 23–25°C, L: 15 cm, pH: 7, D: 3

Asprotilapia leptura   3/690

H: Southern section: rock zone.
SD: Unknown.   S: =
B: ♀♂ Mb ,13 d (very short); N fam. F: O
T: 24–26°C, L: 11 cm, pH: >7, D: 2–3

Aulonocranus dewindti   3/707
Gold-striped aulonocranus
H: Lakewide: transition sand/rock littoral.
♂: Blue and yellow horizontal stripes. S: =
B: ♀ Mb; unsuccessful.   F: C
T: 24–26°C, L: 11 cm, pH: >7, D: 3–4

Benthochromis tricoti ♂   4/584

H: Huge schools in open waters.
♂: Long fins; more colorful.   S: =
B: ♀ Mb; 2–15 young; no reports.   F: C
T: 23–25°C, L: 20 cm, pH: >7, D: 4

CICHLIDS

Boulengerochromis microlepis   3/710
Giant Tanganyika cichlid
H: Throughout the lake.
♂: Larger; more colorful.   S: –
B: Nat.: substrate spawner; 10000 e. F:C
T: 24–26°C, L: 80 cm, pH: ≫7, D: 3

Callochromis macrops ♂   3/712
Large-eyed mouthbrooder
H: S section: sand/rock; shallow water.
♂: More colorful.   S: =
B: ♀ Mb, 20 d; agamic.   F: O
T: 24–26°C, L: 15 cm, pH: >7, D: 2–3

Callochromis melanostigma ♂   3/712
Blackspot callochromis
H: Only in the northernmost section.
♂: More colorful.   S: =
B: ♀ Mb, 19 days; agamic.   F: O
T: 24–26°C, L: 15 cm, pH: >7, D: 3

Callochromis pleurospilus ♂   3/714
Redspot callochromis
H: Sand littoral & sand/rock littoral.
♂: More colorful fringe on anal fin.   S: –
B: ♀Mb, 21d; 20–30y; aga.; M fam.   F:O
T: 23–28°C, L: 15 cm, pH: >7, D: 2–3

Cardiopharynx schoutedeni   4/584
Blue-striped cardio
H: Sand and sand/rock littoral: 3–60 m.
♂: More colorful.   S: =
B: Details unknown; mouthbrooder.   F: C
T: 23–28°C, L: 16 cm, pH: >7, D: 3

Chalinochromis brichardi ♂   2/852

H: Not central E coast: rocky littoral: 2–10 m.
♂: Defined D spot; frontal hump.   S: =
B: Rare. Cs; <120 e; nuclear fam.   F: C
T: 24–27°C, L: <15 cm, pH: >7, D: 2–3

Chalinochromis sp. *"bifrenatus"*　3/716
(Ikola)
H: Rocky littoral.
♂: Larger; with frontal hump.　　S: =
B: Cave sp.; 4–50 e; close N fam.　F: C
T: 24–28°C, L: 11 cm, pH: ≫7, D: 2–3

Ctenochromis benthicola ♂　　5/806
Orange hap
H: Burundi, Zaïre, Tanzania: rock zone.
♀: Brownish yellow to red.　　S: –
B: ♀ Mb, 21 d; 100 e; & 28 d care.　F:O
T: 23–27°C, L: 17 cm, pH: >7, D: 2

Ctenochromis horei ♀　　3/758
Red-spotted mouthbrooder, spothead hap
H: Shallow water: sand and vegetation.
♀: Rather gray.　　　　S: –
B: Not difficult? ♀ Mb.　　F: O
T: 24–26°C, L: 18 cm, pH: >7, D: 3–4

Cunningtonia longiventralis ♂　　5/806

H: Southern section; in several morphs.
♂: More colorful; longer ventral fins.　S: =
B: ♀ Mb; builds nest in the sand.　F: O
T: 24–28°C, L: 15 cm, pH: >7, D: 3

Cyathopharynx furcifer ♂　　2/888
Furcifer
H: Sand littoral & transition to rocky littoral.
♂: More colorful; very long ventrals.　S: =
B: ♀ Mb. 21d; 25 e; maternal fam.　F: O
T: 24–26°C, L: 20 cm, pH: ≫7, D: 3

Cyathopharynx furcifer ♂　　3/760
Furcifer "Karilani"
H: Morph from Tanzania.
♂: More colorful; very long V fins.　S: =
B: ♀ Mb, 21d; 25 e; maternal fam.　F: C,O
T: 24–26°C, L: 20 cm, pH: ≫7, D: 3

643

Cyathopharynx furcifer ♂ 3/760
Furcifer
Spawning coloration (see photo on p. 3/781).

Cyphotilapia frontosa 1/700
Frontosa
H: Sublittoral benthos: rock sub.: 20–30 m.
♂: Slightly larger hump; longer.　S: =
B: ♀ Mb; 50 e; <42 d brood care.　F: C
T: 24–26°C, L: 35 cm, pH: >7, D: 4

Cyprichromis leptosoma ♂ 1/700
Bright-finned slender cichlid
H: Southern end: Kigoma.
♂: Much more colorful.　S: =
B: ♀ mouthbrooder, 21 days.　F: C,O
T: 23–25°C, L: 14 cm, pH: >7, D: 2–3

Cyprichromis microlepidotus 2/890
Small-scaled slender cichlid
H: Rock zone w/ many vertical crevices.
♂: Darker; dark throat when spawn.　S: =
B: ♀ Mb <29 d; 25e; maternal fam. F: C
T: 23–25°C, L: 14 cm, pH: >7, D: 3

Cyprichromis microlepidotus ♂ 3/760
Small-scaled slender cichlid (morph)
H: Open waters of the rock littoral.
♀: Darker; more colorful caudal fin.　S: =
B: ♀Mb <21d; 5–10y; agamic; Mfam. F: C
T: 23–28°C, L: 11 cm, pH: >7, D: 4

Cyprichromis nigripinnis ♂ 2/892
Black-finned slender cichlid
H: Within schools of *C. microlepidotus*.
♂: Yellow anal fin; no pinstripes.　S: =
B: ♀ Mb; maternal family.　F: C
T: 23–25°C, L: 10 cm, pH: >7, D: 3

Cyprichromis pavo ♂   4/614

Cyprichromis pavo ♀   4/614

H: SW section: near rocks: >20 m depth.
♂: More colorful; see photos.   S: =
B: ♀ Mb, <30 d; agamic; M fam.   F: O
T: 24–28°C, L: 12 cm, pH: ≫7, D: 3

Ectodus descampsi ♂   3/762
Descamp's strange-tooth
H: Sand littoral: in open water.
♀: Dorsal spot smaller?   S: =
B: ♀ Mb; rarely successsful.   F: O
T: 24–26°C, L: 10 cm, pH: >7, D: 2

Enantiopus melanogenys   3/762
Black-chinned xenotilapia
H: Sand littoral to 40 m depth.
♂: More colorful.   S: =
B: ♀ Mb, 20 d; aga.; maternal fam.   F: O
T: 24–26°C, L: 16 cm, pH: >7, D: 4

Enantiopus ochrogenys   3/765
Red-striped xenotilapia
H: Sandy littoral.
♂: More colorful; longer dorsal fin. S: =
B: ♀ Mb; maternal family.   F: O
T: 24–26°C, L: 11 cm, pH: >7, D: 3–4

Eretmodus cyanostictus   1/702
Striped goby cichlid
H: The shallow rubble littoral.
♂: Somewhat longer ventral fins.   S: –
B: ♀♂ Mb; 25 e; nuclear family.   F: C
T: 24–26°C, L: 8 cm, pH: ≫7, D: 3

CICHLIDS

645

Gnathochromis pfefferi WC   3/768
Tanganyika hap
H: Zambia: Ndole Bay.
♂: More colorful.   S: –
B: ♀ Mb, 21 d; maternal family.   F: C,O
T: 24–26°C, L: 12 cm, pH: >7, D: 2–3

Gnathochromis permaxilaris ♂   5/818
H: 15–215 m depth. At least 2 color morphs.
♂: Slightly larger.   S: +
B: ♀♂ Mb in cave, 12 d; 60 young.   F: C,O
T: 24–26°C, L: 20–25 cm, pH: >7, D: 3

Grammatotria lemairii   5/820
Lemaire's odd-tooth
H: Entire lake: sand zone.
♂: Spotted when courting.   S: =
B: ♀ Mb, 26 days; 40 eggs.   F: C
T: 23–27°C, L: 25 cm, pH: >7, D: 2

Haplotaxodon microlepis   3/786
Bulldog cichlid
H: Rocky littoral.
♂: Larger; longer fin tips.   S: =
B: Mouthbrooder?   F: C
T: 23–28°C, L: 25 cm, pH: >7, D: 3

Julidochromis dickfeldi   1/726
Dickfeld's julie, brown julie
H: Zambia: rubble/rocky littoral transition.
♂: Probably smaller?   S: =
B: Cave spawner; 300 e; N fam.   F: C,O
T: 22–25°C, L: 8 cm, pH: ≫7, D: 2

Julidochromis marlieri   1/726
Marlier's julie
H: Rocky littoral.
♂: Usually smaller; nuchal hump.   S: =
B: Cave spawner; 100 e; N fam.   F: C,O
T: 22–25°C, L: <15 cm, pH: ≫7, D: 2

CICHLIDS

Julidochromis ornatus 1/726
Yellow julie, ornate julie, southern julie
H: Rocky littoral.
♂: Usually smaller S: –
B: Cave spawner; <100 e; N fam. F: C,O
T: 22–24°C, L: 8 cm, pH: ≫7, D: 2

Julidochromis regani 1/728
Striped julie, four-stripe julie
H: Rocky littoral.
♂: Smaller; pointed gen. papilla. S: =
B: Cave spawner; 300 e; N fam. F: C,O
T: 22–25°C, L: <30 cm, pH: ≫7, D: 2

Julidochromis transcriptus 1/728
Masked julie, black and white julie
H: Rocky littoral.
♂: Genital papilla longer. S: –
B: Cave spawner; 30 e; N fam. F: C,O
T: 22–25°C, L: 7 cm, pH: ≫7, D: 2

Lamprologus callipterus ♂ 3/796
Lamprologus "tempo," callipterus
H: Rubble and rocky littoral and transitional zones to the sandy littoral. Gastropod shells (shell-dweller).

Lamprologus callipterus ♀ 3/796
Lamprologus "tempo", callipterus

♂: About 150% larger. S: –
B: Cave spawner: snail shells. F: C
T: 23–26°C, L: ♂ 15 cm, pH: >7, D: 2

Lamprologus lemairii ♂ 2/934
Lemaire's lamprologus
H: Littoral zone lakewide.
SD: None. S: –
B: Nat.: cave spawner; Pch-M fam? F: C!
T: 23–26°C, L: 24 cm, pH: >7, D: 3

Lamprologus meleagris　　　　5/862

H: Close to Bwasse, S of Moba.
SD: None.　　　　　　　　　　　　S: =
B: Cs: snail shell. <20 e; maternal f.　F: O
T: 24–28°C, L: 7 cm, pH: >7, D: 3

Lamprologus ocellatus ♂　　　　2/942
Ocellated shell-dweller

H: Broadly distributed: sand at 5–30 m.
♂: Longer ventral fins?　　　　　S: –
B: Cs: snail shell. P-M fam.　　　F: C
T: 23–25°C, L: ♂ 6 cm, pH: >7, D: 3–4

Lamprologus ornatipinnis　　　2/944
Ornate shell-dweller

H: Widely distrib.: sand littoral at 0–100 m.
♂: 3 cm larger.　　　　　　　　　S: =
B: Cs: snail shell. Pch-M fam?　　F: O
T: 24–26°C, L: ♂ 8 cm, pH: >7, D: 4

Lamprologus signatus ♂　　　　4/632

H: Moba (Zaïre), Camerone Bay (Zambia).
♂: 2 cm larger; striations.　　　　S: =
B: Cave spawner: snail shell.　　　F: O
T: 24–28°C, L: ♂ 6 cm, pH: >7, D: 3

Lamprologus signatus ♀　　　　4/632

Lamprologus speciosus ♂　　　　4/630

H: Zaïre: sand substrates w/ snail shells.
♂: Slightly larger.　　　　　　　　S: +
B: Cave spawner: snail shell.　　　F: C
T: 23–27°C, L: 5 cm, pH: >7, D: 2

CICHLIDS

Lamprologus speciosus ♀   4/630

Lepidiolamprologus attenuatus   4/634
Marbled lamprologus
H: Rubble/sand transition zone.
♂: Somewhat larger and slimmer.   S: –
B: Cave sp.; 40 e; nuclear family.   F: C
T: 23–27°C, L: 14 cm, pH: >7, D: 2

Lepidiolamprologus cunningtoni 2/928

H: Very common fish of the littoral zone.
♂: Longer ventral fins?   S: –
B: Cs? Paternal-maternal fam?   F: C,O
T: 23–26°C, L: 15 cm, pH: >7, D: 3

Lepidiolamprologus cunningtoni 3/811
Black lamprologus
H: Sandy areas.
♂: Larger by 15 cm.   S: –
B: Nat.: among and under stones. F: O
T: 24–27°C, L: ♂ 25 cm, pH: >7, D: 2–3

Lepidiolamprologus elongatus juv. 2/928
Elongate lamprologus
H: Widely distributed: rocky littoral.
♂: Longer ventral fins?   S: –
B: Cs; >500 e; nuclear family.   F: C!
T: 23–25°C, L: 20 cm, pH: ≫7, D: 3–4

Lepidiolamprologus elongatus   4/636
Elongate lamprologus   adult
H: Widely distributed: rocky littoral.
♂: Larger.   S: –
B: Cs; >500 e; nuclear family.   F: C!
T: 23–27°C, L: 30 cm, pH: >7, D: 2

Lepidiolamprologus kendalli ♂ 4/634

H: Zambia: Mutondwe Island: rocky littoral.
♂: Slightly larger. S: =
B: Cave sp.; >40 e; nuclear family. F: C
T: 23–27°C, L: 16 cm, pH: >7, D: 2

Lepidiolamprologus nkambae 2/942

H: Nkamba Bay: rocky littoral.
SD: None. S: –
B: There are no reports. F: C!
T: 23–25°C, L: 14 cm, pH: ≫7, D: 3–4

Lepidiolamprologus profundicola 3/820
Deep-water lamprologus

H: Rock and rubble zone.
SD: Not described. S: –
B: There are no breeding reports. F: C
T: 24–26°C, L: 30 cm, pH: >7, D: 3

Lestradea perspicax 3/800

H: Littoral zone.
♂: Dorsal fin has 2 longitudinal lines. S: =
B: Unsuccessful; mouthbrooder. F: O
T: 25°C, L: 12 cm, pH: >7, D: 2

Limnochromis auritus 2/948
Auritus

H: Sublittoral sandy benthos: 30–50 m.
♂: Longer ventral fins? S: =
B: ♀♂ Mb; <300 eggs. F: C,O
T: 24–26°C, L: 14 cm, pH: >7, D: 2

Lobochilotes labiatus t. ♂ 1/738
Zebra cichlid

H: Rocky littoral.
♂: Egg spots. S: –
B: Mb? Maternal family? F: C,O
T: 24–27°C, L: 37 cm, pH: >7, D: 2–3

Microdontochromis tenuidentatus 4/638

H: West coast: Zaïre.
SD: Unknown.   **S:** ?
B: Unsuccessful. Mouthbrooder?   **F:** O
T: 24–28°C, **L:** 8 cm, **pH:** >7, **D:** 3

Neolamprologus bifasciatus ♂   4/642
Two-striped lamprologus

H: Rock hab. >30 m; near small caves.
♂: Larger.   **S:** =
B: Cs; <40 e; paternal-maternal fam. **F:** O
T: 24–28°C, **L:** 10 cm, **pH:** ≫7, **D:** 3

Neolamprologus bifasciatus ♀   4/642
Two-striped lamprologus

Neolamprologus boulengeri   3/808
Boulenger's shell-dweller
H: Sand w/ snail shells.
♂: 2 cm larger.   **S:** =
B: Cs; snail shell; 60 e; P-M fam. **F:** O
T: 24–26°C, **L:** ♂7 cm, **pH:** >7, **D:** 3

Neolamprologus brevis t.♂, b.♀ 2/922
Brevis shell-dweller
H: Mud/sand bottom; snail shells.
♂: Larger; more colorful; see photo. **S:** =
B: Snail shell; <30 e; Pch-M/M fam. **F:**C
T: 23–25°C, **L:** ♂ 6 cm, **pH:** >7, **D:** 3–4

Neolamprologus brevis ♂   2/922
Brevis shell-dweller

Neolamprologus brichardi　　1/732
Fairy cichlid, lyretail lamprologus, brichardi
H: Rocky littoral.
♂: Longer dorsal & caudal fin tips.　S: =
B: Cs; 200 e; nuclear family.　F: C,O
T: 22–25°C, L: 10 cm, pH: >7, D: 2

Neolamprologus buescheri　　3/808
Striped lamprologus
H: Southern section.
SD: None visible.　S: =
B: Cs; 200 e; paternal-maternal fam.　F: O
T: 24–28°C, L: 7 cm, pH: >7, D: 3

Neolamprologus caudopunctatus　3/812
H: Southern section.
♂: 1 cm larger.　S: =
B: Unsuccessful; cave spawner.　F: C,O
T: 23–25°C, L: ♂ 7 cm, pH: >7, D: 3

Neolamprologus christyi　　3/812
H: Above sand substrates.
SD: Unknown.　S: –
B: Cs; <150 e; nuclear family.　F: C
T: 23–28°C, L: 12 cm, pH: >7, D: 2–3

Neolamprologus cylindricus　　3/814
H: SE coast: rocky littoral.
♂: Slightly larger.　S: –
B: Cs; 50–200 e; nuclear family.　F: C
T: 23–28°C, L: 12 cm, pH: >7, D: 2

Neolamprologus falcicula juv.　5/888
Long-fin lamprologus
H: N coast: rock/sand: >10 m depth.
SD: Only the genital papilla.　S: –
B: Cs w/ intense brood care.　F: O
T: 23–27°C, L: 8 cm, pH: ≫7, D: 2

Neolamprologus falcicula adult 5/888
Long-fin lamprologus

Neolamprologus furcifer 2/932
Fork-tailed lamprologus
H: Lakewide: rubble and rocky littoral.
♂: Nuchal hump develops w/ age. S: –
B: Cs; 50 eggs; nuclear family. F: C
T: 23–25°C, L: 15 cm, pH: >7, D: 3

Neolamprologus fasciatus 2/930
Barred lamprologus
H: Rubble and rocky littoral: 2–5 m.
SD: None. S: =
B: Cave spawner; N or Pch-M fam? F: C
T: 23–25°C, L: 14 cm, pH: >7, D: 2–3

Neolamprologus gracilis 5/891
Graceful lamprologus
H: SW coast: Moba: 3–40 m depth.
SD: Only the genital papilla. S: +
B: Cave spawner. F: O
T: 24–28°C, L: 9 cm, pH: ≫7, D: 2

Neolamprologus hecqui ♂ 5/892
Hecq's shell-dweller
H: Ndole Bay: sand zone.
♂: Larger. S: +
B: Snail shell; P-M fam. F: O
T: 23–27°C, L: 8 cm, pH: >7, D: 2

Neolamprologus kungweensis ♂ 3/814
Ocellated shell-dweller
H: Maswa.
♂: 3 cm larger. S: =
B: Snail shell? No reports. F: C,O
T: 24–26°C, L: ♂ 7 cm, pH: >7, D: 2–3

CICHLIDS

653

Neolamprologus kungweensis ♀ 3/814
Ocellated shell-dweller

Neolamprologus leleupi 1/734
Lemon cichlid
H: Rocky littoral.
♂: Massive head; slightly larger.　S: =
B: Cs; <150 eggs; nuclear family.　F: C
T: 24–26°C, L: 10 cm, pH: >7, D: 3–4

Neolamprologus leloupi ♂ 4/644
Pearlscale lamprologus
H: Zaïre, Zambia, Tanzania: rubble zone.
♂: Slightly slimmer.　S: +
B: Cs, <30 e; close nuclear family.　F: C
T: 23–27°C, L: 6 cm, pH: >7, D: 2

Neolamprologus longior 2/932
Elongated lemon cichlid
H: E shore: central to lower rocky littoral.
♂: Elongated fins.　S: =
B: Cs; <200 e; P-M fam.　F: C
T: 24–26°C, L: 10 cm, pH: >7, D: 3

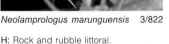

Neolamprologus marunguensis 3/822

H: Rock and rubble littoral.
SD: Virtually indiscernible.　S: =
B: Cs; 10 e (short cycle); N fam.　F: C
T: 24–26°C, L: 30 cm, pH: >7, D: 3

Neolamprologus marunguensis ♂ 4/644

H: Zaïre: S of Kapampa: rubble littoral.
♂: Longer and slimmer.　S: =
B: Cs; 40 e; close pair bond; N fam.　F: C
T: 23–27°C, L: 7 cm, pH: >7, D: 2

CICHLIDS

Neolamprologus meeli ♂ 2/934
Meeli shell-dweller
H: In zones with empty snail shells.
♂: Almost twice as large. **S:** =
B: Cs; paternal-maternal family. **F:** C
T: 23–25°C, **L:** ♂ 7 cm, **pH:** >7, **D:** 3

Neolamprologus modestus 2/938
(morph from Nkamba Bay, Zambia)
H: Shallow rubble and rock zones.
♂: D & A fins slightly more pointed. **S:** –
B: Cs; 50–100 e; nuclear family. **F:** C,O
T: 23–25°C, **L:** ♂ 12 cm, **pH:** >7, **D:** 2–3

Neolamprologus modestus 2/938
Modest lamprologus

Neolamprologus mondabu 4/646
Mondabu lamprologus
H: Rubble and sand zone.
♂: Slightly larger. **S:** =
B: Cave spawner; nuclear family. **F:** C
T: 23–27°C, **L:** 8 cm, **pH:** >7, **D:** 2

Neolamprologus multifasciatus ♂ 3/817
Many-banded shell-dweller
H: At 10m depth w/ empty snail shells.
♂: 1cm larger; reddish dorsal fringe. **S:** =
B: In a snail shell. **F:** C
T: 24–26°C, **L:** ♂ 4.5 cm, **pH:** >7, **D:** 3

Neolamprologus mustax 2/941
Mustax
H: Widely distributed in the SW section.
♂: Larger; cephalic hump w/ age. **S:** +
B: Cs; <80 e; P-M fam. **F:** C,O
T: 24–26°C, **L:** ♂ 10 cm, **pH:** >7, **D:** 2–3

CICHLIDS

Neolamprologus niger ♂   4/648
Muddy lamprologus
H: Zaïre, Tanzania, Zambia.
♂: Slightly larger.   S: +
B: Cave spawner; nuclear family.   F: O
T: 24–28°C, L: 9 cm, pH: >7, D: 3

Neolamprologus nigriventris ♂   4/648
Black-belly lamprologus
H: Kampampa: sand w/ rocks at >15 m.
♂: 2 cm larger.   S: +
B: Cs; 100 e; paternal-maternal fam.   F: O
T: 24–28°C, L: ♂ 12 cm, pH: ≫7, D: 3

Neolamprologus nigriventris ♀   4/648
Black-belly lamprologus

Neolamprologus obscurus   3/819
Mottly lamprologus
H: Rock and rubble littoral.
♂: Slightly larger.   S: =
B: Cs; <50 eggs; nuclear family.   F: C
T: 23–28°C, L: 9 cm, pH: >7, D: 2

Neolamprologus pectoralis   4/650

H: SW section: sand w/ rocks; >15 m.
♂: 2 cm larger.   S: =
B: Cs; <40 e; P-M to N fam.   F: O
T: 24–28°C, L: ♂ 14 cm, pH: ≫7, D: 3

Neolamprologus pectoralis   4/650

Dorsal view: note the black pectoral fins.

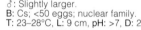

Neolamprologus pleuromaculatus 3/820
Blotched lamprologus
H: N section: muddy and sandy bottoms.
♂: Somewhat larger? S: =
B: Cave spawner; <300 e; N fam. F: C
T: 23–25°C, L: 12 cm, pH: >7, D: 3

Neolamprologus pulcher 3/822
H: Rocky littoral.
♂: Longer dorsal and anal fins? S: =
B: Cs; <100 e; nuclear family. F: C,O
T: 24–26°C, L: 10 cm, pH: >7, D: 1

Neolamprologus savoryi savoryi 2/944

H: Hiding places in the rubble littoral.
♂: More pointed dorsal & anal fins? S: =
B: Cave spawner; nuclear family. F: O
T: 23–26°C, L: 9 cm, pH: >7, D: 2

Neolamprologus sexfasciatus 2/946
Six-bar lamprologus, sexfasciatus
H: S section: rubble & rocky littoral: 2–5 m.
♂: Larger. S: =
B: Cave spawner; nuclear family. F: C
T: 23–26°C, L: 15 cm, pH: >7, D: 2–3

Neolamprologus sexfasciatus 4/652
Yellow six-bar lamprologus yellow form
H: Southern half of the Tanzanian coast.
♂: Larger. S: =
B: Cave spawner; nuclear family. F: O
T: 24–28°C, L: 15 cm, pH: >7, D: 3

Neolamprologus similis ♀ 4/654
H: Zaïre, Zam., Tan.: rock zone at >30 m.
♂: Somewhat larger. S: =
B: Nat.: cave spawner; nuclear fam. F: C
T: 23–28°C, L: 5 cm, pH: >7, D: 2

CICHLIDS

Neolamprologus sp. *"daffodil"*   2/925
Daffodil
H: Rocky littoral.
♂: Slightly more color; pointed fins.   S: +
B: Cs; 200 e; nuclear family.   F: C,O
T: 22–27°C, L: 7 cm, pH: >7, D: 1

Neolamprologus sp. *"magarae"* ♂   2/936

H: Magara: sand littoral w/ snail shells.
♂: 2 cm larger.   S: =
B: Cs; snail shell; Pch-M fam.   F: O
T: 24–26°C, L: ♂ 7 cm, pH: ≫7, D: 3

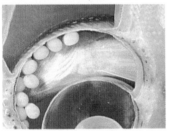

Neolamprologus sp. *"magarae"*   2/936

Spawns in a snail shell. The underside
of the head and throat of the ♀ is visible.

Neolamprologus splendens   4/654

H: SE of Moba: rock/sand: 2–40 m.
♂: Slightly larger.   S: =
B: Cave spawner.   F: O
T: 24–28°C, L: 8 cm, pH: ≫7, D: 2

Neolamprologus tetracanthus   1/734
Pearl-lined lamprologus
H: Common in the littoral zone.
♂: Larger; frontal hump dev. w/ age. S: =
B: Cs; 200 e; nuclear family.   F: C
T: 23–25°C, L: 19 cm, pH: >7, D: 2–3

Neolamprologus tretocephalus   1/736
Five-bar cichlid
H: Rubble and rocky littoral.
♂: Darker fins?   S: =
B: Cs; <400 e; nuclear family.   F: L,O
T: 24–26°C, L: 15 cm, pH: >7, D: 2–3

CICHLIDS

Neolamprologus variostigma   5/894

H: 40 km SE of Moba: rocks at 45 m.
♂: Clearly larger.   S: =
B: Snail shell; nuclear family.   F: C
T: 23–27°C, L: ♂ 8 cm, pH: >7, D: 2

Neolamprologus ventralis   5/894

H: 40 km SE of Moba: 20 to >60 m.
SD: Genital papilla. ♂: Larger.   S: =
B: Cs w/ intense brood care.   F: O
T: 23–27°C, L: 8 cm, pH: ≫7, D: 2

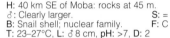

Neolamprologus wauthioni   2/946

H: Sandy littoral w/ snail shells: 35 m depth.
♂: 2.5 cm larger.   S: =
B: Cs; snail shell on sand pile.   F: O
T: 24–26°C, L: ♂ 7 cm, pH: >7, D: 3

Ophthalmotilapia boops ♂   3/826

H: S Tanzania.
♂: Much longer V fins; more colorful. S: =
B: ♀ Mb; modified ESM; aga.; Mfam. F: O
T: 22–26°C, L: 15 cm, pH: >7, D: 3

Ophthalmotilapia heterodonta ♂ 3/826

H: Rock/sand transition zone.
♂: Much longer V fins; more colorful. S: =
B: ♀ Mb; modified ESM; aga.; Mfam. F: O
T: 24–26°C, L: 15 cm, pH: >7, D: 3

Ophthalmotilapia nasuta ♂   2/960
Long-nosed gold-tip cichlid
H: Almost lakewide: rocky littoral; 2–5 m.
♂: Darker; much longer ventral fins. S: =
B: ♀ Mb; modified ESM; aga.; Mfam. F: O
T: 24–26°C, L: 18 cm, pH: >7, D: 3–4

Ophthalmotilapia ventralis ♂   1/746

H: Rock/sand transition zone.
♂: Much longer V fins; more colorful. S: =
B: ♀ Mb; <60 e; modified ESM.   F: C,O
T: 23–25°C, L: 15 cm, pH: >7, D: 2–3

Ophthalmotilapia ventralis ♂   3/824
Blue gold-tip cichlid (Mpimbwe morph)
H: Rock/sand transition zone.
♂: Much longer V fins; more colorful. S: =
B: ♀ Mb; <60 e; modified ESM.   F: C,O
T: 24–26°C, L: ♂ 14 cm, pH: >7, D: 3

Ophthalmotilapia ventralis ♂   4/658
Blue gold-tip cichlid   ("gold" morph)
H: SW coast: Kampapa–Lunangwa: 1–8 m.
♂: Much longer V fins; more colorful. S: =
B: ♀ Mb; modified ESM.   F: O
T: 24–28°C, L: ♂ 12 cm, pH: ≫7, D: 3

Ophthalmotilapia ventralis ♂   1/746
Blue gold-tip cichlid
Chimba.

Ophthalmotilapia ventralis ♂   3/824
Blue gold-tip cichlid
Nominate form.

Ophthalmotilapia ventralis ♂   3/824
Blue gold-tip cichlid
Kabogog white cap.

CICHLIDS

Ophthalmotilapia ventralis ♂   3/824
Blue gold-tip cichlid
Kachese.

Ophthalmotilapia ventralis ♂   3/824
Blue gold-tip cichlid
Kapembe.

Ophthalmotilapia ventralis ♂   3/824
Blue gold-tip cichlid
Maxa.

Oreochromis tanganicae ♂   3/832
Tanganyika tilapia
H: Shallow sand and rock littoral.
♂: More colorful; egg spots.   S: =
B: Nature: ♀ Mb; maternal family.   F: O
T: 24–26°C, L: 40 cm, pH: >7, D: 2–3

Oreochromis tanganicae ♀   3/832
Tanganyika tilapia

Palaeolamprologus toae   3/836

H: Rock and rubble littoral.
♂: Dermal lobe over genital papilla.   S: –
B: ♀ Cs; paternal-maternal family.   F: C
T: 24–26°C, L: 11 cm, pH: >7, D: 2–3

Paracyprichromis brieni ♂   3/838

Paracyprichromis brieni ♀   3/838

H: Open waters of the rocky littoral.
♂: Darker; slightly larger.   S: =
B: ♀ Mb, 21d; 5–10 y; aga.; M fam.   F: C
T: 23–28°C, L: 11 cm, pH: >7, D: 3

Perissodus microlepis   3/846
Blue-spotted perissodus
H: Kigoma.
SD: Unknown.   S: –
B: ♀ Mb; <350 e; nuclear family.   F: P!
T: 24–28°C, L: 11 cm, pH: >7, D: 4

Petrochromis famula ♂   2/968

H: Kigoma and NW coast: rubble littoral.
♂: More colorful; egg spots.   S: –
B: ♀ Mb; <60 e; agamic; M fam.   F: O,H
T: 23–26°C, L: 15 cm, pH: >7, D: 3

Petrochromis famula   2/968

Petrochromis fasciolatus ♂   3/845

Petrochromis fasciolatus ♂ 4/670
Banded petrochromis
H: Widely distributed: rubble a. rock zone.
♂: More colorful during courtship. **S:** =
B: ♀ Mb; <30 e; ♀♂ tend spawn. **F:** O,H
T: 23–27°C, **L:** 16 cm, **pH:** >7, **D:** 3

Petrochromis macrognathus 3/846

H: NW section, Kalemie: rubble littoral.
♀: Light crossbands; smaller. **S:**–
B: Nat: ♀Mb; agamic; maternal fam? **F:**O
T: 24–26°C, **L:** 20 cm, **pH:** >7, **D:** 4

Petrochromis orthognathus ♂ 3/848

H: Rubble and rocky littoral.
♀: Crossbands on sides. **S:** –
B: ♀ Mb; <35 d; agamic; M fam. **F:** O,H
T: 24–26°C, **L:** 12 cm, **pH:** >7, **D:** 3

Petrochromis orthognathus ♂ 4/672

H: Central W coast (Zaïre): rocky littoral.
♂: Some egg spots. **S:** –
B: ♀ mouthbrooder, <30 d. **F:** O,H
T: 23–27°C, **L:** 14 cm, **pH:** ≫7, **D:** 3

Petrochromis polyodon ♂ 2/968
Brown petrochromis
H: Widely distrib.: shallow rubble littoral.
♂: Egg spots. **S:** –
B: ♀ Mb; <15 e; agamic; M fam. **F:** O,H
T: 23–26°C, **L:** 21 cm, **pH:** >7, **D:** 3

Petrochromis sp. 3/845

CICHLIDS

Petrochromis trewavasae 2/970

H: SW coast: upper rubble & rocky littoral.
♂: Egg spots; differences slight.　S: –
B: ♀ Mb; <15 e; agamic; M fam.　F: O
T: 23–25°C, L: 18 cm, pH: >7, D: 2–3

Plecodus straeleni 3/848

H: Rare.
SD: Unknown.　S: –
B: Unsuccessful.　F: P!
T: 24–28°C, L: 16 cm, pH: >7, D: 4

Pseudosimochromis curvifrons ♂ 2/970
Thick-headed pseudosimochromis

H: Rubble zone.
♀: Intense bands; smaller.　S: –
B: ♀ Mb; maternal family.　F: O,H
T: 24–26°C, L: 14 cm, pH: >7, D: 3

Pseudosimochromis curvifrons ♂ 3/852
Thick-headed pseudosimochromis

H: Rubble & rocky littoral.
♀: Intense bands.　S: –
B: ♀ Mb, 25days; agamic; M fam.　F:O,H
T: 24–26°C, L: 12 cm, pH: >7, D: 2

Reganochromis calliurus 3/862
Calliurus

H: At greater depths.
SD: None.　S: =
B: ♀♂ Mb; intense nuclear family.　F: C
T: 23–28°C, L: 15 cm, pH: >7, D: 2–3

Simochromis babaulti ♂ 2/984
Babault's mouthbrooder

H: Rocky littoral.
♂: Black dorsal band; egg spots.　S: –
B: ♀ Mb; <50 eggs; ESM; M fam.　F: O
T: 24–26°C, L: 11 cm, pH: >7, D: 2–3

Simochromis dardennii ♂ 2/986

H: Widely distributed: littoral zone.
♂: Egg spots. S: –
B: Unsuccessful. ♀ Mb; M fam. F: O
T: 23–26°C, L: 26 cm, pH: >7, D: 3

Simochromis diagramma ♂ 3/868
Diagonal bar mouthbrooder

H: Rocky littoral.
♂: 2 cm larger; more colorful fins. S: –
B: ♀ Mb, 25 d; agamic; M fam. F: O
T: 25°C, L: 18 cm, pH: >7, D: 2

Simochromis marginatus 5/948

H: Kigoma, Nyanza Lac: sand bottom
♂: Slightly darker. S: =
B: ♀ Mb? Agamic? Maternal fam? F: O,H
T: 24–28°C, L: 11 cm, pH: >7, D: 2–3

Simochromis pleurospilus ♂ 3/868

H: Rocky littoral & transition to sandy littoral.
♂: Salmon red spots. S: –
B: ♀ Mb 25d; agamic; maternal fam. F: O
T: 25°C, L: 9–12 cm, pH: >7, D: 2

Spathodus erythrodon 2/986
Blue goby cichlid

H: Rubble littoral: 30–50 cm depth.
♂: Larger; longer fins. S: –
B: ♀♂ Mb; <25 e; tight nuclear fam. F: O
T: 25–27°C, L: 8 cm, pH: >7, D: 2–3

Spathodus marlieri 2/989
Plain goby cichlid

H: Northern section of the lake.
♂: Larger; longer fins; cephalic hump. S: –
B: ♀ Mb; <25 e; maternal fam. F: O
T: 25–27°C, L: ♂ <9 cm, pH: >7, D: 3

665

Tanganicodus irsacae 2/997
Speckled goby cichlid
H: North: rubble littoral: <1 m.
♂: Slightly longer ventral fins? S: –
B: ♀Mb, ♂Mb? Nuclear family? F: O
T: 24–28°C, L: 7 cm, pH: >7, D: 3

Telmatochromis bifrenatus ♂ 1/774
Two-banded cichlid, striped telmat
H: At Kigoma: rocky littoral.
♂: Larger; elongated fins. S: +
B: Cs; <80 eggs; P-M fam. F: C,O
T: 24–26°C, L: 6 cm, pH: ≫7, D: 2–3

Telmatochromis burgeoni 5/966

H: Southern half.
♂: Larger; small frontal hump. S: =
B: Snail shell; nuclear family. F: O
T: 24–28°C, L: 7 cm, pH: >7, D: 2–3

Telmatochromis dhonti 1/776

H: Littoral zone.
♂: Larger; prominent forehead. S: –
B: Cs; <500 e; P-M fam. F: C,O
T: 24–26°C, L: 12 cm, pH: ≫7, D: 2–3

Telmatochromis temporalis 2/998
Temporalis cichlid
H: Rubble and rocky littoral.
♂: Larger; prominent forehead. S: =
B: Cs; <60 eggs; nuclear family. F: O
T: 25–27°C, L: 10 cm, pH: ≫7, D: 2–3

Telmatochromis vittatus 1/776
Blunt-headed telmat
H: Mbity Rocks.
♂: Larger; slimmer. S: =
B: Cs; <80 eggs; P-M fam. F: C,O
T: 24–26°C, L: 4 cm, pH: ≫7, D: 2–3

CICHLIDS

Triglachromis otostigma   1/780
Tripod cichlid
H: Mud/sand sublittoral: 20–60 m depth.
SD: Unknown.   **S:** =
B: Mb; details unknown   **F:** C,O
T: 24–26°C, L: 12 cm, pH: ≫7, D: 2

Tropheus brichardi   2/1004
Blue-eyed tropheus
H: N shore: rubble & rock littoral: 2–5 m.
SD: None.   **S:** =
B: Open spawner; Mb; 10 young. **F:** C,H
T: 24–26°C, L: 12 cm, pH: >7, D: 3–4

Tropheus brichardi   2/1004
Blue-eyed tropheus
Kipili   (photo 3/897)

Tropheus duboisi ♂   1/782
White-spotted cichlid, duboisi
H: Rocky substrate: 3–15 m depth.
♂: Larger; longer ventral fins.   **S:** =
B: ♀ Mb; 5–15 e; maternal fam. **F:** L,O
T: 24–26°C, L: 12 cm, pH: ≫7, D: 3

Tropheus duboisi juv.   1/782
White-spotted cichlid, duboisi

Tropheus moorii   1/782
Moorii
H: Rocky littoral.
♂: Longer ventral fins.   **S:** =
B: ♀ mouthbrooder, 5–17 eggs. **F:** O, H
T: 24–26°C, L: 15 cm, pH: >7, D: 4

Tropheus moorii   1/782
Moorii

(photo 2/1005)

Tropheus moorii   1/782
Moorii
Rainbow morph   (photo 2/1005)

Tropheus moorii   1/782
Moorii
Striped morph   (photo 2/1005)

Tropheus moorii   1/782
Moorii
Orange morph   (photo 2/1005)

Tropheus moorii   1/782
Moorii
Green morph   (photo 2/1005)

Tropheus moorii   1/782
Moorii
Double spot morph   (photo 2/1005)

Tropheus moorii 1/782
Moorii
Black-banded morph   (photo 2/1005)

Tropheus moorii 1/782
Moorii
Murango   (photo 3/896)

Tropheus moorii 1/782
Moorii, kaiser moorii
    (photo 2/1005)

Tropheus moorii 1/782
Moorii
Kachese   (photo 3/897)

Tropheus moorii 1/782
Moorii
Kalambo   (photo 3/897)

Tropheus moorii 1/782
Moorii
Chipimbi, Katete   (photo 3/897)

CICHLIDS

Tropheus moorii   1/782
Moorii
Mkombe   (photo 3/897)

Tropheus polli   1/784
Poll's tropheus
H: Bulu Island: S coast and Bulu Point.
♂: More forked caudal fin.   S: =
B: ♀ Mb; 5–15 e; maternal fam.   F: O,H
T: 24–26°C, L: 16 cm, pH: >7, D: 3–4

Tropheus polli   1/784
Poll's tropheus
Yellow rainbow morph   (photo 2/1006)

Tropheus polli   1/784
Poll's tropheus
Wimpel morph   (photo 2/1006)

Tropheus polli   1/784
Poll's tropheus
Frontal stripe   (photo 2/1006)

Tropheus polli   1/784
Poll's tropheus
Green-red morph   (photo 2/1006)

CICHLIDS

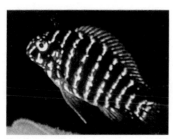

Tropheus polli juv.   1/784
Poll's tropheus
Ikola Island   (photo 3/896)

Tropheus polli   1/784
Poll's tropheus
Mpimbwe   (photo 3/897)

Tropheus polli   1/784
Poll's tropheus
Karilani   (photo 3/897)

Variabilichromis moorii juv.   2/938
Moore's lamprologus
H: S half: rubble & rocky littoral: <3 m.
♂: W/ age fins more pointed.   S: +
B: Cs; <100 e; tight nuclear fam.   F: C,O
T: 24–26°C, L: 10 cm, pH: >7, D: 2–3

Variabilichromis moorii subadult 2/938
Moore's lamprologus

Variabilichromis moorii adult   2/938
Moore's lamprologus

CICHLIDS

671

Xenotilapia boulengeri   2/1007
Boulenger's xenotilapia
H: Sandy bottom: 1–60 m depth.
♂: Anal fin w/ design; more colorful. **S: +**
B: ♀♂ Mb; 20–30 e; nuclear fam. **F: O**
T: 23–26°C, **L:** 15 cm, **pH:** >7, **D:** 3

Xenotilapia flavipinnis   3/898
Yellow-finned xenotilapia
H: Northern section.
♂: More yellow, including ventrals. **S: =**
B: ♀♂ Mb, <16 d; nuclear family. **F: O**
T: 24–27°C, **L:** 8 cm, **pH:** >7, **D:** 3

Xenotilapia papilio   4/706
Butterfly xenotilapia
H: SE of Moba: sandy areas: at 3–50 m.
SD: Only the genital papilla. **S: =**
B: ♀♂ Mb, >32 d; nuclear family. **F: O**
T: 24–26°C, **L:** 16 cm, **pH:** ≫7, **D:** 3

Xenotilapia papilio   4/706
Butterfly xenotilapia
In its natural biotope.

Xenotilapia sima   3/900
Big-eyed xenotilapia
H: Large schools in the sandy littoral.
♂: Larger; more color; pointed fins. **S: +**
B: ♀ Mb, 21 days; agamic. **F: O**
T: 24–26°C, **L:** 16 cm, **pH:** >7, **D:** 3

Xenotilapia spilopterus   3/900
Spot-fin xenotilapia
H: S section: rocks & rock/rubble/sand.
SD: None. **S: =**
B: ♀♂ Mb; nuclear family. **F: C**
T: 26–27°C, **L:** 8 cm, **pH:** >7, **D:** 4

CICHLIDS

Introduction

This subgroup presents the cichlids of lakes Albert, Baringo (Kenya), Barombi (W Cameroon), Bemini (W Cameroon), Bosumtwe (Ghana), Chilwa (Malawi), Edward, Fwa (Zaïre), George, Guinas (N Namibia), Kachira, Kafue (S Zambia), Kariba, Kioga, Kivu, Kwania, Magadi (Kenya), Malombe, Nawampasa (Uganda), Nakavali, Nubugabo, Otjikoto (N Namibia), Salisbury (Zimbabwe), and Victoria as well as the non-endemic cichlids of lakes Malawi and Tanganyika.

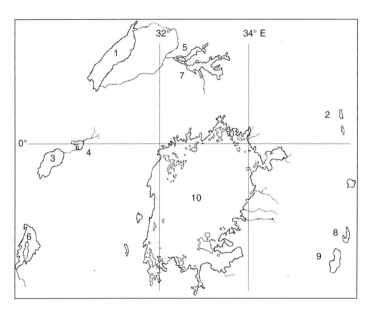

CICHLIDS

Physical Characteristics of Lake Victoria

Located 1134 m above sea level, Lake Victoria is the largest lake in Africa and the second largest lake in the world with a surface area of 68000 km^2 and an approximate diameter of 300 km. It is a flooded lowland with an extremely irregular shore. In comparison to the Great

Rift Lakes, Lake Victoria is young, only coming into existence 250 000 to 750 000 years ago. The hypolimnion has recently become seasonally anaerobic, a problematic situation the piscine fauna.

At its deepest point, the lake has a depth of 85 m (20 m on average). Additional values of interest for the aquarium hobby are: pH: 7.1–9.0; conductivity: 96 µS; temperature: 23.8°–26°C.

Ichthyological Characteristics of Lake Victoria

In the lake, 12 fish families with a total of 288 species in 28 genera can be found.

- Non-cichlids: 20 genera (1 endemic) and 38 species (16 endemic).
- Cichlids: 8 genera (4 endemic) and 250 species (247 endemic).

As is the case in lakes Malawi and Tanganyika, the fish fauna of Lake Victoria is highly endemic. During the 1960's, the predatory nile perch, *Lates niloticus,* was released in Lake Victoria with the aim of improving the diet of the populations of the bordering countries. After an initial increase in captures, species diversity in the lake was severely diminished. Today, many species in the lake are considered extinct. Four tilapine species were also introduced (i.e., *Oreochromis leucostictus*, *O. niloticus*, *Tilapia rendalli,* and *T. zillii*). The native *Oreochromis variabilis* and *O. esculentus* were displaced, and it is suspected that *O. niloticus* and *O. variabilis* are crossbreeding (PITCHER and HART, 1995).

Because a new ecological equilibrium in the lake has not been established since the release of *Lates niloticus,* it is difficult to estimate how many of the endemic species will be extinct in the end. Public aquaria, as well as hobbyists, can make a significant contribution towards the preservation of these threatened species.

Brief Descriptions of Additional Lakes

Lake Albert:
618 m above sea level, 5347 km², 150 km long, 40 km wide, up to 48 m deep (see map).

Lake Chilwa:
600 m above sea level, 1600 km², 50 km long, 25 km wide. Due to fluctuations in water level, it has swampy shores (15°12' S, 35°50' W).

Lake Edward:
913 m above sea level, 2200 km², up to 113 m deep (see map).

Lake Kafue:
A 75 km long and 20 km wide reservoir in southern Zambia.

Lake Kyoga:
130 km long (see map).

Lake Kivu:
1460 m above sea level, 2650 km², over 80 m deep; few fish (see map).

Lake Mayi-Ndombe (Leopold II):
About 130 km long with a surface area of 1300 km². It has fluctuating water level (Zaïre: 2° S, 18°15' W).

Lake Bosumtwi:
With a diameter of approximately 7 km and a depth 70 m, Lake Bosumtwi is the largest lake of Ghana. It is the impact site of a meteorite (6°30' N, 1°25' W).

Subgroup Generalities

The males of most species of this subgroup are aggressive—particularly among themselves. However, they can be readily associated with other fishes such as characins and catfishes. A cichlid community aquarium is also possible as long as the chosen species are of compatible temperament and the aquarium is richly decorated, thereby offering shelter and optical barriers. Because their requirements in regard to water chemistry greatly coincide, cichlids of the various African lakes are easiest to associate.

The most widely employed type of reproduction among these cichlids is the agamic maternal mouthbrooder. For these species, a ratio of 3–4 females for each male is recommended. Even more females per male should be present if the species is unusually aggressive. The presence of heterospecifics will also serve to disperse aggressions.

Not all cichlids in this subgroup are agamic maternal mouthbrooders. *Konia eisentrauti* (p. 680) and *Sarotherodon lohbergeri* (p. 684) are paternal-maternal mouthbrooders, *Nanochromis transvestitus* (p. 681) is a cave spawner, and various *Tilapia* spp. (p. 685) are open spawners and cave spawners.

Pronounced sexual dichromatism characterizes most species: while males often display all the colors of the rainbow, females are usually silver/gray/greenish. Females, juveniles, and subdominant males have the same coloration. Under close scrutiny, the males can be discerned by their slightly larger size and tad more color. *N. transvestitus* is somewhat the exception; females are more colorful than males, enabling one to easily distinguish females and juveniles. Like utaka cichlids of Lake Malawi, the second ranking male will attain its full adult coloration within a few days of the socially dominant male being removed from the aquarium. Females of related species are often indistinguishable.

The species of this subgroup are by and large omnivores; tilapine species have a herbivorous bent, while haplochromines tend to be somewhat carnivorous.

These cichlids are often spectacularly colored and easily maintained in captive environments. The main problem facing aquarists was the acquisition of animals, as their presence in the trade was limited. Thanks to increasing public awareness and popularity, more and more species are being offered. They are proving to be robust and relatively easily bred. With few exceptions, they are medium-sized fishes, which can be kept in appropriately decorated aquaria of moderate dimensions (from 1 m length).

CICHLIDS

Astatoreochromis alluaudi ♂ WC 3/690
Alluaudi cichlid
H: Vict., Edward, George, Nakavali, Kachira.
♂: Egg spots; black ventral fins. S: =
B: ♀ Mb; <40 e; maternal family. F: C,O
T: 24–28°C, L: 15 cm, pH: >7, D: 2–3

Astatoreochromis straeleni ♂ 3/692
Yellow-bellied cichlid
H: Lake Tanganyika and its affluents.
♂: Egg spots; more intense colors. S: =
B: There are no reports. F: C,O
T: 24–28°C, L: 12 cm, pH: >7, D: 2–3

Astatotilapia aeneocolor ♂ 5/730
Papyrus mouthbrooder
H: Lake George and the Kazinga region.
♂: Much more colorful; egg spots. S: =
B: Maternal mouthbrooder. F: C,O
T: 22°C, L: 8.5 cm, pH: 7, D: 2

Astatotilapia brownae ♂ 3/694
Brown's mouthbrooder
H: Lake Victoria. E
♂: More colorful; egg spots. S: =
B: ♀ Mb, 14 d; <40 e; M fam. F: C,O
T: 22–28°C, L: 12 cm, pH: ≫7, D: 2

Astatotilapia burtoni ♂ 1/680
Burton's mouthbrooder
H: Lakes Tanganyika and Kivu.
♂: M. color, egg spots; 5cm larger. S: =
B: ♀ Mb; 35 eggs; M fam; ESM. F: C,O
T: 20–25°C, L: ♂ 20 cm, pH: ≫7, D: 2

Astatotilapia calliptera ♂ 3/694
Callipterus hap
H: Lakes Malawi, Chilwa (also coastal riv.).
♂: More colorful; egg spots. S: =
B: There are no reports. F: C,O
T: 24–28°C, L: 14 cm, pH: ≫7, D: 2–3

Astatotilapia lacrimosa ♂　　　5/732
Tear-drop hap
H: Lake Victoria.　　　　　　　　　　E
♂: Pointed D and A fins; egg spots. S: =
B: Maternal mouthbrooder.　　F: C,O
T: 23–26°C, L: 11 cm, pH: 7, D: 2–3

Astatotilapia limax ♂　　　4/622, 5/732
H: Lakes Edward and George.　　　E
♂: Much more colorful; egg spots. S: –
B: ♀ Mb; agamic; maternal fam. F: O,C
T: 24–28°C, L: 12 cm, pH: >7, D: 3

Astatotilapia limax ♂　　　4/622, 5/732

Astatotilapia martini ♂　　　2/834
H: Lake Victoria: sand & mud bottoms. E
♂: More colorful; egg spots.　　S: =
B: Nature: ♀ Mb; agamic; M fam.　F: O
T: 24–26°C, L: 13 cm, pH: >7, D: 2

Astatotilapia nubila ♂　　　3/696
(K86/12 Nzaiu River)
H: Vic., Ed., Ge., Kioga, Kachira, Nakavali...
♂: More colorful: egg spots.　　S: –
B: ♀Mb, 14d, 40e; aga.; M fam.　F: C,O
T: 21–30°C, L: <13 cm, pH: >7, D: 2–3

Astatotilapia sp. ♂　　　3/697
H: Wembere River, Tanzania.

CICHLIDS

Chromidotilapia guentheri   4/586
Günther's mouthbrooder

H: Ghana: Lake Bosumtwe and affluents.
♀: Dorsal fin with shiny band.   **S:** –
B: Paternal mouthbrooder.   **F:** C
T: 24–26°C, **L:** 15 cm, **pH:** >7, **D:** 2–3

Dimidiochromis kiwinge ♂   5/810
Kiwinga hap

H: Lake Malawi, Lake Malombe.   E
♂: More colorful.   **S:** =
B: Unsuccessful. ♀ Mb; agamic.   **F:** C
T: 24–26°C, **L:** <30 cm, **pH:** >7, **D:** 3–4

Dimidiochromis kiwinge ♀   5/810
Kiwinga hap

Brooding.

Haplochromis chilotes ♂   5/826
Victoria big-lip hap, CH 38

H: Lake Victoria: to 17 m depth. Rare, E
♂: More colorful; egg spots.   **S:** =
B: ♀ mouthbrooder, 21 days.   **F:** C,O
T: 18–24°C, **L:** 15 cm, **pH:** >7, **D:** 3

"Haplochromis" ishmaeli ♂   5/828

H: Lake Victoria, Edward(?).   Endangered
♂: More colorful; larger.   **S:** =
B: ♀ Mb; spawn laid in large crater. **F:** C
T: 25°C, **L:** 14 cm, **pH:** >7, **D:** 3

Haplochromis nyererei ♂   4/622
Nyerere's Victoria cichlid   (Mwanza Bay)

H: Lake Victoria   E
♂: Much more colorful; egg spots. **S:** –
B: ♀ Mb; agamic; maternal fam. **F:** O,C
T: 22–28°C, **L:** 10 cm, **pH:** >7, **D:** 3

Haplochromis obliquidens ♂　　2/913

H: Lake Victoria; rock or sand littoral.　E
♂: Much more colorful; egg spots. S: –
B: ♀Mb, 21d; agamic; maternal fam.　F: O
T: 24–26°C, L: 12 cm, pH: >7, D: 2

Haplochromis sp. "blue red fin" ♂
CH 34　　　　　　　　　　　　5/830

H: Lake Victoria: Kenyan Coast.　　E
♂: Much more colorful; larger.　　S: –
B: ♀Mb, 16d; agamic; maternal fam. F: O
T: 23–26°C, L: 10 cm, pH: 7, D: 2

Haplochromis sp. "fire" ♂　　5/834
Fire mouthbrooder

H: Uganda: Lake Victoria?
♂: Much more colorful; larger.　　S: =
B: ♀ mouthbrooder; <120 young.　F: O
T: 23–26°C, L: 18 cm, pH: 7, D: 2–3

Haplochromis sp. "Kenya gold" ♂　5/830

H: Lake Victoria: Kenyan Coast.　　E
♂: More colorful; egg spots.　　S: =
B: ♀Mb, 16d; agamic; maternal fam. F: C
T: 23–26°C, L: 10 cm, pH: 7, D: 2

Haplochromis sp. "rock kribensis" ♂
　　　　　　　　　　　　　　5/832

H: Lake Victoria; widely distributed.
♂: Much more colorful; egg spots. S: =
B: Unproblematic. ♀ Mb.　　　F: C
T: 23–26°C, L: 12 cm, pH: >7, D: 2

Haplochromis sp. "rock kribensis" ♂
　　　　　　　　　　　　　　5/832

Haplochromis sp. "rock kribensis" ♀
5/832

Haplochromis sp. "thick skin like" ♂
5/828

H: Lake Victoria. E
♂: Much more colorful; larger. S: =
B: ♀ mouhtbrooder; 16 days. F: O
T: 23–26°C, L: 15 cm, pH: >7, D: 2–3

Haplochromis sp. "zebra-obliquidens" ♂
5/834

H: Uganda: Kioga B.: Lake Nawampasa.
♂: More colorful; larger. S: –
B: ♀ Mb, 20 days; <100 young. F: C,O
T: 23–26°C, L: 13 cm, pH: 7, D: 2

Hemichromis frempongi 4/624

H: Ghana: Lake Bosumtwe. E
SD: Unknown. S: –
B: Unknown. F: C,O
T: 24–27°C, L: 20 cm, pH: 7, D: 4

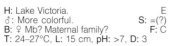

Hoplotilapia retrodens ♀ 3/790

H: Lake Victoria. E
♂: More colorful. S: =(?)
B: ♀ Mb? Maternal family? F: C
T: 24–27°C, L: 15 cm, pH: >7, D: 3

Konia eisentrauti 5/846

H: W Cameroon: Lake Barombi-Ma-Mbu. E
♂: Face mask more intense; larger. S: +
B: ♀♂ mouthbrooder. F: O (also eggs)
T: 25–27°C, L: 10 cm, pH: 7, D: 2–3

CICHLIDS

Nanochromis transvestitus ♂   2/956

Nanochromis transvestitus ♀   2/956

H: Zaïre: Lake Mayi-Ndombe (Leopold II).
♀: Smaller; more color (s. photos). S: +
B: Cs; Pch-M fam? No reports.   F: O
T: 24–26°C, L: ♂ 4 cm, pH: <7, D: 2–3

Neochromis nigricans ♂   2/960

H: Lake Victoria, Victoria-Nile: rock litt. E
♂: Dark red A fin w/ egg spots.   S: ?
B: ♀ Mb? Maternal family? ESM?   F: O
T: 24–26°C, L: 12 cm, pH: >7, D: 2–3

Oreochromis alcalicus grahami ♂ 2/978
Graham's soda tilapia

H: Lake Magadi. pH 10.5!   E
♂: Larger; more colorful.   S: =
B: ♀ Mb, 23 d; >20 e; maternal fam. F: O
T: 24–32°C, L: 12 cm, pH: ≫7, D: 2–3

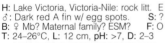

Oreochromis esculentus   4/660

H: Victoria, Kioga, Kwania, Nubugabo.
♂: Long genital papilla.   S: =
B: ♀ Mb, 21 day; agamic; M fam.   F: O
T: 24–26°C, L: 40 cm, pH: 7, D: 2–3

Oreochromis leucostictus ♂   2/982
Iridescent tilapia

H: Lakes Albert, Edward, George.   E
♂: Darker; black when courting.   S: =
B: ♀Mb, 23d; 100e; maternal fam.   F:O,H
T: 26–28°C, L: 28 cm, pH: >7, D: 2

CICHLIDS

681

Oreochromis leucostictus ♀   2/982
Iridescent tilapia

Oreochromis niloticus baringoensis
Baringo Nile tilapia   3/828
H: Kenya: Lake Baringo.
♂: Darker.   S: –
B: Unsuccessful in the aquarium.   F: O
T: 24–28°C, L: 36 cm, pH: 7, D: 2

Oreochromis niloticus eduardianus 4/660
Lake Edward Nile tilapia

H: Lakes Tanganyika to Albert.
♂: Larger fins; differences slight.   S: –
B: ♀ Mb, <28 d; maternal family.   F: O
T: 24–28°C, L: 30 cm, pH: >7, D: 2

Oreochromis variabilis ♂   3/836

H: Vict. & afflu., Kioga, Kwania, Salisbury.
♂: Genital p. long; black iris (♀ red).   S: –
B: ♀ Mb; 500 e; maternal family.   F: O
T: 24–28°C, L: 28 cm, pH: >7, D: 2–3

Platytaeniodus degeni ♂   4/674

Platytaeniodus degeni ♀   4/674

H: Lake Victoria.   E
SD: See photos.   S: –
B: Difficult? ♀ Mb; maternal fam.   F: C
T: 24–26°C, L: 15 cm, pH: >7, D: 3–4

CICHLIDS

Pseudocrenilabrus philander philander ♂ 3/850
Dwarf Egyptian mouthbrooder
H: Kariba, Kafue, Mal., Tan., and rivers.
♂: Much more colorful. S: –
B: ♀ Mb; 70 e; maternal family. F: C
T: 22–25°C, L: 9 cm, pH: 7, D: 2–3

Ptyochromis sauvagei ♂ 3/858
Victoria mottled hap
H: Lake Victoria E
♂: Egg spots; adult is blue. S: =
B: ♀ Mb; maternal family; ESM. F: C
T: 24–27°C, L: 13 cm, pH: >7, D: 2–3

Ptyochromis sauvagei ♀ 3/858
Victoria mottled hap

Ptyochromis xenognathus ♂ 3/861

H: Lake Victoria. E
♂: Egg spots; more colorful. S: +
B: ♀ Mb; egg-spot method; M fam. F: C
T: 24–27°C, L: 15 cm, pH: >7, D: 2–3

Pungu maclareni 5/930

H: W Cameroon: Lake Barombi. rare
♂: Pointed dorsal and anal fins. S: =
B: Largely unknown; Mb. F: C,O
T: 20–28°C, L: 9 cm, pH: >7, D: 2–3

Pyxichromis orthostoma ♂ 5/930

H: Lakes Kioga, Salisbury, Nawampasa.
♂: Slightly more colorful; egg spots. S: =
B: ♀ Mb, 16 d; no spawning pit. F: C
T: 23–27°C, L: >15 cm, pH: 7, D: 3

CICHLIDS

Sarotherodon linnellii 5/938

H: W Cameroon: Lake Barombi.
♂: Darker during courtship. **S:** –
B: ♀(♂) mouthbrooder; agamic. **F:** O
T: 24–26°C, **L:** 25 cm, **pH:** 7, **D:** 2–3

Sarotherodon lohbergeri 4/682

H: W Cam.: Lake Barombi, Creek Kumba.
♂: Slightly larger and more colorful. **S:** =
B: ♀♂ Mb; nuclear family. **F:** H,O
T: 25–27°C, **L:** 18 cm, **pH:** 7, **D:** 2–3

Sarotherodon steinbachi 5/940

H: W Cameroon: Lake Barombi.
SD: Genital papilla. **S:** =
B: ♀ mouthbrooder; agamic. **F:** O
T: 24–26°C, **L:** 15 cm, **pH:** 7, **D:** 2–3

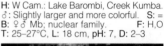

Schwetzochromis neodon ♂ 4/686

H: Zaïre: upper Lac Fwa and springs.
♂: Distinct egg spots. **S:** =
B: ♀ Mb, 21 d; agamic; M fam. **F:** C,O
T: 24–26°C, **L:** 12 cm, **pH:** 7, **D:** 3

Serranochromis robustus robustus 3/866
Southern bass cichlid

H: Lake Malawi & upper Shire River: sand.
♂: Blue-green during courtship. **S:** –
B: Nat.: ♀ Mb; agamic; M fam. **F:** C,O
T: 24–26°C, **L:** <50 cm, **pH:** 7, **D:** 2–4

Stomatepia mariae 5/954
Alkali cichlid

H: W Cameroon: Lake Barombi.
♂: Larger; longer snout. **S:** =
B: ♀ Mb; weak pair bond. **F:** O
T: 25–27°C, **L:** 12 cm, **pH:** 7, **D:** 2–3

Stomatepia pindu ♂   5/954

H: W Cameroon: Lake Barombi.
♂: Larger; more intensely black.   S: =
B: ♀ mouthbrooder; agamic.   F: O
T: 25–27°C, L: 10 cm, pH: 7, D: 4

Thoracochromis brauschi ♂   5/968

H: Fwa River, also called Lake Fwa.   E
♂: More colorful; larger.   S: =
B: Maternal mouthbrooder.   F: O
T: 25–27°C, L: ca.10 cm, pH: 7, D: 2–3

Thoracochromis wingatii ♂   2/998

H: Lakes Albert and Edward; also rivers.
♂: More colorful; egg spots.   S: =
B: Maternal mouthbrooder.   F: C,O
T: 24–26°C, L: 12 cm, pH: 7, D: 2

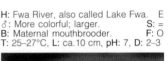

Tilapia bemini   4/690

H: W Cameroon: Lake Bemini.   E?
♂: Larger; otherwise equal.   S: =
B: Nat.: Cs; 200 e; nuclear family.   F: H
T: 27°C, L: 20 cm, pH: 7, D: 2–3

Tilapia guinasana ♀♀   3/890
Guinas tilapia

H: N Namibia: lakes Guinas and Otjikoto.
♂: Pointed genital papilla.   S: =
B: Open spawner; 200 e; P-M fam.   F:O,H
T: 22–26°C, L: 15 cm, pH: >7, D: 2

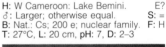

Tilapia kottae ♂   4/694
Kott's tilapia

H: W Cameroon: Lake Barombi Kotto. E
♂: Larger and slimmer.   S: –
B: Easy; open spawner.   F: O,H
T: 24–26°C, L: 25 cm, pH: >7, D: 2

CICHLIDS

Introduction

This subgroup presents the cichlids of African rivers. Part of Asia Minor—Israel, Jordan, and Syria—is included, since distributions of fishes such as tilapines often extend into that region. Cichlids from Madagascar (X) are presented in the subgroup "Remaining World."

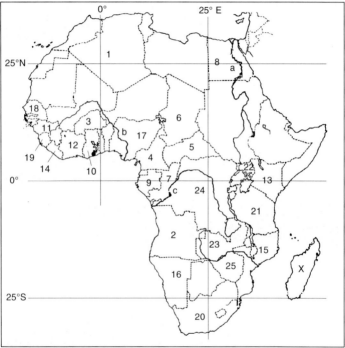

Generalities

From mineral-rich waters (desert and brackish habitats) to extremely soft, acid waters (rain forest habitats), the requirements of species within this sub-group are too varied to be generalized. Each species must be considered on an individual basis.

Tilapine Cichlids

Cichlids of the genera *Oreochromis*, *Sarotherodon*, and *Tilapia* are medium to large species. Several (e.g., *O. niloticus*, *O. mossambicus,* and *O. aureus*) are economically important in aquaculture in Africa as well as Asia and America. These robust, omnivorous species fishes have high quality meat. Most are mouthbrooders, e.g., *Oreochromis* and *Sarotherodon*, but some are open spawners and cave spawners, i.e., *Tilapia*. Deviating from the great majority of cichlids, *S. melanotheron* is a paternal mouthbrooder with a paternal family.

The main problem confronting tilapine aquaculture is the sexual precocity of the fishes; sexual maturity is achieved prior to market weight and is expressed in prolific breeding in culture ponds. The final result is an overpopulation of small, unmarketable animals. This problem is dealt with in various ways:

- Crossbreeding select species and strains yields 100% male offspring (while some hybridizations result in 100% females, they are of secondary economic importance).
- Feeding swim-up fry testosterone-treated feed until they are 12 mm long results in masculine sterile females and normal males.
- Examination of the genital papilla of juveniles of about 20 g to sex them.

A red morph is cultured primarily for the American market, often in brackish water.

The Genus *Pelvicachromis*

There are many color morphs of *Pelvicachromis* spp. Small, colorful, and peaceful, they are popular fishes for community aquaria. With the exception of *P. pulcher*, they are regrettably difficult to find in the trade. In nature, they occur along the western coast of Africa and some species even inhabit brackish waters. Most prefer medium-hard water with a slightly acid pH. With the exception of those species which hail from extremely soft, acid water biotopes—e.g., *P. roloffi* and *P. subocellatus*—recently imported, wild-caught *Pelvicachromis* fare best in slightly saline water (1 teaspoon salt per 5 l of water).

All are paternal-maternal cave spawning cichlids. The young should be left with the parents for quite some time; otherwise the male may "blame" the female for the young's disappearance, attacking and perhaps even killing her.

The Genus *Nanochromis*

Nanochromis spp. are typically found in flowing, oxygen-rich biotopes. Soft, slightly acid waters are preferred. As an inhabitant of a lentic biotope, i.e., Lake Mayi-Ndombe (Leopold II), *N. transvestitus* deviates from its conge-

CICHLIDS

ners; it was presented in the subgroup "Africa—Various Lakes" (p. 681).

Good filtration contributes significantly to the health of those species. Males are aggressive among themselves and towards nonripe females; the aquarium should therefore be richly decorated and contain numerous hiding places.

The Genus *Hemichromis*
Roomy aquaria with abundant shelter are required to diminish the aggressive behavior of *Hemichromis*. Even with optimal infrastructure, problematic behavior is frequently observed with sexually active pairs. Soft, slightly acid water is preferred.

The Genus *Steatocranus*
As bottom-oriented inhabitants of torrential waters, these species have a reduced swimbladder. The water should be medium-hard, neutral, and free of nitrogenous wastes. A strong current is not necessary.

Anomalochromis thomasi 1/748
African butterfly cichlid
H: Sierra Leone, SE Guinea, W Liberia.
♀: Black design; 3 cm smaller.   S: +
B: Os; <500 e; nuclear family.   F: C,O
T: 23–27°C, L: ♂ 10 cm, pH: <7, D: 1

Astatotilapia bloyeti ♂ 3/692
Bloyet's mouthbrooder
H: Tanzania: Wami Basin.
♂: More colorful; egg spots.   S: =
B: ♀Mb; maternal family.   F: C,O
T: 24–28°C, L: 14 cm, pH: ≫7, D: 2

Astatotilapia desfontainii ♂ 5/730
North African mouthbrooder
H: Algiers, Tunesia.
♂: More colorful; egg spots.   S: =
B: Maternal mouthbrooder.   F: C,O
T: 18–28°C, L: 15 cm, pH: 7, D: 2

Chromidotilapia batesii 2/854
Bates's chromidotilapia
H: Equatorial Guinea and SW Cameroon.
♂: Larger. ♀: Wine red ventrally.   S: =
B: ♀ LMb; 100 eggs; P-M fam.   F: C,O
T: 24–26°C, L: 12 cm, pH: <7, D: 2–3

CICHLIDS

Chromidotilapia batesii ♂ "Eseka"   4/586

H: Cameroon: near the city of Eseka.
♀: Smaller; silver dorsal fin base.   S: =
B: ♀♂ larvophile mouthbrooder.   F: C
T: 24–26°C, L: ♂ 12 cm, pH: <7, D: 3–4

Chromidotilapia finleyi   1/684

H: SW Cameroon: Campo Reservation.
♂: Red-fringed D f. ♀: Ventrally red. S: =
B: ♀♂ Mb; role exchange; Nfam. F: C,O
T: 23–25°C, L: 12 cm, pH: ≪7, D: 2

Chromidotilapia kingsleyae ♂   5/744
Kingsley's chromidotilapia

H: P.R. Congo? Gabon: Oogoue River.
SD: See photos.   S: =
B: ♀ Mb; perhaps polygamous.   F: O
T: 23–26°C, L: <15 cm, pH: 7, D: 2–3

Chromidotilapia cavalliensis   4/638

H: Ivory Coast: Cavally River.
♀: Silver dorsal fin base.   S: +
B: ♂ Mb; successful once.   F: C
T: 24–26°C, L: 12 cm, pH: 7, D: 4

Chromidotilapia guentheri   1/686, 4/586
Günther's mouthbrooder

H: Sierra Leone to Cameroon, Gabon.
♀: Dorsal fin w/ shiny band.   S: =
B: ♂♀ Mb; <15 e; nuclear fam. F: C,O
T: 23–25°C, L: <20 cm, pH: 7, D: 2–3

Chromidotilapia kingsleyae ♀   5/744
Kingsley's chromidotilapia

Chromidotilapia linkei ♀   2/856
Linke's chromidotilapia

H: W Cameroon: Mungo River.
♂: Lacks shiny longitudinal band.   **S:** +
B: ♀♂ Mb; strong bond; P-M fam.   **F:**C,O
T: 24–27°C, L: 10 cm, pH: >7, D: 2–3

Ctenochromis polli ♂   3/758

H: Congo at Kinshasa.
♂: Single egg spot; larger.   **S:** =
B: ♀.Mb, 30 days; maternal family.   **F:**C
T: 24–26°C, L: 11.5 cm, pH: 7, D: 2

Hemichromis bimaculatus   1/722
Jewel cichlid

H: S Guinea to central Liberia.
SD: Genital papilla.   **S:** =
B: Os; 200–500 e; nuclear fam.   **F:** C,O
T: 21–23°C, L: <15 cm, pH: 7, D: 3

Hemichromis cerasogaster   3/786

H: Lake Mayi-Ndombe, Zaïre River.
♂: 2 cm larger; more iridesc. spots.   **S:** –
B: Os; nuclear family.   **F:** C,O
T: 22–26°C, L: ♂ 10 cm, pH: 7, D: 2–3

Hemichromis cristatus   2/914
Crown jewel cichlid

H: Guinea, Ghana and Nigeria.
♂: Slightly larger.   **S:** =
B: Os; 200–500 e; nuclear fam.   **F:** C,O
T: 23–26°C, L: 9 cm, pH: <7, D: 3

Hemichromis elongatus   2/914
Elongate jewel cichlid

H: Guinea to Zaïre, Angola, and Zambia.
SD: None.   **S:** –
B: Os; 800 e; nuclear family.   **F:** O
T: 23–25°C, L: 15 cm, pH: 7, D: 4

CICHLIDS

Hemichromis guttatus　　　　4/624

H: Senegal, Ghana, Nigeria, Cameroon.
♂: Slightly larger; longer fins.　　S: =
B: Os; tight nuclear family.　　F: C,O
T: 23–27°C, L: 10 cm, pH: 7, D: 3

Hemichromis letourneuxi　　　2/916
Letourneux's jewel cichlid

H: Egy., Alg., Sud., Gui., Sen., Chad,...
SD: Slight.　　　　　　　　S: =
B: Unsuccessful? Os; N fam.　　F: C,O
T: 22–25°C, L: 15 cm, pH: <7, D: 3

Hemichromis lifalili front ♀　　1/722
Blood-red jewel cichlid, lifalili cichlid

H: Zaïre Basin and Central African Rep.
♂: Spawning colors; see photo.　　S: =
B: Os; nuclear family.　　F: C,O
T: 22–24°C, L: <10 cm, pH: 7, D: 3

Hemichromis paynei　　　　2/916
Faded jewel cichlid

H: Guinea, Sierra Leone, and Liberia.
♂: More colorful when spawning.　S: =
B: Os; nuclear fam; no reports.　F: C,O
T: 23–25°C, L: 10 cm, pH: <7, D: 3

Hemichromis sp. "Guinea II"　　5/836

Hemichromis sp. "Guinea I"　　5/837

H: Nigeria: Niger Delta.
♂: Slightly larger; larger ventral fins.　S: =
B: Open spawner; nuclear family.　F: O
T: 24–26°C, L: <10 cm, pH: 7, D: 2

CICHLIDS

Hemichromis stellifer 3/788

H: Gabon to Zaïre.
♂: Slightly larger and elongated. S: =
B: Open spawner. F: C,O
T: 22–26°C, L: <11 cm, pH: 7, D: 1–2

Lamprologus congoensis ♂ 2/926
Congo lamprologus

H: Rapids of the Zaïre River.
♂: Larger; shiny scales; front. hump. S: –
B: Cs; 80 e; patriarch-maternal fam. F: O
T: 23–25°C, L: 15 cm, pH: <7, D: 2

Lamprologus werneri 1/736
Werner's lamprologus

H: Rapids of the Zaïre River, Stanley Pool.
SD: Unknown. S: –
B: Cs; patriarch-maternal family? F: C,O
T: 22–25°C, L: 12 cm, pH: 7, D: 2–3

Paranochromis caudifasciatus ♂ 2/954
Banded-tail nanochromis

H: S Cameroon: Nyong River tributaries.
♂: Shiny dorsal band; 3 cm larger. S: =
B: Cs;>100e; paternal-maternal fam. F:O
T: 23–25°C, L: ♂ 11 cm, pH: <7, D: 3–4

Nanochromis dimidiatus ♂ 1/744
Dimidiatus

H: Tributary of the Zaïre: Banghi region.
♀: Purple; 2 cm smaller. S: =
B: Cs; 60 eggs; nuclear family. F: C,O
T: 23–25°C, L: ♂ 8 cm, pH: <7, D: 3

Nanochromis dimidiatus ♂ 5/884
Dimidiatus

CICHLIDS

Nanochromis nudiceps ♂   5/886
Bar-tailed dwarf cichlid
H: Zaïre: Stanley Pool, Kasai River.
♂: C fin w/ 7 vertical rows of dots.   S: =
B: Cs; 60 eggs; nuclear family.   F: C,O
T: 24–26°C, L: 8 cm, pH: <7, D: 3

Nanochromis parilus t.♀, b.♂   1/746
Blue Congo dwarf cichlid
H: Zaïre Basin, Stanley Pool.
♀: More color; 1 cm smaller.   S: =
B: Cs; <250 e; Pch-M fam.   F: C
T: 22–25°C, L: ♂ 8 cm, pH: <7, D: 2–3

Limbochromis robertsi   2/956
Robert's Congo dwarf cichlid
H: W central Ghana.
♂: 3 cm larger; fins more yellow.   S: =
B: Cs; Pch-M fam? No reports.   F: C
T: 22–25°C, L: ♂ 11 cm, pH: <7, D: 2–3

Nanochromis sp. "Kisangani" ♂ 3/806
Silverspot nanochromis
H: Zaïre: Kisangani region.
♀: Silver spot; 1.5 cm smaller.   S: +
B: Cs; <50 e; Pch-M fam.   F: C
T: 23–26°C, L: ♂ 6 cm, pH: ≪7, D: 3–4

Nanochromis sp. "Kisangani" ♀ 3/806
Silverspot nanochromis

Nanochromis squamiceps ♂   5/886

H: Zaïre.
♂: C fin w/ rows of dots; slimmer.   S: =
B: Cave spawner; nuclear family.   F: C
T: 23–26°C, L: ♂ 6 cm, pH: <7, D: 3

693

Oreochromis aureus ♂   2/978
Blue tilapia
H: Sen., Niger, Chad, Benue, Nile, Jordan.
♂: More colorful; larger.   S: =
B: ♀ Mb; maternal family?   F: O
T: 17–24°C, L: 40 cm, pH: 7, D: 2

Oreochromis karomo ♂   2/980
H: Tanzania: Malagarasi Swamps.
♂: Colorful; larger; 15 mm gen. pap.   S: –
B: ♀ Mb; 250 e; agamic; M fam.   F: O
T: 22–28°C, L: 30 cm, pH: 7, D: 2–3

Oreochromis mossambicus ♂   1/768
Mozambique tilapia
H: E Africa.
♂: More colorful; larger.   S: =
B: ♀ Mb; 300 e; agamic; M fam.   F: O
T: 20–24°C, L: 40 cm, pH: 7, D: 3–4

Oreochromis niloticus niloticus   3/828
Nile tilapia
H: Widely distributed; also Syria, Israel.
♂: Pointed dorsal and anal fins.   S: =
B: ♀ Mb, 200 e; agamic; M fam.   F: O
T: 14–26°C, L: 35 cm, pH: 7, D: 1–2

Oreochromis pangani pangani ♂ 3/830
Pangani tilapia
H: Tanzania: Pangani River.
♂: Darker; 15 cm larger.   S: –
B: Nat.: ♀ Mb; <1000 e; M fam.   F: O
T: 24–28°C, L: ♂ 47 cm, pH: 7, D: 2–3

Oreochromis spilurus niger   3/830
H: Kenya.
♂: Courtship coloration.   S: =
B: Nat.: ♀ Mb; maternal family.   F: O
T: 24–28°C, L: 33 cm, pH: 7, D: 2–3

CICHLIDS

Oreochromis spilurus spilurus WC 3/832

H: Kenya, N Tanzania.
♂: Courtship coloration.   S: =
B: Nat.: ♀ Mb; maternal family.   F: O
T: 24–28°C, L: <40 cm, pH: 7, D: 2–3

Oreochromis urolepis hornorum   2/980
Wami tilapia

H: Tanzania: Wami River basin.
♂: Darker; more intense coloration. S: =
B: ♀ Mb; maternal family?   F: O
T: 22–26°C, L: 17 cm, pH: 7, D: 2

Oreochromis urolepis urolepis   3/835

H: Tanzania: Rifigi, Kingani, Mbemkuru.
♂: Darker; larger.   S: =
B: ♀ Mb; <500 e. Maternal family? F: O
T: 22–28°C, L: 38 cm, pH: >7, D: 2–3

Schwetzochromis stormsi   2/962

H: Zaïre River, Lake Mweru.
SD: Unknown.   S: =
B: ♀ Mb; agamic; maternal family. F: O
T: 22–25°C, L: 6.5 cm, pH: 7, D: 2–3

Parananochromis gabonicus   4/662

H: Abanga, Okano, and Ntem basins.
♀: Smaller; silver dorsal band.   S: +
B: Cave spawner; pair-forming.   F: C
T: 24–26°C, L: 12 cm, pH: <7, D: 3

Parananochromis longirostris ♂   3/840

H: S Cameroon, N Gabon.
♂: Longer fins; more iridescent spots. S: +
B: Rarely successful; ♀Mb.   F: O
T: 22–26°C, L: ♂ 12 cm, pH: <7, D: 2–3

CICHLIDS

Parananochromis sp. "Belinga" ♂ 4/664

Parananochromis sp. "Belinga" ♀ 4/664

H: Gabon. S Cameroon?
♂: Larger; banded caudal fin.　　　　S: +
B: Cave spawner; pair-forming.　　F: C
T: 24–25°C, L: 12 cm, pH: ≪7, D: 3–4

Pelmatochromis buettikoferi　　　5/906

Pelmatochromis ocellifer　　　5/906

H: Port Guinea to Liberia: coastal rivers.
SD: Genital papilla.　　　　　　　S: =
B: Open spawner; nuclear family.　F: O
T: 24–26°C, L: 25 cm, pH: 7, D: 2–3

H: Central and lower Zaïre Basin.
♂: Slightly longer fins.　　　　　S: =
B: Open spawner?　　　　　　　F: O
T: 25–28°C, L: 20 cm, pH: 7, D: 3

Pelvicachromis humilis ♂　　　2/964
Yellow krib　　　　Kasewe color morph

Pelvicachromis humilis ♂　　　2/964
Yellow krib　　　Kenema color morph

H: Liberia, SE Guinea, Sierra Leone.
♂: Pointed D, A, and V.　　　　　S: +
B: Cs; paternal-maternal family.　F: C,O
T: 24–26°C, L: ♂ 12.5 cm, pH:<7, SG: 2–3

Pelvicachromis pulcher f.♂, b.♀ 1/750
Kribensis, purple cichlid
H: S Nigeria. Fw, (Bw)
♂: Pointed dorsal and anal fins. S: +
B: Cs; <300 eggs; P-M family. F:C,O
T: 24–25°C, L: 10 cm, pH: <7, D: 1

Pelvicachromis roloffi f.♂, b.♀ 2/966
Roloff's kribensis
H: E Guinea, Sierra Leone, W Liberia.
♂: Pointed D, A, and V fins. S: +
B: Cs; paternal-maternal family. F: C,O
T: 24–26°C, L: ♂ 8.5cm, pH: <7, D: 3

Pelvicachromis subocellatus t.♂ 1/750
Eye-spot cichlid, gold-cheek krib
H: Gabon to mouth of Zaïre R. Fw,(Bw)
♂: Pointed dorsal and anal fins. S: +
B: Cs; <200 eggs; P-M family. F:C,O
T: 22–26°C, L: 10 cm, pH: <7, D: 2

Pelvicachromis taeniatus t.♂, b.♀ 1/752
Striped kribensis
H: S Nigeria, Cameroon. Fw, (Bw)
♂: Pointed D and A fins; 2cm larger.S: +
B: Cs; <60 eggs; P-M family. F:C,O
T: 22–25°C, L: ♂ 9 cm, pH: <7, D: 1

Pseudocrenilabrus multicolor r.♂ 1/754
Egyptian mouthbrooder
H: Lower Nile to Uganda and Tanzania.
♀: Paler. S: =
B: ♀ Mb, 10d; 30–80e; M fam. F:C,O
T: 20–24°C, L: 8 cm, pH: 7, D: 2

Pseudocrenilabrus multicolor victoriae ♂
5/913
H: Uganda and Tanzania.
♂: Colorful; orange-tipped A fin. S: =
B: ♀ Mb; agamic; maternal fam. F: O
T: 24–26°C, L: 11 cm, pH: 7, D: 2–3

CICHLIDS

697

Pseudocrenilabrus nicholsi ♂ WC 3/850
Nichols mouthbrooder

H: Zaïre Basin.
♀: Paler.   S: –
B: ♀ Mb; maternal family.   F: C
T: 22–25°C, L: 7 cm, pH: 7, D: 2–3

Pseudocrenilabrus philander dispersus ♂
Dwarf Egyptian mouthbrooder   1/754

H: S.Af., Na., Zam., Moz., Zim., Ang., S.Zaïre.
♂: Much more colorful.   S: –
B: ♀ Mb; <100 e; maternal fam.   F: C,O
T: 20–24°C, L: 11 cm, pH: 7, D: 2–3

Sarotherodon caudomarginatus   4/680
                                                    5/938

H: Guinea to Liberia: coastal rivers.
SD: Almost indiscernible.   S: =
B: ♀ mouthbrooder; agamic.   F: O
T: 24–26°C, L: 30 cm, pH: 7, D: 2–3

Sarotherodon galilaeus   3/864

H: Jordan; E and central Africa to Liberia.
SD: Almost indiscernible.   S: =
B: ♀♂Mb; <1500 e; nuclear family. F: O
T: 22–28°C, L: 40 cm, pH: 7, D: 2

Sarotherodon galilaeus sanagaensis
                                                    4/680

H: Cameroon: Sanaga River.
SD: Almost indiscernible.   S: =
B: Mouthbrooder.   F: O
T: 24–26°C, L: 25 cm, pH: 7, D: 2

Sarotherodon melanotheron ♂   2/984
Black-throat tilapia, black-chin tilapia

H: Ivory Coast to Cameroon.
♂: Larger.   S: =
B: ♂Mb, 21 d; <150 e; paternal fam. F: O
T: 23–25°C, L: 20 cm, pH: 7, D: 2–3

Sarotherodon melanotheron heudelotii
4/682

H: Senegal to Guinea. Fw, (Bw)
♂: Pointed genital papilla. S: =
B: ♂ Mb, 14 d; agamic; paternal fam. F: O
T: 24–26°C, L: 20 cm, pH: >7, D: 2

Sarotherodon melanotheron leonensis
4/684

H: Guinea to Liberia: numerous in Bw.
♂: Pointed genital papilla. S: =
B: ♂ Mb, 14 d; agamic; paternal fam. F: O
T: 24–26°C, L: 20 cm, pH: >7, D: 2

Sarotherodon occidentalis 5/940

H: Guinea to Liberia.
SD: Unknown. S: ?
B: Mouthbrooder? Agamic? F: O?
T: 24–26°C, L: 25 cm, pH: 7, D: 2–3

Sarotherodon tournieri tournieri 4/684

H: Ivory Coast: Cavally River.
SD: Unknown. S: ?
B: Mouthbrooder? Agamic? F: O?
T: 24–26°C, L: 25 cm, pH: 7, D: 3

Schwetzochromis stormsi ♂ 4/686

H: Upper and central Zaïre River.
♂: Stouter; more massive head. S: –
B: Maternal mouthbrooder. F: H!
T: 25–26°C, L: 15 cm, pH: 7, D: 4

Steatocranus casuarius f. ♀, b. ♂ 1/768
African blockhead, lionhead cichlid

H: Lower and central Zaïre River.
♂: 3 cm larger; larger cephalic hump. S: =
B: Cs; 60 e; pairwise; P-M fam. F: O
T: 24–28°C, L: ♂ 11 cm, pH: <7, D: 2

CICHLIDS

Steatocranus gibbiceps ♂   3/870
Blunt head
H: Lower Zaïre River.
SD: None in juveniles.   S: +
B: Cs; <100 e; strong pair bond. F: O
T: 24–27°C, L: 11 cm, pH: 7, D: 1–2

Steatocranus gibbiceps ♀ juv. 3/870
Blunt head

Steatocranus glaber   2/990
False Mpozo lionhead cichlid
H: Rapids of the Zaïre River.
♂: Larger.   S: +
B: Cs? No breeding reports.   F: O
T: 23–27°C, L: 6 cm, pH: 7, D: 2

Steatocranus irvinei ♂   3/872
H: Ghana, Burkina Faso.
♂: Slightly larger.   S: =
B: Cave spawner; 200 eggs.   F: O
T: 24–27°C, L: ca.15 cm, pH: 7, D: 1–2

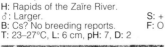

Steatocranus irvinei ♀   3/872

Steatocranus tinanti ♂   2/990
Slender lionhead cichlid
H: Zaïre River: Kinshasa.
♂: Elongated dorsal and anal fins. S: =
B: Cs; 100 e; paternal-maternal fam. F: O
T: 25–27°C, L: 15 cm, pH: 7, D: 2–3

Steatocranus ubanguiensis 3/874
Ubangi lionhead cichlid
H: W Africa: Ubangi tributaries.
♂: Pointed dorsal and anal fins. **S**: +
B: Cs; <25 e; ♂ tends the brood. **F**: O
T: 25–27°C, **L**: 6–7 cm, **pH**: 7, **D**: 1–2

Teleogramma brichardi ♀ 1/774
Brichard's teleo
H: Lower Zaïre betw. Kinshasa & Matadi.
♀: Broad fringed D fin; more color. **S**: =
B: Cs; <30 e; Pch-M fam. **F**: C,O
T: 20–23°C, **L**: ♂ 12 cm, **pH**: <7, **D**: 2–3

Thoracochromis demeusii ♂ 4/688

H: Lower Zaïre.
♂: Egg spots; larger frontal hump. **S**: –
B: Maternal mouthbrooder. **F**: C
T: 24–28°C, **L**: 12 cm, **pH**: 7, **D**: 3

Thysochromis ansorgii ♀ 2/1000
Five-spot African cichlid
H: Nigeria, Ivory Coast, Ghana, Cameroon.
♀: Smaller; round fins; white spot. **S**: +
B: Os–Cs; 500 e, Pch-M to N fam. **F**: O
T: 24–26°C, **L**: 13 cm, **pH**: <7, **D**: 2

Tilapia brevimanus 4/690

H: Guinea-Bissau to E Liberia.
♂: Larger; longer fins. **S**: –
B: Cave spawner; nuclear family. **F**: H,O
T: 24–26°C, **L**: 25 cm, **pH**: 7, **D**: 2–3

Tilapia busumana 2/1000

H: S Ghana: Kumasi area, Lake Volta,...
♂: Lighter; adults have no spot. **S**: =
B: Os; 400 eggs; nuclear family. **F**: O
T: 23–25°C, **L**: 20 cm, **pH**: <7, **D**: 2

CICHLIDS

701

Tilapia buttikoferi   2/1002
Zebra tilapia
H: Guinea-Bissau to W Liberia.
♂: Larger.   S: +,–
B: Os; tight nuclear family.   F: O
T: 23–25°C, L: 25 cm, pH: <7, D: 2

Tilapia cessiana   4/692
Cess tilapia
H: Liberia/Ivory Coast: Cess River.
♂: Slightly more massive; larger. S:+,–
B: Os; tight nuclear family.   F: H,O
T: 24–26°C, L: 35 cm, pH: 7, D: 2

Tilapia dageti   4/692

H: Niger, Benne, Chad, Volta,... basins.
♂: Usually larger and slimmer. S: =
B: Os; tight nuclear family.   F: H,O
T: 24–28°C, L: 30 cm, pH: 7, D: 2

Tilapia guineensis   3/892
Guinea tilapia
H: Senegal to Angola; coastal areas.
♂: Usually larger and slimmer. S: –
B: Os, <1000 e; tight nuclear fam. F: O
T: 22–26°C, L: 25 cm, pH: 7, D: 2

Tilapia joka   2/1002

H: Sierra Leone.
SD: Unknown.   S: +
B: Cave sp.; <200 e; P-M fam. F: O
T: 23–25°C, L: 13 cm, pH: <7, D: 2

Tilapia louka ♂   4/694

H: Sierra Leone, Guinea, Ivory Coast.
♀: Redder throat.   S: –
B: Os; intense nuclear family. F: O,H
T: 26–30°C, L: ca. 25 cm, pH: 7, D: 1–2

Tilapia mariae ♂   1/778
Tiger tilapia
H: Ivory Coast to Cameroon: Niger.
♂: Long D and A fins; steep forehead.   S: −
B: Os–Cs; <2000 e; P-M fam.   F: L,O
T: 20–25°C, L: <35 cm, pH: <7, D: 3–4

Tilapia mariae juv.   1/778
Tiger tilapia

Tilapia nyongana   4/696
Nyong tilapia
H: S Cameroon: Nyong and Dja rivers.
♂: Slightly larger?   S: −?
B: Os? Nuclear family?   F: O?
T: 24–26°C, L: 30 cm, pH: ≪7, D: 4

Tilapia rendalli   3/892
Rendall's tilapia
H: Zaïre: Zambezi & Limpopo; Tan., Mal.,...
♂: More pointed dorsal & anal fins.   S:−
B: Nat.: Os; P-M to N family.   F: O,H
T: 24–28°C, L: 30 cm, pH: >7, D: 2

Tilapia sparrmanii   3/894
Sparrman's tilapia
H: Angola to Zaïre and South Africa.
SD: Almost indiscernible.   S: =
B: Os; <500 e; nuclear family.   F: O
T: 22–25°C, L: 20 cm, pH: 7, D: 1–2

Tilapia tholloni   4/696
Thollon's tilapia
H: Gabon to Zaïre.
♂: Pointed genital papilla.   S: −
B: Open spawner; nuclear family.   F: H,O
T: 24–26°C, L: 30 cm, pH: 7, D: 2

Tilapia walteri   4/698
Walter's tilapia
H: W Africa: Cavally and Cess rivers
♂: Pointed D and A fins; larger.   S: =
B: Nat.: Os; nuclear family.   F: H,O
T: 24–26°C, L: 30 cm, pH: 7, D: 2

Tilapia zillii   1/778
Zilli's tilapia
H: Jordan, Syria; Sahara.   Fw, (Bw)
SD: Slight; genital papilla.   S: –
B: Os; <1000 e; nuclear family.   F: O
T: 20–24°C, L: <30 cm, pH: 7, D: 4

Tilapia zillii ♀, adult   3/894
Zilli's tilapia   (different color)
H: Jordan, Syria; Sahara.   Fw,(Bw)
SD: Slight; genital papilla.   S: –
B: Os; >1000 e; nuclear family. F: O,H
T: 18–24°C, L: 30 cm, pH: 7, D: 1

Tylochromis intermedius   3/898

H: Sierra Leone.
SD: Unknown.   S: ?
B: Unknown.   F: C? O?
T: 24–28°C, L: 15 cm, pH: 7, D: 3

Tylochromis lateralis   5/970
Congo tylochromis
H: Lower Zaïre.
SD: Unknown. Genital papilla?   S: =?
B: Mouthbrooder? Unknown.   F: C
T: 24–26°C, L: 25 cm, pH: 7, D: 3

Tylochromis leonensis   4/700
Sierra Leone tylochromis
H: Sierra Leone, W Liberia: coastal rivers.
SD: Unknown. Genital papilla?   S: =
B: Mouthbrooder? Unknown.   F: C
T: 24–26°C, L: 30 cm, pH: 7, D: 3

CICHLIDS

Introduction

The subgroup "North and Central America" deals with cichlids from the southern United States (*Cichlasoma cyanoguttatum*) to Panama. The natural habitat of some cichlids in this region, namely *Cichlasoma atromaculatum* and *C. umbriferum*, includes northern Colombia, but since their primary area of distribution is Central America, they are included in this subgroup rather than with the South American cichlids. Species which primarily occur from Colombia southward, even if their natural habitat includes areas of Panama, are presented in the subgroup "South America." (For instance, *Aequidens coeruleopunctatus*, which occurs from southern Costa Rica to northwestern Ecuador.) The endemic species of the Caribbean—Cuba, Hispaniola—are presented in the subgroup "Remaining World."

With a little practice it is not difficult to place the natural habitat of most cichlids.

Geographic Distribution

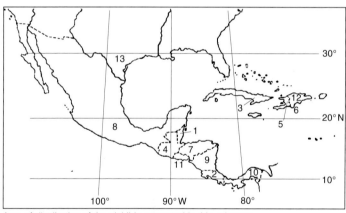

Area of distribution of the cichlids presented in this subgroup.

Belize (Bel.)	1	Mexico (Mex.)	8
Costa Rica (C.R.)	2	Nicaragua (Nic.)	9
Cuba	3	Panama (Pan.)	10
Guatemala (Gua.)	4	El Salvador (Sal.)	11
Haiti	5	Santo Domingo	12
Hispaniola	6	Texas, United States	13
Honduras (Hon.)	7		

Cuba, Haiti, and Santo Domingo (Hispaniola) are presented with Madagascan endemics and Indian species in the subgroup "Remaining World."

705

Generalities

Virtually all the cichlids of this subgroup are medium-large to large (20–35 cm); the fire mouth and its relatives are notable exceptions. At a length of 70 cm for males and 50 cm for females, *Cichlasoma dovii* is one of the largest of all cichlids.

The larger species are appreciated food fishes, but they are rarely cultured. Tilapine species of Africa, particularly *Oreochromis* spp., totally dominate cichlid aquaculture today, since they are comparatively robust and fast-growing. Perhaps further investigation will identify a Central American cichlid as a comparable alternative.

A large spacious aquarium is a prerequisite for successful care, and neutral to alkaline, medium-hard water is preferred. They are adept at rearranging their environment to meet their "personal tastes," an activity in which they seem to be constantly consumed. A few judiciously placed large rocks and a fine-meshed grating buried halfway in the substrate will curtail the damage. The latter measure will prevent the fish from exposing the bottom pane or, worse, the undergravel filter.

Aside from a few cave spawners and *"Geophagus" crassilabris*, a mouthbrooder, these cichlids can be characterized as prolific open spawners with a nuclear family. The males usually distinguish themselves through more color, larger size, and elongated and pointed fins. Oftentimes these features are only present in adults; hence, the genital papilla must be examined to reliably sex subadults.

Although most are omnivores with a carnivorous bent, some will nibble tender plant shoots or uproot plants as they sieve the substrate looking for edibles. As long as there is adequate plant fare in the diet and the plants are potted or have a few strategically placed rocks around their base, vegetation can be included in the decor.

Thanks to their striking colors and interesting social behavior, Central American cichlids are popular among hobbyists. Provided the aquarium is spacious and the water well-filtered, maintenance is straightforward. The aquarium's infrastructure should take their propensity for digging into account. Any rock edifications must be firmly based on the bottom pane of the aquarium so they will not come crashing down as the cichlids dig around the foundation. Most *Thorichthys* species are suitable for "normal" community aquaria as long as they are not breeding.

Archocentrus spinosissimus ♂   4/590
5/726

H: Guatemala.
♂: Longer fins.   S: =
B: Cs, Ös? Only successful once. F: C,O
T: 25–30°C, L: ♂ 12 cm, pH: >7, D: 3

Archocentrus spinosissimus ♂   4/590
5/726

Chuco godmanni ♂   3/726, 5/746
Godmann's cichlid
H: Guatemala, Belize.
♂: Red throat,shoulder; blue posterior.   S: =
B: Open spawner; nuclear family.   F: O
T: 26°C, L: ♂ 25 cm, pH: >7, D: 1

Chuco intermedius   3/732
Jordan's cichlid   Rio Chamata
H: S Mexico, Guatemala.
♂: Larger; more color. ♀: Dark throat.   S: =
B: Open spawner.   F: O,H
T: 25–27°C, L: ♂ 30 cm, pH: >7, D: 1–2

Chuco intermedius   3/732
Jordan's cichlid   Rio Nototum

Chuco microphthalmus   3/738

H: Guatemala and Honduras.
♂: Larger; more color; frontal hump.   S: =
B: Open spawner.   F: O
T: 22–28°C, L: 25 cm, pH: >7, D: 2

Chuco microphthalmus ♂   5/746

H: Guatemala: Motagua Basin,...
♂: Red dots, metallic blue.   S: –
B: Open spawner; nuclear family.   F: O
T: 25–30°C, L: ♂ 25 cm, pH: >7, D: 3

CICHLIDS

Chuco sp. "Rio Guarumo"   5/748

H: Panama: Rio Guarumo Basin.
♂: Darker brown fins; slightly larger.   S: =
B: Open spawner? Unsuccessful.   F: O
T: 26°C, L: ♂ 20 cm, pH: >7, D: 1

Cichlasoma alfari t.♂, b.♀   2/860
Pastel cichlid

H: Nicaragua, Costa Rica, Panama.
♂: Larger; boxy forehead.   S: –
B: Open spawner; nuclear family.   F: O
T: 23–27°C, L: 22 cm, pH: 7, D: 2–3

Cichlasoma altifrons   2/859
Hi-head cichlid

H: Costa Rica, Panama, Colombia.
♂: Larger; more colorful.   S: –
B: Open spawner; nuclear family.   F: O
T: 23–27°C, L: 22 cm, pH: 7, D: 2

Cichlasoma atromaculatum ♂   2/860
Rust-belly cichlid

H: Panama (Pacific), W Colombia.
♂: Larger.   S: –
B: Os; >1000 e; nuclear family.   F: O
T: 23–25°C, L: 25 cm, pH: >7, D: 3

Cichlasoma atromaculatum ♀   2/860
Rust-belly cichlid

"Cichlasoma" bartoni ♂   3/718
Barton's cichlid

H: N Mexico: Rio Panuco   E
♂: Larger; cepahlic hump w/ age.   S: –
B: Os; <300 e; nuclear family.   F: C,O
T: 21–27°C, L: 18 cm, pH: >7, D: 2

"Cichlasoma" bartoni ♀ 3/718
Barton's cichlid

"Cichlasoma" beani 3/720
Bean's cichlid
H: N Mexico.
SD: Unknown. S: –
B: Open spawner? Nuclear fam? F: O
T: 23–25°C, L: 30 cm, pH: >7, D: 1–2

Cichlasoma bifasciatum 2/862
Red-spotted cichlid
H: Mexico, Guatemala.
♀: Smaller; darker at spawning time. S: –
B: Os, 500 e; nuclear family. F: H,O
T: 22–27°C, L: 25 cm, pH: >7, D: 2

"Cichlasoma" calobrense 3/722
Red-spotted cichlid
H: Panama.
♂: Larger; more colorful. S: –
B: Os; <500 e; N or Pch-M fam. F: O
T: 22–27°C, L: <25 cm, pH: >7, D: 2

"Cichlasoma" centrarchus 3/722
Flier cichlid
H: Nicaragua to Costa Rica.
♂: Larger. S: =
B: Os; <500 e; nuclear family. F: O
T: 25–27°C, L: 15 cm, pH: 7, D: 1–2

Cichlasoma citrinellum 2/864
Midas cichlid
H: S Mex., Nicaragua, Costa Rica, Hon.
♂: Longer fins; frontal hump. S: –
B: Os; >1000 e; nuclear family. F: O
T: 22–25°C, L: 30 cm, pH: 7, D: 1–2

CICHLIDS

709

Cichlasoma cyanoguttatum 1/724
Texas cichlid, Rio Grande cichlid
H: NE Mexico, Texas.
♂: Larger; more colorful. S: –
B: Os; <500 e; nuclear family. F: C,O
T: 20–24°C, L: <30 cm, pH: 7, D: 3

Cichlasoma cyanoguttatum 1/724
Texas cichlid, Rio Grande cichlid

"Cichlasoma" diquis 3/724

H: Costa Rica: Pacific affluents.
♀: D fin often has a dark blotch. S: –
B: Os? Nuclear family? F: O
T: 25–28°C, L: 20 cm, pH: >7, D: 2–3

Cichlasoma dovii ♂ 2/866
Dow's cichlid, "lagunero"
H: E Honduras, Nicaragua, Costa Rica.
♂: 20 cm larger; more colorful. S: –
B: Os; >1000 e; nuclear family. F: C
T: 22–28°C, L: ♂ 70 cm, pH: 7, D: 3–4

"Cichlasoma" fenestratum 3/726

H: S Mexico.
♀: Darker; dorsal fin w/ design. S: =
B: Os; >1000 y; nuclear family. F: O
T: 25–28°C, L: 30 cm, pH: >7, D: 1–2

Cichlasoma friedrichsthalii ♂ 2/869
Friedrichsthal's cichlid
H: Mex., Gua., Hon., Bel., Nic., C.R.
♂: Less yellow; larger; darker. S: =
B: Os; nuclear family. F: C,O
T: 22–28°C, L: <25 cm, pH: 7, D: 1–2

"Cichlasoma" (or *Herichthys*?) *geddesi* (?)
4/588

H: S Mexico.
Species insufficiently defined.

"Cichlasoma" grammodes ♂ 3/728
Many-pointed cichlid
H: S Mexico.
♂: Longitudinal rows of spots. S: –
B: Cave spawner. F: O
T: 25°C, L: ♂ 25 cm, pH: >7, D: 2

"Cichlasoma" guttulatum ♂ 3/728
Gold-cheeked cichlid
H: Mexico and Guatemala.
♀: Dark zone on dorsal fin. S: =
B: Open spawner; >1000 young. F: O
T: 25–28°C, L: 30 cm, pH: >7, D: 1

"Cichlasoma" heterospilum ♂ 3/730
Candelaria cichlid
H: Mexico, Guatemala.
♀: Darker; pale dorsal spot. S: =
B: Open spawner. F: O,H
T: 25–30°C, L: <25 cm, pH: >7, D: 2

"Cichlasoma" hogaboomorum ♂ 3/730
Hogaboom cichlid
H: Honduras.
♀: Darker; smaller; dorsal spot? S: –
B: Open spawner. F: O
T: 25–30°C, L: 30 cm, pH: >7, D: 2

"Cichlasoma" istlanum 3/734
Papagallo cichlid
H: S Mexico.
♂: Larger; lighter; light blue. S: –
B: Open spawner. F: C
T: 27–30°C, L: 20 cm, pH: >7, D: 2

CICHLIDS

711

Cichlasoma labiatum 2/870
Red devil
H: Nic.: Lakes Nicaragua, Managua, Xiloa.
♂: Larger. S: –
B: Os; 600–700 e; P-M family. F: O
T: 24–26°C, L: 25 cm, pH: 7, D: 3

"Cichlasoma" labridens 3/734
Curve-bar cichlid
H: N Mexico: Panuco River.
♂: Larger; longer D and A fins. S: –
B: Open spawner; 300–600 eggs. F: O
T: 22–26°C, L: ♂ 25 cm, pH: >7, D: 2

"Cichlasoma" labridens ♀ 3/734
Curve-bar cichlid

"Cichlasoma" labridens ♀ 3/734
Curve-bar cichlid

Parapetenia loisellei ♀ 5/752
Yellow guapote
H: E Hon., Nicaragua, Costa Rica, Pan.
♀: Smaller; more yellow. S: =
B: Open spawner. F: C
T: 26–30°C, L: ♂ 25 cm, pH: >7, D: 1–2

Parapetenia loisellei ♂ 5/752
Yellow guapote

Cichlasoma longimanus 2/872
Longfin cichlid 3 pops. (data for C.R.)
H: 1) Hon.–N Nic. 2) Gua.–C.R. 3) Lakes Nic.
♂: Larger; lighter. S: =
B: Open spawner; nuclear family. F: O
T: 24–28°C, L: 22 cm, pH: 7, D: 2

"Cichlasoma" lyonsi 3/737

H: Costa Rica. Panama?
♂: Larger; slimmer. S: –
B: Open spawner. F: O
T: 25–28°C, L: 30 cm, pH: 7, D: 2–3

"Cichlasoma" macracanthum ♂ 3/738
High-spine cichlid
H: S Mexico, Gua., El Salvador, NW Hon.
♂: Longer D and A fins; larger. S: =
B: Open spawner. F: O
T: 25–28°C, L: 25 cm, pH: >7, D: 1–2

Cichlasoma maculicauda 2/872
Black belt cichlid
H: S Mexico, Gua., Belize, C.R., Pan.
♂: Larger; more colorful. S: –
B: Os; < 600 e; nuclear family. F: H,O
T: 22–27°C, L: 30 cm, pH: 7, D: 3

"Cichlasoma" minckleyi 5/754
Minkley's cichlid
H: N Mexico: Cuatro Cienegas Basin. E
♂: Boxy head; slimmer; larger. S: –
B: Open spawner; nuclear family. F: O
T: 26–30°C, L: ♂ 25 cm, pH: 7, D: 3

"Cichlasoma" motaguense ♀ 3/740
Motaguense
H: Guatemala, Honduras, El Salvador.
♂: Lighter; more greenish. S: –
B: Os; 2000 e; nuclear family. F: O
T: 25–30°C, L: >30 cm, pH: 7, D: 3

CICHLIDS

"Cichlasoma" nanoluteus ♀   4/590

H: Panama.
♂: Dark markings on dorsal fin.   **S:** =
B: Cs; paternal-maternal family.   **F:** C,O
T: 24–28°C, **L:** ♂ 9 cm, **pH:** 7, **D:** 1

Cichlasoma nicaraguense l.♂, r.♀   2/874
Nicaragua cichlid, spilotum

H: Nicaragua, Costa Rica.
♂: Dark markings on fins.   **S:** =
B: Os; non-adhesive eggs; P-M fam.   **F:** O
T: 23–27°C, **L:** ♂ 25 cm, **pH:** >7, **D:** 2

Cichlasoma nicaraguense ♂   2/874
Nicaragua cichlid, spilotum

"Cichlasoma" nigrofasciatum ♂   1/690
Zebra cichlid, convict cichlid

H: Gua., Sal., NW Hon., Nic., C.R., Pan.
♀: Shorter fins; red ventrally.   **S:** –
B: Cs–Os; paternal-maternal fam.   **F:** O
T: 20–23°C, **L:** 15 cm, **pH:** 7, **D:** 3

"Cichlasoma" octofasciatum   1/692
Jack Dempsy

H: S Mexico, Guatemala, and Honduras.
♂: More pointed D and A fin.   **S:** –
B: Os, <800 e; nuclear family.   **F:** C,O
T: 22–25°C, **L:** <20 cm, **pH:** <7, **D:** 3

"Cichlasoma" panamense ♂   3/742
Panama cichlid   red morph

H: Panama: Atlantic affluents = red morph.
♀: Dark blotch on dorsal fin.   **S:** =
B: Cave spawner.   **F:** C
T: 23–26°C, **L:** 15 cm, **pH:** 7, **D:** 3–4

CICHLIDS

"Cichlasoma" panamense   3/742
Panama cichlid

Brown morph, courtship coloration.
H: Panama: Pacific = brown morph.

"Cichlasoma" pantostictum ♂   3/744

H: N Mexico.   Fw (Bw)
SD: Unknown.   S: –
B: Open spawner? Saline water. F: C
T: 23–26°C, L: >20 cm, pH: >7, D: 2

"Cichlasoma" robertsoni ♂   3/746
Robertson's cichlid

H: S Mexico, Honduras.
♂: Larger; more sparkling dots.   S: –
B: Os; <400 e; nuclear family.   F: C
T: 22–26°C, L: 20 cm, pH: >7, D: 2–3

"Cichlasoma" rostratum   3/746

H: Nicaragua to N Costa Rica.
♂: Larger; more dots on the fins. S: =
B: Os; nuclear family.   F: C,O
T: 24–28°C, L: ♂ 24 cm, pH: 7, D: 2

Cichlasoma sajica ♂   2/878
T-bar cichlid

H: Costa Rica: in rivers.
♂: Pointed D and A fins; larger.   S: =
B: Cs; 300 e; N to P-M fam.   F: O
T: 23–26°C, L: ♂ 22 cm, pH: 7, D: 2

"Cichlasoma" salvini ♂   1/692
Salvin's cichlid

H: S Mexico, Guatemala, Honduras.
♂: Pointed D and A fins; w/ blue. S: –
B: Os; <500 e; nuclear family.   F: C,O
T: 22–26°C, L: 15 cm, pH: 7, D: 2

CICHLIDS

Cichlasoma septemfasciatum ♂   2/878
Cutter's cichlid

H: Costa Rica; several morphs.
♂: Pointed D and A fins; larger.   S: =
B: Open spawner; nuclear family.   F: O
T: 24–26°C, L: ♂ 12 cm, pH: 7, D: 2

Cichlasoma septemfasciatum ♀   2/878
Cutter's cichlid

Cichlasoma sieboldii b. ♀, t. ♂   2/880
Siebold's cichlid

H: Costa Rica to Panama.
♀: Smaller; black areas on D fin.   S: =
B: Cave spawner.   F: H,O
T: 23–25°C, L: 25 cm, pH: 7, D: 2–3

"*Cichlasoma*" sp. "Usumacinta"   3/750

H: S Mexico and Guatemala.
♂: Frontal hump develops w/ age.   S: =
B: Unknown.   F: O
T: 24–28°C, L: ca. 25 cm, pH: >7, D: 2

"*Cichlasoma*" sp.   3/750

H: Panama.
♂: Larger.   S: –
B: Open spawner.   F: O
T: 23–28°C, L: 18 cm, pH: 7, D: 3

"*Cichlasoma*" spilurum ♂   1/694
Blue-eyed cichlid

H: Guatemala.
♂: Pointed D & A fins; frontal hump. S: =
B: Cs; <300 e; nuclear family.   F: C,O
T: 22–25°C, L: ♂ 12 cm, pH: 7, D: 2

"Cichlasoma" steindachneri　　3/752,
5/756

H: N Mexico.
♂: Boxy head; larger; slimmer.　　S: =
B: Open spawner; nuclear family.　F: C
T: 23–26°C, L: ♂ 20 cm, pH: >7, D: 2

Cichlasoma synspilum ♂　　2/880
Redheaded cichlid

H: Guatemala to Belize.
♂: Cephalic hump develops w/ age.　S: =
B: Os; >1000 e; nuclear family.　　F: O
T: 24–28°C, L: 35 cm, pH: >7, D: 3

Cichlasoma synspilum ♀　　2/880
Redheaded cichlid

Cichlasoma trimaculatum　　2/882
Three-spot cichlid

H: Mexico to El Salvador.
♂: 11 cm larger.　　S: –
B: Os; >1000 e; nuclear family.　　F: O
T: 21–30°C, L: ♂ 36 cm, pH: 7, D: 2–3

"Cichlasoma" tuba　　3/754

H: Costa Rica.
♂: Larger.　　S: =
B: Open spawner; nuclear family.　F: O
T: 24–30°C, L: 35 cm, pH: 7, D: 3

"Cichlasoma" tuyrense　　3/754
Tuyre cichlid

H: Panama: Rio Bayano, Rio Tuyra.
♀: Smaller; dark blotch on D fin.　S: =
B: Os; <5000 e; nuclear family.　F: O,H
T: 25–30°C, L: <25 cm, pH: 7, D: 4

CICHLIDS

Cichlasoma umbriferum ♂   2/884
Umbriferum
H: Panama to Colombia.
♂: Filamentous D and A fins.   S: –
B: Open spawner.   F: C
T: 23–27°C, L: <80 cm?, pH: 7, D: 2–3

Cichlasoma urophthalmus   2/884
Eight-banded cichlid
H: Mexico, Belize, Honduras, Gua., Nic.
♂: Larger; more colorful.   S: =
B: Os; <600 e; nuclear family.   F: C,O
T: 20–27°C, L: 20 cm, pH: 7, D: 1–2

"Geophagus" crassilabris ♂   3/766
Thick-lipped eartheater
H: Panama.
♂: Larger; different colors.   S: =
B: ♀Mb; maternal family.   F: O
T: 25–30°C, L: 15 cm, pH: 7, D: 2–3

"Geophagus" crassilabris ♀   3/766
Thick-lipped eartheater

Herotilapia multispinosa   1/724
H: Nicaragua to Panama.
♂: Pointed D and A fins; larger.   S: =
B: Os; <1000 e; nuclear family.   F: C,O
T: 22–25°C, L: 13 cm, pH: 7, D: 2

Herichthys bocourti   5/838
H: Guatemala, Belize.
♂: Larger; orange (♀ more yellow).   S: =
B: Open spawner.   F: O,H
T: 26–30°C, L: 40 cm, pH: 7, D: 1

CICHLIDS

Herichthys carpintis 3/788
Pearlscale cichlid

H: N Mexico.
♂: Larger. S: =
B: Open spawner; nuclear family. F: O
T: 24–26°C, L: 30 cm, pH: 7, D: 1–2

Herichthys pearsei ♂ 4/626

H: Mexico, Guatemala.
♂: Frontal hump; larger; shinier. S: =
B: Nature: Os; very fertile. F: C,O
T: 26–30°C, L: ca. 40 cm, pH: 7, D: 1–2

Herichthys pearsei ♀ 3/790

H: S Mexico, N Guatemala.
♂: More colorful (green-yellow). S: –
B: Nature: Os; very prolific. F: O
T: 25–29°C, L: ca. 30 cm, pH: 7, D: 1–2

Herichthys sp. "Rio Nautla/Misautla"
5/840

H: Mexico.
♀: Dark blotch on D fin. S: =
B: Os; nuclear family. F: C,O
T: 24–27°C, L: ♂ 18 cm, pH: >7, D: 1–2

Herichthys sp. "Rio Tuxpán/Rio Pantepec"
5/840

H: Mexico: Rio Tuxpán Basin.
♀: Dark blotch on dorsal fin; smaller. S: –
B: Os; >1000 e; nuclear family. F: C,O
T: 24–27°C, L: ♂ 22 cm, pH: >7, D: 1–2

Herichthys tamasopoensis 5/842

H: Mexico: San Luis Postosi.
♀: Dark blotch on dorsal fin; smaller. S: –
B: Os; 200–300 e; nuclear fam. F: C,O
T: 23–26°C, L: ♂ 18 cm, pH: >7, D: 1

CICHLIDS

719

Neetroplus nematopus 2/958
Little lake cichlid normal coloration
H: Nicaragua, Costa Rica.
♂: Pointed D & A fins; 3 cm larger. S: –
B: Cs; <60 e; 6 d to hatch; N fam. F: O
T: 24–26°C, L: ♂ 11 cm, pH: >7, D: 2

Neetroplus nematopus 2/958
Little lake cichlid courtship coloration

Paraneetroplus bulleri 3/840

H: S Mexico: upper Coatzacoalcos.
♂: More intensely red. S: –
B: Nat.: Os; the few eggs are large. F: O
T: 25–27°C, L: 25 cm, pH: >7, D: 1–2

Paraneetroplus gibbiceps ♂ 4/664

H: S Mexico.
♂: Larger; steeper forehead. S: –
B: Os; relatively large eggs. F: C,O
T: 24–30°C, L: ♂ 30 cm, pH: >7, D: 3

Paraneetroplus nebulifer ♂ 4/666
Chonga cichlid
H: S Mexico.
♂: Larger; steeper forehead. S: =
B: Open spawner. F: O
T: 24–28°C, L: ♂ >30 cm, pH: >7, D: 4

Paraneetroplus omonti ♂ 4/668

H: S Mexico.
♂: Larger; steeper forehead. S: –
B: Os; relatively large eggs. F: C,O
T: 24–30°C, L: ♂ 30 cm, pH: >7, D: 4

CICHLIDS

Parapetenia managuensis 1/688
Managua cichlid
H: E Honduras, Nicaragua, Costa Rica.
♂: Pointed D & A fins; more colorful. **S:** –
B: Os; <5000 e; nuclear family. **F:** C,O
T: 23–25°C, **L:** <30 cm, **pH:** >7, **D:** 2

Paratheraps breidohri ♂ 3/842
Angostura cichlid
H: S Mexico: Angostura Reservoir.
♀: Black blotch on dorsal fin. **S:** =
B: Open spawner. **F:** O,H
T: 22–28°C, **L:** 21 cm, **pH:** >7, **D:** 2

Paratheraps hartwegi ♂ 3/842
Hartweg's cichlid
H: Mexico: Chiapas Highlands.
♀: Smaller; smaller dots; see photos. **S:** –
B: Os; many small eggs; N fam. **F:** O
T: 24–27°C, **L:** ♂ 16 cm, **pH:** >7, **D:** 1–2

Paratheraps hartwegi ♂ 3/842
Hartweg's cichlid

Paratheraps hartwegi ♀ 3/842
Hartweg's cichlid

Petenia splendida 2/966
Red snook
H: SE Mex., Guatemala, Belize, Nicaragua.
SD: None. **S:** –
B: Nature: Os; nuclear family. **F:** C
T: 24–26°C, **L:** <50 cm, **pH:** >7, **D:** 4

CICHLIDS

721

Theraps coeruleus ♀   3/879

Theraps irregularis   3/876

H: S Mexico, Guatemala.
♂: Cephalic hump; more colorful.   S: –
B: Open spawner.   F: O
T: 25–27°C, L: <25 cm, pH: >7, D: 3–4

Theraps lentiginosus ♀   3/876

Theraps lentiginosus ♂   3/876

H: S Mexico (Atlantic side), Guatemala.
♂: Larger; many brown dots.   S: =
B: Cave spawner.   F: C,O
T: 24–27°C, L: ♂ 25 cm, pH: >7, D: 3

H: Guatemala.

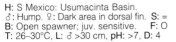

Theraps nourissati   5/968

Theraps rheophilus ♀   3/879

H: S Mexico: Usumacinta Basin.
♂: Hump. ♀: Dark area in dorsal fin. S: =
B: Open spawner; juv. sensitive.   F: O
T: 26–30°C, L: ♂ >30 cm, pH: >7, D: 4

H: Mexico: Panaque.

Thorichthys affinis ♂   3/881

H: Mexico, Guatemala, Belize.
♂: Pointed D & A fins; more colorful. **S:** =
B: Os; 100–500e; nuclear family. **F:**C,O
T: 21–27°C, **L:** 14 cm, **pH:** >7, **D:** 2

Thorichthys aureus b.♀, t.♂   3/882
Aureum

H: S Belize, Guatemala, Honduras.
♂: More pointed D and A fins.   **S:** =
B: Open spawner.   **F:** C
T: 24–28°C, **L:** 15 cm, **pH:** >7, **D:** 3–4

Thorichthys aureus ♀   3/882
Aureum

Thorichthys callolepis ♂   4/688

H: S Mexico.
♂: Pointed D and A fins; lighter.   **S:**–
B: Open spawner.   **F:** C
T: 25–28°C, **L:** ♂<12 cm, **pH:** >7, **D:** 3

Thorichthys ellioti   3/884

Thorichthys ellioti ♀   3/884

H: S Mexico.
♂: Pointed D & A fins; more colorful. **S:** =
B: Os;100–300 e; nuclear family.   **F:**C,O
T: 20–27°C, **L:** 13 cm, **pH:** >7, **D:** 2

CICHLIDS

Thorichthys helleri ♂ 3/886

Thorichthys helleri ♂ 3/886

H: S Mexico, Guatemala.
♂: Pointed D & A fins; more colorful. S: =
B: Os; 100–300 e; nuclear family. F: C,O
T: 22–27°C, L: 16 cm, pH: >7, D: 2

Thorichthys meeki ♂ 1/690
Firemouth cichlid

Thorichthys pasionis ♂ 3/888

H: Mexico, Guatemala.
♂: Pointed D & A fins; more colorful. S: =
B: Os; 100–500 e; nuclear fam. F: C,O
T: 21–24°C, L: 15 cm, pH: 7, D: 2

H: Guatemala.
♀: Reddish dots on ventrum. S: =
B: Os; nuclear family. F: C
T: 25–28°C, L: ♂16 cm, pH: ≫7, D: 1–2

Thorichthys pasionis ♂ 3/888

Thorichthys socolofi 3/890

H: SE Mexico.
♀: Smaller; dorsal fin spot. S: =
B: Os; 100–200 e; nuclear family. F: C
T: 22–26°C, L: 14 cm, pH: 7, D: 2–3

Tomocichla tuba ♀ 4/698

H: Nicaragua, Costa Rica, Panama.
♂: Head & body dark while courting. **S:** =
B: Os; eggs relatively large. **F:** C,O
T: 24–30°C, **L:** >30 cm, **pH:** >7, **D:** 3

Vieja argentea ♀ 4/702
Silver cichlid
H: S Mexico, Guatemala.
♂: Frontal hump develops w/ age. **S:** =
B: Open spawner? **F:** O
T: ca. 27°C, **L:** 27 cm, **pH:** >7, **D:** 1–2

Vieja heterospila 4/702
Pozolera cichlid
H: Mexico, Guatemala.
♀: Smaller; dark blotch on dorsal fin. **S:** =
B: Os; large eggs; nuclear fam. **F:** H,O
T: ca. 27°C, **L:** <22 cm, **pH:** >7, **D:** 1–2

Vieja melanurus 4/705

H: Guatemala: Lake Petén.
♂: Larger; protruding forehead. **S:** –
B: Os; easier w/ young breeders. **F:** O
T: ca. 27°C, **L:** 35 cm, **pH:** <7, **D:** 1–2

Vieja regani 3/744
Regan's cichlid
H: S Mexico.
♂: Larger; more colorful? **S:** =
B: Os; 300–500 e; nuclear family. **F:** O
T: 24–27°C, **L:** 25 cm, **pH:** >7, **D:** 1–2

Vieja zonata 5/976

H: Mexico: Chiapas: Pacific side.
♀: Darker dorsal fin. **S:** =
B: Open spawner; nuclear fam. **F:** O,H
T: 25–28°C, **L:** 25 cm, **pH:** >7, **D:** 2

CICHLIDS

725

SOUTH AMERICA

Introduction

The area of distribution of the cichlids in the subgroup "South America" includes South America in its entirety and, in some cases such as *Aequidens coeruleopunctatus*, southern Central America.

After catfishes (Siluriformes—Group 4) and characins (Characiformes—Group 2), cichlids have the greatest presence in South America.

Geographic Distribution

The morphological adaptation to various biotopes is highly developed, ranging from the torpedo-shaped bodies of riffle-dwelling fishes—e.g., *Retroculus* spp. and *Teleocichla* spp.—to the very unusual discoidal bodies of angelfishes and discus (*Pterophyllum* spp. and *Symphysodon* spp., respectively). The latter have evolved to better maneuver between the submersed branches of trees so commonly found in the tranquil backwaters they inhabit. As can be seen by the much greater species diversity, calm waters are the preferred biotope of cichlids. They are tropical fishes; *Gymnogeophagus* spp. are part of a very small minority of South American cichlids which live in subtropical regions. Therefore, most cichlids are unable to tolerate a temperature of 15°C for extended periods of time in the aquarium. They should not be maintained at temperatures less than 20°C.

Generalities

South American waters are predominantly soft and slightly acid. Fishes from the Rio Negro Basin even prefer extremely soft and acid waters. Such species are often prone to bacterial diseases in other types of water, and reproduction and long term health depend on the slightly antiseptic qualities of acidic waters. In rivers along the edge of the Amazon Basin, hardness and pH constantly fluctuate with the water level. In the aquarium, cichlids from such biotopes readily adapt to different pH and hardness values, but require oxygen-rich, well-filtered water. Fishes from the lowlands depend more on a relatively constant hardness and pH, while being more tolerant of dissolved metabolic wastes (nitrates, etc.).

South American cichlids are mostly omnivorous with a carnivorous bent. Few are specialized herbivores. The wide seasonal fluctuations of water levels that characterize so many biotopes of the region (p. 65) inhibit the establishment of an aquatic plant population. Furthermore, that trophic level is efficiently filled at present by catfishes and characins. As a planktivore, *Chaetobranchopsis orbicularis* is the exception. Its long-term maintenance has proven unsuccessful, even with a diet of plankton. *Cichla* spp. require live foodstuffs, live fishes in particular, and pieces of meat. They are difficult if not impossible to train to pelleted foods. *Crenicichla* are not as inflexible, displaying interest in dry commercial diets. Although often belligerent among themselves, either of the latter two genera can be associated with other fishes provided they are too large to be considered prey.

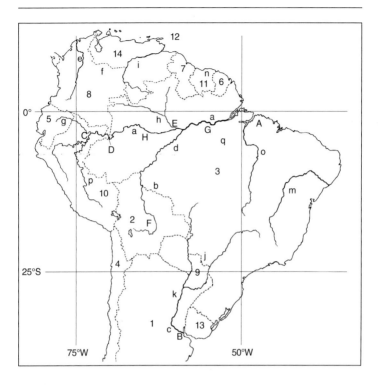

CICHLIDS

727

Larger species such as *Cichla* spp. are popular food fishes throughout their habitat. Although growth rate and pond breeding show promise, the problem of an economical diet for aquaculture is still unresolved (FISCHER, 1991).

Several reproductive strategies are represented: *Cichla* are prolific open spawners with a nuclear family; *Apistogramma* are polygamous cave spawners which can often be successfully bred in pairs (several will only breed in very soft, acid water); many in the *"Geophagus* group" are ovophile mouthbrooders; and some *Aequidens* and *Bujurquina* are larvophile mouthbrooders, laying their eggs on the substrate in a manner consistent to that of open spawners (sometimes on something they will move, like a leaf). Often the parents assist the larvae to hatch by "chewing" the eggs. The larvae are then mouthbrooded until they are free-swimming. The fry are commonly readmitted to either parent's mouth at night or when danger threatens for several days following their initial release.

One of the most unusual forms of brood care is practiced by the genera *Symphysodon* and *Uaru*. These open spawners adhere their eggs on vertical surfaces. Soon the parents begin to secrete copious amounts of mucus from their skin. The nutrition of the free-swimming fry is based on this mucus for the first couple of weeks; growth is rapid. Unfortunately, young which must be separated from their parents during this critical time often perish.

Apistogramma sp. aff. *payaminonis* ♀ with spawn.

Apistogramma sp. aff. *payaminonis* ♂. An offspring of parents captured in the Napo-Payamino Basin, Ecuador. Note the shape and color of the caudal fin.

Acarichthys geayi 1/666
Bandit cichlid
H: Guyana, N Brazil.
♂: 2 cm larger; steeper forehead. **S:** =
B: Cs, 500 e; P-M family. **F:** C,O
T: 22–25°C, **L:** ♂ 15 cm, **pH:** 7, **D:** 2

Acarichthys heckelii 2/812
Thread-finned cichlid
H: Guyana, Suriname, Brazil, Peru.
♀: Slightly fuller at spawning time. **S:** +
B: Cs; paternal-maternal family. **F:** O
T: 23–26°C, **L:** 20 cm, **pH:** 7, **D:** 2–3

Acaronia nassa 2/812
Big-eyed cichlid
H: Guyana, Brazil, Bolivia.
♂: Pointed D & A fins; more colorful. **S:** –
B: Open spawner; nuclear family. **F:** C
T: 25–28°C, **L:** 25 cm, **pH:** 7, **D:** 3

Aequidens coeruleopunctatus 2/814
Blue-point flag cichlid
H: NW Ecuador to S Costa Rica.
♂: Longer D & A fins; larger. **S:** =
B: Open spawner; nuclear family. **F:** O
T: 22–27°C, **L:** 15 cm, **pH:** 7, **D:** 2

Aequidens diadema 2/814

H: Brazil/Venezuela: upper Rio Negro.
♂: Larger; pointed genital papilla. **S:** +
B: ♀ ♂ LMb; nuclear family. **F:** O
T: 23–28°C, **L:** <25 cm?, **pH:** 7, **D:** 2–3

Aequidens mariae 1/668
Red-top green cichlid, Mary's cichlid
H: Colombia, W and N Brazil.
♂: Longer D and A fins; larger. **S:** +
B: ♀ ♂ LMb; nuclear family. **F:** C,O
T: 24–26°C, **L:** 15 cm, **pH:** <7, **D:** 2

Aequidens metae　　　3/680
Twin-spot flag cichlid
H: Colombia: Rio Meta.
SD: Virtually indistinguishable.　　S: +
B: Open spawner.　　F: O
T: 24–28°C, L: <20 cm, pH: 7, D: 1–2

Aequidens pallidus　　　1/664, 2/816
Pale flag cichlid
H: Amazon at Manaus.
SD: Only the genital papilla.　　S: =
B: ♀♂LMb; nuclear family.　　F: C,O
T: 23–28°C, L: ♂ 30, ♀ 20 cm, pH: 7, D: 3

Aequidens pallidus　　　1/664, 2/816
Pale flag cichlid

Aequidens patricki ♀　　　4/576

H: Peru: Ucayali region.
♀: Fins redder, also elongated.　　S: =
B: Os; N fam; pairing problematic.　F:C,O
T: 24°C, L: 17 cm, pH: 7, D: 2–3

Aequidens pulcher　　　1/670
Blue acara
H: Trinidad, Panama, N Venezuela, Col.
♂: Longer dorsal and anal fins.　　S: +
B: Open spawner; nuclear family.　F: C
T: 18–23°C, L: <20 cm, pH: 7, D: 1

Aequidens rivulatus ♂　　　1/672
Green terror
H: W Ecuador, central Peru.
♂: Larger; frontal hump.　　S: –
B: Open spawner; nuclear family.　F: C
T: 20–24°C, L: 20 cm, pH: 7, D: 2–3

Aequidens sapayensis ♂ 2/816
Sapayo cichlid
H: Ecuador: Rio Sapayo.
♂: Larger. S: =
B: Open spawner; <400 e; N fam. F: O
T: 24–26°C, L: ♂ <20 cm, pH: 7, D: 2–3

Aequidens syspilus 2/818
Somber flag cichlid
H: Peru: upper Amazon, Rio Ucayali.
♂: Longer fins; larger. S: =
B: ♀♂ LMb; nuclear family. F: O
T: 23–27°C, L: 15 cm, pH: 7, D: 2–3

Aequidens tetramerus ♂ 1/672
Saddle cichlid, blue-scale flag cichlid
H: Central and NE South America.
♂: Longer D and A fins; more color. S:=,–
B: Os; <1000; nuclear family. F: C
T: 24–26°C, L: 25 cm, pH: <7, D: 2–3

Aequidens sp. (*tetramerus* group) 3/680
Saddle cichlid, blue-scale flag cichlid
H: Peru: Yarina Cocha (Rio Ucayali).
♂: Elongated dorsal fin; larger. S: =
B: Os; <500 e; nuclear family. F: O
T: 25°C, L: ♂ 15 cm, pH: 7, D: 2

Aequidens vittatus ♂ 2/818
Half-banded cichlid
H: Brazil, N Argentina.
♂: Slightly larger. S: =
B: ♀♂ LMb; 200 e; nuclear family. F: O
T: 23–26°C, L: 15 cm, pH: 7, D: 2–3

Apistogramma agassizii ♂ 1/674
Agassiz's dwarf cichlid
H: Brazil: Amazon: S tributaries.
♂: Larger; more colorful. S: +
B: Cs; 150 e; Pch-M fam. F: C,O
T: 22–24°C, L: 8 cm, pH: <7, D: 3

731

Apistogramma cf. *agassizii* ♂ Tefé
"Tefé" dwarf cichlid   5/660
H: Brazil: Rio Tefé Basin.
♂: Larger; more colorful.   S: +
B: Cave sp.; 150 e; Pch-M fam. F: C,O
T: 23–29°C, L: ♂ 8 cm, pH: <7, D: 2

Apistogramma cf. *agassizii* ♂   5/660
Agassiz' dwarf cichlid
Orange morph.

Apistogramma cf. *agassizii* ♂   5/660
Agassiz' dwarf cichlid
Blue morph.

Apistogramma bitaeniata ♂   1/674
Two-striped dwarf cichlid
H: Peru, Brazil: Amazon.
♂: Larger; more colorful.   S: +
B: Cs; 40–60 eggs; Pch-M family. F: C
T: 23–25°C, L: ♂ 6 cm, pH: ≪7, D: 3

Apistogramma bitaeniata ♂   2/820
Two-striped dwarf cichlid
H: Central Amazon: Leticia.
♂: Larger; more colorful.   S: +
B: Cave sp.; <100 e; Pch-M fam.   F:C
T: 26–28°C, L: ♂ 6 cm, pH: <7, D: 3–4

Apistogramma borelli ♂   1/676
Borelli, umbrella dwarf cichlid
H: Brazil: Matto Grosso, Rio Paraguay.
♂: Larger; more colorful.   S: +
B: Cs; <70 e; Pch-M family.   F:C
T: 24–25°C, L: ♂ 8 cm, pH: <7, D: 3–4

Apistogramma borelli ♂ 3/682
Borelli, umbrella dwarf cichlid
Blue morph from the Rio Paraguay Basin.

Apistogramma cacatuoides ♂ 1/676
Cockatoo dwarf cichlid
H: Amazon Basin: 69°–71° west.
♂: Larger; more colorful.   S: +
B: Cs; <80 e; Pch-M family.   F: C,O
T: 24–25°C, L: ♂ 9 cm, pH: 7, D: 3

Apistogramma cacatuoides ♂ 3/684
Cockatoo dwarf cichlid
Color morph.

Apistogramma cacatuoides ♂ 3/684
Cockatoo dwarf cichlid
Color morph.

Apistogramma caetei ♂ 2/820
Caete dwarf cichlid
H: Brazil.
♂: Larger; more colorful.   S: +
B: Cave sp.; 200 e; Pch-M fam.   F: C
T: 23–30°C, L: ♂ 6 cm, pH: 7, D: 3

Apistogramma commmbrae ♂ 2/822
Corumba dwarf cichlid
H: Brazil, Paraguay.
♂: Reddish opercular spots.   S: +
B: Cs; 80 e; Pch-M to N fam.   F: C
T: 23–28°C, L: ♂ 5 cm, pH: 7, D: 3

CICHLIDS

733

Apistogramma cruzi ♂   3/682, 5/662

Apistogramma cruzi ♀   5/662

H: Colombia, Ecuador, Peru, Brazil.
♂: Larger; longer fins.   S: +
B: Cs; <150 e; Pch-M family.   F: C
T: 22–29°C, L: ♂ 8 cm, pH: <7, D: 2–3

Apistogramma cruzi ♀   3/682, 5/662

Apistogramma diplotaenia ♂   5/664
Double-band dwarf cichlid

H: Brazil, Venezuela.
♂: Larger; more colorful.   S: +
B: Cave spawner; Pch-M fam.   F: C,O
T: 24–29°C, L: ♂ 5.5 cm, pH: <7, D: 2–4

Apistogramma diplotaenia ♀   5/664
Double-band dwarf cichlid

Apistogramma elizabethae ♂   5/666
Elizabeth's dwarf cichlid

H: Venezuela, Colombia, Brazil: Uaupés R.
♂: Larger; more colorful; longer fins. S: +
B: Cs; 250 young; Pch-M family. F: C,O
T: 22–29°C, L: ♂ 10 cm, pH: ≪7, D: 4

Apistogramma elizabethae ♂   5/666
Elizabeth's dwarf cichlid

Apistogramma elizabethae ♀   5/666

Apistogramma eunotus ♂   2/822
Blue cheek dwarf cichlid

H: Peru: Rio Ucayali Basin.
♂: Larger; more colorful.   S: +
B: Cave spawner; 100 e; Pch-M fam. F: C
T: 23–30°C, L: ♂ 8.5 cm, pH: 7, D: 3

Apistogramma eunotus ♀   2/822
Blue cheek dwarf cichlid

Apistogramma geissleri ♂   5/670

H: Brazil: NW from Santarém.
♂: Larger; longer D and A fins.   S: +
B: Cs; patriarch-maternal family.   F: O
T: 21–29°C, L: ♂ 7 cm, pH: 7, D: 3

Apistogramma gephyra ♂ 2/824, 5/672
Mottled dwarf cichlid

H: Brazil: Rio Negro to Santarém.
♂: Larger; more colorful.   S: +
B: Cs; 120 e; patriarch-maternal fam. F:C
T: 23–30°C, L: ♂ 6 cm, pH: ≪7, D: 3–4

CICHLIDS

Apistogramma gephyra ♂ 2/824, 5/672
Mottled dwarf cichlid

Apistogramma gephyra ♀ 2/824, 5/672
Mottled dwarf cichlid

Apistogramma gephyra ♂ 2/824, 5/672
Mottled dwarf cichlid

Apistogramma gibbiceps ♂ 2/824, 5/675
Yellow-cheeked dwarf cichlid

H: Brazil: Rio Negro.
♂♀:Larger; double-tipped caudal fin. S: +
B: Cs; 200 e; patriarch-maternal fam. F:C
T: 27–29°C, L: ♂ 8 cm, pH: ≪7, D: 4

Apistogramma gibbiceps ♂ 2/824, 5/675
Yellow-cheeked dwarf cichlid

Apistogramma gibbiceps ♀ 2/824, 5/675
Yellow-cheeked dwarf cichlid

Apistogramma gossei ♂ 5/676
Brilliant dwarf cichlid

Apistogramma gossei ♀ 5/676
Brilliant dwarf cichlid

H: French Guiana/Brazil.
♂: Larger; more color; longer D & A. S: +
B: Cs; patriarch-maternal family. F: C!
T: 22–29°C, L: ♂ 6 cm, pH: <7, D: 2–3

Apistogramma guttata ♂ 5/678

H: Venezuela: Rio Morichal Largo Basin.
♂: Larger; more color; longer D & A. S: =
B: Cave spawner; Pch-M family. F: C!
T: 23–29°C, L: ♂ 6 cm, pH: <7, D: 4

Apistogramma hippolytae ♂ 2/826
Empress or two spotted dwarf cichlid

H: Brazil: Amazon, Rio Negro.
♂: Larger; more colorful. S: +
B: Cs; <200 e; Pch-M family. F: C!
T: 23–30°C, L: ♂ 6.5 cm, pH: 7, D: 3

Apistogramma hippolytae ♀ 2/826
Empress or two spotted dwarf cichlid

Apistogramma hoignei ♂ 5/678

H: Venezuela: Rio Apuré, Rio Portuguesa.
♂: Larger; more color; longer D & A. S: +
B: Cave spawner; Pch-M family. F: C,O
T: 22–24°C, L: ♂ 8 cm, pH: <7, D: 3

Apistogramma hoignei ♀   5/678

Apistogramma hongsloi ♂   2/826, 5/680
Red-lined dwarf cichlid
H: Ven., Col.: Orinoco, Rio Vichada, Meta.
♂: Larger; more colorful.   S: +
B: Cs; 60–90 eggs; Pch-M family.   F: C
T: 23–30°C, L: ♂ 7.5 cm, pH: ≪7, D: 3–4

Apistogramma hongsloi ♂   2/826, 5/680
Red-lined dwarf cichlid   red

Apistogramma hongsloi ♀   2/826, 5/680
Red-lined dwarf cichlid

Apistogramma inconspicua ♂   3/685
Undistinguished dwarf cichlid
H: Bolivia, Brazil, Paraguay.
♂: Larger; more pointed fins.   S: +
B: Cave spawner; Pch-M fam.   F: C
T: 23–28°C, L: ♂ 8 cm, pH: <7, D: 3

Apistogramma inconspicua ♀   3/685
Undistinguished dwarf cichlid
See photo on p. 5/683.

Apistogramma iniridae ♂   2/828
Thread-finned dwarf cichlid
H: Colombia: Rio Inirida.
♂: Larger; more colorful.   S: +
B: Cs; 150 e; patriarch-maternal fam. F: C
T: 23–30°C, L: ♂ 7.5 cm, pH: ≪7, D: 4

Apistogramma juruensis ♂   5/684
Juruá dwarf cichlid
H: Brazil, Peru: Rio Juruá.
♂: 3 cm larger; long D and A fins. S: +
B: Cave spawner; Pch-M fam.   F: C
T: 22–29°C, L: ♂ 8 cm, pH: <7, D: 2–3

Apistogramma juruensis ♀   5/684
Juruá dwarf cichlid

Apistogramma linkei ♂   3/686
Linke's dwarf cichlid
H: Bolivia: Santa Cruz.
♂: Larger; more colorful.   S: +
B: Cave spawner; 100 e; Pch-M fam. F: O
T: 24–26°C, L: ♂ 6 cm, pH: >7, D: 2

Apistogramma linkei ♀   3/686

See photo on p. 5/683.

Apistogramma luelingi ♂   3/686
Lüling's dwarf cichlid, golden apisto
H: Bolivia: Rio Chapore.
♂: Larger; longer fins.   S: +
B: Cs; 60 e; patriarch-maternal fam. F: O
T: 22–26°C, L: ♂ 7 cm, pH: 7, D: 2

CICHLIDS

Apistogramma luelingi ♂ 3/686
Lüling's dwarf cichlid, golden apisto
See photo on p. 5/687.

Apistogramma luelingi ♀ 3/686
Lüling's dwarf cichlid, golden apisto
See photo on p. 5/688.

Apistogramma macmasteri ♂ 1/678
Macmaster's or red-tailed dwarf cichlid
H: Brazil: Amazon: S tributaries.
♂: Larger; more colorful. S: +
B: Cs; <120 e; Pch-M family. F: C!
T: 23–30°C, L: ♂ 8 cm, pH: <7, D: 3

Apistogramma macmasteri ♀ 1/678
Macmaster's or red-tailed dwarf cichlid
See photo on p. 5/688.

Apistogramma meinkeni t.♂,b.♀ 5/689
Meinken's dwarf cichlid
H: Brazil: Rio Uaupés.
♂: More elongated fins. S: =
B: Cave spawner; 30y; Pch-M fam. F: C
T: 22–29°C, L: ♂ 5 cm, pH: ≪7, D: 3–4

Apistogramma meinkeni ♂ 5/689
Meinken's dwarf cichlid

CICHLIDS

Apistogramma mendezi ♂   5/694

Apistogramma mendezi ♀   5/694

H: NW Brazil: upper Rio Negro.
♂: Larger; more colorful.   S: +
B: Cave spawner; Pch-M family.   F: C
T: 22–29°C, L: ♂ 10 cm, pH: ≪7, D: 3–4

Apistogramma moae ♂   5/697
Moa dwarf cichlid
H: Brazil: state of Acre: Rio Moa.
♂: Larger; D and A longer.   S: ?
B: Unknown.   F: O
T: 21–29°C, L: ♂ 7 cm, pH: <7, D: 2–3

Apistogramma nijsseni ♂   2/828
Panda dwarf cichlid, Nijssen's dwarf cich.
H: Peru: lower Ucayali region.
♂: Larger; more colorful.   S: +
B: Cave spawner; Pch-M family.   F: C
T: 23–30°C, L: ♂ 6.5 cm, pH: ≪7, D: 3–4

Apistogramma norberti ♂   4/576
Norbert's dwarf cichlid
H: Peru: Loreto.
♂: More colorful; larger.   S: +
B: Cs? 150 eggs; Pch-M fam?   F: C
T: 24°C, L: 7 cm, pH: ≪7, D: 2–3

Apistogramma ortmanni ♂   5/698
"Tumuremo" apistogramma
H: E Venezuela, Guyana, Suriname.
♂: Larger; longer D and A fins.   S: +
B: Cs; patriarch-maternal family.   F: C!
T: 23–29°C, L: ♂ 7 cm, pH: <7, D: 2–3

741

Apistogramma ortmanni ♀   5/698
"Tumuremo" dwarf cichlid

Apistogramma paucisquamis ♂   5/700
orange morph
H: NW Brazil: Rio Negro.
♂: Larger; more colorful.   S: +
B: Cave spawner; Pch-M fam.   F: C
T: 22–29°C, L: ♂ 10 cm, pH: ≪7, D: 4

Apistogramma paucisquamis ♀   5/700

H: Brazil: Rio Preto.

Apistogramma pertensis ♂   2/830
Amazon dwarf cichlid
H: Brazil: Rio Negro, Amazon.
♂: Larger; sail-like dorsal fin.   S: +
B: Cs; 120 e; patriarch-maternal fam. F: C
T: 23–30°C, L: ♂ 6.5 cm, pH: ≪7, D: 3–4

Apistogramma cf. *pertensis* ♂   5/702
Amazon dwarf cichlid
H: Brazil: Rio Negro, Amazon.
♂: Larger; sail-like dorsal fin.   S: +
B: Cave spawner; 120 e; Pch-M fam. F: C
T: 23–30°C, L: ♂ 6.5 cm, pH: ≪7, D: 3–4

Apistogramma cf. *pertensis* ♀   5/702
Amazon dwarf cichlid

CICHLIDS

Apistogramma piauensis ♂   5/704

Apistogramma piauensis ♀   5/704

H: E Brazil: Rio Itapicuru and Paranaiba.
♂: Larger; more color; longer D fin.   S: +
B: Cs; 150 e; patriarch-maternal fam. F: C
T: 20–29°C, L: ♂ 6 cm, pH: <7, D: 3

Apistogramma regani ♂   2/830
Regan's dwarf cichlid

Apistogramma regani ♀   2/830
Regan's dwarf cichlid

H: Brazil: Rio Negro, Amazon.
♂: Larger; larger fins.   S: +
B: Cave spawner? Pch-M fam?   F: C
T: 23–30°C, L: ♂ 7 cm, pH: <7, D: 3–4

Apistogramma resticulosa ♂   3/688
Reticulated dwarf cichlid
H: Brazil: Rio Madeira.
♂: Larger; more colorful.   S: +
B: Cs; 100 young; Pch-M family. F: O
T: 26°C, L: ♂ 5 cm, pH: <7, D: 2

Apistogramma rupununi ♂   5/706

H: Brazil, Guyana: Rio Branco & Rupununi.
♂: Larger; more colorful.   S: +
B: Cs; patriarch-maternal family. F: C,O
T: 22–30°C, L: ♂ 9 cm, pH: <7, D: 3

Apistogramma sp. "Tiquié 1" ♂ 5/692
"Tiquié 1" (with 3 spots)
H: Brazil: Rio Uaupés, Rio Tiquié.
♂: Larger; yellowish. ♀: 3–5 spots. **S:** +
B: Cs; 15 young; Pch-M fam. **F:** C
T: 22–29°C, **L:** ♂ 5 cm, **pH:** ≪7, **D:** 3–4

Apistogramma sp. "Tiquié 1" ♀ 5/692
"Tiquié 1" (with 3 spots)

Apistogramma sp. "Tucurui" ♂ juv. 5/706

H: Brazil: Rio Tocantins.
♂: Larger; fins w/ blue sheen. **S:** +
B: Cave spawner; Pch-M fam. **F:** C,O
T: 22–30°C, **L:** ♂ 6 cm, **pH:** <7, **D:** 2–3

Apistogramma sp. "Tucurui" ♀ 5/706

Apistogramma sp. ♂ 5/716
"Broad-band" dwarf cichlid
H: Venezuela, Brazil: Uaupés, Orinoco.
♂: Larger; more colorful; longer fins. **S:** +
B: Cs; patriarch-maternal family. **F:** C
T: 23–29°C, **L:** ♂ 10 cm, **pH:** ≪7, **D:** 2–4

Apistogramma sp. ♀ 5/716
"Broad-band" dwarf cichlid

Apistogramma sp. ♀ 5/718

H: Unknown.
SD: Only ♀♀ have been found! S: +
B: Unknown. F: C!
T: 23–29°C, L: ♀ 6 cm, pH: <7, D: 4

Apistogramma sp. ♂ 5/720

H: Brazil: around Manaus.
♂: Larger; longer D and A fins. S: +
B: Cave spawner; Pch-M family. F: O
T: 21–29°C, L: ♂ 8 cm, pH: 7, D: 2

Apistogramma sp. ♀ 5/720

Apistogramma sp. ♂ 5/722

H: Venezuela, Brazil: Orinoco, Uaupés.
♂: Larger fins. S: +
B: Patriarch-maternal family. F: C
T: 22–30°C, L: 8 cm, pH: <7, D: 3–4

Apistogramma sp. ♀ 5/722

Apistogramma sp. ♂ 5/724
"Pandurini," blue sky, or azure dwarf cichlid
H: Ecuador? Peru: Rio Napo Basin.
♂: Larger; see photos. S: +
B: Unknown. F: C,O
T: 20–32°C, L: ♂ 8 cm, pH: <7, D: 3–4

Apistogramma sp. ♀ 5/724
"Pandurini," blue sky, or azure dwarf cichlid

Apistogramma staecki ♂ 3/688
Staeck's dwarf cichlid
H: N Bolivia.
♂: Larger; double-tipped C fin. S: +
B: Cave spawner; 80 e; Pch-M fam. F: O
T: 24–28°C, L: ♂ 5 cm, pH: <7, D: 2–3

Apistogramma steindachneri ♂ 1/678
Steindachner's dwarf cichlid
H: Guianas.
♂: Larger; longer fins. S: +
B: Cs; patriarch-maternal family. F: C
T: 20–25°C, L: ♂ 12 cm, pH: <7, D: 2

Apistogramma trifasciata ♂ 1/680
Three-stripe dwarf cichlid, blue apistogr.
H: Rio Paraguay, Rio Guaporé.
♂: Larger; 3rd–5th D fin rays longer. S: +
B: Cave spawner; 100 e; Pch-M fam. F: C
T: 26–29°C, L: ♂ 6 cm, pH: <7, D: 3

Apistogramma uaupesi ♂ 5/710

Apistogramma uaupesi ♀ 5/710

H: Venezuela, Colombia, Brazil.
♂: Sail-like D fin; double-tipped C. S: +
B: Cave sp.; <2°dGH, pH 4–5. F: C!
T: 23–29°C, L: ♂ 9 cm, pH: ≪7, D: 4

CICHLIDS

Apistogramma uaupesi ♂   5/710

Apistogramma uaupesi ♀   5/710

Apistogramma urteagai ♂   5/714

Apistogramma urteagai ♀   5/714

H: Peru: Rio Madre de Dios, Rio Tambopata.
♂: Longer D & A fins; more colorful. **S:** +
B: Cs; patriarch-maternal family. **F:** C,O
T: 22–29°C, **L:** ♂ 6 cm, **pH:** ≪7, **D:** 2

Apistogramma viejita ♂   2/832
Viejita dwarf cichlid
H: Colombia: Rio Meta.
♂: Larger; elongated dorsal fin.   **S:** +
B: Cave sp.; 100 e; Pch-M family.   **F:** C
T: 23–30°C, **L:** ♂ 7.5 cm, **pH:** ≪7, **D:** 4

Apistogrammoides pucallpaensis ♂   2/832
T-bar dwarf cichlid
H: Peru: Amazon Basin.
♂: Longer D & A fins; more color.   **S:** +
B: Cs; 80 e; Pch-M to N fam.   **F:** C
T: 23–30°C, **L:** ♂ 4.5 cm, **pH:** <7, **D:** 3–4

CICHLIDS

Astronotus ocellatus   1/682
Oscar
H: Amaz., Paraná, Rio Paraguay, Rio Negro.
SD: Only the genital papilla.   S: =
B: Os; 2000 eggs; nuclear family.   F: C
T: 22–25°C, L: 33 cm, pH: 7, D: 4

Batrachops semifasciatus ♀   2/848
H: Paraguay, Uruguay, Argentina.
♂: Dark spots.   S: =
B: Cave spawner?   F: O
T: 23–27°C, L: 27 cm, pH: 7, D: 3–4

Batrachops semifasciatus ♂   2/848

Biotodoma cupido   1/684
Cupid cichlid
H: Central Amazon, W Guyana.
♂: More pointed D and A fins.   S: –
B: Os; 100 e; nuclear family.   F: C
T: 23–25°C, L: 13 cm, pH: 7, D: 3

Biotodoma cupido ♂   3/708
Cupid cichlid
H: Peru to SE Brazil.
♂: Much more colorful.   S: –
B: Open spawner; 400 e; N family.   F: C
T: 22–25°C, L: 12 cm, pH: 7, D: 3

Biotodoma cf. *cupido* ♂   3/708
Cupid cichlid
See photo on p. 5/738.

Biotodoma wavrini   3/708
Wavrin's cichlid
H: Upper Rio Orinoco, Rio Negro,...
♂: Longer C & V fins; more colorful. S: +
B: Probably unsuccessful.   F: C
T: 26–30°C, L: 15 cm, pH: <7, D: 4

Biotoecus opercularis ♀   5/738
Green dwarf cichlid
H: At Santarém: Amazon tributaries.
♂: Longer ventral fins.   S: +
B: Cs; almost maternal family.   F: C
T: 28°C, L: 5 cm, pH: <7, D: 4

Biotoecus opercularis ♂   5/738
Green dwarf cichlid

Caquetaia kraussii ♂   2/850
Krauss' cichlid
H: Colombia, Venezuela.
♂: More pointed D & A fins; larger. S: –
B: Os; <400 e; nuclear family.   F: C,O
T: 22–27°C, L: 25 cm, pH: 7, D: 2–3

Caquetaia kraussii juv.   2/850
Krauss' cichlid

Caquetaia myersi ♂   5/740

H: Colombia, Ecuador: Caquetá, Napo.
♂: Dark blue fins. ♀: Yellow.   S: =
B: Open spawner; <700 e; N fam.   F: C
T: 24–27°C, L: 27 cm, pH: 7, D: 2–3

Caquetaia spectabilis 3/714

H: Central and lower Amazon.
♂: Larger; sexes otherwise equal. S: =
B: Open spawner; nuclear family. F: C
T: 26–27°C, L: ♂ 25 cm, pH: 7, D: 1–2

Chaetobranchopsis orbicularis ♂ 2/850
Two-striped cichlid

H: Amazon.
SD: Unknown. S: +
B: Unknown. F: C! (filtering planktivore)
T: 23–27°C, L: 12 cm, pH: 7, D: 4

Chaetobranchopsis orbicularis juv. 2/850
Two-striped cichlid

Chaetobranchus flavescens 2/852
Red-eye cichlid

H: Guyana, Brazil, Peru, Bolivia.
♂: Longer D and A fins; larger. S: ?
B: Mouthbrooder? F: O
T: 24–26°C, L: 28 cm, pH: 7, D: 3

Cichla monoculus ♀ 5/750
Peacock cichlid, tucunare

H: Fr. Guiana, Brazil, Ecuador, Peru, Bol.
♂: Nuchal hump develops w/ age. S: =
B: Nat.: Os; 2000 e; nuclear fam. F: C!
T: 25–28°C, L: 50 cm, pH: <7, D: 2

Cichla ocellaris 2/856
Peacock cichlid

H: Venezuela, Guyana, Brazil, Peru, Bolivia.
♂: Nuchal hump develops w/ age. S: =
B: Nat.: Os; 10000e; nuclear fam. F: C!
T: 24–27°C, L: 60 cm, pH: 7, D: 3–4

CICHLIDS

Cichla orinocensis 5/750
Orinoco peacock cichlid
H: Venezuela, Colombia, Brazil.
♂: Nuchal hump develops w/ age. **S**: =
B: Nat.: spawns in a pit. **F**: C!
T: 27–29°C, **L**: <70 cm, **pH**: <7, **D**: 2

Cichla temensis 5/748
Spot-line peacock cichlid
H: Brazil: Rio Negro, Orinoco.
♂: Larger; nuchal hump w/ age. **S**: =
B: Nat.: spawns in a pit. **F**: C!
T: 27–29°C, **L**: <70 cm, **pH**: <7, **D**: 2

Cichlasoma amazonarum 3/716
Amazon cichlid
H: Amazon Basin.
♂: Longer D and A fins. **S**: =
B: Open spawner; 300 e; N fam. **F**: C,O
T: 22–27°C, **L**: 14 cm, **pH**: <7, **D**: 1

Cichlasoma araguaiense ♂ 4/588
Araguaia cichlid
H: S Amaz. trib.: Araguaia, Tocantins, Xingú.
♂: Longer D and A fins. **S**: =
B: Open spawner; nuclear family. **F**: O
T: 23–27°C, **L**: ♂ 16 cm, **pH**: 7, **D**: 1–2

Cichlasoma bimaculatum ♂ 2/862
Twin-spot cichlid
H: E Peru to the Guianas.
♂: Slightly larger. **S**: =
B: Open spawner; nuclear family. **F**: O
T: 22–27°C, **L**: 20 cm, **pH**: 7, **D**: 1–2

Cichlasoma boliviense ♂ 3/720
Bolivian cichlasoma
H: Bolivia: Amazon Basin.
♂: Longer D and A fins. **S**: =
B: Open spawner; nuclear family. **F**: O
T: 23–27°C, **L**: 17 cm, **pH**: 7, **D**: 1–2

CICHLIDS

751

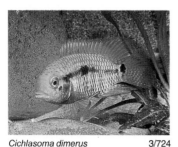

Cichlasoma dimerus 3/724
Dimerus cichlid
H: Rio Paraguay, Rio Paraná.
♂: Longer D and A fins; larger.   S: =
B: Open spawner; nuclear family.   F: O
T: 23–27°C, L: 17 cm, pH: 7, D: 1

"Cichlasoma" facetum 1/688
Chanchito, chameleon cichlid
H: S Brazil, N Arg., Paraguay, Uruguay.
SD: Genital papilla.   S: –
B: Os; 300–1000 e; nuclear fam. F: C,O
T: 27–30°C, L: Nat: 70 cm, pH: <7, D: 2

Cichlasoma festae ♀ 2/866
Red terror
H: W Ecuador.
♂: Blue dotted D, A, and C fins.   S: –
B: Os; 3000 e; nuclear family.   F: C,O
T: 26–28°C, L: 50 cm, pH: 7, D: 3

Cichlasoma festae ♂ 2/866
Red terror

Cichlasoma orinocoense ♂ 5/754
Orinoco cichlid
H: Venezuela: Rio Orinoco.
♂: Larger; elongated D and A fins. S: =
B: Unknown.   F: C,O
T: 26–30°C, L: 50 cm, pH: 7, D: 2

"Cichlasoma" ornatum 3/740
Esmeraldas cichlid
H: NW Ecuador, SW Colombia?
SD: Unknown.   S: = (to 14 cm length)
B: Open spawner? Nuclear family? F: O
T: 24–27°C, L: >20 cm?, pH: >7, D: 2

CICHLIDS

Cichlasoma portalegrense 1/670
Black acara, port acara
H: S Brazil, Bolivia, Paraguay.
♀: Dark brown to reddish. S: =
B: Os; <500 e; nuclear family. F: C
T: 16–24°C, L: 15 cm, pH: <7, D: 2

Cichlasoma taenia 3/752
H: Trinidad; Venezuela: Orinoco Basin.
SD: None. S: =
B: Open spawner; nuclear family. F: O
T: 24–27°C, L: ♂ 14 cm, pH: 7, D: 2

Cleithracara maronii adult 1/668
Keyhole cichlid
H: Guyana.
♂: Longer D and A fins; larger. S: +
B: Os; 350 e; nuclear family. F: C,O
T: 22–25°C, L: 15 cm, pH: 7, D: 1–2

Cleithracara maronii juvenil 1/668
Keyhole cichlid

Crenicara filamentosa ♂ 1/696
Chessboard or lyre-tailed checkerboard c.
H: Rio Negro, Orinoco.
♂: Double-tipped C fin; more color. S: =
B: Os; 60–120 e; nuclear family. F: C!
T: 23–25°C, L: ♂ 9 cm, pH: ≪7, D: 2–3

Crenicara latruncularium ♂ 5/764
H: Brazil, Bolivia: Rio Guaporé & Mamoré.
♂: Slightly pointed fins. S: =
B: Open spawner; polygamous. F: O
T: 20–30°C, L: 15 cm, pH: 7, D: 4

753

Crenicara latruncularium ♀   5/764

Crenicara punctulata ♂   1/696
Red-finned checkerboard cichlid
H: Guyana, N Brazil, Ecuador, Peru.
♂: Longer fins; more colorful.   S: =
B: Open spawner; nuclear family.   F: C!
T: 23–25°C, L: 12 cm, pH: <7, D: 3

Crenicichla acutirostris ♂   5/766

Crenicichla acutirostris ♀   5/766

H: Brazil: at Santarém.
♂: Finely spotted caudal fin.   S: =
B: Nat.: Cs; nuclear family.   F: C!
T: 26–28°C, L: ♂ 35 cm, pH: <7, D: 3–4

Crenicichla albopunctata ♂   5/768
White-spotted pike cichlid
H: Guyana, French Guiana.
♂: Shiny spots.   S: =
B: Cave spawner; nuclear family.   F: C!
T: 24–27°C, L: ♂ 25 cm, pH: 7, D: 1–2

Crenicichla albopunctata ♀   5/768
White-spotted pike cichlid

CICHLIDS

Crenicichla alta ♂   4/596

Crenicichla alta ♀   4/596

H: Guyana, Brazil.
♀: Beautifully fringed D fin.   S: –
B: Cs; paternal-maternal family.   F: C
T: 24–27°C, L: ♂ 25 cm, pH: ≪7, D: 1–2

See photo on p. 5/789.

Crenicichla anthurus ♀   3/756

Crenicichla cametana subadult ♂   4/596
Star-gazing pike cichlid

H: E Ecuador, Peru.
♀: Red stomach; no iridescent spots. S:=
B: Cs; paternal-maternal family.   F: C
T: 25–27°C, L: ♂ <25 cm, pH: 7, D: 3

H: Brazil: Rio Tocantins.
♀: Reddish ventrum.   S: –
B: Cs; paternal-maternal family.   F: C
T: 24–27°C, L: 25 cm, pH: 7, D: 3

Crenicichla cametana ♀   4/596
Star-gazing pike cichlid

Crenicichla cardiostigma ♂   5/770
Heart-spot pike cichlid

H: Brazil: Rio Branco/Rio Mucajai.
♂: Iridescent spots.   S: =
B: Cave spawner; nuclear family.   F: C!
T: 24–27°C, L: ♂ 25 cm, pH: 7, D: 1

CICHLIDS

755

Crenicichla cardiostigma ♀ 5/770
Heart-spot pike cichlid

Crenicichla cincta 4/598

H: Brazil, Peru.
SD: Unknown. S: –
B: Cave spawner? F: C,O
T: 24–27°C, L: ♂45 cm, pH: <7, D: 1–2

Crenicichla compressiceps ♂ 4/600

H: Brazil: Tocantins, Araguaia.
♂: Striped, yellow fins. S: –
B: Cs; paternal-maternal family. F: C,O
T: 24–27°C, L: ♂7 cm, pH: 7, D: 1–2

Crenicichla cyanonotus ♀ 5/772

Crenicichla cyanonotus ♂ 5/772

H: Venezuela?, Brazil.
♀: More colorful; smaller. S: =
B: Cave sp.; ♀ tends the spawn. F: C
T: 24–27°C, L: 25 cm, pH: 7, D: 1

Crenicichla cyclostoma ♂ 4/600

H: Brazil: Tocantins Basin.
♂: Elongated dorsal fin; larger. S: =
B: Cs; not very fecund; P-M fam. F: C
T: 24°C, L: 15 cm, pH: <7, D: 1–2

Crenicichla edithae b.♀, t.♂   4/602

Crenicichla edithae ♀   4/602

H: S Amazon Basin.
♀: Golden dots; larger.   S: =
B: Cave spawner; P-M family.   F: C
T: 24–27°C, L: ♂ 22 cm, pH: 7, D: 1–2

Crenicichla geayi b.♀, t.♂   4/604
Half-barred pike cichlid

Crenicichla geayi ♀   4/604
Half-barred pike cichlid

H: Venezuela, Colombia.
♂: Red stripe running along flanks. S: =
B: Cs; paternal-maternal family.   F: C
T: 24–27°C, L: 20 cm, pH: 7, D: 1–2

Crenicichla jegui ♂ (?)   5/774

H: Brazil: Rio Tocantins.   E
♀: Red-blotched D fin; smaller.   S: =
B: Unknown.   F: C!
T: 27–29°C, L: >30 cm, pH: 7, D: 4

Crenicichla johanna ♀   2/886
Red-finned pike cichlid, gray pike cichlid

H: Ven., Guyana, Braz., Peru, Paraguay.
♂: Dorsal fin w/ dark/light margin.   S: =
B: Cave spawner; P-M family?   F: C
T: 23–26°C, L: >35 cm, pH: 7, D: 3–4

CICHLIDS

Crenicichla labrina ♂   5/776

Crenicichla labrina ♀   5/776

H: Brazil: Rio Tocantins.
♂: Larger; vertical rows of spots.   S: =
B: Cave spawner.   F: C!
T: 24–27°C, L: 25 cm, pH: 7, D: 3–4

Crenicichla lenticulata ♂   5/778
Spot-faced pike cichlid
H: Colombia, Brazil, Venezuela.
♀: Pale submarginal fringe on D fin.   S: =
B: Unsuccessful.   F: C!
T: 26–29°C, L: ♂ 38 cm, pH: <7, D: 4

Crenicichla lepidota ♂   2/886
Two-spot pike cichlid, comb pike cichlid
H: Brazil, Bolivia.
♂: Spotted body; larger.   S: =
B: Open spawner; P-M fam.   F: C
T: 23–28°C, L: ♂ <45 cm, pH: 7, D: 3–4

Crenicichla cf. *lugubris* ♀   5/792
"Atabapo-red" pike cichlid
H: Colombia: upper Orinoco basin.
♀: White-banded dorsal fin.   S: =
B: Unsuccessful.   F: C
T: 27–29°C, L: ♂ 40 cm, pH: <7, D: 2

Crenicichla marmorata ♀   5/778
Marbled pike cichlid
H: Brazil: Rio Madeira Basin.
♀: Light submarginal fringe on D fin.   S: –
B: Cave spawner; nuclear family.   F: C
T: 26–28°C, L: ♂ 38 cm, pH: <7, D: 2–4

Crenicichla multispinosa ♂   5/780

H: Suriname, French Guiana.
♂: Dotted posterior body.   **S:** =
B: Unsuccessful.   **F:** C!
T: 26–28°C, **L:** ♂ 32 cm, **pH:** <7, **D:** 3–4

Crenicichla notophthalmus ♂   1/698
(see photo on p. 5/782)

H: Brazil: Amazon.
♂: D spot; creme-colored ventrum.   **S:**+
B: Cs; paternal-maternal family.   **F:** C
T: 24–27°C, **L:** <16 cm, **pH:** <7, **D:** 3–4

Crenicichla notophthalmus ♀   1/698
See photo p. 5/782.

Crenicichla percna   5/786

H: Brazil: Rio Xingú.   E
♀: Pale sublateral band when spaw. **S:** =
B: Unsuccessful.   **F:** C!
T: 28–30°C, **L:** 35 cm, **pH:** <7, **D:** 3

Crenicichla phaiospilus ♂   5/784

H: Brazil: Rio Xingú: scarse in the lower.
♀: Reddish; white band on D fin.   **S:** =
B: Cave spawner?   **F:** C
T: 27–30°C, **L:** ♂ 35 cm, **pH:** <7, **D:** 2

Crenicichla phaiospilus ♀   5/784

Crenicichla punctata ♂ 5/786
Spotted pike cichlid
H: SE Brazil: at Porto Alegre.
♂: Larger; area betw. eyes greater. S: =
B: Cs? Not accomplished. F: C!
T: 22–25°C, L: ♂ 25 cm, pH: 7, D: 2

Crenicichla punctata ♀ 5/786, (5/791)
Spotted pike cichlid

Crenicichla regani ♂ 4/606
Regan's pike cichlid
H: Amazon region: broadly distributed.
♂: Longer D and A fins; see photos. S: +
B: Cs; paternal-maternal family. F: C
T: 24–27°C, L: ♂ 14 cm, pH: <7, D: 1–2

Crenicichla regani ♀ 4/606
Regan's pike cichlid

Crenicichla reticulata subadult ♀ 4/606

H: Peru? Brazil.
♀: More colorful. S: =
B: Open spawner? F: C,O
T: 24–25°C, L: ♂ 25 cm, pH: 7, D: 1–2

Crenicichla saxatilis ♂ 3/756
White-spotted pike cichlid
H: Suriname: Surinam Basin.
♂: Silver dots. S: =
B: Cave spawner; P-M family. F: C
T: 25–30°C, L: 25 cm, pH: 7, D: 3

Crenicichla sp. aff. *sedentaria* ♂   5/794

Crenicichla sp. aff. *sedentaria* ♀   5/794

H: Colombia: Rio Meta Basin.
♂: Larger. ♀: Dorsal spot.   **S:** =
B: Cs; paternal-maternal family.   **F:** C!
T: 24–26°C, **L:** ♂ <22 cm, **pH:** 7, **D:** 3

Crenicichla semifasciata ♀   4/608

H: Brazil.
♀: Red-banded dorsal fin.   **S:** =
B: Cave spawner; P-M family.   **F:** C,O
T: 24–27°C, **L:** ♂ 25 cm, **pH:** 7, **D:** 1–2

Crenicichla sp. "Jabuti/Santarém" ♀
5/788

H: Brazil: southern Santarém.
♂: Larger. ♀: More colorful.   **S:** =
B: Cs; paternal-maternal family.   **F:** C!
T: 25–30°C, **L:** ♂ 22 cm, **pH:** 7, **D:** 1

Crenicichla sp. "Orinoco" ♂   5/796

Crenicichla sp. "Orinoco" ♀   5/796

H: Venezuela, Colombia: Orinoco Basin.
♂: Long D & A fins. ♀: Spot on D fin. **S:** =
B: Cave spawner.   **F:** C!
T: 24–29°C, **L:** ♂ 12 cm, **pH:** ≪7, **D:** 1–2

CICHLIDS

761

Crenicichla sp. "Puerto Gaitán" ♀ 5/790

H: Colombia: Rio Meta Basin.
♂: Long D & A fins. ♀: Spot on D fin. **S**: =
B: Cs; paternal-maternal family.　**F**: C!
T: 24–27°C, **L**: ♂ 25 cm, **pH**: <7, **D**: 2

Crenicichla sp. "red spot Inirida" ♂
5/792

H: Colombia: upper Orinoco: Rio Inirida.
♀: Blue/black/red fringe on D, A, C.　**S**: =
B: Cave spawner.　**F**: C
T: 25–30°C, **L**: ♂ >20 cm, **pH**: <7, **D**: 2

Crenicichla sp. "Sinóp" t. ♀, b. ♂　5/796

H: Brazil: Mato Grosso: Rio Teles Pires.
♂: Larger. ♀: Colorful fringe on D fin. **S**: =
B: Cs; paternal-maternal family.　**F**: C!
T: 24–29°C, **L**: ♂ <12 cm, **pH**: 7, **D**: 3

Crenicichla sp. "Xingú I" t. ♀,b. ♂　5/798
Orange pike cichlid

H: Brazil: Rio Xingú.
♀: Red ventrum; white-fringed D fin.　**S**: =
B: Cave spawner; nuclear family.　**F**: C!
T: 24–27°C, **L**: 35 cm, **pH**: <7, **D**: 3

Crenicichla sp. "Xingú I"　5/798
Orange pike cichlid
Subadult.

Crenicichla sp. "Xingú I" ♀　5/798
Orange pike cichlid
Courtship coloration.

Crenicichla sp. "Xingú II" ♂   5/802

Crenicichla sp. "Xingú II" ♀   5/802

H: SE Brazil: Rio Xingú.
♀: Redder fins; white-banded D fin.   **S:** =
B: Unsuccessful.   **F:** C
T: 28–30°C, **L:** ♂ 35 cm, **pH:** <7, **D:** 3

Crenicichla sp. "Xingú III" ♂   5/804

Crenicichla sp. "Xingú III" ♀   5/804

H: SE Brazil: Rio Xingú.
♂: Long D fin. ♀: White-banded D f.   **S:** =
B: Unsuccessful.   **F:** C
T: 28–30°C, **L:** ♂ 35 cm, **pH:** <7, **D:** 3

Crenicichla stocki   4/610

H: Brazil: Rio Tocantins and tributaries.
♀: More red?   **S:** =
B: Cave spawner? P-M family?   **F:** C,O
T: 24–27°C, **L:** 25 cm, **pH:** <7, **D:** 1–2

Crenicichla strigata   1/698
Striped pike cichlid

H: Guyana, N Brazil.
♀: Red-violet ventral area.   **S:** =
B: Cave spawner? P-M family?   **F:** C
T: 23–27°C, **L:** >40 cm, **pH:** 7, **D:** 4

CICHLIDS

763

Crenicichla sveni ♀ 4/610

H: Colombia: Rio Meta.
♂: Longer D and A fins; larger. S: =
B: Cs; paternal-maternal family. F: C,O
T: 24–27°C, L: ♂ 30 cm, pH: <7, D: 1–2

Crenicichla vittata ♀ 4/612

H: Brazil: Rio Paraguay.
♀: Red ventral area. S: =
B: Cs; paternal-maternal family. F: C,O
T: 24–27°C, L: ♂ 30 cm, pH: 7, D: 1–2

Crenicichla vittata ♂ 4/612

This coloration is also seen in brood caring ♀♀.
See photo on p. 5/781.

Crenicichla wallacii 2/888
Slender pike cichlid

H: Guyana, Brazil.
♂: Slimmer. S: =
B: Cave spawner; P-M family. F: C
T: 24–27°C, L: 15 cm, pH: <7, D: 3–4

Dicrossus maculatus ♂ 5/808
Checkerboard cichlid

H: Brazil: Amazon tributaries.
♂: More colorful; longer fins (V!). S: +
B: Os under plants; 150 eggs. F: C
T: 22–25°C, L: 7 cm, pH: ≪7, D: 2–3

Geophagus acuticeps 2/906
Sparkling geophagus

H: Amazon Basin.
♂: Longer D and A fins. S: +
B: Open spawner? Nuclear family. F: O
T: 24–26°C, L: 25 cm, pH: <7, D: 2–3

CICHLIDS

Geophagus argyrosticus   4/618

H: Brazil: Rio Xingú.
♂: Longer D and A fins; larger.   S: =
B: Open spawner; nuclear fam.   F: C,O
T: 25–30°C, L: ♂ 15 cm, pH: <7, D: 1–2

Geophagus brasiliensis   1/704
Pearl cichlid

H: E Brazil: also brackish water.
♂: D and A fins elongate w/ age.   S: =
B: Os; 600–800 e; nuclear fam.   F: C,O
T: 20–23°C, L: 10–28 cm, pH: <7, D: 3

Geophagus daemon ♂   2/908
Three-spotted eartheater

H: Orinoco, Amazon, Rio Negro.
♂: Threadlike elongation of D fin.   S: =
B: Nat.: open spawner.   F: O
T: 27–30°C, L: 30 cm, pH: <7, D: 2–3

Geophagus grammepareius ♂   5/814

H: Venezuela: Rio Caura/Rio Caroni.
♂: Larger; elongated fins.   S: =
B: Open sp.? Nuclear family?   F: C,O
T: 25–30°C, L: ♂ 14 cm, pH: <7, D: 1

Geophagus hondae ♂   1/706
Redhump geophagus

H: Colombia: Rio Magdalena.
♂: Cephalic hump; longer fins.   S: +
B: Mouthbrooder; maternal fam. F: C,O
T: 24–26°C, L: ♂ 25 cm?, pH: <7, D: 2

Geophagus pellegrini ♂   4/620

H: W Colombia.
♂: Red fins; cephalic hump.   S: =
B: Maternal mouthbrooder.   F: C,O
T: 25–30°C, L: ♂ >15 cm, pH: ≪7, D: 1–2

CICHLIDS

Geophagus proximus 1/706
Suriname eartheater

H: Guyana to the Amazon River.
SD: Very slight. S: =
B: LMb; 250 e; nuclear family. F: C,O
T: 22–25°C, L: 30 cm, pH: 7, D: 3

Geophagus sp. 5/814

H: Unknown.
♂: Larger; elongated fins. S: =
B: Unknown. F: C,O
T: 23–27°C, L: 13 cm, pH: <7, D: 2–3

Geophagus sp. 3/766

H: Venezuela: Orinoco.
GU: Unknown. S: =
B: Mouthbrooder? F: O
T: 22–26°C, L: 20 cm, pH: <7, D: 3

Geophagus sp. "Orinoco" 5/816

H: Venezuela: Rio Caroni/Rio Caura.
♂: Larger; more massive head. S: =
B: ♀♂ larvophile mouthbrooder. F: C,O
T: 27–30°C, L: ♂ 30 cm, pH: ≪7, D: 1–2

Geophagus sp. "Rio Areões" 5/816

H: Brazil: Rio Araguaia Basin.
♂: Larger; elongated fins. S: =
B: ♀Mb eggs; ♀♂Mb the larvae. F: O
T: 25–30°C, L: ♂ 15 cm, pH: <7, D: 1–2

Geophagus taeniopareius t.♀, b.♂ 5/818

H: Venezuela: Rio Orinoco.
♂: Larger; longer fins. S: =
B: Open spawner. F: O
T: 25–30°C, L: ♂ 15 cm, pH: 7, D: 1–2

CICHLIDS

Guianacara cf. *geayi* ♂?   5/822
Red-cheek cichlid

H: Unknown.
♂: Larger; more massive head.   S: +
B: Cs; paternal-maternal family.   F: O
T: 24–27°C, L: ♂ 15 cm, pH: 7, D: 2

Guianacara sp. "Orinoco" t.♂, b.♀ 5/820

H: Venezuela: Rio Orinoco.
♂: Larger; more massive head.   S: +
B: Cave spawner.   F: C,O
T: 27–30°C, L: ♂ 16 cm, pH: <7, D: 1–2

Guianacara sp. "Owroeweti" (?) ♂   5/822

Guianacara sp. "Owroeweti" (?) ♀   5/822

H: Suriname.
♂: Larger; more massive head.   S: +
B: Cave spawner.   F: C,O
T: 27–30°C, L: ♂ 16 cm, pH: <7, D: 1–2

Guianacara sp. "red cheek" ♂   5/824

H: Venezuela?
♂: Slightly larger; longer fins.   S: =
B: Cave spawner.   F: O
T: 23–30°C, L: ♂ 14 cm, pH: <7, D: 1–2

Gymnogeophagus australis   1/708
Southern eartheater

H: Argentina: La Plata region.
SD: Only the genital papilla.   S: =
B: Open spawner; ca. 400 e; N fam.   F: O
T: 22–24°C, L: 18 cm, pH: 7, D: 2

CICHLIDS

Gymnogeophagus balzanii ♂   1/708
Paraguay mouthbrooder

H: Paraguay: Rio Paraná.
♂: Long D & A fins; cephalic hump.   S: +
B: ♀Mb; <500 e; maternal fam.   F: C,O
T: 22–26°C, L: 20 cm, pH: 7, D: 3

Gymnogeophagus gymnogenys ♂   2/910
Squarehead geophagus

H: S Brazil, Uruguay, Argentina.
♂: Cephalic hump w/ age; larger.   S: =
B: Open spawner? Nuclear family?   F: O
T: 21–24°C, L: 25 cm, pH: 7, D: 2–3

Gymnogeophagus labiatus ♂   5/824
Pouty eartheater

H: S Brazil: Rio Cadeia,...
♂: More colorful; larger.   S: +
B: ♀ larvophile mouthbrooder.   F: O
T: (15°) 24°C, L: ♂ 15 cm, pH: 7, D: 1–2

Gymnogeophagus rhabdotus ♂   2/910
Pearl-striped geophagus

H: S Brazil, Uruguay, Argentina.
♂: More colorful; larger.   S: +
B: Open spawner; 300 e; N fam.   F: O
T: 20–25°C, L: 15 cm, pH: 7, D: 2

Heros appendiculatus ♂   4/626

H: Colombia, Brazil, Peru.
♂: Larger; pale colored.   S: =
B: Open spawner; nuclear family.   F: C,O
T: 25–32°C, L: 25 cm, pH: 7, D: 1–2

Heros cf. *notatus* ♂   5/844
Spotted heros

H: N slope of the Guiana Highlands.
♀: More yellow; unspotted fins.   S: +
B: Open spawner; nuclear family.   F: O
T: 25–32°C, L: 25 cm, pH: 7, D: 1

Heros cf. *notatus* ♀   5/844
Spotted heros

Heros cf. *notatus* juv.   5/844
Spotted heros

Heros severus   1/694
Banded cichlid, severum
H: N South America to Amazon Basin.
SD: Only the genital papilla.   S: =
B: Os, >1000 e; nuclear family.   F: C
T: 23–25°C, L: 20 cm, pH: <7, D: 2

Heros severus juv.   1/694
Banded cichlid, severum

Hoplarchus psittacus juv.   2/876
Parrot cichlid
H: Brazil: Rio Negro, Orinoco, Paduari.
♂: Pointed genital papilla.   S: =
B: Open spawner; nuclear family.   F: O
T: 24–28°C, L: 35 cm, pH: ≪7, D: 2–3

Hoplarchus psittacus WC ♂   2/876
Parrot cichlid

CICHLIDS

769

Hypselecara coryphaenoides 2/864
Chocolate cichlid
H: Amazon, Rio Negro.
♂: Longer D & A fins; adipose hump. S:–
B: Unknown. F: C
T: 22–25°C, L: 25 cm, pH: <7, D: 2

Hypselecara temporalis b.♀, t.♂ 1/686
F-cichlid
H: Brazil: upper & central Amazon region.
♂: Distinct cephalic hump; larger. S: =
B: Open spawner; nuclear family. F: C,O
T: 25–28°C, L: ♂ 30 cm, pH: 7, D: 2–3

Krobia guianensis 1/666, 5/846
Dolphin cichlid
H: Guianas.
♂: Longer D & A fins; more colorful. S: =
B: Os; 500 e; nuclear family. F: C,O
T: 23–25°C, L: ♂ 15 cm, pH: <7, D: 3

Krobia guianensis 1/666, 5/846
Dolphin cichlid

Laetacara curviceps ♀ 1/662
Dwarf flag cichlid (w/ eggs)
H: Amazon region.
♂: Longer D & A fins. S: =
B: Os; 300 e; nuclear family. F: C,O
T: 22–26°C, L: ♂ 10 cm, pH: <7, D: 2

Laetacara dorsigera ♀ 1/662
Red-breasted flag cichlid (w/ eggs)
H: Bolivia.
♂: Longer D and A fins; larger. S: +
B: Open spawner; nuclear family? F: C,O
T: 23–26°C, L: ♂ 10 cm, pH: 7, D: 3–4

CICHLIDS

Laetacara cf. *flavilabris* ♂   5/862
Orange-fin flag cichlid
H: Ecuador, Peru, Brazil.
♂: Longer fins; larger.   S: +
B: Open spawner; 150 e; N fam.   F: O
T: 24–28°C, L: ♂ 13 cm, pH: <7, D: 3

Laetacara sp. "humpback" ♀   5/861

Laetacara sp. "humpback" ♂   5/861

Laetacara thayeri   1/664
Red-bellied flag cichlid
H: Peru: upper Amazon.
♂: Longer D and A fins.   S: =
B: Open spawner; nuclear family.   F: C
T: 22–26°C, L: 15 cm, pH: 7, D: 2

Mazarunia mazarunii ♂   5/866
Mazaruni cichlid
H: Guyana: Mazaruni River.
♂: Pointed dorsal fin; larger.   S: +
B: Successful, but no report.   F: C,O
T: 20–30°C, L: 8 cm, pH: <7, D: 3–4

Mazarunia mazarunii ♀   5/866
Mazaruni cichlid

CICHLIDS

771

Mesonauta festivus   1/742
Festivum
H: W Guyana, Brazil.
SD: Slight.   S: +
B: Os; 200–500e; nuclear family.   F: C,O
T: 23–25°C, L: 15 cm, pH: <7, D: 2–3

Mesonauta insignis   5/871
Flag cichlid
H: Brazil, Venezuela: Rio Negro/Orinoco.
♂: Larger; more blue/yellow.   S: +
B: Os; <1000 e; nuclear family.   F: C,O
T: 26–30°C, L: ♂ 20 cm, pH: <7, D: 2

Microgeophagus altispinosa ♂   3/802
Bolivian ram
H: Bolivia, Brazil: Guaporé.
♀: Slightly fuller with age.   S: +
B: Os; <200 e; nuclear family.   F: C,O
T: 22–26°C, L: 8 cm, pH: 7, D: 2

Microgeophagus altispinosa ♀   3/802
Bolivian ram

Microgeophagus ramirezi t.♂, b.♀   1/748
Butterfly cichlid, blue ram
H: W Venezuela, Colombia.
♀: Reddish ventral zone.   S: +
B: Os; 150–200 e; nuclear fam.   F: C,O
T: 22–26°C, L: 7 cm, pH: 7, D: 3

Nannacara adoketa ♂   5/878

H: Brazil: upper Rio Negro, Rio Uaupés.
♂: More colorful; longer fins.   S: +
B: Os (Cs); 350 y; nuclear family.   F: C
T: 22–28°C, L: ♂ 12 cm, pH: ≪7, D: 3–4

Nannacara adoketa ♀ 5/878

Nannacara anomala ♂ 1/744
Golden dwarf cichlid
H: W Guyana.
♂: More colorful; 4 cm larger. S: +
B: Cave sp.; 50–300 e; P-M fam. F: C
T: 22–26°C, L: 9 cm, pH: <7, D: 2

Nannacara aureocephalus ♂ 3/804
Golden-head dwarf cichlid
H: French Guiana.
♂: Larger, more colorful, longer fins. S: =
B: Cs; 50–300 e; P-M family. F: C!
T: 22–25°C, L: ♂ 9 cm, pH: <7, D: 2

Nanacara aureocephalus ♀ 3/804
Golden-head dwarf cichlid

Nannacara ["*Aequidens*"] *hoehnei* ♂
4/640, 5/880
H: Brazil: Mato Grosso.
♂: White-fringed dorsal fin. S: =
B: Open spawner;<600 e; N fam. F:C,O
T: 24°C, L: ♂ <15 cm, pH: <7, D: 1–2

Nannacara taenia ♂ 5/882
Banded dwarf cichlid
H: NE Brazil: at Belém.
♂: Pointed dorsal and anal fins. S: +
B: Cave spawner. F: C,O
T: 22–30°C, L: 4 cm, pH: <7, D: 3

CICHLIDS

773

Nannacara taenia ♀ 5/882
Banded dwarf cichlid

Pterophyllum dumerilii 2/976
Long-nosed angelfish
H: Guyana, Brazil: Belém to Solimões.
SD: Only the genital papilla. S: +
B: Open spawner; nuclear family. F: C,O
T: 26–30°C, H: 10 cm, pH: <7, D: 2–3

Pterophyllum scalare 1/766
Angelfish marbled
H: Peru, E Ecuador.
♂: Pointed genital papilla. S: +
B: Os; <1000 e; nuclear family. F: C,O
T: 24–28°C, H: 15 cm, pH: <7, D: 2

Pterophyllum altum 1/765
Altum angelfish
H: Orinoco.
♂: Steeper dorsum? S: +
B: More than 500 young; pH 4.4. F: C,O
T: 28–30°C, H: 18 cm, pH: <7, D: 3

Pterophyllum scalare 1/766
Angelfish
Half black lacefin.

Pterophyllum scalare   5/928
Angelfish   pearl
H: Peru, E Ecuador.
♂: Pointed genital papilla.   S: +
B: Open sp.; <1000 e; N fam.   F: C,O
T: 20–32°C, H: <25 cm, pH: <7, D: 3–4

Pterophyllum scalare   1/766
Angelfish
Golden morph.

Retroculus lapidifer   3/862
Riffle eartheater
H: Brazil: Tocantins.
SD: Unknown.   S: +
B: Open sp. or mouthbrooder?   F: C,O
T: 22–27°C, L: 25 cm, pH: 7, D: 3–4

Retroculus xinguensis   5/933

H: Brazil: Rio Xingú, Rio Tapajos?
♂: Larger; larger fins.   S: +
B: Nat: nest on sand or rock.   F: C,O
T: 27–30°C, L: <25 cm, pH: <7, D: 4

Satanoperca jurupari   1/704
Eartheater
H: Guyana, Brazil.
SD: Genital papilla.   S: =
B: ♀♂ Mb; 150–400e; nuclear fam. F: C,O
T: 24–26°C, L: 25 cm, pH: <7, D: 2–3

CICHLIDS

Satanoperca cf. *jurupari*   5/942

H: Brazil: at Puerto Ayacucho.
♂: Longer fins?   S: +
B: Mb; otherwise unknown.   F: C,O
T: 24–27°C, L: 20 cm, pH: 7, D: 2–3

Satanoperca leucosticta   3/864

H: Guyana, Suriname.
♂: Slightly larger.   S: +
B: ♀♂ LMb; nuclear family.   F: C,O
T: 27–30°C, L: 20 cm, pH: <7, D: 3

Satanoperca lilith front ♂   5/942

H: Brazil: Amazonia.
♂: Fins elongate with age.   S: +
B: Substrate spawner? N family?   F: C
T: 23–30°C, L: 25 cm, pH: <7, D: 4

Satanoperca pappaterra   3/866

H: Brazil, Bolivia: Rio Guaporé.
♂: Slightly larger.   S: =
B: Mouthbrooder.   F: C
T: 24–27°C, L: ♂ 25 cm, pH: <7, D: 3

Symphysodon aequifasciatus aequifasciatus
Green discus   1/770
H: Amazon at Santarém and Tefé.
SD: Genital papilla.   S: +
B: Os; 300e; Nfam.; dermal secretions. F: C
T: 26–30°C, L: 15 cm, pH: <7, D: 4

Symphysodon aequifasciatus axelrodi
Brown discus   1/770

Symphysodon aequifasciatus haraldi
Blue discus ("royal blue")   1/770

Symphysodon aequifasciatus aequifasciatus
Green discus   2/994
Bred form.

Symphysodon aequifasciatus haraldi
Blue discus   2/994
Bred male with complete striation.

Symphysodon aequifasciatus aequifasciatus
Green discus   2/994
A beautifully striated specimen.

Symphysodon aequifasciatus   2/996
Giant discus   (w/ selective breeding)
H: Brazil: Rio Jurna (original stock).

Symphysodon discus   1/772
Heckel discus
H: Brazil: Rio Negro.
SD: Genital papilla while spawning.   S: +
B: Os; N fam; dermal secretions.   F: C
T: 26–30°C, L: 20 cm, pH: <7, D: 4

Symphysodon discus ∞   2/992
Symphysodon aequifasciatus

Taeniacara candidi ♂   3/874
Black-stripe dwarf cichlid
H: Brazil: around Manaus.
♂: More colorful; lanceolate C fin.   S: =
B: Cs; Pch-M to N family.   F: C
T: 25–28°C, L: ♂ 7 cm, pH: ≪7, D: 3

Tahuantinsuyoa macantzatza   5/956
"Inca stone cichlid"
H: Peru: Rio Ucayali Basin.
♂: Larger; slender; more colorful.   S: =
B: ♀♂LMb; spawns on leaves, etc.   F: O
T: 25–28°C, L: ♂ 12 cm, pH: 7, D: 2

Teleocichla cinderella ♂   5/958
Cinderella cichlid
H: Brazil: lower Rio Tocantins/Araguaia.
♂: Larger; elongated dorsal fin.   S: =
B: Cave spawner? Nuclear family?   F: C!
T: 24–27°C, L: 14 cm, pH: <7, D: 3

Teleocichla cinderella ♀   5/958
Cinderella cichlid

Teleocichla gephyrogramma ♂   5/960

H: Brazil: Rio Xingú.   E
♂: Red/blue fringed caudal fin.   S: =
B: Cave spawner; <50 e; P-M fam.   F: C!
T: 26–30°C, L: 8 cm, pH: <7, D: 2–3

CICHLIDS

Teleocichla monogramma ♀   5/960

H: Brazil: Rio Xingú.
♂: Larger; paler; longer fins.   S: =
B: Cave spawner?   F: C
T: 27–33°C, L: ♂ 11 cm, pH: 7, D: 1

Teleocichla proselytus t. ♂, b. ♀   5/962

H: Brazil: Rio Tapajos, Arapiuns, Cupari.
♂: Larger; paler; longer fins.   S: =
B: Cave spawner; "maternal fam."   F: C
T: 27–33°C, L: ♂ 11 cm, pH: <7, D: 1

Teleocichla sp. "Xingú I" ♂   5/964

H: Brazil: Rio Xingú at Altamira.
♂: Longer fins. ♀: Red belly.   S: +
B: Cave spawner; "maternal fam."   F: C
T: 27–33°C, L: ♂ 5 cm, pH: <7, D: 1

Teleocichla sp. "Xingú II" ♀   5/964
"Black" teleo

H: Brazil: Rio Xingú at Altamira.
♂: Larger?   S: +
B: Cave spawner?   F: C
T: 27–33°C, L: ♂ 15 cm, pH: <7, D: 1

Teleocichla sp. IV ♂   5/966
"Goby" teleo

H: Brazil: Rio Xingú at São Felix.
♀: Black-spotted D fin; smaller   S: +
B: Cave spawner; P-M family.   F: C
T: 27–33°C, L: ♂ 7 cm, pH: <7, D: 3

Uaru amphiacanthoides   1/784
Waroo, triangle cichlid

H: Guyana, Brazil.
SD: Genital papilla.   S: =
B: Os; 300 e; dermal secretions; Nfam.   F: C
T: 24–26°C, L: 30 cm, pH: <7, D: 3–4

CICHLIDS

Introduction

This subgroup presents the cichlids of India, Sri Lanka, Madagascar, and the Caribbean. There are no cichlids indigenous to either Florida or Puerto Rico, although there are some on Cuba and Hispaniola. Cichlids that are distributed in Asia Minor (i.e., Israel, Jordan, and Syria) can be found in the subgroup "Africa—Flowing Waters."

Geographic Distribution

India/Sri Lanka
As cyprinids dominate the fish fauna in this region, hardly any cichlids can be found. Only two species of the salt-tolerant (euryhaline) genus *Eutroplus* have found a niche in coastal waters over the course of evolution.

Caribbean
Here, too, there are few endemic cichlids. Some of the species of Hispaniola (Haiti/Dominican Republic) and Cuba are euryhaline, inhabiting brackish waters. Cuba has only two endemic species, but one—*Cichlasoma tetra-canthus*—has five subspecies.

Lac Bempazawa, a crater lake on Nosy Be, Madagascar; habitat of *Paratilapia bleekeri*.

Madagascar

The situation of native fishes on Madagascar seems to be reaching a critical point: in many places, tilapine cichlids such as *Tilapia rendalli* and *Oreochromis mossambicus* and other exotic species have been released. Consequently, some bodies of water are now exclusively inhabited by exotic species. A total of 20 endemic cichlids are presently known, but further discoveries are expected in the future (O. LUCANUS, DATZ 11/96).

Cichlasoma tetracanthus 2/882
Cuban cichlid
H: Cuba. Fw, Bw
♂: Larger. S: =
B: Os; <600 e; nuclear family. F: C,O
T: 20–27°C, L: 25 cm, pH: 7, D: 1

Etroplus maculatus 1/702
Orange chromide
H: W India and Sri Lanka. Fw,(Bw)
♂: Red fin fringes? S: =
B: Os; <300 e; N fam; 5% Mw. F: C,O
T: 20–25°C, L: 8 cm, pH: >7, D: 2–3

Etroplus suratensis 2/906
Banded chromide, banded chromide
H: W India and Sri Lanka. Bw,Fw,(Mw)
♂: Larger? S: –
B: Os or Cs; nuclear family. F: O,H
T: 23–26°C, L: 46 cm, pH: >7, D: 3

Nandopsis haitiensis ♂ 5/876
Haiti cichlid
H: Haiti: Cul-de-Sac Plateau. Bw
♂: Larger and lighter; frontal hump. S: –
B: Open spawner; 150 eggs. F: H,O
T: 24–27°C, L: ♂ 25 cm, pH: >7, D: 1

Nandopsis haitiensis ♀ 5/876
Haiti cichlid

Paratilapia bleekeri ♂   5/902
Fimanga cichlid, Bleeker's cichlid
H: Madagascar.   E
♂: Larger; otherwise similar.   S: =
B: A cluster of <5000 e; ♀ tends. F: C,O
T: 15–30°C, L: ♂ 18 cm, pH: 7, D: 3

Paratilapia polleni ♂   4/668
Marakeli cichlid, Pollen's cichlid
H: Madagascar.   E
♂: Larger; otherwise similar.   S: =
B: A cluster of <5000 e; ♀ tends. F: C,O
T: 24–28°C, L: ♂ 25 cm, pH: 7, D: 3

Paratilapia polleni I   4/668
Marakeli cichlid, Pollen's cichlid
See photo on p. 5/903.

Paratilapia polleni II   4/668
Marakeli cichlid, Pollen's cichlid
See photo on p. 5/903.

Paretroplus kieneri   5/905
Kotsovato cichlid
H: Madagascar, western section.   E
SD: Only the genital papilla.   S: –
B: Open spawner; 200 e; N fam.   F:C,O
T: 24–28°C, L: 20 cm, pH: >7, D: 2–4

Ptychochromis oligacanthus   3/858
Madagascar cichlid
H: Madagascar.   E
SD: Unknown.   S: =
B: Open spawner; nuclear family.   F: O
T: 24–30°C, L: 27 cm, pH: 7, D: 2–3

Perca fluviatilis in the Rhine in Switzerland.

Hypseleotris compressa (see p. 809), one of the most colorful sleeper gobies.

PERCHES

Introduction

Some Perciformes where presented previously, i.e., Group 7 (Suborder Anabantoidei—Labyrinth Fishes) and Group 8 (Family Cichlidae—Cichlids). From an aquaristic point of view, both groups contain popular, very familiar fishes that are easily distinguished by the layperson. Group 9 presents the following additional families of the Perciformes:

Group 9

Geographic Distribution

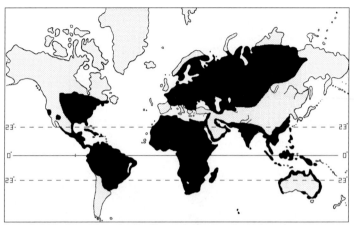

Area of distribution of the order Perciformes (without marine biotopes).

Generalities

The Perciformes are the largest order of vertebrates, dominating the seas and many tropical and subtropical freshwaters. A total of 9300 species are distributed among almost 150 families; of those, close to 2200 are associated with freshwater. Only the Siluriformes (Group 4—Catfishes) with almost 2300 species and the Cypriniformes (Group 3—Carplike Fishes) with over 2600 species are more diverse (NELSON, 1994).

A group of such magnitude is difficult to characterize, since virtually all sizes and trophic levels are represented and they occur in all but the most inhospitable environments. Nevertheless, all share the following attributes:

- There are true spiny rays within the dorsal fin, the ventral fins, and the anal fin.
- The dorsal fin has an anterior spiny-rayed section and a posterior soft-rayed section. These two parts can be connected within one fin or form two separate dorsal fins (e.g., Gobiidae—Gobies).
- An adipose fin is lacking.
- For the food fish industry, it is interesting to note that Perciformes have no small intramuscular Y-bones like, e.g., trout and carp.
- These fishes normally have ctenoid scales, but some families have resduced scales.
- The swimbladder has no connection to the intestine (physoclists).

PERCHES

785

Family Ambassidae (Chandidae)

Glassfishes inhabit fresh, brackish, and marine waters of the Indian and western Pacific regions. Freshwater species are primarily found from India and Madagascar to the Australian region.

Eight families and a total of 41 species are recognized; of these, just over 20 species are found in freshwater.

There are two dorsal fins. Due to the transparent body and visible internal anatomy, these fish enjoy a certain degree of popularity among aquarists. Most species do not attain their maximum size in aquaria. With few exceptions, these are small fishes which are suitable for community aquaria.

Some of the species have been successfully reproduced, a few in freshwater, but most in marine water. Depending on species, the eggs are either pelagic or adhesive. The latter are usually adhered to aquatic plants, although all types of substrates has been used. Typically the fry are very small, which complicates rearing.

Ambassis gymnocephalus   4/711
Bald glassfish
H: E African coast.
♂: Black-tipped on C and D fins.   S: =
B: Egg scatterer; marine water!   F: C!
T: 22–28°C, L: 10 cm, pH: >7, D: 3–4

Ambassis cf. *gymnocephalus*   4/711
Bald glassfish
See photo on p. 4/708.

Ambassis cf. *gymnocephalus*   4/711
Bald glassfish
See photo on p. 5/978.

Chanda agramma   2/1020

H: Australia.
♂: Slightly brighter and slimmer.   S: +
B: Unsuccessful.   F: C
T: 20–28°C, L: 7 cm, pH: 7, D: 3

Chanda baculis   3/906
Burmese glassfish
H: Asia: India, Burma, Thailand.
SD: Unknown.   S: +
B: Unsuccessful.   F: C!
T: 18–25°C, L: 4.5 cm, pH: 7, D: 2–3

Chanda buruensis ♂   3/908
Buru glassfish
H: SE Asia.
♂: Swimbladder pointed posteriorly. S: +
B: On aquatic plants; >100 eggs.   F: C
T: 22–30°C, L: 7 cm, pH: 7, D: 3

Chanda buruensis ♀   3/908
Buru glassfish

Chanda commersonii   2/1020
Commerson's glassfish
H: Africa, Asia, N Australia.
♂: Black-tipped D and C fins.   S: +
B: Unsuccessful.   F: C!
T: 22–26°C, L: 10 cm, pH: 7, D: 3–4

Chanda elongata   2/1022
Elongated glassfish
H: N Australia.
♀: Slightly fuller?   S: +
B: Unsuccessful.   F: C!
T: 20–32°C, L: 7.5 cm, pH: 8, D: 2

Chanda macleayi   2/1022
Macleay's glassfish
H: Australia, New Guinea.
♀: Slightly fuller?   S: +
B: Unsuccessful.   F: C
T: 20–32°C, L: 10 cm, pH: 7, D: 2

PERCHES

Chanda ranga   1/800
Indian glassfish
H: SE Asia: India, Burma, Thailand.
♂: Blue-edged D, A; pointed swimbl. S: +
B: On aquatic plants; 150 eggs.   F: C
T: 20–30°C, L: 8 cm, pH: 7, D: 3

Chanda sp. ♂   3/905

H: Asia: India, Assam.

Chanda sp. ♀   3/905

H: Asia: India, Assam, Dibru River.

Chanda wolfii   1/800
Wolf's glassfish
H: SE Asia: Thailand, Sumatra, Borneo.
SD: Unknown.   S: +
B: Unsuccessful.   F: C
T: 18–25°C, L: 20 cm, pH: 7, D: 3–4

Denariusa bandata   2/1024
Penny fish
H: Australia.
♂: Slimmer; somewhat larger.   S: +
B: Unsuccessful.   F: C
T: 20–30°C, L: 8 cm, pH: 7, D: 3

Gymnochanda filamentosa   2/1026
Filament glassfish
H: SE Asia: Malaysia, Singapore.
♂: Very elongated D₂ and A fins.   S: +
B: Occasionally successful; Bw.   F: C!
T: 23–26°C, L: 5 cm, pH: 7, D: 3–4

PERCHES

Parambassis confinis   4/712
Papuan perchlet
H: New Guinea: Sepik River.   E
♂: More pronounced colors.   S: +
B: Egg scatterer; Mw(!).   F: C,O
T: 22–28°C, L: 12 cm, pH: >7, D: 4

Parambassis gulliveri   4/712
Giant perchlet
H: S New Guinea, N Australia.
♂: More colorful; slimmer.   S: –
B: Brackish water?   F: C!
T: 23–28°C, L: 28 cm, pH: >7, D: 4

Tetracentrum apogonoides ♂   4/714
Four-spined perchlet
H: SE Papua New Guinea.
♂: Sometimes darker.   S: +
B: Unsuccessful.   F: C
T: 23–28°C, L: 18 cm, pH: 7, D: 3

Tetracentrum apogonoides ♀   4/714
Four-spined perchlet

Tetracentrum caudovittatus   4/716
Stripe-tail perchlet
H: New Guinea.   Fw
♂: More colorful.   S: +
B: Pelagic eggs; marine water(!).   F: C
T: 22–26°C, L: 9 cm, pH: >7, D: 4

Tetracentrum honessi   4/716
Honess's perchlet
H: New Guinea.   Fw
SD: Unknown.   S: +
B: Egg scatterer. Marine water?   F: C,O
T: 22–26°C, L: 8.5 cm, pH: >7, D: 3

PERCHES

Family Apogonidae

The family of cardinalfishes consists of 22 genera and about 122 species. Most inhabit marine biotopes, but the 9 *Glossamia* species solely live in freshwaters of New Guinea and Australia. Some *Apogon* can be found in brackish water and in lower river courses.

Apogonidae are peaceful schooling fishes which can readily be associated with fishes such as rainbows. They have two dorsal fins.

Glossamia aprion aprion   2/1012
Northern Quensland mouthbrooder
H: Australia.
SD: Unknown.   S: +
B: Nat.: mouthbrooder; paternal fam. F: C
T: 23–25°C, L: 12 cm, pH: >7, D: 2

Australia: coastal Queensland, Cattle Creek. Habitat of glassfishes, gobies, and rainbowfishes (for the last see Group 10).

PERCHES

Family Badidae

Badidae are considered by some to be a subfamily (Badinae) of the Nandidae. A certain relation to the Anabantoidei (Group 7) is also suspected. The family Badidae is monotypic, i.e., it only contains the one species presented below (NELSON, 1994). Depending on subspecies it occurs in freshwaters of Pakistan, India, Burma (Myanmar), and Thailand. It is famous for its ability to quickly change its bright, beautiful colors, earning it the common name of chameleonfish in Germany.

The aquarium should have an abundance of hiding places and a sandy substrate. A layer of floating plants will attenaute the illumination, thereby lending a proper ambience to the aquarium.

Breeding can be accomplished even in small aquaria. The water should be soft and slightly acid. Peat filtration may be advantageous.

Unfortunately, *Badis badis* rarely accepts flake foods.

Badis badis   1/790
Badis
H: Asia: India.
♂: More colorful; ventrally concave. S: +
B: Cs; 30–100 e; paternal family. F: C!
T: 23–26°C, L: 8 cm, pH: 7, D: 4

Badis badis burmanicus   2/1013
Burmese badis
H: SE Asia: Burma.
♂: More colorful; ventrally concave. S: +
B: Cs; <150 eggs; paternal fam. F: C!
T: 24–26°C, L: 8 cm, pH: <7, D: 4

Badis badis siamensis   3/902
Siamese badis
H: SE Asia: Thailand: Phuket.
♂: More colorful; ventrally concave. S: +
B: Cs; 30–100 e; paternal family. F: C
T: 22–26°C, L: 6 cm, pH: 7, D: 4

PERCHES

Family Blenniidae

Combtooth blennies are distributed in the Atlantic, the Indian Ocean, and the Pacific. Few inhabit freshwater biotopes; some live in brackish water. There are 53 genera and 345 species within the family.

Since they are bottom-oriented, they lack a swimbladder. The body is naked or covered by small scales.

Salaria fluviatilis requires optimum oxygen concentrations. For long-term maintenance, *S. basilisca* requires a marine aquarium; it is a suitable tankmate for marine fishes and invertebrates.

Salaria basilisca   5/1004
Labyrinth blenny
H: Meditarranean.   Very rare; Mw, Bw
♂: Yellow comb.   S: =
B: Cs; paternal fam;add 1% salt.   F:O
T: 18–22°C, L: 18 cm, pH: >7, D: 2–4

Salaria fluviatilis   1/825
H: Meditarranean.   Fw
♂: Larger cepahlic comb.   S: (–)
B: Cs; 200–300 e; paternal fam.   F:C,O
T: 18–24°C, L: 15 cm, pH: 7, D: 2–3

Bovichthyidae   Icefishes

Family Bovichthyidae

Icefishes are inhabitants of marine waters of southern Australia, South America, and New Zealand as well as freshwaters of Australia and Tasmania. Three genera and approximately 11 species are found in the family.

Only one species migrates into freshwaters of southeastern Australia; the remaining species occur in Antarctica, hence the name icefishes.

Although *P. bursinus* is a benthic predator, it can be associated with coldwater fishes of similar size.

Pseudaphritis bursinus   2/1058
Congolli, Tupong
H: SE Australia, Tasmania.   Bw,Fw,Mw
SD: Unknown.   S: =
B: Unsuccessful.   F: C
T: 5–20°C, L: 20 cm, pH: >7, D: 3

Family Centrarchidae

The family of sunfishes consists of 8 genera and a total of 29 species, all of which occur in freshwaters of North America.

Since some species are important game fishes and some are used in physiological laboratory research, certain members of the family are cultured commercially.

From the 60 cm popular game fish *Micropterus salmoides*—better known as the largemouth bass—to the diminutive *Elassoma* spp., Centrarchidae occur in a wide array of sizes. The latter are suitable for tropical aquaria, while the other species require cooler waters. However, all species must be overwintered at cool temperatures to maintain their overall health and reproductive capacity.

Either the eggs are deposited in a fanned out depression or haphazardly scattered among plants (e.g., *Elassoma*). *Micropterus* is the only nesting genus of centrarchids with a nuclear family, i.e., both parents care for their offspring. In the remainder, it is the male alone that cares for the spawn (paternal family).

With the exception of *Elassoma* spp., these species are very sensitive in front of pH and temperature fluctuations and suboptimal water conditions. A large filter and conscientious maintenance are therefore necessary.

The aquarium's infrastructure should provide numerous hiding places and three-dimensionality; less centrarchids, especially the small species, adopt a cryptic lifestyle. At the same time, all sunfishes need open swimming space in the middle and lower water strata.

Acantharchus pomotis   4/720, 5/979
Mud sunfish
H: N America: USA: New York to Florida.
♂: Metallic at spawning time?   S: =
B: Pit dug in sand; ♂ tends spawn.   F: C!
T: 5–25°C, L: 21 cm, pH: 7, D: 4

Acantharchus pomotis   4/720, 5/979
Mud sunfish

Ambloplites rupestris   2/1014, 5/980
Rock bass
H: N Am.: S Canada to USA (Louisiana).
♂: Black V fins; opercula w/ gold edge. S:–
B: Eggs laid in pit; paternal family. F: C
T: 10–25°C, L: 43 cm, pH: 7, D: 4

PERCHES

Ambloplites rupestris   2/1014, 5/980
Rock bass

Centrarchus macropterus   1/791
Flier, round sunfish, peacock sunfish
H: N America: E USA.
♂: Black anal fin. ♀: White anal fin.   S: =
B: Pit; 200 eggs; ♂ tends spawn.   F: C,O
T: 12–22°C, L: 16 cm, pH: 7, D: 2

Lepomis gulosus   1/792, (4/722)
Warmouth
H: North America.
♂: More colorful and slimmer.   S: =
B: Pit; 1000 e; ♂ tends spawn.   F: C,O
T: 10–20°C, L: 20 cm, pH: >7, D: 2

Lepomis gulosus   1/792, (4/722)
Warmouth

Elassoma evergladei 2♂ 1♀   1/792
Everglades or Florida pigmy sunfish
H: N Am.: USA: North Carolina to Florida.
♂: Black fins at spawning time.   S: +
B: Among plants; <60 eggs.   F: C,O
T: 10–30°C, L: 3.5 cm, pH: >7, D: 2

Elassoma okefenokee ♀   2/1014
Okefenokee pigmy sunfish
H: N Am.: USA: SW Georgia: Okefenokee.
♂: Darker during spawning season. S: =
B: Spawns among plants.   F: C
T: 4–30°C, L: 4 cm, pH: <7, D: 2–3

Elassoma zonatum ♂   4/722
Banded pygmy sunfish
H: N America: E and SE USA.
♂: More colorful; larger.   S: +
B: Among plants.   F: C,O
T: 10–25°C, L: 3.8 cm, pH: 7, D: 2–3

Elassoma zonatum ♂   4/722
Banded pygmy sunfish
Northern Florida.

Enneacanthus chaetodon   1/794
Black-banded sunfish
H: N America: NE USA.
♀: Usually fuller; more colorful.   S: +
B: Pit; <500 eggs; paternal fam.   F: C
T: 4–22°C, L: 10 cm, pH: 7, D: 3

Enneacanthus gloriosus   1/794
Blue-spotted sunfish
H: N America: E USA.
♂: Deeper body; longer fins.   S: +
B: Pit near plants; <500 eggs.   F: C
T: 10–22°C, L: 8 cm, pH: >7, D: 2

Enneacanthus obesus   1/796
Diamond sunfish, little sunfish
H: N America: E USA.
♂: More colorful; longer D & A fins.   S: +
B: Pit; plants; 500 e; ♂ tends sp.   F:C,O
T: 10–22°C, L: 10 cm, pH: >7, D: 2

Lepomis auritus   2/1016
Golden sunfish, redbreast sunfish
H: N America: USA: Maine to Virginia.
♂: More colorful.   S: –
B: Pit; 1000 eggs; ♂ tends spawn.   F: C
T: 4–22°C, L: 20 cm, pH: >7, D: 2

PERCHES

795

Lepomis cyanellus   1/796
Green sunfish
H: N America: Canada to Mexico.
♀: Fuller; deeper-bodied.   S: =
B: Pit; 1000 eggs; ♂ tends spawn. F: C,O
T: 18–22°C, L: 20 cm, pH: >7, D: 2

Lepomis gibbosus   1/798
Pumkinseed, kiver
H: N America.
♂: More colorful.   S: =
B: Pit; 1000 eggs; ♂ tends spawn.   F: C
T: 4–22°C, L: 20 cm, pH: >7, D: 1–2

Lepomis humilis   4/720
Orange-spotted sunfish
H: N America: Canada, USA.
♂: More colorful, darker.   S: =
B: In a pit, ♂ guards the spawn.   F: C
T: 10–28°C, L: 10 cm, pH: >7, D: 2

Lepomis macrochirus   1/798
Bluegill   Rare
H: N America: USA: Ohio Valley, AK, KY.
SD: Very slight.   S: =
B: Unknown.   F: C
T: 4–22°C, L: 13 cm, pH: >7, D: 2

Micropterus dolomieui   2/1016
Smallmouth bass
H: N Am.: S Canada to USA (Arkansas).
♂: Slightly slimmer and darker.   S: –
B: Unsuccessful.   F: C
T: 10–18°C, L: 50 cm, pH: >7, D: 2–3

Micropterus salmoides   2/1018
Largemouth bass
H: N America: S Canada to Mexico.
♂: Somewhat slimmer and darker.   S: –
B: Unsuccessful.   F: C!
T: 10–18°C, L: 60 cm, pH: >7, D: 4

Family Centropomidae

Snooks, or giant perches, inhabit marine, brackish, and freshwater biotopes of the Atlantic, Indian, and Pacific oceans. Most freshwater species are found in Africa.

Of the approximately 3 genera and 22 species, 7 *Lates* species live in African freshwaters.

At the most, juvenile giant perches are suitable for home aquaria. Adults are even problematic for public show aquaria; aside from their monstrous proportions, they are also aggressive predators (see the species descriptions).

Lates niloticus has come into the spotlight in recent years (see p. 673). In an attempt to improve the protein level in the diet of populations in bordering countries, this fish was released into Lake Victoria. While initially there was a lack of suitable fishing gear for such large fishes, it was quickly adapted and the capture rates improved significantly over the short term. But now there are smaller harvests because the piscivorous Nile perch is dominating the food web, placing such pressure on the endemic cichlid populations of the lake that many species are extinct or on the brink of extinction. The final state of equilibrium in the lake has not been achieved, but it is hoped that several species, including some now considered extinct, will reestablish from relict populations.

The members of this family are popular as food and game fishes, but utterly unsuitable as aquarium fishes.

Lates angustifrons   juv.   4/724

H: Africa: Lake Tanganyika.   E
♀: Fuller.   S: –
B: Too large; pelagic eggs.   F: C
T: 24–28°C, L: 135 cm, pH: >7, D: 4

Lates calcarifer   2/1019
Barramundi, giant perch

H: Asia, Australia.   Fw,Bw,Mw
SD: Sexual transformation?   S: –
B: Unsuccessful. Too large.   F: C
T: 15–28°C, L: 180 cm, pH: >7, D: 3–4

Lates microlepis   3/904
Small-scaled Nile perch

H: Africa: Lake Tanganyika.   E
SD: Unknown.   S: –
B: Too large for aquarium breeding.   F: C
T: 24–28°C, L: 135 cm, pH: 7, D: 4

Family Channidae

Snakeheads inhabit freshwaters of tropical Africa and southern Asia. There are 2 genera and a total of 21 species—the Asian *Channa* with 18 species and the African genus *Parachanna* with 3 species.

Due to the presence of a suprabranchial accessory breathing organ (labyrinth), snakeheads are often grouped with the labyrinth fishes (suborder Anabantoidei—Group 7). However, few consider the two closely related despite the common labyrinth organ, since it seems to have evolved independently in each group.

Two types of reproduction have been observed:

- Floating nest. The floating eggs rise to the water surface, where they are guarded by the male. However, they are not incorporated into a bubble nest.
- Oral incubation. Inhabitants of flowing waters are paternal mouthbrooders. In comparison to those that lay floating eggs, these snakeheads are much less fecund, producing just 1% of the eggs typically found in a floating nest.

All snakeheads are intolerant of saline water, which restricts treatment options for infirmities such as ectoparasites. On the other hand, the fact that they possess an air breathing organ means oxygen levels are of secondary importance. They are robust fishes overall, even capable of enduring turbid waters. Not surprisingly, these attributes combined with their delicious meat mean they are frequently cultured in ponds as food fishes, predominantly in Asia but also in Africa. They are raised in conjunction with tilapine species, controlling the undesired reproduction of those fishes and at the same time alimenting themselves. Even with training, commercial diets are rarely accepted.

Smaller species grow to a length of 30 cm. As predatory loners, they can only be associated with large species that are capable of defending themselves. Heterogenic tankmates are recommended, since snakeheads have a tendency to quarrel among themselves and those maintained alone become reclusive. A few species are relatively peaceful outside the spawning season and can be associated with conspecifics in the interim. When well-fed, snakeheads are less aggressive and easier to house with other fishes.

As previously mentioned, no particular demands are placed on water chemistry, but given their high metabolic rate, good filtration is needed, especially for their tankmates. The aquarium should have refuges and free swimming space. Tough plants are not damaged.

Channa argus   2/1060
Spotted snakehead
H: Asia: China: Amur and northward.
♀: Fuller at spawning time.   S: =
B: N.: floating nest; P fam; 50000e.   F:C!
T: 14–22°C, L: <85 cm, pH: 7, D: 1–4

Channa asiatica   3/671
Northern green snakehead
H: Asia: S China, SE Asia.
SD: None.   S: –
B: Floating nest; <2000 eggs.   F: C
T: 22–28°C, L: 30 cm, pH: 7, D: 2

Channa gachua   3/672
Ceylonese green snakehead
H: SE Asia.
SD: Very slight.   S: =
B: ♂ mouthbrooder; 50–80 eggs.   F: C
T: 22–26°C, L: 35 cm, pH: <7, D: 2–3

Channa lucius   3/674
Shiny snakehead
H: SE Asia.
SD: Almost indiscernible.   S: –
B: Unsuccessful.   F: C
T: 22–26°C, L: 50 cm, pH: 7, D: 2–4

Channa marulia juv.   5/1005
Ocellated snakehead
H: Asia: India.
SD: Almost indiscernible.   S: =
B: Unknown.   F: C
T: 22–26°C, L: 120 cm, pH: 7, D: 4

Channa micropeltes juv.   1/827
Red snakehead
H: Asia: India to W Malaysia.
♀: Fuller during spawning season?   S: –
B: <3000 eggs; ♂ tends spawn.   F: C!
T: 25–28°C, L: <100 cm, pH: 7, D: 4

Channa orientalis   1/828
Ceylonese green snakehead
H: Asia: Sri Lanka.
♀: Fuller.   S: –
B: ♂ mouthbrooder; <40 eggs.   F: C
T: 23–26°C, L: 30 cm, pH: 7, D: 4

PERCHES

Channa punctata   3/676
Spotted snakehead
H: Asia: India, Sri Lanka, China.
SD: Unknown.   S: –
B: Nature: floating eggs.   F: C
T: 22–28°C, L: >100 cm, pH: 7, D: 1–4

Channa striata   1/830
Striped snakehead
H: SE Asia.
SD: Unknown.   S: –
B: Floating eggs; ♂ tends spawn.   F: C!
T: 23–27°C, L: 90 cm, pH: >7, D: 4

Parachanna africana   2/1059
African snakehead
H: W Africa: Nigeria, Cameroon.
♂: More colorful when spawning?   S: =
B: Floating eggs; ♂ cares; light sen. F: C!
T: 25–28°C, L: 32 cm, pH: 7, D: 1–2

Parachanna insignis   3/674
Square-spotted African snakehead
H: Tropical Africa: Congo Basin.
♂: Larger.   S: =
B: <3000 floating eggs.   F: C
T: 22–28°C, L: 40 cm, pH: <7, D: 2–4

Parachanna obscura   1/828
Dark snakehead
H: Central Africa: Senegal to White Nile.
♀: Fuller during spawning season?   S: –
B: <3000 e; ♂ tends the spawn.   F: C!
T: 26–28°C, L: 35 cm, pH: 7, D: 4

Parachanna obscura juvenile   1/828
Dark snakehead

A typical biotope in Zaïre, western Africa.

Family Coiidae

Datnioides has been separated from the family Lobotidae, renamed *Coius*, and placed into the family Coiidae. It contains 3 species which inhabit brackish water and freshwater biotopes from India to Borneo and New Guinea.

Tripletails need 2–3 tablespoons of marine salt per 10 l water. Though peaceful among themselves, they are aggressive towards heterospecifics.

Coius microlepis   1/802
Siamese tigerfish   Bw
H: Asia: Thai., Cambodia, Borneo, Sum.
SD: Unknown.   S: –
B: Unknown.   F: C
T: 22–26°C, L: 40 cm, pH: 7, D: 3–4

Coius quadrifasciatus   1/802
Four-lined tigerfish   Bw, (Fw)
H: Asia: India to Indo-Australia.
SD: Unknown.   S: –
B: Unknown.   F: C
T: 22–26°C, L: 30 cm, pH: 7, D: 3–4

Family Gobiidae

In the INDEX, the goby family includes the sleeper gobies as the subfamily Eleotrinae, though they are often considered a family in and of themselves (Eleotridae). The species of the Gobiidae were ordered alphabetically by subfamily to maintain the unity of the Eleotrinae (and other subfamilies).

Close to 250 genera and more than 2000 species are found worldwide in tropical and subtropical regions. Their greatest species richness is found in marine habitats, but many species inhabit brackish water and freshwater biotopes. The Gobiidae are the largest family of marine fishes; the freshwater ichthyofauna of islands often is predominantly gobies. Overall, the Gobiidae contain more species than either the Cyprinidae (Group 3) or the Cichlidae (Group 8).

Many of the freshwater inhabitants of this group lay their eggs in freshwater. The hatching planktonic larvae are swept into estuaries. There and in the sea they develop, returning to the rivers to breed once they have attained sexual maturity (anadromous). Some species are catadromous; i.e., they abandon their riverine habitats and enter the littoral zone of marine waters to breed, subsequently returning to the rivers.

Gobies have two dorsal fins. The anterior dorsal fin (D_1) has hard spines, whereas the posterior dorsal fin (D_2) consists of soft rays. Within this family, size is very divergent, varying from less than a centimeter to more than a half meter in length. The great majority are less than 10 cm in length. The smallest freshwater fish, *Pandaka pygmaea* (p. 823), as well as the smallest vertebrate of the world, the slightly smaller *Trimmatom nanus* (a marine species—not presented here), are part of this family. Some of the larger freshwater species are primitively cultured as food fishes in ponds. For example, *Dormitator latifrons*—a sleeper goby of western Ecuador—is cultured in that country. It is famous for its hardiness, surviving unfavorable water conditions and up to a day outside water; the latter ability is of great benefit in tropical countries where refrigeration is not common.

Mudskippers (p. 826) are a peculiar group among the gobies. As indicated by their common name, these species live amphibiously along shorelines of estuaries and mangrove swamps. They can move over land at astounding speed. The superiorly located eyes provide good vision outside the water.

Most brackish and freshwater gobies are cave spawners with a paternal family, but a few are open spawners (substrate spawners). There are two basic impediments to reproduction in the aquarium: the dependence on brackish or marine waters for oviposition and the extremely minute size of the larvae upon hatching. The latter is particularly serious, as it greatly complicates initial feeding. Fortunately, the larvae of gobies that live and breed in freshwater are typically larger. Sexual dimorphism and dichromatism are not always apparent. In such cases, the genital papilla must be examined to reliably identify sex. Males have a long, flat, pointed genital papilla, whereas in females it is short and blunt.

For most species, salt added to the water is beneficial. With the exception of predacious species—namely, sleeper gobies of the subfamily Butinae—gobies are shy fishes which can be associated with peaceful tankmates. However, as halophiles, the list of suitable tankmates is reduced.

The ventral fins of many gobies are fused, forming a suction cup which allows these bottom-oriented fishes to maintain their position in the strong currents of their riverine habitats. The two distinct ventral fins found in most sleeper gobies is not sufficient to place them into a given subfamily.

Gobioides broussonnetii   2/1090
Violet goby, dragonfish   Bw
H: America: USA (Georgia) to Brazil.
SD: Unknown.   S: −
B: Unknown.   F: C
T: 23–25°C, L: 63 cm, pH: >7, D: 4

Gobioides grahamae   3/984
                                     Bw
H: S America: Amazona Delta, uyana.
SD: Unknown.   S: −
B: Unknown.   F: O,C
T: 25°C, L: 22 cm, pH: >7, D: 4

Gobioides peruanus   3/984
Peruvian goby   Fw,Bw
H: America: Costa Rica to N Peru.
♂: Smaller, flat genital papilla.   S: =
B: Unknown.   F: O
T: 25°C, L: 38 cm, pH: 7, D: 4

Odontamblyopus rubicundus   4/776
Eel goby   Bw
H: India to Japan, China, Indonesia.
♂: Pointed genital papilla.   S: −
B: W/ hormone injection; in tunnels. F:C,O
T: 20–30°C, L: 33 cm, pH: >7, D: 4

Bunaka gyrinoides   4/750

H: W Indo-Pacific region.   Fw
SD: Unknown.   S: =
B: Unknown. Diadromous?   F: C!
T: 22–28°C, L: 40 cm, pH: 7, D: 3

Butis amboinensis   4/750
Slender bony-snouted gudgeon
H: India to Indonesia and New Guinea.
♂: Elongated D_2 and anal fins.   S: –
B: Unknown.   F: C!
T: 22–28°C, L: 13 cm, pH: 7, D: 3

Butis butis   2/1063
Bony-snouted gudgeon
H: Indo-Pacific.   Mw, Bw, Fw.
SD: Unknown.   S: –
B: Unsuccessful.   F: C!
T: 22–28°C, L: 15 cm, pH: >7, D: 3

Butis gymnopomus   3/954

H: India to Philippines, Indonesia,...
♂: Elongated D_2 and anal fins.   S: –
B: On rocks; ♂ tends the spawn.   F: C
T: 25°C, L: 11.5 cm, pH: 7, D: 3

Butis melanostigma   3/958

H: Asia: India to Indochina.   Bw
♂: Elongated D_2 and anal fins.   S: –
B: Unknown.   F: C!
T: 25°C, L: 14 cm, pH: 7, D: 3

Kribia kribensis   4/754

H: W Africa: Guinea to Zaïre.
SD: Unknown.   S: =
B: Unknown.   F: C!
T: 22–28°C, L: 5.7 cm, pH: 7, D: 3

Kribia nana 4/756
West African dwarf sleeper
H: W Africa: Nile, Lake Chad, Zaïre Basin.
♂: Darker; lighter fin fringes. S: (–)
B: Cave spawner; ♂ tends spawn. F: C!
T: 24–26°C, L: 4 cm, pH: <7, D: 3

Oxyeleotris lineolata 4/764
H: Australia. Fw
♂: Small, flat, slender genital papilla. S: –
B: N: cave spawner; <70000 eggs. F: C!
T: 20–28°C, L: 40 cm, pH: 7, D: 3

Oxyeleotris marmoratus 1/832
Marbled sleeper Fw
H: Asia: Indonesia, Malay Pen., Thailand.
♂: Elongated D₂ and A fins. S: –
B: Unknown. F: C,O
T: 22–28°C, L: 50 cm, pH: 7, D: 4

Oxyeleotris urophthalmoides 4/766
H: Asia: Sumatra, Borneo. Fw
♂: Small, flat, slender genital papilla. S: –
B: Unknown. F: C!
T: 23–28°C, L: 20 cm, pH: 7, D: 3

Oxyeleotris urophthalmus 4/766
Fw
H: Asia: Bor., Malay Pen. Thai.? New Gui.?
♂: Small, flat, slender genital papilla. S: –
B: Unsuccessful. F: C!
T: 23–28°C, L: 28 cm, pH: 7, D: 3

Dormitator lebretonis ♂ 2/1070, 3/954
Clay goby Bw,Fw
H: W Africa: Senegal to S Angola.
♂: Elongated D₂ and A fins. S: =
B: In caves and on plants. F: O
T: 25°C, L: 12 cm, pH: >7, D: 2–3

PERCHES

805

Dormitator lebretonis ♀   2/1070, 3/954
Clay goby

Dormitator lebretonis ♂   3/954
Clay goby
Fright coloration.

Belobranchus belobranchus   5/1012
Long-head goby   Fw,Bw
H: Philippines to New Guinea.
SD: Unknown.   S: =
B: Unknown.   F: C
T: >25°C, L: 20 cm, pH: >7, D: 3

Dormitator maculatus ♂   1/832, 3/958
Spotted sleeper, fat sleeper Fw,Bw,Mw
H: Am.: USA (North Carolina) to Brazil.
♂: Elongated D_2 and A fins.   S: =
B: Stimulated w/ water exchange. F: H,O
T: 20–27°C, L: 25 cm, pH: >7, D: 3–4

Dormitator maculatus ♀   1/832, 3/958
Spotted sleeper, fat sleeper Fw,Bw,Mw

Eleotris amblyopsis   4/752
                                                Bw, Fw
H: America: Costa Rica to Suriname.
♂: Elongated D_2 and A fins.   S: –
B: Unknown.   F: C,O
T: 23–28°C, L: 10 cm, pH: >7, D: 3

Eleotris fusca   3/960
Fw, Bw
H: Indo-Pacific btw. E Af., Melanesia, Polyn.
♂: Elongated D₂ and A fins.   S: –
B: Planktonic larvae.   F: C
T: 25°C, L: 26 cm, pH: >7, D: 3

Eleotris melanosoma   3/960
Brown sleeper   Bw, Fw
H: From E Africa to Tahiti.
♂: Elongated D₂ and A fins.   S: –
B: Unknown; ♂ tends spawn.   F: C,O
T: 25°C, L: 20 cm, pH: >7, D: 3

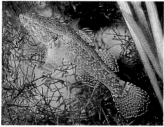

Eleotris pisonis   4/752
Bw, Fw
H: Am.: USA: South Carolina to Brazil.
SD: Unknown.   S: =
B: Unknown.   F: O
T: 20–27°C, L: 20 cm, pH: >7, D: 3

Eleotris vittata   5/1012
Banded sleeper   Bw, Fw
H: Africa: Senegal, Namibia, Nigeria.
♂: Larger, flatter genital papilla.   S: –
B: Unknown.   F: C!
T: 22–28°C, L: 24 cm, pH: >7, D: 3–4

Gobiomorphus australis   2/1064
Stripe gudgeon   Fw,Bw
H: Austl.: E Queensland, New South Wales.
SD: None known.   S: =
B: Unsuccessful.   F: C!
T: 18–25°C, L: 22 cm, pH: >7, D: 2

Gobiomorphus basalis ♂   5/1018

H: Australia, New Zealand.
♂: Elongated D₂ and A fins.   S: +
B: Overwinter at 10°C; 5.7 mm y.   F: C
T: 4–22°C, L: 9 cm, pH: 7, D: 3

PERCHES

Gobiomorphus basalis ♀ 5/1018

Gobiomorphus cotidianus 5/1020
Fw, Bw

H: New Zealand.
♂: Elongated D₁, D₂, and A fins. S: +
B: Cave or open spawner; <2000 e. F: C!
T: 4–22°C, L: 15 cm, pH: 7, D: 3

Gobiomorphus huttoni ♂ 5/1022
Red-fin sleeper Fw, Bw
H: Australia, New Zealand.
♂: Long D₁, D₂, & A fins; more color. S: =
B: Cs; <20000 e; in the sea. F: C!
T: 4–20°C, L: 12 cm, pH: 7, D: 3

Gobiomorphus huttoni ♀ 5/1022
Red-fin sleeper

Gobiomorus dormitor 5/1024
Giant sleeper Fw,Bw
H: Americas: Florida, Texas to Suriname.
♂: Elongated D₂ and A fins. S: –
B: Too large for aquarium breeding. F: C!
T: 4–22°C, L: 90 cm, pH: 7, D: 4

Gobiomorus dormitor juv. 5/1024
Giant sleeper

PERCHES

Gobiomorus maculatus   5/1026
Spotted sleeper   Fw,Bw
H: America: N Mexico to N Peru.
♂: Long D₂ & A fins; more colorful.   S: –
B: Unknown.   F: C!
T: 22–30°C, L: 32 cm, pH: 7, D: 4

Hannoichthys africanus   5/1030
African sleeper   Fw,Bw
H: Africa: Senegal to S Angola.
SD: Unknown.   S: =
B: Unknown.   F: C!
T: >28°C, L: 20 cm, pH: 7, D: 3

Hemieleotris latifasciatus ♂   2/1064
Broad-band sleeper
H: C & S Am.: W Costa Rica to Ecuador.
♂: Longer D₂ & A; shiny spot on D₁. S: +
B: In narrow caves.   F: C
T: 22–26°C, L: 12 cm, pH: 7, D: 2

Hemieleotris latifasciatus juv. ♀ 2/1064
Broad-band sleeper

Hypseleotris compressa ♂   2/1066
Empire gudgeon   spawning coloration
H: Australia and New Guinea.   Fw,Bw
♂: More color; bright red spawning. S: +
B: Unknown; ♂ tends spawn.   F: C,O
T: 10–30°C, L: 11 cm, pH: 7, D: 2

Hypseleotris cyprinoides ♂   5/1032
Minnow gudgeon
H: Indo-West Pacific region.   Fw,Bw
SD: See photos.   S: +
B: On leaves, stones; rearing failed. F:C
T: 22–28°C, L: 7 cm, pH: 7, D: 2

PERCHES

809

Hypseleotris cyprinoides ♀   5/1032
Minnow gudgeon

Hypseleotris galii   2/1066
Fire-tailed gudgeon   Fw
H: Australia: SE Queensland, E NSW.
♂: Larger fins; more colorful.   S: =
B: Hard subtrates; 100 eggs.   F: C,O
T: 10–30°C, L: 8 cm, pH: 7, D: 2

Hypseleotris guentheri ♂   2/1068
Gunther's gudgeon
H: SE Asia: Sulawesi.   Fw
♂: Larger; more colorful.   S: +
B: Attempts to rear young failed. F: C,O
T: 25–27°C, L: 7 cm, pH: 7, D: 1–2

Hypseleotris cf. *guentheri* ♂   5/1034
Gunther's gudgeon
H: N New Guinea.   Fw
♂: Long D_2 & A fins; more colorful. S: +
B: On roots.   F: C
T: 22–28°C, L: 7 cm, pH: 7, D: 2

Hypseleotris klunzingeri ♂   2/1068
Western carp gudgeon
H: Australia: Murray Darling Basin. Fw
♂: Larger; longer fins.   S: +
B: Nat.: small eggs; ♂ tends sp. F: C,O
T: 10–30°C, L: 6.5 cm, pH: 7, D: 1–2

Hypseleotris swinhornis t.♂,b.♀ 3/962

H: Asia: China (N of Hong Kong). Fw
♂: Elongated D_2 and A fins; darker. S: +
B: Unknown; ♂ tends spawn.   F: C,O
T: 18–22°C, L: <8 cm, pH: 7, D: 2

Madagascar: Matsabory, Maintimaso.

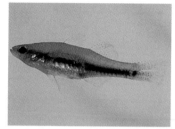

Hypseleotris tohizonae   4/754

H: Madagascar.   Fw
♂: Long D₂ & A fins; more colorful.   **S:** ?
B: Unknown.   **F:** C
T: 22–26°C, **L:** 10 cm, **pH:** 7, **D:** 2

Mogurnda adspersa   3/962
Purple-spotted gudgeon

H: Australia.   Fw
♂: Pointed genital pap.; more color.   **S:** =
B: Os/Cs; ♂ tends spawn.   **F:** C
T: 16–20°C, **L:** 14 cm, **pH:** 7, **D:** 3

Mogurnda kutubuensis ♀   4/756
Kutubu gudgeon

H: Papua New Guinea: Lake Kutubu. Fw
♂: Pointed, flat, long genital pap.   **S:** =
B: Unknown.   **F:** C,O
T: 23–28°C, **L:** 11 cm, **pH:** 7, **D:** 3

Mogurnda mogurnda   2/1070
Purple-striped gudgeon

H: Australia and New Guinea.   Fw
♂: Slightly darker ventrum.   **S:** –
B: Cs, <200 e; paternal family.   **F:** C,O
T: 24–26°C, **L:** <17 cm, **pH:** 7, **D:** 3

Mogurnda nesolepis ♂   4/758
Yellow-belly gudgeon

H: N New Guinea.   Fw
♂: Long D₂ & A fins; larger C fin.   **S:** =
B: Cave ceiling; <80 e; ♂ tends sp.
                                                    F: C
T: 22–27°C, **L:** 5.6 cm, **pH:** 7, **D:** 3

PERCHES

Mogurnda nesolepis ♀ 4/758
Yellow-belly gudgeon

Mogurnda pulchra ♂ 4/760
Moresby gudgeon
H: SE Papua New Guinea. Fw
♂: Elongated D_2 and A fins. S: =
B: Os; <200 e; ♂ tends spawn. F: C
T: 23–28°C, L: 10 cm, pH: 7, D: 3

Mogurnda pulchra ♀ 4/760
Moresby gudgeon

Mogurnda sp. "Papuan" 4/762

H: E Papua New Guinea.
♂: Elongated D_2 and A fins. S: =
B: Cave spawner; ♂ tends spawn. F: C
T: 22–27°C, L: 8 cm, pH: 7, D: 3

Mogurnda spilota ♀ 4/762
Spotted Kutubu gudgeon
H: Papua New Guinea: Lake Kutubu. Fw
♂: Pointed, flat, long genital papilla. S: =
B: Unknown. F: C,O
T: 23–28°C, L: 15 cm, pH: 7, D: 3

Mogurnda variegata ♀ 4/764
Mottled gudgeon
H: Papua New Guinea: Lake Kutubu. Fw
♂: Pointed, flat, long genital papilla. S: =
B: Unknown. F: C,O
T: 23–28°C, L: 15 cm, pH: 7, D: 3

PERCHES

Ophieleotris aporos   2/1072
Snakehead gudgeon
H: Indo-Pacific region.   Bw,Mw
♂: More colorful.   S: –
B: Successful; there are no reports.   F: C!
T: 20–30°C, L: 40 cm, pH: >7, D: 2

Ophiocara porocephala   2/1072
Flat-head sleeper
H: Indo-Pacific region.   Bw
SD: Unknown.   S: –
B: Unknown.   F: C!
T: 20–30°C, L: 30 cm, pH: >7, D: 2

Padogobius martensi   5/1021

Perccottus glehni   3/964
Amur sleeper   Fw
H: Asia: CIS States, China, NE Korea.
♂: Larger?   S: =
B: N: Os; <1000 eggs; ♂ tends sp.   F: C!
T: 15–30°C, L: 25 cm, pH: 7, D: 3

Ratsirakia legendrei   5/1043

H: Madagascar.   Fw
♂: Elongated D₂ and A fins.   S: =
B: Nat.: 2000 eggs on plants.   F: C
T: 25°C, L: 17 cm, pH: 7, D: 3

Tateurndina ocellicauda t. ♀, b. ♂   2/1074
Peacock goby, eye-spot sleeper   Fw
H: New Guinea: E Papua New Guinea.
♂: Lighter anal and dorsal fins.   S: +
B: Cave spawner; ♂ tends spawn.   F: O
T: 22–26°C, L: 7.5 cm, pH: 7, D: 2

PERCHES

Acentrogobius audax   3/972

H: Mozambique, Ryukyu Islands.   Bw
♂: 3 slender crossbands anteriorly. S: =
B: Unknown.   F: C!
T: 25°C, L: 9 cm, pH: >7, D: 3

Acentrogobius cyanomos ♂   5/1008
                                          Bw

H: Asia: India to Thailand and Indonesia.
♂: Elongated D_1, D_2, and A fins.   S: =
B: Cave spawner?   F: C
T: 22–28°C, L: 12 cm, pH: >7, D: 3

Acentrogobius pflaumii   5/1016

Acentrogobius viridipunctatus   3/972
Gold-spot goby
H: Indian Ocean, W Pacific.   Bw
♂: Long, spine-shaped genital pap.   S: =
B: Nat.: cave spawner.   F: C
T: 25°C, L: 16.5 cm, pH: >7, D: 3

Benthophilus macrocephalus   3/976

H: Coasts of the Caspian Sea.   Fw,Bw
♂: Long D_2 and A fins; larger.   S: =
B: Unsuccessful.   F: C
T: 4–20°C, L: 12 cm, pH: >7, D: 3

Bentophilus stellatus   3/978

H: Black Sea Basin.   Fw,Bw
♂: Elongated D_2 and A fins; larger. S: =
B: Nat: <2500 e at 30–35 m depth.   F: C
T: 4–20°C, L: ♂ 13.5 cm, pH: >7, D: 3

Brachygobius doriae   1/836
Golden-banded goby   spawning color
H: Asia: E Malaysia: Sarawak.   Bw,Fw
♂: More colorful.   S: (–)
B: Cs; 150–200 e; ♂ tends spawn.   F: C!
T: 22–29°C, L: 4.2 cm, pH: >7, D: 3

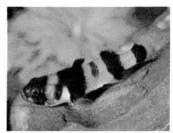

Brachygobius doriae   1/836
Golden-banded goby   normal coloration

Brachygobius kabiliensis   3/978

H: Asia: N Borneo.   Bw,Fw
♂: Pointed genital papilla.   S: (–)
B: Unknown.   F: C!
T: 25°C, L: 2.5 cm, pH: 7, D: 2

Chlamydogobius eremius ♂   2/1090
Desert goby
H: Australia: central and S Australia.
♂: Larger; much more colorful.   S: =
B: Cave spawner; paternal fam.   F: C,O
T: 10–35°C, L: 6 cm, pH: >7, D: 2

Evorthodus lyricus ♂   3/980
Lyra goby   Bw,(Fw)
H: America: USA (Virginia) to Brazil.
♂: Elongated D₁ and C fins.   S: =
B: In cave; 100 e; paternal family.   F: O
T: 20–30°C, L: 10 cm, pH: >7, D: 4

Evorthodus lyricus ♀   3/980
Lyra goby   Bw,(Fw)

Exyrias belissimus   5/1014

Exyrias puntang ♂   5/1014
Silver-spotted goby   Bw
H: Andaman Is., Japan, China, N Australia.
♂: Pointed and flat genital papilla.   S: =
B: Unknown.   F: O
T: 23–28°C, L: 16 cm, pH: >7, D: 3

Exyrias puntang   5/1014
Silver-spotted goby

Glossogobius bicirrhosus   3/982
Two-bristle goby   Bw,(Fw)
H: Asia: Ryukyu Is., Philippines, Indonesia.
♂: Filamentous D₁.   S: =
B: Unknown.   F: C
T: 25°C, L: 8.5 cm, pH: >7, D: 3

Glossogobius biocellatus   5/1017
Twin-spot gudgeon   Bw
H: SE Africa to S China, Japan, N Australia.
♂: Pointed genital papilla.   S: =
B: Unsuccessful.   F: C
T: 22–28°C, L: 11 cm, pH: >7, D: 3–4

Glossogobius giuris   3/982
Flathead goby   Bw,Fw
H: India, E Africa, Red Sea to W Pacific.
♂: Pointed genital papilla.   S: =
B: Rearing unsuccessful? Fw, Bw.   F: O
T: 25°C, L: 42 cm, pH: 7, D: 3

PERCHES

Gobiosoma bosci   5/1030
Naked gudgeon   Bw
H: N&C Am.: E USA (Long Island) to Mex.
♂: Darker; pointed genital papilla.   S: =
B: In mussel and oyster shells.   F: C
T: 25°C, L: 6.4 cm, pH: >7, D: 3

Hypogymnogobius xanthozona   1/836
Bumblebee goby
H: SE Asia: Indonesia.   Bw,Fw
♂: More intensely colored.   S: (–)
B: Cs; 150–200 e; paternal family. F: C!
T: 25–30°C, L: 4.5 cm, pH: >7, D: 3

Knipowitschia longecaudata ♂   3/986
Long-tailed goby   Fw,Bw
H: Black and Caspian Seas, Sea of Azov.
♂: Dark bands; D & A fins larger.   S: (–)
B: Cave spawner; paternal family.   F: C
T: 22–28°C, L: 11 cm, pH: >7, D: 3–4

Knipowitschia longecaudata ♀   3/986
Long-tailed goby   Fw,Bw

Lophogobius cyprinoides ♂ WC   3/988
                                               Bw, Mw
H: N–S America: S Florida to Venezuela.
♂: Colorful D₁; darker.   S: ?
B: Cave spawner; marine water.   F: O
T: 24–28°C, L: 10 cm, pH: >7, D: 3

Mesogobius batrachocephalus   3/988
Toad goby   Bw,(Fw)
H: Black and Caspian seas, Sea of Azov.
♂: Larger; pointed genital papilla.   S: –
B: Cave spawner; paternal family.   F: C!
T: 4–18°C, L: 37 cm, pH: >7, D: 3

Gobiidae (Gobiinae)

Nematogobius maindroni 4/772

H: W Africa: Senegal to Angola. Bw,Fw
SD: Unknown. S: +
B: Unknown. F: C!
T: 20–25°C, L: <8 cm, pH: 7, D: 3

Neogobius cephalarges constructor
3/992

H: Asia: CIS States: S Caspian Sea.
SD: None known. . S: ?
B: Unknown. F: C!
T: 16–22°C, L: 13 cm, pH: 7, D: 3

Neogobius eurycephalus 5/1036
Bw,Fw

H: Sea of Azov, NW Black Sea.
♂: Darker and larger. S: =
B: Nature: December to April. F: C!
T: 4–20°C, L: 20 cm, pH: >7, D: 3

Neogobius fluviatilis ♂ 3/992
Fluvial goby Fw

H: Black and Caspian seas.
♂: Larger fins; yellow while spaw. S: =
B: May–Sep.; Os; ♂ tends spawn. F: C!
T: 4–20°C, L: 20 cm, pH: 7, D: 3

Neogobius fluviatilis ♀ 3/992
Fluvial goby

Neogobius gymnotrachelus 3/995
Fw,Bw

H: Black and Caspian seas, Sea of Azov.
♂: Darker; pointed genital papilla. S: =
B: April–June; Cs; ♂ tends spawn. F: C!
T: 4–20°C, L: 16 cm, pH: >7, D: 3

PERCHES

Neogob. gymnotrachelus macrophthalmus
5/1036

H: Asia: Caspian Sea.   Bw
SD: Unknown.   S: =
B: April–August; Os; <570 e.   F: C!
T: 4–18°C, L: 6.7 cm, pH: >7, D: 3–4

Neogobius kessleri ♂   3/996
Kessler's goby   Fw,Bw

H: NW Black Sea, Caspian Sea, Iran.
♂: Pointed genital papilla.   S: =
B: Mar.–Apr. (May); ♂ tends spawn. F: C!
T: 4–20°C, L: 22 cm, pH: 7, D: 3

Neogobius melanostomus ♂   3/996
Blackmouth goby   Fw,Bw

H: Black and Caspian seas, Sea of Azov.
♂: Larger; dark when spawning.   S: =
B: Os; <5000 e; ♂ tends spawn.   F: C!
T: 4–20°C, L: 25 cm, pH: >7, D: 3

Neogobius ratan goebeli   4/774

Neogobius ratan ratan ♂   4/774
                                                              Bw

H: N Black Sea & N Sea of Azov.
♂: Dark during spawning season.   S: =
B: March to May; cave spawner.   F: C!
T: 4–20°C, L: 23 cm, pH: >7, D: 3

Neogobius ratan ratan ♀   4/774

PERCHES

819

Oligolepis acutipennis ♂   2/1092

H: S and SE Asia.   Mw,Bw,(Fw)
♂: Longer fins; larger.   S: =
B: Cs; pelagic larvae; unsuccessful. F:O
T: 22–26°C, L: 12 cm, pH: >7, D: 3

Padogobius martensii   2/1094

H: Europe: N Italy.   Fw
♂: Slimmer; spotted D_1 fin.   S: +
B: Simple; Os; ♂ tends spawn.   F: C!
T: 10–18°C, L: 6 cm, pH: >7, D: 2–3

Pomatochistus marmoratus   4/778
Marbled goby   Bw

H: E Atl., Mediterranean, Black S., S. of Azov.
♂: 4 crossbands; dark chest.   S: =
B: Nat.: cave spawner; <1200 e.   F: C,O
T: 20–28°C, L: 6.5 cm, pH: >7, D: 3

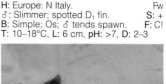

Porogobius schlegelii   5/1041

H: W Africa: Senegal to Zaïre.   Bw,Fw
♂: Pointed, longer genital papilla.   S: =
B: Unknown.   F: C!
T: >25°C, L: 15 cm, pH: >7, D: 3

Proterorhinus marmoratus ♂   2/1096
Amur tube-nose   Fw,Bw

H: Austria, Black and Caspian seas.
♂: Red spot on D_1 when spawning. S: =
B: Nature: open spawner.   F: C!
T: 10–18°C, L: <11 cm, pH: >7, D: 2–3

Pseudapocryptes lanceolatus   4/778
Lanceolate goby   Bw

H: As.: India, Burma, Thai., Viet., Kal., Java.
♂: Pointed genital papilla.   S: =
B: Unsuccessful.   F: C!
T: 23–28°C, L: 22 cm, pH: >7, D: 4

Redigobius balteatus   2/1088
Balteata goby   Bw
H: SE Asia: Kal., Viet., Sri L., Philippines...
♂: Elongated D₂ and A fins.   S: =
B: Cs; ♂ tends sp.; rearing difficult. F: C!
T: 25–28°C, L: 5 cm, pH: >7, D: 3–4

Redigobius bikolanus ♂   4/780
                                          Fw,Bw
H: South Africa–Japan, Guam, NE Austl.
♂: Elongated D₂ and A fins; larger. S: =
B: Cs; 1000 e; rearing failed.   F: C!
T: 21–28°C, L: 4.5 cm, pH: 7, D: 3

Redigobius bikolanus ♀   4/780

Redigobius chrysosoma   4/776
Pretty-fin goby   Fw,Bw
H: Borneo, New Guinea, N Australia.
♂: Pointed and flat genital papilla.   S: +
B: Unknown.   F: C!
T: 23–28°C, L: 6.2 cm, pH: 7, D: 3

Redigobius chrysosoma   4/776
Pretty-fin goby
See photo on p. 5/1016.

Stenogobius gymnopomus   3/1000

PERCHES

H: Asia: India, Indonesia.   Fw,Bw
♂: Elongated D₁ and C fins.   S: =
B: Unknown.   F: O
T: 25°C, L: 13.5 cm, pH: >7, D: 3

Gobiidae (Gobiinae[1])
Gobiidae (Gobionellinae[2–6])

Gobies
Dwarf Gobies

Yongeichthys thomasi   5/1050
                            Bw,Fw

H: W Africa: Guinea-Bissau to Zaïre.
♂: Pointed genital papilla.   S: =
B: Unknown.   F: C!
T: 25°C, L: 6 cm, pH: >7, D: 3

Gobiopterus chuno   2/1092
Glass goby

H: SE Asia: India, Bngl., Thai., Singapore.
SD: Unknown.   S: +
B: Unknown.   F: C
T: 23–26°C, L: 2.5 cm, pH: ?, D: 4

Mugilogobius chulae   3/990
                            Bw,Mw

H: Asia: Thai., Phil., Taiwan, Ryukyu.
♂: Elongated D₁, D₂, and, A fins.   S: +
B: Cs; ♂ tends, rearing possible.   F: C!
T: 25–28°C, L: 5 cm, pH: >7, D: 2–3

Gobiopterus brachypterus   5/1028

H: Sumatra, Java, Australia, Philippines.
♂: Slender and pointed papilla.   S: ?
B: Unknown.   F: C
T: 25°C, L: 3 cm, pH: 7, D: 4

Mugilogobius adeia ♂   4/772
                            Fw

H: Asia: Sulawesi: Lake Matano.
♂: Elongated D₁, D₂, and A fins.   S: =
B: Cs; ♂ tends sp.; rearing failed. F: C!
T: 22–28°C, L: 4.3 cm, pH: 7, D: 3

Mugilogobius inhacae   3/990
                            Bw

H: W Indian O.: Mozambique, Seychelles.
♂: Elongated D₂ and A fins.   S: ?
B: Unknown.   F: C?
T: 22–25°C, L: 4 cm, pH: >7, D: 3

PERCHES

822

Mugilogobius valigouva   5/1034
Mullet-headed goby   Bw
H: Asia: Sri Lanka, India, Pakistan.
♂: Elongated D₁, D₂, and A fins.   S: ?
B: Unknown.   F: C!
T: 22–28°C, L: 2.5 cm, pH: >7, D: 2–3

Pandaka trimaculata   2/1094
Pygmy goby
H: SE Asia: Philippines.   Bw
♀: 15 mm; fuller during spawning. S: =
B: Unsuccessful.   F: C,O
T: 24–30°C, L: ♂ 9 mm, pH: >7, D: 3

Pseudogobius javanicus   2/1100
Pug-nose goby   Fw
H: Asia: trop. W Pacific, India to Ryukyu Is.
♂: Pointed genital papilla.   S: =
B: Open spawner; ♂ tends spawn.   F: O
T: 23–25°C, L: 3 cm, pH: 7, D: 3

Rhinogobius lindbergi   2/1098

H: Asia: Russia: Amur Basin.   Fw
SD: Unknown.   S: (–)
B: Unknown.   F: C!
T: 16–20°C, L: 4.5 cm, pH: 7, D: 3

Rhinogobius sp. 1   5/1044

H: Asia: Taiwan.   Fw
♂: Longer D₁, D₂, A fins; more color. S: =
B: Cave spawner.   F: C!
T: 25°C, L: 8 cm, pH: 7, D: 3

Rhinogobius sp. 1   5/1044
See photo on p. 5/1040.

PERCHES

823

Rhinogobius sp. 1　　　　　　5/1044
See photo on p. 5/1040.

Rhinogobius sp. 2　　　　　　5/1044

H: E Russia: Peter the Great Bay.　　Fw
♂: Longer D_1, D_2, A; more colorful. **S:** =
B: Cave spawner.　　　　　　　**F:** C!
T: 4–20°C, **L:** 6.5 cm, **pH:** 7, **D:** 3

Northern Borneo: Regang River at Song
Sarawak.

Rhinogobius wui ♂　　2/1100, 3/998
White-cheek goby　　　　　　(5/1026)

H: S China: mountains, Hong Kong.　　Fw
♂: Longer D_2, A fins; broader head. **S:** (–)
B: Cs; <50 large eggs; ♂ tends sp. **F:** C!
T: 15–25°C, **L:** 4.5 cm, **pH:** 7, **D:** 2

Rhinogobius wui ♂　　2/1100, 3/998
White-cheek goby　　　　　　(5/1026)

♂: Branchial membranes with red mark-
　ings.

Rhinogobius wui ♀　　2/1100, 3/998
White-cheek goby　　　　　　(5/1026)

Schismatogobius deraniyagalai ♂   5/1046

Schismatogobius deraniyagalai ♀   5/1046

H: Asia: Sri Lanka.   Fw
♂: Large red mouth.   S: (–)
B: Cs; ♂ tends sp.; rearing failed.   F: C!
T: 22–27°C, L: 4.6 cm, pH: 7, D: 3

Schismatogobius deraniyagalai ♂?   5/1046

Stigmatogobius sadanundio   1/838
Knight goby   Fw,Bw
H: SE Asia: Sumatra, Borneo, Java.
♂: Larger fins.   S: (–)
B: Cs; <1000 e; ♂ tends sp.; Bw. F:C,H
T: 20–26°C, L: 8.5 cm, pH: >7, D: 3

Tridentiger bifasciatus   5/1048
Two-striped goby   Bw,Fw
H: Asia: China, Taiwan, Korea, Japan.
♂: Pointed papilla; broader head.   S: –
B: Unsuccessful.   F:C
T: 10–25°C, L: 12 cm, pH: >7, D: 3

Apocryptes bato   5/1008

H: India, Bengal, Bangladesh, Burma.   Bw
♂: Very long C fin; pointed papilla.   S: =
B: During the monsoon season.   F: O
T: 23–28°C, L: 17 cm, pH: >7, D: 4

PERCHES

825

Boleophthalmus pectinirostris   2/1088
Mw,Bw,(Fw)
H: SE Asia: Japan, China, Thailand, Burma.
SD: Unknown.   S: =
B: Unknown; amphibious.   F: C
T: 26–30°C, L: 20 cm, pH: >7, D: 4

Parapocryptes serperaster   3/998
Slim mudskipper   Bw
H: Asia: S China, Thailand, Malaysia, India.
SD: Unknown.   S: =
B: Unknown.   F: O,H
T: 25°C, L: 22 cm, pH: >7, D: 3–4

Periophthalmus barbarus   1/838
Mudskipper   Bw (amphibious)
H: Red Sea to Madag., SE Asia, Australia.
SD: Unknown.   S: (–)
B: Unsuccessful.   F: C
T: 25–30°C, L: 15 cm, pH: ≫7, D: 4

Periophthalmus barbarus   2/1096
Butterfly mudskipper
H: W Africa: coasts.   Bw (amphibious)
SD: Unknown.   S: =
B: Unsuccessful.   F: C!
T: 26–30°C, L: 25 cm, pH: >7, D: 4

Awaous lateristriga   5/1010
Side-band river goby
H: Africa: Senegal to Angola.   Fw,Bw
♂: Longer, pointed genital papilla. S: =
B: Prob. Fw & larvae wash downriver. F:C
T: 22–28°C, L: 26 cm, pH: 7, D: 3–4

Awaous lateristriga juv.   5/1010
Side-band river goby

Awaous strigatus ♂ 3/974
Striated river goby

H: S America: Col. to Brazil: coast. Fw
♂: Elongated D_2 and anal fins. S: =
B: Cs; ♂ tends sp.; rearing. unsucc. F:O
T: 25–27°C, L: 10 cm, pH: 7, D: 3

Awaous strigatus ♀ 3/974
Striated river goby

Awaous taiasica WC 3/976

H: America: Florida to SE Brazil. Fw,Bw
♂: Genital papilla long and spinelike. S: =
B: Unknown; diadromous. F: C
T: 22–30°C, L: 30 cm, pH: 7, D: 4

Sicydium punctatum ♂ 5/1038
Fw

H: America: Martinique, Trinidad, Col., Ven.
♂: D_1, D_2, A longer; pointed papilla. S: =
B: Cs; diadromous; rear. unsuccessful. F: O
T: 22–27°C, L: 8 cm, pH: 7, D: 3

Sicyopus jonklaasi ♂ 3/1000
Lipstick goby

H: SE Asia: Sri Lanka. Fw
♂: Red upper lip & C peduncle. S: =
B: Unknown; diadromous. F: C!
T: 23–25°C, L: 5 cm, pH: 7, D: 3

Stiphodon ornatus 2/1098
Emerald river goby Fw

H: Indo., Philipp., New Guinea, Japan,...
SD: Sexual dichromatism. S: +
B: Partially successful. F: O
T: 24–28°C, L: 4.5 cm, pH: 7, D: 3

PERCHES

827

Family Kuhliidae

Flagtails colonize marine, brackish, and freshwater biotopes of the Indo-Pacific region. After the genera *Edelia* and *Nannoperca* were reclassified into the family Percichthyidae (p. 832), the family Kuhliidae was left with just 8 species. The presented species is the only one that spends most of its life in freshwater; other species occasionally enter rivers.

Kuhlia rupestris can be maintained in a freshwater aquarium. A decor based on stones and roots is appropriate, and vegetation can be waived. In accordance to conditions in its natural biotope—i.e., swiftly flowing creeks—the aquarium must be equipped with a strong, current-producing filtration system.

Kuhlia rupestris   2/1028
Jungle perch
H: Indo-Pacific coastal areas.
SD: Unknown.   S: =
B: Unsuccessful.   F: C!
T: 20–26°C, L: 45 cm, pH: 7, D: 4

Family Kurtidae

The family consists of just one genus and two species. They are inhabitants of brackish water and freshwater habitats, rarely marine biotopes. They colonize the Indomalayan region to Australia.

To our knowledge, *Kurtus gulliveri* has not been maintained in an aquarium. However, it is known to be susceptible to fungal infection and, upon capture, prone to fatal seizures. The egg clump is carried around on the male's nuchal hook. Developmental stages or other details of brood care are still unknown.

Kurtus gulliveri   3/910
Nursery fish
H: New Guinea, Australia.
♂: Nuchal hook.   S: +
B: Nature: egg clump on hook.   F: C!
T: 20–28°C, L: 60 cm, pH: 7, D: 3–4

PERCHES

Family Lutjanidae

The family of snappers contains 5 subfamilies, 21 genera, and a total of 125 species. They inhabit brackish and marine waters of tropical and subtropical regions. As exceptions, *Lutjanus fuscescens*, *L. goldiei*, and possibly *L. maxweberi* solely occur in freshwater and estuarine biotopes (NELSON, 1994).

They are popular food fishes. When a certain dinoflagellate multiplies explosively in their biotope, a toxin concentrates in the fish, causing ciguatera poisoning in humans.

Lutjanus argentimaculatus   2/1033
Mangrove jack
H: Tropical Indo-Pacific.   Bw, Mw, Fw
SD: Unknown.   S: –
B: Unknown.   F: C
T: 16–30°C, L: 100 cm, pH: >7, D: 3

Family Monodactylidae

Moonfishes or fingerfishes inhabit brackish and marine biotopes of western Africa and the Indo-Pacific. At times its members seek freshwater, but successful long-term aquarium maintenance is contingent on brackish or marine water. The family is composed of 2 genera and a total of 5 species.

Fingerfishes are schooling fishes which have not yet been bred in an aquarium.

Monodactylus argenteus   1/804
Fingerfish, mono
H: Africa, Asia.   Bw
SD: Unknown.   S: =
B: Unsuccessful.   F: O
T: 22–28°C, L: 25 cm, pH: >7, D: 3–4

Psettus sebae   2/1034
Seba mono
H: W Africa: Senegal to Zaïre.   Mw, Bw.
SD: Unknown.   S: =
B: Unsuccessful.   F: O
T: 24–28°C, L: 20 cm, pH: >7, D: 3–4

PERCHES

Amazon tributary at Santarém, Brazil.

Family Nandidae

Leaf-fishes can be found in freshwaters of western Africa, southern Asia, and northeastern South America. According to some authorities, the badis are actually classified in their own subfamily—the Badinae—within this family. In the INDEX, the badis have been placed in the autonomous family Badidae(p. 791) and the Nandidae is solely composed of the two subfamilies Nandinae and Pristolepidinae and their 6 genera and 9 species.

As indicated by their large, extremely protrusile mouth, leaf-fishes are largely specialized predators. Their uncanny resemblence to a leaf drifting in the current allows them to ambush their unsuspecting prey.

While the fringes of the aquarium should be densely planted with tough vegetation, the center must be left free to provide needed swimming space. A sand substrate and hiding places among stones and roots complete the furnishings.

Monocirrhus polyacanthus   1/805
South American leaf-fish
H: South America: Peru.
♀: Sometimes fuller.   S: =
B: Substrate sp.; <300 e; P fam.   F: C!
T: 22–26°C, L: 12 cm, pH: <7, D: 3–4

PERCHES

Nandus nandus   1/806
Nandus
H: SE Asia: India, Burma, Thailand.
♂: Darker; larger fins.   S: –
B: Egg scatterer; <300 eggs.   F: C!
T: 22–26°C, L: 20 cm, pH: 7, D: 2–3

Nandus nebulosus   2/1035
Fog nandus
H: SE Asia: Thai., Malay Pen., Indonesia.
SD: Unknown.   S: –
B: Egg scatterer; <300 eggs.   F: C!
T: 22–26°C, L: 12 cm, pH: 7, D: 2–3

Polycentropsis abbreviata   3/911
African leaf-fish
H: Africa: Nigeria, Cameroon, Gabon.
♀: Slightly convex and paler.   S: –
B: Bubble nest; <100 e; P fam.   F: C!
T: 26–30°C, L: 8 cm, pH: <7, D: 3–4

Polycentrus punctatus   1/806
Schomburgk's leaf-fish
H: NE South America.
♂: Darker.   S: =
B: Cave; <600 eggs; paternal fam.   F: C!
T: 22–26°C, L: 10 cm, pH: <7, D: 2

Pristolepis grooti juv.   3/912
Tiger leaf-fish
H: SE Asia: Burma, Thailand to Indonesia.
SD: Unknown.   S: =
B: Unknown.   F: O
T: 23–28°C, L: 21 cm, pH: 7, D: 3

Polycentropsis abbreviata.   3/911
African leaf-fish

PERCHES

831

Family Percichthyidae

There are 11 genera and approximately 22 species within the family of temperate perches; they inhabit freshwaters and occasionally brackish waters of Australia and South America, where they are particularly common in Argentina and Chile.

According to some experts, the genus *Gadopsis* should be placed into its own family and even its own order, the Gadopsidae and Gadiformes, respectively. The genera *Edelia* and *Nannoperca*, previously part of the family Kuhliidae (p. 828), are now considered part of the family Percichthyidae (NELSON, 1994).

The smaller species (genera *Edelia*, *Nannatherina,* and *Nannoperca*) are commonly called pygmy perches because of their diminutive stature. They are popular aquarium fishes in Australia, largely because their amiable nature permits them to be associated with congeners, cichlids, and other fishes of similar size. In species aquaria, breeding proceeds without further ado. Spawning can be fomented through a partial water exchange. Brood care has not been observed within this family.

As long as extreme values are avoided, maintenance is straightforward. The aquarium should have abundant vegetation, a sand substrate, and a few hiding places among stones and roots. Freeze-dried and flake foods are accepted, but like most carnivores, small live foods are relished.

A few of the large species have been studied as possible aquaculture subjects in Australia. Results obtained with *Gadopsis marmoratus* were clearly inferior to those of trout. A more promising fish of this family is *Plectoplites ambiguus.* It is bred in ponds, and an economically feasible aquaculture diet is being sought (BARDACH et al., 1972).

Edelia obscura   2/1027
Yarra pygmy perch
H: Australia.
♂: Slimmer.   S: +
B: Unknown.   F: C,O
T: 10–30°C, L: 7.5 cm, pH: 7, D: 2

Edelia vittata   2/1028
West Australian pygmy perch
H: Australia.
♂: Darker fins; slimmer.   S: +
B: 20–60 sinking adhesive eggs.   F: C,O
T: 10–30°C, L: 7 cm, pH: 7, D: 2

Gadopsis marmoratus   2/1075
River blackfish, freshwater cod
H: SE Australia: freshwater.
♂: Smaller and slimmer.   S: =
B: Cave spawner; demersal eggs. F: C
T: 5–20°C, L: <60 cm, pH: 7, D: 3

Macquaria australasica   2/1036
Macquarie perch
H: Australia.
SD: Unknown.   S: +
B: Nat.: Sept.–Nov.; <200 000 e. F: C
T: 4–25°C, L: 35 cm, pH: 7, D: 3

Nannatherina balstoni   2/1030
Balston's perchlet
H: Australia.
♂: Slimmer; more color (spawning). S: +
B: Unknown.   F: C
T: 15–30°C, L: 8 cm, pH: <7, D: 2

Nannoperca australis   2/1030
South Australian pygmy perch
H: Australia.
♂: Slimmer; more color (spawning). S: +
B: Simple; no brood care. F: C,O
T: 10–30°C, L: 8 cm, pH: 7, D: 2

Nannoperca oxleyana   2/1032
Northern pygmy perch
H: Australia.
♂: Slimmer; black (spawning time). S: +
B: Simple.   F: C,O
T: 16–30°C, L: 7.5 cm, pH: 7, D: 2

Plectoplites ambiguus   2/1036
Australian golden perch
H: Australia.
SD: Unknown.   S: =
B: In ponds.   F: C
T: 10–30°C, L: 75 cm, pH: 7, D: 4

PERCHES

Family Percidae

The family of true perches consists of 2 subfamilies—Percinae and Luciopercinae—10 genera, and a total of 162 species. They inhabit freshwaters of the Northern Hemisphere. With 102 species, the North American darters of the genus *Etheostoma* are the most specious of the family.

Darters are bottom-oriented fishes that have a degenerate swimbladder and live in lotic (flowing) biotopes. In many species, the males become very colorful during the spawning season; some even develop nuptial tubercles like the cyprinids. The genders can be distinguished by the shape of the genital papilla: males have a triangular, pointed genital papilla, whereas females have a round, blunt genital papilla.

Outside the United States, *Etheostoma* are rarely maintained. It is important to know the biotope the fish originated from to meet its requirements appropriately. Species hailing from current-rich waters require gravel and stone substrates, a current, clear and oxygen-rich water, a neutral pH, and a moderate hardness. A strong pump dedicated exclusively to water movement is sometimes unavoidable. The requirements of species originating from lentic waters, e.g., the swamp darter (p. 835), largely correspond to those of fishes from the Amazon Basin—but a little cooler, of course.

Information about their reproductive biology stems from observations in nature. The eggs are laid under stones, in gravel substrates and, in the case of species such as the swamp darter, on aquatic plants. Sexually active males are territorial.

For economic reasons, repeated attempts to commercially culture *Perca fluviatilis,* the river perch (p. 837), have failed. Because of its pronounced carnivorous diet, alimentation is too expensive. Other large Percidae are popular game fishes; hence, they are bred to stock lakes and rivers for recreational fishing.

Etheostoma blennoides, one of over 100 species of darters.

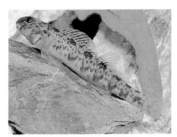

Etheostoma blennioides   3/914
Greenside darter
H: N America: E USA.
♂: Short, pointed genital papilla.   S: =
B: Nat.: April–May; 460–1830 eggs.   F: C
T: 4–18°C, L: 15 cm, pH: 7, D: 3

Etheostoma blennioides newmanii
Greenside darter   3/914

Etheostoma caeruleum   3/916
Rainbow darter
H: N America: E USA, SE Canada.
♂: Much more colorful.   S: =
B: Nature: 800 eggs.   F: C
T: 4–18°C, L: 8 cm, pH: 7, D: 2–3

Etheostoma flabellare   3/918
Fantail darter
H: N Am.: S Canada, central to E USA.
♂: Very small genital papilla.   S: =
B: Nat.: underside of rocks; 450 e.   F: C
T: 4–18°C, L: 8 cm, pH: 7, D: 3

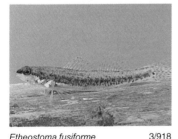

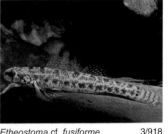

Etheostoma fusiforme   3/918
Swamp darter
H: N America: E USA.
♂: Very small genital papilla.   S: =
B: Nat.: on aquatic plants.   F: C
T: 14–26°C, L: 6 cm, pH: 7, D: 2

Etheostoma cf. *fusiforme*   3/918
Swamp darter
H: N America: E USA: N Florida.

Etheostoma maculatum   4/726
Spotted darter
H: N America: USA.
♂: More colorful; larger V & P fins.   S: =
B: Like its congeners.   F: C
T: 10–24°C, L: 6.5 cm, pH: 7, D: 2–3

Etheostoma microperca   4/726
Least darter
H: N America: USA.
♂: Slightly more colorful.   S: (−)
B: Unknown.   F: C
T: 10–22°C, L: 3.5 cm, pH: >7, D: 3

Etheostoma nigrum   3/920
Johnny darter
H: N America: E USA.
♂: Dark during spawning season.   S: =
B: Nat.: April–June; paternal fam.   F: C
T: 4–18°C, L: 6 cm, pH: 7, D: 2–3

Etheostoma olmstedi   4/728
Tesselated darter
H: N America: USA.
♂: More colorful.   S: (−)
B: Like its congeners.   F: C
T: 10–24°C, L: 5 cm, pH: 7, D: 1–2

Etheostoma spectabile   3/920
Orangethroat darter
H: N America: USA.
♂: More colorful; triangular gen.pap. S: =
B: Nat.: April, May; <1200 e.   F: C
T: 4–18°C, L: 8 cm, pH: 7, D: 2–3

Etheostoma tetrazonum   4/728
Missouri saddled darter
H: N America: USA.
♂: More colorful.   S: −
B: Gravel substrate or in algae mats. F: C
T: 10–28°C, L: 6 cm, pH: 7, D: 2–3

PERCHES

Gymnocephalus acerina   4/730

H: N affluents of the Black Sea.
SD: Unknown.   S: =
B: Unsuccessful?   F: C
T: 10–24°C, L: 12–21 cm, pH: 7, D: 3

Gymnocephalus baloni   4/730

H: Europe: lower Danube Basin.
SD: Not described.   S: =
B: In rock crevices?   F: C,O
T: 10–20°C, L: 12 cm, pH: 7, D: 3

Gymnocephalus cernuus   1/808
Ruffe, blacktail

H: Europe, Asia.
SD: None.   S: –
B: Mar.–May; on plants, stones. F: C!
T: 10–20°C, L: 25 cm, pH: 7, D: 2–3

Gymnocephalus schraetser   3/922

H: Europe: Danube and tributaries.
SD: None.   S: =
B: Nat.: April, May.   F: C
T: 4–18°C, L: 25 cm, pH: >7, D: 3

Perca fluviatilis   1/808
River perch

H: Throughout Europe.
♂: Often more colorful.   S: =
B: N: Mar–June; "perch cords." F: C!
T: 10–22°C, L: 45 cm, pH: >7, D: 4

Percina caprodes caprodes   5/981
Logperch

H: N America: Canada, E USA.
♂: Red-fringed D₁ fin; A fin larger. S: =
B: Groupwise in pits; adhesive e. F: C
T: 4–20°C, L: 18 cm, pH: 7, D: 3

Percina sciera   4/732
Dusky darter
H: N America: USA.
♂: More colorful; nuptial tubercles.   S: =
B: Like *Etheostoma* spp.   F: C!
T: 10–24°C, L: 13 cm, pH: 7, D: 2–3

Romanichthys valsanicola   4/734
H: Europe: Romania.
SD: Unknown.   S: (–)
B: Among small-grained gravel.   F: C
T: 10–20°C, L: ca.12 cm, pH: 7, D: 4

Stizostedion lucioperca   3/922
European pikeperch
H: Central and eastern Europe.
SD: Very slight.   S: –
B: Apr.–May; gravel, plants; ♂ tends. F: C!
T: 6–22°C, L: 70 cm, pH: 7, D: 3

Stizostedion volgensis   4/734
H: Europe: N Black Sea.
SD: Very slight.   S: –
B: N.: April–May; among stones.   F: C!
T: 8–22°C, L: 35 cm, pH: >7, D: 4

Zingel streber   4/736
H: Europe: Danube.   Rare
SD: None.   S: –
B: Unknown.   F: C!
T: 5–20°C, L: 20 cm, pH: 7, D: 3

Zingel zingel   3/924
H: Europe.   Rare
SD: Unknown.   S: –
B: Nat.: March–May; on gravel.   F: C!
T: 4–18°C, L: <50 cm, pH: 7, D: 3

PERCHES

Family Polynemidae

The family of threadfins consists of
7 genera and a total of 33 species.
With the exception of 4 species
which are limited to freshwater biotopes (especially Borneo), all threadfins live in tropical and subtropical
seas (NELSON, 1994).

The pectoral fins are divided into
two sections, whereby the anterior
part consists of up to 15 independent, long rays (= threadfins).

These fishes are unsuitable for
home aquaria.

Polynemus borneensis   5/1085
Borneo threadfin
H: Malaysia, Borneo: estuaries.   Bw
SD: Unknown.   S: –?
B: In the sea: pelagic eggs.   F: C
T: 24–28°C, L: 35 cm, pH: >7, D: 4

Family Pomacentridae

Damselfishes are predominantly marine inhabitants; a few occur in brackish
water biotopes. While damselfishes enjoy a worldwide distribution, the greatest concentration is found in the Indo-Pacific.

The systematics of Pomacentridae is confounded by intraspecific and habi-
tat-dependent variations in coloration. According to ALLEN (1991), there are
4 subfamilies, 28 genera, and about 315 described species and 6 undescribed species.

This family is a favorite of marine aquarists, since many of its species live
symbiotically with sea anemones.

Neopomacentrus taeniurus ♂   4/738
Freshwater damsel
H: W Indian Ocean.   Bw
♂: Longer fin rays.   S: –
B: Cave sp.; ♂ tends the 1800 e. F: C,O
T: 23–28°C, L: 9 cm, pH: >7, D: 3

Stegastes otophorus   4/738
H: Caribbean: Cuba.   Bw
SD: Unknown.   S: –
B: Nat.: Cs; ♂ tends the spawn.   F: O
T: 21–28°C, L: 14 cm, pH: >7, D: 3

PERCHES

Family Scatophagidae

The scats are a small family of only 2 genera and about 4 species. Although *Scatophagus tetracanthus* breeds in freshwater, scats are primarily found in marine and brackish water biotopes. They occur in the Indo-Pacific region (NELSON, 1994).

Scats are peaceful, lively schooling fishes. As juveniles they can be maintained in brackish waters, but adults need marine water for long-term care. They are very sensitive in front of nitrites; therefore, a good filtration system is a requisite for successful care. Ample free swimming space is necessary. Over the course of their development, they undergo a metamorphosis. Scats are unselective omnivores, readily consuming flake foods, live foods, and vegetable fare.

Due to their required water chemistry, the maintenance of these fishes is not easy.

Scatophagus argus argus   1/810
Argusfish, scat
H: Tropical Indo-Pacific.   Bw
SD: Unknown.   S: +
B: Reproductive biology unknown.   F: O
T: 20–28°C, L: 30 cm, pH: >7, D: 4

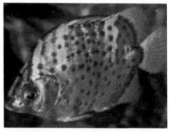

Scatophagus argus atromaculatus 1/810
Red scat   adult
H: Sri Lanka and New Guinea to Australia.

Scatophagus tetracanthus   1/810
African scat
H: E Africa.   Mw, Bw, Fw
SD: Unknown.   S: +
B: Unsuccessful.   F: O
T: 22–30°C, L: 40 cm, pH: >7, D: 3

Selenotoca multifasciata   5/982
Spot-stripe scat, butterfish
H: Australia, Indonesia.   Bw
SD: Unknown.   S: +,!
B: Unsuccessful.   F: O,H
T: 20–28°C, L: <40 cm, pH: >7, D: 1–4

Family Serranidae

Sea basses consist of 3 subfamilies, 62 genera, and almost 450 species (Nelson, 1994). Few species inhabit freshwater. Many are hermaphrodites.

These predators oftentimes display intraspecific aggressions. Nevertheless, *Siniperca chua-tsi* is a popular aquarium fish in countries of the former Soviet Union (CIS States). In Australia, *Maccullochella macquariensis* is an important pond-cultured food fish.

Maccullochella macquariensis   2/1038
Trout cod, Murray cod
H: Australia.
SD: None known.   S: –
B: Nat.: substr. spawer, 20 000 e.   F: C!
T: 18–28°C, L: 80 cm, pH: 7, D: 3–4

Maccullochella macquariensis var. *peelii*
2/1038

Siniperca chua-tsi   3/925
Chinese perch
H: Asia: central and lower Amur.   Fw
♂ : Slightly larger and darker.   S: –
B: Nature: June and July.   F: C!
T: 4–22°C, L: 30 cm, pH: >7, D: 2–3

Siniperca chua-tsi   3/925
Chinese perch

Siniperca kawamebari   4/742
Silla
H: Japan, South Korea.   Fw
♂ : Larger; red anal fin.   S: –
B: Unknown.   F: C
T: 10–23°C, L: 13 cm, pH: 7, D: 3

Family Sillaginidae

Sillagos, or whitings, are largely littoral marine species. Only rarely do they venture into adjacent freshwater. There are 3 genera and a total of 32 species within the family.

The species *Sillaginopsis pannijus* has no swimbladder. Up to a length of 18 cm, it can be maintained in freshwater, then it requires brackish water. It is a popular game fish with finely flavored white meat.

Sillaginopsis panijus   4/824

H: Asia: India: coastal waters.   Bw
♂ : Slightly smaller & more colorful.   S: =
B: Nat.: juv. spend 2–3 m. in Fw.   F:C,O
T: 22–28°C, L: 44 cm, pH: >7, D: 4

Family Teraponidae (previously also Theraponidae)

Tigerfishes and grunters are inhabitants of the littoral zone of marine waters, of brackish waters, and freshwaters. There are 16 genera and about 45 species. Most freshwater species are found in Australia and New Guinea (NELSON, 1994).

Even though they are bellicose and predacious, moderate-sized species can be associated with fishes such as cichlids, especially as juveniles. *Hephaestus carbo* often becomes very tame in an aquarium.

The large species are all popular game and food fishes throughout their native range, and *Bidyanus bidyanus* has been bred in aquaculture ponds.

Amniataba percoides   2/1040
Black-striped grunter
H: N Australia.
SD: None known.   S: –
B: Unsuccessful.   F: C
T: 22–28°C, L: 20 cm, pH: 7, D: 3

PERCHES

Bidyanus bidyanus   2/1040
Australian silver perch
H: Australia.
SD: None known.   S: –
B: Aquaculture: 500000 eggs.   F: C,O
T: 10–30°C, L: 50 cm, pH: 7, D: 4

Hephaestus carbo   2/1042
Coal grunter
H: N Australia.
SD: None known.   S: –
B: Unsuccessful.   F: C
T: 25–30°C, L: <33 cm, pH: 7, D: 3

Hephaestus fuliginosus   2/1042
Sooty grunter
H: Australia.
SD: None known.   S: –
B: Unsuccessful.   F: C
T: 25–30°C, L: 50 cm, pH: 7, D: 4

Leiopotherapon unicolor   2/1044
Jewel perch
H: N Australia.
SD: None known.   S: =
B: Nature: prolific egg scatterer.   F: H
T: 15–30°C, L: 15 cm, pH: 7, D: 2

Pingalla midgleyi   3/928
Black-blotch grunter
H: N Australia.
SD: None known.   S: =
B: Unsuccessful.   F: H,O
T: 23–35°C, L: 14.5 cm, pH: <7, D: 3

Scortum barcoo   2/1044
Barcoo grunter
H: Australia.
SD: None known.   S: –
B: Nature: egg scatterer.   F: C,O
T: 10–30°C, L: 30 cm, pH: 7, D: 2

Family Toxotidae

The family of archerfishes only consists of 1 genus and 6 species. They are inhabitants of littoral marine water, brackish water, and freshwater biotopes from India to the Philippines, Australia, and Polynesia.

The common name "archerfishes" is a result of their method of food acquisition: they spit a stream of water at insects sitting on plants above the water, thereby knocking them into the water where they are summarily consumed. These are surface-oriented fishes.

In nature, *Toxotes* species are encountered in groups, but they are preferably associated with heterogeners in the aquarium. As long as all are equal-sized, a group of conspecifics can be maintained.

The aquarium should have a large surface area and plants that thrive in brackish water. Warm temperatures are required.

Toxotes chatareus   1/812
Seven-spotted archerfish
H: Asia.   Bw
SD: None known.   S: =
B: Unknown.   F: C!
T: 25–30°C, L: 27 cm, pH: >7, D: 3–4

Toxotes jaculatrix   1/812
Archerfish
H: Asia.   Mw,Bw, Fw
SD: Unknown.   S: =
B: Unsuccessful.   F: C!
T: 25–30°C, L: 24 cm, pH: >7, D: 3–4

Toxotes lorentzi   2/1046
Primitive archerfish
H: Australia and New Guinea.   Fw
SD: None known.   S: =
B: Unknown.   F: C!
T: 24–32°C, L: <23 cm, pH: 7, D: 3–4

Toxotes oligolepis   2/1046
Few-scaled archerfish
H: Australia and New Guinea.   Fw
SD: Unknown.   S: =
B: Unknown.   F: C!
T: 24–30°C, L: 15 cm, pH: 7, D: 3–4

Tetraodon fangi; puffers (p. 919 ff.) look "cute," but are unsuitable for beginners.

Iriatherina werneri; rainbowfishes (p. 850 ff.) continue gaining in popularity.

Division Teleostei

Group 10 is a collective group for all true bony fish orders which could not be classified into one of the previous groups. Therefore, the orders contained herein are highly divergent, and some are poorly suited for the aquarium (e.g., salmonids and mullets).

True bony fishes probably originated during the Triassic Era—i.e., 200–220 million years ago in the Earth's Middle Ages. Today the Teleostei are the most specious group among the vertebrates. About 96% of all fishes are true bony fishes. According to NELSON (1994), there are 38 orders, 426 families, and more than 4000 genera and 23500 species of true bony fishes. Of the 38 orders, 26 contain approximately 10000 species which are in some way affiliated with freshwater.

To present related species together, we have alphabetized the families within their respective orders. This arrangement deviates somewhat from the format of the AQUARIUM ATLAS, but in view of the quantity of species presented in the INDEX, the result is a collection of coherent "mini-groups."

The orders of particular interest to the hobbyist have been addressed in greater detail.

Not all families within an order are presented: for the most part, only those families which contain freshwater or brackish water inhabitants are contained within the AQUARIUM ATLAS.

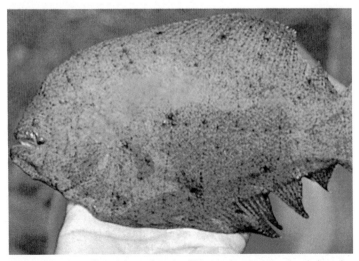

Trinectes fasciatus (?), a righteye flounder. This specimen was captured along the Ecuadorian edge of the Amazon Basin.

Systematic overview of the families in Group 10 (alphabetized by order).
Please note that all Perciformes—including those presented in Group 10 in the AQUARIUM ATLAS—have been placed in Group 9 of the INDEX.

BONY FISHES

ANGUILLIFORMES
Anguillidae[2-4]
Muraenidae[5]
Ophichthidae[6]

Freshwater Eels
Moray Eels
Snake Eels and Worm Eels

Order Anguilliformes

This order consists of 15 families, 141 genera, and 738 species (NELSON, 1994). It is often difficult to determine the identity of the larvae.

Eels undergo long-distance migrations to breed (e.g., *Anguilla anguilla* migrates from Europe to the Sargasso Sea). Eel blood contains a powerful neurotoxin. Nevertheless, eels are highly appreciated food fishes which are cultured commercially.

Anguilla anguilla 3/935
European eel
H: Europe.
♀: 60 cm longer. S: −
B: Nat.: long distance migrations. F: C,O
T: 4–20°C, L: ♀ 150 cm, pH: 7, D: 1–4

Anguilla japonica 4/744
Asian eel
H: W USA, Japan, China.
♀: 60 cm longer. S: −
B: At 7–10 years of age; in the sea. F: C,O
T: 4–27°C, L: ♀ 120 cm, pH: 7, D: 1–4

Anguilla rostrata 4/744
American eel
H: E Canada, E USA, Caribbean.
♀: 60 cm longer. S: −
B: Long distance migration; sea. F: C,O
T: 4–25°C, L: ♀ 120 cm, pH: 7, D: 1–4

Gymnothorax tile 5/1080
Freshwater moray eel 1% Bw
H: Philippines, Indonesia, Sum., Bor., Sing.
SD: None. S: =
B: Pelagic eggs? In the sea. F: C
T: 23–28°C, L: 60 cm, pH: >7, D: 4

Dalophis boulengeri 5/1081
Dolphin eel
H: NW Africa: Mauretania to the Congo.
SD: Unknown. S: =
B: Long distance migration; sea. F: C,O
T: 23–28°C, L: 60 cm, pH: >7, D: 4

BONY FISHES

Order Atheriniformes

This order consists of 3 suborders, 8 families, 47 genera, and in excess of 280 species. Two families consist solely of marine inhabitants and as such have not been included here.

As aquarists, we automatically think of the rainbowfishes and blue-eyes of Australia and Papua New Guinea in relation to this order. These families are strongly emphasized in the AQUARIUM ATLAS and therefore the INDEX. However, please note that the Atheriniformes include 2 families of purely marine species—Dentatherinidae and Notocheiridae—and subfamilies within the Atherinidae from America.

Geographic Distribution

Most Atheriniformes of aquaristic interest are inhabitants of Australia and Papua New Guinea.

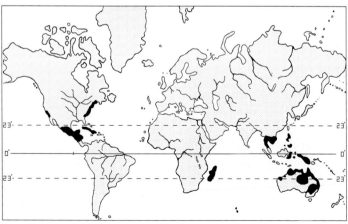

Area of distribution of the order Atheriniformes (freshwater).

Individual Families

What the characins (Group 2) are to South America, the rainbowfishes are to the Australian region. Their beautiful coloration, active and pacific lifestyle, and moderate size in conjunction with their frequently easy maintenance make them ideal candidates for community aquaria. With so many new, beautiful rainbowfishes appearing in pet stores, they are becoming more popular every day.

As omnivores with carnivorous tendencies, atherinids' nutritional requirements are easily met. Flake and freeze-dried foods are accepted. They scatter their eggs among plants or adhere them to the roots of floating plants. Dense vegetation, stones, and roots should be used to decorate the aquarium. Since the majority are schooling fishes, ample free swimming space is needed. In accordance to conditions in their natural habitat—that is, clear, moving, and oxygen-rich waters—an ample dimensioned filter is a prerequisite for the successful husbandry of most species. Sand is the best substrate.

Family Atherinidae
The family of silversides contains 4 subfamilies, about 25 genera, and a total of 165 species. These are mostly marine inhabitants, though approximately 50 species occur in freshwater. They are distributed through the southern Mexican Plateau, the eastern United States, Cuba (*Alepidomus evermanni*), Australia, and New Guinea (about 20 species in the genus *Craterocephalus*).

Although *Craterocephalus lacustris* (p. 852) is peaceful, it is extremely sensitive to stress; therefore, a species tank is recommended in this case.

Family Bedotiidae
This family consists of 2 genera and a total of 9 species. Their area of distribution is limited to Madagascar.

Family Melanotaeniidae
Melanotaeniidae are the rainbowfishes proper. The family consists of 6 genera and 53 species. They can be found on northern and eastern Australia and on New Guinea as well as some area islands. Males are usually deeper-bodied and more colorful, though some species need a year and longer to display their full coloration.

Most species prefer neutral to slightly alkaline and moderately hard water, but are not exacting in this regard.

Family Phallostethidae
There are 2 subfamilies, 4 genera, and a total of 19 species within this family. They inhabit the brackish waters and freshwaters of Southeast Asia. Characteristically, the males possess a priapium, an organ very similar to the andropodium of livebearers. Even though fertilization is internal, phallostethids are oviparous (egg-laying). They are asymmetrical: the priapium is either located to the left or right side of the body and the anal opening on the opposite side.

BONY FISHES

Family Pseudomugilidae

The family of blue-eyes consists of 3 genera and 15 species of fresh- and brackish waters as well as some marine species of the Indoaustralian region.

Family Telmatherinidae

Within the family there are 4 genera and 17 species which inhabit fresh- and brackish waters of Sulawesi and islands west of New Guinea. Sulawesi rainbowfishes are readily recognized by their extremely unorthodox finnage, a feature which greatly contributes to their popularity.

Craterocephalus eyresii   2/1054

H: S Australia and Northern Territoy.
SD: Unknown.   S: +
B: There are no reports.   F: C,O
T: 24–30°C, L: 10 cm, pH: 7, D: 2–3

Craterocephalus kailolae   5/998
Kailola hardyhead

H: E Papua New Guinea.
SD: Unknown.   S: +
B: Eggs scattered over plants?   F: C,O
T: 22–24°C, L: 7 cm, pH: 7, D: 4

Craterocephalus lacustris   5/998
Kutubu hardyhead

H: E Papua New Guinea: Lake Kutubu.
SD: None.   S: +(–,stress)
B: Unknown.   F: C,O
T: 22–24°C, L: <13 cm, pH: >7, D: 4

Craterocephalus marjoriae   2/1054
Marjorie's hardyhead, straw man

H: Australia: S Queensland: coastal rivers.
SD: Unknown.   S: +
B: There are no reports.   F: C,O
T: 24–30°C, L: 8 cm, pH: 7, D: 2

Craterocephalus nouhuysi   5/1000
Fly hardyhead

H: Australia.
SD: None.   S: +
B: Eggs scattered over plants?   F: C,O
T: 22–24°C, L: 12 cm, pH: >7, D: 3

Craterocephalus stercusmuscarum   2/1056
Fly-speckled hardyhead
H: Australia: Queensland.
SD: Unknown.   S: +
B: There are no reports.   F: O
T: 24–30°C, L: 10 cm, pH: <7, D: 2

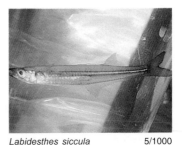

Labidesthes siccula   5/1000
Brook silverside
H: N America: USA, Canada.
♂: More colorful; blood-red mouth. S: =
B: Eggs scattered over plants?   F: C,O
T: 10–20°C, L: 13 cm, pH: 7, D: 3–4

Menidia menidia   5/1002
Moon silverside
H: E Coast of USA.   Bw
♀: Fuller during spawning season.   S: +
B: Tidal zone; on grass.   F: C,O
T: 8–24°C, L: 10 cm, pH: >7, D: 3–4

Quirichthys stramineus   2/1056
Straw man
H: Austl.: Queensland, Northern Territory.
SD: Unknown.   S: +
B: There are no reports.   F: C,O
T: 25–30°C, L: 7 cm, pH: 7, D: 2–3

Bedotia madagascariensis   1/822
Madagascar rainbow
H: Madagascar.
♂: More colorful; pointed D₁.   S: +
B: Eggs scattered among plants.   F: C,O
T: 20–24°C, L: 15 cm, pH: 7, D: 2

Rheocles sikurae   5/1002

H: Madagascar: Andasibe.
SD: Unknown.   S: =
B: Eggs scattered among plants?   F: C,O
T: 18–22°C, L: 8 cm, pH: 7, D: 3

BONY FISHES

Cairnsichthys rhombosomoides   2/1108
Cairns rainbowfish

H: Australia: N Queensland.
♂: Deep-bodied; yellow-edged fins. **S:** +
B: Eggs scattered among plants. **F:** C,O
T: 21–25°C, **L:** ♂ 8 cm, **pH:** >7, **D:** 3–4

Cairnsichthys rhombosomoides ♂   5/1063
Cairns rainbowfish

Chilatherina axelrodi ♂   3/1012
Axelrod's rainbowfish

H: Papua New Guinea: at Bewani.
♂: Higher back; pointed fins.   **S:** +
B: Eggs scattered among plants.   **F:** O
T: 27–30°C, **L:** ♂ 10 cm, **pH:** >7, **D:** 2

Chilatherina bleheri ♂   2/1108
Bleher's rainbowfish

H: New Guinea: Irian Jaya.
♂: Slimmer; more colorful.   **S:** +
B: Eggs scattered among plants. **F:** C,O
T: 23–27°C, **L:** 10 cm, **pH:** >7, **D:** 2

Chilatherina bulolo ♀   4/789
Bulolo rainbowfish

H: Papua New Guinea: Markham Basin.
♂: Deeper-bodied; more colorful. **S:** =
B: Eggs scattered among plants. **F:** O
T: 24–26°C, **L:** 8 cm, **pH:** 7, **D:** 2

Chilatherina campsi   2/1110
Highland rainbowfish

H: Papua New Guinea: central highlands.
♂: Slightly deeper-bodied; more color. **S:** +
B: N.: continuous spawner; plants. **F:** C,O
T: 21–26°C, **L:** ♂ 10 cm, **pH:** >7, **D:** 2–3

Chilatherina crassispinosa ♂   4/790
Silver rainbowfish

H: N New Guinea.
♂: Deeper-bodied; more colorful.   S: +
B: Spawns continuously on plants.   F: O
T: 25–30°C, L: ♂ 9 cm, pH: >7, D: 2

Chilatherina crassispinosa ♀   2/1110
Silver rainbowfish

Chilatherina fasciata ♂   2/1112
Barred rainbowfish

H: Papua New Guinea: Lake Wanam.
♂: More colorful; lighter.   S: +
B: Eggs scattered among plants.   F: C,O
T: 28–32°C, L: ♂ 11 cm, pH: >7, D: 2

Chilatherina lorentzi ♀   3/1012
Lorentz's rainbowfish

H: N Papua New Guinea.
♂: Deep-bodied; pointed D & A fins. S: +
B: Eggs scattered among plants.   F: O
T: 26–30°C, L: ♂ 12 cm, pH: >7, D: 2

Chilatherina sentaniensis   2/1112
Sentani rainbowfish

H: New Guinea: Lake Sentani?
♀: 1.5 cm smaller.   S: =
B: Unknown.   F: C,O
T: 24–28°C, L: ♂ 11.5 cm, pH: 7, D: 2–3

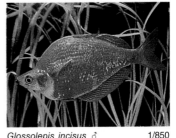

Glossolepis incisus ♂   1/850
Red rainbowfish

H: New Guinea: Lake Sentani.
♂: Deeper-bodied; more red.   S: +
B: Eggs scattered among plants.   F: C,O
T: 22–24°C, L: 15 cm, pH: >7, D: 2

Bony Fishes

Glossolepis maculosus 2/1114
Spotted rainbowfish
H: New Guinea: Omsis River.
♂: Slightly deeper-bodied; more color. S: +
B: Spawns continuously on plants. F: C,O
T: 23–27°C, L: 6 cm, pH: >7, D: 2

Glossolepis multisquamatus ♂ 2/1114
Sepik rainbowfish
H: New Guinea: lower Sepik River.
♂: Deeper-bodied; more colorful. S: +
B: Eggs scattered among plants. F: C,O
T: 26–30°C, L: ♂ 13 cm, pH: 7, D: 2

Glossolepis multisquamatus ♂ 4/790
Sepik rainbowfish

Glossolepis multisquamatus ♂ 4/790
Sepik rainbowfish

Glossolepis ramuensis ♂ 4/792
Ramu rainbowfish
H: Papua New Guinea: Ramu Basin.
♂: Deep-bodied; more colorful. S: +
B: Eggs scattered among plants. F: O
T: 24–27°C, L: 8 cm, pH: 7, D: 1

Glossolepis wanamensis ♂ 2/1116
Lake Wanam rainbowfish
H: Papua New Guinea: Lake Wanam. E
♂: Deep-bodied; D₁ & A fins larger. S: +
B: Eggs scattered among plants. F: C,O
T: 26–30°C, L: ♂ 10 cm, pH: >7, D: 2

Iriatherina werneri t.♂, b.♀　　　2/1116
Threadfin rainbowfish
H: S New Guinea, N Australia.
♂: Larger fins; more colorful.　　S: +
B: Eggs scattered on Java moss.　F: C,O
T: 24–28°C, L: ♂ 5 cm, pH: 7, D: 2–3

Melanotaenia affinis ♂　　　2/1118
North New Guinea rainbowfish
H: N New Guinea.
♂: Pointed D & A fins; more colorful. S: +
B: Egg scatterer.　　　　　　F: C,O
T: 20–30°C, L: 12 cm, pH: >7, D: 2

Melanotaenia angfa ♂　　　4/792
Yakati rainbowfish
H: New Guinea: Yakati River.
♂: Deep-bodied and more colorful? S: +
B: Eggs scattered among plants?　F: O?
T: 24–26°C, L: 13 cm, pH: 7, D: 3

Melanotaenia arfakensis　　　4/794
Arfak rainbowfish
H: New Guinea: Prafi Basin.
♂: Distinct lateral band; darker fins.　S: +
B: Slightly difficult; egg scatterer.　F: O
T: 24–28°C, L: 9 cm, pH: 7, D: 2–3

Melanotaenia boesemani ♂　　　2/1118
Boesemani rainbow
H: New Guinea: Ajamaru Lakes.
♂: Deep-bodied; colorful; orange.　S: +
B: Spawns continuously on plants. F: C,O
T: 27–30°C, L: ♂ 10 cm, pH: >7, D: 2

Melanotaenia boesemani ♂　　　2/1118
Boesemani rainbow
Fully colored.

Melanotaenia eachamensis ♂   2/1120
Lake Eacham rainbowfish

H: Australia: Lake Eacham.   E
♂: Deeper-bodied; more colorful.   S: +
B: Unknown.   F: C,O
T: 24–30°C, L: 8 cm, pH: >7, D: 2

Melanotaenia exquisita ♂   2/1120

H: Australia: Edith River, Lake Malkyllumbo.
♂: Deeper-bodied; more colorful.   S: +
B: Unknown.   F: C,O
T: 24–30°C, L: ♂ 7 cm, pH: 7, D: 2

Melanotaenia fluviatilis ♂   1/850
Australian rainbowfish

H: Austl.: New South Wales, Queensland.
♂: Red lines on caudal peduncle.   S: +
B: Eggs scattered among plants.   F: C,O
T: 22–25°C, L: 10 cm, pH: >7, D: 2

Melanotaenia fredericki   4/794
Sorong rainbowfish

H: New Guinea: Irian Jaya.
♂: More colorful; ♀♂ fins rounded! S: +
B: Eggs scattered among plants.   F: O
T: 24–28°C, L: 10 cm, pH: 7, D: 2–3

Melanotaenia goldiei t.♀, b.♂   2/1122
Goldie River rainbowfish

H: New Guinea & Aru Islands. Common
♂: Deep-bodied; more color; larger. S: +
B: Eggs scattered among plants.   F: C,O
T: 25–28°C, L: 12 cm, pH: >7, D: 2

Melanotaenia gracilis   2/1122
Slender rainbowfish

H: Australia: N Western Australia.
♂: Deep-bodied; larger.   S: +
B: Unknown.   F: C,O
T: 22–28°C, L: ♂ 7.5 cm, pH: >7, D: 2

Melanotaenia herbertaxelrodi ♂   2/1124
Lake Tebera rainbowfish
H: Papua New Guinea: Lake Tebera Basin.
♂: Deep-bodied; more colorful.   S: +
B: Eggs scattered among plants.   F: C,O
T: 20–26°C, L: 9 cm, pH: >7, D: 2

Melanotaenia irianjaya ♂   4/796
West New Guinea rainbowfish
H: New Guinea: Irian Jaya.
♂: Slightly more colorful.   S: +
B: Eggs scattered among plants.   F: O
T: 23–26°C, L: <10 cm, pH: <7, D: 2

Melanotaenia irianjaya ♀   4/796
West New Guinea rainbowfish

Melanotaenia lacustris   3/1015
Lake Kutubu rainbowfish
H: S New Guinea: Lake Kutubu.   E
♂: Darker and longer fins; more color. S: +
B: Eggs scattered among plants.   F: O
T: 20–24°C, L: 12 cm, pH: >7, D: 2–3

Melanotaenia macullochi   1/852
Dwarf or black-lined rainbowfish
H: NE Australia, south to Sydney.
♂: More pointed fins; more colorful.   S: +
B: Eggs scattered among plants.   F: C,O
T: 20–25°C, L: 7 cm, pH: >7, D: 1

Melanotaenia macullochi ♂   3/1016
McCulloch's rainbowfish, dwarf rainbowfish
H: S Papua New Guinea strain.
♂: More colorful; slimmer.   S: +
B: Eggs scattered among plants.   F: O
T: 24–30°C, L: <7 cm, pH: 7, D: 1

BONY FISHES

Melanotaenia maccullochi ♂   3/1016
McCulloch's rainbowfish, dwarf
rainbowfish
H: Australia: Harvey Creek.

Melanotaenia monticola b.♀,t.♂   3/1018
Mountain rainbowfish
H: Papua New Guinea: at Mendi.
♂: Deep-bodied, more pointed fins.   S: +
B: Eggs scattered among plants.   F: O
T: 18–22°C, L: 9 cm, pH: 7, D: 3

Melanotaenia nigrans ♂   2/1124
Dark Australian rainbowfish
H: SW Papua New Guinea.
♂: Black-fringed A and D_2 fins.   S: +
B: Eggs scattered among plants.   F: C,O
T: 18–24°C, L: ♂ 7 cm, pH: >7, D: 1

Melanotaenia oktediensis ♂   4/798
Oktedi rainbowfish
H: S Papua New Guinea: Ok Tedi River.
♂: Longer D_2 and A fins.   S: +
B: Eggs scattered among plants.   F: O
T: 23–26°C, L: 11 cm, pH: 7, D: 2–3

Melanotaenia papuae ♂   2/1126
Papuan rainbowfish (var?)
H: New Guinea: at Port Moresby.
♂: Larger; more colorful.   S: +
B: Eggs scattered among plants.   F: C,O
T: 22–32°C, L: ♂ 6.5 cm, pH: >7, D: 2

Melanotaenia papuae ♂   4/798
Papuan rainbowfish
H: New Guinea: at Port Moresby.
♂: Slightly larger; more colorful.   S: +
B: Eggs scattered among plants.   F: O
T: 24–30°C, L: ♂ 7.5 cm, pH: >7, D: 1–2

Melanotaenia parkinsoni ♂   2/1126
Parkinson's rainbowfish
H: New Guinea: Kamp Welsh River.
♂: Deep-bodied; more colorful.   S: +
B: Eggs scattered among plants.   F: C,O
T: 26–30°C, L: ♂ 12 cm, pH: >7, D: 2–3

Melanotaenia praecox ♂   4/796
Neon rainbowfish
H: New Guinea: Irian Jaya.
♂: Deep-bodied; more color; larger. S: +
B: Eggs scattered among plants.   F: C,O
T: 22–28°C, L: 6 cm, pH: <7, D: 2–3

Melanotaenia sexlineata ♂   4/800
Fly River rainbowfish
H: Papua New Guinea: upper Fly River.
♂: Deep-bodied; yellow.   S: +
B: Eggs scattered among plants.   F: O
T: 24–26°C, L: 7 cm, pH: >7, D: 2

Melanotaenia splendida australis ♂
Western splendid rainbowfish   2/1128
H: W Australia.
♂: More colorful; longer fins.   S: +
B: Eggs scattered among plants.   F: C,O
T: 22–28°C, L: ♂ 10 cm, pH: 7, D: 2

Melanotaenia splendida australis ♀
Western splendid rainbowfish   4/800

Melanotaenia splendida inornata t. ♀
2/1131

861

Melanotaenia splendida rubrostriata ♂
Red-striped splendid rainbowfish 2/1128
H: New Guinea: central Irian Jaya.
♂: Deep-bodied; colorful; larger.   S: +
B: Eggs scattered among plants. F: C,O
T: 24–28°C, L: ♂ 13 cm, pH: >7, D: 2–3

Melanotaenia splendida splendida ♂
Cape York rainbowfish   1/852
H: Australia: Cape York Peninsula.
♂: Deeper-bodied; more colorful.   S: +
B: Eggs scattered among plants.   F: C
T: 20–25°C, L: 15 cm, pH: 7, D: 2

Melanotaenia splendida tatei ♂   3/1018

H: Central Australia.
♂: Deep-bodied; pointed A & D_2 fins. S: +
B: Eggs scattered among plants.   F: O
T: 20–30°C, L: <10 cm, pH: 7, D: 2

Melanotaenia trifasciata ♂   2/1132
Banded rainbowfish
H: Austl.: Northern Territory, Cape York.
♂: More colorful; pointed A & D_2 fins. S: +
B: Eggs scattered among plants.   F: C,O
T: 25–30°C, L: 12 cm, pH: 7, D: 2

Melanotaenia trifasciata ♂   2/1132
Banded rainbowfish
H: Australia: Giddy River, Arnhemland.

Melanotaenia trifasciata ♂   2/1132
Banded rainbowfish
H: NE Australia: Coen, Cape York Pen.

ATHERINIFORMES
Melanotaeniidae I–3
Phallostethidae[4]
Pseudomugilidae[5–6]

Rainbowfishes

Blue-Eyes

Melanotaenia trifasciata ♂   2/1132
Banded rainbowfish

Rhadinocentrus ornatus ♂   2/1140
Southern soft-spined rainbowfish
H: Austl.: N New South Wales, S Queensl.
♂: Pointed D_2; more color; 3 cm larger. S: +
B: Easy; continuous spawner.   F: C,O
T: 20–30°C, L: ♂ 7 cm, pH: <7, D: 2

Rhadinocentrus ornatus ♂   2/1140
Southern soft-spined rainbowfish
Blue strain.

Gulaphallus mirabilis ♂   5/1082
Phallus miraclefish
H: Philippines.   1%–2% Bw
♂: Priapium (copulatory organ).   S: +
B: Internal fertilization; egg layer. F: C
T: 23–28°C, L: 3.3 cm, pH: >7, D: 4

Kiunga ballochi   3/1026
Kiunga blue-eye
H: Papua New Guinea: upper Fly River.
SD: Unknown.   S: +
B: Unknown.   F: O
T: 24–26°C, L: 3 cm, pH: >7, D: 3

Pseudomugil connieae ♂   2/1134
Popondetta rainbowfish
H: Papua New Guinea: at Popondetta.
♂: D_1 fin taller; more colorful.   S: =
B: Eggs scattered among plants. F: C,O
T: 25–28°C, L: ♂ 5.5 cm, pH: >7, D: 2

Pseudomugil furcatus t.♀, b.♂   2/1134
Forktail blue-eye
H: E New Guinea.
♂: Long D₁ fin; more colorful.   S: +
B: Eggs scattered among plants.   F: C,O
T: 24–26°C, L: ♂ 5.5 cm, pH: >7, D: 2

Pseudomugil gertrudae ♂   2/1136
Gertrud's blue-eye, spotted blue-eye
H: Australia, New Guinea, Aru Islands.
♂: More colorful; longer fins.   S: +
B: Continuous spawner: 4 ws.   F: C,O
T: 25–30°C, L: 3 cm, pH: <7, D: 2

Pseudomugil mellis ♂ ♂   2/1136
Honey blue-eye
H: Australia: Queensland.
♂: More colorful; longer fins.   S: +
B: Spawns continuously on plants. F: C,O
T: 24–28°C, L: 3 cm, pH: <7, D: 2

Pseudomugil novaeguineae   4/820
New Guinea blue-eye
H: New Guinea.
♂: More colorful; more pointed fins. S: +
B: Eggs scattered among plants. F: C,O
T: 26–30°C, L: 3.5 cm, pH: 7, D: 2–3

Pseudomugil paludicola   3/1026
Swamp blue-eye
H: W Papua New Guinea.
SD: Unknown.   S: –
B: Eggs scattered among plants? F: O
T: 26–30°C, L: 3.0–3.5 cm, pH: >7, D: 3

Pseudomugil paskai ♂   4/820
Paska's blue-eye
H: Papua New Guinea: near Kiunga.
♂: Elongated fins; more colorful. S: +
B: Eggs scattered among plants. F: C,O
T: 22–26°C, L: 3 cm, pH: 7, D: 3–4

Pseudomugil signifer ♂ 1/822
Australian blue-eye, southern blue-eye
H: Australia: N and E Queensland.
♂: Larger; more colorful. S: +
B: Eggs scattered among plants. F: C,O
T: 23–28°C, L: 4.5 cm, pH: 7, D: 2

Pseudomugil signifer Cairns form 2/1138
Southern blue-eye, Pacific blue-eye
H: Australia: N and E Queensland.
♂: More colorful; longer fins S: +
B: Spawns continuously on plants. F: C,O
T: 23–28°C, L: 4 cm, pH: <7, D: 2

Pseudomugil tenellus 2/1138
Delicate blue-eye
H: Australia: E Alligator River system.
♂: Colors slightly more intense. S: +
B: Spawns continuously on plants. F: C,O
T: 28–35°C, L: 4 cm, pH: <7, D: 2

Telmatherina celebensis 3/938
Towoeti rainbowfish
H: Indonesia: Sulawesi: Lake Towoeti.
♂: Slightly elongated fins. S: +
B: Eggs scattered among plants. F: O
T: 24–26°C, L: 8 cm, pH: 7, D: 3–4

Telmatherina ladigesi t.♂, b.♀ 1/824
Celebes rainbowfish
H: Indonesia: Sulawesi.
♂: Elongated fins; more colorful. S: +
B: Eggs scattered among plants. F: C,O
T: 22–28°C, L: 7.5 cm, pH: 7, D: 2–3

Tominanga sanguicauda 5/1100
Blood-tail rainbowfish
H: Indonesia: Sulawesi.
♂: Elongated fins; more colorful. S: =
B: Not described. F: C,O
T: 20–26°C, L: 6 cm, pH: 7, D: 3

Order Batrachoidiformes

The order of toadfishes is comprised of just one family, 3 subfamilies, 19 genera, and a total of 69 species. They are largely bottom-oriented fishes of littoral marine biotopes, but some species are inhabitants of brackish waters and a few of freshwater.

Some toadfishes (like the species presented) can emit quaking sounds. The spines of the anterior dorsal fin (D_1) and the operculum are sometimes toxic. Unless one is allergic to the poison, however, the effect is not more serious than a wasp sting. Many species are very hardy, surviving in waters that have very little dissolved oxygen or even out of the water for periods of up to several hours.

These lethargic, benthic predators "inhale" their prey with strong suction. The aquarium must have hiding places and a salinity of 2.5%–3.0%. Long-term maintenance in freshwater is not possible.

Batrachomoeus trispinosus 3/939
Toadfish Mw,Bw
H: Indian Ocean and estuaries.
SD: Unknown. S: –
B: Unknown. F: C
T: 23–28°C, L: 20 cm, pH: >7, D: 4

BELONIFORMES

Order Beloniformes

This order is comprised of 5 families, 38 genera, and 191 species. About 51 species live in freshwater and slightly brackish water. They were previously classified into the Cyprinodontiformes (NELSON, 1994).

Since they consist solely of marine members, Scomberesocidae and Exocoetidae—the sauries and flying fishes, respectively—are not presented in the INDEX.

The following families are of interest to the freshwater aquarist:

Family Adrianichthyidae
Adrianichthyidae—also called ricefishes or Asian lampeyes—colonize freshwater and brackish water biotopes from India to Japan and the Indo-Australian Archipelago. The family is comprised of 3 subfamilies, 4 genera, and 18 species.

In keeping with the tendency towards brackish water habitats, several species benefit from salt in the water. There are also species which are very sensitive to dissolved nitrogenous wastes and therefore require an effective filtration system. Dense vegetation around the fringes of the aquarium will provide adequate shelter for animals dominated during the occasional intraspecific aggressions.

Being relatively colorless, this family has found little dissemination in the aquarium hobby. Their reproductive biology is unusual: the fertilized eggs are initially carried by the female on her ventrum until they are scattered among plants or even until the young hatch.

Family Belonidae
Among the 32 species within 10 genera, there are about 11 species of needlefishes, which are confined to freshwaters of South America, India, and Southeast Asia.

With little provocation, these skittish fishes crash into the aquarium's infrastructure or glass, injuring themselves. They are proficient jumpers. Little is known about their maintenance needs.

Family Hemiramphidae
There are 12 genera and 85 species contained within this family. Of these, 24 species are found in freshwaters of the Indo-Australian region and South America. Four genera of halfbeaks—i.e., *Dermogenys, Hemiramphus, Nomorhamphus,* and *Zenarchopterus*—have an andropodium, a modified anal fin analogous to the gonopodium of the livebearing toothcarps (Group 6). Fertilization is internal. The first three genera are livebearers, whereas the fourth lays fertilized eggs (oviparous).

Oryzias celebensis ♀ ♀   1/572
Celebes medaka
H: E Asia: Indonesia, S Celebes.
♂: Ragged A fin; longer D fin.   S: =
B: E. cluster placed among plants. F:C,O
T: 22–30°C, L: 5 cm, pH: >7, D: 3

Oryzias latipes ♂   2/1148
Japanese ricefish, medaka
H: E Asia: Japan, China, South Korea.
♂: More colorful; larger fins.   S: +
B: E. cluster placed among plants. F:O,C
T: 18–24°C, L: 3.5 cm, pH: 7, D: 2

Oryzias latipes ♀   2/1148
Japanese ricefish, medaka
With egg cluster.

BONY FISHES

Oryzias latipes iliensis ♂   5/462
Caspian medaka
H: Asia: affluents of the Caspian Sea.
♂: Longer anal fin. ♀: Egg cluster.   S: +
B: Egg cluster laid into plant thicket. F: C
T: 12–24°C, L: 4 cm, pH: 7, D: 2

Oryzias melastigmus ♂   1/572
Java medaka
H: S Asia: Sri Lanka, India, Java.
♂: Frayed anal fin; longer dorsal fin. S: +
B: Egg cluster laid into plant thicket. F: C
T: 22–26°C, L: 5 cm, pH: 7, D: 2–3

Oryzias minutillus ♂   3/579
Minute ricefish
H: SE Asia: SE Thailand to Malaysia.
♂: Somewhat larger and slimmer.   S: +
B: Egg cluster laid into plant thicket. F: C
T: 22–26°C, L: 2 cm, pH: 7, D: 4

Oryzias nigrimas ♂   5/462
Black-coat ricefish
H: Indonesia: Sulawesi: Lake Poso.
♂: Darker; elongated fins.   S: (–)
B: Egg cluster laid into plant thicket. F: C
T: 20–26°C, L: 6 cm, pH: >7, D: 2–3

Oryzias sp. "Bentota" ♂ *O. melastigmus*?
Bentota ricefish   5/464
H: Sri Lanka: at Beruwala.
♂: More colorful, larger fins; smaller. S: +
B: Egg cluster laid into plant thicket. F: C
T: 18–25°C, L: 4 cm, pH: ≫7, D: 4

Xenopoecilus sarasinorum   5/464
Sarasin's ricefish
H: Sulawesi: Lake Lindu.   E
♂: Longer fins; slightly larger.   S: +
B: Eggs in cluster until hatching.   F: C
T: 24–30°C, L: 8 cm, pH: >7, D: 2

Xenopoecilus oophorus ♂   5/466   *Xenopoecilus oophorus* ♀   5/466

H: Sulawesi: Lake Poso.   E
♂: Shorter ventral fins.   S: +
B: Eggs in cluster until hatching.   F: C
T: 23–28°C, L: 6.5 cm, pH: >7, D: 3

This is a needlefish from the Rio Suno, a clear-water river with a rock/sand bottom which flows into the Rio Napo west of Coca (eastern Ecuador, South America). It was seen coincidentally at night as it swam along the surface of shallow water over an open sand substrate a few meters from shore. It was captured using a hand net. Unfortunately, it did not survive the trip back to the ranch.

Potamorrhapis guianensis   3/940
Freshwater needlefish
H: S Am.: Amazonia, Guianas, Paraguay.
SD: Unknown.   S: =
B: Unsuccessful.   F: C
T: 23–26°C, L: <40 cm, pH: 7, D: 3–4

Xenentodon cancila   1/826
Silver needlefish
H: Asia: India, Sri Lanka, Thai., Burma,...
♂: Black-fringed D and A fins.   S: =
B: On plant leaves; <15 eggs daily.   F: C
T: 22–28°C, L: 32 cm, pH: 7, D: 4

BONY FISHES

Xenentodon cancila　　　　　　1/826
Silver needlefish

Dermogenys ebrardtii　　　　　　3/1002
Ebrardt's halfbeak
H: SE Asia: Celebes.
♂: Anal fin as andropodium.　　　　S: =
B: 28–42 dg; 20 young, 20 mm.　　F: C
T: 24–26°C, L: 9 cm, pH: 7, D: 3

Dermogenys pusilla ♂　　　　　　1/841
Malayan halfbeak
H: SE Asia: Thai., Sing., Indo., Malay Pen.
♂: Anal fin as andropodium.　　　　S: =
B: Not easy; 20–60 dg; 10–30 y.　　F: C
T: 18–30°C, L: 7 cm, pH: 7, D: 3

Dermogenys pusilla sumatrana t.♂, b.♀
Sumatra halfbeak　　　　　　　　2/1102
H: SE Asia: Indonesia, Singapore.
♂: A fin as andropodium; smaller.　S: =
B: Not easy; 42–56 dg; <30 young. F: C
T: 26–30°C, L: ♂ 5 cm, pH: 7, D: 3

Dermogenys viviparus ♂　　　　　4/782
Luzon halfbeak
H: Philippines: Luzon.
♂: A fin as andropod.; 2 cm smaller. S: +
B: 42 days of gestation; 25 y.　　F: C,O
T: 23–28°C, L: ♀ 8.5 cm, pH: 7, D: 3

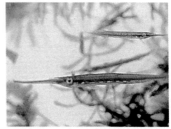

Hemirhamphodon chrysopunctatus
Gold-spot halfbeak　　　　　　　3/1002
H: SE Asia: S Borneo: near Benjarmasin.
♂: Anal fin as andropodium.　　　　S: –
B: Unknown.　　　　　　　　　　F: C
T: 24–28°C, L: 8.5 cm, pH: <7, D: 4

Hemirhamphodon pogonognathus 2/1102
Long-snout halfbeak
H: SE Asia: Thai., Sing., Indo., Malay Pen.
♂: Andropodium. **S: =**
B: Within 21 d; 30–40 y, 12 mm. **F: C,O**
T: 22–28°C, L: ♂ 9 cm, pH: >7, D: 3

Hemirhamphodon (?) sp. 5/1052
Egg-laying halfbeak (!)
H: SE Asia: Indonesia.
♀: Broad anal fin; roundish. **S: +**
B: Spawns continuously on plants. **F: C**
T: 22–26°C, L: 6 cm, pH: <7, D: 2

Nomorhamphus liemi liemi l. ♀, r. ♂ 1/842
Celebes halfbeak
H: Indonesia: S Sulawesi: Maros Highland.
♂: Andropodium; 3 cm smaller. **S: +**
B: 42–56 dg; <11 y, 18 mm. **F: C**
T: 24–26°C, L: ♀ 9 cm, pH: 7, D: 3

Nomorhamphus liemi snijdersi 1/842

H: Indonesia: Sulawesi: east of Maros.
♂: Andropodium. **S: +**
B: 42–56 dg; <11 y, 18 mm. **F: C**
T: 23–26°C, L: ♀ 9 cm, pH: 7, D: 3

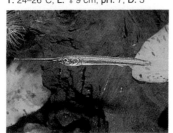

Zenarchopterus dispar ♀ 4/782
Spoon-fin garfish
H: SE Asia: widely distributed.
♂: Modified anal fin. **S: –**
B: Facultatively livebearing? **F: C**
T: 24–28°C, L: 15 cm, pH: >7, D: 3–4

Zenarchopterus kampeni ♀ 5/1053
New Guinea garfish
H: New Guinea: lower Sepik, Ramu,....
♂: Modified anal fin. **S: =**
B: Internal fertilization? Oviparous. **F: C**
T: 24–28°C, L: 18 cm, pH: 7, D: 3–4

BONY FISHES

Order Clupeiformes

Herrings are largely marine inhabitants, familiar to most as the main course on the dinner table. The entire order consists of 5 families, 83 genera, and almost 360 species. Of these, 80 species require freshwater at least part of their life (NELSON, 1994).

Ample free swimming space is a prerequisite for successful care. Some species such as *Denticeps clupoides* drown when not allowed to actively swim. Since a school should always be kept, the aquarium must be large. *Nematolosa erebi* is very intolerant of stress.

Nematolosa erebi   2/1062
Bony bream
H: Australia, New Guinea.
♂: Red snout while spawning.   S: =
B: Unknown.   F: O
T: 15–25°C, L: 47 cm, pH: 7, D: 4

Denticeps clupeoides ♀   5/1006
Denticle herring
H: Africa: SW Nigeria, SE Benin, SW Cam.
♂: More colorful fins.   S: +
B: Unknown; prone to diseases.   F: C
T: 20–25°C, L: 5 cm, pH: <7, D: 3–4

ELOPIFORMES
Megalopidae

Tarpons

Order Elopiformes

With only 2 families, 2 genera, and 8 species, Elopiformes is a relatively small order.

Most species are large marine fishes. For the home aquarium, only juveniles are suitable. The presented species should be maintained at least in brackish water. Although it can be associated with other brackish water species (e.g., *Monodactylus* spp.), appropriate care of this schooling fish demands a huge species aquarium.

Megalops cyprinoides   2/1107
Indo-Pacific tarpon
H: Indo-Pacific region: <100 km upriver.
SD: Unknown.   S: –
B: Nature: spring/summer.   F: C
T: 22–24°C, L: 150 cm, pH: >7, D: 3–4

Order Esociformes

The order of pikes and mudminnows consists of just 2 families, 4 genera, and 10 species. All are found in the Northern Hemisphere. While they are coldwater fishes, *Dallia pectoralis* (p. 874) is an extreme case: it survives until its visceral fluids become frozen.

Family Esocidae

The pike family contains one genus and 5 species. Among pikes, *Esox lucius* is the most frequently cultured. In North America it is almost exclusively bred to be released as a game fish, while in Europe it is used in carp aquaculture to control unwanted reproduction and to keep the carp actively moving in the pond. Pikes are ambush predators.

In aquaria, they must be maintained individually, lest they prey on each other. No particular demands are placed on water values. Shelters from which they can ambush passing prey are a necessity.

Family Umbridae

The family of mudminnows consists of 3 genera and 5 species. The genus *Dallia* deviates somewhat from the rest, but the tendency in recent years has been to include it in the family Umbridae (NELSON, 1994).

Umbridae bury themselves in the muddy bottoms of their natural habitat, hence the name "mudminnows." Virtually all their oxygen requirement is fulfilled through the accessory breathing organ associated with their swimbladder which allows them to breathe atmospheric air. If precluded from reaching the water surface, they will drown, regardless of the oxygen concentration of the water.

The aquarium should have dense vegetation around the fringes, an open swimming area, and a substrate of fine sand. Maintenance requirements of *Dallia pectoralis* are unknown, but a chiller is probably needed.

Esox lucius   3/965
Northern pike
H: Europe and Siberia, North America.
♂: 60 cm smaller.   S: –
B: Feb. to May on aquatic plants.   F: C
T: 10–22°C, L: ♀150 cm, pH: 7, D: 1

Esox niger   3/966
Chain pickerel
H: North America: S Canada, USA.
♂: Slightly smaller.   S: –
B: Unsuccessful.   F: C
T: 10–20°C, L: 80 cm, pH: 7, D: 1–2

Dallia pectoralis   3/1044
Alaska blackfish
H: Arctic and subarctic biotopes.
♂: Pale red fins at spawning time.   S: +,–
B: Nat.: May–August; 40–300 e.   F: C
T: 4–14°C, L: <33 cm, pH: 7, D: 4

Novumbra hubbsi ♂   4/830
Olympic mudminnow
H: N America: USA: Olympic Peninsula.
♂: Darker.   S: =
B: Nat.: in the spring on plants.   F: C,O
T: 4–25°C, L: 8 cm, pH: 7, D: 2

Novumbra hubbsi ♀   4/830
Olympic mudminnow

Umbra krameri   3/1044
Eurasian mudminnow
H: Europe: lower Danube.   Endangered
♂: Smaller; paler at spawning time.   S: =
B: Pit; 200–300 e; maternal family.   F: C
T: 10–23°C, L: 11.5 cm, pH: <7, D: 1–2

Umbra limi   1/870
Central mudminnow
H: North America: Canada, USA.
♂: Smaller; yellow/red at spawning.   S: =
B: Pit; 200–300 e; maternal family.   F: C
T: 17–22°C, L: ♀ 15 cm, pH: <7, D: 2

Umbra pygmaea   1/870
Eastern mudminnow
H: North America: USA: Long Island.
♂: Smaller.   S: +
B: Pit; 200–300 e; maternal family.   F: C
T: 17–23°C, L: ♀ 15 cm, pH: <7, D: 2

Order Gadiformes

The order of codfishes is comprised of 12 families, 85 genera, and approximately 482 species. Codfishes are cosmopolitan and constitute over 25% of the world's marine fisheries catch. The systematics within the order are still under review; for example, the subfamily Lotinae is often considered to be the family Lotidae (NELSON, 1994). Only a handful of species are found in brackish water, and only one lives in freshwater. Some marine species have populations that inhabit freshwater.

From the point of view of water composition, only *Lota lota* is suitable for a freshwater aquarium. Because of its predatory lifestyle and large adult size, however, only a single juvenile can be kept in a species aquarium. A chiller may be required to lower the temperature during the summer (coldwater fish). These burdensome aspects combined with the fact that it is nocturnal and has little to recommend itself in the way of coloration translate into its rare presence in the aquarium hobby. Aquarium breeding has not been successful.

Gaidropsaurus mustellaris is a marine species which can be maintained in a brackish water aquarium. Although juveniles tolerate freshwater, the aquarium should be planned for brackish water from the start. It is peaceful towards conspecifics, but heterospecific tankmates are limited to brackish water fishes of larger size. Like the previously described species, *G. mustellaris* is not very attractive and a chiller may be required during the summer months.

Neither species is recommended for the aquarium.

Lota lota 3/967
Burbot
H: Europe: N of the Balkans and Pyrenees.
SD: Unknown. S: =
B: Nov.–Mar.; eggs with oil sphere. F: C!
T: 4–18°C, L: 60 cm, pH: >7, D: 3

Gaidropsarus mustellaris 4/768
Five-bearded rockling Rare
H: Baltic & Atlantic affluents. Mw,1%Bw
SD: Unknown. S: =
B: Planktonic larvae in estuaries. F: C!
T: 5–18°C, L: 50 cm, pH: >7, D: 4

BONY FISHES

875

Order Gasterosteiformes

This order has a worldwide tropical and subtropical distribution. Most species are marine inhabitants. The systematic classification of the order is somewhat controversial. Like most of the INDEX, here, too, we follow NELSON (1994). Accordingly, the order is made up of two suborders—the sticklebacks (Gasterosteoidei) and the pipefishes and seahorses (Syngnathoidei)—with a total of 11 families, 71 genera, and 257 species. Of these, there are approximately 19 freshwater species and 40 brackish water species.

Suborder Gasterosteoidei

The freshwater and brackish water species are contained within the family Gasterosteidae. The kidneys of sticklebacks secrete a sticky fluid which is used by the males to construct a nest from pieces of plants. They are cold-water species which must be overwintered at cool temperatures (5°–8°C) to stimulate them to spawn the following spring.

Suborder Syngnathoidei

The majority of freshwater and brackish water species are contained within the families Indostomidae and Syngnathidae (pipefishes and seahorses). Their tubular mouth has a small opening.

The family Indostomidae is monotypic; i.e., it only contains one species, *Indostomus paradoxus* (p. 878). This diminutive fish should be maintained in a species tank, although small, peaceful community fishes such as rasboras are suitable tankmates. It has the unusual ability to move its head up and down.

One genus within the family Syngnathidae (subfamily Hippocampinae) is very familiar to us all: *Hippocampus*—the seahorses. All 25 species, unfortunately, are exclusively found in marine biotopes.

Of the 51 genera and 190 species of pipefishes (Syngnathinae), there are a few species that live in freshwater and brackish water biotopes which are suitable for freshwater or brackish water aquaria.

Like seahorses, male pipefishes have a broodpouch, where they brood the eggs. Some species have been successfully reproduced in the aquarium. Feeding the breeders is laborious: normally only small live foods are accepted.

Apeltes quadracus   3/968
Fourspine stickleback
H: N America: Labrador to Virginia.
♂: More colorful at spawning time. **S:** =
B: 1% salt; nest; paternal family.   **F:** C!
T: 4–20°C, **L:** 6 cm, **pH:** 7, **D:** 2

Culaea inconstans inconstans 3/968
Brook stickleback
H: N America: S Canada, NE USA.
♂: Black during spawning season. S: =
B: Nest; polygamous; paternal fam. F: C!
T: 4–18°C, L: 7 cm, pH: 7, D: 3

Culaea inconstans pygmaeus ♂ 3/968
Brook stickleback

Culaea inconstans pygmaeus 3/968
Brook stickleback

Culaea inconstans pygmaeus 3/968
Brook stickleback
Nest.

Gasterosteus aculeatus ♂ w/ eggs 1/834
Threespine stickleback
H: All of Europe except Danube region.
♂: Livelier; courtship coloration. S: =
B: Nest; <50 e; polygamous; P fam. F: C!
T: 4–22°C, L: 12 cm, pH: <7, D: 2

Pungitius platygaster aralensis 4/770
Aral stickleback
H: Asia: coasts of Aral Sea, Lake Teniz,...
♂: Courtship coloration. S: =
B: Nat.: nest; polygamous; P fam. F: C
T: 4–20°C, L: 5.3 cm, pH: 7, D: 2

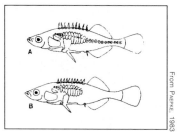

From Paepke, 1983

Pungitius platygaster platygaster (A)
Pungitius platygaster aralensis (B) 4/770

Pungitius pungitius   1/834
Ten-spined stickleback
H: Eu.: except Danube & Mediterranean.
♂: More colorful at spawning time. S: =
B: Nest; <50 e; polygamous; P fam. F: C!
T: 10–20°C, L: 7 cm, pH: <7, D: 2

Indostomus paradoxus ♂   3/1004
Paradox fish
H: SE Asia: N Burma, Thai., Camb., Malay.
♂: Slimmer; D fin is broader black. S: +
B: 20 eggs on rock; paternal fam.   F: C
T: 24–28°C, L: 3 cm, pH: <7, D: 2–3

Indostomus paradoxus ♀   3/1004
Paradox fish

Doryichthys deokhatoides ♂   3/1038

H: SE Asia: Malaysia, Indonesia.
♂: 2 ventral ridges.   S: +
B: Unsuccessful; paternal family.   F: C!
T: 24–28°C, L: 13 cm, pH: 7, D: 4

Enneacampus ansorgii   1/864
African freshwater pipefish
H: W Africa: Cameroon to Gabon.
♂: Ventral groove.   S: +
B: In brooding pouch; paternal fam. F: C!
T: 24–28°C, L: 15 cm, pH: 7, D: 4

Hippichthys spicifer   4/828
Black-barred freshwater pipefish
H: Red Sea to Indonesia.
♂: Brooding pouch.   S: =
B: 10 g/l salt; ♂ broods in pouch.   F: C!
T: 23–28°C, L: 18 cm, pH: >7, D: 4

Syngnathus lineatus   3/1039

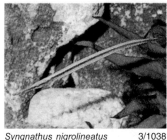

Syngnathus nigrolineatus   3/1038
Black-line pipefish
H: Europe, Asia: Sea of Azov and Black Sea.
♂: Ventral groove; smaller.   S: +
B: Unsuccessful; paternal family.   F: C!
T: 22–24°C, L: 21.5 cm, pH: >7, D: 4

Microphis brachyurus aculeatus   1/865
Red-line pipefish
H: Africa: coastal waters Senegal–Angola.
♂: Ventral pouch.   S: (–)
B: 10 g/l salt; ♂ broods in pouch.   F: C!
T: 22–26°C, L: 20 cm, pH: >7, D: 4

BONY FISHES

879

Order Gonorhynchiformes

This order is comprised of 4 suborders, 4 families, 7 genera, and approximately 35 species—28 of which are freshwater inhabitants (NELSON, 1994).

Because it is exclusively marine, the family Gonorhynchidae is not presented in the INDEX.

As a monotypic family, the Chanidae solely contains the algivorous species *Chanos chanos*. It is an economically important food fish of Southeast Asia, where it is cultured in saltwater ponds. The young metamorphose in brackish water. Juveniles are then captured from the wild and transferred to ponds for growout. It is not bred in captivity, and it is not a suitable aquarium fish. An algae-based diet called lab-lab is fed.

The family Kneriidae contains 27 species, all inhabitants of freshwaters of tropical Africa and the Nile. Several species of the genera *Kneria* and *Parakneria* are presented in the INDEX. The presence (*Kneria*) or absence (*Parakneria*) of an occipital organ in males is the main distinguishing characteristic between the two genera. The function of this organ is not fully understood. In an aquarium, a male *Kneria* has been observed joining with a female, but no gametes were released. In all probability, some of the *Kneria* species should actually be classified in the genus *Parakneria* (SEEGERS, DATZ 9/96). Another feature which can be used to differenciate these two genera is the position of the dorsal fin in relation to the ventral fins: the anterior edge of the dorsal fin is always even with or posterior to the base of the ventral fins of *Kneria* spp., whereas in *Parakneria* spp. the anterior edge of the dorsal fin clearly precedes the base of the ventral fins (SEEGERS, DATZ 11/96).

These species are found in clear, oxygen-rich, flowing waters. Like most fishes from such biotopes, they demand a powerful filter, a current, and rather cool temperatures. Strong illumination to foment algae growth is recommended. The algae are grazed from all smooth surfaces. They are bottom-oriented, peaceful fishes which can be associated with like-natured species with similar demands. Reproduction ranges from simple to unsuccessful, depending on the species.

The family Phractolaemidae—or African mudfishes—is monotypic, comprising the single species, *Phractolaemus ansorgei*. Its modified lunglike swimbladder allows the fish to utilize atmospheric oxygen. The mouth is very small. Since it has a penchant for digging, a soft substrate is beneficial and vegetation must be protected. Moderate illumination and numerous plants are recommended. It is peaceful.

Kneria sp. WC   (3/1005)

H: Africa: Zaïre: Shaba.

Kneria sp.   1/844

H: Africa: Angola to E Africa.
♂: Occipital organ.   S: +
B: After joining, e. scattered; N fam.   F: O
T: 18–22°C, L: 7 cm, pH: 7, D: 1–2

Kneria sp. aff. *spekii*   3/1006

H: Africa: Tanzania.
♂: Occipital organ.   S: +
B: No brood care.   F: O
T: 20–22°C, L: 5.5 cm, pH: 7, D: 2

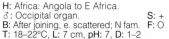

Parakneria tanzaniae   5/1054

H: E Africa: central Tanzania (highland).
♂: Slimmer; smaller?   S: +
B: Unknown.   F: O
T: 18–22°C, L: 7 cm, pH: >7, D: 3

Parakneria sp. aff. *tanzaniae*   3/1006

H: E Africa: Tanzania.
♂: Slimmer.   S: +
B: Unknown.   F: O
T: 22–24°C, L: 7.5 cm, pH: 7, D: 2–3

Parakneria thysi   5/1054

H: Africa: Zaïre system.
SD: Unknown.   S: +
B: Spawning migraton?   F: O
T: 18–22°C, L: 5 cm, pH: 7, D: 3

Phractolaemus ansorgei   1/861
African mudfish

H: W Africa: Niger Delta, Ethiope, Zaïre.
♂: White nodules on head.   S: +
B: Unsuccessful.   F: C
T: 25–30°C, L: 15 cm, pH: 7, D: 2

BONY FISHES

881

Order Gymnotiformes

This order consists exclusively of freshwater fishes of Central and South America. Of the 6 families, only the Gymnotidae inhabit Central America. There are 23 genera and over 62 species described at the present time. Many new discoveries are anticipated (NELSON, 1994).

Gymnotiformes have a very characteristically shaped body. Ventral fins are lacking, the dorsal and caudal fins are either absent or rudimentary, and the anal fin has more than 140 rays. Wavelike motions of the anal fin propel the fish both forward and backward. These fishes, also known as South American knifefishes, can regenerate part of their caudal region.

All species have a fairly well-developed electric organ, but it is particularly well-developed in the case of *Electrophorus electricus*. They use the electricity to communicate and navigate, althought *E. electricus* also uses it to stun prey.

Their cryptic and nocturnal lifestyle is not the ideal for an aquarium fish. However, since they use changing electrical fields to "see," the aquarist can trick the animal to remain visible: he/she can provide a transparent tube. The tube is readily accepted as a refuge, unbeknown to the fish that it is in full view. Numerous hiding places are required. Tankmates must be chosen carefully. Intraspecifically they are usually waspish, but specimens introduced at the same time get along somewhat better. Heterospecific tankmates must exceed in size what could be considered suitable prey, lest inexplicable dents in the aquarium's fish population occur every night.

Reproduction of knifefishes is occasionally successful. Water chemistry seems to be of secondary importance as long as the water is soft and slightly acid. Breeding can be induced by simulating conditions prevailing during the rainy season: vary the water temperature and conductivity by replacing part of the water with cool, distilled water, sprinkle the water surface with water ("rain"), and create a slight current.

The family Apteronotidae (ghost knifefishes) can easily be distinguished from all other Gymnotiformes, as all its members have a disjointed caudal and anal fin.

Electrophorus electricus belongs to the monotypic family Electrophoridae. It is capable of producing sufficient energy to kill or stun its prey with one discharge, i.e., 300–500 V and little current (<1 A). Unlike other knifefishes, it grows to the incredible size of more than 2 m.

Rhamphichthyidae distinguish themselves as the only species which bury themselves in soft substrates.

Adontosternarchus devenanzii   5/988

H: Venezuela: Rio Portuguesa.
♂: Slightly slimmer.   S: =
B: Simulate the rainy season.   F: C!
T: 20–30°C, L: 20 cm, pH: 7, D: 3

GYMNOTIFORMES
Apteronotidae[1-4]
Electrophoridae[5]
Gymnotidae[6]

Ghost Knifefishes
Electric Knifefishes
Naked-Back Knifefishes

Apteronotus albifrons　　1/821
Black ghost knifefish
H: S Am.: Ven., Guyana, Brazil, Ec., Peru.
SD: Unknown.　　　　　　　　S: =
B: See introduction of order.　　F: C,O
T: 23–28°C, L: <50 cm, pH: 7, D: 3

Apteronotus albifrons　　1/821
Black ghost knifefish
See photo on p. 3/937.

Apteronotus leptorhynchus　　3/936
Long-nosed black ghost knifefish
H: S America: Guianas, Brazil, Peru.
SD: Unknown.　　　　　　　　S: =
B: Unknown.　　　　　　　　F: C,O
T: 24–28°C, L: 40 cm, pH: 7, D: 3

Platyurosternarchus macrostomus　　5/988
H: S Am.: Venezuela, Guyana, Brazil, Peru.
SD: Unknown.　　　　　　　　S: ?
B: Unsuccessful.　　　　　　　F: C
T: 22–28°C, L: 40 cm, pH: 7, D: 3

Electrophorus electricus　　1/831
Electric eel
H: S Am.: Ven., Guy., Brazil, Ecuador, Peru.
SD: Unknown.　　　　　　　　S: –,!
B: Unknown.　　　　　　　　F: C
T: 23–28°C, L: 230 cm, pH: 7, D: 3

Gymnotus anguillaris　　5/994
Slant-bar knifefish
H: S Am.: Sur., Brazil, Guyana. Peru? Ven.?
SD: Unknown.　　　　　　　　S: =
B: Unsuccessful.　　　　　　　F: C
T: 22–30°C, L: 30 cm, pH: 7, D: 3

BONY FISHES

Gymnotus carapo 1/840
Banded knifefish
H: C & S Am.: Guat., Amazon, Rio de la Plata.
SD: Unknown. S: =
B: Unknown. F: C
T: 22–28°C, L: 60 cm, pH: 7, D: 2–3

Gymnotus coatesi 5/994
H: S America: Venezuela, Brazil.
SD: Unknown. S: =
B: Unsuccessful. F: C
T: 22–30°C, L: 30 cm, pH: 7, D: 3

Gymnotus pedanopterus 5/996
H: S America: Venezuela, Brazil.
SD: Unknown. S: =
B: Unsuccessful. F: C
T: 22–28°C, L: 30 cm, pH: 7, D: 3

Gymnotus sp. 5/996
H: Tropical S America.
SD: Unknown. S: –
B: Unsuccessful. F: C
T: 20–30°C, L: 30 cm, pH: 7, D: 3

Brachypopomus sp. 5/992
H: S America: Venezuela, Brazil.
SD: Unknown. S: =
B: See introduction of order. F: C,O
T: 22–28°C, L: 30 cm, pH: <7, D: 3

Steatogenes elegans 1/862
H: S America: Guyana, Brazil, Peru.
SD: Unknown. S: =
B: Unsuccessful. F: C
T: 22–26°C, L: 20 cm, pH: <7, D: 3

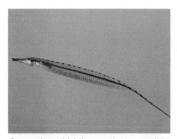

Gymnorhamphichthys rondoni   5/990
Mousetail knifefish
H: S Am.: Ven., Col., Sur., Brazil, Peru, Par.
SD: Unknown.   S: (–)
B: Unknown.   F: C
T: 25–28°C, L: 15 cm, pH: <7, D: 3–4

Gymnorhamphichthys cf. *rondoni*   5/990
Mousetail knifefish
Possibly a juvenile.

Eigenmannia lineata   4/827

H: Tropical S America: broadly distributed.
♂: Testis appear whitish; larger.   S: =
B: Simulation of rainy season.   F: C!
T: 20–30°C, L: ♂ 35 cm, pH: 7, D: 3

Eigenmannia cf. *lineata*   5/992

H: Tropical S America.
♂: Testis appear whitish; larger.   S: =
B: Unsuccessful.   F: C!
T: 20–30°C, L: ♂ 35 cm, pH: 7, D: 3

Eigenmannia virescens   1/862
Green knifefish
H: Broadly distributed in the tropics.
♂: 25 cm larger.   S: =
B: Simulation of rainy season.   F: C
T: 22–28°C, L: ♂ 45 cm, pH: <7, D: 2–3

Sternopygus macrurus   3/1029
Variable ghost knifefish
H: S Am.: Guianas, Brazil, Peru, Bolivia.
♂: Larger.   S: –
B: Unknown.   F: C!
T: 22–28°C, L: 90 cm, pH: <7, D: 3–4

BONY FISHES

At the edge of the Amazon Basin in a tributary of the Rio Napo along the eastern Andean slopes of Ecuador, the waters are swift and relatively poor in fishes. Some Loricariidae, Characiidae, and Lebiasinidae can be found.

Order Mugiliformes

The order of mullets is only comprised of the family Mugilidae and its 17 genera and at least 66 species. Whether the family should actually be classified into the order Mugiliformes or Perciformes or Atheriniformes is still debated (NELSON, 1994). Mugiliformes are found in all tropical and temperate marine and brackish water biotopes.

This family has little to offer for the aquarium, but as food fishes, the striped mullet (*Mugil cephalus*) and *Chanos chanos* (see p. 880) are the most important species cultured in coastal ponds of Southeast Asia. It has been artificially bred with hormones.

Using its superiorly placed eyes, *Rhinomigil corsula* peers above the water surface, appearing as if it had four eyes.

Crenimugil labrosus juv.   (5/1074)

Crenimugil labrosus   (5/1074)

Liza dumerili   5/1075

H: Coastal waters of W Africa.   2% Bw
SD: Unknown.   S: +
B: Marine water.   F: C
T: 20–25°C, L: 28 cm, pH: >7, D: 4

Mugil cephalus   5/1076
Striped mullet   Mw,Bw

H: Atlantic coasts, India to Hong Kong.
♂: Courtship colors; ⅓ smaller.   S: =
B: Marine water.   F: C
T: 5–25°C, L: <90 cm, pH: >7, D: 4

Rhinomugil corsula   5/1078
Indian mullet   0.5% Bw
H: Asia: India, Burma, Bengal.
SD: Unknown.   S: +
B: N: planktonic eggs & larvae.   F: C,O
T: 22–30°C, L: 48 cm, pH: >7, D: 4

Rhinomugil corsula   5/1078
Indian mullet   0.5% Bw

OSMERIFORMES

Order Osmeriformes

This order consists of 2 suborders, 13 families, and 74 genera with 236 species. All the freshwater and brackish water families presented here—Galaxiidae, Lepidogalaxiidae, and Retropinnidae—belong to the suborder Osmeroidei (NELSON 1994). MOYLE and CECH (1988) consider Galaxiidae and Retropinnidae part of the Salmoniformes and place the Lepidogalaxiidae into the Esociformes.

The family Lepidogalaxiidae is monotypic. *Lepidogalaxias salamandroides*, the sole species of the family, buries itself into moist sand to endure dry periods. Fertilization is internal, but it is oviparous (PUSEY and STEWARD, 1989).

In contrast to the otherwise very similar Retropinnidae, Galaxiidae do not have an adipose fin. The geographic distribution of the Galaxiidae in the Southern Hemisphere is interpreted as an indication that the continents were previously connected (see also Characiformes, p. 40).

Few details are known about these small- to medium-sized fishes. They are considered the southern ecological counterpart to the salmonids.

Galaxiids are characteristically peaceful, active fishes that school in midwater. *Galaxias cleaveri,* as one of the few exceptions, is a solitary-natured nocturnal fish which spends much of its time buried in the substrate.

The reproductive biology largely remains a mystery, but some species have spawned spontaneously in species aquaria without any special effort on the part of the aquarist; for example, *Galaxiella pusilla* is known to be an open spawner.

Brachygalaxias bullocki b.♂, t.♀ 2/1076

H: S America: S Chile.
♂: White spot. S: ?
B: Unsuccessful. F: C!
T: 15–20°C, L: <6 cm, pH: 7, D: 4

Brachygalaxias gothei b.♀, t.♂ 2/1076

H: S America: S Chile.
♂: Red band. S: ?
B: Fortuitous; several ♂♂ follow 1♀. F: C
T: 15–22°C, L: 5 cm, pH: 7, D: 3–4

Galaxias auratus 2/1078
Golden galaxias
H: Australia: Tasmania.
SD: Unknown. S: +
B: Unsuccessful. F: C,O
T: 10–28°C, L: 24 cm, pH: 7, D: 2–3

Galaxias cleaveri 2/1078
Mud galaxias
H: Australia: Tasmania, Victoria. Rare
SD: Unknown. S: (–)
B: Unknown. F: C!
T: 10–20°C, L: 14 cm, pH: 7, D: 4

Galaxias maculatus 2/1080
Common jollitail
H: S and W Australia to Chile.
SD: Unknown. S: (–)
B: Nat.: Bw, among sea grasses. F: C!
T: 10–22°C, L: 19 cm, pH: 7, D: 3

Galaxias olidus 2/1080
Mountain galaxias
H: Australia: Victoria.
SD: Unknown. S: +
B: Unknown. F: C,O
T: 4–30°C, L: 13.5 cm, pH: 7, D: 3–4

BONY FISHES

Galaxias "fuscus" olidus　　2/1080
Mountain galaxias

Galaxias rostratus　　2/1082
Murray jollytail
H: Australia: Murray River.　　Very rare
SD: Unknown.　　S: +
B: Unknown.　　F: C,O
T: 10–26°C, L: 13 cm, pH: 7, D: 3–4

Galaxias tanycephalus　　2/1082
Saddled galaxias
H: Australia: Tasmania.
♂: More colorful; larger.　　S: +
B: Unknown.　　F: C!
T: 10–26°C, L: 15 cm, pH: 7, D: 3

Galaxias truttaceus　　2/1084
Spotted mountain trout
H: SW Australia to Tasmania.
SD: Unknown.　　S: +
B: Unknown.　　F: C
T: 6–20°C, L: 13 cm, pH: 7, D: 3

Galaxias zebratus　　4/769
Cape Galaxias
H: South Africa: Cape region.
♂: More colorful; larger.　　S: =
B: Unknown.　　F: C,O
T: 24–26°C, L: 20 cm, pH: 7, D: 2–3

Galaxiella munda　　2/1084
Swamp pygmy galaxias
H: W Australia.
♂: More colorful; smaller.　　S: +
B: Unknown.　　F: C,O
T: 8–24°C, L: 5 cm, pH: 7, D: 2

OSMERIFORMES
Galaxiidae[1-3]
Lepldogalaxiidae[4]
Retropinnidae[5,6]

Galaxiids
Salamanderfishes
New Zealand Smelts

Galaxiella nigrostriata   2/1086
Black-striped dwarf galaxias
H: W Australia.
♂: More colorful; slimmer.   S: (−)
B: Unknown.   F: C,O
T: 10–25°C, L: 3.5 cm, pH: 7, D: 3

Galaxiella pusilla   2/1086
Eastern dwarf galaxias
H: Australia: S Victoria.
♂: More colorful; 1.5 cm smaller. S: (−)
B: Substrate spawner.   F: C,O
T: 10–30°C, L: ♀ 4.5 cm, pH: 7, D: 2

Paragalaxias mesotes   2/1086
Arthur's paragalaxias
H: Australia: Tasmania.
SD: Unknown.   S: (−)
B: Unknown.   F: C,O
T: 5–20°C, L: 8 cm, pH: 7, D: 3

Lepidogalaxias salamandroides   2/1104
Salamander mudminnow
H: Australia: southern coast.
♂: Anal fin w/ dermal lobe.   S:(−)
B: Unknown.   F: C!
T: 8–25°C, L: 6.5 cm, pH: <7, D: 3

Prototroctes maraena   2/1053
Grayling, cucumber herring
H: Australia: coastal rivers. Threatened
♂: Slimmer?   S: −
B: Spawns in freshwater.   F: C,O
T: 10–25°C, L: 30 cm, pH: 7, D: 3

Retropinna semoni   3/1028
Australian smelt
H: Austl.: S Queensl., New South Wales,...
♂: Larger fins.   S: (−)
B: Spawning grid; static water. F: C,O
T: 10–25°C, L: 8 cm, pH: 7, D: 2

BONY FISHES

891

Order Osteoglossiformes

The order of bonytongue fishes consists of two suborders: the Notopteroidei and the Osteoglossoidei. The former consists of Nile pikes (p. 893), African elephantfishes (pp. 893–900), featherfin knifefishes (pp. 900, 901), and the mooneyes (*Hiodon* with 2 species; not yet introduced in the Atlas). The Osteoglossoidei contain the bonytongues (pp. 901, 902) and butterflyfishes (p. 902). In summary, there are 6 families, 29 genera, and 217 species in this order. The Mormyridae are the most specious family of the order with 18 genera and almost 200 species.

Geographic Distribution

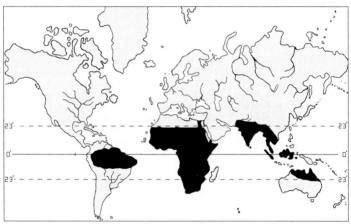

Area of distribution of the order Osteoglossiformes (excluding Hiodontidae, which inhabit North America).

The Families

Family Gymnarchidae

This monotypic family has in *Gymnarchus niloticus* (next page) its only representative. Due to its extremely large size and pronounced predacious behavior, the Nile pike is not recommended for the aquarium. It is capable of stunning even large prey with its electric discharges. In nature, the male uses plant material to build a nest which is suspended about 1 m below the water surface. Approximately 1000, 1 cm diameter eggs are deposited therein. When the young leave the nest, they are already 10 cm long.

Soft substrates are preferred, since this fish scours the bottom for worms. Aside from pectoral fins and a many-rayed dorsal fin, the Nile pike has lost its fins. Both forward and backward propulsion are provided by sinuate movements of the dorsal fin.

OSTEOGLOSSIFORMES
Gymnarchidae[b]
Mormyridae[6]

BONYTONGUE FISHES
Nile Pikes
Elephantfishes

Family Mormyridae

The African elephantfishes, also referred to as mormyrids, colonize tropical Africa and the Nile River. Their common name is in reference to the trunklike mouth of some species. Elephantfishes have thick, glandular skin and an electric organ on the caudal peduncle, which is used to delineate territories.

Ranging from 6 to 50 cm—or 150 cm in extreme cases—there is a suitable species for practically any size aquarium. Most are social and nocturnal. Breeding is difficult: simulating conditions prevailing during the rainy season seems to be essential (see also p. 882).

Family Notopteridae

The featherfin knifefishes have a many-rayed anal fin which, in conjunction with the caudal fin, forms a long continuous fin fringe. The ventral fins and the dorsal fin are vestigial or totally lacking. Using the swimbladder, featherfin knifefishes are able to breathe atmospheric air.

With age, they often turn aggressive and territorial among themselves, but they are usually peaceful towards heterospecifics.

Family Osteoglossidae

The family of bonytongues contains 5 genera with a total of 7 species. Providing these large, stately predators are well-fed, they can be associated with fellow large, peaceful fishes such as *Geophagus* spp. and *Leporinus* spp. The large scales give them an ancient appearance. *Arapaima gigas*, an obligate air-breather, is the largest scaled freshwater fish of all. All species are popular food fishes in their respective habitats, though some are absent from the aquarium trade because they are protected (CITES, p. 964).

Family Pantodontidae

This monotypic family only contains the species presented: *Pantodon buchholzi*, the butterflyfish (p. 902). It is a surface-oriented predator which can be associated with appropriate-sized fishes that inhabit the middle and lower water strata.

Gymnarchus niloticus   5/1051
Nile pike, aba aba
H: Africa: Nile, Niger, Chad, Gambia Basin.
SD: Unknown.   S: –
B: Nest; 1000 eggs, 10 mm Ø.   F: C
T: 23–28°C, L: 150 cm, pH: 7, D: 4

Brienomyrus brachyistius   5/1064
Whale-faced marcusenius
H: Africa: Nigeria, Liberia, Gambia to Zaïre.
♂: Larger anal fin?   S: =
B: Rainy season: eggs laid on A fin. F: C
T: 20–28°C, L: 28 cm, pH: 7, D: 4

Brienomyrus longianalis 5/1064
Slender elephantnose
H: Africa: Lower Nile, S Cameroon.
♂: Larger anal fin? S: =
B: Unsuccessful. F: C
T: 22–26°C, L: 15 cm, pH: 7, D: 4

Brienomyrus niger 4/802
H: Africa: Zaïre, Niger, Volta, Chad Basin,
   Senegal, Gambia, White Nile.
♂: Base of anal fin concave. S: =
B: Simulation of rainy season. F: C
T: 22–28°C, L: 13 cm, pH: ≪7, D: 4

Campylomormyrus alces 4/802

H: Africa: Zaïre, Angola: Zaïre Basin.
♂: Base of anal fin concave. S: =
B: Unsuccessful. F: C
T: 22–28°C, L: 36 cm, pH: ≪7, D: 4

Campylomormyrus elephas 3/1020
Blunt-jaw elephant nose
H: Africa: Zaïre Basin.
SD: Unknown. S: =
B: Unsuccessful. F: C
T: 26–28°C, L: 40 cm, pH: 7, D: 3–4

Campylomormyrus numenius 5/1066

H: Africa: Zaïre Basin.
♂: Elongated anal fin. S: ?
B: In flooded areas. F: C
T: 22–25°C, L: 65 cm, pH: 7, D: 4

Campylomormyrus rhynchophorus 4/804

H: Africa: Zaïre Basin.
♂: Concave anal fin. S: =
B: Simulation of rainy season. F: C
T: 22–28°C, L: 22 cm, pH: <7, D: 3–4

Campylomormyrus tamandua　1/854

Campylomormyrus tamandua　4/804

H: Africa: Volta, Niger, Chad, Zaïre Basin.
♂: Base of anal fin concave.　　　S: =
B: Simulation of rainy season.　　F: C
T: 22–24°C, L: 43 cm, pH: <7, D: 4

Gnathonemus petersii　1/854
Peter's elephantnose
H: Africa: Zaïre Basin, Nigeria, Cameroon.
♂: Base of anal fin concave.　　　S: =
B: Unsuccessful.　　　　　　　F: C,O
T: 22–28°C, L: 23 cm, pH: 7, D: 3

Gnathonemus schilthuisiae　2/1142
Schilthuis' elephantnose
H: Africa: Central Congo River.
SD: Unknown.　　　　　　　　S: =
B: Unsuccessful.　　　　　　　F: C,O
T: 24–28°C, L: 10 cm, pH: 7, D: 3

Hippopotamyrus discorhynchus　4/806

H: Af.: Zaïre B., lakes Tanganyika, Malawi,...
♂: Base of anal fin concave.　　　S: =
B: Simulation of rainy season.　　F: C
T: 22–28°C, L: <30 cm, pH: <7, D: 3–4

Hippopotamyrus paugyi ♂　5/1066
Spoon-bill elephant nose
H: Africa: Zaïre Basin.
♂: Concave, longer anal fin.　　　S: +
B: Unknown.　　　　　　　　　F: C
T: 23–27°C, L: 18 cm, pH: 7, D: 3

Hippopotamyrus pictus ♀ 4/806

H: Af.: White Nile, Gold C., B. Faso, Nig.
♂: Base of anal fin concave. S: =
B: Simulate the rainy season. F: C,O
T: 22–28°C, L: 30 cm, pH: <7, D: 3–4

Hippopotamyrus psittacus 5/1068
Parrot elephantnose

H: Africa: upper Zaïre, upper Niger.
♂: Larger anal fin? S: =
B: Among stones and rock crevices. F: C
T: 20–24°C, L: 18 cm, pH: 7, D: 3

Hyperopisus bebe 4/808

H: Africa: Nile B., Eth., Sen., Volta, Chad.
♂: Base of anal fin slightly concave. S: =
B: Unsuccessful. F: C
T: 22–28°C, L: 51 cm, pH: 7, D: 3–4

Isichthys henryi 4/808

H: Af.: Sierra L. to Nigeria, Cam., Gabon.
♂: Base of anal fin concave. S: =
B: Simulate rainy season. F: C
T: 22–28°C, L: 29 cm, pH: <7, D: 3–4

Marcusenius brachyistius 2/1142

H: Africa: Sierra Leone, Liberia, Ivory C.
SD: Unknown. S: =
B: Unsuccessful. F: C
T: 25–28°C, L: 18 cm, pH: 7, D: 3

Marcusenius longianalis 2/1144
Slender elephantnose

H: Africa: Nigeria, Cameroon.
SD: Unknown. S: –
B: Unsuccessful. F: C,O
T: 25–30°C, L: 15 cm, pH: 7, D: 3

Marcusenius macrolepidotus 2/1144
Large-scaled elephantnose
H: SE Africa.
SD: Unknown. S: =
B: Unsuccessful. F: C
T: 22–26°C, L: 25 cm, pH: 7, D: 3

Marcusenius macrolepidotus 4/810
Large-scaled elephantnose
H: Af.: Ghana, Zaïre B., Tan., Kenya, L. Mal.,...
♂: Base of anal fin concave. S: =
B: Simulate the rainy season. F: C
T: 22–28°C, L: <15 cm, pH: <7, D: 3–4

Mormyrops anguilloides 4/810
H: Af.: Sen., Gam., Nig., Volta, Chad, Zaïre &
Zambezi basins, lakes Tangan. & Malawi.
♂: Base of anal fin concave. S: –
B: Simulate the rainy season. F: C
T: 22–28°C, L: 150 cm!, pH: 7, D: 3–4

Mormyrops curtus 4/812

H: Africa: Zaïre: lower Zaïre.
♂: Base of anal fin concave. S: =
B: Unsuccessful. F: C
T: 22–28°C, L: 40 cm, pH: <7, D: 3–4

Mormyrus boulengeri 5/1068
Slender-nosed elephantfish
H: Africa: Central Zaïre Basin.
♂: Larger anal fin. S: –
B: N.: in rock crevices or on algae. F: C
T: 23–26°C, L: 25 cm, pH: 7, D: 4

Mormyrus bozasi 4/812

H: Africa: Republic of Congo.
♂: Base of anal fin concave. S: =
B: Simulate the rainy season? F: C
T: 22–28°C, L: 36 cm, pH: 7, D: 3–4

Mormyrus caballus   4/814

H: Africa: Zaïre Basin, Cameroon, Angola.
♂: Base of anal fin concave.   S: =
B: Simulate the rainy season?   F: C
T: 22–28°C, L: 20 cm, pH: <7, D: 3–4

Mormyrus caschive   4/814

H: Af.: Nile B., lakes Edw., Alb., George,...
♂: Base of anal fin concave.   S: =
B: Simulate the rainy season?   F: C
T: 22–28°C, L: 52 cm, pH: <7, D: 3–4

Mormyrus kannume   3/1020

H: Af.: Nile and many of the mayor lakes.
SD: Unknown.   S: –
B: Unknown   F: C
T: 22–26°C, L: 50 cm, pH: 7, D: 3

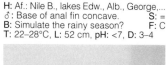

Mormyrus proboscirostris   4/816

H: Africa: Zaïre: upper Zaïre.
♂: Base of anal fin concave.   S: =
B: Simulate the rainy season?   F: C
T: 22–28°C, L: 20 cm, pH: <7, D: 3–4

Mormyrus rume proboscirostris   3/1022

H: Africa: Angola, Zaïre: upper Zaïre.
SD: Unknown.   S: =
B: Unsuccessful.   F: C
T: 24–28°C, L: 60 cm, pH: <7, D: 3–4

Petrocephalus bane ansorgii   5/1070

H: Africa: upper Niger. Nominate form: Nile.
♂: Larger anal fin.   S: =
B: Builds a nest in flooded areas. F: C!
T: 20–25°C, L: 20 cm, pH: 7, D: 3

Petrocephalus bovei   2/1146

H: Af.: lower Nile, Senegal R., Gambia R.
SD: Unknown.   S: =
B: Nest of plant pieces in dark areas. F: C
T: 23–26°C, L: 12 cm, pH: 7, D: 4

Petrocephalus catostoma ♂   2/1146
Big-nosed whale

H: E and S Africa; broadly distributed.
♂: Anal fin wavelike.   S: –
B: Unknown.   F: C
T: 23–26°C, L: 13 cm, pH: 7, D: 3

Petrocephalus christyi   4/816
Christy's whale

H: Africa: Zaïre Basin.
♂: Anal fin more concave.   S: =
B: Simulate the rainy season.   F: C
T: 22–28°C, L: 11 cm, pH: <7, D: 3–4

Petrocephalus keatingii   5/1070
(possibly *Petrocephalus catostoma*)

H: Africa: Zaïre Basin, Nigeria.
♂: Anal fin more concave.   S: =
B: Simulation of rainy season.   F: C!
T: 20–30°C, L: 12 cm, pH: 7, D: 3

Petrocephalus levequei   5/1072

Petrocephalus simus   3/1022
Dorsal-band whale

H: Africa: from Lybia to Zaïre.
♂: Anal fin more concave.   S: –
B: Unsuccessful.   F: C
T: 24–28°C, L: 12 cm, pH: 7, D: 3

BONY FISHES

Osteoglossiformes
Mormyridae[1-5]
Notopteridae[6]

Bonytongue Fishes
Elephantfishes
African knifefishes, Featherfin Knifefishes

Petrocephalus soudanensis   5/1072
Sudanese whale

Pollimyrus adspersus   4/818

H: Africa: Zaïre Basin, Cameroon, Nigeria.
♂: Anal fin more concave.   S: =
B: By simulating the rainy season? F: C
T: 22–28°C, L: 8 cm, pH: <7, D: 3–4

Pollimyrus isidori   4/818
H: Africa: Nile, Gambia, Niger, Volta,
   Chad basins; Ivory Coast.
♂: Anal fin more concave.   S: =
B: By simulating the rainy season. F: C
T: 22–28°C, L: 10 cm, pH: <7, D: 3–4

Pollimyrus macularius   5/1073

H: Af.: Senegal, Gambia, Burkina Faso,...
♂: Anal fin more concave.   S: =
B: By simulating the rainy season. F: C
T: 22–28°C, L: 6 cm, pH: <7, D: 3–4

Pollimyrus nigripinnis   3/1024
Dusky whale
H: Africa: Zaïre: central Zaïre Basin.
SD: Unknown.   S: –
B: Unsuccessful.   F: C
T: 24–26°C, L: 12 cm, pH: 7, D: 3–4

Chitala ornata   2/1150
Clown knifefish
H: SE Asia: Thai., Bur., Greater Sunda Is.
SD: Unknown.   S: –
B: Substrate spawner; paternal fam. F: C
T: 24–28°C, L: <100 cm, pH: <7, D: 3

OSTEOGLOSSIFORMES
Notopteridae[1-3]
Osteoglossidae[4-6]

BONYTONGUE FISHES
African knifefishes, Featherfin Knifefishes
Bonytongues

Notopterus notopterus　　　1/856
Asiatic knifefish
H: SE Asia: India, Burma, Thai., Malay.,...
SD: Unknown.　　　　　　　　S: –
B: Open spawner; paternal family. F: C!
T: 24–28°C, L: 35 cm, pH: <7, D: 3

Papyrocranus afer　　　3/1025
African featherfin
H: Africa: W Africa and Zaïre Basin.
SD: Unknown.　　　　　　　　S: –
B: Successful; paternal family.　　F: C
T: 24–30°C, L: <62 cm, pH: <7, D: 3

Xenomystus nigri　　　1/856
African knifefish
H: Africa: Zaïre, Gabon, Niger, Liberia.
SD: Unknown.　　　　　　　　S: –
B: Nat.: 150–200, 2 mm Ø eggs.　F: C!
T: 22–28°C, L: 30 cm, pH: <7, D: 2–3

Arapaima gigas　　　2/1151
Paiche, piracurú, arapaima
H: South America: Amazonia. Protected
♂: Head darker at spawning; colorful.　S: –
B: Nat.: in pits; P–N fam.　　F: C!
T: 25–29°C, L: <300 cm, pH: <7, D: 4

Heterotis niloticus　　　2/1152
African bonytongue
H: Western & central Africa.
SD: Indistinguishable.　　　　S: =
B: N: plant nest; maternal family. F: C,O
T: 25–30°C, L: 90 cm, pH: 7, D: 4

Osteoglossum bicirrhosum　　　1/858
Arowana, arahuana
H: S America: Amazonia.
♂: Lower mandible & A fin longer.　S: =
B: ♂ Mb, 60 d; y 8–10 cm long.　F: C
T: 24–30°C, L: <120 cm, pH: <7, D: 4

OSTEOGLOSSIFORMES
Osteoglossidae[1-5]
Pantodontidae[6]

BONYTONGUE FISHES
Bonytongues
Butterflyfishes

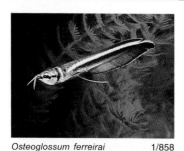

Osteoglossum ferreirai　　　　1/858
Black arowana
H: S America: Rio Negro.
SD: Unknown.　　　　　　　　　S: =
B: ♂ Mb, 56 days; y 9 cm long.　F: C
T: 24–30°C, L: 100 cm, pH: <7, D: 4

Scleropages formosus　　　　2/1152
Asian arowana
H: Australia, SE Asia.　　　Protected
SD: Unknown.　　　　　　　　　S: =
B: Nat.: ♀ Mb; maternal family.　F: C
T: 24–30°C, L: 90 cm, pH: <7, D: 2–3

Scleropages jardini　　　　　2/1154
Spotted barramundi
H: N Australia, New Guinea.
SD: Unknown.　　　　　　　　　S: =
B: Nat.: ♂ Mb? Paternal family?　F: C
T: 24–30°C, L: 80 cm, pH: <7, D: 3

Scleropages leichardtii　　　2/1154
Spotted barramundi
H: Australia: Queensland: Fitzroy River.
SD: Unknown.　　　　　　　　　S: =
B: Nat.: ♂ Mb? Paternal family?　F: C
T: 24–30°C, L: 80 cm, pH: <7, D: 3

Scleropages leichardtii　　　2/1154
Spotted barramundi

Pantodon buchholzi　　　　　1/860
Butterflyfish
H: Africa: Nigeria, Cameroon, Zaïre.
♂: Posterior edge of A fin concave.　S: =
B: <220 floating eggs.　　　　　F: C
T: 23–30°C, L: 10 cm, pH: <7, D: 3

Order Percopsiformes

The Percopsiformes consist of 3 families, all inhabitants of freshwater. Aphredoderidae is a monotypic family, *Aphredoderus sayanus* (right) its only species.

The position of the anal opening is normal in juveniles, but with advancing age it moves forward; additionally, one anal fin ray turns into a third spine.

The species should be overwintered at cool temperatures.

Aphredoderus sayanus　　　　4/718
Pirate perch
H: N America: USA: Minnesota to Texas.
SD: Slight.　　　　　　　　　　　S: –
B: Nest; parents guard the spawn.　F: C!
T: 5–26°C, L: 13 cm, pH: 7, D: 3–4

Order Pleuronectiformes

Flounderlike fishes primarily inhabit marine biotopes. Of 11 the families, 123 genera, and 570 species, only 20 species pass at least part of their life in freshwater (NELSON, 1994). The INDEX presents species of 2 families, Achiridae and Soleidae. Both are righteye flounders; i.e., it is the left eye that moves to the right side of the initially symmetrical, "normal" larva as it metamorphs into a benthic juvenile that lives with its left side against the substrate.

Achirus achirus　　　　4/826
Dwarf freshwater flounder
H: S Am.: Suriname, Brazil, Peru, Uruguay.
SD: Unknown.　　　　　　　　　S: +
B: Unknown.　　　　　　　　　　F: C
T: 25–28°C, L: 10 cm? pH: <7, D: 3–4

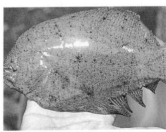

Trinectes fasciatus (?)　　　　5/984
American freshwater flounder
H: S North Am., South America: Ecuador.
SD: Unknown.　　　　　　　　　S: +
B: Unsuccessful.　　　　　　　　F: O
T: 20–24°C, L: 25 cm, pH: 7, D: 3–4

BONY FISHES

Trinectes fasciatus (?) 5/984
American freshwater flounder
Juvenile.

Trinectes maculatus 5/984
Spotted flounder, hogshocker
H: N America: coastal areas to Florida.
SD: Unknown. S: +
B: Successful. F: C,O
T: 5–22°C, L: 45 cm, pH: 7, D: 1–4

Trinectes maculatus 5/984
Spotted flounder, hogshocker
Juvenile.

Brachirus salinarum 2/1157
Salt-pan sole (Bw)
H: Australia: Gulf of Carpentaria affluents.
SD: Unknown. S: =
B: Unknown. F: C,O
T: 22–30°C, L: 15 cm, pH: >7, D: 3–4

Platichthys flesus 5/1084
Common flounder (2% salt)
H: North, Baltic, Black S., Medit., NAm. coast.
SD: Unknown. S: =
B: Pelagic eggs in the sea. F: C,O
T: 5–25°C, L: 60 cm, pH: >7, D: 4

Solea selheimi 4/825
Australian freshwater sole Mw, (Bw)
H: Australia: Gulf of Carpentaria affluents.
SD: Unknown. S: =
B: Unknown. F: C
T: 22–26°C, L: <15 cm, pH: >7, D: 2–4

Order Salmoniformes

The systematics of the salmonid fishes are not universally accepted. The subfamilies Coregoninae and Thymallinae are also considered families—Coregonidae and Thymallidae. Here they have been classified as subfamilies after Nelson (1994).

Although they now enjoy a worldwide distribution, salmonids originally only inhabited the Northern Hemisphere. Salmon and trout have been introduced in streams and lakes as game fishes, cultured as food fishes in temperate and cold waters, and simply bred and released to replenish fisheries populations. Trout are even raised successfully in tropical countries at high elevations, where temperatures are cooler. Chile is presently emerging as one of the largest producers of salmon. Salmon, the king of fishes! Unlike the discus, salmon have not earned the title by an aesthetically pleasing form, coloration, or stately elegance, but rather through their marvelous culinary qualities. All Salmoniformes are coldwater species—salmon are very intolerant of elevated temperatures—requiring a chiller for summer months. As large, very active schooling fishes with a high oxygen requirement, aquarium maintenance is not recommended. Only specialized aquarists, food markets, and restaurants should consider such a difficult undertaking.

Salmon are famous for their spawning migrations, a spectacle to behold. Thousands of these fishes migrate from the sea into the rivers where they

Oncorhynchus nerka, during a spawning migration, British Columbia, Canada.

were spawned (see photo on previous page). They show incredible perseverance to achieve their goal. Even waterfalls are scaled. Once they have reached their "native gravel bed," they spawn. Most succumb to exhaustion, as salmon do not feed during migration. Some nonanadromous species spawn several times. During the spawning migration, males are easily recognized by their enlarged upper mandible (salmon hook).

All Salmoniformes are carnivores, unable to metabolize carbohydrates for energy.

In food fish aquaculture, salmon are primarily cultured in fjords and protected bays using cages. Norway, the United States, Canada, and Chile are the largest producers. The removal of metabolites by marine currents is an ecological production constraint.

Trout are mostly cultured inland in rectangular and circular cement tanks with constant water flow-through. The most favorable temperature for growth is 15°C, whereas 9°C is best to spawn species such as rainbow trout.

Coregonus albula pereslavicus   4/748
European cisco
H: N Europe, N Asia.
SD: Unknown.   S: =
B: N.: on sand and gravel banks.   F: C
T: 4–18°C, L: 34 cm, pH: 7, D: 4

Coregonus autumnalis migratorius 3/944
Arctic cisco
H: Asia: Russia: Lake Baikal.   E
SD: Unknown.   S: =
B: Nat.: in rivers; <47000 benthic e.   F: C
T: 4–16°C, L: 56 cm, pH: >7, D: 4

Coregonus lavaretus   3/944
Common whitefish
H: Europe, Asia.
SD: Unknown.   S: =
B: Nat.: egg scatterer.   F: C
T: 4–16°C, L: 57 cm, pH: >7, D: 4

Coregonus muksun   4/748
Muksun
H: N Europe, N Asia.
SD: Unknown.   S: =
B: N: over sand and gravel beds.   F: C
T: 4–18°C, L: 15–75 cm, pH: 7, D: 4

Coregonus oxyrhynchus 3/941

H: N Europe, N Asia. Endangered
SD: None. S: =
B: Nat.: egg scatterer. F: C
T: 4–20°C, L: <50 cm, pH: 7, D: 3

Coregonus pidschian 4/748
Humpback whitefish

H: N Europe, N Asia.
SD: Unknown. S: =
B: N.: over sand and gravel beds. F: C
T: 4–18°C, L: 25–52 cm, pH: 7, D: 4

Coregonus sardinella 4/748
Least cisco

H: N Europe, N Asia.
SD: Unknown. S: =
B: N: over sand and gravel beds. F: C
T: 4–18°C, L: 15–33 cm, pH: 7, D: 4

Coregonus ssp. 4/748
Cisco (photo on p. 4/747)

H: N Europe, N Asia.
SD: Unknown. S: =
B: N: over sand and gravel beds. F: C
T: 4–18°C, L: 15–85 cm, pH: 7, D: 4

Hucho hucho 3/1030
Danube salmon

H: Europe: Danube.
♂: "Hook" present when spawning. S: –
B: Migrates in Mar.–May to spawn. F: C
T: 6–18°C, L: <150 cm, pH: 7, D: 3

Oncorhynchus gorbuscha ♀♀,♂♂ 5/1087
Pink salmon

H: NW USA, NE Asia.
♂: Has "hook" when spawning; pink. S: –
B: Migrates to birth site. F: C
T: 4–12°C, L: 76 cm, pH: 7, D: 4

BONY FISHES

Oncorhynchus keta ♂　　5/1088
Chum salmon
H: N America, Asia.
♂: White-tipped V and A fins.　　S: –
B: Migrates to birth site to spawn.　F: C
T: 4–10°C, L: 102 cm, pH: 7, D: 4

Oncorhynchus kisutch yearlings　5/1088
Coho salmon, silver salmon
H: N America, SE Asia.
♂: Bright red flanks.　　S: –
B: Migrates to birth site to spawn.　F: C
T: 4–10°C, L: 98 cm, pH: 7, D: 4

Oncorhynchus mykiss　　3/1030
Rainbow trout, steelhead
H: N America, now also Europe.
♂: "Hook" forms when spawning.　S: –
B: Gravel pits; young hatch in 90 d.　F: C
T: 10–20°C, L: 50 cm, pH: 7, D: 4

Oncorhynchus nerka ♂　　5/1091
Sockeye salmon, red salmon　(4/823)
H: N America, NE Asia.
♂: "Hook" when spawning; red.　S: –
B: Migrates to birth site to spawn.　F: C
T: 4–10°C, L: 85 cm, pH: 7, D: 4

Oncorhynchus tschawytscha　5/1096
Chinook salmon, king salmon　(4/823)
H: N America: USA: Alaska.
♂: Red-brown during spawning time. S: –
B: Migrates to birth site to spawn.　F: C
T: 4–12°C, L: 147 cm, pH: 7, D: 4

Salmo salar ♂　　3/1033
Atlantic salmon
H: N Europe.
♂: "Hook" develops with age.　　S: –
B: Migrates Sep.–Feb. to spawn.　F: C
T: 6–18°C, L: <150 cm, pH: 7, D: 4

Salmo salar juvenile   3/1033
Atlantic salmon

Salmo salar   3/1033
Atlantic salmon

Salmo trutta f. *fario* juvenile   3/1034
Brown trout

H: Europe, N Africa.
♂: "Hook" forms at spawning time. S: –
B: In gravel pits; January–March. F: C
T: 2–16°C, L: 50 cm, pH: 7, D: 4

Salmo trutta × *Salvelinus fontinalis* 4/822
Tigerfish

H: Europe. Hybrid.
♂: "Hook" forms at spawning time. S: –
B: Sterile natural hybrid. F: C
T: 5–15°C, L: 50 cm, pH: 7, D: 3

Salvelinus alpinus salvelinus ♂   3/1035
Arctic char

H: Europe: deep lakes of the N Alps.
♂: More colorful. S: –
B: Over gravel; 20–80 m depth. F: C
T: 4–16°C, L: 15 cm, pH: 7, D: 4

Salvelinus fontinalis ♂ ♂   3/1036
Brook trout

H: E N America, and now Europe.
♂: More colorful? S: –
B: October to March. F: C
T: 10–14°C, L: 40 cm, pH: 7, D: 4

BONY FISHES

Salvelinus fontinalis 3/1036
Brook trout

Salvelinus lepechini 5/1098

H: N Asia: Siberia.
♂: More colorful. S: –
B: Migrates to spawn. F: C
T: 5–18°C, L: 75 cm, pH: 7, D: 4

Salvelinus malma 5/1098
Dolly varden
H: N America, Asia.
♂: More colorful. S: –
B: Anadromous; migrates to spawn. F: C
T: 4–18°C, L: 63 cm, pH: 7, D: 4

Thymallus thymallus 3/1042
Grayling
H: Europe.
♂: Larger fins; larger. S: –
B: In gravel pits; March to June. F: C
T: 6–18°C, L: 50 cm, pH: 7, D: 3–4

Thymallus thymallus l.♀, r.♂ 5/1108
Grayling

Thymallus thymallus ♂ 5/1108
Grayling spawning

Order Scorpaeniformes

The systematic arrangement of this order is not universally recognized; according to NELSON (1994), the order contains 25 families and 266 genera. Only 62 of the 1270 species are associated with freshwater, 52 of which are sculpins.

The family Comephoridae (Baikal oilfishes) only contains the two live-bearing oilfishes presented below. Both are coldwater species that live at great depths (750–1000 m). As the name indicates, their meat is very oily. Ventral fins are lacking. Almost all females die after giving birth.

The family Cottidae (sculpins) exclusively consists of coldwater fishes. The Baikal sculpins belong to this family (subfamily Cottocomephorinae).

The Platycephalidae are mostly marine species; very few enter brackish water. They are bottom-oriented predators which burrow into the substrate.

Scorpaenidae (subfamily Tetraroginae) possess very poisonous fin spines.

In general, Scorpaeniformes are unsuitable aquarium fishes. Maintenance should be reserved for specialists.

Comephorus baicalensis   3/942
Large oilfish
H: Asia: Russia: Lake Baikal.   E
♂: Smaller; only 3%–4% are ♂.   S: ?
B: Livebearer; July–October.   F: C
T: 4–18°C, L: ♀ 19 cm, pH: 7, D: 3–4

Comephorus dybowskii   3/942
Small oilfish
H: Asia: Russia: Lake Baikal.   E
♂: 5 cm smaller; 12%–21% are ♂. S: ?
B: Livebearer; February–March.   F: C
T: 4–18°C, L: ♀ 14 cm, pH: 7, D: 3–4

Batrachocottus baicalensis   3/950
Large-headed Baikal sculpin
H: Asia: Russia: Lake Baikal.   E
♂: Thin fin rays.   S: =
B: March, April; paternal family.   F: C
T: 4–20°C, L: 19 cm, pH: 7, D: 3

Cottocomephorus comephoroides   3/950
Long-finned Baikal sculpin juv.
H: Asia: Russia: Lake Baikal, Angara R.
♂: Dark brown pectoral fins.   S: =
B: February–April; paternal family.   F: C
T: 4–20°C, L: 19 cm, pH: 7, D: 3

Cottocomephorus grewingki ♂ 3/952
Yellow-finned Baikal sculpin

H: Asia: Russia: Lake Baikal. E
♂: Nuptial tubercles: larger. S: =
B: Coast; <2400 e; paternal family. F: C
T: 4–20°C, L: 19 cm, pH: 7, D: 2–3

Cottocomephorus grewingki ♀ 3/952
Yellow-finned Baikal sculpin

Cottus cognatus 5/1007
Slimy sculpin

H: E Siberia, N North America.
SD: Unknown. S: =
B: Among stones; paternal family. F: C,O
T: 4–16°C, L: 8 cm, pH: 7, D: 3

Cottus gobio 3/947
Miller's thumb

H: Europe.
♂: More colorful; larger head. S: =
B: Successful; Cs; <1000 e; P fam. F: C
T: 10–16°C, L: 15 cm, pH: >7, D: 2–3

Cottus gobio 3/947
Miller's thumb

Paracottus kessleri adult ♂ 3/948
Sand sculpins

H: Asia: Russia: Lake Baikal and rivers.
♂: Flat head; thick pectoral fin rays. S: =
B: May, June; paternal family. F: C
T: 4–20°C, L: 14 cm, pH: 7, D: 2–3

BONY FISHES

Scorpaeniformes
Cottidae[1, 2]
Platycephalidae[3]
Scorpaenidae[4–6]

Sculpins
Flatheads
Scorpionfishes

Paracottus kneri 3/948
Rock sculpin
H: Asia: Russia: lakes Baikal and Baunt.
♂: Larger; thicker fin rays. S: =
B: May–July; among stones; P fam. F: C
T: 4–20°C, L: <14 cm, pH: 7, D: 2–3

Procottus jeittelesi 3/952
Red Baikal sculpin
H: Asia: Russia: Lake Baikal. E
♂: Larger; thicker fin rays; darker. S: =
B: Nov.–Feb.; paternal family. F: C
T: 4–20°C, L: 35 cm, pH: 7, D: 3

Platycephalus indicus 4/724
Indian flathead
H: Coasts of India, Madagascar.
SD: Unknown. S: –
B: Pelagic eggs are laid in the sea. F: C
T: 22–28°C, L: 45 cm, pH: >7, D: 4

Nothestes robusta 2/1156
Bullrout Mw, Bw
H: Austl.: Queensland, New South Wales.
SD: Unknown. S: =,!
B: Unsuccessful. F: C
T: 10–30°C, L: 35 cm, pH: >7, D: 4

Vespicula depressifrons 4/740
Waspfish Mw, Bw
H: Indonesia, Philippines, New Guinea.
SD: Unknown. S: =,!
B: Pelagic eggs; 0.8% salinity. F: C
T: 22–28°C, L: 10 cm, pH: 7, D: 3

Vespicula depressifrons 4/740
Waspfish
Atypical coloration.

Order Synbranchiformes

This order consists of 3 families, 12 genera, and approximately 87 species. All but 3 species are found in freshwater. They inhabit the tropics and subtropics. Two of the families are presented below.

Family Mastacembelidae

Spiny eels occur from tropical Africa to Southeast Asia. Their body is eel- to ribbon-shaped and their head is pointed with a trunk-shaped, mobile "nose" (rostrum). The common name "spiny eels" is derived from the row of 9–42 individual spines anterior to the dorsal fin. The anal fin is many-rayed. It, the dorsal fin, and the caudal fin form a largely continuous fringe. Ventral fins and a swimbladder are lacking.

As bottom-oriented, nocturnal fishes, many species spend the day buried in the substrate. A loose, smooth-edged substrate is therefore required. In accordance to conditions in their natural biotope, the aquarium should be dimly illuminated and densely planted. When danger is perceived, these fishes quickly dive into the substrate. The large species are regional food fishes. A detailed report about maintenance and breeding of *Mastacembelus* sp. aff. *circumcinctus* can be found in the AQUARIUM ATLAS Vol. 5, pages 1056 ff. It scatters approximately 30 eggs among Java moss.

Lake Tanganyika in Africa; habitat of countless cichlids, but also of several endemic spiny eels.

Family Synbranchidae

Swamp eels occur in tropical South America, Africa, Southeast Asia including Indonesia, and Australia. Despite their gross similarity to eels, they are not related. Dorsal, caudal, and anal fins form a fin fringe which is commonly very short-rayed. Both ventral and pectoral fins as well as a swimbladder are lacking. The gills are vestigial and would actually be of little use in the swampy, oxygen-poor biotopes where these "eels" are found. Through various modifications, synbranchids are able to utilize atmospheric oxygen: richly vascularized membranes in their throat, a lunglike appendage in the brachial cavity, or the large intestine.

Swamp eels are bottom-oriented predators; hence, tankmates must be large enough not to become a convenient mouthfull. A species aquarium is also appropriate. As nocturnal, retiring fishes, they are rarely seen.

Aethiomastacembelus loennbergii 4/786
Loennberg's spiny eel
H: Africa: Chad: Benue and Niger basins.
SD: Unknown.   S: =
B: Unsuccessful.   F: C
T: 25–30°C, L: 26 cm, pH: 7, D: 3

Aethiomastacembelus cf. *moori* 5/1060
Mottled spiny eel
H: Africa: Lake Tanganyika.   E
SD: Unknown.   S: =
B: Unsuccessful; prob. too large.   F: C
T: 20–24°C, L: 44 cm, pH: >7, D: 4

Aethiomastacembelus praesens 5/1060

H: Africa: Ghana: Prah River system.
SD: Unknown.   S: =
B: Unsuccessful.   F: C,O
T: 23–26°C, L: <20 cm, pH: <7, D: 2–3

Aethiomastacembelus shiranus 4/786
Shiran spiny eel
H: Africa: Lake Malawi.   E
SD: Unknown.   S: ?
B: Unsuccessful.   F: C
T: 23–27°C, L: 26 cm, pH: >7, D: 3

Afromastacembelus flavidus 3/1008

H: Africa: Lake Tanganyika. Very rare, E
SD: Unknown. S: =
B: Unsuccessful. F: C
T: 24–28°C, L: 27 cm, pH: >7, D: 3

Afromastacembelus moorii 2/1105
Mottled spiny eel

H: Africa: Lake Tanganyika.
SD: Unknown. S: –
B: Unsuccessful. F: C
T: 25–28°C, L: 44 cm, pH: >7, D: 3–4

Afromastacembelus plagiostomus 2/1106

H: Africa: Lake Tanganyika.
SD: Unknown. S: ?
B: Unsuccessful. F: C
T: 25–28°C, L: 35 cm, pH: >7, D: 3–4

Afromastacembelus tanganicae 3/1008
Tanganyikan spiny eel

H: Africa: Lake Tanganyika. E
SD: Unknown. S: =
B: Unsuccessful. F: C
T: 24–28°C, L: 19 cm, pH: >7, D: 3

Caecomastacembelus cryptacanthus
4/784

H: Africa: Cam., Nig., central Zaïre Basin.
SD: Unknown. S: –?
B: Algae nests? No brood care. F: C
T: 24–30°C, L: 25 cm, pH: 7, D: 3

Caecomastacembelus frenatus 4/784
Ladder-back spiny eel

H: Africa: Lake Tanganyika. E
SD: Unknown. S: –?
B: Unsuccessful. F: C
T: 23–27°C, L: 25 cm, pH: >7, D: 3

Macrognathus aculeatus 1/848

H: SE Asia: Thai., Sum., Moluccas, Bor., Java.
SD: Unknown. S: =
B: >1000 e; 1% salinity. F: C
T: 23–28°C, L: 35 cm, pH: 7, D: 3

Mastacembelus armatus 1/846
White-spotted spiny eel

H: SE Asia: India, Sri L., Thai., S China, Sum.
♀: Much fuller when ripe. S: =
B: Unsuccessful. 1% salinity. F: C
T: 22–28°C, L: 75 cm, pH: 7, D: 3

Mastacembelus armatus favus 5/1062
White-spotted spiny eel

Macrognathus circumcinctus 1/846
Half-banded spiny eel

H: SE Asia: SE Thailand.
SD: Unknown. S: =
B: See introduction of order. F: C
T: 24–27°C, L: 16 cm, pH: 7, D: 3

Macrognathus circumcinctus 5/1056
Half-banded spiny eel

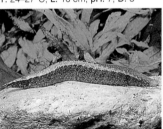

Macrognathus circumcinctus 5/1062
Half-banded spiny eel

Macrognathus circumcinctus   1/846
Half-banded spiny eel (yellow form)
H: SE Asia: SE Thailand.
SD: Unknown.   S: =
B: See introduction of order.   F: C
T: 24–28°C, L: 16 cm, pH: 7, D: 3

Mastacembelus erythrotaenia   1/848
Fire eel
H: SE Asia: Thai., Burma, Sumatra, Borneo.
♀: Fuller when ripe.   S: =
B: Unsuccessful. 1% salinity.   F: C
T: 24–28°C, L: 100 cm, pH: 7, D: 3

Mastacembelus zebrinus   1/848
Short-finned spiny eel, zebra spiny eel
H: SE Asia: Thailand: at Trang.
SD: Unknown.   S: =
B: Unsuccessful. 1% salinity.   F: C
T: 23–28°C, L: 9 (31) cm, pH: 7, D: 3

Mastacembelus zebrinus   3/1010
Short-finned spiny eel, zebra spiny eel

Monopterus albus   2/1158
East Asian swamp eel
H: Asia: from Japan to Thailand & Burma.
SD: Unknown.   S: −
B: Nat.: bubble nest; brood care.   F: C
T: 25–28°C, L: 90 cm, pH: 7, D: 3–4

Synbranchus marmoratus   2/1158
American swamp or American marbled eel
H: C and S America: S Mex. to S Brazil.
SD: Unknown.   S: −
B: Unknown.   F: C
T: 20–22°C, L: 150 cm, pH: 7, D: 3–4

Order Tetraodontiformes

The order of pufferlike fishes consists of 9 families, approximately 100 genera, and 339 species. Only 20 species are in some way affiliated with freshwater, 12 of them exclusively found in freshwater biotopes (NELSON, 1994).

Some families within the Tetraodontiformes such as the Tetraodontidae have developed a rather unique way to defend themselves: they fill their stomach with water, thereby inflating the body into a sphere so that it is too large for prospective predators. This defense mechanism makes them easily recognized, even to laypersons. Puffers removed from the water (e.g., while being handled in the aquarium) often fill their stomach with air. Caution! For some species this can have fatal consequences.

Eating puffer—fugu—is one of the great Japanese culinary traditions and one fraught with risk. The viscera and, at certain times of the year, the musculature are highly poisonous (tetrodotoxin = a nerve toxin). While chefs are especially trained to correctly eviscerate and prepare puffers, fatal accidents do occur.

The freshwater and brackish water species within the Tetraodontidae make interesting and exotic aquarium subjects. Unlike most fishes, puffers propel themselves with their pectorals. The dorsal and anal fins contribute when speed is of the essence. The caudal fin solely acts as a rudder and there are no ventral fins. The cute "facial expressions," the humanlike eye movements, and the ability to interact with the aquarist insure their continued popularity. Unfortunately, their intraspecific waspishness oftentimes spills over towards heterospecifics. Many species school while young, but turn territorial with age. Some species depend on brackish water for long-term care.

Triplespines, the family Triacanthidae, play an insignificant role in food fish and aquarium fish markets. *Triacanthus biaculeatus* (p. 922) should be kept in a marine aquarium as an adult.

Carinotetraodon lorteti t. ♀, b. ♂   1/866
Red-bellied puffer
H: SE Asia: Thailand.
♂: See photo.   S: –
B: Java moss; 350 e; remove ♂♀.   F: C
T: 24–28°C, L: 6.5 cm, pH: <7, D: 3

Chelichthys asellus   5/1101
Brazilian freshwater puffer
H: South America: W Brazil.
SD: Unknown.   S: =
B: Unsuccessful.   F: C
T: 22–28°C, L: 14 cm, pH: <7, D: 3

Chelonodon patoca 2/1160
Milk-spotted puffer
H: SE Africa to SE Asia, Australia,...
SD: Unknown. S: =
B: Unsuccessful. Brackish water. F: C!
T: 23–28°C, L: 25 cm, pH: >7, D: 3

Chonerhinus modestus 3/1040
Modest puffer
H: E Asia: S Thai., Malaysia, and Indonesia.
SD: Unknown. S: –
B: Unsuccessful. F: C,O
T: 23–28°C, L: 13 cm, pH: 7, D: 3

Colomesus psittacus 2/1160
South American puffer
H: S Am.: Venezuela, Guyana, Brazil, Peru.
SD: Unknown. S: =
B: Unsuccessful. F: C,O
T: 23–26°C, L: 25 cm, pH: 7, D: 3

Tetraodon biocellatus 1/868
Palembang puffer
H: SE Asia: Thailand, Malay Pen., Bor., Sum.
♂: Smaller, slimmer. S: –
B: Unknown. F: C
T: 22–26°C, L: 6 cm, pH: 7, D: 2–3

Tetraodon cf. *biocellatus* 5/1104
Palembang puffer

Tetraodon cutcutia 3/1040
Sea frog
H: Asia: India, Sri Lanka, Bangladesh.
♂: Larger, darker; nuptial coloration. S: –
B: Substrate spawner; P fam. F: C,O
T: 24–28°C, L: 8 cm, pH: 7, D: 3

Tetraodon fahaka 2/1162
Nile puffer
H: Africa: Sen., Gam., Nig., Nile, Chad,...
SD: Unknown. S: –
B: Nat.: at greater depths. F: C
T: 24–26°C, L: 45 cm, pH: 7, D: 3

Tetraodon fangi 5/1102
Fang's puffer
H: Asia.
♂: More colorful? S: –
B: N.: substrate spawner; P fam. F: C
T: 20–25°C, L: 10 cm? pH: 7, D: 3–4

Tetraodon fangi 5/1102
Fang's puffer
Spawning.

Tetraodon leiurus brevirostris 2/1162
Twin-spot puffer
H: SE Asia: probably Thailand.
♀: Opposite colors when spawning. S: –
B: Open spawner; 300–500 e; P fam. F: C
T: 24–28°C, L: 12 cm, pH: 7, D: 3

Tetraodon mbu 2/1164
Giant puffer
H: Africa: central and lower Congo.
SD: Unknown. S: –
B: Unsuccessful. F: C
T: 24–26°C, L: 75 cm, pH: 7, D: 4

Tetraodon miurus 2/1164
Congo puffer
H: Africa: central and lower Congo.
SD: Unknown. S: –
B: Unsuccessful. F: C
T: 24–28°C, L: 15 cm, pH: 7, D: 4

BONY FISHES

921

Tetraodon nigroviridis　　　　1/866
Green puffer
H: SE Asia: Indonesia, Sumatra, Borneo.
SD: Unknown.　　　　　　　　　S: –
B: Substrate spawner; Bw; P fam.　F: C,O
T: 24–28°C, L: 17 cm, pH: 7, D: 3

Tetraodon schoutedeni　　　　1/868
Spotted Congo puffer
H: Africa: lower Zaïre: Stanley Pool.
♂: Much smaller.　　　　　　　S: =
B: Open/substrate spawner; P fam.　F: C
T: 22–26°C, L: 10 cm, pH: 7, D: 3

Tetraodon sp.　　　　　　　　5/1102
Puffer
H: Asia.　　　　　　　　　　0.5% Bw
SD: Unknown.　　　　　　　　　S: –
B: Unsuccessful.　　　　　　　　F: C
T: 20–25°C, L: 12 cm, pH: 7, D: 3–4

Tetraodon sp.　　　　　　　　5/1106
Dwarf puffer
H: Asia: India: Ganges and its tributaries.
SD: Unknown.　　　　　　　　　S: –
B: Unsuccessful.　　　　　　　　F: C
T: 24–26°C, L: 8 cm, pH: >7, D: 3–4

Tetraodon travancorius　　　　5/1105
Malabar puffer
H: Asia: India, Burma.　　　　Fw, Bw.
SD: Unknown.　　　　　　　　　S: =
B: Unsuccessful.　　　　　　　　F: C
T: 22–28°C, L: 15 cm, pH: 7, D: 3

Triacanthus biaculeatus　　　　5/1109
H: Persian Gulf, Gulf of Oman, China, Ja-
pan, Philippines, Australia. >0.5% Bw.
SD: Unknown.　　　　　　　　　S: =
B: Unknown.　　　　　　　　　　F: C
T: 20–30°C, L: 20 cm, pH: >7, D: 4

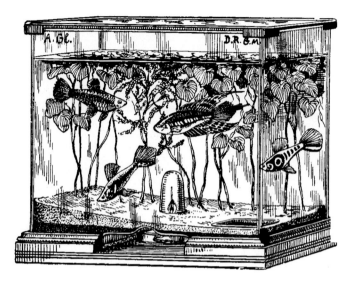

General Abbreviations

Striving to provide high informational content in a limited space without having to recur to pictographs, the repeated use of abbreviations became unavoidable. Abbreviations typical of a certain group, are listed at the introduction to that group.
In the INDEX the following abbreviations are used under the various headings:

Scientific name:
cf.: [confero = compare] it is most likely the pictured specimen corresponds to this species, but there is no total certainty, because there are some differences.
sp. aff.: [species, affinis = close to , affinity] The pictured specimen is very similar to the named species, but it is a different, not yet described species.

t.: top   b.: bottom   l.: left   r.: right

Breeding:					Habitat:	
e	eggs	Cs	Cave spawner		N	north, northern
y	young	Os	Open spawner		E	east, eastern
d	days	N fam	Nuclear family		S	south, southern
dg	days gestation	P fam	Paternal family		W	west, western
ws	weeks storage	M fam	Maternal family			

Abbreviations

Habitat:

CIS States. The commonwealth of independent states (the states of the former Sowiet Union, located in Europe and Asia).

Africa (Af.):

B.F.	Burkina Faso	Ivory C.	Ivory Coast
Cam.	Cameroon	Lib.	Liberia
C.Af.Rep.	Central African Republic	Moz.	Mozambique
		Nig.	Nigeria
Eq.Gui.	Equatorial Guinea	S. Af.	South Africa
Egy.	Egypt	Sen.	Senegal
Eth.	Ethiopia	S.L.	Sierra Leone
Gab.	Gabon	Sud.	Sudan
Gam.	Gambia	Tan.	Tanzania
Gold C.	Gold Coast	Zam.	Zambia
Guin.	Guinea	Zim.	Zimbabwe

America (Am.):

Arg.	Argentina	Mex.	Mexico
Bol.	Bolivia	Nic.	Nicaragua
Col.	Colombia	Pan.	Panama
C.R.	Costa Rica	Par.	Paraguay
Ec.	Ecuador	Sal.	El Salvador
Fr. Gu.	French Guiana	Sur.	Suriname
Gua.	Guatemala	Tri.	Trinidad
Guy.	Guyana	Uru.	Uruguay
Hond.	Honduras	Ven.	Venezuela

Asia:

Bngl.	Bangladesh	Malay Pen.	Malay Peninsula
Bor.	Borneo	Pak.	Pakistan
Bur.	Burma (Myanmar)	Sing.	Singapore
Camb.	Cambodia	Sri L.	Sri Lanka
Indon.	Indonesia	Sum.	Sumatra (Sumatera)
Kal.	Kalimantan	Thai.	Thailand
Mala.	Malaysia	Viet.	Vietnam

Fins (f.):

A	Anal fin
D	Dorsal fin
D_1	Anterior dorsal fin
D_2	Posterior dorsal fin
C	Caudal fin
P	Pectoral fins
V	Ventral fins

Others:

&	and
E	Endemic
N. or Nat.	In nature
WC	wild caught
Fw	Freshwater
Bw	Brackish water
Mw	Marine water

Temperature

$$°F = (°C \times 1.8) + 32 \qquad °C = (°F - 32) \div 1.8$$

°C	°F	°C	°F	°C	°F	°C	°F	°C	°F
0	32	15	59	21	70	27	81	50	122
10	50	16	61	22	72	28	82	60	140
11	52	17	63	23	73	29	84	70	158
12	54	18	64	24	75	30	86	80	176
13	55	19	66	25	77	35	95	90	194
14	57	20	68	26	79	40	104	100	212

Volume

$$gal = l \div 3.785 \qquad l = 3.785 \times gal$$

l	gal	l	gal	l	gal	l	gal	l	gal
1	0.26	15	3.96	70	18.5	250	66	550	145
2	0.53	20	5.28	80	21.1	300	79	600	158
3	0.79	30	7.93	90	23.8	350	92	700	185
4	1.06	40	10.57	100	26.4	400	106	800	211
5	1.32	50	13.21	150	39.6	450	119	900	238
10	2.64	60	15.85	200	79.3	500	132	1000	379

Length

$$1m = 100 \text{ cm} = 1000 \text{ mm} \qquad 1yd = 3 \text{ ft} = 36 \text{ in}$$
$$in = cm \div 2.54 \qquad cm = in \times 2.54 \qquad ft = m \div 0.305 \qquad m = 0.305 \times ft$$

mm	in	cm	in	cm	in	m	ft	m	ft
0.5	0.02	1	0.4	30	12	1	3.3	70	230
1	0.04	2	0.8	35	14	2	6.6	80	262
2	0.08	3	1.1	40	16	3	9.8	90	295
3	0.12	4	1.6	45	18	4	13.1	100	328
4	0.16	5	2.0	50	20	5	16.4	200	656
5	0.20	6	2.4	60	24	10	32.8	300	984
6	0.24	7	2.8	70	28	15	49.2	400	1310
7	0.28	8	3.1	80	31	20	65.6	500	1640
8	0.32	9	3.5	90	35	25	82.0	600	1970
9	0.35	10	3.9	100	39	30	98.4	700	2300
		15	5.9	125	49	40	131.1	800	2620
		20	7.9	150	59	50	163.9	900	2950
		25	9.8	175	69	60	196.7	1000	3280

General Glossary

Some of the terms in this glossary are not used in the INDEX. These are terms used in the various volumes of the AQUARIUM ATLAS.

Abdomen: Body cavity containing the viscera. In arthropods, the body section behind the thorax or cephalothorax (the "tail").

Adhesive spawner: Mode of reproduction where the eggs are adhered randomly among plants (e.g., killifishes). Sometimes also called ʌǀ egg scatterer (especially in regard to characins and cyprinids).

Agamic: Without pair bond; fish which do not form attachments with their mates before, during, or after spawning. This type of reproductive behavior is common in ʌǀ mbuna cichlids.

Amoeba: Microscopic, one-celled animal consisting of a naked mass of protoplasm constantly changing in shape as it moves and engulfs food (extending pseudopodia). Under unfavorable conditions it forms a ʌǀ cyst. They can be both harmless inhabitants of the intestine as well as parasites. The amoeba reproduces by partition.

Anadromous: Fish that live most of its adult life in the sea, but migrates to freshwater to spawn (e.g., salmon). ʌǀ Catadromous

Andropodium: Gonopodium. A modified fin that acts as a copulatory organ for some species of male fishes. Commonly found in Poeciliidae.

Anemia: A condition marked by a significant decrease in the hemoglobin concentration and in the number of circulating red blood cells. Oxygen transport is impaired. Anemia can be caused by loss of blood, an unbalanced production of red blood cells, removal of red blood cells, and vitamin and/or iron deficiency. Iron is a constituent of hemoglobin.

Antibiotic: Any of a large group of chemicals, e.g., penicillin or streptomycin, produced by various microorganisms and fungi, which have the capacity in dilute solutions to inhibit the growth or destroy bacteria and other microorganisms; used chiefly in the treatment of infectious diseases

Ascites: An abnormal accumulation of serous fluid in the abdominal cavity. Dropsy of the peritoneum.

Ascorbic Acid: Vitamin C. This vitamin is a water soluble substance that is essential for most fish species. While it serves many function in the body and symptoms of deficiency are manifest differently from species to species, some of the more common symptoms are ʌǀ lordosis, ʌǀ scoliosis, reduced hematocrit, hemorrhages, ʌǀ ascites, and deformed opercula. Vitamin C is very heat labile. Storage, alkaline media, and oxidation also act to decrease the potency of this substance.

Asphyxia: Suffocation due to lack of oxygen. It can be caused by certain infirmities or chemical substances that impair oxygen uptake or transport. Physically preventing an organism from breathing also results in asphyxiation.

Assimilation: Conversion of nutritive materials into protoplasm.

Atrophy: Wasting away or degeneration of the body or an organ or part thereof, as from defective nutrition or other cause.

Aufwuchs: Biocover. Largely, the layer of filamentous algae growing on hard substrates and the associated tiny invertebrates living within. Many fishes have specialized morphological adaptations that allow them to efficiently feed upon this layer.

Bacteria: Any of a group of single-celled microorganisms of the kingdom Monera characterized by their lack of a nucleus. Their cell wall is mainly composed of peptidoglycan, unlike plants whose cell walls are of cellulose. Bacteria are one of three shapes: bacillus (rod-shaped), coccus (spherical), or spirillum (spiral). Depending on the bacteria, they are either beneficial (e.g., fermentation, intestinal flora), harmless, or pathogenic (disease causing).

Benthic: Of, pertaining to, or living on the bottom or at the greatest depths of a large body of water. Also benthonic.

Biotope: A particular ecological area a species inhabits.

Black Water: Waters that are dark brown, appearing black from a distance. The color is due to dissolved organic humic substances. This water is characteristically poor in dissolved ions with an acidic pH of approximately 4.5. The Rio Negro, the largest tributary of the Amazon, is a black water river.

Bottom Spawner: Mode of reproduction where the eggs are deposited in the bottom substrate and there is no associated brood care. Usually called ^| substrate spawner in killifishes.

Brackish Water: Water with a salinity between 0.05% and 1.7%. It contains less salt than marine water, but is still undrinkable. This type of water is mostly found in estuaries and in general close to the sea.

Brood Care: Care of eggs and offspring which may include guarding, guiding the young, fanning the eggs, and/or mouthbrooding. Which gender (one or both) preforms what duties is generally a standard characteristic of the species.

By-Catch: Fishes inadvertently packed with shipments of other species.

Carapace: A chitinous shield (^| chitin) or shell that covers the ^| cephalothorax of many arthropods.

Catadromous: Fish that live most of their adult lives in freshwater, but enter the sea to spawn (e.g., American eel). ^| Anadromous

Catalyst: A substance that alters the speed of a reaction, and may be recovered essentially unaltered in form and amount at the end of the reaction. ^| Enzyme

Caudal: Toward, belonging to, or pertaining to the tail or posterior end, especially in regard to fishes.

Cave Spawner: A species that lays its eggs inside a cave or similarly protected site. The eggs are typically adhered by their pole or side, colorful, relatively large, and few in number (rarely over 200). Males are usually larger and more colorful than females.

Cephalothorax: The body segment found in spiders and some crustacea consisting of a fused head and thorax.

Chitin: A white or colorless amorphous (without shape) polysaccharide (multiple sugar) that forms a base for the hard outer layers of crustacea, insects, and other invertebrates. The rigid exoskeleton (shell) the organism creates with chitin cannot grow with the animal; therefore, the animal must shed the exoskeleton in a periodical process called molting.

Cilia: Relatively short, centriole-based, hairlike processes on certain anatomical cells and mobile organisms. Some unicellular and small multicellular organisms move by beating cilia.

Ciliates: Members of the phylum Ciliata. All are unicellular organisms and, as implied by their name, have numerous ^\l cilia. Unlike other protozoans, ciliates have two types of nuclei—a ^\l macronucleus and a ^\l micronucleus.

Commensalism: A relationship between two different species, whereby one is benefited and the other is neither benefited nor harmed.

Congener: A member of a different species or not, but within the same genus.

Conspecific: A member of the same species.

Contagious: In relation to infirmities, one that is transmissible either by direct or indirect contact.

Cosmopolitan: Having a worldwide distribution where ever the habitat is suitable, with reference to the geographical distribution of a ^\l taxon.

Cranial: The anterior end of an organism (toward the cranium = skull)

Cyclops: A freshwater copepod of the genus *Cyclops*, that has a median eye in front of the body. These crustacea are often cultured or harvested from ponds or lakes as food for fish fry.

Cyst: A normal or pathologic sac with a distinct wall that contains gas, a semisolid, or a fluid substance; sometimes, the larval stage of an organism.

Demersal: Organisms (generally fishes and/or their eggs) that exist on or near the bottom in aquatic environments.

Detergent: A synthetic cleansing agent resembling soap in its ability to emulsify oil and hold dirt. Do not use to clean aquaria or its accessories, as it damages the surface mucous layer of fishes.

dGH: Total hardness measured on the scale of degrees of German hardness. This value is a reflection of the amount of calcium and magnesium ions. One degree of German hardness is equivalent to 17.9 ppm $CaCO_3$.

Diadromous: An ability to migrate between freshwater and seawater or vice versa.

Diapause: A period of suspended development (very low metabolic rate) known to occur during the embryonal development of many egg-laying Cyprinodontiformes (and other organisms). There it is caused by changes in oxygen concentration. An initial lowering of the concentration stops metabolism (1st diapause) after some initial development. It is reinitiated when oxygen levels rise (air into the substrate as the dry season is entered). Prior to hatching (into a dry environment) a second diapause occurs. It concludes with a lowering in oxygen concentration as water returns to the habitat and microbial activity begins to deplete the available oxygen.

Dichromatism: Within a species, the occurrence of two forms distinct in coloration but similar in other aspects, particularly gender related (sexual dichromatism).

Diffuser: Porous terminal section of an airline to break the continuous airstream into small bubbles to increase the air-water interface and contact time.

Digenetic Worms: Parasitic, hermaphroditic flatworms or flukes of the class Trematoda. They have both sexual and asexual reproductive phases in their life cycle, hence the name digenetic.

Dimorphism: The occurrence of two forms distinct in structure, coloration, etc., among animals of the same species, particularly due to sex (sexual dimorphism).

Dinoflagellates: Members of the division Pyrrhophyta. These unicellular organisms have two flagella, one of which propels the organism forward while the other, transverse to the first, spins the cell. Present in both fresh and salt water. They reproduce through cellular division.

Diurnal: Active during the day.

DNA: Deoxyribonucleic Acid. A nucleic acid which forms genes. Hence, it is the substance by which genetic characteristics are passed on from a parent organism to its offspring and, on a cellular level, maintains the information when cells undergo division. Chiefly found in the nucleus of cells.

Dorsal: Located on or near the back (e.g., dorsal fin). ⁁| Ventral

Dropsy: The abnormal accumulation of fluids in body cavities, cells, and tissues. May be caused by certain infirmities that disrupt the normal fluid exchange processes of the organism.

Ectoparasite: External ⁁| parasite (e.g. *Ichthyophthirius multifiliis* = white spot).

General Glossary

Egg scatterer: Mode of reproduction where the eggs are scattered randomly, usually among fine-leaved plants. There is no associated brood care. ^l adhesive spawner

Egg Spot Method: Many cichlid species have a design on their anal fin which is reminiscent of eggs (e.g., mbuna in Lake Malawi). As a mouthbrooding female tries to collect those "eggs" as part of the spawning sequence, she inhales sperm, thereby fertilizing the eggs already contained in her mouth.

Endemic: Indigenous. Particular to a certain, relatively restricted, geographical range (e.g., endemic to a particular lake).

Enzyme: A protein that acts as a ^l catalyst. Since it is a protein, an enzyme can be denatured by heat, certain chemicals, etc. Its function is then lost, as its shape is often the key to its catalytic nature.

Epidermis: The outer nonsensitive, nonvascular portion of the skin comprised of two strata of cells. The outermost layer of cells of an animal or plant.

Epithelium: A primary animal tissue, distinguished by it having tightly packed cells with little ^l intercellular substance; covers free surfaces and lines body cavities and ducts.

Estuary: Where the river's mouth meets the sea. This biotope is typically nutrient rich, supporting many organisms. But due to salt water meeting freshwater, it is a difficult environment for organisms to live in because of its fluctuating chemical and physical characteristics.

Facultative: Not required, optional. A few fishes are facultative parasites, for example, some scale-eaters. In an aquarium, where food is readily available, they may change their diet and leave tankmates alone.

Flagellum (*pl.* flagella): A long hairlike locomotory organelle that emerges off centrioles.

Flagellate: An organism that has flagella. A member of the protozoan superclass Mastigophora.

Gill Rakers: Bony or cartilaginous structures on the inner margins of the gill arches. They are generally adapted to the species' main diet. For example, planktivores typically have long, fine, closely placed gill rakers, while piscivores have short, widely spaced structures.

Gamete: A cell which participates in fertilization and development of a new organism. Also known as a germ cell or sex cell.

Gram's Stain: A differential bacteriological stain; a fixed smear is stained with a slightly alkaline solution of basic dye, treated with a solution of iodine in potassium iodide, then with a neutral decolorizing agent, and usually counterstained. Bacteria stain either blue (gram-positive) or red (gram-negative). Many gram-positive bacteria are successfully treated with penicillin and sulfonamide based drugs, while gram-negative bacteria are generally combated with tetracycline, streptomycin, and chloramphenicol.

Granuloma: A discrete nodular lesion of inflammatory tissue in which granulation is significant.

Hemoglobin: The iron-containing, oxygen-carrying molecule of red blood cells of vertebrates.

Hermaphrodites: An individual with both male and female reproductive organs.

Heterogener: Members of different genera. ^| Congeners

Heterospecific: Different species of the same or different genera.

Histology: Biological science dedicated to the study of tissues.

Hormone: A chemical messenger produced by endocrine glands and secreted in minute quantities directly into the bloodstream to exert a specific effect on a distant part of the body. Every hormone has an "antihormone," the balance between the two is the regulatory mechanism (e.g., adrenaline, noradrenaline; insulin, glucagon). In aquaculture, the injection of hormones of the hypophysis into fishes in order to artificially breed them is a common practice and a conditions sine qua non for most of the migratory species (*Colossoma* sp., some cyprinids, catfishes, etc.)

Host: An organism on or in which a ^| parasite lives. The dominant partner in a ^| symbiotic or ^| commensal relationship.

Immunity: The ability of a living organism to resist and overcome an infection or a disease.

Infection: Invasion of the body by a pathogenic organism, with or without disease manifestation.

Infusoria: Any of various microscopic organisms found in infusions of decaying organic matter. They are motile and feed on bacteria, microscopic algae, and microorganisms. The hobbyist can produce his own infusions at home with made with banana peels or hay. Infusoria represent a necessary first food for tiny fry, which cannot yet feed on ground flake food or brine shrimp nauplii.

Intercellular: Between the cells.

Interspecific: Interaction between different species.

Intraspecific: Interaction among the members of one species.

KH or dKH: The German scale to measure carbonate hardness or the quantitative amounts of carbonate or bicarbonate. One degree of German hardness is equivalent to 17 ppm $CaCO_3$.

Lacustrine: Living or growing in lakes.

Larvophile Mouthbrooder: Fish species that incubates its larvae in its buccal cavity. In general the eggs are laid and fertilized on hard ^| substrates. The fish then guards the spawn until the larvae hatch, or frees the larvae from the egg membrane, then takes the spawn into its buccal cavity to incubate them until they are free-swimming. ^| Ovophile Mouthbrooder

Latent: Present but not visible or apparent. Existing in concealed or dormant form, but potentially able to achieve expression.

Lentic: Of or pertaining to still waters such as lakes, reservoirs, ponds, and bogs. ^| Lotic

Lifecycle: The series of changes an organism goes through from its initial stages of life until maturity or death.

Littoral Zone: The shore of a lake, sea, or ocean.

Lotic: Pertaining to or living in flowing water. ^| Lentic

Macronucleus: The larger nucleus found in multinucleated protozoans that controls the cell's metabolism.

Macroscopic: Large enough to be observed by the naked eye. ^| Microscopic

Maternal Family: This family structure is only found among mouthbrooders. Brood care is fully the responsibility of the female and is fulfilled outside the male's territory. The bond of the breeding pair is limited to the reproductive act itself (^| agamic). The majority of Lake Malawi cichlids have a maternal family structure.

Mbuna: A group of Lake Malawi cichlids which generally live in close association to a rocky biotope. Other characteristics include comparatively fewer scales about the head, ocelli (egg spots) on the anal fin (most notably on males), and one functional ovary.

Membrane: Thin layer that limits the ^| cytoplasm and gives a certain independence to the cell. It maintains the hydric (water) and ionic (potassium, sodium, chlorine) equilibrium. A thin layer of tissue surrounding a part of the body, separating adjacent cavities, lining cavities, or connecting adjacent structures.

Meristic Values: The values obtained after an organism has been divided into measurable segments; they can be used to characterize a species.

Micronucleus: The smaller nucleus concerned with reproduction in multinucleated protozoans.

Microscopic: Visible only under a microscope. ^| Macroscopic

Mimicry: A system of protection gained through adaptation when one species resembles another in behavior and appearance. The species being mimicked generally has an unpleasant, protective property in the face of predators—e.g., venom, spines, or an unpalatable flavor. Hence, the mimic is avoided because of the attributes of the species it is mimicking.

Miracida: A ciliated larval stage of digenetic worms that penetrates the tissue of an intermediate host (e.g., snails) and develops into a second larval stage, a sporocyst, therein. This stage can then infect a fish.

Monogenetic Fluke: Parasitic flukes which are most commonly found on the gills and skin of fish. Unlike digenetic flukes, these animals do not have an intermediate host, hence the name monogenetic. Some species are egg layers, while others are viviparous. The entire life of the latter is spent on its host.

Monotypic: A taxon whose immediate subordinate taxon is not divided (i.e., a monotypic genus is made up of only one species).

Morph: Form. A group of individuals within a species that share common characteristics—such as a particular coloration pattern—but generally separated from other morphs by geographic barriers and not genetics. The differences are not relevant enough to confer the state of subspecies to the population.

Mouthbrooder: A fish which takes its eggs (^| ovophile) and/or larvae (^| larvophile) into its buccal cavity and cares for them in such a manner, generally until they are free-swimming.

Nauplii (*sin.* nauplius): The first free-swimming larval stage of some crustacea.

Necrosis: Pathologic death of living plant or animal tissue.

Niche: The role or position of an organism in an ecosystem. A cranny or crevice.

Nocturnal: Active at night.

Nominate Species: The species which served as the basis for the establishment of subspecies. Its subspecies name is a repetition of its species name (e.g., *Symphysodon aequifasciatus aequifasciatus*, the brown discus)

Nuclear Family: Both sexes participate in brood care, whereby the male's activity is mostly centered in defending the territory. After the young are free-swimming, both parents guide the offspring. Typically, these species are monogamous (e.g., *Symphysodon, Geophagus*) and the sexual differences are slight.

Nuptial Tubercles: The presence of dermal nodules, generally on the ^| cranial region of a cyprinid male, during the period of sexual activity. Their appearance is similar to the white spots caused by ich, but usually much larger and localized.

Obligatory: Required, compulsory.

Odontodes: Bristlelike appendages found on the body scutes and fin spines mostly of catfishes in the family Loricariidae and Callichthyidae. They cover most of the body or are concentrated in patches (e.g., giving the appearance of a beard).

Oocysts: Encysted zygote found in some Sporozoa.

Oospore: A diploid spore produced by heterogamous fertilization. It then passes through meiosis to produce haploid spores which produce the gametophytes.

General Glossary

Open Spawner: A species which adheres its eggs onto an exposed substrate (sometimes also called ⌃I substrate spawner). The eggs are relatively small, cryptically colored, and numerous (up to 10000). They are adhered by their long axis. ⌃I Sexual dimorphism is slight, e.g., *Symphysodon, Pterophyllum*) and there is associated brood care.

Ovophile Mouthbrooder: Fish species that incubates its eggs and larvae in its buccal cavity until the fry are free-swimming. The eggs are usually grabbed in mid-water and fertilization occurs intrabuccally. ⌃I Larvophile Mouthbrooder

Paedogenesis: The process by which gametes produced by one protozoan can fertilize each other—a type of autogamy.

Papilla (*pl.* papillae): A small, nipplelike eminence. Often the morphology of the genital papilla is the only external feature that permits males to be distinguished from females.

Parasite: Organism which lives on or in another organism (⌃I host) to its detriment. An organism that generally derives its nutrients from another organism.

Parasitism: Relationship between two organisms, where the benefit of one (⌃I parasite) is in detriment of the other (⌃I host).

Paternal Family: This family is the "sexual opposite" of the ⌃I maternal family. To date, only few species—e.g., the mouthbrooding cichlid *Sarotherodon melanotheron*—has been found to have a true paternal family structure. Following oviposition, the female relinquishes all responsibility of the spawn to the male.

Paternal-Maternal Family: A family structure very much like that of the ⌃I nuclear family, but the eggs are the exclusive responsibility of the female. After the young are free-swimming, both sexes guide the offspring (e.g., *Pelvicachromis*).

Pathogenic: Disease causing.

Patriarch-Maternal Family: Social order in which the male claims a super-territory that encompasses several small female spawning territories. The polygamous male defends all the territories, but does not participate directly in the care of the individual spawns. Males are larger and more colorful (e.g., *Apistogramma* and *Nannacara*).

Pelagic: Inhabiting the open water column, beyond the limits of the ⌃I littoral zone.

Petricolous: Organisms which live in or among rocks.

Pigment: Any coloring matter in animal and plant cells.

Pharyngeal Teeth: Teeth found on the pharyngeal bone (throat) of many fishes. It aids in the grinding of foodstuffs.

Planaria: Any flatworm of the turbellarian order Tricladida; the body is broad and dorsoventrally flattened, with anterior lateral projections, the auricles, and a pair of eyespots on the anterior dorsal surface. Planarians can turn into a pest in aquaria, particularly in breeding setups, since they will feed on the eggs.

Plankton: Organisms that drift or weakly swim in oceanic or freshwater currents. They are incapable of any but the most nominal directional mobility.

Polygamy (*adj.* polygamous): Having more than one sexual partner. This mating system has two forms—polyandry and polygyny. In the former, one female mates with many males, while in the latter, one male mates with many females. Polygamy is by far the more common of the two in the animal world.

Proboscis: A long, flexible snout or trunk; a nose.

Procercariae: The product of the asexual reproductive phase of digenetic worms which penetrates fish. They in turn become metacercariae.

Procercoid: A parasitic larvae of certain eucestodes (tapeworms) that develops in the body of an intermediate host.

Protein: Chemical compounds essential for life. The animal body ^l assimilates them for growth. Some groups of fishes (carnivores such as salmonids) cannot use proteins of vegetal origin, requiring those of animal origin, mainly fish. Other have a digestive system highly adapted (i.e., long intestines) to digest vegetable sources of protein (herbivores such as many tilapia and loricariids). The most expensive component of commercial fish diets.

Purulent: Containing or secreting pus.

Pyridoxine: Vitamin B_6. Essential for all fish. Vitamin B_6 is synthesized by plants and some microorganisms. Deficiency symptoms include nervous disorders, poor swimming coordination, convulsions, and rapid breathing.

Riboflavin: Vitamin B_2. Essential for all nonruminant animals. Sources include yeast, green plants, and grains. Deficiencies are manifested in abnormalities of the eyes, poor growth, and dark pigmentation.

Riverine: Of or pertaining to a river.

Scoliosis: Lateral curvature of the spine.

Scutes: Bony plates along the body of some species of fishes, i.e., catfishes and sturgeons. They are more firmly attached than scales.

Sporangium (*pl.* sporangia): A structure in which spores are produced.

Spore: A unicellular or multicellular, asexual resting body that is resistant to unfavorable environmental conditions and produces a new vegetative individual when the environment is favorable.

General Glossary

Substrate: The base or material on which an organism lives.

Substrate Spawner: Also called ^l Open spawner for cichlids and characins. In killifishes it denotes the laying of eggs into the bottom substrate (usually a layer of peat in the aquarium) not on it.

Subterritory: A territory, generally established by a female dwarf cichlid for breeding, within a larger, usually male, ^l superterritory.

Superterritory: Some fishes, i.e., dwarf cichlids, establish several small territories (^l subterritories) within the framework of one large superterritory. In the case *Apistogramma caetei*, several sexually active females maintain territories within the large superterritory of the male. These females are considered part or the male's harem.

Symbiosis: A mutually beneficial association of two dissimilar organisms. Generally one individual receives protection in exchange for providing food for its partner.

Sympatric: Occupying the same range as another species but maintaining identity by not interbreeding.

Taxon: A taxonomic entity such as genus, species, etc.

Thiamine: Vitamin B_1. Essential for all animals except ruminants, as the microbes in their digestive tract synthesize it for them. Synthesized by higher plants, microorganisms, and some lower plants. Since thiamine has been isolated in nerve membranes and is suspected of participating in sodium transport, deficiency symptoms include convulsions, loss of equilibrium, edema, and poor growth.

Trematodes: A term for parasitic flatworms of the phylum Platyhelminthes.

Type Species: Species on which the definition of a genus is based.

Ulcer: An inflamed lesion on the skin or internal mucous surface of the body, typified by tissue necrosis.

Ulcerated: Having ^l ulcers or ulcerlike lesions.

Unicellular: A one-celled organism.

Variety: A taxonomic group or category inferior in rank to a subspecies.

Ventral: On or belonging to the lower surface of a fish (e.g., ventral fins), that is, opposite to the back. ^l Dorsal.

Virulent: Extremely poisonous or pathogenic.

Viviparous: Bearing live offspring.

Xanthochroism or Xanthochromism: A variation in color in which an organism's normal pigmentation is replaced by yellow pigments.

Zoospores: Mobile, ciliated or flagellated asexual spores.

The botanical section of the glossary refers to technical terms used in the aquarium plant descriptions contained in the AQUARIUM ATLAS, Vols. 1–3.

The INDEX does not present these plant species.

Acuminate: In reference to a ↑ blade, one that gradually tapers to a prolonged point.

Acute: In reference to a ↑ blade, one that ends in a sharp point.

Adventitious plants: Plants that develop on an unusual site, e.g., on ⌐| stolons or ↑ rhizomes. Also ↑ daughter plants.

Alternate: Having one leaf or bud at a node. Placed singly at different heights on the stem. ⌐| Opposite

Apex: Tip or extremity.

Axil: The superior angle where a leaf or twig emerges from the main stem.

Axis: The main or central line of development of a plant or organ; the stem.

Blade: The expanded portion of a leaf. The "leaf" without its "stem" (⌐| petiole).

Bract: A much-reduced leaf, particularly one of the small or scalelike leaves of a flower cluster or one of those associated with an ↑inflorescence.

Bullate: Having a wafflelike or blistered appearance.

Calyx: Outer whorl of floral envelopes. Collective term for sepals.

Capitate: Aggregated into a dense or compact cluster or head.

Carpel: One of the foliar units of a compound pistil. A simple pistil has one carpel.

Clasping: Property of the basal portion of a leaf or other organ that partly or entirely surrounds a stem or other structure.

Cleistogamous: Fertilization occurring within an unopened flower.

Collar: Part of a cryptocoryne flower. Rim on the ⌐| spathe between the ⌐| flag and ⌐| throat.

Compound leaf: A blade that is divided into distinct parts.

Cordate: A blade having the shape of a heart, with the point away from the base.

Corolla: Collectively the ⌐| petals of a flower.

Crown: Corona. A crownlike appendage, especially one on the inner part of a corolla.

Curvinervate: Leaf venation that is arched or curved.

Cuspidate: Tipped with a sharp point.

Botanical Glossary

Cutting: A section of a plant, usually a stem, used to propagate a plant.

Cyme: A flat-topped inflorescence in which the central section of flowers opens first or lateral branches continue to grow, adding to the inflorescence concentrically.

Daughter plants: Form of asexual reproduction, where a small plant develops on a mother plant. Later, as the new plant grows its own roots, the connection between the two plants degenerates. ^| Adventitious plants

Dioeceous: Unisexual with staminate and pistillate flowers on different plants.

Dentate: Margin of a ^| blade that is toothed, with teeth pointing outward.

Elliptical: Oval or oblong with rounded ends.

Entire: A ^| blade with an even margin.

Fimbriate: Having a margin of hairs or filiform processes.

Flag: Part of a cryptocoryne flower. The superior part of the spathe above the collar when present.

Gibbous: Swollen on one side.

Glabrous: Without hairs, nude.

Glands: A swollen section or projection.

Hypha: One of the filaments composing the ^| mycelium of a fungus.

Inflorescence: A flower cluster.

Internode: The section of stem between two nodes.

Kettle: The basal part of the flower that sits upon the peduncle of cryptocorynes. It houses the stamens and ovaries.

Lamina (*pl.* Laminae): The ^| blade of a leaf.

Lanceolate: Narrow, tapering at both ends, with the widest point closer to the base.

Leaflets: One of the blades of a compound leaf.

Linear: Long and narrow with parallel margins.

Mycelium: A mass of filaments or hyphae composing the vegetative body of many fungi.

Natant: Floating.

Obtuse: Blunt or rounded at the end.

Opposite: Bearing two leaves or buds at one node 180° from each other. ↑Alternate.

Ovary: The section of the ^| pistil within which the seeds develop.

Ovate: Shaped like the outline of a chicken egg with the broad end towards the base.

Botanical Glossary

Paliform: Spade-shaped, ^l spatulate.

Papillose: Having many tiny, nipple-shaped projections.

Pedicel: Stalk of a flower.

Peduncle: Stem of a solitary flower or the main stem of an inflorescence.

Pedunculate: Borne on a ^l peduncle.

Peltate: Attached to its petiole inside the leaf margin.

Petal: One unit of a corolla.

Petiole: The stem of a leaf.

Phyllodia: A ^l petiole with the form and function of a leaf.

Pilose: Having hairs.

Pinna: A leaflet of a fern leaf or a main division of a pinnate leaf.

Pinnate: Featherlike. Having leaflets arranged on opposite sides of an axis.

Pistil: The female part of the flower that contains the ovule. Made up of the ^l sigma, ^l style, and ^l ovary.

Postrate: Lying flat on the ground.

Procumbent: Trailing or lying flat upon the ground but not rooting.

Rhizome: An underground stem.

Rosette: A circular cluster of leaves, usually at or near the ground.

Runner: A slender stem that lies prostrate upon the ground with roots at the nodes. It serves to vegetatively propagate the plant.

Serrate: Characteristic of a ^l blade having forward-pointing teeth along its margin.

Serrulate: Finely ^l serrate.

Sepal: One of the units of a ^l calyx. Basal flower part.

Seta (*pl.* setae): A bristlelike structure.

Sessile: Without a stalk or ^l petiole.

Sheath: A long or more or less tubular structure surrounding an organ or part.

Shoot: A young stem or sprout.

Simple Leaves: ^l Blade in one piece.

Sinuous: Having a wavy margin.

Spadix: A fleshy spike with tiny flowers surrounded or subtended by a ^l spathe.

Spathe: The sheath (bract) surrounding or subtending a ^l spadix.

Spatulate: A leaf with a rounded, obtuse tip that tapers towards the base with its widest part near the apex.

Botanical Glossary

Spike: An inflorescence consisting of a central stalk with ↗ sessile or nearly sessile flowers.

Stalked: Having a ↗ petiole (leaves) or a ↗ peduncle (flowers).

Stamen: The male, pollen-bearing part of a flower made up of a filament and an anther.

Staminoides: A sterile stamen or stamenlike organ.

Stigma: The part of the pistil that receives the pollen.

Stolon: A slender branch or runner that gives rise to a new plant when it produces roots and leaves. A form of ↗ vegetative propagation.

Style: The part of the ↗ pistil that lies between the ↗ ovary and ↗ stigma. Generally elongated.

Throat: Part of a cryptocoryne flower. A section of the ↗ spathe below the ↑collar, when present, but above the ↗ kettle.

Tuber: Enlarged, fleshy underground stem.

Umbel: A form of an indeterminate inflorescence in which the pedicels all emerge from the top of the peduncle and radiate outward, similar to the supports of an umbrella.

Undulate: Having a wavy margin.

Urtricle: A small capture bladder such as those found on bladderworts.

Vegetative Propagation (Reproduction): A form of asexual reproduction in which stems or other plant parts are capable of growing into complete plants.

Whorl: When several parts, e.g., leaves, all emerge from one point.

Bibliography

The following bibliography refers directly to the information contained in the INDEX. A more extensive reference can be found at the end of each AQUARIUM ATLAS. As a source of the individual species information, the five volumes of the AQUARIUM ATLAS are listed below (English editions are available):

Mergus Verlag GmbH, P.O. Box 86, 49302 Melle, Germany:

Riehl, R. and Baensch, H. A., 1997. Aquarien Atlas Vol. 1, 11th edition.

Baensch, H. A. and Riehl, R., 1993. Aquarien Atlas Vol. 2, 6th edition.

Riehl, R. and Baensch, H. A., 1996. Aquarien Atlas Vol. 3, 4th edition.

Baensch, H. A. and Riehl, R., 1995. Aquarien Atlas Vol. 4, 1st edition.

Baensch, H. A. and Riehl, R., 1997. Aquarien Atlas Vol. 5, 1st edition.

Allen, G.R., 1995. Rainbowfishes. Tetra Verlag, 49324 Melle, Germany.

Allen, G.R., 1991. Damselfishes of the World. Mergus Verlag GmbH, 49302 Melle, Germany.

Burgess, W.E., 1989. Freshwater and Marine Catfishes. T.F.H. Publications Inc., Neptune City, NJ 07753, USA.

Estevez, M., 1990. La Cachama – Cultivo en estanques. 4th edition. Litografía Cafetera Ltda, Manizales, Colombia.

Ferraris, C., Jr., 1991. Catfish in the Aquarium. Tetra Press, Morris Plains, NJ 07950, USA.

Fink, S.V. and Fink, W.L., 1981. Interrelationships of the ostariophysan fishes (Teleostei). J. Linn. Soc. (Zool.) 72(4): 297–353.

Fischer, G.W., 1991. Acclimation to captivity, predatory characteristics and production economics of Tucunare, *Cichla monoculus* (Spiz, 1831) (Pisces: Cichlidae), including polyculture with tilapia, *Oreochromis niloticus* (L.), in Amazonian Ecuador. Doctoral Diss., Texas A&M University, College Station, TX, USA.

Franke, H.J., 1985. Handbuch der Welskunde. Landbuch-Verlag GmbH, Hannover, Germany.

Konings, A., 1988. Tanganyika Cichlids. Verduijn Cichlids & Lake Fish Movies. 2761 DL Zevenhuizen, Holland, and 4352 Herten 6, Germany.

Konings, A., 1989. Malawi Cichlids in their natural habitat. Verduijn Cichlids & Lake Fish Movies. 2761 DL Zevenhuizen, Holland, and 4352 Herten 6, Germany.

Linke, H., 1990. Labyrinthfische – Farbe im Aquarium. 3rd revised edition, Tetra Verlag, 4520 Melle 1, Germany.

Meyer, M.K., Wischnath, L., and Foerster, W., 1985. Lebendgebärende Zierfische: Arten der Welt. Mergus Verlag GmbH, P.O. Box 86, 49302 Melle, Germany.

Moyle, P.B. and Cech, Jr., J.J., 1988. Fishes—An Introduction to Ichthyology. 2nd edition. Prentice Hall, New Jersey 07632, USA.

Bibliography

Nelson, J.S., 1994. Fishes of the World, 3rd edition. John Wiley & Sons, Inc., New York, United States.

Paepke, H.-J.,1983. Die Hechtlinge – Gasterosteidae. A. Ziemsen Verlag. Wittenberg, Germany.

Pinter, H., 1983. Handbuch der Aquarienfisch-Zucht, 4th edition. Alfred Kernen Verlag, Stuttgart, Germany.

Pitcher, T. J. and Hart, P. J. B., (eds.), 1995. The Impact of Species Changes in African Lakes. Chapman & Hill, Fish and Fisheries Series 18, New York, United States.

Pusey, B.J. and Steward, T., 1989. Internal fertilization in *Lepidogalaxias salamandroides* Mees (Pisces: Lepidogalaxiidae). Zool. J. Linn. Soc. 97(1): 69–79.

van Ramshorst, J.D., (ed.), 1995/1978. The complete Aquarium Encyclopedia of Tropical Freshwater Fish. Chartwell Books, Inc., P.O.Box 7100, Edison New Jersey 00818-7100, USA/Elsevier Publishing Projects, S, A, Lausanne, Switzerland.

Roberts, T.R., 1992. Systematik revision of the Southeast Asian anabantoid fish genus *Osphronemus*, with description of two new species. Ichthyol. Explor. Freshwaters 2(4): 351–360.

Seegers, L., 1980. Killifishe. Eugen Ulmer Verlag, 7000 Stuttgart, Germany.

Sterba, G., 1987. Süßwasserfische der Welt. Urania-Verlag, Leipzig, Jena, Berlin, Germany.

World Conservation Monitoring Center – Redlist (Fishes)

Animal Redlist – Version: 11th October 1996
World Conservation Monitoring Centre, Cambridge, UK.
Internet Address: http://iucn.org/themes/ssc

The scientific names are taken directly from the Redlist; therefore, there may be some discrepancy in regard to the nomenclature used in the INDEX.
Only freshwater and brackish water species are listed.

Symbology:
Ex: Extinct
Exw: Extinct in the wild
CE: Critically endangered
E: Endangered
V: Vulnerable
NT: Near threatened
CD: Conservation dependant

CEPHALASPIDOMORPHI
PETROMYZONTIFORMES
PETROMYZONTIDAE

Eudontomyzon danfordi (NT)
H: Austria, Bosnia and Herzegovina, Bulgaria, Croatia, Czech Republic, Hungary, Moldova, Romania, Slovakia, Ukraine, Yugoslavia

Eudontomyzon hellenicus (V)
H: Greece

Eudontomyzon vladykovi (NT)
H: Austria, Bulgaria, Romania, Yugoslavia

Lampetra fluviatilis (NT)
H: Albania, Austria, Belgium, Czech Republic, Denmark, Estonia, Finland, France, Germany, Ireland, Italy, Latvia, Lithuania, Luxembourg, Netherlands, Norway, Poland, Portugal, Russia, Slovakia, Spain, Sweden, Switzerland, United Kingdom

Lampetra hubbsi (NT)
H: USA

Lampetra minima (Ex)
H: USA

Lampetra planeri (NT)
H: Austria, Belgium, Bulgaria, Czech Republic, Estonia, Finland, France, Germany, Ireland, Italy, Latvia, Lithuania, Luxembourg, Netherlands, Norway, Portugal, Russia, Slovakia, Spain, Sweden, Switzerland, United Kingdom

Lethenteron zanandreai (E)
H: Croatia, Italy, Slovenia

Mordacia praecox (V)
H: Australia

ELASMOBRANCHII
PRISTIFORMES
PRISTIDAE

Pristis microdon (E)
H: Australia, India, Indonesia, eastern Indian Ocean, Papua New Guinea, South Africa, Thailand, western central Pacific.

ACTINOPTERYGII
ACIPENSERIFORMES
ACIPENSERIDAE

Acipenser baerii (V)
H: Russia

Acipenser baerii baerii (E)
H: Russia

Acipenser baerii baikalensis (E)
H: Russia

Acipenser baerii stenorrhynchus (V)
H: Russia

Acipenser brevirostrum (V)
H: Atlantic northwest, Atlantic western central, Canada, USA

Acipenser dabryanus (CE)
H: China

Acipenser fulvescens (V)
H: Canada, USA

Acipenser guldenstaedti (E)
H: Mediterranean and Black Sea , Azerbaijan, Bulgaria, Hungary, Iran, Kazakhstan, Moldova, Romania, Russia, Turkey, Turkmenistan, Ukraine, Yugoslavia

Acipenser gueldenstaedti (E)
H: Mediterranean and Black Sea , Azerbaijan, Hungary, Romania, Ukraine, Iran, Kazakhstan, Russia, Turkmenistan, Yugoslavia

Acipenser medirostris (V)
H: Pacific northeast, Canada, USA

Acipenser mikadoi (E)
H: Pacific northwest, Japan, Russia

Acipenser naccarii (V)
H: Albania, Croatia, Italy, Yugoslavia

Acipenser nudiventris (Ex)
H: Mediterranean and Black Sea, Kazakhstan, Uzbekistan

Acipenser nudiventris (E)
H: Mediterranean and Black Sea , Azerbaijan, Bulgaria, Hungary, Iran, Kazakhstan, Moldova, Romania, Russia, Ukraine, Uzbekistan

Acipenser nudiventris (CE)
H: Hungary, Romania

Acipenser oxyrinchus oxyrinchus (NT)
H: Atlantic northwest, Atlantic western central, Canada, Mexico, USA

Acipenser persicus (E)
H: Mediterranean and Black Sea , Azerbaijan, Georgia, Iran, Russia, Turkey

Acipenser persicus (V)
H: Mediterranean and Black Sea , Azerbaijan, Iran, Russia

Acipenser ruthenus (V)
H: Austria, Bosnia and Herzegovina, Czech Republic, Germany, Hungary, Kazakhstan, Latvia, Lithuania, Romania, Russia, Slovakia, Switzerland, Ukraine, Yugoslavia

Acipenser schrencki (E)
H: China, Russia

Acipenser sinensis (E)
H: China

Acipenser stellatus (E)
H: Mediterranean and Black Sea , Azerbaijan, Bulgaria, Georgia, Hungary, Iran, Kazakhstan, Moldova, Romania, Russia, Turkmenistan, Ukraine, Yugoslavia

Acipenser stellatus (V)
H: Mediterranean and Black Sea , Azerbaijan, Iran, Kazakhstan, Russia, Turkmenistan

Acipenser sturio (CE)
H: Atlantic northeast, Mediterranean and Black Sea , Albania, Algeria, Belgium, Estonia, Finland, France, Georgia, Germany, Greece, Hungary, Ireland, Italy, Morocco, Netherlands, Norway, Poland, Portugal, Romania, Russia, Spain, Sweden, Switzerland, Turkey, Ukraine, United Kingdom, Yugoslavia

Acipenser transmontanus (NT)
H: Pacific northeast, Canada, USA

Acipenser transmontanus (E)
H: USA

Huso dauricus (E)
H: China, Russia

Huso huso (Ex)
H: Mediterranean and Black Sea, Italy

Huso huso (E)
H: Mediterranean and Black Sea, Azerbaijan, Bulgaria, Hungary, Iran, Italy, Kazakhstan, Moldova, Romania, Russia, Turkmenistan, Ukraine, Yugoslavia

Huso huso (CE)
H: Mediterranean and Black Sea , Russia

Pseudoscaphirhynchus fedtschenkoi (CE)
H: Kazakhstan

Pseudoscaphirhynchus hermanni (CE)
H: Turkmenistan, Uzbekistan

Pseudoscaphirhynchus kaufmanni (E)
H: Tajikistan, Turkmenistan, Uzbekistan

Scaphirhynchus albus (E)
H: USA

Scaphirhynchus platorynchus (V)
H: USA

Scaphirhynchus suttkusi (CE)
H: USA

POLYODONTIDAE

Polyodon spathula (V)
H: USA

Psephurus gladius (CE)
H: China

OSTEOGLOSSIFORMES
OSTEOGLOSSIDAE

Scleropages formosus (E)
H: Brunei, Cambodia, Indonesia, Malaysia, Philippines, Singapore, Thailand, Vietnam

Scleropages leichhardti (NT)
H: Australia

NOTOPTERIDAE

Chitala blanci (NT)
H: Cambodia, Thailand

CLUPEIFORMES
CLUPEIDAE

Alosa alabamae (E)
H: USA

Alosa macedonia (V)
H: Greece

Clupeonella abrau muhlisi (V)
H: Turkey

Jenkinsia parvula (V)
H: Atlantic western central, Venezuela

Tenualosa thibaudeaui (E)
H: Cambodia, Laos, Thailand, Vietnam

CYPRINIFORMES
CYPRINIDAE

Acanthobrama hulensis (Ex)
H: Israel

Acheilognathus elongatus (E)
H: China

Acheilognathus longipinnis (V)
H: Japan

Alburnus akili (V)
H: Turkey

Alburnus albidus (V)
H: Croatia, Italy, Turkey

Anabarilius polylepis (E)
H: China

Anaecypris hispanica (E)
H: Portugal, Spain

Aulopyge hugeli (V)
H: Bosnia and Herzegovina, Croatia

Balantiochoilos melanopterus (E)
H: Indonesia, Malaysia, Thailand

Barbopsis devecchi (V)
H: Somalia

Barbus andrewi (V)
H: South Africa

Barbus brevipinnis (V)
H: Mozambique, South Africa

Barbus calidus (E)
H: South Africa

Barbus caninus (NT)
H: Italy, Switzerland

Barbus capensis (V)
H: South Africa

Barbus comizo (V)
H: Portugal, Spain

Barbus erubescens (CE)
H: South Africa

Barbus euboicus (CE)
H: Greece

Barbus guiraonis (V)
H: Spain

Barbus haasi (V)
H: Spain

Barbus hospes (NT)
H: Namibia, South Africa

Barbus kimberleyensis (V)
H: South Africa

Barbus microcephalus (V)
H: Portugal, Spain

Barbus motebensis (V)
H: South Africa

Barbus plebejus (NT)
H: Croatia, Italy, Slovenia, Switzerland

Barbus prespensis (V)
H: Albania, Greece, Macedonia

Barbus sclateri (NT)
H: Portugal, Spain

Barbus serra (E)
H: South Africa

Barbus steindachneri (V)
H: Portugal

Barbus treurensis (CD)
H: South Africa

Barbus trevelyani (CE)
H: South Africa

Barbus tyberinus (NT)
H: Italy

Caecobarbus geertsi (V)
H: Zaire

Caecocypris basimi (V)
H: Iraq

Capoeta pestai (NT)
H: Turkey

Carassius carassius (NT)
H: Austria, Belarus, Belgium, Bosnia and Herzegovina, Bulgaria, Croatia, Czech Republic, Denmark, Estonia, Finland, France, Germany, Greece, Hungary, Italy, Latvia, Lithuania, Luxembourg, Moldova, Netherlands, Poland, Romania, Russia, Slovakia, Slovenia, Sweden, Switzerland, Turkey, Ukraine, United Kingdom, Yugoslavia

Cephalakompsus pachycheilus (CE)
H: Philippines

Chalcalburnus belvica (NT)
H: Albania, Greece, Macedonia

Chela caeruleostigmata (CE)
H: Cambodia, Thailand

Chondrostoma genei (NT)
H: Italy, Slovenia

Chondrostoma holmwoodii (V)
H: Turkey

Chondrostoma lusitanicum (V)
H: Portugal

Chondrostoma prespensis (NT)
H: Albania, Greece, Macedonia

Chondrostoma scodrensis (CE)
H: Albania, Yugoslavia

Cyprinella alvarezdelvillari (CE)
H: Mexico

Cyprinella bocagrande (CE)
H: Mexico

Cyprinella caerulea (V)
H: USA

Cyprinella callitaenia (NT)
H: USA

Cyprinella formosa (V)
H: Mexico, USA

Cyprinella monacha (NT)
H: USA

Cyprinella panarcys (E)
H: Mexico

Cyprinella proserpina (V)
H: Mexico, USA

Cyprinella santamariae (V)
H: Mexico

Cyprinella xanthicara (V)
H: Mexico

Cyprinus carpio (CE)
H: Austria, Bulgaria, Croatia, Hungary, Romania, Slovakia, Slovenia, Yugoslavia

Cyprinus micristius (E)
H: China

Cyprinus yilongensis (Ex)
H: China

Danio pathirana (CE)
H: Sri Lanka

Dionda diaboli (V)
H: Mexico, USA

Dionda dichroma (V)
H: Mexico

Dionda mandibularis (CE)
H: Mexico

Epalzeorhynchos bicolor (Exw)
H: Thailand

Eremichthys acros (V)
H: USA

Erimystax cahni (V)
H: USA

Evarra bustamantei (Ex)
H: Mexico

Evarra eigenmanni (Ex)
H: Mexico

Evarra tlahuacensis (Ex)
H: Mexico

Garra barreimiae (V)
H: Oman, United Arab Emirates

Garra dunsirei (V)
H: Oman

Garra longipinnis (V)
H: Oman

Gibbibarbus cyphotergous (V)
H: China

Gila alvordensis (V)
H: USA

Gila boraxobius (V)
H: USA

Gila crassicauda (Ex)
H: USA

Gila cypha (V)
H: USA

Gila ditaenia (V)
H: Mexico, USA

Gila elegans (E)
H: Mexico, USA

Gila intermedia (NT)
H: Mexico, USA

Gila modesta (CE)
H: Mexico

Gila nigrescens (CE)
H: Mexico, USA

Gila purpurea (V)
H: Mexico, USA

Gobio hettitorum (V)
H: Turkey

Hampala lopezi (CE)
H: Philippines

Hybognathus amarus (E)
H: USA

Iberocypris palaciosi (E)
H: Spain

Iotichthys phlegethontis (V)
H: USA

Iranocypris typhlops (V)
H: Iran

Labeo fisheri (E)
H: Sri Lanka

Labeo lankae (CE)
H: Sri Lanka

Labeo seeberi (CE)
H: South Africa

Ladigesocypris ghigii (V)
H: Greece, Turkey

Lepidomeda albivallis (CE)
H: USA

Lepidomeda altivelis (Ex)
H: USA

Lepidomeda vittata (V)
H: USA

Leuciscus illyricus (V)
H: Croatia

Leuciscus koadicus (V)
H: Greece

Leuciscus lucumontis (NT)
H: Italy

Leuciscus microlepis
H: Croatia

Leuciscus polylepis (E)
H: Croatia

Leuciscus svallize (V)
H: Croatia

Leuciscus turskyi (Ex)
H: Croatia

Leuciscus ukliva (CE)
H: Croatia

Lythrurus snelsoni (V)
H: USA

Macrhybopsis gelida (V)
H: USA

Macrhybopsis meeki (NT)
H: USA

Mandibularca resinus (CE)
H: Philippines

Meda fulgida (V)
H: USA

Moapa coriacea (CE)
H: USA

Neolissochilus theinemanni (V)
H: Indonesia

Notropis aguirrepequenoi (V)
H: Mexico

Notropis amecae (Ex)
H: Mexico

Notropis aulidion (Ex)
H: Mexico

Notropis buccula (V)
H: USA

Notropis cahabae (CE)
H: USA

Notropis imeldae (V)
H: Mexico

Notropis mekistocholas (CE)
H: USA

Notropis melanostomus (V)
H: USA

Notropis moralesi (CE)
H: Mexico

Notropis orca (Ex)
H: Mexico, USA

Notropis perpallidus (CD)
H: USA

Notropis saladonis (Ex)
H: Mexico

Notropis simus (E)
H: Mexico, USA

Onychostoma alticorps (E)
H: Taiwan

Opsaridium peringueyi (V)
H: South Africa

Oregonichthys crameri (V)
H: USA

Oregonichthys kalawatseti (CD)
H: USA

Ospatulus palaemophagus (E)
H: Philippines

Ospatulus truncatus (CE)
H: Philippines

Pachychilon pictum (NT)
H: Albania, Greece, Yugoslavia

Paraphoxinus alepidotus (V)
H: Croatia

Paraphoxinus croaticus (V)
H: Croatia

Paraphoxinus ghetaldi (V)
H: Croatia

Paraphoxinus metohiensis (V)
H: Croatia

Phenacobius teretulus (V)
H: USA

Phoxinellus anatolicus (E)
H: Turkey

Phoxinellus egridiri (CE)
H: Turkey

Phoxinellus handlirschi (CE)
H: Turkey

Phoxinellus pleurobipunctatus (NT)
H: Greece

Phoxinellus zeregii (NT)
H: Turkey

Phoxinellus zeregii fahirae (V)
H: Turkey

Phoxinellus zeregii meandri (NT)
H: Turkey

Phoxinus cumberlandensis (V)
H: USA

Phoxinus tennesseensis (NT)
H: USA

Phreatichthys andruzzi (V)
H: Somalia

Plagopterus argentissimus (V)
H: USA

Pogonichthys ciscoides (Ex)
H: USA

Pogonichthys macrolepidotus (E)
H: USA

Poropuntius tawarensis (V)
H: Indonesia

Probarbus jullieni (E)
H: Cambodia, Laos, Malaysia, Thailand, Vietnam

Pseudobarbus afer (NT)
H: South Africa

Pseudobarbus asper (V)
H: South Africa

Pseudobarbus burchelli (E)
H: South Africa

Pseudobarbus burgi (CE)
H: South Africa

Pseudobarbus phlegethon (E)
H: South Africa

Pseudobarbus quathlambae (CE)
H: Lesotho

Pseudobarbus tenuis (E)
H: South Africa

Pseudophoxinus beoticus (E)
H: Greece

Pseudophoxinus stymphalicus (NT)
H: Greece

Ptychocheilus lucius (V)
H: USA

Puntius amarus (CE)
H: Philippines

Puntius asoka (E)
H: Sri Lanka

Puntius bandula (CE)
H: Sri Lanka

Puntius baoulan (CE)
H: Philippines

Puntius clemensi (CE)
H: Philippines

Puntius cumingii (CD)
H: Sri Lanka

Puntius disa (CE)
H: Philippines

Puntius flavifuscus (CE)
H: Philippines

Puntius hemictenus (V)
H: Philippines

Puntius herrei (CE)
H: Philippines

Puntius katalo (CE)
H: Philippines

Puntius lanaoensis (CE)
H: Philippines

Puntius lindog (V)
H: Philippines

Puntius manalak (CE)
H: Philippines

Puntius manguaoensis (V)
H: Philippines

Puntius martenstyni (E)
H: Sri Lanka

Puntius nigrofasciatus (CD)
H: Sri Lanka

Puntius pleurotaenia (CD)
H: Sri Lanka

Puntius sirang (V)
H: Philippines

Puntius speleops (V)
H: Thailand

Puntius titteya (CD)
H: Sri Lanka

Puntius tras (CE)
H: Philippines

Puntius tumba (V)
H: Philippines

Rasbora baliensis (V)
H: Indonesia

Rasbora tawarensis (V)
H: Indonesia

Rasbora vaterifloris (CD)
H: Sri Lanka

Rasbora wilpita (E)
H: Sri Lanka

Relictus solitarius (E)
H: USA

Rhinichthys cobitis (V)
H: USA

Rhinichthys deaconi (Ex)
H: USA

Rhodeus ocellatus smithi (CE)
H: Japan

Rutilus lemmingii (V)
H: Portugal, Spain

Rutilus macedonicus (NT)
H: Greece

Rutilus macrolepidotus (V)
H: Portugal

Rutilus meidingeri (E)
H: Austria, Germany, Slovakia

Scardinius graecus (V)
H: Greece

Schizothorax lepidothorax (E)
H: China

Sinocyclocheilus anatirostris (V)
H: China

Sinocyclocheilus angularis (V)
H: China

Sinocyclocheilus anophthalmus (V)
H: China

Sinocyclocheilus hyalinus (V)
H: China

Sinocyclocheilus microphthalmus (V)
H: China

Spratellicypris palata (CE)
H: Philippines

Stypodon signifer (Ex)
H: Mexico

Tanakia tanago (V)
H: Japan

Tor yunnanensis (E)
H: China

Typhlobarbus nudiventris (V)
H: China

Typhlogarra widdowsoni (V)
H: Iraq

Vimba melanops (V)
H: Greece, Macedonia

COBITIDAE

Botia sidthimunki (CE)
H: Laos, Thailand

Cobitis calderoni (V)
H: Portugal, Spain

Cobitis meridionalis (NT)
H: Albania, Greece, Macedonia

Cobitis paludica (NT)
H: Portugal, Spain

Lepidocephalichthys jonklaasi (E)
H: Sri Lanka

Misgurnis fossilis (NT)
H: Austria, Belarus, Belgium, Bosnia and Herzegovina, Bulgaria, Croatia, Czech Republic, Estonia, France, Germany, Hungary, Latvia, Lithuania, Luxembourg, Moldova, Netherlands, Poland, Romania, Russia, Slovakia, Slovenia, Switzerland, Ukraine, Yugoslavia

Protocobitis typhlops (V)
H: China

Sabanjewia larvata (NT)
H: Italy

BALITORIDAE

Acanthocobitis urophthalmus (CD)
H: Sri Lanka

Hemimyzon taitungensis (V)
H: Taiwan

Homaloptera thamicola (V)
H: Thailand

Nemacheilus smithi (V)
H: Iran

Nemacheilus troglocataractus (V)
H: Thailand

Nemacheilus tschaiyssuensis (V)
H: Turkey

Oreonectes anophthalmus (V)
H: China

Schistura jarutanini (V)
H: Thailand

Schistura oedipus (V)
H: Thailand

Schistura sijuensis (V)
H: India

Sinogastromyzon puliensis (V)
H: Taiwan

Sphaerophysa dianchiensis (V)
H: China

Sundoreonectes tiomanensis (V)
H: Malaysia

Triplophysa gejiuensis (V)
H: China

Triplophysa xiangxensis (V)
H: China

Yunnanilus macrogaster (V)
H: China

Yunnanilus niger (V)
H: China

Yunnanilus nigromaculatus (E)
H: China

CATOSTOMIDAE

Catostomus bernardini (V)
H: Mexico, USA

Catostomus cahita (V)
H: Mexico

Catostomus conchos (V)
H: Mexico

Catostomus leopoldi (V)
H: Mexico

Catostomus microps (E)
H: USA

Chasmistes muriei (Ex)
H: USA

Catostomus santaanae (V)
H: USA

Catostomus snyderi (NT)
H: USA

Catostomus warnerensis (V)
H: USA

Catostomus wigginsi (V)
H: Mexico

Chasmistes brevirostris (E)
H: USA

Chasmistes cujus (CE)
H: USA

Cycleptus elongatus (NT)
H: Mexico, USA

Deltistes luxatus (E)
H: USA

Lagochila lacera (Ex)
H: USA

Moxostoma hamiltoni (NT)
H: USA

Moxostoma hubbsi (V)
H: Canada

Xyrauchen texanus (E)
H: USA

CHARACIFORMES
CHARACIDAE

Astyanax mexicanus jordani (V)
H: Mexico

Gymnocharacinus bergi (E)
H: Argentina

SILURIFORMES
DIPLOMYSTIDAE

Diplomystes chilensis (E)
H: Chile

ICTALURIDAE

Ictalurus mexicanus (V)
H: Mexico

Ictalurus pricei (V)
H: Mexico

Noturus baileyi (CE)
H: USA

Noturus flavipinnis (V)
H: USA

Noturus gilberti (V)
H: USA

Noturus lachneri (V)
H: USA

Noturus munitus (NT)
H: USA

Noturus placidus (NT)
H: USA

Noturus stanauli (V)
H: USA

Noturus taylori (V)
H: USA

Noturus trautmani (CE)
H: USA

Prietella lundbergi (V)
H: Mexico

Prietella phreatophila (E)
H: Mexico

Satan eurystomus (V)
H: USA

Trogloglanis pattersoni (V)
H: USA

BAGRIDAE

Austroglanis barnardi (CE)
H: South Africa

Austroglanis gilli (V)
H: South Africa

Coreobagrus ichikawai (V)
H: Japan

Pseudobargus medianalis (E)
H: China

SILURIDAE

Silurus mento (E)
H: China

PANGASIIDAE

Pangasianodon gigas (E)
H: Cambodia, China, Laos, Myanmar

AMBLYCIPITIDAE

Liobagrus nigricauda (E)
H: China

SISORIDAE

Oreoglanis siamensis (V)
H: Thailand

CLARIIDAE

Clarias cavernicola (CE)
H: Namibia

Clarias maclareni (CE)
H: Cameroon

Encheloclarias curtisoma (CE)
H: Malaysia

Encheloclarias kelioides (CE)
H: Indonesia, Malaysia

Encheloclarias prolatus (V)
H: Malaysia

Encheloclarias tapeinopterus (V)
H: Indonesia

Horaglanis krishnai (V)
H: India

Uegitglanis zammaranoi (V)
H: Somalia

HETEROPNEUSTIDAE

Heteropneustes microps (V)
H: Sri Lanka

ARIIDAE

Arius bonillai (E)
H: Western central Atlantic, eastern central Pacific, Colombia

PLOTOSIDAE

Oloplotosus torobo (V)
H: Papua New Guinea

MOCHOKIDAE

Chiloglanis bifurcus (E)
H: South Africa

PIMELODIDAE

Rhamdia reddelli (V)
H: Mexico

Rhamdia zongolicensis (V)
H: Mexico

TRICHOMYCTERIDAE

Rhizosomichthys totae (Ex)
H: Colombia

Trichomycterus chungarensis (V)
H: Chile

Trichomycterus laucaensis (NT)
H: Chile

Trichomycterus rivulatus (NT)
H: Chile

SALMONIFORMES
UMBRIDAE

Novumbra hubbsi (NT)
H: USA

Umbra krameri (V)
H: Austria, Bosnia and Herzegovina, Bulgaria, Croatia, Czech Republic, Hungary, Moldova, Romania, Slovakia, Slovenia, Ukraine, Yugoslavia

LEPIDOGALAXIIDAE

Lepidogalaxias salamandroides (NT)
H: Australia

OSMERIDAE

Hypomesus transpacificus (E)
H: USA

PLECOGLOSSIDAE

Plecoglossus altivelis ryukyuensis (E)
H: Japan

SALANGIDAE

Neosalanx regani (V)
H: Japan

RETROPINNIDAE

Prototroctes maraena (V)
H: Australia

Prototroctes oxyrhynchus (Ex)
H: New Zealand

GALAXIIDAE

Galaxias argenteus (V)
H: New Zealand

Galaxias fontanus (CE)
H: Australia

Galaxias fuscus (CE)
H: Australia

Galaxias gracilis (V)
H: New Zealand

Galaxias johnstoni (CE)
H: Australia

Galaxias pedderensis (CE)
H: Australia

Galaxias postvectis (V)
H: New Zealand

Galaxias rekohua (V)
H: New Zealand

Galaxias rostratus (V)
H: Australia

Galaxias tanycephalus (V)
H: Australia

Galaxias zebratus (NT)
H: South Africa

Galaxiella munda (NT)
H: Australia

Galaxiella nigrostriata (NT)
H: Australia

Galaxiella pusilla (V)
H: Australia

Neochanna apoda (NT)
H: New Zealand

Neochanna burrowsius (V)
H: New Zealand

Paragalaxias mesotes (V)
H: Australia

SALMONIDAE

Acantholingua ohridana (V)
H: Albania, Macedonia

Coregonus alpenae (Ex)
H: Canada, USA

Coregonus hoyi (V)
H: Canada, USA

Coregonus huntsmani (V)
H: Canada, USA

Coregonus johannae (Ex)
H: Canada, USA

Coregonus kiyi (V)
H: Canada, USA

Coregonus nigripinnis (Ex)
H: Canada

Coregonus reighardi (CE)
H: Canada

Coregonus zenithicus (V)
H: Canada, USA

Hucho hucho (E)
H: Austria, Bosnia and Herzegovina, Croatia, Czech Republic, Germany, Hungary, Poland, Romania, Slovakia, Slovenia, Ukraine, Yugoslavia

Oncorhynchus apache (CE)
H: USA

Oncorhynchus chrysogaster (V)
H: Mexico

Oncorhynchus formosanus (CE)
H: Taiwan

Oncorhynchus gilae (E)
H: USA

Oncorhynchus ishikawai (E)
H: Japan

Salmo carpio (V)
H: Italy

Salmo letnica (V)
H: Albania, Macedonia

Salmo platycephalus (CE)
H: Turkey

Salmothymus obtusirostris (E)
H: Croatia, Yugoslavia

Salvelinus agassizi (Ex)
H: USA

Salvelinus confluentus (V)
H: Canada, USA

Salvelinus japonicus (E)
H: Japan

Salvethymus svetovidovi (V)
H: Russia

Stenodus leucichthys leucichthys (E)
H: Azerbaijan, Kazakhstan, Russia

PERCOPSIFORMES
AMBLYOPSIDAE

Amblyopsis rosae (V)
H: USA

Amblyopsis spelaea (V)
H: USA

Speoplatyrhinus poulsoni (NT)
H: USA

Typhlichthys subterraneus (V)
H: USA

OPHIDIIFORMES
BYTHITIDAE

Lucifuga simile (V)
H: Cuba

Lucifuga spelaeotes (V)
H: Bahamas

Lucifuga subterranea (V)
H: Cuba

Lucifuga teresinarum (V)
H: Cuba

Saccogaster melanomycter (V)
H: Atlantic western central, Colombia

Stygicola dentata (V)
H: Cuba

Typhliasina pearsei (V)
H: Mexico

BATRACHOIDIFORMES
BATRACHOIDIDAE

Batrachoides manglae (V)
H: Western central Atlantic, eastern central Pacific, Colombia, Venezuela

Sanopus astrifer (V)
H: Western central Atlantic, Belize

Sanopus greenfieldorum (V)
H: Western central Atlantic, Belize

Sanopus reticulatus (V)
H: Western central Atlantic, Belize

Sanopus splendidus (V)
H: Western central Atlantic, Belize, Mexico

ATHERINIFORMES
ATHERINIDAE

Basilichthys australis (NT)
H: Chile

Cairnsichthys rhombosomoides (V)
H: Australia

Cauque mauleanum (NT)
H: Chile

Chilatherina bleheri (V)
H: Indonesia

Chilatherina sentaniensis (CE)
H: Indonesia

Chirostoma bartoni (V)
H: Mexico

Craterocephalus amniculus (V)
H: Australia

Craterocephalus centralis (NT)
H: Australia

Craterocephalus dalhousiensis (V)
H: Australia

Craterocephalus fluviatillis (E)
H: Australia

Craterocephalus gloveri (V)
H: Australia

Craterocephalus helenae (NT)
H: Australia

Craterocephalus lacustris (V)
H: Papua New Guinea

Craterocephalus lentiginosus (NT)
H: Australia

Glossolepis incisus (V)
H: Indonesia

Glossolepis wanamensis (CE)
H: Papua New Guinea

Kiunga ballochi (CE)
H: Papua New Guinea

Melanotaenia arfakensis (V)
H: Indonesia

Melanotaenia boesemani (E)
H: Indonesia

Melanotaenia eachamensis (V)
H: Australia

Melanotaenia gracilis (NT)
H: Australia

Melanotaenia lacustris (V)
H: Papua New Guinea

Melanotaenia oktediensis (V)
H: Papua New Guinea

Melanotaenia parva (V)
H: Indonesia

Melanotaenia pygmaea (NT)
H: Australia

Menidia conchorum (NT)
H: USA

Menidia extensa (V)
H: USA

Paratherina cyanea (V)
H: Indonesia

Paratherina labiosa (V)
H: Indonesia

Paratherina lineata (V)
H: Indonesia

Paratherina striata (V)
H: Indonesia

Paratherina wolterecki (V)
H: Indonesia

Poblana alchichica (CE)
H: Mexico

Poblana letholepis (E)
H: Mexico

Poblana squamata (E)
H: Mexico

Pseudomugil mellis (E)
H: Australia

Rheocles sikorae (Ex)
H: Madagascar

Rheocles wrightae (CE)
H: Madagascar

Scaturiginichthys vermeilipinnis (CE)
H: Australia

Telmatherina abendanoni (V)
H: Indonesia

Telmatherina antoniae (V)
H: Indonesia

Telmatherina celebensis (V)
H: Indonesia

Telmatherina ladigesi (V)
H: Indonesia

Telmatherina obscura (V)
H: Indonesia

Telmatherina opudi (V)
H: Indonesia

Telmatherina prognatha (V)
H: Indonesia

Telmatherina sarasinorum (V)
H: Indonesia

Telmatherina wahjui (V)
H: Indonesia

Tominanga aurea (V)
H: Indonesia

Tominanga sanguicauda (V)
H: Indonesia

PHALLOSTETHIDAE

Phallostethus dunckeri (V)
H: Malaysia

CYPRINODONTIFORMES
APLOCHEILIDAE

Campellolebias brucei (V)
H: Brazil

Cynolebias boitonei (V)
H: Brazil

Cynolebias constanciae (V)
H: Brazil

Cynolebias marmoratus (V)
H: Brazil

Cynolebias minimus (V)
H: Brazil

Cynolebias opalescens (V)
H: Brazil

Cynolebias splendens (V)
H: Brazil

Nothobranchius sp. (E)
H: Namibia

Pachypanchax sakaramyi (V)
H: Madagascar

CYPRINODONTIDAE

Aphanius anatoliae (E)
H: Turkey

Aphanius burduricus (E)
H: Turkey

Aphanius splendens (CE)
H: Turkey

Aphanius sureyanus (CE)
H: Turkey

Aphanius transgrediens (CE)
H: Turkey

Crenichthys baileyi (V)
H: USA

Crenichthys nevadae (V)
H: USA

Cualac tessellatus (E)
H: Mexico

Cyprinodon alvarezi (Exw)
H: Mexico

Cyprinodon beltrani (E)
H: Mexico

Cyprinodon bovinus (CE)
H: USA

Cyprinodon ceciliae (Ex)
H: Mexico

Cyprinodon diabolis (V)
H: USA

Cyprinodon elegans (E)
H: USA

Cyprinodon fontinalis (E)
H: Mexico

Cyprinodon inmemoriam (Ex)
H: Mexico

Cyprinodon labiosus (E)
H: Mexico

Cyprinodon latifasciatus (Ex)
H: Mexico

Cyprinodon longidorsalis (Exw)
H: Mexico

Cyprinodon macrolepis (E)
H: Mexico

Cyprinodon maya (E)
H: Mexico

Cyprinodon meeki (CE)
H: Mexico

Cyprinodon pachycephalus (CE)
H: Mexico

Cyprinodon pecosensis (CE)
H: USA

Cyprinodon radiosus (E)
H: USA

Cyprinodon simus (E)
H: Mexico

Cyprinodon spp. (Ex)
H: Mexico

Cyprinodon tularosa (V)
H: USA

Cyprinodon verecundus (CE)
H: Mexico

Cyprinodon veronicae (CE)
H: Mexico

Fundulus albolineatus (Ex)
H: USA

Fundulus julisia (V)
H: USA

Fundulus waccamensis (V)
H: USA

Lucania interioris (CE)
H: Mexico

Megupsilon aporus (Exw)
H: Mexico

Orestias chungarensis (V)
H: Chile

Orestias laucaensis (NT)
H: Chile

Pantanodon madagascariensis (E)
H: Madagascar

Valencia hispanica (E)
H: Spain

Valencia letourneuxi (E)
H: Albania, Greece

GOODEIDAE

Ameca splendens (Exw)
H: Mexico

Allotoca maculata (CE)
H: Mexico

Ataeniobius toweri (E)
H: Mexico

Characodon audax (V)
H: Mexico

Characodon garmani (Ex)
H: Mexico

Characodon lateralis (E)
H: Mexico

Empetrichthys merriami (Ex)
H: USA

Girardinichthys multiradiatus (V)
H: Mexico

Girardinichthys viviparus (CE)
H: Mexico

Goodea gracilis (V)
H: Mexico

Hubbsina turneri (CE)
H: Mexico

Ilydon whitei (CE)
H: Mexico

Skiffia francesae (Exw)
H: Mexico

Xenoophorus captivus (E)
H: Mexico

POECILIIDAE

Gambusia alvarezi (V)
H: Mexico

Gambusia amistadensis (Ex)
H: USA

Gambusia eurystoma (CE)
H: Mexico

Gambusia gaigei (V)
H: USA

Gambusia georgei (Ex)
H: USA

Gambusia heterochir (V)
H: USA

Gambusia hurtadoi (V)
H: Mexico

Gambusia krumholzi (V)
H: Mexico

Gambusia longispinis (V)
H: Mexico

Gambusia nobilis (V)
H: USA

Gambusia senilis (NT)
H: Mexico, USA

Poecilia latipunctata (CE)
H: Mexico

Poecilia sulphuraria (CE)
H: Mexico

Poeciliopsis occidentalis (NT)
H: Mexico, USA

Poeciliopsis occidentalis sonorensis (V)
H: Mexico

Priapella bonita (Ex)
H: Mexico

Xiphophorus couchianus (CE)
H: Mexico

Xiphophorus gordoni (E)
H: Mexico

Xiphophorus meyeri (E)
H: Mexico

BELONIFORMES
ADRIANICHTHYIDAE

Adrianichthys kruyti (CE)
H: Indonesia

Oryzias celebensis (V)
H: Indonesia

Oryzias marmoratus (V)
H: Indonesia

Oryzias matanensis (V)
H: Indonesia

Oryzias nigrimas (V)
H: Indonesia

Oryzias orthognathus (E)
H: Indonesia

Oryzias profundicola (V)
H: Indonesia

Xenopoecilus oophorus (E)
H: Indonesia

Xenopoecilus poptae (CE)
H: Indonesia

Xenopoecilus sarasinorum (E)
H: Indonesia

HEMIRAMPHIDAE

Dermogenys megarramphus (NT)
H: Indonesia

Dermogenys weberi (V)
H: Indonesia

Nomorhamphus towoeti (V)
H: Indonesia

Tondanichthys kottelati (V)
H: Indonesia

GASTEROSTEIFORMES
GASTEROSTEIDAE

Pungitius hellenicus (CE)
H: Greece

SYNGNATHIFORMES
SYNGNATHIDAE

Solegnathus dunckeri (V)
H: Southwest Pacific, western central Pacific, Australia

Solegnathus hardwickii (V)
H: Pacific northwest, western central Pacific

Syngnathus watermayeri (CE)
H: South Africa

SYNBRANCHIFORMES
SYNBRANCHIDAE

Ophisternon infernale (E)
H: Mexico

SCORPAENIFORMES
COTTIDAE

Cottus asperrimus (V)
H: USA

Cottus echinatus (Ex)
H: USA

Cottus extensus (V)
H: USA

Cottus greenei (V)
H: USA

Cottus leiopomus (V)
H: USA

Cottus petiti (CE)
H: France

Cottus pygmaeus (CE)
H: USA

PERCIFORMES
PERCICHTHYIDAE

Edelia obscura (V)
H: Australia

Maccullochella ikei (E)
H: Australia

Maccullochella macquariensis (E)
H: Australia

Maccullochella peelii mariensis (NT)
H: Australia

Nannoperca oxleyana (E)
H: Australia

Nannoperca variegata (V)
H: Australia

TERAPONTIDAE

Bidyanus bidyanus (V)
H: Australia

Hephaestus adamsoni (V)
H: Papua New Guinea

Hephaestus epirrhinos (NT)
H: Australia

Leiopotherapon aheneus (NT)
H: Australia

Leiopotherapon macrolepis (NT)
H: Australia

Pingalla midgleyi (NT)
H: Australia

Syncomistes kimberleyensis (NT)
H: Australia

Syncomistes rastellus (NT)
H: Australia

Varia jamoerensis (V)
H: Indonesia

CENTRARCHIDAE

Ambloplites cavifrons (V)
H: USA

Micropterus notius (NT)
H: USA

ELASSOMATIDAE

Elassoma boehlkei (NT)
H: USA

Elassoma okatie (V)
H: USA

PERCIDAE

Crystallaria asprella (V)
H: USA

Etheostoma acuticeps (NT)
H: USA

Etheostoma aquali (V)
H: USA

Etheostoma australe (V)
H: Mexico

Etheostoma boschungi (E)
H: USA

Etheostoma cinereum (V)
H: USA

Etheostoma cragini (NT)
H: USA

Etheostoma ditrema (V)
H: USA

Etheostoma fonticola (V)
H: USA

Etheostoma grahami (V)
H: Mexico, USA

Etheostoma kanawhae (NT)
H: USA

Etheostoma luteovinctum (NT)
H: USA

Etheostoma maculatum (NT)
H: USA

Etheostoma moorei (V)
H: USA

Etheostoma nianguae (V)
H: USA

Etheostoma nuchale (E)
H: USA

Etheostoma okaloosae (E)
H: USA

Etheostoma osburni (NT)
H: USA

Etheostoma pallididorsum (V)
H: USA

Etheostoma pellucidum (V)
H: Canada, USA

Etheostoma pottsi (V)
H: Mexico

Etheostoma rubrum (NT)
H: USA

Etheostoma sellare (Ex)
H: USA

Etheostoma striatulum (V)
H: USA

Etheostoma trisella (V)
H: USA

Etheostoma tuscumbia (V)
H: USA

Etheostoma wapiti (V)
H: USA

Gymnocephalus schraetzer (V)
H: Austria, Bulgaria, Croatia, Czech Republic, Germany, Hungary, Moldova, Romania, Slovakia, Ukraine, Yugoslavia

Percarina demidoff (V)
H: Moldova, Russia, Ukraine

Percina antesella (V)
H: USA

Percina aurolineata (V)
H: USA

Percina burtoni (V)
H: USA

Percina cymatotaenia (E)
H: USA

Percina jenkinsi (V)
H: USA

Percina lenticula (V)
H: USA

Percina macrocephala (NT)
H: USA

Percina nasuta (NT)
H: USA

Percina pantherina (V)
H: USA

Percina rex (V)
H: USA

Percina tanasi (V)
H: USA

Percina uranidea (NT)
H: USA

Romanichthys valsanicola (CE)
H: Romania

Zingel asper (CE)
H: France, Switzerland

Zingel streber (V)
H: Austria, Bosnia and Herzegovina, Bulgaria, Croatia, Czech Republic, Germany, Greece, Hungary, Italy, Moldova, Slovakia, Slovenia, Switzerland, Ukraine, Yugoslavia

Zingel zingel (V)
H: Austria, Bosnia and Herzegovina, Bulgaria, Croatia, Czech Republic, Germany, Hungary, Moldova, Romania, Slovakia, Slovenia, Ukraine, Yugoslavia

CICHLIDAE

Allochromis welcommei (CE)
H: Uganda

Astatotilapia dwarf bigeye scraper (CE)
H: Kenya

Astatotilapia martini (Ex)

Astatotilapia megalops (Ex)

Astatotilapia shovelmouth (E)
H: Uganda

Astatotilapia barbarae (E)
H: Uganda

Astatotilapia brownae (E)
H: Tanzania

Astatotilapia latifasciata (CE)
H: Uganda

Astatotilapia piceata (E)
H: Tanzania

Astatotilapia velifer (V)
H: Uganda

Chetia brevis (V)
H: Mozambique, South Africa

Cichlasoma bartoni (V)
H: Mexico

Cichlasoma labridens (E)
H: Mexico

Cichlasoma minckleyi (V)
H: Mexico

Cichlasoma pantostictum (V)
H: Mexico

Cichlasoma steindachneri (V)
H: Mexico

Enterochromis paropius (CE)
H: Tanzania

Gaurochromis obtusidens (Ex)

Gaurochromis simpsoni (E)
H: Uganda

Haplochromis lividus (Exw)

Haplochromis ruby (CE)
H: Uganda

Haplochromis annectidens (CE)
H: Uganda

Haplochromis obliquidens (E)
H: Tanzania, Uganda

Harpagochromis artaxerxes (Ex)

Harpagochromis boops (Ex)

Harpagochromis cavifrons (Ex)

Harpagochromis frogmouth (V)
H: Kenya, Uganda

Harpagochromis guiarti complex (CE)
H: Uganda

Harpagochromis maculipinna (Ex)

Harpagochromis michaeli (Ex)

Harpagochromis nyanzae (Ex)

Harpagochromis pachycephalus (Ex)

Harpagochromis paraplagiostoma (Ex)

Harpagochromis pectoralis (Ex)

Harpagochromis plagiostoma (CE)
H: Uganda

Harpagochromis spekii (Ex)

Harpagochromis thuragnathus (Ex)

Harpagochromis victorianus (Ex)

Harpagochromis worthingtoni (CE)
H: Uganda

Hoplotilapia retrodens (Ex)

Konia dikume (CE)
H: Cameroon

Konia eisentrauti (CE)
H: Cameroon

Labrochromis ishmaeli (Exw)

Labrochromis mylergates (Ex)

Labrochromis pharyngomylus (Ex)

Labrochromis teegelaari (Ex)

Lipochromis backflash *cryptodon* (CE)
H: Uganda

Lipochromis black *cryptodon* (CE)
H: Tanzania

Lipochromis parvidens-like (CE)
H: Uganda

Lipochromis small *obesoid* (CE)
H: Uganda

Lipochromis maxillaris (CE)
H: Kenya

Lipochromis melanopterus complex (CE)
H: Tanzania

Lipochromis microdon (Ex)

Macropleurodus bicolor (CE)
H: Tanzania

Myaka myaka (CE)
H: Cameroon

Oreochromis esculentus (V)
H: Kenya, Tanzania, Uganda

Oreochromis variabilis (V)
H: Kenya, Uganda

Oxylapia polli (V)
H: Madagascar

Paralabidochromis beadlei (CE)
H: Uganda

Paralabidochromis chilotes complex (V)
H: Kenya, Tanzania, Uganda

Paralabidochromis chromogynos (V)
H: Kenya, Tanzania, Uganda

Paralabidochromis crassilabris (V)
H: Kenya, Tanzania, Uganda

Paralabidochromis victoriae (CE)
H: Kenya

Paretroplus dami (V)
H: Madagascar

Paretroplus kieneri (V)
H: Madagascar

Paretroplus maculatus (CE)
H: Madagascar

Paretroplus petiti (CE)
H: Madagascar

Platytaeniodus degeni (Exw)

Prognathochromis arcanus (Ex)

Prognathochromis argenteus (Ex)

Prognathochromis bartoni (Ex)

Prognathochromis bayoni (Ex)

Prognathochromis decticostoma (Ex)

Prognathochromis dentex (Ex)

Prognathochromis estor (Ex)

Prognathochromis flavipinnis (Ex)

Prognathochromis gilberti (Ex)

Prognathochromis gowersi (Ex)

Prognathochromis howesi complex (E)
H: Tanzania

Prognathochromis long snout (E)
H: Uganda

Prognathochromis longirostris (Ex)

Prognathochromis macrognathus (Ex)

Prognathochromis mandibularis (Ex)

Prognathochromis mento (CE)
H: Tanzania

Prognathochromis nanoserranus (Ex)

Prognathochromis nigrescens (Ex)

Prognathochromis paraguiarti (Ex)

Prognathochromis percoides (Ex)

Prognathochromis perrieri (Exw)

Prognathochromis prognathus (Ex)

Prognathochromis pseudopellegrini (Ex)

Prognathochromis venator (E)
H: Uganda

Prognathochromis vittatus (Ex)

Prognathochromis worthingtoni (CE)
H: Uganda

Prognathochromis xenostoma (Ex)

Psammochromis acidens (V)
H: Kenya, Tanzania, Uganda

Psammochromis aelocephalus (V)
H: Kenya, Tanzania, Uganda

Psammochromis cassius (Ex)

Ptychochromoides sp. (V)
H: Madagascar

Ptychochromoides betsileanus (CE)
H: Madagascar

Ptyochromis Rusinga oral sheller (CE)
H: Kenya

Ptyochromis rainbow sheller (CE)
H: Kenya, Tanzania

Ptyochromis annectens (E)
H: Kenya

Ptyochromis granti (E)
H: Kenya

Ptyochromis sauvagei (V)
H: Kenya, Tanzania

Pungu maclareni (CE)
H: Cameroon

Pyxichromis orthostoma (V)
H: Uganda

Pyxichromis parorthostoma (Ex)

Sarotherodon caroli (CE)
H: Cameroon

Sarotherodon galileus Ejagham (V)
H: Cameroon

Sarotherodon linnellii (CE)
H: Cameroon

Sarotherodon lohbergeri (CE)
H: Cameroon

Sarotherodon steinbachi (CE)
H: Cameroon

Serranochromis meridianus (CD)
H: South Africa

Stomatepia mariae (CE)
H: Cameroon

Stomatepia mongo (CE)
H: Cameroon

Stomatepia pindu (CE)
H: Cameroon

Tilapia jewel (V)
H: Cameroon

Tilapia little black (V)
H: Cameroon

Tilapia yellow-green (V)
H: Cameroon

Tilapia bakossiorum (V)
H: Cameroon

Tilapia bemini (V)
H: Cameroon

Tilapia bythobathes (V)
H: Cameroon

Tilapia deckerti (V)
H: Cameroon

Tilapia flava (V)
H: Cameroon

Tilapia guinasana (CE)
H: Namibia

Tilapia gutturosa (V)
H: Cameroon

Tilapia imbriferna (V)
H: Cameroon

Tilapia kottae (V)
H: Cameroon

Tilapia snyderae (V)
H: Cameroon

Tilapia spongotroktis (V)
H: Cameroon

Tilapia thysi (V)
H: Cameroon

Xystichromis bayoni (Ex)

Xystichromis Kyoga flameback (CE)
H: Uganda

Xystichromis nuchisquamulatus (E)
H: Kenya

Xystichromis phytophagus (CE)
H: Kenya

Yssichromis argens (Exw)

Yssichromis pyrrhocephalus (V)
H: Kenya, Tanzania

ELEOTRIDAE

Boroda expatria (V)
H: Philippines

Butis butis (NT)
H: Mozambique, South Africa

Eleotris melanosoma (NT)
H: Mozambique, South Africa

Gobiomorphus alpinus (V)
H: New Zealand

Hypseleotris dayi (NT)
H: South Africa

Hypseleotris ejuncida (NT)
H: Australia

Hypseleotris kimberleyensis (NT)
H: Australia

Hypseleotris regalis (NT)
H: Australia

Kimberleyeleotris hutchinsi (NT)
H: Australia

Kimberleyeleotris notata (NT)
H: Australia

Mogurnda furva (V)
H: Papua New Guinea

Mogurnda spilota (V)
H: Papua New Guinea

Mogurnda variegata (V)
H: Papua New Guinea

Mogurnda vitta (V)
H: Papua New Guinea

Typhleotris madgascarensis (V)
H: Madagascar

Typhleotris pauliani (V)
H: Madagascar

GOBIIDAE

Chlamydogobius gloveri (V)
H: Australia

Chlamydogobius micropterus (CE)
H: Australia

Chlamydogobius squamigenus (CE)
H: Australia

Croilia mossambica (NT)
H: Mozambique, South Africa

Economidichthys pygmaeus (V)
H: Greece

Economidichthys trichonis (V)
H: Greece

Eucyclogobius newberryi (V)
H: USA

Glossgobius flavipinnis (V)
H: Indonesia

Glossogobius ankaranensis (CE)
H: Madagascar

Glossogobius biocellatus (NT)
H: Mozambique, South Africa, Tanzania

Glossogobius intermedius (V)
H: Indonesia

Glossogobius matanensis (V)
H: Indonesia

Knipowitschia croatica (V)
H: Croatia

Knipowitschia punctatissima (V)
H: Italy

Knipowitschia thessala (V)
H: Greece

Lentipes whittenorum (V)
H: Indonesia

Mistichthys luzonensis (CD)
H: Philippines

Mugilogobius adeia (V)
H: Indonesia

Mugilogobius latifrons (V)
H: Indonesia

Oligolepis keiensis (NT)
H: Mozambique, South Africa

Padogobius martensii (NT)
H: Croatia, Italy, Slovenia, Switzerland

Padogobius nigricans (V)
H: Italy

Pandaka pygmaea (CE)
H: Philippines

Papillogobius melanobranchus (NT)
H: Mozambique, South Africa

Papillogobius reichei (NT)
H: Mozambique, South Africa, Tanzania

Priolepis robinsi (NT)
H: Western central Atlantic

Redigobius bikolanus (NT)
H: Mozambique, South Africa

Redigobius dewaali (NT)
H: Mozambique, South Africa

Sicydium stimpsoni (NT)
H: USA

Sicyopus axillimentus (V)
H: Philippines

Silhouettea sibayi (NT)
H: Mozambique, South Africa

Stiphodon surrrufus (V)
H: Philippines

Stupidogobius flavipinnis (V)
H: Indonesia

Taenioides jacksoni (NT)
H: South Africa

Tamanka sarasinorum (V)
H: Indonesia

Weberogobius amadi (CE)
H: Indonesia

ANABANTIDAE

Sandelia bainsii (E)
H: South Africa

BELONTIIDAE

Belontia signata (CD)
H: Sri Lanka

Betta burdigala (V)
H: Indonesia

Betta chini (V)
H: Malaysia

Betta chloropharynx (V)
H: Indonesia

Betta hipposideros (V)
H: Malaysia

Betta livida (E)
H: Malaysia

Betta macrostoma (V)
H: Brunei

Betta miniopinna (CE)
H: Indonesia

Betta persephone (CE)
H: Malaysia

Betta simplex (V)
H: Thailand

Betta spilotogena (CE)
H: Indonesia

Betta tomi (V)
H: Malaysia

Malpulutta kretseri (CD)
H: Sri Lanka

Parosphromenus harveyi (E)
H: Malaysia

CITES

CONVENTION ON INTERNATIONAL TRADE IN ENDANGERED SPECIES
OF WILD FAUNA AND FLORA (CITES)

Version: Appendices I and II: 16 February 1995
        Appendix III: 16 November 1995
Internet address: http://www.wcmc.org.uk/CITES

PISCES

CERATODIFORMES
    Ceratodidae
        Neoceratodus forsteri

COELACANTHIFORMES
    Coelacanthidae
        Latimeria chalumnae

ACIPENSERIFORMES
    Acipenseridae
        Acipenser brevirostrum
        Acipenser oxyrhynchus
        Acipenser sturio
    Polyodontidae
        Polyodon spathula

OSTEOGLOSSIFORMES
    Osteoglossidae
        Arapaima gigas
        Scleropages formosus

CYPRINIFORMES
    Cyprinidae
        Caecobarbus geertsi
        Probarbus jullieni
    Catostomidae
        Chasmistes cujus

SILURIFORMES
    Schilbeidae
        Pangasianodon gigas

PERCIFORMES
    Sciaenidae
        Cynoscion macdonaldi

Comprehensive Index

Scientific names are in **bold**, species and genera are in *italics* and while higher taxa (families, etc.) are listed in SMALL CAPS.
Synonyms and other "scientific" denominations (e.g., trade names) are in *italics* and light. The superscript refers to the position of the species on the indicated page; for spatial reasons the individual species descriptions could not include such identifiers.
Common names are listed in normal, light font.

A

Comprehensive Index

Comprehensive Index

Comprehensive Index

Comprehensive Index

Comprehensive Index

Comprehensive Index

973

Comprehensive Index

Comprehensive Index

Comprehensive Index

Comprehensive Index

Comprehensive Index

Comprehensive Index

Comprehensive Index

Comprehensive Index

Comprehensive Index

Comprehensive Index

Comprehensive Index

Comprehensive Index

"Bentota", *Oryzias* sp. — 5/464, 868
- ricefish — 5/464, 868
bequaerti, Alestes — 1/216, 47[2]
-, *Gobius* — 5/1050, 822[1]
berdmorei, Botia — 1/366, 163
-, *Syncrossus* — 1/366, 163[5]
bergi, Abramis sapa — 5/118, 174
-, *Gymnocharacinus* — 3/110, 77
Bergia altipinnis — 1/250, 88[2]
bergianus, Nemachilus — 3/280, 152[1]
Berg's bream — 5/118, 174
Berkenkamp's panchax — 2/642, 421
berkenkampi, Epiplatys — 2/642, 5/474, 420[5,6], 421[1-3], 421
berlandieri, Lepidosteus — 2/212, 32[6]
Berney's shark cat — 2/434, 251
berneyi, Arius — 2/434, 251[5]
-, *Hexanematichthys* — 2/434, 251[5]
Berthold's killie — 1/580, 398
bertholdi, Aphyosemion — 1/580, 398
-, *Roloffia* — 1/580, 398[3]
bertoni, Corydoras — 2/468, 282[2]
Betta akarensis — 5/640, 575, 577
- *anabatoides* — 2/794, 2/794, 578[5], 575
- *anabantoides* — 2/794, 578[5]
betta, Balung — 5/642, 576
Betta balunga — 5/642, 576
betta, Banded — 2/798, 585
Betta bellica — 1/628, 3/642, 576
betta, Black — 3/654, 581
Betta bleekeri — 3/642, 576[3-5]
betta, Breder's — 3/644, 576
Betta brederi — 3/644, 576
- *brownorum* — 4/566, 577
- *burdigala* — 5/644, 577
- *chini* — 5/640, 575[4,5]
- *climacura* — 3/644, 5/640, 575[4,5], 577[3]
- - "Matang" — 3/644, 577[4]
- - "Spitzkopf" — 3/644, 577[5,6]
- *coccina* — 1/628, 3/646, 5/645, 578
- sp. aff. *coccina* — 4/566, 577[1]
betta, Dark — 3/648, 579, 580
-, Dwarf — 3/656, 581, 582
-, Edith's — 2/794, 578
Betta edithae — 2/794, 578
betta, Emerald — 1/632, 583
Betta enisae — 5/648, 578, 579
- *fasciata* — 1/628, 3/642, 576[3-5]
betta, Foersch's — 2/796, 579
Betta foerschi — 2/796, 579
- - "Nataisedawak" — 4/570, 579
- - "Tarantang" — 4/570, 579
- *fusca* — 3/648, 5/646, 578, 579
betta, Giant — 3/653, 580, 581
Betta imbellis — 1/630, 3/650, 5/646, 5/650, 583[1], 580
betta, Ladder-finned — 3/644, 577
Betta livida — 5/645, 578[1-4]
betta, Long-finned — 3/644, 577
Betta macrophthalma — 2/798, 3/653, 5/647, 585[1], 580, 581
- *macrostoma* — 2/796, 581
- *miniopinna* — 5/645, 581[5,6], 582[1,2]

betta, Mouthbrooding — 1/630, 582
Betta ocellara — 2/800, 585[4]
betta, One-spot — 2/800, 585
-, Painted — 2/798, 582
Betta patoti — 3/654, 581
betta, Peaceful — 1/630, 3/650, 580, 583
-, Pearly — 2/794, 575
Betta persephone — 3/656, 5/645, 581, 582
- *phuket* — 3/650, 580[4]
- *picta* — 2/798, 3/648, 579[5,6], 580[1,2], 582
- *prima* — 5/651, 582
- *pugnax* — 1/630, 1/632, 3/644, 3/648, 5/648, 576[6], 579[5,6], 580[1,2], 584[1-6], 582
- *rubra* — 1/630, 1/632, 2/798, 5/646, 5/650, 582[3], 584[1-6], 583
- *rutilans* — 4/566, 583
betta, Sarawak — 5/640, 575
Betta schalleri — 5/646, 579[5,6], 580[1,2]
- *simplex* — 4/568, 583
betta, Slender — 1/628, 3/642, 583
Betta smaragdina — 1/632, 583
- sp. "Anjungan" — 4/566, 583[2]
- - "Krabi" — 4/568, 583[3-5]
- *spilotogena* — 5/647, 580[5,6], 581[1]
- *splendens* — 1/632, 3/650, 4/565, 580[3,4], 584
- *"splendens"* — 1/630, 583[1]
betta, Striped fighting — 1/628, 3/642, 576
Betta strohi — 4/570, 579[3]
- *taeniata* — 2/794, 2/798, 3/644, 5/640, 575[4,5], 577[3-6], 578[5], 585
- *tomi* — 5/647, 580[5,6], 581[1]
- *trifasciata* — 1/632, 2/798, 3/648, 579[5,6], 580[1,2], 582[3], 584[1-6], 585[1]
betta, Tussy's — 3/658, 585
Betta tussyae — 3/658, 585
- *unimaculata* — 2/800, 585
- *waseri* — 3/653, 580[5,6], 581[1]
betta, Wine-red — 1/628, 3/646, 5/645, 578
biaculeata, Acantopsis — 1/366, 163[2]
biaculeatus, Balistes — 5/1109, 922[6]
-, *Gasterosteus* — 1/834, 877[5]
-, *Triacanthus* — 5/1109, 922
Biafra panchax — 4/384, 421, 422
biafranus, Aplocheilus — 4/384, 421[6], 422[1]
-, *Epiplatys* — 4/384, 421, 422
bibie, Barilius — 4/192, 199[2]
-, *Chelaethiops* — 4/192, 199
-, *Leuciscus* — 4/192, 199[2]
-, *Pelecus* — 4/192, 199[2]
bibroni, Anguilla — 3/935, 849[2]
bicarinatus, Chaenothorax — 1/458, 270[3], 3/326, 270[4]
bichir, Armored — 2/216, 30
-, Cuvier's — 2/218, 30
-, Marbled — 2/216, 30
-, Senegal — 2/218, 30
bicirrhis, Cryptopterichthys — 1/515, 382[4]
-, *Silurus* — 1/515, 382[4]
bicirrhosa, Illana — 3/982, 816[4]
bicirrhosum, Ischnosoma — 1/858, 901[6]
-, *Osteoglossum* — 1/858, 901

Comprehensive Index

Comprehensive Index

Comprehensive Index

Comprehensive Index

Comprehensive Index

Comprehensive Index

Comprehensive Index

Comprehensive Index

Comprehensive Index

Comprehensive Index

Comprehensive Index

Comprehensive Index

Comprehensive Index

Comprehensive Index

Comprehensive Index

Comprehensive Index

Comprehensive Index

Comprehensive Index

Comprehensive Index

Comprehensive Index

Comprehensive Index

Comprehensive Index

Comprehensive Index

Comprehensive Index

Comprehensive Index

Comprehensive Index

Comprehensive Index

Comprehensive Index

Comprehensive Index

Comprehensive Index

Comprehensive Index

Comprehensive Index

Comprehensive Index

Comprehensive Index

Comprehensive Index

Comprehensive Index

1041

Comprehensive Index

Comprehensive Index

Comprehensive Index

Comprehensive Index

Comprehensive Index

Comprehensive Index

Comprehensive Index

Comprehensive Index

Comprehensive Index

Comprehensive Index

Comprehensive Index

Comprehensive Index

Comprehensive Index

Comprehensive Index

Comprehensive Index

Comprehensive Index

Comprehensive Index

Comprehensive Index

Comprehensive Index

Comprehensive Index

Comprehensive Index

Comprehensive Index

Comprehensive Index

Comprehensive Index

Comprehensive Index

Comprehensive Index

Comprehensive Index

Comprehensive Index

Comprehensive Index

Comprehensive Index

Comprehensive Index

Comprehensive Index

Comprehensive Index

Comprehensive Index

Comprehensive Index

Comprehensive Index

Comprehensive Index

Comprehensive Index

Comprehensive Index

Comprehensive Index

Comprehensive Index

Comprehensive Index

Comprehensive Index

Comprehensive Index

Comprehensive Index

Comprehensive Index

Comprehensive Index

Comprehensive Index

Comprehensive Index

Comprehensive Index

Comprehensive Index

Comprehensive Index

Comprehensive Index

Comprehensive Index

1118

Comprehensive Index

Comprehensive Index

Comprehensive Index

Comprehensive Index

Comprehensive Index

Comprehensive Index

Comprehensive Index

Comprehensive Index

Comprehensive Index

1130

Comprehensive Index

Comprehensive Index

Comprehensive Index

Comprehensive Index

Comprehensive Index

Comprehensive Index

Comprehensive Index

Comprehensive Index

Comprehensive Index

Comprehensive Index

Comprehensive Index

Comprehensive Index

Comprehensive Index

Comprehensive Index

Comprehensive Index

Comprehensive Index

Comprehensive Index

Comprehensive Index

Comprehensive Index

Comprehensive Index

Comprehensive Index

Comprehensive Index

Comprehensive Index

Comprehensive Index

Comprehensive Index

Comprehensive Index

Comprehensive Index

Comprehensive Index

1173

Comprehensive Index

Comprehensive Index

1176

Comprehensive Index

1180

Comprehensive Index

Comprehensive Index

Comprehensive Index

Comprehensive Index

Comprehensive Index

Comprehensive Index

Comprehensive Index

Comprehensive Index

Comprehensive Index

Comprehensive Index

Comprehensive Index

Comprehensive Index

Hans A. Baensch,

born 1941 in Flensburg, Germany, grew up in the vicinity of Hannover. The native aquatic fauna and flora were introduced early to the biologist's son by his father. After an apprenticeship as a zoological wholesaler, he joined the family's aquarium fish food factory (Tetra). He traveled to most mayor aquarium fish centers of the world and participated in two Amazon expeditions, during which three new fish species were discovered. He has a passion for diving in and photographing tropical waters. His first book —"Kleine Seewasser Praxis"—was published in 1974.

In 1977 he opened his own publishing house. Today, he lives on a small farm near Melle, immersed in forest and water, where he actively protects the native amphibian, reptile, and fish populations. He writes and publishes books which bring joy and knowledge to naturalists. With the book series AQUARIUM ATLAS and MARINE ATLAS, he has acquired a worldwide reputation for the authors of the MERGUS VERLAG.

Dr. Gero W. Fischer,

born 1961 in Saarbrücken, Germany, moved overseas with his parents during his early childhood. There he has lived since 1968 in Ecuador, South America. During his studies in the German School Quito, most of his free time was spent at his parents' beef cattle ranch at the edge of the Amazon Basin. Both the aquaria of his early childhood and the colorful schools of coral fishes of Bora Bora in Polynesia he observed while snokeling enticed him to set out with a sieve and bucket to the creeks and rivers of his home in Ecuador. His interest grew, and he graduated to a canoe and then a motor boat and began exploring the rivers and lagoons throughout his adopted country. His interest cemented, he began collecting broodstock to start a breeding program.

After graduating in animal science (B.S.) and agricultural economics (M.S.), he concluded his years of study in the United States in 1991 with a doctorate in aquaculture (Ph.D.) from Texas A&M University; the necessary field work he performed in ponds, vats, and aquaria at his ranch, which he expanded from beef cattle production to aquaculture. Food fishes are produced with weekly harvests year-round and several dozen aquarium and food fishes are being investigated in regard to their production economies.

For the past few years, Dr. Fischer and his wife Shellie (M.S.—fish nutrition) have worked as translators, taking MERGUS ATLASES from German into English and Spanish.

Otto Böhm

was born 1922 in Vienna, Austria. At the age of eight, he had his first frame aquarium with the obligatory heating cone. He built himself small terraria from fruit shipping crates and maintained lizards, frogs, and blindworms therein. Otto Böhm returned from Sunday excursions with aquatic snails, minnows, fire salamanders and newts, which he cared for successfully. Later he made his first aquaristic experiences with sticklebacks and paradise fishes. Livebearers were followed by egg-laying characins, and in 1959, he successfully bred the cardinal tetra.

Starting in 1970, killifishes caught his attention, and he joined the German Killifish Association (Deutsche Killifisch Gemeinschaft). Numerous novel species were being imported then from Africa. After successfully breeding most, he distributed them to fellow aquarists. His photographs and valuable sixty years of experience are shared in numerous national and foreign publications.

Dieter Bork,

born 1945 in Hanau, Germany, has been a dedicated aquarist since 1956. His aquaristic activities were interrupted by the military service and subsequent studies in engineering (Dipl. Ing.). In his capacity as an engineer, he is responsible for the acquisition and maintenance of production lines.

In 1972 he joined the German Killifish Association (Deutsche Killifisch Gemeinschaft). For over 25 years he has devotedly bred aquarium fishes. His interest centers on killies, dwarf cichlids, rare livebearers, and various dwarf rasboras.

Since 1988 he has traveled regularly to the natural biotopes of aquarium fishes to collect and study them. The results are expressed in seminars and publications in aquarium magazines.

Heinz H. Büscher,

born 1942 in Bielefeld, Germany, has worked for over 30 years as a biotechnician at a pharmaceutical company in Switzerland.

In his early childhood he began observing native aquatic organisms in bomb craters. The magnifying glass and the microscope, his most important tools, were discovered early on, and his aquaristic development began. His exceptional talents have been demonstrated over the years.

After many years of maintaining and breeding characins and South American dwarf cichlids as well as invertebrates and blennies from the Mediterranean, he developed an interest in fishes hailing from lakes Malawi and Tanganyika during the late 60's. In numerous expeditions to Lake Tanganyika he discovered more than 14 unknown cichlid species. The study of a section of Zaïrean coast yielded data rich in information on lifestyles and species communities. This in turn led to new discoveries, 10 of which he has described.

Hans-Georg Evers

was born 1964 in Hamburg, Germany, where he still lives today. After getting his high school diploma, he completed his training to be a shipping merchant. He has maintained an aquarium and an occasional terrarium since his 11th birthday. So far he has successfully bred over 200 fish species. The catfishes and, more recently, the characins are especially interesting to him. In the VDA work-group "barbs, characins, loaches, catfishes" he leads the division "characins" and is the regional group chairman.

Aside from nomenclatural problems and their introduction and significance for the aquarium hobby, he has dedicated his attentions on the reproduction of these fishes and publishes his results in more than 100 different national and foreign publications.

In 1994, his book "Panzerwelse" [Armored Catfishes] was published, and in 1996 he coauthored the BSSW special publication "Maulbrütende Harnischwelse" [Mouthbrooding Suckermouth Catfishes] with Ingo Seidel. He has collaborated in various other books, especially with his photographs.

He has traveled several times to South America since 1992, introducing new species to the aquarium hobby and science.

Dr. Jörg Freyhof

was born the 4th of November 1964, in Ludwigshafen at the Rhein, Germany.

He studied biology at the universities of Heidelberg and Bonn, where he received a doctorate in biology with emphasis on limnological ecology and fisheries sciences concerning the deterministic and coincidental structuring of a piscine community in a Rhein tributary.

His interests largely center on the biology of fishes of the Palearctic and African regions.

Raised in a family of aquarists, he has dealt with many fish groups and traveled to western, central, and northern Africa, South America, and European countries in search of fishes.

He is presently on staff at the Ichthyology Department of the Alexander König Zoological Research Institute and Museum in Bonn.

Steffen E. P. Hellner

was born 1961 in Rendsburg/Holstein. After graduating from high school in 1981, he served in the armed forces until 1983 as a liaison officer to the US Army, first lieutenant of the reserve.

He studied political science and philosophy in Munich, Stuttgart, and Tübingen. From 1989 to 1993 he was employed as a conceptual copywriter in advertising agencies. Now he has his own copywriting firm for advertising and PR. Besides his wife Godja and son Moritz (born June 1996), good friends and nature are of primary importance to him.

He has maintained an aquarium since the age of 12. At the age of 14, his interest was captured by killifishes and he has concentrated on that fish group ever since. In 1977 he joined the German Killifish Association (Deutsche Killifisch Gemeinschaft) where he has been an editor since 1996.

His 1989 monograph about killifishes has been translated into English. Subsequently he has been coauthor/advisor for several books. He has participated in international symposia in England, Belgium, Austria, and Switzerland as well as the United States.

From collecting trips to Sierra Leone, the United States, and thrice to Brazil, he has imported many killifishes for the first time and discovered several unknown species. A collection trip to Cameroon and two scientific descriptions of killifishes are planned.

Harro Hieronimus,

born 1956 in Krefeld, Germany, has been an aquarist since childhood. During his studies (chemistry/geography Sek. II), his aquaristic interests intensified, giving birth to his first publications. This trend did not alter with the beginning of his activities as a consultant for teaching aids of natural sciences. From the beginning, it was the livebearing toothcarps and the Mexican goodeids that were particularly appealing to him. It is no surprise that his collecting trips led him to Mexico and other areas of Central America. Nevertheless, in the mid 80's, two additional fish groups began to interest him: the rainbowfishes and the catfishes, especially the corydoras.

In 1986, he founded and has since headed the International Rainbowfish Association (IRG = Internationale Gesellschaft für Regenbogenfische), and since 1992 he also heads the German Livebearer Association (DGLZ = Deutsche Gesellschaft für Lebendgebärende Zahnkarpfen).

Meanwhile, he has authored several books dealing with aquaristic subjects and several hundred articles in German and foreign magazines and presented numerous public presentations regarding the aquarium hobby. He has described two new corydoras species. Additional species are in the works.

Martin Hoffmann

was born 1970 in Salzgitter, Germany. Son of an aquarium hobbyist, he soon became interested in decorative fishes. At the same time he explored the native aquatic fauna (sticklebacks, frogs, salamanders, etc.). He received his first aquarium at the age of 10. Two additional aquaria were quickly attained. Livebearing toothcarps and corydoras were the first fishes he successfully bred. His interest now centers on small South American characins as well as armored catfishes and dwarf cichlids. Martin Hoffmann graduated from high school in 1990 and absolved the civil service in a hospital. In 1991 he began his studies in medicine at the Medical University of Hannover. He expects to attain his license in early 1998 after a 2 year experimental doctoral dissertation in internal medicine.

In 1994 he realized one of his dreams: a trip to Brazil (Tefé). There he captured several fishes for his aquaria back home, including the Tefé apistogramma. For some years he and his father, Peter Hoffmann, have published articles in DATZ.

Peter Hoffmann

was born 1942 in Liegnitz, Silesia, present day Poland. Following elementary school, an 1956 apprenticeship in casting, a 1959 journeyman examination, and a 1963 casting technician examination at the metallurgical school in Duisburg, he is now employed as a production designer.

At seven years of age he kept sticklebacks in a marmalade jar; at the age of nine he kept goldfish in his first all-glass aquarium. From there he developed into an avid aquarist, until now he has a basement with approximately 40 aquaria.

Peter Hoffman breeds and photographs aquarium fishes as a hobby, particularly characin, dwarf cichlid, and armored catfish by-catches from South America.

For the past 20 years, he has written breeding reports and other informative articles and provided photographic material to the DATZ magazine.

On two separate occasions he collected fishes from the Rio Negro and Lake Tefé of Brazil, importing them into Germany.

Hans Horsthemke

was born the 17th of December of 1952 in Bochum, Germany. He studied Germanistics and geography. Since 1982, he has taught at a secondary school in Dortmund.

An aquarist from childhood, he became interested in brackish water fishes during the mid 70's. His attention has centered on brackish water and freshwater gobies (Gobioidei). His experiences with almost 150 exotic goby species have resulted in numerous essays in journals, principally dealing with the reproductive biology of these fishes.

For the past few years he has been working on a monograph about gobies for the brackish water and freshwater aquarium, which will appear shortly.

Prof. Dr. Frank Kirschbaum,

born 1942 in Hilden, Germany, began breeding fishes and amphibians at the age of 10.

After attaining his high school diploma in 1961, he studied biology and biochemistry with a mayor in zoology in Cologne and Tübingen. His dissertation with the title "Untersuchungen zum Farbmuster der Zebrabarbe" [Analyses of the color schemes in zebra barbs] shows that henceforth he dealt with fishes in science.

During a research stay of almost five years in France, he was the first to successfully breed weakly electrical fishes (Nile pikes and knifefishes). These successes were the starting point for research into the development and evolution of electrical organs, resulting in the discovery of electrical organs in larvae. This research served as a foundation for his dissertation that was concluded in 1984.

From 1978 to 1988 he was an assistant at the Zoological Institute of Cologne; from 1988 to 1992 he lead the work group at the Institute for Toxicology and Embryonal Pharmaceutics at the Freie Universität Berlin. Since 1992 he has headed the section of fish biology and ecology at the prestigious Institute for Aquatic Ecology and Inland Fisheries at the Müggelsee in Berlin (an institute on the "blue list").

Several research expeditions have taken him to South and Central America, Africa, and Southeast Asia, where his interests centered on ecological questions and systematics of knifefishes.

Magister Anton Lamboj

was born 1956 in Baden near Vienna, Austria. The goldfish of his grandfather's garden pond represented his first childhood contact with fishes. At the age of ten, he received his first aquarium with tropical fishes.

After his qualifying exam, he began his professional career at the Austrian railway, where he is still employed today.

In the later half of the 70's he mostly specialized in west African dwarf cichlids and their systematics. This led to studies in biology in 1988 and eventually to a masters in 1993. His doctoral dissertation, a monograph including a revision of the genus *Chromidotilapia*, is close to completion. Since 1983 he has traveled ten times to western and central Africa to study in detail habitat and distribution of the dwarf cichlids in detail.

So far he is the author of over fifty publications—both of aquaristic and scientific nature. Numerous presentations—both national and international—as well as the collaboration on various books and magazines are part of his regular activities.

Authors – Aᴛʟᴀꜱᴇꜱ

Manfred K. Meyer,

born 1952 in Friedberg, Hessen, Germany, studied mathematics and by the age of 10 had his first aquarium of guppies. In the early 70's, he specialized in livebearers. Since the mid 80's he has also developed an interest towards cichlids from the east African Rift Valley Lakes—Malawi and Tanganyika in particular—and other fishes from west African habitats.

He has written two books dealing with livebearing aquarium fishes and over 100 articles in foreign and national zoological papers and aquarium magazines. In cooperation with numerous authors he has described over 20 new fish species from Africa and Central America.

Besides dealing with aspects of the aquarium hobby and phylogenesis in fishes, the author practices his profession dealing with AI research in computers with emphasis on the development of neural networks.

Gerhard Ott

was born in 1954 along the lower Rhein. From his elementary school days, he had a small "zoo" at home. Aquaria were added to his menagerie at the age of 12. After finishing high school, he studied educational science (andragogics), philosophy, theology, and biology in Hamburg, where he graduated with a thesis about "Ethology and Pedagogics." For over 10 years he traveled the seas, and presently he is a lieutenant commander in the fleet of the Baltic Sea at Glücksburg.

Gerhard Ott's aquaristic interests are centered on the ichthyological fauna of Sri Lanka and the south Indian area as well as in the Cypriniformes of southern and southeastern Asia, particularly the Cobitoidea. He directs the VDA division "fish identification" and is responsible for the loach chapter of the VDA work group BSSW (Barben Salmler Schmerlen Welse = barbs, characins, loaches, catfishes). He is an active member of the aquarium and terrarium association "Aǫᴜᴀᴛʀᴏᴘɪᴄ 1990 e.V." Since 1971 he has written articles for trade magazines and books. His first book "Schmerlen" [Loaches] appeared in 1988.

1204

Kurt Paffrath,

born 1931 in Cologne, Germany, is the author of the plant sections in the AQUARIUM ATLASES.

His intense interest in aquarium plants came from his profession. After WW II he entered an agricultural apprenticeship with a farmer in the Eifel. In 1948 he continued his gardening studies at a cloister garden. Since 1953 he worked at the Botanical Garden of Cologne. Because of his previous experience with aquarium plants, he was assigned to the bog and aquatic plants as well as to the maintenance of exhibition aquaria. In 1958 he passed his masters exam in botanical gardening. He began working at the Department for Green Areas in Cologne in 1965, where he is a garden construction technician.

He has shared his extensive experience with aquarium plants in almost 300 slide presentations for aquarium associations. Additionally he has published numerous articles in many German and foreign aquarium magazines. His book about the care of aquarium plants was published in 1978 by Landbuch of Hannover.

Dr. Rüdiger Riehl,

born 1949 in Gombeth at Kassel, Germany, was maintaining and observing native fishes in canning jars from the early age of six. Soon followed an aquarium and the switch to exotic fishes. After high school graduation in 1967, he began studying biology at Gießen. In his masters thesis and doctoral dissertation he studied the various mechanisms of ovogenesis of native freshwater fishes. He received his doctorate (Dr. rer. nat.) in 1976 at Gießen.

From 1974 to 1979 he worked as a scientist at the Institute for General and Applied Zoology of Gießen. Subsequently he moved to the skin clinic at the University of Heidelberg (1979–1982) where he researched skin cancer. At the end of 1982 Dr. Riehl moved to Düsseldorf and became the head advisor for electron microscopy at the biology institutes. In Düsseldorf he remains heavily involved with fishes; over 130 articles in scientific journals and six books bear witness to his activities. Since 1977 he has participated at numerous national and international symposia with presentations and poster sessions. He spent research time in Israel, Austria, Liechtenstein, and the Antarctic. Additionally, he is an active participant in two international fish programs: one about eggs of Antarctic species and the other about aquaculture of economically important fishes.

Dipl. Biol. Uwe Römer,

born in 1959, has been a nature enthusiast since early childhood. As a youth, he dealt with specific questions concerning the protection and biology of native fishes, amphibians, and reptiles. During high school, he specialized in ornithology and made an intensive commitment to nature conservation.

Several scientific long-term studies are the result of this phase. His involvement with birds lead to an active travel schedule, with an emphasis on the bird islands in the North Atlantic, Scandinavia, and North America. The professional specialization brought about extensive consulting for planning agencies and administrative bodies which he accomplished during his studies. At present, he is a biologist at a biological station. Concurrently he is concluding his dissertation which deals with the biology of dwarf cichlids of the genus *Apistogramma*.

At the beginning of his studies in Bielefeld, his interest became focused on neotropical fishes—particularly *Apistogramma* spp.—as well as ecological and ethnological problems of Amazonia. During the 1990's several trips were undertaken to the Rio Negro region, where he was even able to reach the very unaccessible Rio Uaupés. The main subject of the enthusiastic nature photographer are birds, cichlids, and ethnological themes. The majority of his 100 publications and numerous presentations in Europe and North America are illustrated with his own photographs from his extensive archives.

Dr. Jürgen Schmidt,

born 1959 in Kamen, Germany, had his first aquarium and other domestic pets as a kindergartner.

In the 70's he specialized in labyrinth fishes and other fishes of Southeast Asia.

He studied biology and geography with a major in ethology (behavioral studies) and landscape ecology at Münster and received his doctorate. His dissertation is titled "Vergleichende Untersuchungen zum Fortpflanzungsverhalten der *Betta*-Arten (Belontiidae, Anabantoidei" [Comparative studies in the reproductive behavior of *Betta* species (Belontiidae, Anabantoidei]. The theses of Dr. Schmidt dealt with fighting fishes for biology and the aquatic ecology of a valley in the Sauerland for the subject of geography.

He worked in an internship at the WWU Münster, in various publishing houses, and as a nature correspondent. He has collaborated on books and written numerous articles for aquarium and scientific magazines.

Erwin Schraml

was born 1957 in Augsburg, Germany. Based on his close bond with nature and fascination with the unknown, he soon developed an intense interest in native ichthyofaunal populations. He was particularly enthused by the limited spatial requirements of aquaria and the ease with which they allowed him to observe the fish's natural behavior. Soon every nook and crevice in his surroundings was filled with "aquatic microcosms."

This led to textual and photographic documentation, which was expressed in a multitude of articles in trade journals and a study of photography. Today, his archives of thousands of photos enable him to contribute his photographic material to numerous books and magazines. Because even published information on fishes is easily forgotten or difficult to retrieve, he developed data base applications to index and store aquaristic and ichthyological articles.

As an amateur diver he observed the behavior of fishes in their natural habitat, complementing his aquarium experiences. Taxonomic questions are largely resolved through his contacts with ichthyologists, and his relations with fish importers keep him supplied in new species, thereby providing him with subject matter for his photography. Fishes have become a large part of his life. In parallel, for the past number of years he has supported himself and his family through his activities as an independent social pedagogue.

Ingo Seidel

was born in 1967 in Delmenhorst, Germany. Because of his childhood fascination with everything that creeped, flew, or swam, his father introduced him to the aquarium hobby. He received his first aquarium at the tender age of 10 and has been an enthusiastic aquarist ever since. His professional development, however, went in a totally different direction. After graduating from high school, he began training to become a mathematical/technical assistant and is now working in software development at an electronics company in Bremen in the area of simulation technology.

The fish fauna of South America particularly interests him; he initially dealt intensively with the genus *Apistogramma*. Later his focus began to shift towards catfishes, until today his interests are firmly centered on the reproductive biology of that group. He has specialized in the suckermouth catfishes (Loricariidae), but he has also successfully bred over 30 *Corydoras* spp. During his travels to South America he learned quite a lot concerning this interesting fish group. Since 1992 he has headed the catfish chapter of the VDA work group "barbs, characins, loaches, catfishes."

Dr. Andreas Spreinat,

born 1960 in Lemgo, Germany, had his first aquarium at the age of six. In the early 70's, he became particularly interested in the cichlids of Lake Malawi. After graduating from high school in 1979, he served for two years as a navigation NCO on a submarine. He then studied biology with an emphasis in microbiology/biochemistry in Göttingen. His doctoral dissertation was titled "Thermostabile stärke-abbauende Enzyme von thermophilen anaeroben Mikroorganismen" [Heat stable carbohydrate-reducing enzymes of thermophile anaerobic microorganisms]. Since 1991 he has held a position in an engineering office in Göttingen as area manager in charge of biological-chemical analyses, environmental reports, and environmental reclamation.

He has visited Lake Malawi 6 times in the last 13 years, taking many of his 32,000 fish photographs during his 600 dives in the lake. Two books about Lake Malawi cichlids, contributions to trade journals, and numerous national and international presentations are accredited to his name.

Dr. Wolfgang Staeck,

born 1939 in Berlin, Germany, studied biology at the Freie Universität Berlin. Following the state examination, he joined the research staff at the Technische Universität Berlin. He received his doctorate in zoology and botany in 1972.

Dr. Staeck is widely known through his presentations and publications. Since 1966 he has published numerous essays on aquarium fishes in German and foreign magazines as well as several books. Because of his interest in the behavioral biology of cichlids, he has remained active in the hobby. He is a highly accomplished, experienced aquarist.

He has traveled repeatedly to South and Central America and the lakes Tanganyika and Malawi in eastern Africa in the last 25 years. These numerous research expeditions were dedicated to the study of cichlids in their natural habitats and lead to the discovery of many new species, subspecies, and color races. He observed and photographed fishes underwater while visiting lakes Tanganyika and Malawi in the early 70's and later Central and South America. He was the first to successfully photograph many cichlids in their natural biotope. As a result of his travels, he has described approximately a dozen new fish species.

Helmut Stallknecht,

born 1935 in Mühlhausen/Thüringen, Germany, has been an aquarist for over 50 years. Just after World War II, he began breeding fishes. He studied geography, geology, biology, and fisheries biology, and has been a teacher, a wholesaler in the former DDR, a professional breeder, an editor, and an author.

His numerous contributions to trade magazines emphasize maintenance, breeding, and reproductive behavior. The broad range of aquarium expertise was born through necessity; successful care and breeding programs were vital to the hobby in the former DDR due to the lack of imports.

Since 1960 he has written more than 800 essays and communications. The 17 brochures and books he has written since 1969 largely aim to introduce readers to biological processes that can be observed in the limited confines of an aquarium.

Only recently has he been able to visit Venezuela, Costa Rica, Sri Lanka, and Thailand to observe aquarium fishes in their natural habitat. Collecting fishes himself and new species mean constant new challenges, invigorating his drive for further study.

Frank Warzel,

born 1960 in Koblenz, Germany, grew up near Mainz and developed an interest in the fauna of his neighborhood as a very young child. His childhood expeditions to nearby bodies of water filled his parents' balcony with numerous aquatic organisms. At the age of seven he had his first tropical aquarium. After his civil service in 1983, he trained as a climate technician. For over 5 years he abandoned the hobby, but he never completely lost touch or his fascination with aquaria. With his renewed interest in aquarium keeping, he began amassing aquarium literature; today he possess virtually all the original cichlid descriptions, including synonyms.

Since his first publication in 1988, he has written over 50 articles and given several national and international presentations. He has made several trips to South America and has introduced new species of pike cichlids—his primary area of interest—from Brazil and Colombia to the aquarium hobby as well as to science. Some of these species he was able to successfully breed.

Uwe Werner,

born in 1948, is a foreign language teacher and, since 1958, an aquarist. His experiences include many varied fish families and have been summarized in his book "Aquarienpraxis—Süßwasser" [The practical freshwater aquarium] (1987). His special knowledge on Central and South American cichlids and his talent as an aquarium photographer led to a two-volume standard reference (1985, 1988), of which a new edition is currently in the works.

He has written numerous articles for national and foreign trade magazines. He published two additional books, "Fischfangabenteuer Südamerika" [South American fishing adventure] and "Ausgefallene Aquarienpfleglinge" [Exotic aquarium charges] in 1992 and 1993, respectively. Since the early 80's, Uwe Werner has undertaken many collection trips to South and Central America. He has imported many unknown fishes (mostly cichlids) for the first time (or anew) from Ecuador, Venezuela, Brazil, Colombia, Costa Rica, Guatemala, Honduras, and especially Mexico.

Rudolf Hans Wildekamp,

born in 1945 in Putten, Netherlands, received his first aquarium at the age of five. He graduated from high school in 1962 and then became a career soldier in the Dutch Air Force, where he was an airplane electronics technician and, for the last twelve years, an airport environmental officer. His duties involve reducing the danger of bird/airplane collisions by using, in part, radar to study bird migrations.

Since 1970 he has concentrated his attentions on killifishes, traveling several times to southern Europe, Turkey, the United States, Mexico, Brazil, Thailand, Nigeria, Somalia, Kenya, Tanzania, and Uganda. As a result of these travels, he has described 19 new killifish species, written numerous magazine articles, and made many national and international presentations.

In 1993 he authored three parts of a six part series, "A World of Killies," published in the United States. All relevant aspects of all the killifishes of the world are introduced therein.

Photographs

Dr. Gerald R. Allen, David Allison, Aqua Medic, Dr. Herbert R. Axelrod, Herbert Bader, Hans A. Baensch, Dr. Ulrich Baensch, H.-J. Bäselt, P.G. Bianco, Rudi Bischoff, Friedrich Bitter, Heiko Bleher, Dr. Rüdiger Bless, Jörg Bohlen, Otto Böhm, Dieter Bork, Sven Brun, Gerhard Brünner, Horst Büscher, Ingo Carstensen, Maurice Chauche, Helmut Debelius, Horst Dieckhoff, Norbert Dokoupil, Dupla Aquaristik, Jaroslav Eliás, Udo Essmann, Dr. Vollrad Etzel, Hans-Georg Evers, Dr. Gero W. Fischer, Dr. Walter Foersch, Dr. Stanislav Frank, Dr. Hanns Joachim Franke, Jörg Freyhof, Karl Albert Frickhinger, Joachim Frische, Heiner Garbe, J. Geck, S. Gehmann, M. Göbel, Jaap-Jan de Greef, Hans-Jürgen Günther, Werner Gutekunst, Hilmar Hansen, Klaus Hansen, Andreas Hartl, Horst Haunert, Steffen Hellner, Dr. Hans-J. Herrmann (Hamburg), Dr. Hans-J. Herrmann (Melle), Wolfgang Herzog, Harro Hieronimus, Martin Hoffmann, Peter Hoffmann, Kerstin Holota, Hans Horsthemke, Kurt Huwald, Stefan Inselmann, Heinrich Jung, Juwel Aquarium, Burkhard Kahl, Horst Kipper, Dr. Frank Kirschbaum, Karl Knaack, Alexander M. Kochetov, Dr. Sergei M. Kochetov, Joachim Kollo, Dr. A. Konings, Edith Korthaus, Ingo Koslowski, Dr. Maurice Kottelat, René Krummenacher, Dr. Friedhelm Krupp, Axel Kulbe, Mr. Lagdon, J. Lake, Anton Lamboj, Horst Linke, Karl-Heinz Lübeck, Oliver Lucanus, Peter Lucas, Dr. Volker Mahnert, Olaf Manzischke, Hans Joachim Mayland, Manfred K. Meyer, Ulrich Minde, Friedrich Müller, Arend van den Nieuwenhuizen, J. Nikolas, Aaron Norman, Roland Numrich, Gerhard Ott, Kurt Paffrath, Klaus Paysan, A. Pieter, Alan Pinkerton, Helmut Pinter, Eduard Pürzl, Hans Reinhard, Günter Reitz, Dr. Patrick de Rham, Hans Joachim Richter, Dr. Rüdiger Riehl, Michel Roggo, Manfred Rogner, Dr. Uwe Römer, Hans Jürgen Rösler, Lucas Rüber, Mike Sandford, David D. Sands, Hiromichi Sasakawa, Ingo Schindler, Ulrich Schliewen, Günther Schmelzer, Werner Schmettkamp, Gunther Schmida, Dr. Jürgen Schmidt, Dr. Eduard Schmidt-Focke, Erwin Schraml, Ulrich Schramm, Roland Schreiber, Dr. Gottfried Schubert, Thomas Schulz, Lothar Seegers, Ingo Seidel, Werner Seuss, Wolfgang Sommer, Ernst Sosna, Dr. Andreas Spreinat, Dr. Wolfgang Staeck, Rainer Stawikowski, B. Stemmer, Klaus Szafranek, Tetra Archiv, W. A. Tomey, F. Vermeulen, Dr. Jörg Vierke, Prof. Dr. W. Villwock, Vogelsänger-Studios, Frank Warzel, Berthold Weber, Frans Wennmacker, Uwe Werner, G. Westdörp, Ruud Wildekamp, Klaus Wilkerling, Wolfgang A. Windisch, Lothar Wischnath, Kai Erich Witte, Tonnie Woeltjes, Dr. Axel Zarske, Rudolf Zukal, Georg Zurlo.

THE
CORNERSTONE OF THE
AQUARIUM HOBBY

Available in most pet stores and in the book trade.
When not available please contact the distributor
(page 2 of this book).

AQUARIUM ATLAS

The AQUARIUM ATLAS Series has become the standard for the aquarium hobby. Each of the approximately 4000 fish species found in the five volumes is represented by a beautiful color photograph and information given on its care, association, breeding, diet, etc. In a similar format, Volumes 1, 2, and 3 additionally introduce approximately 330 plants.

Thanks to the best photographers and scientists, the AQUARIUM ATLAS has become renown worldwide. Your pet shop uses it daily as a reference! All volumes come in the same handy 12.5 x 19 cm format.

Available in English.

VOLUME 1
DR. RÜDIGER RIEHL AND HANS BAENSCH

992 pages, over 800 photos—
There are 600 fish species and 100 plant species presented.
The book that started it all. For beginners as well as advanced hobbyists!
ISBN 1-890087-12-2 (hardcover)
ISBN 1-890087-05-X (softcover)

VOLUME 2
HANS BAENSCH AND DR. RÜDIGER RIEHL

1216 pages, ca. 1150 photos—
900 fish species and 150 aquatic plants are introduced.
ISBN 1-890087-13-0 (hardcover)
ISBN 1-890087-06-8 (softcover)

VOLUME 3
DR. RÜDIGER RIEHL AND HANS BAENSCH

1104 pages, ca. 1100 photos—
This volume contains ca. 850 new fish species and 80 plant species.
ISBN 1-890087-14-9 (hardcover)
ISBN 1-890087-07-6 (softcover)

CICHLID ATLAS

Dr. Uwe Römer

1216 pages, ca. 1400 color photos, 150 drawings, 12.5 x 19 cm format—
This CICHLID ATLAS is a must-have for every enthusiast of South American dwarf cichlids. All of the described *Apistogramma* species, many of which are novelties, are presented. An original key to identify *Apistogramma* spp. has been included as well as explanations on maintenance, breeding, and factors determinig sex. Species identification of juvenile and female *Apistogramma* spp. gives aquarists assurance that he/she is maintaining pure blood lines. Numerous drawings, distribution charts, and the most extensive bibliography ever assembled for the genus complete this reference.
ISBN 3-88244-056-2 (hardcover)

MARINE ATLAS

For Aquarists and Divers
Available in English

VOLUME 1
HELMUT DEBELIUS AND HANS A. BAENSCH

1216 pages, ca. 1000 fishes and invertebrates, and over 1100 color photos and drawings—
The MARINE ATLAS addresses the joint aquarium care of invertebrates and tropical marine fishes. Aquarium decoration, care, technology, and chemistry are clearly explained. Great detail has been devoted to *Caulerpa* and other marine algae. Crustacea, sea anemones, and fishes are presented with photographs and descriptive text.
ISBN 1-890087-09-2 (hardcover)
ISBN 1-890087-08-4 (softcover)

VOLUME 2
DR. HARRY ERHARDT, DR. HORST MOOSLEITNER,
DR. ROBERT PATZNER

736 pages, more than 670 color photos and over 600 invertebrates—
Volumes 2 and 3 are complementary books with consecutively numbered pages.
Sponges, hydrozoans, corals, sea pens, comb jellies, turbellarians, bryozoans, gastropods, and nudibranchs constitute this volume. It is a valuable identification aid for every aquarist, biologist, and diver!
ISBN 1-890087-11-4 (hardcover)
ISBN 1-890087-10-6 (softcover)

VOLUME 3
DR. HARRY ERHARDT, DR. HORST MOOSLEITNER,
DR. ROBERT PATZNER

592 pages, 500 species, and about 530 color photos—
Volumes 2 and 3 are complementary books with consecutively numbered pages.
The bivalves, squid, octopi, bristleworms, sea stars, sea urchins, sea cucumbers, and tunicates are introduced in this volume.
It is a valuable identification aid for every aquarist, biologist, and diver!
ISBN 1-890087-20-3 (hardcover)
ISBN 1-890087-43-2 (softcover)

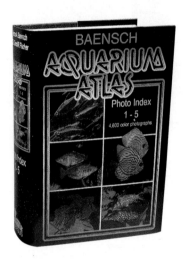